ISBN 978-1-5285-3592-2
PIBN 10915974

Forgotten Books is a registered trademark of FB &c Ltd.
Copyright © 2018 FB &c Ltd.
FB &c Ltd, Dalton House, 60 Windsor Avenue, London, SW19 2RR.
Company number 08720141. Registered in England and Wales.

For support please visit www.forgottenbooks.com

English
Français
Deutsche
Italiano
Español
Português

www.forgottenbooks.com

Mythology Photography **Fiction**
Fishing Christianity **Art** Cooking
Essays Buddhism Freemasonry
Medicine **Biology** Music **Ancient
Egypt** Evolution Carpentry Physics
Dance Geology **Mathematics** Fitness
Shakespeare **Folklore** Yoga Marketing
Confidence Immortality Biographies
Poetry **Psychology** Witchcraft
Electronics Chemistry History **Law**
Accounting **Philosophy** Anthropology
Alchemy Drama Quantum Mechanics
Atheism Sexual Health **Ancient History**
Entrepreneurship Languages Sport
Paleontology Needlework Islam
Metaphysics Investment Archaeology
Parenting Statistics Criminology
Motivational

ANNUAL REPORT

OF THE

AMERICAN HISTORICAL ASSOCIATION

FOR

THE YEAR 1919

IN TWO VOLUMES
AND A SUPPLEMENTAL VOLUME

VOL. I

WASHINGTON
GOVERNMENT PRINTING OFFICE
1923

1427473

LETTER OF SUBMITTAL.

SMITHSONIAN INSTITUTION,
Washington, D. C., December 14, 1920.

To the Congress of the United States:

In accordance with the act of incorporation of the American Historical Association approved January 4, 1889, I have the honor to submit to Congress the annual report of the association for the year 1919. I have the honor to be,

Very respectfully, your obedient servant,

CHARLES D. WALCOTT, *Secretary.*

3

ACT OF INCORPORATION.

Be it enacted by the Senate and House of Representatives of the United States of America in Congress assembled, That Andrew D. White, of Ithaca, in the State of New York; George Bancroft, of Washington, in the District of Columbia; Justin Winsor, of Cambridge, in the State of Massachusetts; William F. Poole, of Chicago, in the State of Illinois; Herbert B. Adams, of Baltimore, in the State of Maryland; Clarence W. Bowen, of Brooklyn, in the State of New York, their associates and successors, are hereby created, in the District of Columbia, a body corporate and politic by the name of the American Historical Association, for the promotion of historical studies, the collection and preservation of historical manuscripts, and for kindred purposes in the interest of American history and of history in America. Said association is authorized to hold real and personal estate in the District of Columbia so far only as may be necessary to its lawful ends to an amount not exceeding $500,000, to adopt a constitution, and make by-laws not inconsistent with law. Said association shall have its principal office at Washington, in the District of Columbia, and may hold its annual meetings in such places as the said incorporators shall determine. Said association shall report annually to the Secretary of the Smithsonian Institution concerning its proceedings and the condition of historical study in America. Said secretary shall communicate to Congress the whole of such report, or such portions thereof as he shall see fit. The Regents of the Smithsonian Institution are authorized to permit said association to deposit its collections, manuscripts, books, pamphlets, and other material for history in the Smithsonian Institution or in the National Museum at their discretion, upon such conditions and under such rules as they shall prescribe.

[Approved, January 4, 1889.]

5

LETTER OF TRANSMITTAL.

AMERICAN HISTORICAL ASSOCIATION,
Washington, D. C., September 28, 1920.

SIR: We have the honor to transmit herewith, as provided by law, the Annual Report of the American Historical Association for 1919. This report includes the proceedings of the association for the thirty-fourth annual meeting at Cleveland on December 29–31, 1919, and the proceedings of the Pacific Coast Branch of the American Historical Association at its fifteenth annual meeting held in San Francisco, Calif., on November 28–29, 1919. There is also transmitted as Volume II of this report the fifteenth report of the Historical Manuscripts Commission containing the first installment of the Stephen B. Austin papers concerning the affairs relating to Texas and the Southwest.

Very respectfully yours,

H. BARRETT LEARNED,
Chairman of the Committee on Publications.
ALLEN R. BOYD, *Editor.*

To the SECRETARY OF THE SMITHSONIAN INSTITUTION,
Washington, D. C.

CONTENTS.

VOLUME I.

CONSTITUTION.

I.

The name of this society shall be The American Historical Association.

II.

Its object shall be the promotion of historical studies.

III.

Any person approved by the executive council may become a member by paying $3, and after the first year may continue a member by paying an annual fee of $3. On payment of $50 any person may become a life member, exempt from fees. Persons not resident in the United States may be elected as honorary or corresponding members and be exempt from the payment of fees.

IV.

The officers shall be a president, two vice presidents, a secretary, a treasurer, an assistant secretary-treasurer, and an editor.

The president, vice presidents, secretary, and treasurer shall be elected by ballot at each regular annual meeting in the manner provided in the by-laws.

The assistant secretary-treasurer and the editor shall be elected by the executive council. They shall perform such duties and receive such compensation as the council may determine.

V.

There shall be an executive council, constituted as follows:

1. The president, the vice presidents, the secretary, and the treasurer.

2. Elected members, eight in number, to be chosen annually in the same manner as the officers of the association.

3. The former presidents; but a former president shall be entitled to vote for the three years succeeding the expiration of his term as president, and no longer.

VI.

The executive council shall conduct the business, manage the property, and care for the general interests of the association. In the exercise of its proper functions, the council may appoint such committees, commissions, and boards as it may deem necessary. The council shall make a full report of its activities to the annual meeting of the association. The association may by vote at any annual meeting instruct the executive council to discontinue or enter upon any activity, and may take such other action in directing the affairs of the association as it may deem necessary and proper.

VII.

This constitution may be amended at any annual meeting, notice of such amendment having been given at the previous annual meeting or the proposed amendment having received the approval of the executive council.

BY-LAWS.

I.

The officers provided for by the constitution shall have the duties and perform the functions customarily attached to their respective offices with such others as may from time to time be prescribed.

II.

A nomination committee of five members shall be chosen at each annual business meeting in the manner hereafter provided for the election of officers of the association. At such convenient time prior to the 15th of September as it may determine, it shall invite every member to express to it his preference regarding every office to be filled by election at the ensuing annual business meeting and regarding the composition of the new nominating committee then to be chosen. It shall publish and mail to each member at least one month prior to the annual business meeting such nominations as it may determine upon for each elective office and for the next nominating committee. It shall prepare for use at the annual business meeting an official ballot containing, as candidates for each office or committee membership to be filled thereat, the names of its nominees and also the names of any other nominees which may be proposed to the chairman of the committee in writing by 20 or more members of the association at least one day before the annual business meeting, but such nominations by petition shall not be presented until after the committee shall have reported its nominations to the association, as provided for in the present by-law. The official ballot shall also provide under each office a blank space for voting for such further nominees as any member may present from the floor at the time of the election.

III.

The annual election of officers and the choice of a nominating committee for the ensuing year shall be conducted by the use of an official ballot prepared as described in By-law II.

IV.

The association authorizes the payment of traveling expenses incurred by the voting members of the council attending one meeting of that body a year, this meeting to be other than that held in connection with the annual meeting of the association.

The council may provide for the payment of expenses incurred by the secretary, the assistant secretary-treasurer, and the editor in such travel as may be necessary to the transaction of the association's business.

12

AMERICAN HISTORICAL ASSOCIATION.

Organized at Saratoga, N. Y., September 10, 1884. Incorporated by Congress, January 4, 1889.

ALBERT BUSHNELL HART, Ph. D., LL. D., Litt. D.,
Harvard University.

FREDERICK JACKSON TURNER, Ph. D., LL. D., Litt. D.,
Harvard University.

WILLIAM MILLIGAN SLOANE, Ph. D., L. H. D., LL. D.,
Columbia University.

WILLIAM ARCHIBALD DUNNING, Ph. D., LL. D.,
Columbia University.

ANDREW C. McLAUGHLIN, A. M., LL. B., LL. D.,
University of Chicago.

GEORGE LINCOLN BURR, LL. D., Litt. D.,
Cornell University.

WORTHINGTON C. FORD, A. M.,
Massachusetts Historical Society.

WILLIAM ROSCOE THAYER, LL. D., Litt. D., L. H. D.,
Cambridge.

(Elected Councillors.)

HENRY E. BOURNE, L. H. D.,
Western Reserve University.

GEORGE M. WRONG, M. A., F. R. S. C.,
University of Toronto.

HERBERT E. BOLTON, B. L., Ph. D.,
University of California.

WILLIAM E. DODD, Ph. D.,
University of Chicago.

WALTER L. FLEMING, M. S., Ph. D.,
Vanderbilt University.

WILLIAM E. LINGELBACH, Ph. D.,
University of Pennsylvania.

JAMES T. SHOTWELL, Ph., D.,
Columbia University.

RUTH PUTNAM, B. Litt.,
Washington.

PACIFIC COAST BRANCH.

TERMS OF OFFICE.

(Deceased officers are marked thus : †.)

---

†CHARLES FRANCIS ADAMS, LL. D., 1900.
†HERBERT BAXTER ADAMS, Ph. D., LL. D., 1901.
†ALFRED THAYER MAHAN, D. C. L., LL. D., 1901.
†HENRY CHARLES LEA, LL. D., 1902.
†GOLDWIN SMITH, D. C. L., LL. D., 1902, 1903.
†EDWARD McCRADY, LL. D., 1903.
JOHN BACH McMASTER, Ph. D., Litt. D., LL. D., 1904.
SIMEON E. BALDWIN, LL. D., 1904, 1905.
J. FRANKLIN JAMESON, Ph. D., LL. D., Litt. D., 1905, 1906.
GEORGE BURTON ADAMS, Ph. D., Litt. D., 1906, 1907.
ALBERT BUSHNELL HART, Ph. D., LL. D., Litt. D., 1907, 1908.
FREDERICK JACKSON TURNER, Ph. D., LL. D., Litt. D., 1908, 1909.
WILLIAM MILLIGAN SLOANE, Ph. D., L. H. D., LL. D., 1909, 1910.
†THEODORE ROOSEVELT, LL. D., D. C. L., 1910, 1911.
WILLIAM ARCHIBALD DUNNING, Ph. D., LL. D., 1911, 1912.
ANDREW C. McLAUGHLIN, A. M., LL. B., LL. D., 1912, 1913.
†H. MORSE STEPHENS, M. A., Litt. D., 1913, 1914.
GEORGE LINCOLN BURR, LL. D., Litt. D., 1914, 1915.
WORTHINGTON C. FORD, A. M., 1915, 1916.
WILLIAM ROSCOE THAYER, LL. D., Litt. D., L. H. D., 1916, 1917.
EDWARD CHANNING, Ph. D., 1917, 1918–1919.

SECRETARIES.

†HERBERT BAXTER ADAMS, Ph. D., LL. D., 1884–1900.
†A. HOWARD CLARK, A. M., 1889–1908.
CHARLES HOMER HASKINS, Ph. D., 1900–1913.
WALDO GIFFORD LELAND, A. M., 1908–1919.
EVARTS BOUTELL GREENE, Ph. D., 1914–1919.
JOHN SPENCER BASSETT, Ph. D., 1919–

TREASURERS.

CLARENCE WINTHROP BOWEN, Ph. D., 1884–1917.
CHARLES MOORE, Ph. D., 1917–

CURATOR.

†A. HOWARD CLARK, A. M., 1889–1918.

EXECUTIVE COUNCIL.

†WILLIAM BABCOCK WEEDEN, A. M., 1884–1886.
†CHARLES DEANE, LL. D., 1884–1887.
†MOSES COIT TYLER, L. H. D., LL. D., 1884–1885.
EPHRAIM EMERTON, Ph. D., 1884–1885.
FRANKLIN BOWDITCH DEXTER, A. M., Litt. D., 1885–1887.
†WILLIAM FRANCIS ALLEN, A. M., 1885–1887.
†WILLIAM WIRT HENRY, LL. D., 1886–1888.
†RUTHERFORD BIRCHARD HAYES, LL. D., 1887–1888.
JOHN W. BURGESS, Ph. D., LL. D., 1887–1891.
†ARTHUR MARTIN WHEELER, A. M., LL. D., 1887–1889.
†GEORGE PARK FISHER, D. D., LL. D., 1888–1891.
†GEORGE BROWN GOODE, LL. D., 1889–1896.
JOHN GEORGE BOURINOT, C. M. G., D. C. L., LL. D., 1889–1894.
JOHN BACH McMASTER, Ph. D., Litt. D., LL. D., 1891–1894.
GEORGE BURTON ADAMS, Ph. D., Litt. D., 1891–1897; 1898–1901.
†THEODORE ROOSEVELT, LL. D., D. C. L., 1894–1895.
†JABEZ LAMAR MONROE CURRY, LL. D., 1894–1895.
†H. MORSE STEPHENS, M. A., Litt. D., 1895–1899.
FREDERICK JACKSON TURNER, Ph. D., LL. D., Litt. D., 1895–1899; 1901–1904.
†EDWARD MINOR GALLAUDET, Ph. D., LL. D., 1896–1897.
†MELVILLE WESTON FULLER, LL. D., 1897–1900.
ALBERT BUSHNELL HART, Ph. D., Litt. D., 1897–1900.
ANDREW C. McLAUGHLIN, A. M., LL. B., LL. D., 1898–1901; 1903–1906.

WILLIAM ARCHIBALD DUNNING, Ph. D., LL. D., 1899–1902.
†PETER WHITE, A. M., 1899–1902.
J. FRANKLIN JAMESON, Ph. D., LL. D., Litt. D., 1900–1903.
A. LAWRENCE LOWELL, Ph. D., LL D., 1900–1903.
HERBERT PUTNAM, Litt. D., LL. D., 1901–1904.
GEORGE LINCOLN BURR, LL. D., 1902–1905.
EDWARD POTTS CHEYNEY, LL. D., 1902–1905.
†EDWARD G. BOURNE, Ph. D., 1903–1906.
†GEORGE P. GARRISON, Ph. D., 1904–1907.
†REUBEN GOLD THWAITES, LL. D., 1904–1907.
CHARLES McLEAN ANDREWS, Ph. D., L. H. D., 1905–1908.
JAMES HARVEY ROBINSON, Ph. D., 1905–1908.
WORTHINGTON CHAUNCEY FORD, A. M., 1906–1909.
WILLIAM MacDONALD, Ph. D., LL. D., 1906–1909.
MAX FARRAND, Ph. D., 1907–1910.
FRANK HEYWOOD HODDER, Ph. M., 1907–1910.
EVARTS BOUTELL GREENE, Ph. D., 1908–1911.
CHARLES HENRY HULL, Ph. D., 1908–1911.
FRANKLIN LAFAYETTE RILEY, A. M., Ph. D., 1909–1912.
EDWIN ERLE SPARKS, Ph. D., LL. D., 1909–1912.
JAMES ALBERT WOODBURN, Ph. D., LL. D., 1910–1913.
FRED MORROW FLING, Ph. D., 1910–1913
HERMAN VANDENBURG AMES, Ph. D., 1911–1914.
DANA CARLETON MUNRO, A. M., 1911–1914.
ARCHIBALD CARY COOLIDGE, Ph. D., 1912–1914.
JOHN MARTIN VINCENT, Ph. D., LL. D., 1912–1915.
FREDERIC BANCROFT, Ph. D., LL. D., 1913–1915.
CHARLES HOMER HASKINS, Ph. D., 1913–1916.
EUGENE C. BARKER, Ph. D., 1914–1917.
GUY S. FORD, B. L., Ph. D., 1914–1917.
ULRICH B. PHILLIPS, Ph. D., 1914–1917.
LUCY M. SALMON, A. M., L. H. D., 1915–1919.
SAMUEL B. HARDING, Ph. G., 1915–1919.
HENRY E. BOURNE, A. B., B. D., L. H. D., 1916–
CHARLES MOORE, Ph. D., 1916–1817.
GEORGE M. WRONG, M. A., 1916–
HERBERT E. BOLTON, B. L., Ph. D., 1917–
WILLIAM E. DODD, Ph. D., 1917–
WALTER L. FLEMING, M. S., Ph. D., 1917–
WILLIAM E. LINGELBACH, Ph. D., 1917–
JAMES T. SHOTWELL, Ph. D., 1919–
RUTH PUTNAM. B. Litt., 1919–

OFFICERS AND COMMITTEES, 1920.

President.—Edward Channing, Harvard University, Cambridge, Mass.

First vice president.—Jean Jules Jusserand, French Embassy, Washington, D. C.

Second vice president.—Charles H. Haskins, Harvard University, Cambridge, Mass.

Secretary.—John Spencer Bassett, Smith College, Northampton, Mass.

Treasurer.—Charles Moore, Library of Congress, Washington, D. C.

Assistant secretary-treasurer.—Patty W. Washington, 1140 Woodward Building, Washington, D. C.

Editor.—Allen R. Boyd, Library of Congress, Washington, D. C.

EXECUTIVE COUNCIL.

(In addition to above.)

Elected members.—Henry E. Bourne, Western Reserve University, Cleveland, Ohio (1916); George M. Wrong, University of Toronto, Toronto, Ontario (1916); Herbert E. Bolton, University of California, Berkeley, Calif. (1917); William E. Dodd, University of Chicago, Chicago, Ill. (1917); Walter L. Fleming, Vanderbilt University, Nashville, Tenn. (1917); William E. Lingelbach, University of Pennsylvania, Philadelphia, Pa. (1917); James T. Shotwell, Columbia University, New York, N. Y. (1919); Ruth Putnam, 2025 O Street NW., Washington, D. C. (1919).

Ex-presidents.—James Ford Rhodes, 392 Beacon Street, Boston, Mass.; John Bach McMaster, 2109 De Lancey Place, Philadelphia, Pa.; Simeon E. Baldwin, 69 Church Street, New Haven, Conn.; J. Franklin Jameson, 1140 Woodward Building, Washington, D. C.; George Burton Adams, 57 Edgehill Road, New Haven, Conn.; Albert Bushnell Hart, Harvard University, Cambridge, Mass.; Frederick J. Turner, 7 Phillips Place, Cambridge, Mass.; William M. Sloane, Princeton, N. J.; William A. Dunning, Columbia University, New York, N. Y.; Andrew C. McLaughlin, University of Chicago, Chicago, Ill.; George L. Burr, Cornell University, Ithaca, N. Y.; Worthington C. Ford, 1154 Boylston Street, Boston, Mass.; William Roscoe Thayer, 8 Berkeley Street, Cambridge, Mass.

STANDING EXECUTIVE COMMITTEES OF THE COUNCIL.

Committee on docket.—Edward Channing, chairman; John S. Bassett, W. E. Dodd, A. C. McLaughlin, J. T. Shotwell.

Committee on meetings and relations.—John S. Bassett, chairman; Charles H. Haskins, J. F. Jameson, G. M. Wrong, Ruth Putnam.

Committee on finance.—Charles Moore, chairman; John S. Bassett, Herbert E. Bolton, W. C. Ford, W. E. Lingelbach.

Committee on appointments.—Edward Channing, chairman; John S. Bassett, H. E. Bourne, W. L. Fleming, G. L. Burr.

SPECIAL COMMITTEES TO REPORT TO THE COUNCIL.

Committee on policy.—Charles H. Haskins, chairman, Harvard University, Cambridge, Mass.; Carl Becker, Cornell University, Ithaca, N. Y.; William E. Dodd, University of Chicago, Chicago, Ill.; Guy Stanton Ford, University of Minnesota, Minneapolis, Minn.; Dana C. Munro, 119 Fitz Randolph Road, Princeton, N. J.

Committee on London headquarters.—J. Franklin Jameson, chairman, 1140 Woodward Building, Washington, D. C.; Charles H. Haskins, Harvard University, Cambridge, Mass.; Charles M. Andrews, 424 St. Ronan Street, New Haven, Conn.

Committee on disposition of records.—Waldo G. Leland, chairman, 1140 Woodward Building, Washington, D. C.; H. Barrett Learned, 2123 Bancroft Place, Washington, D. C.; C. O. Paullin, 1801 K Street NW., Washington, D. C.

Committee on nominations.—Victor H. Paltsits, chairman, 48 Whitson Street, Forest Hills Gardens, Long Island, N. Y.; Carl Russell Fish, 244 Lake Lawn Place, Madison, Wis.; J. G. de Roulhac Hamilton, University of North Carolina, Chapel Hill, N. C.; Frank H. Hodder, University of Kansas, Lawrence, Kans.; Eloise Ellery, Vassar College, Poughkeepsie, N. Y.

STANDING COMMITTEES OF THE ASSOCIATION.

Board of editors of the American Historical Review.—J. Franklin Jameson, managing editor, 1140 Woodward Building, Washington, D. C. (term expires 1925); Edward P. Cheyney, chairman, University of Pennsylvania, Philadelphia, Pa. (1924); Williston Walker, Yale University, New Haven, Conn. (1923); Carl Becker, Cornell University, Ithaca, N. Y. (1922); Claude H. Van Tyne, 1942 Cambridge Road, Ann Arbor, Mich. (1921); James Harvey Robinson, Columbia University, New York, N. Y. (1920).

Board of editors of the Historical Outlook.—Albert E. McKinley, managing editor, 1619 Ranstead Street, Philadelphia, Pa. The following appointed to serve for one year: Edgar Dawson, Hunter College, New York, N. Y.; Laurence M. Larson, University of Illinois, Urbana, Ill.; Lucy M. Salmon, Poughkeepsie, N. Y.; St. George L. Sioussat, Brown University, Providence, R. I.; William L. Westermann, University of Wisconsin, Madison, Wis.

Historical manuscripts commission.—Justin H. Smith, chairman, 7 West Forty-third Street, New York, N. Y.; Eugene C. Barker, University of Texas, Austin, Tex.; Mrs. Amos G. Draper, The Richmond, Washington, D. C.; Logan Esarey, Bloomington, Ind.; Gaillard Hunt, Department of State, Washington, D. C.; Charles H. Lincoln, 22 Dean Street, Worcester, Mass.

Public archives commission.—Suspended for 1920.

Committee on Justin Winsor prize.—Frederic L. Paxson, chairman, 2122 Van Hise Avenue, Madison, Wis.; Arthur C. Cole, 706 Michigan Avenue, Urbana, Ill.; C. H. Haring, 339 Williow Street, New Haven, Conn.; Frank H. Hodder, University of Kansas, Lawrence, Kans.; Nathaniel W. Stephenson, College of Charleston, Charleston, S. C.

Committee on Herbert Baxter Adams prize.—Conyers Read, chairman, University of Chicago, Chicago, Ill.; C. J. H. Hayes, Columbia University, New

York, N. Y.; Charles H. McIlwain, 3 Concord Avenue, Cambridge, Mass.; Nellie Neilson, Mount Holyoke College, South Hadley, Mass.; Bernadotte E. Schmitt, 1938 East One hundred and sixteenth Street, Cleveland, Ohio.

· *Committee on bibliography.*—Suspended for 1920.

Committee on publications.—H. Barrett Learned, chairman, 2123 Bancroft Place, Washington, D. C.; Allen R. Boyd, secretary, Library of Congress, Wash-. ington, D. C.; John S. Bassett, Smith College, Northampton, Mass.; J. Franklin Jameson, 1140 Woodward Building, Washington, D. C.; Justin H. Smith, 7 West Forty-third Street, New York, N. Y.; Rayner W. Kelsey, Haverford College, Haverford, Pa.

Committee on membership.—Thomas J. Wertenbaker, chairman, 111 Fitz Randolph Road, Princeton, N. J.; Louise Fargo Brown, 263 Mill Street, Poughkeepsie, N. Y.; Eugene H. Byrne, 240 Lake Lawn Place, Madison, Wis.; A. C. Krey, University of Minnesota, Minneapolis, Minn.; Frank E. Melvin, 737 Maine Street, Lawrence, Kans.; Richard A. Newhall, 253 Ellsworth Avenue, New Haven, Conn.; Charles W. Ramsdell, University of Texas, Austin, Tex.; James G. Randall, Richmond College, Richmond, Va.; Arthur P. Scott, University of Chicago, Chicago, Ill.; J. J. Van Nostrand, jr., University of California, Berkeley, Calif.; George F. Zook, Bureau of Education, Washington, D. C.

Conference of historical societies.—George S. Godard, chairman, Connecticut State Library, Hartford, Conn.; John C. Parish, secretary, State Historical Society of Iowa, Iowa City, Iowa. -

Committee on national archives.—J. Franklin Jameson, chairman, 1140 Woodward Building, Washington, D. C.; Charles Moore, Library of Congress, Washington, D. C.; Lieut. Col. Oliver L. Spaulding, jr., historical branch, General Staff, Washington Barracks, Washington, D. C.

Committee on program, thirty-fifth annual meeting, Washington, D. C.—C. J. H. Hayes, chairman, Columbia University, New York, N. Y.; John C. Parish, State Historical Society of Iowa, Iowa City, Iowa; William K. Boyd, Trinity College, Durham, N. C.; Marshall S. Brown, 19 Fairview Street, Yonkers, N. Y.; Lyman Carrier, secretary of Agricultural History Society, Department of Agriculture, Washington, D. C.; William R. Shepherd, Columbia University, New York, N. Y.; George F. Zook, Bureau of Education, Washington, D. C.

Committee on local arrangements, thirty-fifth annual meeting, Washington, D. C.—Thomas Nelson Page, chairman, 1759 R Street, Washington, D. C.; H. Barrett Learned, secretary, 2123 Bancroft Place, Washington, D. C.; Charles Moore, Library of Congress, Washington, D. C. Others to be appointed.

SPECIAL COMMITTEES OF THE ASSOCIATION.

Committee on bibliography of modern English history.—Edward P. Cheyney, chairman, University of Pennsylvania, Philadelphia, Pa. Others to be appointed.

Committee on military history prize.—Milledge L. Bonham, jr., chairman, Hamilton College, Clinton, N. Y.; Frank Maloy Anderson, Dartmouth College, Hanover, N. H.; Allen Richards Boyd, Library of Congress, Washington, D. C.; Albert Bushnell Hart, Harvard University, Cambridge, Mass.; Fred M. Fling, University of Nebraska, Lincoln, Nebr.

Committee on the historical congress at Rio de Janeiro.—Bernard Moses, chairman, University of California, Berkeley, Calif.; Julius Klein, secretary, Department of Commerce, Washington, D. C.; Charles Lyon Chandler, Corn Exchange National Bank, Philadelphia, Pa.; Charles H. Cunningham, University of Texas, Austin, Tex.; Percy A. Martin, Leland Stanford University, Stanford University, Calif.

Committee on history and education for citizenship in the schools.—Joseph Schafer, chairman, State Historical Society of Wisconsin, Madison, Wis.; Daniel C. Knowlton, secretary, Lincoln School, New York, N. Y.; William C. Bagley, Carnegie Foundation, 576 Fifth Avenue, New York, N. Y.; Frank S. Bogardus, 2312 North Tenth Street, Terre Haute, Ind.; Julian A. C. Chandler, College of William and Mary, Williamsburg, Va.; Guy Stanton Ford, University of Minnesota, Minneapolis, Minn.; Samuel B. Harding, 5413 Woodlawn Avenue, Chicago, Ill.; Andrew C. McLaughlin, University of Chicago, Chicago, Ill.

Committee on manual of historical literature.—George M. Dutcher, chairman, Wesleyan University, Middletown, Conn.; Sidney B. Fay, 32 Paradise Road, Northampton, Mass.; Augustus H. Shearer, Grosvenor Library, Buffalo, N. Y.; Henry R. Shipman, 27 Mercer Street, Princeton, N. J.

Committee on a primer of archives.—Victor H. Paltsits, chairman, 48 Whitson Street, Forest Hills Gardens, Long Island, N. Y.; Waldo G. Leland, 1140 Woodward Building, Washington, D. C.

ORGANIZATION AND ACTIVITIES.

The American Historical Association is the national organization for the promotion of historical writing and studies in the United States. It was founded in 1884 by a group of representative scholars, and in 1889 was chartered by Congress. Its national character is emphasized by fixing its principal office in Washington and by providing for the publication of its annual reports by the United States Government through the secretary of the Smithsonian Institution. The membership of the association, at present about 2,500, is drawn from every State in the Union, as well as from Canada and South America. It includes representatives of all the professions and many of the various business and commercial pursuits. To all who desire to promote the development of history—local, national, or general—and to all who believe that a correct knowledge of the past is essential to a right understanding of the present the association makes a strong appeal through its publications and other activities.

The meetings of the association are held annually during the last week in December in cities so chosen as to accommodate in turn the members living in different parts of the country, and the average attendance is about 400. The meetings afford an opportunity for members to become personally acquainted and to discuss matters in which they have a common interest.

The principal publications of the association are the Annual Report and the American Historical Review. The former, usually in two volumes, is printed for the association by the Government and is distributed free to all members who desire it. It contains the proceedings of the association, including the more important papers read at the annual meetings, as well as valuable collections of documents, edited by the historical manuscripts commission; reports on American archives, prepared by the public archives commission; bibliographical contributions; reports on history teaching, on the activities of historical societies, and other agencies, etc.; and an annual group of papers on agricultural history contributed by the Agricultural History Society. The American Historical Review is the official organ of the association and the recognized organ of the historical profession in the United States. It is published quarterly, each number containing about 200 pages. It presents to the reader authoritative articles, critical reviews of important new works on history, notices of inedited documents, and the news of all other kinds of historical activities. The Review is indispensable to all who wish to keep abreast of the progress of historical scholarship, and is of much value and interest to the general reader. It is distributed free to all members of the association.

For the encouragement of historical research the association offers two biennial prizes, each of $200, for the best printed or manuscript monograph in the English language submitted by a writer residing in the Western Hemisphere who has not achieved an established reputation. The Justin Winsor prize, offered in the even years, is awarded to an essay in the history of the Western Hemisphere, including the insular possessions of the United States.

In odd years the Herbert Baxter Adams prize is awarded for an essay in the history of the Eastern Hemisphere.

To the subject of history teaching the association has devoted much and consistent attention through conferences held at the annual meetings, the investigations of committees and the preparation of reports. The association appoints the board of editors of The Historical Outlook thus assuming a certain responsibility for that valuable organ of the history-teaching profession. At the close of the war a special committee was appointed on the revision of the historical program in all schools under college grade.

The association maintains close relations with the State and local historical societies through a conference organized under the auspices of the association and holds a meeting each year in connection with the annual meeting of the association. In this meeting of delegates the various societies discuss such problems as the collection and editing of historical material, the maintenance of museums and libraries, the fostering of popular interest in historical matters, the marking of sites, the observance of historical anniversaries, etc. The proceedings of the conference are printed in the Annual Reports of the association.

The Pacific Coast Branch of the association, organized in 1904, affords an opportunity for the members living in the Far West to have meetings and an organization of their own while retaining full membership in the parent body. In 1915 the association met with the branch in San Francisco, Berkeley, and Palo Alto in celebration of the opening of the Panama Canal. The proceedings of this meeting, devoted to the history of the Pacific and the countries about it, have been published in a separate volume.

From the first the association has pursued the policy of inviting to its membership not only those professionally or otherwise actively engaged in historical work, but also those whose interest in history or in the advancement of historical science is such that they wish to ally themselves with the association in the furtherance of its various objects. Thus the association counts among its members lawyers, clergymen, editors, publishers, physicians, officers of the Army and Navy, merchants, bankers, and farmers, all of whom find material of especial interest in the publications of the association.

Membership in the association is obtained through election by the executive council, upon nomination by a member or by direct application. The annual dues are $3, there being no initiation fee. The fee for life membership is $50, which secures exemption from all annual dues.

Inquiries respecting the association, its work, publications, prizes, meetings, memberships, etc., should be addressed to the assistant secretary of the association at 1140 Woodward Building, Washington, D. C., from whom they will receive prompt attention.

HISTORICAL PRIZES.

WINSOR AND ADAMS PRIZES.

For the purpose of encouraging historical research, the American Historical Association offers two prizes, each prize of $200—the Justin Winsor prize in American history and the Herbert Baxter Adams prize in the history of the Eastern Hemisphere. The Winsor prize is offered in the even years (as heretofore), and the Adams prize in the odd years. Both prizes are designed to encourage writers who have not published previously any considerable work or obtained an established reputation. Either prize shall be awarded for an excellent monograph or essay, printed or in manuscript, submitted to or selected by the committee of award. Monographs must be submitted on or before July 1 of the given year. In the case of a printed monograph the date of publication must fall within a period of two years prior to July 1. A monograph to which a prize has been awarded in manuscript may, if it is deemed in all respects available, be published in the annual report of the association. Competition shall be limited to monographs written or published in the English language by writers of the Western Hemisphere.

In making the award the committee will consider not only research, accuracy, and originality, but also clearness of expression and logical arrangement. The successful monograph must reveal marked excellence of style. Its subject matter should afford a distinct contribution to knowledge of a sort beyond that having merely personal or local interest. The monograph must conform to the accepted canons of historical research and criticism. A manuscript—including text, notes, bibliography, appendices, etc.—must not exceed 100,000 words if designed for publication in the annual report of the association.

The Justin Winsor prize.—The monograph must be based upon independent and original investigation in American history. The phrase "American history" includes the history of the United States and other countries of the Western Hemisphere. The monograph may deal with any aspect or phase of that history.

The Herbert Baxter Adams prize.—The monograph must be based upon independent and original investigation in the history of the Eastern Hemisphere. The monograph may deal with any aspect or phase of that history, as in the case of the Winsor prize.

Inquiries regarding these prizes should be addressed to the chairmen of the respective committees, or to the secretary of the association, 1140 Woodward Building, Washington, D. C.

The Justin Winsor prize (which until 1906 was offered annually) has been awarded to the following:

1896. Herman V. Ames: "The proposed amendments to the Constitution of the United States."

1900. William A. Schaper: "Sectionalism and representation in South Carolina"; with honorable mention of Mary S. Locke: "Antislavery sentiment before 1808."

1901. Ulrich B. Phillips: "Georgia and State rights"; with honorable mention of M. Louise Green: "The struggle for religious liberty in Connecticut."

1902. Charles McCarthy: "The Anti-Masonic Party"; with honorable mention of W. Roy Smith: "South Carolina as a royal province."

1903. Louise Phelps Kellogg: "The American colonial charter: A study of its relation to English administration, chiefly after 1688."

1904. William R. Manning: "The Nootka Sound controversy"; with honorable mention of C. O. Paullin: "The Navy of the American Revolution."

1906. Annie Heloise Abel: "The history of events resulting in Indian consolidation west of the Mississippi River."

1908. Clarence Edwin Carter: "Great Britain and the Illinois country, 1765–1774"; with honorable mention of Charles Henry Ambler: "Sectionalism in Virginia, 1776–1861."

1910. Edward Raymond Turner: "The Negro in Pennsylvania: Slavery—servitude—freedom, 1639–1861."

1912. Charles Arthur Cole: "The Whig Party in the South."

1914. Mary W. Williams: "Anglo-American Isthmian diplomacy, 1815–1915."

1916. Richard J. Purcell: "Connecticut in transition, 1775–1818."

1918. Arthur M. Schlesinger: "The Colonial Merchants and the American Revolution, 1763–1776." (Columbia University Studies in History, etc., No. 182.)

From 1897 to 1899 and in 1905 the Justin Winsor prize was not awarded.

The Herbert Baxter Adams prize has been awarded to:

1905. David S. Muzzey: "The Spiritual Franciscans"; with honorable mention of Eloise Ellery: "Jean Pierre Brissot."

1907. In equal division, Edward B. Krehbiel, "The Interdict: Its history and its operation, with especial attention to the time of Pope Innocent III"; and William S. Robertson: "Francisco de Miranda and the revolutionizing of Spanish America."

1909. Wallace Notestein: "A history of witchcraft in England from 1558 to 1718."

1911. Louise Fargo Brown: "The political activities of the Baptists and Fifth Monarchy men in England during the Interregnum."

1913. Violet Barbour: "Henry Bennet, Earl of Arlington."

1915. Theodore C. Pease, "The leveler movement"; with honorable mention of F. C. Melvin, "Napoleon's system of licensed navigation, 1806–1814."

1917. Frederick L. Nussbaum: "G. J. A. Ducher: An essay on the political history of mercantilism during the French Revolution."

The essays of Messrs. Muzzey, Krehbiel, Carter, Notestein, Turner, Cole, Pease, Purcell, Miss Brown, Miss Barbour, and Miss Williams have been published by the association in a series of separate volumes. The earlier Winsor prize essays were printed in the annual reports.

MILITARY HISTORY PRIZE.

The American Historical Association offers a prize of $250 for the best unpublished essay in American military history submitted to the military history prize committee before July 1, 1920.

The essay may treat of any event of American military history—a war, a campaign, a battle; the influence of a diplomatic or political situation upon military operations; an arm of the service; the fortunes of a particular command; a method of warfare historically treated; the career of a distinguished soldier. It should not be highly technical in character, for the object of the contest is to extend the interest in American military history, but it must be a positive contribution to historical knowledge and the fruit of original research. The essay is not expected to be less than 10,000 or more than 100,000 words in length. It should be submitted in typewritten form, unsigned, and should be accompanied by a sealed envelope marked with its title and containing the name and address of the author and a short biographical sketch. Maps, diagrams, or other illustrative materials accompanying a manuscript should bear the title of the essay.

The committee, in reaching a decision, will consider not only research, accuracy, and originality but also clearness of expression and literary form. It reserves the right to withhold the award if no essay is submitted attaining the required degree of excellence.

For further information address the chairman of the military history prize committee.

Committee on military history prize.—Prof. Milledge L. Bonhan, jr., chairman, Hamilton College, Clinton, N. Y.; Prof. F. M. Anderson, Hanover, N. H.; Mr. Allen R. Boyd, Library of Congress, Washington, D. C.; Prof. Albert Bushnell Hart, Harvard University, Cambridge, Mass.; Maj. Fred M. Fling.

AMERICAN HISTORICAL ASSOCIATION STATISTICS OF MEMBERSHIP.

DECEMBER 18, 1919.

I. General.

Total membership	2,445
Life	107
Annual	2,128
Institutions	210
Total paid membership, including life members	2,032
Delinquent (total)	413
Since last bill	368
For one year	45
Loss (total)	282
Deaths	35
Resignations	58
Dropped	189
Gain (total)	208
Life	2
Annual	198
Institutions	8
Total number of elections	225
Net gain or loss	74

II. By Regions.

New England: Maine, New Hampshire, Vermont, Massachusetts, Rhode Island, Connecticut	397
North Atlantic: New York, New Jersey, Pennsylvania, Delaware, Maryland, District of Columbia	779
South Atlantic: Virginia, North Carolina, South Carolina, Georgia, Florida	132
North Central: Ohio, Indiana, Illinois, Michigan, Wisconsin	477
South Central: Alabama, Mississippi, Tennessee, Kentucky, West Virginia	72
West Central: Minnesota, Iowa, Missouri, Arkansas, Louisiana, North Dakota, South Dakota, Nebraska, Kansas, Oklahoma, Texas	278
Pacific coast: Montana, Wyoming, Colorado, New Mexico, Idaho, Utah, Nevada, Arizona, Washington, Oregon, California	232
Territories: Porto Rico, Alaska, Hawaii, Philippine Islands	5
Other countries	83
	2,445

III. By States.

	Members.	New members, 1919.		Members.	New members, 1919.
Alabama	6	1	New Jersey	78	5
Alaska			New Mexico	9	2
Arizona	5	4	New York	356	22
Arkansas	8	6	North Carolina	25	3
California	137	15	North Dakota	6	1
Colorado	13	2	Ohio	105	8
Connecticut	89	5	Oklahoma	12	3
Delaware	11		Oregon	17	1
District of Columbia	106	16	Pennsylvania	177	15
Florida	5		Philippine Islands	3	
Georgia	20		Porto Rico	2	
Hawaii		1	Rhode Island	21	2
Idaho	6		South Carolina	20	
Illinois	182	14	South Dakota	10	4
Indiana	46	7	Tennessee	20	2
Iowa	44	3	Texas	44	2
Kansas	23	1	Utah	9	2
Kentucky	23	4	Vermont	8	1
Louisiana	16	1	Virginia	52	2
Maine	16		Washington	24	1
Maryland	51	1	West Virginia	19	3
Massachusetts	236	12	Wisconsin	64	6
Michigan	80	7	Wyoming	3	
Minnesota	48	8	Canada	28	3
Mississippi	4		Cuba	2	
Missouri	43	2	South America	5	
Montana	5		Foreign	48	4
Nebraska	24	2			
Nevada	4		Total	2, 445	208
New Hampshire	27	4			

I. PROCEEDINGS OF THE THIRTY-FOURTH ANNUAL MEETING OF THE AMERICAN HISTORICAL ASSOCIATION.

CLEVELAND, OHIO, DECEMBER 29–31, 1919.

1427473

THE MEETING OF THE AMERICAN HISTORICAL ASSOCIATION AT CLEVELAND, OHIO.[1]

The meeting of the American Historical Association at Cleveland, December 29–31, 1919, was designated on the program as the " Thirty-fourth–Thirty-fifth Annual Meeting," because the meeting planned for December, 1918, as the thirty-fourth was postponed for a year. But the annual meetings of the association have not taken place with perfect regularity (there was, for instance, no meeting in 1892) and the meeting of December, 1919, was properly the thirty-fourth. So many annual meetings have now been held that henceforth many a city must enjoy or suffer its second meeting rather than its first.

This was the second time the association had met in Cleveland. It had held a meeting there in 1897 when the presidential address was delivered by Dr. James Schouler. That meeting was a notable one, held west of the Alleghanies as a consequence of that mild revolution or infusion of new life which had marked the New York meeting of 1896, and typifying in many ways the new spirit then evoked. It was the first meeting in which the discussion of practical professional problems, chiefly educational, as distinguished from the mere reading of substantive historical papers, took the chief place. The report of the committee of seven on the teaching of history in schools, presented in a provisional form, was made the subject of consideration at one of the sessions; at others, the teaching of economic history, the use of sources in teaching, the opportunities for historical study in Europe, and the functions of State and local historical societies. The Annual Report for 1896, published at about the same time as that of the meeting, brought out the first report of the Historical Manuscripts Commission, the first of those standing committees through which the association has done so much of its best work for the profession.

From these significant beginnings it is not difficult to measure the progress which the association has made between the dates of the first Cleveland meeting and the second. Progress of another sort may be measured by the fact that the membership, which in December, 1896, had been less than 600, and in December, 1897, stood at 928, stands now at 2,445, and by the contrast, respecting means for useful works, between assets of $10,885 in 1897 and of $35,581 in 1919.

[1] This account of the Cleveland meeting is taken, with some modifications and abridgments, from the American Historical Review for April, 1920.

That the registration at the recent meeting should have reached a total of 316—a figure quite as large as that which has usually been attained when meeting in cities comparable with Cleveland—was especially gratifying in view of the present status of professional salaries, the high cost of railroad travel as well as of everything else, and the regrettable refusal of the Railroad Administration to grant those reductions of railroad fares which were customary in happier times. It was noticeable that an unusual number of the younger members of the association were present. The Mississippi Valley Historical Association, the Agricultural History Society, the American Political Science Association, the National Municipal League, and the American Association of University Professors met at the same time and place. A joint session was held with each of the first three, and at one of the luncheons the work of the American Association of University Professors was explained by its president, Prof. Arthur O. Lovejoy, of the Johns Hopkins University.

The general opinion seems to have been that the meeting was exceptionally pleasant and successful. That it was so was mainly due to the interesting program provided by a committee of which Prof. Elbert J. Benton, of the Western Reserve University, was chairman, and to the excellent arrangements made for all these societies by a committee of local arrangements, of which the secretary was his colleague, Prof. Samuel B. Platner. All the sessions of the association were held under one roof, that of the Hollenden Hotel, and indeed on one floor of that hotel, which makes it unnecessary this year to say a word on the banal theme of December weather. Even the excellent luncheons to which with generous hospitality the trustees of the Western Reserve Historical Society and of the Western Reserve University, on successive days, invited the members of the association, were served in the ballroom of the hotel. The trustees of the Cleveland Museum of Art and of the Historical Society provided special occasions for visiting their remarkable collections. The privileges of the Union Club and of the University Club, of the Women's City Club and of the College Club, were extended to the members of the association, men and women, respectively, during the days of the meeting. The College Club gave a reception to the women, the Union Club a "smoker" for the men. Appropriate votes of thanks showed the gratitude of the members for all this hospitable kindness.

At one of the luncheons there was a most interesting address by Mr. Alexander Whyte, M. P. for Perth, 1910–1918; and at another Mr. A. Percival Newton, of the University of London, who since then has been elected to the chair of imperial and colonial history in that institution, spoke of the new developments in historical instruction in London and other British universities, especially of the new provisions for advanced degrees, of the work of the British Universities Bureau and the British division of the American University Union in Europe, and of the possibilities and advantages of mutual exchange of teachers and students between the two nations.

Of the dinner conferences which of late have become characteristic of the meetings, three were held on the present occasion. One was composed of members specially interested in Hispanic-American history; another of those specially interested in the history of the Far East; a third of those specially interested in the history of the Great War. The last was addressed by Hon. Albert J. Beveridge, formerly Senator from Indiana. All three performed a useful function in promoting acquaintance and the interchange of plans and suggestions among Fachgenossen. There was also a dinner of the National Board for Historical Service, at which that body, organized in April, 1917, to do whatever service historians as such could perform for government and public in war time, now brought its labors to an end and adjourned sine die. Finding itself at the conclusion of its work in possession of a fund of somewhat more than a thousand dollars, the board offered that sum to the association, to be maintained as a separate fund, to be called the Andrew D. White Fund in memory of the association's first president, and to be used, appropriately to that title, for international historical undertakings, through the association's representatives in the American Council of Learned Societies.

One of the noteworthy events of the Cleveland meeting was the organization of the American Catholic Historical Association. The initiative in calling such a society into existence was taken by the energetic editor of the Catholic Historical Review, Prof. Peter Guilday, of the Catholic University of America. The meeting for organization, attended by some 60 or 70 persons, was presided over by Mgr. T. C. O'Reilly, rector of St. John's Cathedral, Cleveland. Prof. Guilday, in an interesting address, reviewed the history of Catholic historical societies in the United States and outlined the possibilities of usefulness that lay before the new organization. Dr. J. F. Jameson, of the Carnegie Institution of Washington, speaking as one of the elder members of the American Historical Association, welcomed cordially the formation of the new society, which expects to hold one of its meetings each year at the same time and place as the American Historical Association. Dr. Laurence Flick, of Philadelphia, was elected its first president; Rev. Richard Tierney, S. J., and Rev. Victor O'Daniel, O. P., vice presidents; Prof. C. J. H. Hayes, of Columbia University, secretary; Mgr. O'Reilly, treasurer; and Dr. Guilday, archivist. Its beginnings are made under excellent auspices.

The program of the American Historical Association was composed, as has been usual, on the one hand, of conferences, and, on the other hand, of sessions devoted to the reading of formal papers; and too often, as has also been usual, the simultaneous occurrence of three different conferences or sessions brought confusion or dismay to those auditors who allow themselves to be interested in more than one field of history. In some instances the term conference meant nothing else than a series of four or five related papers, but in some there was real discussion. Of these, that which excited the widest interest was the one called for consideration of the report of the committee on history and education for citizenship in the schools. Under the chairmanship of Prof. Joseph Schafer, of the University of Oregon, this committee had been at work for more than a year, at first under the auspices of the National Board for Historical Service, but since February as a committee of the American Historical Association. It had held many conferences with representative bodies of school-teachers and had published, in the Historical Outlook and elsewhere, much preliminary matter respecting its deliberations and conclusions. The number of that periodical for June, 1919, had contained the fullest statement of the committee's proposals, and the audience at the conference (somewhat more than 200 in number) had copies of that statement before them. In the elementary school, beginning with the making of the community, the plan provides for the first six grades a progressive study of the making of the United States. For the junior high school, which must now be reckoned with, it provides a study of the history of the world and of American history in that setting, culminating in the ninth grade in a study of community and national activities which involves a combination of recent economic and social history with commercial geography and civics. For the senior high school it provides a maturer study of modern European and American history and of social, economic, and political principles and problems. Like all programs of educational improvement, it calls for completer preparation of the teacher in a world which is constantly making the teacher's career more difficult to enter upon or to sustain; and Prof. Frank S. Bogardus, of the Indiana State Normal School, in a capital paper, approving the program in general, showed what teachers' training schools could and should do to meet its requirements. The remainder of the discussion is fully reported in the Historical Outlook for February. To an external observer not versed in the problems of the schools it seemed much like other educational discussions he had heard, wherein A and B and C urge that in the framing of a new curriculum more emphasis should have been laid on this or that or the other element, while on the other hand all agree that the new scheme already contains too much, that it will be difficult to introduce, and that it should be worked out in greater detail. Such an observer was inclined to think that the new program, so carefully planned by the committee and so ably and open-mindedly defended on the floor by Prof. Schafer, was a good one, well adapted to its purpose of meeting the exigencies of a rapidly altered world, and that if it did not include all desiderata it was not for want of having taken them into account.

There was also a joint conference of representatives of State and local historical societies and of State organizations formed to deal with each State's part in the history of the Great War.[2] The theme was the preservation and publication of war material. Mr. Wallace H. Cathcart, of the Western Reserve Historical Society, presided. Mr. Frank H. Severance, of the Buffalo Historical Society, described the various lists, records, books, collections of newspaper clippings, printed ephemera, and the like, which the average historical society, not State-aided, in the average city, might well accumulate; and Mr. Frank M. Gregg, of Cleveland, described his own remarkable collection of posters, post cards, broadsides, pieces of music, and other fugitive printed matter, brought together primarily with a view to the illustration of mass psychology and the workings of propaganda and emotional appeal. Others described systems for dealing with material, and the kinds of data embraced in official State surveys and State war records. The proceedings concluded with a formal session of the National Association of State War History Organizations; a body formed to secure greater uniformity and cooperation in the work of such organizations. The intelligence with which its plans have been developed has deserved for them a greater measure of cooperation than they have received. The chief feature of the present occasion was an elaborate report by Dr. Newton D. Mereness, the agent employed by the association to carry out in military and other achives in Washington the great work which the common purposes of the constituent organizations require.

Another body, the Agricultural History Society, allied with the American Historical Association, held on this occasion for the first time sessions conjoint with those of the annual meeting. In its discussions the one paper of general purport was that of Prof. Rayner W. Kelsey, of Haverford College, on "Possibilities of intensive research in agricultural history." His main thesis was that many of the important influences of agriculture cannot be discovered until a large amount of intensive research has been applied to circumscribed fields of agricultural history. Various methods and sources and forms of presentation were suggestively considered. New light could be thrown upon many critical periods

---

[2] The proceedings of the conference are printed in the present volume.

of political history, showing the reaction of the farming community to and upon the events of the time. Social histories could be written, compassing the whole round of country life, economic, social, educational, and religious. Finally, one could rewrite the general history of a State or a section by filling in the important background of rural life, so fundamental to the picture yet so largely omitted in most histories. The other papers read before this new society may better be described in the place into which they will naturally fall in our brief report of the papers read before the main society.

Another novelty in the program and one greatly to be commended was the provision of a session for papers on the history of science. That studies in that field, either on the part of men of science or on that of historical students, have increased to such a degree that those who pursue them are conscious of an important common purpose and seek opportunities of fruitful mutual acquaintance is of itself exceedingly gratifying, and the meeting was of a character to augur well for the continuance of such occasions in future programs.[3] The leading subject of discussion was that of the place and treatment of the history of science in the college curriculum. The discussion began with a paper by Dr. Henry Crew, professor of physics in Northwestern University, who showed ways in which the history of science might be made interesting and profitable to even quite young minds, and how general courses and courses special to the history of physics and chemistry, zoology and botany might be combined and conducted by the teachers having charge of those disciplines. Other points brought out in the discussion were the need that students should not be tempted to undertake courses in the history of science until they knew something of the nature of science itself by at least one laboratory course preceding, and that those whose function it is to teach general history in various epochs should not fail to lay appropriate emphasis on the relation of scientific progress to the advance of civilization.

Three papers on portions of the history of science were also read in this session. The first, by Prof. T. Wingate Todd, of the medical school of the Western Reserve University, was an illustrated address on Egyptian medicine, showing its relation to ritual and superstition and the primitive practice prevalent in modern Africa, and the extent of the advance it achieved in dentistry, general surgery, therapeutics, and pharmacology. Prof. Lynn Thorndike, of the same university, read a paper on the medieval scientist, Peter of Abano, setting forth the facts of his life and writings and the extent of his contributions to astronomy, to medicine, and to the knowledge of Aristotle. Prof. Louis C. Karpinski, of the University of Michigan, traced the history of the development of algebra through Egyptian, Greek, and Arabic mathematical thinking.

The association and American historical students generally have been disposed to give so little attention, relatively, to the intellectual history of mankind that we most cordially wish great success to the new movement thus happily inaugurated.

We pass from the conferences of organized groups to the review of individual papers. The presidential address of Mr. William R. Thayer on Fallacies in History dealt largely with German interpretations of history.[4] Another paper of general character was that of Prof. N. S. B. Gras, of the University of Minnesota, on the Present Condition of Economic History.[5] As against the inclination of historians to concentrate their attention on periods of economic history, and of economists to pursue it by topics, and the general tendency to make it dependent on either history or economics, he suggested the possibilities lying in the pursuit of what he called genetic economics, or the general theory of economic historical development.

Four papers, in addition to that of Dr. Todd, already mentioned, were to be classed as falling in the domain of ancient history. In one, Mr. Oscar C. Stine, of the Department of Agriculture at Washington, described the characteristics of Egyptian agriculture in Ptolemaic times. In another, Dr. John R. Knipfing, of the Ohio State University, reviewed the writings of German historians on Macedonian imperialism, showing how the views of Niebuhr and Droysen were influenced by the changing political currents of their day, and how those of the present generation of German writers of Greek history, almost without exception ardent for Philip and bitterly hostile to Demosthenes, have been formed by the experiences of the period of Bismarck, the political conclusions deducible from his statecraft, and the rising tide of nationalistic imperialism. In a third paper, written apropos of the present Greek claim to a part of southern Albania, as historically Epeirote, Prof. Herbert Wing, jr., of Dickinson College, discussed the Epeiros-Albania boundary dispute in ancient times. In the fourth, Prof. David Magie, of Princeton University, sketched the history of Roman policy in Armenia and its significance. The subsequent discussion revealed much difference of opinion as to whether Armenia was chiefly valued by the Romans as a commercial or as a military highway between east and west.

Three papers dealt with the history of the British Empire. Prof. Edward P. Cheyney, of the University of Pennsylvania, under the title "England's earliest empire," treated of the acquisition and status of that commercial empire which was composed of outlying trading posts, with extraterritorial and other rights, and somewhat

[4] Printed in the American Historical Review for January, 1920.
[5] Printed in the Quarterly Journal of Economics, February, 1920.

of the process by which this began to grow into a political empire. Prof. A. Percival Newton, of the University of London, discussed the organization of the dependent British Empire, using that term to characterize the relations to the British Crown of those territories that can neither be included among the self-governing Dominions, nor among the Crown colonies enjoying some measure of representative government, nor with the Indian empire. The criterion suggested for the classification of a dependency within the British realms was that its inhabitants could make no valid treaties with external powers except through the medium of the King's government at Westminster. Attention was called to the way in which experience gained in dealing with the native States of India has guided the policy of the empire in its relations with protectorates.

Finally, in a paper on "Some problems of British imperial federation," Prof. Arthur L. Cross, of the University of Michigan, prefaced his account of present-day arrangements and of the various plans for the future with a narrative of the stages of development through which the empire has advanced from the paternalistic exploitation prevalent in early days and the laissez-faire policy of the middle period of the nineteenth century, to the colonial and imperial conferences of 1887–1911 and the imperial war conference and imperial war cabinet instituted in 1917.

A great part of the interest, distinctly unusual in degree, with which the proceedings of the annual meetings were invested arose from the frank dedication of large parts of the program to consideration of present politics. Many of the papers in modern history ran well into the future; some lay entirely there. It will not be thought inappropriate if the present very condensed chronicle confines itself practically to such portions of the material as were strictly historical in character. Thus, in the session devoted to Russia, a joint session of the historical and political science associations, Mr. Jerome Landfield's paper on the "Revolution of November, 1917," was a piece of history, while that of Baron Korff, formerly professor of law in the University of Helsingfors, related to the "Future constitution of Russia as seen by Russian liberals."[6] Mr. Landfield described the democratic traits of monarchial Russia and the social and economic conditions which led to the November revolution, and showed how an unscrupulous minority, carefully organized, took advantage of war weariness, hunger, and want, to bring itself into supreme power.

In an evening session which aroused more general interest than any other, Profs. Charles H. Haskins and Robert H. Lord, of Harvard University, spoke on the Franco-Prussian frontier and the New

[6] Printed in the American Political Science Review for May, 1920.

Poland, respectively, and Mr. A. F. Whyte reviewed the "Operations of the main forces at the peace conferences of 1919." Mr. Haskins and Mr. Lord had had an important part in assisting at Paris the work of that conference; Mr. Whyte had watched it as representative of one of the chief London newspapers. Mr. Haskins's principal endeavor was to relate the history of Alsace and Lorraine and neighboring lands, and the old linguistic boundaries, to the recent arrangement, to show the connection of the latter with problems of strategy and mineral resources, and to explain the manner in which international interests were influential in shaping the settlement as respects especially the left bank of the Rhine, the Saar Valley, and the mines. Mr. Lord dwelt little upon the previous history of Poland, but discussed the new Poland, its boundaries and its future, from the point of view of race, language, and religion. Mr. Whyte in a brilliant address, sympathetic to the liberals of the world, but premising that they had expected too much from the peace conferences, described the main currents of force at work there—the overmastering desire of the French for security, the attachment of Baron Sonnino to the old principles of the balance of power, the new conceptions of international order put forward by President Wilson, conceptions grateful to millions in Europe, and the dubious position occupied by the British prime minister in view of an election in which the "war-mind" had predominated, and the consequent necessity that the result should be a compromise. Yet it was a compromise which, thanks to President Wilson, contained the means of its own betterment.

In a conference devoted to the recent history of the Far East, Prof. Stanley K. Hornbeck, of the University of Wisconsin, reviewed the technical aspects of the Shantung question in the light of the historical events of the last 25 years, and criticized adversely the provisions of the recent treaty on the subject. Prof. Kenneth S. Latourette, of Denison University, read a valuable paper on the "Missionary factor in the Chinese situation," the historical portion of which appraised the results of Catholic and Protestant missionary endeavors in China in mediating between east and west, in accelerating the adoption in China of elements from western civilization, in increasing the influence of western nations and in some respects weakening the empire politically, in furthering political and social reform, in "westernizing" the educational system and democratizing learning, and in improving physical health. The paper of Prof. Edmund D. Soper, of Northwestern University, on "Democracy and progress in present-day Japan" gave rise to an unusual amount of discussion, relating to the degree in which militarism and the democratic spirit, respectively, prevail or are likely to prevail in the Japanese Empire.

On the colonial period of American history three papers were presented. That óf Prof. M. W. Jernegan, of the University of Chicago, on "Slavery and the beginnings of industrialism in the American Colonies," has been printed in the American Historical Review.[7] That of Prof. Herbert C. Bell, of Bowdoin College, on "Materials for study in West Indian archives," was based on the labors of its author in the West Indian classes of the Colonial Office Papers at London, in preparing an inventory of that material for the department of historical research in the Carnegie Institution of Washington. The period to which the paper related was that between 1708, the date reached by the last-published volume of the Calendars of State Papers, Colonial, and the year 1775. The material consists mostly of correspondence between colonial officials and the secretary of state and board of trade. Its uses for the student of the history of the British Empire rest on its value for the study of the commercial and diplomatic, and in a less degree the military and naval, relations between that Empire and the other powers possessing colonies in the West Indies. To the student of the mainland colonies the West Indian correspondence offers material not only for the knowledge of intercolonial trade, but also for the better understanding, by comparison and contrast, of many elements in the development of the different communities on the continent.

To the history of colonial relations with the mother country Prof. Beverley W. Bond, jr., of Purdue University, contributed a paper on the "Colonial agent as a popular representative," tracing in detail the development of that official, in the southern colonies, as a representative of the lower house in controversies with the governor and council, and showing how the necessity for the consent of governor and council in order to secure appropriations for the agent's salary and expenses limited the power of the lower houses to use him, and by what means and how far they prevailed.

In a later period of American history the foreign policy of Alexander Hamilton was expounded from materials in the archives of the British foreign office, by Dr. Samuel F. Bemis, of Colorado College, in a paper read in a joint session with the Mississippi Valley Historical Association. Hamilton's genius had created American credit. American nationality depended on the ability of the new Government to meet its financial obligations. Thirteen-fifteenths of American revenues came from customs duties on imports from England. This was the reason why Hamilton made peace with Great Britain fundamental in his policy, and why he "went behind" Jefferson's office in secret negotiations which Dr. Bemis described.

In the same session Dr. Reginald C. McGrane, of the University of Cincinnati, set forth the "American position on the Revolution of 1848

---

[7] January, 1920.

in Germany," first with respect to the strict observance of neutrality by A. J. Donelson, minister to Prussia and to Germany, and secondly with respect to the efforts of Baron von Roenne, Prussian minister in Washington, to create a navy for Prussia and Germany—efforts considerably helped by the Polk administration, but abruptly checked by Taylor and Clayton. Another aspect of foreign relations in the same troubled period was covered by a paper of Dr. Chauncey S. Boucher, of the Ohio State University, on "Southern opinion in regard to the Mexican War and the accession of territory." From his study of speeches, newspapers, and correspondence, published and unpublished, he concluded that the South did not support the Mexican War in its earlier period for the sake of conquest of future slave States, but was forced by the Wilmot proviso to become interested, in a negative and defensive way, in preventing the war from being used to serve an aggressive purpose by the enemies of slavery, and thus toward the end of the war there developed a strong southern sentiment against acquisition of territory.

The paper by Prof. Thomas M. Marshall, of the University of Colorado, on the miners' laws of the region now embraced in that State, is printed in the American Historical Review.[8]

Three papers bore on the history of the Civil War. One, in the military field, was that of Mr. Alfred P. James, of the University of Pittsburgh, on the "Strategy of concentration on the part of the Confederates in the Mississippi Valley in the spring of 1862," in which the drastic concentration effected by Gen. A. S. Johnston at Corinth was described, and the effects of concentration unaccompanied by unity of command and followed by defeat were analyzed. The second of the Civil War papers was one of Prof. Louis B. Schmidt, of the Iowa State College, on the "Internal grain trade of the United States" during that period.[9] The third, figuring in a series concerning "Nationalism in American history," was that of Prof. Nathaniel W. Stephenson, of the College of the City of Charleston, on "Lincoln and the progress of nationality in the North." He discussed with much acuteness the hindrances to the development of a complete nationalism which were presented by the anti-Lincoln secret societies (Sons of Liberty, Knights of the Golden Circle, and the like) rhetorical and infirm of purpose; by the profiteering element whose patriotism did not rise above the level of zeal for the American woolen industry; by the otherwise mindedness and emotional individualism of Greeley and Wendell Phillips and the Cleveland convention. Loyalty to the smaller territorial units had been broken down in the North, but it was still far from a complete nationalism. In Lincoln's influence in helping forward that consummation, char-

---

[8] April, 1920.
[9] Printed in the Iowa Journal of History for January, 1920.

acteristic elements were his acceptance of federalism and the representative system as permanent features of our political science, and his belief that the laboring masses were the part of the Nation entitled to the greatest share of its benefits.

Continuing the subject of nationalism, in a paper entitled "Fifty years of American nationalism, 1865–1918," Dr. Charles A. Beard, of the Bureau of Municipal Research, New York, set forth nationalism as working in an economic pattern; capitalism first of all showing those national and international tendencies which were natural to it, then agrarianism, and then labor adopting nationalistic principles. Finally, "American nationality and recent statecraft" were considered by Prof. William E. Dodd, of the University of Chicago, in a brilliant and thought-provoking paper on the history of the last six years. Substantially, it was an explanation and defense of President Wilson's course from the time when the outbreak of the Great War in Europe endangered his large program of economic reform. He compared the President's delays upon decision and action in a divided country, in which neither party convention of 1916 advanced beyond neutrality, to the wise delays for which Lincoln was so warmly abused in March and April, 1861; described his effort after entrance into the war as essentially an effort to incite the Nation to victory by emotional appeals and yet to preserve the world from subsequent delivery to the forces of economic imperialism; and emphasized the reactionary quality of the opposition which had tied his hands in peace making.

Of two papers in the history of the labor movement, that of Dr. Selig Perlman, of the University of Wisconsin, on the "Historical basis of the tactics of the American Federation of Labor," argued that history showed action through trade unions as more likely to be potent under American conditions than action through a labor party. The paper by Prof. Frank T. Carlton, of De Pauw University, on "Three upheavals in the American labor movement," dealt with the premature but brilliant flare of unionism that marked the "thirties," extinguished by the panic of 1837; the extraordinary development of the Knights of Labor in the "eighties," its rise out of excess of immigration and its disintegration; and the movement of the last four years, in which the American Federation of Labor has grown from 2,000,000 members in 1915 to 3,250,000 in 1919; and he analyzed those elements in the present situation which forbid argument from earlier analogies.[10]

In the sessions of the Agricultural History Society, besides the papers of Messrs. Kelsey, Stine, and Schmidt, already mentioned, Mr. Lyman Carrier, of the Bureau of Plant Industry, at Washington, read a paper on the "Colonial agriculture of Rhode Island," and Mr. Herbert A. Kellar, of the Cyrus McCormick Library in Chicago, one on

[10] See his book, Organized Labor in American History, New York, 1920.

" Some aspects of the agricultural revolution of the United States in the first half of the nineteenth century." The former described particularly those traits of Rhode Island agriculture that flowed from the peculiarities of the Narragansett country. The latter gave attention mainly to the rise and increase, especially between 1830 and 1850, of agricultural journals and societies and fairs, books and libraries, and State institutions helpful to agricultural progress.

Three papers were read in a session or conference devoted to Hispanic-American affairs, of which two were historical in character— that of Prof. W. S. Robertson, of the University of Illinois, on " Latin-American appreciations of the Monroe Doctrine," [11] especially at the time of the Venezuela-Guiana boundary dispute of 1895–1896, and that of Prof. W. W. Pierson, jr., of the University of North Carolina, on the views respecting the Monroe Doctrine expressed by the conservative Argentine publicist Alberdi.

The business meeting of the association, which took place on the second afternoon, was notable among the annual meetings for the variety and importance of the matters which were laid before the members.[12] In the absence of the secretary, Mr. Leland, kept away from the meetings by illness, Prof. St. George L. Sioussat acted as secretary pro tempore. From the secretary's report it appeared that the total membership of the association was 2,445, a decrease of 74 from a year ago and of 481 from the figures of 1915, when the membership of the association reached its highest point. The net loss, however, was smaller than in any of the three preceding years in which a loss had been sustained, being less by 61 than the loss of a year ago, while the number of members whose dues had been paid was over 200 greater than the corresponding number last year. It would appear that while a certain decline in membership has been inevitable because of the war—a decline which it may be said is not confined to the historical association—there are many reasons for believing that the downward tendency has now ceased and for expecting a substantial increase in members during the coming year. The secretary promised that a directory of the association, in process of compilation, would soon be published as a part of the annual report for 1918. Attention was called to the refusal of the Railroad Administration to grant reduced fares on account of the meetings of learned societies, and members were warned to be on their guard against certain so-called historical societies which are in fact commercial organizations, and which, because of similarity in names, are likely to be confused with the American Historical Association.

The report of the treasurer, Mr. Moore, showed the finances of the association to be in a most satisfactory condition; the net receipts of

[11] Printed in the Hispanic-American Review for February, 1920.
[12] See below for minutes of business meeting, with reports of officers and committees.

the year were $10,833; the net disbursements, $8,120, an excess of receipts over disbursements of $2,713. The assets of the association in cash and in Liberty bonds amounted to $33,476, an increase since 1918 of $2,716. The American Historical Review fund was reported as amounting to $2,105 in addition. The treasurer reported that the voluntary contributions of $1 which had been requested from the members had amounted to $1,432. Nothing gives clearer evidence of a healthy condition of sentiment in the association than so abundant a response to such a request, which it has been thought expedient to make each year rather than to propose to increase the annual dues to $5, as so many societies have done.

The secretary of the council, Prof. Greene, reported, as required by the constitution, the decisions and recommendations of that body. A committee of three had been named to examine the records of the association in Washington, destroy those of no value, arrange the others for permanent preservation, and prepare for publication such of the more important records of the council and association as might be deemed suitable. The council had voted to take over in the name of the association the associate membership in the American Council on Education previously held by the National Board for Historical Service; and it had voted to suspend the public archives commission and the standing committee on bibliography for the current year and to refer the question of the future of these two committees to the committee on policy for consideration and report. Two special committees, however, took the place of the two standing committees thus suspended—a committee on the preparation of a primer of archives, consisting of Mr. Victor H. Paltsits and Mr. Leland, and a committee, headed by Prof. George M. Dutcher, to cooperate with the American Library Association in the preparation of a manual of historical literature on the same general plan as that of C. K. Adams (1882). The council voted to rule that only essays formally submitted to the Winsor and Adams prize committees should be considered as having been entered in the competition.

Other votes of the council may be summarized as follows: The committee on publications was authorized to dispose of the unbound copies of the prize essays in stock; the council committee on London headquarters was directed because of the institution in London of the British division of the American University Union in Europe to give legal notice of the termination of the present agreement with the Royal Historical Society for the rental of the room, to make such payments as might be necessary to meet the legal obligations of the association in connection with the London branch, to dispose of the furniture and books on hand, and to express the thanks of the association to the officers of the branch for their services.

Prof. Cheyney, chairman of the committee on the bibliography of modern English history, was authorized to take such preliminary steps as may be necessary, in conjunction with the British committee, for the resumption of the committee's work. It was voted to omit the customary meeting of the council at Thanksgiving time. It was voted to discontinue the present board of advisory editors of the Historical Outlook and in its place to create a new body to be called the board of editors, composed of five members, who should serve for one year, who should cooperate with the present managing editor, and who should report such proposals respecting the future relations of the association and the Outlook as might seem desirable at the end of a year.

Upon recommendation by the council the association voted to join the newly organized American Council of Learned Societies and to authorize the treasurer to pay as the annual dues of the association in the council a sum not exceeding 5 cents per member. The association also voted to adopt the following amendments to the constitution and to the by-laws:

For Article IV substitute the following:

ART. IV. The officers shall be a president, two vice presidents, a secretary, a treasurer, an assistant secretary-treasurer, and an editor. The president, vice presidents, secretary, and treasurer shall be elected by ballot at each regular annual meeting in the manner provided by the by-laws. The assistant secretary-treasurer and the editor shall be elected by the executive council. They shall perform such duties and receive such compensation as the council may determine.

For Article V. 1, substitute the following:

ART. V. There shall be an executive council, constituted as follows:
1. The president, the vice presidents, the secretary, and the treasurer.

To by-law IV add the following paragraph:

The council may provide for the payment of expenses incurred by the secretary, the assistant secretary-treasurer, and the editor in such travel as may be necessary to the transaction of the association's business.

The association voted that the next annual meeting should be held at Washington in the last days of December, 1920. It also voted to adopt an agreement which had been concerted with the Agricultural History Society, and which is printed on a later page, providing for a certain measure of affiliation between the two organizations.

The committee on the Adams prize reported that it had awarded the prize to Asst. Prof. William T. Morgan, of the Indiana State University, for his essay entitled "English political parties and leaders during the reign of Queen Anne, 1702–1710," which is to be published as Volume VII of the Yale Historical Publications.

The association adopted expressions of regret at the retirement of the secretary of the association, Mr. Leland, and the secretary of the council, Mr. Greene, who had served since 1908 and 1913, respectively, and whose services have indeed been of inestimable value. Memorials of Ex-Presidents White, Henry Adams, Roosevelt, and Stephens, who had died since the last meeting of the association, were adopted. The gift of $1,000 from the National Board for Historical Service, already mentioned, and designated as the Andrew D. White fund, was accepted by the association.

A report of the committee on nominations was presented by its chairman, Prof. Charles H. Ambler, of the University of West Virginia. In accordance with its recommendations Prof. Edward Channing, first vice president of the association, was elected president; Dr. J. J. Jusserand, first vice president; Prof. Charles H. Haskins, second vice president; Prof. John S. Bassett, secretary; and Mr. Charles Moore, treasurer. The new members chosen to the council were Prof. James T. Shotwell, of Columbia University, and Miss Ruth Putnam, of Washington. A full list of officers and members of the council and committees appears on a later page. In accordance with the provisions of the constitution as amended, the council elected Miss Patty W. Washington assistant secretary-treasurer, and Mr. Allen R. Boyd, of the Library of Congress, editor. The council reelected Dr. J. Franklin Jameson to the board of editors of the American Historical Review, for the term 1920–1925, and elected Prof. Dana C. Munro to the vacancy in the board caused by the resignation of Prof. Charles H. Haskins, the newly elected second vice president. Dr. Jameson and Prof. Haskins were elected delegates of the association to the American Council of Learned Societies.

PROGRAM OF THE THIRTY-FOURTH ANNUAL MEETING OF THE
AMERICAN HISTORICAL ASSOCIATION, HELD IN CLEVELAND,
OHIO, DECEMBER 29-31, 1919.

Saturday, December 27.

10.30 a. m. Meeting of the executive council. Parlor J.

Monday, December 29.

8 a. m. Breakfast session of the executive committee of the Mississippi Valley
Historical Association.

10 a. m. American history. Joint conference with the Mississippi Valley
Historical Association. Assembly hall. Chairman, Milo M. Quaife, president
of the Mississippi Valley Historical Association. The Transylvania project:
the last phase; Archibald Henderson, University of North Carolina. The
foreign policy of Alexander Hamilton; Samuel F. Bemis, Colorado College.
The American position on the Revolution of 1848 in Germany; Reginald C.
McGrane, University of Cincinnati. Southern opinion in regard to the Mexican War and the accession of territory; Chauncey S. Boucher, Ohio State
University. The strategy of concentration in the Mississippi Valley in the
spring of 1862; Alfred P. James, University of Pittsburgh.

10 a. m. Joint conference with the historical societies and the National Asso-
ciation of State War Historical Organizations. New lounge. Chairman, Thomas
L. Montgomery, State librarian of Pennsylvania. The preservation of war
material. Discussion: Frank H. Severance, Buffalo Historical Society; Burd S.
Patterson, Historical Society of Western Pennsylvania; Wallace H. Cathcart,
Western Reserve Historical Society; Frank M. Gregg, Cleveland. The publi-
cation of war material. Discussion: Arthur K. Davis, chairman of Virginia
War History Commission; Benjamin F. Shambaugh, superintendent of the
Iowa Historical Society; Albert E. McKinley, University of Pennsylvania.

10 a. m. Session of the Agricultural History Society. Assembly lounge.
The home market in New England, 1810–1860; Percy W. Bidwell, Yale University. Possibilities of intensive research in agricultural history; R. W.
Kelsey, Haverford College. Jared Eliot's essays on husbandry in New England—1760; Rodney H. True, Bureau of Plant Industry, Washington.

12.30 p. m. Luncheon session, jointly with the American Association of Uni-
versity Professors. Ballroom. The work of the Association of University
Professors; Arthur O. Lovejoy, president of the Association of University
Professors.

2.30 p. m. Conference on the report of the committee on history and education
for citizenship in the schools. Assembly hall. Chairman, Andrew C. McLaughlin,
University of Chicago. Presentation of the committee's report; Joseph Schafer,
University of Oregon. Presentation of the course for the teachers' training
schools; Frank S. Bogardus, Indiana State Normal School. Discussion (10 minutes for each): The elementary grades; Charles A. Coulomb, district superintendent of schools, Philadelphia. The junior high-school grades; Henry E.

Bourne, Western Reserve University. The senior high-school grades; James Sullivan, University of the State of New York. Application of the course to conditions in the South; Milledge L. Bonham, jr., Hamilton College. Application to conditions in New England; Herbert D. Foster, Dartmouth College. Application to conditions in the Middle West; James A. James, Northwestern University. The standpoint of the National Education Association's committee; Daniel C. Knowlton, Lincoln School of Teachers' College. General discussion from the floor, under the 5-minute rule.

2.30 p. m. Conference on economic history. New lounge. Chairman, Frederick L. Paxson, University of Wisconsin. The miners' courts of Colorado; Thomas M. Marshall, University of Colorado. The historical basis of the tactics of the American Federation of Labor; Selig Perlman, University of Wisconsin. Three upheavals in the American labor movement; Frank T. Carlton, De Pauw University. The present condition of economic history; Norman S. B. Gras, University of Minnesota.

6 p. m. Dinner session of the National Board for Historical Service. One hundred suite.

8.15 p. m. Presidential addresses. Joint session with the Political Science Association. Ballroom. Chairman, Paul L. Feiss, president of the Cleveland Chamber of Commerce. Recent fallacies in history; William R. Thayer, president of the American Historical Association. Present tendencies in American politics; Henry J. Ford, president of the American Political Science Association.

10 p. m. Smoker, American Political Science and American Historical Associations. Union Club.

Tuesday, December 30.

10 a. m. Joint conference with the Political Science Association on the Russian Revolution. Statler Hotel, ballroom. Chairman, Henry J. Ford, Princeton University. The November revolution in Russia; Jerome Landfield, Russian Economic League, New York City. The Soviet Government in Russia; Edward A. Ross and Selig Perlman, University of Wisconsin. The future Russian constitution as seen by Russian liberals, Baron S. A. Korff.

10 a. m. Joint conference with the Agricultural History Society. New lounge. Chairman, Rodney H. True, president of the Agricultural History Society. The internal grain trade of the United States during the Civil War decade; Louis B. Schmidt, Iowa State College. Colonial agriculture of Rhode Island; Lyman Carrier, Bureau of Plant Industry, Washington, D. C. Some aspects of the agricultural revolution of the United States in the first half of the nineteenth century; Herbert A. Kellar, Cyrus McCormick Library, Chicago. Notes on Egyptian agriculture in Ptolemaic times; Oscar C. Stine, Department of Agriculture, Washington, D. C.

10 a. m. Conference on Hispanic-American History. Assembly hall. Latin American appreciations of the Monroe doctrine; William S. Robertson, University of Illinois. The changed attitude of Latin America toward the United States; W. E. Dunn, University of Texas. The recent attitude of the Brazilian press toward the United States and the Monroe doctrine; William R. Manning, Department of State. The future of the Monroe doctrine; Hiram Bingham, Yale University. Alberdi's views on the Monroe doctrine; W. W. Pierson, jr., University of North Carolina. Discussion: James A. Robertson, Hispanic-American Review; Charles E. Chapman, University of California.

12.30 p. m. Luncheon given by the trustees of the Western Reserve Historical Society to the members of the American Historical Association. Ballroom. Luncheon session. Chairman, William P. Palmer, president of the Western Reserve Historical Society. Publicity at the peace conference; Ray Stannard

Baker, member of the American Peace Mission. The aims of the National Association of State War Historical Organizations; James Sullivan, State historian of New York.

2.30 p. m. Annual business meeting. Assembly hall.

4 to 6 p. m. A reception to the women of the association by the College Club. 1958 East Ninety-third Street.

6 p. m. Dinner conferences. Two groups can be announced; one of those interested in the history of the war; another of those interested in the history of the Far East. Those wishing to attend the former will make reservations through Bernadotte E. Schmitt, Western Reserve University; the latter through Kenneth S. Latourette, Denison University, or at the headquarters of the association not later than 9 a. m. of the day of the conference. Other groups by arrangement.

8.15 p. m. General session. Ballroom. Chairman, William Roscoe Thayer. The Franco-German frontier; Charles H. Haskins, Harvard University. The new Poland; Robert H. Lord, Harvard University. The peace treaty of Versailles, 1919; Alexander F. Whyte, M. P., 1910–1918, London.

Wednesday, December 31.

10 a. m. Conference on modern European history. New lounge. Chairman, Carl L. Becker, Cornell University. England's earliest empire; Edward P. Cheyney, University of Pennsylvania. Some problems of the British Crown Colonies and Dependencies, Arthur Percival Newton, University of London. Some problems of British Imperial Federation; Arthur L. Cross, University of Michigan.

10 a. m. Conference on American Colonial History. Assembly lounge. Chairman, Herman V. Ames, University of Pennsylvania. Materials for study in West Indian archives; Herbert C. Bell, Bowdoin College. Slavery and the beginnings of industrialism in the American Colonies; Marcus W. Jernegan, University of Chicago. The Colonial Agent as a popular Representative; Beverly W. Bond, jr., Purdue University. Factors and forces involved in the control of colonies and commerce in the central administration; Winfred T. Root, University of Wisconsin.

10 a. m. Conference on the history of science. Assembly hall. Chairman, George L. Burr, Cornell University. History of Egyptian medicine (illustrated); T. Wingate Todd, Medical School, Western Reserve University. Peter of Abano, a medieval scientist; Lynn Thorndike, Western Reserve University. The history of algebra; Louis C. Karpinski, University of Michigan. The problem of the history of science in the college curriculum; Henry Crew, Northwestern University. Discussion: William A. Locy, Northwestern University; Harry E. Barnes, New School for Social Research.

12.30 p. m. Luncheon given to the members of the Political Science Association and the American Historical Association by the president and trustees of Western Reserve University. Ballroom. Luncheon conference on world conditions and college training. Chairman, Charles F. Thwing, president of Western Reserve University; Andrew C. McLaughlin, University of Chicago; Arthur Percival Newton, University of London.

2 p. m. Ancient History Conference. Assembly lounge. Subject: The historical background of some of the issues before the Peace Conference. Chairman, A. E. R. Boak, University of Michigan. German historians and Macedonian imperialism; John R. Knipfing, Ohio State University. The Epirus-Albania boundary dispute in ancient times; Herbert Wing, jr., Dickinson College.

Roman policy in Armenia and its significance; David Magie, Princeton University.

2 p. m. Conference on the recent history of the Far East. Assembly hall. Chairman, Evarts B. Greene, University of Illinois. Russian colonization and policy in Eastern Asia; David P. Barrows, University of California. Internal development of the Chinese Republic since 1911; Paul S. Reinsch, Washington, D. C. The missionary factor in the Chinese situation; Kenneth S. Latourette, Denison University; Democracy and progress in present-day Japan; Edmund D. Soper, Northwestern University. Discussion: William J. Hail, Yale College in China; Sidney L. Gulick, formerly Imperial University, Kioto, Japan.

2 p. m. Conference on nationalism in American history. New lounge. Chairman, Edward Channing, Harvard University. The psychology of nationalism; Max S. Handman, University of Texas. Lincoln and the sense of nationality in the North; Nathaniel W. Stephenson, College of the city of Charleston. Fifty years of American nationalism, 1865–1918; Charles A. Beard, Bureau of Municipal research, New York. Reason and emotion in recent American history. William E. Dodd, University of Chicago.

4.30 p. m. Visits to the Cleveland Museum of Art and the Western Reserve Historical Society.

6 p. m. Subscription dinner of the Mississippi Valley Historical Association. Address by Albert J. Beveridge.

MINUTES OF THE ANNUAL BUSINESS MEETING OF THE AMERICAN HISTORICAL ASSOCIATION, HELD IN THE ASSEMBLY HALL OF THE HOLLENDEN HOTEL, CLEVELAND, OHIO, DECEMBER 30, 1919.

The meeting was called to order at 2.30 p. m., President William Roscoe Thayer presiding.

The president appointed Messrs. J. R. H. Moore and Daniel C. Knowlton as a committee to inspect the report of the treasurer and the report of the American Audit Co. thereon.

The president called attention to the absence, on account of illness, of the secretary of the association, and appointed as secretary pro tempore, Mr. St. George L. Sioussat.

The report of the secretary of the association was then read by the secretary pro tempore. This report, which is printed in full below, gave statistics as to the membership of the association; described the progress made in the compilation of a directory of the association; commented on the refusal of the United States Railroad Administration to grant concessions in rates for the annual meeting; called attention to so-called historical societies of a commercial type which have adopted names similar to that of the association; and referred to the members whom the association had lost by death during the year just past.

It was voted that the report of the secretary be received and placed on file.

The treasurer of the association presented an informal explanation of the treasurer's report and of the abstract thereof which had been placed in the hands of the members present. On motion, the report of the treasurer was accepted and placed on file.

The treasurer made a preliminary statement as to the budget proposed for the coming year.

The committee upon audit reported that they had examined the records submitted to them and found them to be correct. The report was accepted and placed on file.

The secretary of the council presented a summary of the actions of the executive council, with the recommendations of the council to the association. This was prefaced with the reading by the secretary of the council of a memoir on the late Henry Morse Stephens, former president of the association, which had been adopted by the council.

Upon the motion of Mr. C. L. Burr, the association, by a rising vote, expressed its approval of the memoir.

The secretary of the council read parts of a letter received from Dr. Henry Schouler, a former president of the association, in which he expressed regret at his inability to be present at this meeting.

At the suggestion of the secretary of the council, Mr. E. P. Cheyney, for the board of editors of the American Historical Review, and Mr. H. Barrett Learned, for the committee on publications, made brief statements as to the work of the board and the committee, respectively, during the period since the last meeting and as to the plans for the future.

Upon the motion of the secretary of the council, the budget for the ensuing year, which had been read by the treasurer, was adopted, as follows:

Secretary and treasurer	$2,500
Pacific Coast Branch	50
Nominating committee	25
Membership committee	150
London headquarters	75
Program committee	150
Conference of historical societies	25
American Council of Education	10
American Council of Learned Societies	125
Rio Janeiro congress	25
Committee on publications	750
American Historical Review	4,400
Committee on bibliography	75
Writings on American History	200
Committee on bibliography of modern English history	150
Historical Manuscripts Commission	150
Herbert Baxter Adams prize	200
Military history prize	250
Committee on policy	150
Committee on history and education for citizenship in the schools	350
Legal services	500
	10,310

ESTIMATED INCOME.

Annual dues	6,800
Sale of publications	200
Royalties	75
Interest	1,350
Registration fees	125
Miscellaneous	75
	8,625

Mr. G. E. Fellows moved that, in view of the definite refusal of the United States Railroad Administration to grant concessions in rates for this meeting, and in view of a late report to the effect that this ruling had been rescinded, the secretary of the association be requested hereafter, in sending out notices of the annual meeting, to urge all members who should attend the meeting to secure certificates from the railroads, whether prior notice of reduced rates should have been given or not. The motion was adopted.

After further discussion, in which Messrs. Charles Moore, Schafer, Jameson, Gipson, G. S. Ford, and Paltsits participated, it was voted, upon the motion of Mr. Charles Moore, that a committee be appointed by the president to take up the matter of railroad rates and see if the reduction could not even now be obtained. The president appointed as members of this committee Messrs. Charles Moore, Fellows, and G. S. Ford.

The secretary of the council resumed the reading of his summary and the recommendations of the executive council.

Upon the motion of the secretary of the council it was voted to approve the recommendation of the council to the effect that the next annual meeting of the association—that for 1920—be held in Washington, D. C.

The secretary of the council read the following recommendations submitted by the council to the association, and moved their adoption:

1. That the American Historical Association hereby ratifies the convention establishing the American Council of Learned Societies devoted to the humanistic studies and authorizes and directs the president and the secretary to sign the constitution of said council in the name of the association.

2. That the executive council of the American Historical Association be, and hereby is, authorized and directed to maintain the representation of the Association in the American Council of Learned Societies by the election of delegates as provided for in the constitution of that body.

3. That the treasurer of the American Historical Association be, and hereby is authorized to pay annually to the secretary-treasurer of the American Council of Learned Societies a sum not to exceed 5 cents for each person or institution which was a member of the American Historical Association on the 1st of January preceding each such annual payment.

Brief statements in elucidation of these recommendations of the executive council were made by Mr. C. H. Haskins and Mr. J. F. Jameson.

The recommendations were approved by the association.

The secretary of the council read the following agreement with the Agricultural History Society, the ratification of which was recommended by the council:

It is agreed:

I. That the Agricultural History Society shall hold its principal literary meeting at the same time and in the same city as selected by the American Historical Association.

II. The Board of Editors of the American Historical Review agree to carry a special rubric, "Agricultural History Society," in the section devoted to historical news, whenever a sufficient number of appropriate items shall be furnished by the society.

III. It is further agreed that a maximum of 300 pages in the Annual Report of the American Historical Association be allotted to the Agricultural History Society, with the full autonomy to act in the choice of material for that report, subject to the approval of the committee on publications of the American Historical Association and of the proper officials of the Smithsonian Institution.

IV. Separate reprints of the section of the Annual Report devoted to the Agricultural History Society shall be furnished to the society at the cost of the same to the American Historical Association.

V. That the American Historical Association shall allow the following representation of the Agricultural History Society:

1. The president of the Agricultural History Society, or a representative chosen by that official, may attend the meetings of the council of the American Historical Association and discuss matters pertaining to the welfare of the Agricultural History Society, but will not be granted a vote in the council.

2. The chairman of the publications committee of the Agricultural History Society shall be ex officio a member of the committee on publications of the American Historical Association.

3. The secretary-treasurer of the Agricultural History Society shall be a member of the program committee of the American Historical Association and shall assist in arranging for the program of the joint annual meeting.

VI. That the terms of this agreement shall be in force until January 1, 1920, but may extend for a definite or indefinite period by the mutual consent at the annual business meetings in 1919 of the two organizations.

Mr. J. F. Jameson moved that the terms of the agreement be extended to January 1, 1921, subject to extension at the annual business meeting of 1920 and that the agreement be approved.

Mr. R. W. Kelsey spoke in support of the agreement.

The motion was adopted.

Mr. Hiram Bingham moved that the executive council inquire into the reasons for the withdrawal by the Department of State of Mr. W. R. Manning's paper, and take whatever action may seem to them to be appropriate thereon.

Mr. G. L. Burr seconded the motion of Mr. Bingham.

Mr. Coleman inquired if Mr. Manning's connection with the Department of State might not afford a sufficient explanation of the withdrawal of his paper.

The matter was further discussed by Messrs. Anderson, Robertson, and Bonham, after which the motion of Mr. Bingham was carried.

Upon motion by the secretary of the council it was voted to approve the action of the council in voting that hereafter competition for the Winsor and Adams prizes should be limited to essays submitted by the contestants.

The secretary of the council presented the following proposed amendments to the constitution and by-laws, which had been approved by the council, with the recommendation that they be adopted by the association:

For Article IV, substitute the following:

ARTICLE IV. The officers shall be a president, two vice presidents, a secretary, a treasurer, an assistant secretary-treasurer, and an editor.

The president, vice presidents, secretary, and treasurer shall be elected by ballot at each regular annual meeting in the manner provided by the by-laws.

The assistant secretary-treasurer and the editor shall be elected by the executive council; they shall perform such duties and receive such compensation as the council may determine.

For Article V, 1, substitute the following:

ARTICLE V. There shall be an executive council, constituted as follows:
1. The president, the vice presidents, the secretary, and the treasurer.

To by-law IV add the following paragraph:

The council may provide for the payment of expenses incurred by the secretary, the assistant secretary-treasurer, and the editor in such travel as may be necessary to the transaction of the association's business.

On motion the amendments to articles IV and V of the constitution were severally adopted.

On motion the amendment to article IV of the by-laws was adopted.

The president read the following resolution, which, upon the motion of Mr. G. L. Burr, had been adopted by the executive council:

Resolved, That, before considering the proposed amendment to the constitution and by-laws, the council desires to express its deep regret that the two secretaries find it necessary to withdraw, and its high appreciation of their long and efficient service.

Upon motion by Mr. I. J. Cox it was voted that the hearty endorsement of the association be given to the resolution as read.

Mr. L. H. Gipson moved that the thanks of the association be extended to Mr. Learned for his services as chairman of the committee on publications. The motion was adopted.

Mr. C. H. Ambler, for the committee on nominations, after explaining the necessity for changes in the nominations as originally printed and distributed to members of the association, presented the following nominations for officers, members of the council, and members of the committee on nominations for the ensuing year:

President, Edward Channing.
First vice president, Jean Jules Jusserand.
Second vice president, Charles H. Haskins.
Secretary, John Spencer Bassett.
Treasurer, Charles Moore.
Members of the executive council: Henry E. Bourne, George M. Wrong, Herbert E. Bolton, William E. Dodd, Walter L. Fleming, William E. Lingelbach, James T. Shotwell, Ruth Putnam.
Committee on nominations: Victor H. Paltsits, Carl Russell Fish, J. G. de Roulhac Hamilton, Frank H. Hodder, Eloise Ellery.

The president called for nominations from the floor. There being none, it was voted by unanimous consent that the secretary pro tempore be instructed to cast the ballot of the association for the nominees presented by the committee on nominations.

The secretary pro tempore reported that he had cast the ballot as directed, and the persons whose names appeared in the report of the nominating committee were declared elected.

President William R. Thayer thanked the association for the honor which he had enjoyed and yielded the chair to the incoming president, Mr. Edward Channing, who made a brief acknowledgment.

The secretary of the council moved that the secretary of the association be requested to frame suitable expressions of appreciation upon the part of the association to those individuals and bodies in Cleveland to whose hospitality the association was indebted. The motion was adopted.

Mr. J. F. Jameson, on behalf of Mr. Schafer, vice chairman of the National Board for Historical Service, which, on December 29, 1919, adjourned without day, reported the following minute and resolution of the board:

The National Board for Historical Service, finding itself in possession of a considerable sum of money derived from royalties on a book prepared under its auspices, adopted on December 29, 1919, the following resolution:
That the board offer to the American Historical Association the sum of $1,000, derived from the royalties of the board, together with an assignment of all future royalties, to be kept, together with all interest which may accrue from these sums, as a separate trust fund, to be called the Andrew D. White fund, from which expenditures shall be made, in such manner as the council shall direct, for historical undertakings of an international character through the American Council of Learned Societies or through such other methods as the council may order.

The secretary of the council read the memoirs adopted by the executive council at its meeting of January 31, 1919, respecting the late Andrew D. White, the late Henry Adams, and the late Theodore Roosevelt.

The secretary of the council announced the following appointments by the executive council to the standing committees of the association for the ensuing year, with preliminary observations as to the essential changes in some of the committees:

Historical manuscripts commission.—Justin H. Smith (chairman), E. C. Barker, Mrs. Amos G. Draper, Logan Esarey, Gaillard Hunt, C. H. Lincoln.

Public archives commission.—Commission suspended for 1920.

Special committee on a primer of archives.—Victor H. Paltsits (chairman), W. G. Leland; these two to select one or more additional members.

Committee on the Justin Winsor prize.—Frederic L. Paxson (chairman), A. C. Cole, C. H. Haring, F. H. Hodder, N. W. Stephenson.

Committee on the Herbert Baxter Adams prize.—C. J. H. Hayes (chairman), C. H. McIlwain, Nellie Neilson, Bernadotte E. Schmitt.

Editor of American Historical Review (to serve six years from Jan. 1, 1920).—J. F. Jameson.

Committee on bibliography.—Committee suspended for 1920.

Special committee to cooperate with the American Library Association in the preparation of a manual of historical literature.—G. M. Dutcher, S. B. Fay, A. H. Shearer, H. R. Shipman.

Committee on publications.—H. B. Learned (chairman); other members ex officio.

Secretary conference of historical societies.—John C. Parish.

Committee on national archives.—J. F. Jameson (chairman), Charles Moore, Lieut. Col. O. L. Spaulding.

Committee on membership.—T. J. Wertenbaker (chairman), Louise Brown, E. H. Byrne, A. C. Krey, F. E. Melvin, R. A. Newhall, Julia S. Orvis, C. W. Ramsdell, J. G. Randall, A. P. Scott, J. J. Van Nostrand, jr., G. F. Zook.

Board of editors, Historical Outlook (to serve in cooperation with A. E. Mc-Kinley, managing editor, for one year from Jan. 1, 1920).—Edgar Dawson, L. M. Larson, Lucy M. Salmon, St. George L. Sioussat, W. L. Westermann.

Committee on program, thirty-fifth annual meeting.—C. J. H. Hayes, chairman; other members to be selected by the council in consultation with the chairman.

There being no further business, the meeting adjourned.

ANNUAL REPORT OF THE SECRETARY OF THE AMERICAN HISTORICAL ASSOCIATION AT THE ANNUAL MEETING IN CLEVELAND, DECEMBER 30, 1919.

As most of the more important matters which come before the association at this time will be presented by the secretary of the council or by the chairmen of various committees, the report of the secretary deals only with the membership of the association and with one or two other matters which call for especial emphasis.

Membership.—The total membership of the association on December 18 was 2,445, of which 107 are life members. This figure shows a decrease of 74 from a year ago and of 481 from 1915, when the membership of the association reached its highest point. There are various reasons, however, why the showing this year is encouraging rather than otherwise. The net loss is smaller than in any of the three preceding years in which a loss has been sustained, being less by 61 than the loss of a year ago. The number of members whose dues are paid to date is 2,032, which is 225 more than a year ago. The total loss during the year of 282 is the smallest total loss since 1915, while the total number of new members is 208, which compares favorably with recent years and is 58 more than last year. This increase in the number of new members is particularly encouraging in view of the fact that no systematic campaign for new members has been conducted during the last two years. With the revival of the membership committee and the individual cooperation of the members of the association there is every reason to expect that the association will quickly make good the losses which it, in common with similar associations, has sustained during the war years.

Directory.—The compilation of a directory of the association is being carried forward rapidly, although some delay is experienced by reason of the failure of more than a third of the members to make prompt returns. At present about 1,500 of the blanks have been returned. A month ago the secretary's office had occasion to compile the occupational statistics of the association so far as the 1,200 questionnaires then on hand permitted this to be done. The results of this compilation were as follows: Teachers in universities and colleges, 506; teachers in schools, 248; archivists, librarians, secretaries, etc., 83; research, editing, and writing, 63; students, 31. That is, 931 out of 1,205 members are professionally or chiefly engaged in historical work. Of the remaining 274, there are 80 lawyers, 69 business men, 25 clergymen, 17 publishers, 15 in public service, 9 physicians, 8 farmers, 7 engineers, and 7 Army officers. The remaining 37 are retired or engaged in miscellaneous occupations.

The directory will be published as part of the annual report for 1918, and those members who have made a voluntary contribution of $1 to the funds of the association, as well as those who have specially requested a copy at 30 cents, will receive separate reprints of it. It is expected that these will be distributed early in February. It had been expected to include the record of war services of members in the directory, but this does not appear to the officials of the Smithsonian Institution to be appropriate to the annual report, and these records will be printed separately as a special supplement of the Historical Outlook.

Railroad rates.—In the course of preparation for the present meeting application was made to the United States Railroad Administration for the concessions in rates authorized for the meetings of religious, educational, charitable, and fraternal organizations. This application was refused on the ground that the American Historical Association, as well as the other learned and scientific societies meeting at this time, was not an educational body according to the definition of the term educational adopted by the Railroad Administration. Appeal made in person from this decision was unavailing. The correspondence with the Railroad Administration has been printed and sent to all members of the association. It seems to the secretary that this decision of the Railroad Administration constitutes an unjust discrimination against learned societies and calls for vigorous protest on their part.

Questionable societies.—Once more the members of the association are warned to be on their guard, and to give similar warning to their friends, against one or two so-called historical societies which are in fact commercial organizations and which have adopted names similar enough to that of our association to cause confusion. Numerous complaints have reached the offices of the association during the past year of the practices of the representatives of these corporations.

Deceased members.—During the last two years the association has lost 74 members by death. Their names will be recorded in the annual report, but I can not refrain from calling the names of those who have served the association in conspicuous fashion: Andrew D. White, the first president of the association; Henry Adams, Theodore Roosevelt, and H. Morse Stephens, all former presidents; and A. Howard Clark, assistant secretary, secretary, and curator.

Respectfully submitted.

WALDO G. LELAND, *Secretary.*

DECEASED MEMBERS, 1919.

Joseph Ashbrook, Philadelphia, Pa.
Hubert Howe Bancroft (life member), San Francisco, Calif.
Edmund Mills Barton (life member), Worcester, Mass.
Kemp Plummer Battle, Chapel Hill, N. C.
Nathan W. Blanchard, Santa Paula, Calif.
Henry Lewis Cannon, Stanford University, Calif.
French Ensor Chadwick, Newport, R. I.
Albert Hayden Chatfield, Cincinnati, Ohio.
A. Howard Clark, Washington, D. C.

Percy Robert Colwell, Lawrenceville, N. J.
Hazel Louise Edgerly, Wollaston, Mass.
George Taylor Files, Brunswick, Me.
Wilson M. Foulk, Charleston, W. Va.
Louis F. Frank, Milwaukee, Wis.
Charles Lang Freer, Detroit, Mich.
Samuel Abbott Green (life member), Boston, Mass.
Charles Francis Himes, Carlisle, Pa.
Charles Sumner Holt, Chicago, Ill.
William Roscoe Livermore, Boston, Mass.
Calvin Morgan McClung, Knoxville, Tenn.
Minnie Elizabeth McKenzie, Cincinnati, Ohio.
William W. Manning, Boston, Mass.
Francis Martin, Chattanooga, Tenn.
Gempachi Mitsukuri, Tokyo, Japan.
Theodore Roosevelt (life member), Oyster Bay, N. Y.
George A. Root, New Haven, Conn.
Eben Greenough Scott, Wilkes-Barre, Pa.
Emory Speer, Macon, Ga.
Mrs. Samuel (Louisa V.) Spencer, Washington, D. C.
Henry Morse Stephens (life member), Berkeley, Calif.
Richard Taylor Stevenson, Delaware, Ohio.
Frank Arthur Updyke, Hanover, N. H.
W. H. Williams, Kansas City, Mo.
Mrs. H. M. (Mary J.) Wilmarth, Chicago, Ill.
Henry Ernest Woods, Boston, Mass.

ANNUAL REPORT OF THE TREASURER, NOVEMBER 29, 1919.

Balance Dec. 1, 1918		$3,253.28
Receipts to date:		
Annual dues	$6,780.38	
Partial dues of members in war service	25.35	
Voluntary contributions paid with dues	1,432.00	
Life membership dues	150.00	
Interest on investments	[1] 1,729.86	
Sales of publications—		
Prize essays	$255.24	
Papers and reports	72.68	
Writings on American history	72.95	
	400.87	
Royalties	85.72	
Advance payments for directory	17.00	
Gift for London headquarters	140.00	
Interest on bank account	52.60	
Miscellaneous	19.02	
		10,832.80
Total ordinary receipts		14,086.08
Sale of bank stock	4,500.00	
Payment of mortgage	20,000.00	
		24,500.00
Total receipts to date		38,586.08
Total disbursements to date		33,401.36
Balance on hand Nov. 29, 1919		5,184.72

[1] This item includes $518.57 received from accrued interest on Liberty bonds.

Disbursements December 1, 1918, to November 29, 1919.

Secretary and treasurer, vouchers 79, 80, 81, 82, 88, 89,
92, 94, 95, 97, 98, 101, 111, 112, 113, 114, 114a, 116,
117, 118, 121, 124, 127, 128, 129, 130, 135, 139, 140, 145,
150, 151, 152, 153, 154, 157, 158, 159, 160, 161, 162, 166,
171, 172, 173, 174, 175, 177, 180, 181, 183, 184, 185, 191,
192, 193, 194, 195:

Salary of assistant	$1,200.00	
Additional assistance and services	143.75	
Postage	210.65	
Telegrams, messenger service, express, money order fees	29.81	
Notary fees	5.50	
Stationery and supplies	113.60	
Printing and duplicating	157.20	
Furnishings	20.18	
Auditing treasurer's report, 1918	30.00	
Rent of hall for organization of Agricultural History Society	15.00	
Flowers	57.62	
Miscellaneous	8.85	
Postage and services, office of the secretary of the council	11.60	
Publications for use of Adams prize committee	5.07	
		$2,008.83

Executive council, vouchers 102, 103, 104, 105, 106, 107,
123, expense of travel to attend meeting of executive
council in New York, Jan. 31–Feb. 2, 1919:

H. E. Bourne	45.76	
W. L. Fleming	74.76	
E. B. Greene	66.22	
Lucy M. Salmon	4.96	
S. B. Harding	38.12	
Charles Moore	16.32	
Edward Channing	18.28	
		264.42
Committee on program, voucher 196, printing and stationery		24.00

Committee on publications, vouchers 85, 99, 115, 122, 125, 131,
137, 141, 142, 155, 167, 168, 169, 178, 187, 188, 189, 197, 198,
199:

Wrapping and mailing	$5.34	
Postage and express	17.64	
Storing and insuring	163.79	
Advertising	11.00	
Printing and supplies	25.75	
Editorial services and proof reading	176.40	
Miscellaneous	4.50	
		404.42

American Historical Review, vouchers 132, 133, 134, 143, 144, 156, 163, 170, 179, 186, 190, 200, 201, 202		4,206.25
Historical manuscripts commission, vouchers 108, 120, transcription of Calhoun papers		100.00
Herbert Baxter Adams prize, voucher 100, payment of prize for 1917		200.00
Justin Winsor prize, voucher 110, payment of prize for 1918		200.00

London headquarters, vouchers 109, 165, 176:

Rent	$140.00	
Doorplate	4.40	
		144.40
Writings on American history, vouchers 146, 182		200.00

Committee on history and education for citizenship, vouchers
126, 136, 138, 147, 164:

Postage	$33.35	
Printing and supplies	70.25	
		103.60

Bills payable Dec. 1, 1918, vouchers 78, 83, 84, 86, 87, 90, 91, 93, 96:

Secretary and treasurer, services	$3.68	
Committee on program, printing and supplies	38.75	
Conference of historical societies, postage and printing	26.58	
Committee on publications, postage	17.48	
Winsor prize committee, final payment on prize for 1918	50.00	
Abandoning meeting—		
Services	$6.80	
Postage and telegrams	105.03	
Printing and supplies	15.75	
		127.58
		$264.07

Total ordinary disbursement		8,119.99

Investments, vouchers 119, 148, 149, Liberty bonds (par value, $26,200; accumulated interest, $518.57), 4¼ per cent of 1927–1942 (registered):

Amount paid for bonds	$24,703.80	
Accumulated interest	518.57	
Commission	59.00	
		25,281.37
Total disbursements		33,401.36
Net ordinary receipts		10,832.80
Net ordinary disbursements		8,119.99
Excess of receipts over disbursements		2,712.81

Assets of the association in cash and securities.

Cash on hand in Union Trust Co		$5,184.72
Liberty bonds (par value, $29,450):		
4¼ per cent of 1928, registered	$2,100.00	
Coupon	350.00	
4¼ per cent of 1933–1938, registered	5,197.25	
Coupon	300.00	
4¼ per cent of 1927–1942, registered	20,065.55	
		28,012.80
Accrued interest on Liberty bonds		90.05
Cash in Central Trust Co. of New York (endowment fund)		188.91
		33,476.48

(Increase during year, $2,716.54.)

Assets of the American Historical Review in cash and securities		2,105.44
Total combined assets		35,581.92

(Increase during year, $3,508.70.)

The association has other assets in the form of personal property, the estimated value of which is:

Publications in stock	$7,280.00	
Furniture, office equipment, books	425.00	
		7,705.00
Grand total, all assets		43,286.92

AMERICAN HISTORICAL REVIEW—ANNUAL REPORT OF THE TREASURER, Nov. 29, 1919.

Balance Dec. 1, 1918		1,358.28
Receipts to date:		
Payments by Macmillan for editorial expenses	$2,400.00	
Refund by The Athenaeum	1.00	
Interest	53.03	
		2,454.03
		3,812.31

Disbursements Dec. 1, 1918, to Nov. 29, 1919:

Petty cash, warrants 30, 36, 38, 41, 42, 47, 48, 56, 57, 58, 61, 64, 66_____		$157. 62
Stationery, printing, supplies, warrants 31, 33, 37, 52_		41. 75
Contributions to Review, warrants 34, 43, 55, 60—		
January, 1919_____	$218. 75	
April, 1919_____	320. 75	
July, 1919_____	392. 50	
October, 1919 _____	306. 00	
		1, 238. 00
Transcription of documents for the Review, warrants 53, 59_____		50. 00
Binding, warrants 45, 49, 67_____		11. 00
Publications, warrants 32, 35, 44, 46, 54, 63, 65_____		71. 53
Travel, warrants 39, 40, 50, 51_____		115. 98
Investments, warrant 62—		
Liberty bonds (par value, $1,200; accumulated interest $24.37), 4¼ per cent of 1933–1938 (registered)—		
Amount paid for bonds_____	$1, 131.64	
Accumulated interest_____	24. 37	
Commission _____	3. 00	
		1, 159. 01
		$2, 844. 89
Balance November 29, 1919_____		967. 42

The assets of the Review in cash and securities are:

Cash on hand in Union Trust Co_____	967. 42
Liberty bonds, 4¼ per cent of 1933–1938 (registered)_____	[1]1, 131. 64
Accrued interest on bonds_____	6. 38
Total _____	2, 105. 44

CHARLES MOORE, Treasurer.

WASHINGTON, D. C., *November 29, 1919.*

REPORT OF THE AMERICAN AUDIT CO.

Mr. CHARLES MOORE,   DECEMBER 16, 1919.
     Treasurer American Historical Association,
                         Washington, D. C.

DEAR SIR: We have audited the accounts of the American Historical Association from December 1, 1918, to November 30, 1919, and submit our report, including the following exhibits:

Exhibit A.—Assets as at November 30, 1919.

Exhibit B.—Statement of receipts and disbursements, general, from December 1, 1918, to November 30, 1919.

Exhibit C.—Statement of receipts and disbursements, American Historical Review, from December 1, 1918, to November 30, 1919.

We verified the cash receipts, as shown by the records, and the cash disbursements with the receipted vouchers on file and found the same to agree with the treasurer's report.

The cash on hand in the different funds was reconciled with the bank statements.

---

[1] Par value $1,200.

The securities of the association were submitted for our inspection and found to be as called for by the records.

Respectfully submitted.

THE AMERICAN AUDIT COMPANY,
by C. R. CRANMER,
Resident Manager.

[SEAL.]

Approved:

    F. W. LAFRENTZ, *President.*

Attest:

    A. F. LAFRENTZ, *Secretary.*

EXHIBIT A.—Assets as at Nov. 30, 1919.

General:

Cash on hand	$5,184.72	
Liberty bonds (par value $29,450)	28,012.80	
Accrued interest on Liberty bonds	90.05	
Inventories (not verified by the American Audit Co.)—		
Publications (estimate)	7,280.00	
Furniture, office equipment (estimate)	425.00	
		$40,992.57
American Historical Review:		
Cash on hand	967.42	
Liberty bonds (par value $1,200)	1,131.64	
Accrued interest on Liberty bonds	6.38	
		2,105.44
Endowment fund:		
Cash on hand	188.91	188.91
		43,286.92

NOTE.—No liabilities are reported other than small current bills, the amount of which is not known at this time.

EXHIBIT B.—Receipts and disbursements, Dec. 1, 1918, to Nov. 30, 1919.

Receipts:

Annual dues	$6,805.73	
Life memberships	150.00	
Voluntary contributions	1,432.00	
Publications	400.87	
Royalties	85.72	
Advance payments for directory	17.00	
Interest—		
Investments	[1] 1,729.86	
Bank account	52.60	
		1,782.46
Gift for London headquarters		140.00
Miscellaneous receipts		19.02
		10,832.80
Sale of American Exchange National Bank stock		4,500.00
Payment of mortgage		20,000.00
Total receipts		35,332.80
Cash on hand Dec. 1, 1918		3,253.28
		38,586.08

[1] This item includes $518.57 received from accrued interest on Liberty bonds.

Disbursements:
```
Secretary and treasurer-------------------------------------- $2,008.83
Committee on publications----------------------------------      404.42
Committee on program---------------------------------------       24.00
Committee on history and education-------------------------      103.60
Executive council------------------------------------------      264.42
Historical Manuscripts Commission--------------------------      100.00
Writings on American history-------------------------------      200.00
The Macmillan Co., American Historical Review furnished to
    members ----------------------------------------------    4,206.25
London headquarters ---------------------------------------      144.40
Winsor prize ----------------------------------------------      200.00
Adams prize------------------------------------------------      200.00
Accounts payable Dec. 1, 1918------------------------------      264.07
Liberty bonds purchased (par value, $26,200)--------------   24,762.80
Accrued interest Liberty bonds to date of purchase--------       518.57
```

```
    Total disbursements------------------------------------   33,401.36
Cash on hand Nov. 30, 1919----------------------------------    5,184.72
```

                                                               38,586.08

EXHIBIT C.—*American Historical Review, receipts and disbursements, Dec. 1, 1918, to Nov. 30, 1919.*

Receipts:
```
The Macmillan Co., per contract---------------------------- $2,400.00
Refund from E. G. Lang-------------------------------------        1.00
Interest—
    Liberty bonds -----------------------------    $25.51
    Bank account-------------------------------     27.52
```

                                                               53.03
```
    Total receipts ----------------------------------------    2,454.03
Cash on hand Dec. 1, 1918-----------------------------------    1,358.28
```

                                                                3,812.31

Disbursements:
```
Petty cash-------------------------------------------------  $157.62
Stationery, printing, and supplies-------------------------     41.75
Contributions to Review------------------------------------  1,238.00
Transcription of documents---------------------------------     50.00
Binding----------------------------------------------------     11.00
Publications-----------------------------------------------     71.53
Traveling expenses ----------------------------------------    115.98
Liberty bonds purchased (par value, $1,200)---------------   1,134.64
Accrued interest on Liberty bonds to date of purchase------     24.37
```

```
    Total disbursements------------------------------------    2,844.89
Cash on hand Nov. 30, 1919----------------------------------     967.42
```

                                                             3,812.31

REPORT OF THE HISTORICAL MANUSCRIPTS COMMISSION.

I beg leave to state that the publications committee decided to bring out the Santa Anna letters with the report for 1917. This made it incumbent on the Historical Manuscripts Commission to offer something else for the 1918 report, and the autobiography of Martin Van Buren, edited by Mr. Fitzpatrick, of the Library of Congress, was proposed and accepted.

The rest of the commission's program is expected to work out as it was presented to the council last February. (See Annual Report, 1918.)

Respectfully submitted.

JUSTIN H. SMITH, *Chairman.*

NOVEMBER 11, 1919.

REPORT OF THE PUBLIC ARCHIVES COMMISSION.

The Public Archives Commission being without appropriation for the year 1919 made no formal report. The chairman of the commission, Mr. Victor H. Paltsits, offered, with the approval of the other members of the commission, the following plan for the reorganization of the Public Archives Commission:

PLAN FOR REORGANIZATION.

ART. 1. There shall continue to be a Public Archives Commission, under the auspices of the American Historical Association.

ART. 2. The commission shall consist of a chairman, a secretary, and a commissioner for each State of the United States. Said persons must be members of the American Historical Association.

ART. 3. The officers and commissioners mentioned in article 2 shall be appointed by the executive council of the American Historical Association.

ART. 4. Each commissioner appointed as aforesaid for his State shall have authority to appoint two "adjunct commissioners" in his State, to associate with him in promoting the interests of the archives of his State; and each commissioner shall report annually, or oftener when requested so to do, to the chairman of the commission, with respect to the progress of archival matters in his jurisdiction. The "adjunct members" need not be members of the American Historical Association. The respective State commissioners shall coordinate their work with the national work of archives by their reports and correspondence with the chairman and secretary of the commission.

ART. 5. The chairman shall cooperate in advancing the general interests of archives in the Nation and shall preside at all conferences or other assemblies that are organized by the commission.

ART. 6. The secretary shall keep the records of conferences and other meetings organized by the commission and conduct the correspondence in cooperation with the chairman and aid him in the preparation of reports, papers, or other materials for publication by the American Historical Association under the usual methods prescribed by the association for its publications.

The chairman also recommended that a special committee should be appointed to proceed with the preparation of the Primer on Archives.

REPORT OF THE COMMITTEE ON PUBLICATIONS.

The annual meeting of the association, which was planned to be held at Cleveland, Ohio, December 26–28, 1918, was omitted. The omission of this meeting has reduced somewhat the work of your committee during 1919.

The two volumes of the Annual Report for 1916 have been distributed—Volume I was distributed in July, and Volume II (correspondence of R. M. T. Hunter, 1826–1876, edited by C. H. Ambler), in October. The single volume for 1917 (Philadelphia meeting) is now being indexed.

The Annual Report for 1918 (at present in galley proof) will consist of two volumes. Its contents were partially arranged at the time of the meeting in New York City (Feb. 1, 1919) of the council. Readjustments and additions of materials have been made since that date. Aside from Mr. William Roscoe Thayer's presidential address, "Vagaries of Historians," printed, but never delivered; it was proposed to include (i) reports, council minutes, and other matter respecting various activities of the association; (ii) a list of historical societies over the country and pertinent data relating to such societies; (iii) "Letters of Santa Anna" (thirteenth report of the Historical Manuscripts Commission), edited by Dr. Justin H. Smith; and (iv) an account, extending over about 150 pages, of the war activities of historians working either under the direction of the National Board for Historical Service or otherwise engaged. In order to push Dr. Smith's careful work on the Santa Anna letters more promptly into print, it has been possible to add them to the contents of the annual report for 1917. The detailed report of war activities it now seems best to postpone to the report for 1919. Besides other items, above listed, Volume I, for 1918, will include four papers and a document, all bearing on the history of American agriculture, as follows: "A Brief History of the Sheep Industry in the United States," by Dr. L. G. Connor; "Dr. John Mitchell, Naturalist, Cartographer, and Historian," by Lyman Carrier; "Historical Aspects of the Surplus Food Production of the United States, 1862–1902," by Dr. William Trimble; "Early Days of the Albemarle Agricultural Society," by Dr. Rodney H. True; Minute Book of the Albemarle (Va.) Agricultural Society, prepared for publication by Dr. Rodney H. True. The volume is to be concluded by a much-needed directory of members of the American Historical Association for 1919, the last directory having been printed as a separate pamphlet in 1911.

The Autobiography of Martin Van Buren, issued as the fourteenth report of the Historical Manuscripts Commission, constitutes Volume II of the Annual Report for 1918. It has been printed from a manuscript now and for years past in the possession of the Library of Congress. Editorial work necessary to make the manuscript available in print to scholars or readers was begun some years ago by Mr. Worthington C. Ford. Only about a fifth of the manuscript was prepared by Mr. Ford. Completion of the task of editing was more recently entrusted to the competent hand of Mr. John C. Fitzpatrick, assistant chief of the manuscripts division. To the courtesy of Mr. Appleton P. C. Griffin, acting librarian in the absence overseas of Dr. Herbert Putnam, librarian, and to Mr. Fitzpatrick's patient industry, the association is indebted for the privilege of being able to bring this important contribution to political history to the light of print.

The autobiography was begun in 1854, when Van Buren was 71 years old. It was abandoned—far from being completed—in 1860. Van Buren died, it may be recalled, on July 24, 1862. Opening the story of his life with some account of his forebears, Van Buren concluded it with reflections on the attempt of the senatorial triumvirate (Webster, Clay, and Calhoun) to demoralize and degrade him in the eyes of the Senate in 1834, while he was acting as presiding officer of that body. It must be regarded as a distinct loss to political history that the author took no account of affairs during his term as President. Among matters of minor interest will be found the record of a visit to Jefferson at Monticello, an explanation of the election of John Quincy Adams in 1824, and reflections on the Senate's refusal in 1832 to confirm his nomination as minister to England. The important portions of the autobiography are concerned with Andrew Jackson in his relations to his cabinet and the men of his epoch. Close attention is given to the nullification and bank controversies. The character sketch of Jackson is remarkable. There will also be found fresh judgments on Clay, Calhoun, Webster, De Witt Clinton, Rufus King, John Randolph of Roanoke, Louis McLane, John Quincy Adams, William J. Duane, Levi Woodbury, and others. The old man's sense of chronology was erratic and at times confused. Nevertheless his skill in estimating men and in discovering their motives reveals an extraordinary knowledge of human nature.

The annual report for 1919 may now be in part forecast. There will be two volumes. Volume I will comprise such papers as come from the Cleveland meeting, the minutes and proceedings of the association recorded during the earlier years and now being gathered by Messrs. E. B. Greene and W. G. Leland, and a directory of local historical societies, which is in process of compilation by Dr. Augustus H. Shearer, librarian of the Grosvenor Library of Buffalo,

N. Y. Volume II will consist of the first instalment of the papers of Stephen F. Austin, edited by Prof. Eugene C. Barker, and designed as the Fifteenth Report of the Historical Manuscripts Commission. The Austin papers are sufficiently elaborate to make three volumes when the editorial work has been completed. The scope of the materials in these papers is, it is believed, broad enough to make their publication of rather general interest.

A recommendation recently made by the docket committee of the council suggests to the association a new officer, to be termed editor, such an officer to be appointed by the council and presumably to be paid an annual salary. If the plan meets with the approval of council and association, the duties of the officer will be defined and his compensation indicated. At the risk of appearing to be premature, I wish to record my approval of the proposed position. To have a reliable editor interested in the arrangement of materials for the printer, in proof reading, and such other details as naturally arise in connection with the publications of the association would facilitate the work of the chairman and his collegues on the publications committee. Might it not be desirable to utilize the editor as secretary of the committee on publications?

Last January the committee on the Justin Winsor prize announced the award of the prize to Dr. Arthur M. Schlesinger, of Columbus, Ohio, for his essay printed as volume LXXVIII of the Columbia University Studies in History, Economics, and Public Law, and entitled " The colonial merchants and the American Revolution, 1763–1776." This, it may be observed, is the first award of this prize for a printed work in accordance with a revision of the rules governing the Justin Winsor and the Herbert Baxter Adams prizes—a revision decided upon and carefully set forth at the Philadelphia meeting of the association in December, 1917. (See Annual Report for 1917, p. 59.)

In this connection it should be noted that the association still remains under the obligation to promote the publication of Lieut. F. L. Nussbaum's essay which was awarded the Adams prize in March, 1918, and entitled, " G. J. A. Ducher: An essay in the political history of mercantilism during the French Revolution." In my report last year (Vol. I, p. 56) I referred to this matter. An effort was made to interest a publisher in Lieut. Nussbaum's manuscript. At present it is in the hands of the author, now connected with the Temple University at Philadelphia. It has been slightly revised as a result of new evidence discovered by the author while serving with the American Army in France. It would seem only fair to appropriate a sum of money for the publication of this essay as the concluding volume in the series of prize essays.

Sales of publications (including royalties) during the past three years brought in the following amounts: 1916–17, $542; 1917–18, $260.06; 1918–19, $503.59. The falling off in the amount during 1917–18 was chiefly owing to the fact that during that year the association published no prize essay. Out of the appropriation made to this committee last year of $500, the expenditure by November 30, 1919, was $404.42. The conspicuous cost item, visibly increasing from year to year, is that for storing and insuring the bound and unbound copies of the prize essays. Our latest payment for storage and insurance called for $163.79. Several times before this I have called attention to this same matter. Toward the reduction of this annual payment I request that authority be granted to the chairman of the publications committee in consultation with the treasurer and secretary of the association to dispose of all unbound copies of the prize essays—at present 2,783 in number—on the best terms that can be made. The association will still hold 1,039 bound copies of the essays in varying lots—a supply that will meet the customary demand for some years to come.

The need of advertising our publications was brought again to the attention of the council at its meeting in New York City on Saturday, February 1. " The proper place regularly to advertise our publications," I then said, "would appear to be the American Historical Review, now the recognized organ of the association. If two pages of the Review were devoted to this purpose we should be able to keep the titles of the prize essays and those of other association publications regularly before the public." This suggestion proved to be acceptable to the council after consultation with the board of editors of the Review. Moreover, it met with the generous encouragement of Mr. George P. Brett, president of the Macmillan Co., who assigned two pages gratuitously for the purpose. The April and July numbers of the Review, accordingly, carried a brief summary of the organization and objects of the association, together with titles of all the prize essays and of some other publications. The October and January (1920) numbers contain similar but slightly revised lists. It would be desirable in future, I think, to work into these two pages lists of officers in the association, together with the names of chairmen of all important committees. Another year the chairman of this committee should be able to indicate certain tangible results, I hope, in the way of increased sales arising from this new project of advertising.

We are indebted to Mr. Brett for another matter that should at this time be given as wide publicity as possible in and outside the association. I refer to his encouragement of the project, first outlined last February in my report, of publishing this coming year a volume of historical essays or papers selected chiefly from the volumes of the American Historical Review or the annual reports, and especially designed to signalize the twenty-fifth anniversary (October, 1895–October, 1920) of the founding of the Review. The plan was stated originally in this way:

In October, 1920, the American Historical Review will have completed its twenty-fifth year. To members of the association it is needless to dwell at length upon the significance of the Review in directing, vitalizing, and lending encouragement to careful methods of formulating and presenting historical problems. It would be impossible briefly to state its value in establishing correct standards of research or to estimate the aid that it must frequently have given toward the proper solution of difficult historical problems. Is it not time to consider the question of making a collection of selected essays taken from the files of the Review, in the hope of strengthening the Review, gaining for it and the association together a larger group of readers and members? * * * Such a volume of essays might yield notable results. At any rate, the accomplishments of a quarter of a century should give both the Review and the association a permanent place not merely among historical scholars but among a class of readers constantly growing and interested in historical themes and activities. * * *

The council, after consultation with the board of editors of the Review, and with the board's approval of the plan as above set forth, authorized the publication of the volume, provided it could be issued without expense to the association. It referred the plan to a special committee of three, consisting of the chairman of the committee on publications, a member of the board of editors of the Review (the latter to be named by Prof. E. P. Cheyney, chairman of the board), and a third member to act as chairman of the special committee and to be selected by the other two members. The special committee, as thus provided for, is composed of Prof. Dana C. Munro, chairman; Dr. J. Franklin Jameson of the Review; and H. Barrett Learned, of the Publications Committee. When the plan was brought to the attention of Mr. Brett last June he gave it his prompt support, subject to a few conditions, to only one of which I need call attention—viz, that in his judgment only such papers as are likely to be reckoned of permanent interest should find places in the volume. The book will be issued without expense to the association.

'The special committee has nearly completed its unenviable task of selecting out' of some 500 articles about 25 for the projected anniversary volume. Outwardly such a volume might well conform in size, page, and type to a volume of Rhodes's History of the United States. It will contain about 500 pages of reading matter. In making the selections the committee has kept in mind a variety of considerations. Attention has been paid not merely to intrinsic value, but also to breadth of treatment and general interest. Technical articles have been avoided. As a rule it has not seemed best to print articles that have appeared later as parts of a book or as chapters of a continuous narrative. While some of the best known writers are represented by characteristic work, less well known and younger scholars have not been overlooked. We have been at some pains to discover articles characteristic of the best work that during the past quarter of a century has been done in the different fields of ancient, medieval, modern European, and American history.

In conclusion, I wish to bespeak the interest of members of the association in this anniversary volume. It should be useful not only as a record of admirable work accomplished, but as a source of inspiration toward other work to be as well done in the years that are ahead.

Respectfully submitted.

H. BARRETT LEARNED, *Chairman.*

REPORT OF THE COMMITTEE ON BIBLIOGRAPHY.

By action of the council of the association on February 1, 1919, the committee as heretofore existing was abolished, and instead there was appointed only a chairman, with the understanding that he would choose additional members of special committees to cooperate with him in the conduct of special pieces of work. At the same meeting the council referred to the committee the question of cooperation with a committee of the American Library Association in preparing a revised edition of C. K. Adams's Manual of Historical Literature. The American Library Association, through its president, Mr. Bishop, of Ann Arbor, Mich., has appointed Dr. Augustus H. Shearer, of the Grosvenor Library, Buffalo, N. Y.; Mr. H. H. B. Meyer, chief bibliographer, Library of Congress, Washington, D. C.; and Mr. C. W. Reeder, of Ohio State University, Columbus, Ohio. The chairman has asked, in addition to Dr. Shearer, Prof. Sidney B. Fay, of Smith College, Northampton, Mass., and Prof. Dana C. Munro, Princeton University, Princeton, N. J., to cooperate with him in this undertaking. It will, of course, be necessary in addition to the above-named individuals to enlist the services of a considerable number of individuals as reviewers of the various books.

The chairman and Dr. Shearer have twice undertaken to arrange conferences in connection with their other engagements when no additional traveling expenses would be involved but each time the project fell through. The chairman is now inviting the members of the committee to meet with him at breakfast during the Cleveland meeting. As far as the chairman is aware, the committee of the American Library Association has done nothing, but the chairman and Dr. Shearer have exchanged a considerable number of letters with regard to the plans of work, and it is hoped that definite arrangements for the regular prosecution of the undertaking may be put underway early in the new year. We seem to be in reasonable agreement as to the general outlines of the work. As soon as definite work is begun there will be a considerable amount of expenditure, and the chairman has already requested the secretary of the council of the association to arrange for a grant of at least $100 for this work next year. This will perhaps meet the immediate needs, but the serious question in the undertaking has to do with the compensation of the contributors of the reviews of various books which are included. The committee ought to receive authorization from the council of the association if they are to be able to promise any compensation, and it would be scarcely possible to promise less than $100 per title, if there should be any compensation at all, and that would be obviously inadequate to the amount of time and work that would be involved. Even at the rate of $100 per title, the amount involved will run to several hundred dollars.

The only other project of significance which is now under way is the work on the Bibliography of American Travel, which has long been in process. During the past year Dr. Shearer, who has the work in charge, has added some 300 new titles. The question has been raised as to the publication of this bibliography, but the considerable expenditure of money involved has made necessary the postponement of the project from year to year. Would it be possible to spread the publication over a series of years and so spread out the necessary amount to be appropriated? In making this suggestion Dr. Shearer and I have in mind the possibility of publishing installments of the bibliography in the volumes of the annual reports of the association. The chairman has written—some months ago—to the chairman of the committee on publications, raising this question, but has received no response with regard to it. If the project of publication in this fashion should be approved there would need to be an appropriation of at least $100, possibly $200, to cover the preparation of the material for the present.

The chairman may be permitted to report the continuation of his services in preparing materials on recent publications for the successive issues of the American Historical Review, and also to mention his review of American historical publications during the past decade, which was published in the Historical Outlook for December, 1919.

Respectfully submitted.

GEORGE M. DUTCHER, *Chairman.*

REPORT OF THE BOARD OF EDITORS OF THE AMERICAN HISTORICAL REVIEW.

The board of editors beg to report that three numbers of the Review have been published since their last report, and that the number for January 1, 1920, will appear in a few days. In accordance with the plans for retrenchment formerly announced, the total size of the Review for the year has been considerably reduced. But three body articles have appeared in each number, and this will continue usually to be the practice. As a result of this restriction the funds of the board of editors are in much better shape, and it is hoped that the board will be able to pay an appreciable sum into the treasury of the association.

In accordance with the recommendation of the council, the board arranged with the Macmillan Co. for the printing in each number of the Review of a certain amount of advertising of the publications of the association. Mr. Brett readily agreed that this should be without expense to the Review or the association, and, indeed, offered two pages instead of the single page asked for. Beginning with the number for April, 1919, these advertising pages have regularly appeared, the first two numbers giving certain general information concerning the association and a brief list of all publications of the association. The October advertisement has been devoted and that of January will be devoted more particularly to the Review and the prize essays.

The council may be interested to know that the board has secured an agreement from Prof. Antoine Guilland, of L'Ecole Polytechnique Suisse, to prepare a survey of the historical work done in Germany during the last four years not especially connected with the war itself, so much of which, because of war conditions, has not been adequately reported abroad.

A meeting of the board of editors has been arranged for 4.30 o'clock in the afternoon of December 29.

Respectfully submitted,

E. P. CHEYNEY, *Chairman.*

REPORT OF THE SECRETARY OF THE CONFERENCE OF HISTORICAL SOCIETIES.

The situation of the conference of historical societies is as follows:

First. Subscriptions from historical societies in the United States and Canada to the conference of historical societies in 1918 amounted to $34. The increasing absorption in war matters, however, caused the subscriptions to cease, even some which were promised. Consequently the handbook which has been the hope of the conference for some years could not be produced. A large part of the material was at hand, and after consultation with Mr. Leland it was thought best to publish this in the American Historical Association Report for 1917. I understand that this has been done and the material will appear in that form. It, however, shares the disadvantage of other subject material in appearing so long after the facts were secured. Consequently, an up-to-date handbook is still to be desired.

Second. Personal conditions make it impossible for me to continue as secretary according to the plan adopted in 1916. I am no longer in such close touch with the societies and have not the same time to give.

Third. No attempt has been made since the cancellation of the conference at Cleveland in 1918 to secure further subscriptions or to send out a questionnaire for further information from the societies. This is mainly owing to conditions noted in paragraphs 1 and 2.

Fourth. If it is not possible to secure a secretary in my place by action of the conference, who will carry out the plans of 1916-17, I am willing to continue as secretary for another year, but will not feel justified in asking for further contributions from the societies as yet. Hence, as notices are to be sent out, and especially questionnaires, there must be a subsidy of $25 to $50 from the American Historical Association.

The above points seem to indicate the complete failure of the plan adopted in 1916, due to the circumstances mentioned. There will be some who will say that they predicted such a failure, but the secretary is sure that the plan could have been carried out if the conditions had been the same as they were in 1916. As a constructive plan the secretary suggests a return to conditions as they previously existed. These are by no means perfect, but, perhaps, are the best that we can expect at the present time.

The following notice has been sent to historical societies calling the conference to be held in Cleveland:

CONFERENCE OF HISTORICAL SOCIETIES.

The fifteenth annual conference of historical societies will be held at Cleveland, Ohio, December 29, at 10 a. m., at the Hollenden Hotel, in connection with the meetings of the American Historical Association. The conference will be a joint one with the National Association of State War Historical Organizations to discuss the general after-the-war questions.

On the subject of "The care and preservation of war material," which touches every historical society in the country to some degree, the discussion will be led by Mr. Frank H. Severance, of the Buffalo Historical Society; Mr. Burd S. Patterson, of the Historical Society of Western Pennsylvania;

and Mr. Wallace H. Cathcart, of the Western Reserve Historical Society. Poster collections will be discussed by Mr. Frank Gregg, of Cleveland.

The subject of publication of war material affects mainly large societies and specially created commissions. The discussions will be led by Prof. B. F. Shambaugh, of the State Historical Society of Iowa; Hon. Arthur Kyle Davis, of the Virginia commission; Prof. Albert E. McKinley, of the Pennsylvania commission; and Dr. James Sullivan, New York State historian.

The conference two years ago outlined a plan for a handbook, and subscriptions were received and promises of further subscriptions made. Then we went into the war, and no further subscriptions were received, no further attempts made, and the cost of printing went up. The best arrangement possible was to place all the available material in the American Historical Association Report for 1917. This report is to appear shortly, and will give the best and most complete list of historical societies published in recent years.

The secretary has been in active correspondence with many societies in the past two years, and hopes to continue the work of the conference and to give further announcements from time to time.

Respectfully submitted.

                                          AUGUSTUS H. SHEARER,
                                                    Secretary.

DECEMBER 20, 1919.

REPORT OF THE COMMITTEE ON THE HERBERT BAXTER ADAMS PRIZE.

The committee on the Herbert Baxter Adams prize for 1919 announces that 32 essays have been examined, all but 2 of which were in print, and that the award has been given to William T. Morgan, of Indiana University, for his essay on "English Political Parties in the Reign of Queen Anne, 1702–1710."

Respectfully submitted.

                                          RUTH PUTNAM, *Chairman.*

DECEMBER 28, 1919.

REPORT OF THE COMMITTEE ON THE MILITARY HISTORY PRIZE.

At the Charleston meeting (1913) of the association it was announced that a friend, who wished to remain unknown, had donated $250 for a prize for the best essay in American military history. The association accepted the offer and appointed the following committee to formulate conditions of award and conduct the contest: Capt. A. L. Conger, Army Service Schools, Fort Leavenworth; Milledge L. Bonham, jr., Louisiana State University; Allen R. Boyd, Library of Congress; Fred M. Fling, University of Nebraska; Albert B. Hart, Harvard University.

This committee drafted a circular, which was widely distributed, and held a contest in 1915. It was the unanimous opinion of the committee that none of the four essays submitted was worthy of the prize, so on its recommendation the association withheld the award and the committee was continued in service to hold another contest.

Arrangements were being perfected to hold the contest in 1918, when in May, 1916, due to the disturbances on the Mexican border, Capt. Conger was called into active service. He was succeeded as chairman of the committee by Prof. R. M. Johnston, of Harvard. Prof. Johnston pushed to completion the announcement for the 1918 contest, but shortly after it appeared he was drawn into the service of the General Staff of the United States Army (historical section) and sent to France. Mr. Bonham was appointed chairman to succeed him, and the vacancy on the committee was filled by the appointment of Prof. Frank M. Anderson, of Dartmouth.

As all of the members of the committee were doing war work of one sort or another, it was decided to postpone the contest until peace. The two essays which had been submitted were returned to the authors for possible revision and submission later.

In 1919 the chairman removed from Louisiana State University to Hamilton College. Because of Prof. F. M. Anderson's protracted absence in France with the Peace Commission, Prof. D. R. Anderson, of Richmond College, was appointed a member of the committee in his place.

The committee decided to hold the contest in 1920, and, at the suggestion of Mr. Boyd, had its announcement published not only in the historical and military periodicals of this country, but in the leading American and European dailies, in order to give soldiers of the United States and Allied armies an opportunity to compete. A circular was printed in September and has been distributed by the committee and the secretary of the association. The response has been very encouraging. Numerous inquiries from soldiers and civilians have come in and the prospects for a profitable competition appear good.

It is planned to hold a meeting of the committee at Cleveland this month.

Respectfully submitted.

M. L. BONHAM, JR., *Chairman.*

DECEMBER 5, 1919.

REPORT OF THE COMMITTEE OF ARCHIVES IN WASHINGTON.

The committee on the national archive building, charged to do what can be done to bring about the erection in Washington of the building, has labored individually with various Members of Congress upon the subject, and has had frequent informal consultations between members of the committee. The situation last February was as follows: The site had been selected by the Treasury and approved by the members of the commission constituted for that duty by the act of March 3, 1913. The square selected is that bounded by Twelfth and Thirteenth and B and C streets NW. It lies southwest of the Post Office Department and northwest of the National Museum; is a suitable lot and is inexpensive, the buildings now upon it being unimportant. The Treasury has secured options on all the property, and awaits appropriations.

All efforts to secure appropriations in last summer's sundry civil appropriation act were unsuccessful. The feeling of the majority members of the House subcommittee on the pending sundry civil bill is such, with reference to the necessity of cutting from the estimates everything not deemed vitally necessary, in order to reduce six billions of estimates to four billions of appropriations, that your committee see little hope of securing in the bill as it passes the House any appropriation for the purchase of the site or beginning of construction. At the same time the pressure for space for the storage of documents is being so heightened by the return from France of the archives of the American Expeditionary Force that possibly the needful appropriation may be obtained by means of the Senate.

Respectfully submitted.

J. F. JAMESON, *Chairman.*

DECEMBER 11, 1919.

REPORT OF THE COMMITTEE ON HISTORY AND EDUCATION FOR CITIZENSHIP IN THE SCHOOLS.

The original committee of the National Board for Historical Service was organized January 17, 1919. This committee, with the addition of three members, was adopted by the council at its midwinter meeting in New York. Its organization as a committee of eight was effected at a 2-day meeting in Chicago, February 28–March 1.

During the next three months the burden of the work was borne by the chairman and secretary, the former devoting most of his time to the work of the committee, the latter giving half his time to the secretarial duties involved. Most of the correspondence passed through the hands of the secretary. Every effort was made to get in touch with those interested in the problem throughout the country. State and local committees working on the problem, State superintendents of public instruction, selected lists of city superintendents, heads of department in many of our eastern colleges and universities, all the members of the Middle States Association, the New England Association, and many of the members of the Mississippi Valley Association were written and sent copies of our preliminary circular. This also appeared in the Historical Outlook, which placed its columns at our disposal.

Further publicity was given the committee through notices in educational journals and the presentation of its ideas before all the associations mentioned at their meetings and conferences elsewhere with smaller groups.

Committees at work in the related fields of civics, political science, sociology, geography, etc., have been written, with a view to harmonizing our programs if possible.

Meetings were held for two days—morning, afternoon, and evening—in Washington, of the whole committee, to prepare a tentative report as a basis for its final report to the association. This appeared in the pages of the Historical Outlook and was given wide circulation. The chairman and the secretary devoted several weeks of the summer to presenting this before summer schools. A report of the chairman's itinerary and success appeared in the Outlook for November. The secretary was able to visit eight colleges in the East, holding one or more conferences at each, besides interviewing several of the most prominent teachers interested in the solution of the history situation. The committee's program was also presented by other members of the committee at various gatherings of interested educators in different parts of the country. In some cases the program was presented by a person not a member of the committee, but closely in touch with its work.

At the end of June the secretary dismissed his stenographer, and from that time forward simply answered such inquiries as were addressed to him, completing the arrangements for this canvass of the summer schools, to which reference has already been made. The expense of this part of the committee's work was borne by the colleges interested, with the exception of a very small sum.

Contributions were made to the committee from the treasuries of the Middle States and New England Associations.

As to the work still before the committee: The secretary has already submitted a report on the nature and content of the tenth year, but this has not been acted upon. A tentative report has been submitted on the training of teachers. This phase of our program is in the hands of a subcommittee, consisting of Profs. Bagley and Bogardus. The exact content of Grades IX–XII must be fixed or approximately determined. The chairman has been intrusted with blocking out the ninth and eleventh grades. Prof. Johnson has agreed to prepare for the committee the content and an introduction to the first six grades. The work of the twelfth year is perhaps farthest from a definition of any part of the program. Electives in history have not been considered. The relation of the work of this committee to the committee on the definition of the ancient history field, of the New England Association must be determined. The secretary has the manuscript of their report, which they would like the association to publish as a part of the work of our committee. Proposals from the American Sociological Association for a reorganization of the high-school field must be considered, and the relation of this committee to the committee on social studies of the New England Association. In connection with the latter, subcommittees representing our committee and theirs have been at work and a program prepared by them will come before our committee for consideration.

No formal questionnaires have been sent out by the committee except in a few instances. Points of contact have been established with key men and women, and personal correspondence has placed a great deal of material in our hands. The chairman and secretary have spent much time together trying to get this material in shape for the rest of the committee.

The task of bringing all this data together for publication and the problem of what shall go into the report—whether it would not be advisable to secure the cooperation of groups of teachers throughout the country to work out or try out these proposed courses with a view to a more satisfactory definition—must be considered at the coming meetings of the committee in Cleveland. Three meetings of the committee besides the public meeting advertised are planned.

Respectfully submitted.

DANIEL C. KNOWLTON, *Secretary.*

COMMITTEE OF COUNCIL TO ACT ON REPORT OF COMMITTEE ON AMERICAN SCIENTIFIC AND EDUCATIONAL INTERESTS IN THE OTTOMAN EMPIRE.

Your committee, appointed by the executive council February 1, 1919, found that all essential action had already been taken by members of the committee originally appointed, consisting of Profs. Edward C. Moore, James H. Breasted, and Albert H. Lybyer, who in February, March, and April were in a much more favorable position for acting on the American and other representatives in the Peace Conference than anyone could be who remained in Washington and attempted to act through the Department of State there.

It appeared that Prof. E. C. Moore, chairman of the special committee, had already made a general statement to the Secretary of State urging that the attention of the peace delegation be directed toward the general subject of the committee's report. Those parts of the special committee's report which consisted of memoranda respecting educational laws in the Ottoman Empire and the practices of various countries respecting explorations had already been presented to the experts connected with the American mission to negotiate peace. Prof. Lybyer, a member of the special committee, was one of these experts and was present in Paris. Furthermore, the Archæological Institute of America was effectively presenting the whole matter to the peace conference through the activities of Mr. W. H. Buckler. It seemed, therefore, to the committee of the council that there was no appropriate action to be taken other than to inform the Archæological Institute of America of the vote of the council associating itself with that body in presenting to the peace conference the importance of insuring the preservation of the monuments of western Asia. Since, then, however, further developments have taken place which should be noted.

Acting upon a suggestion from the British Academy, the British secretary of state for foreign affairs invited that body to form an archæological committee, composed of representatives of all the principal societies interested in the matter, for the purpose of presenting their views to the various departments of state. With this committee those members of the American commission to negotiate peace who were especially interested in the subject, cooperated, with the result that a small international committee was formed by the Peace Conference, consisting of Monsieur R. Cagnat, permanent secretary of the Academy of Inscriptions and Belles-Lettres; Mr. D. C. Hogarth, representing the British Academy, Signor R. Paribeni, of Rome; and Mr. W. H. Buckler, representing American interests.

This committee in March drew up suggestions for a convention for the protection of antiquities in the Ottoman Empire, providing for the establishment of a subcommission on historical monuments and antiquities which should be attached to the commission on mandates arranged for in Article XXII of the constitution of the League of Nations. The committee also recommended articles to add to the treaty with Turkey, and to conventions to be drawn up between the League of Nations and each of the mandatory powers. Finally, the committee drew up a series of regulations respecting excavations and the disposal of antiquities which in its opinion should be adopted by the mandatory powers. These regulations were intended to secure the preservation of ancient monuments and of archæological objects; to guard against unauthorized exportation and unskillful excavation; to insure an equitable partition of results between the country in question and the explorers; and to prevent monopoly or selfish policy on the part of mandatory powers.

Translations of all these documents are annexed to this report.

The report of this International Archæological Committee was presented at the October session of the International Academic Union in Paris and approved by the delegates present, subject to final approval by their respective principals. The following modifications were, however, suggested:

1. That the scheme proposed should apply only to the portions of the Ottoman Empire placed under mandates, and not to such portions as might be given in full ownership to an independent State.

2. That the members of the proposed subcommission of the League of Nations be appointed by the council of the league upon the nomination of the duly qualified academies of the several States to which such members might belong.

What effects have proceeded from these recommendations is not known to your committee. Messrs. Moore and Lybyer, a majority of the membership of the original committee, having now returned to this country, the present committee respectfully requests to be discharged.

Respectfully submitted for the committee.

J. F. JAMESON, *Chairman.*

RECOMMENDATIONS OF THE INTERNATIONAL COMMITTEE ÓN HISTORICAL MONUMENTS AND ANTIQUITIES.

I. Recommendation for the establishment of a subcommission of the commission on mandatories under Article XXII of the constitution of the League of Nations:

1. The commission on mandatories of the League of Nations shall establish a subcommission on history and archæology, the duty of which shall be to insure the preservation of historical monuments and the antiquities existing within the territory of the Ottoman Empire as it was in 1914, and to encourage search for and study of such monuments and objects.

This subcommission shall be composed of nine persons, eight of whom shall be archæologists, to be named by the commission on mandatories, fot a term of five years, and to be approved by the council of the league. This subcommission shall meet at the seat of the league. Its expenses shall be included in those of the commission on mandatories.

(NOTE.—It was suggested at the October session of the International Academic Union that this be modified in such a way that the functions of the subcommission should extend over only those parts of the Ottoman Empire placed under mandates, and that the members of the subcommittee should be appointed by the council of the league upon nomination by the duly qualified academies of the several States.)

2. The said subcommission shall take cognizance of the reports made to the league by the mandatory powers with respect to historical monuments and archæology. It shall examine all questions which may come before the commission on mandatories relating to this subject, and shall supervise the execution of the regulations and the functioning of the administration of antiquities established by each of the mandatory powers in the territory which shall be assigned to it.

II. Draft of an article to be added (1) to the treaty between Turkey and the associated powers and (2) to the convention between the League of Nations and each of the mandatory powers.

The Ottoman Government (or the mandatory power) shall, within a year after the deposit of ratifications of the present treaty, adopt regulations respecting antiquities, which shall be based upon the principles set forth in Annex A of the present treaty.

The text of the said regulations shall be previously approved by the commission on mandatories, which shall have power to amend it.

Annex A.

Principles of regulations which should be adopted by each of the mandatory powers:

1. The term "antiquity" shall mean any construction or any product of human activity prior to the year 1700.

2. Any person who shall discover an antiquity and shall give notice of such discovery to an employee of the department of antiquities of the country shall be rewarded according to the value of the object found, the principle adopted being the use of encouragement rather than threats.

3. No antiquity shall be sold except to the department of antiquities of the country; but if that department shall decline its acquisition it may then be sold without restrictions. No antiquity shall be taken out of the country without a permit from the said department.

4. Anyone who, either intentionally or through negligence, shall destroy or damage an antiquity or an ancient construction shall become liable to punishment, to be determined by the authority of the country.

5. No clearing or excavation for the purpose of searching for antiquities shall be permitted, under penalty of a fine, except to such persons as have been authorized by the department of antiquities of the country.

6. It shall be the duty of each mandatory power to establish equitable rules for the temporary or permanent expropriation of ground appearing to possess historical or archæological interest.

7. Authorizations for excavations are not to be granted except to persons who furnish sufficient guarantees of archæological experience. None of the mandatory powers shall be entitled, in giving such authorizations, to act in such a way as to exclude, without a proper motive, the scholars of other countries.

8. The products of excavations may be divided between the excavator and the department of antiquities of each country, according to a proportion fixed by that department. If for scientific reasons a division does not seem possible, the excavator shall be entitled to a just compensation in lieu of a portion of the objects found.

DECEMBER 27, 1919.

MINUTES OF THE MEETING OF THE EXECUTIVE COUNCIL OF THE
AMERICAN HISTORICAL ASSOCIATION, HELD AT THE HOLLEN-
DEN HOTEL, CLEVELAND, OHIO, DECEMBER 27, 1919.

The council met at 10.30 a. m. Present: President Thayer, Messrs. Bolton,
Bourne, Burr, Jameson, Lingelbach, Miss Salmon, and the secretary of the
council. Mr. H. B. Learned, chairman of the committee on publications, and Mr.
Joseph Schafer, chairman of the committee on history and education for citizenship in the schools, also attended.,

The illness of the secretary of the association having prevented his attendance,
various items of his report were presented by the secretary of the council and Mr.
Jameson.

The secretary's report showed a total membership on December 18, 1919, of
2,445, as against 2,517 a year ago. The number of members whose dues were
paid was reported as 2,032—an increase of 225 during the past year.

On recommendation of the secretary of the association it was voted to refer to
the committee on policy a proposal respecting membership in the American
Academy of History at Buenos Aires.

The secretary of the council presented the following recommendation from the
secretary of the association respecting the older records of the association in
Washington:

I recommend that a committee of three, residing in Washington, be authorized
to go through the records and destroy all those that are of no conceivable value
or interest and cause the others to be arranged for permanent preservation and
place them on deposit with the Manuscript Division of the Library of Congress,
provided the latter is willing to receive such a deposit. I recommend that this
action apply only to the records prior to December 31, 1908; that the records
since that time be retained in the Washington offices. I further recommend that
this same committee cause to be prepared for publication in the annual report for
1919 such of those records, especially the minutes of the council and reports of
officers and committees, from the organization of the association on to the present
time, as have not yet been printed, and which in the opinion of the committee
should be permanently preserved in printed form.

This recommendation was approved, and Messrs. Leland and Learned were appointed members of the committee for this purpose, with authority to choose the
third member of the committee.

It was voted that the association should take over the associate membership
in the American Council on Education previously held by the National Board for
Historical Service.

On recommendation of the committee on meetings and relations it was voted
to recommend the following votes to the American Historical Association:

1. That the American Historical Association hereby ratifies the convention
establishing the American Council of Learned Societies devoted to the Humanistic Studies, and authorizes and directs the president and secretary to sign the
constitution of said council in the name of the association.

2. That the executive council of the American Historical Association be, and
hereby is, authorized and directed to maintain the representation of the association in the American Council of Learned Societies by the election of delegates
as provided for in the constitution of that body.

3. That the treasurer of the American Historical Association be and hereby
is authorized to pay annually to the secretary-treasurer of the American Council of Learned Societies a sum not to exceed 5 cents for each person or institution which was a member of the American Historical Association on the first
of January preceding each such annual payment.[1]

The secretary of the association reported that a question had arisen as to the
interpretation of the council vote of February 1, 1919, respecting members en-

[1] For organization and constitution of American Council of Learned Societies, see
appendix to these minutes.

gaged in war service. His ruling, that the vote was intended to apply " only to those members whose dues had lapsed or remained unpaid on January 31, 1919," was approved by the council.

Mr. Bolton presented a brief report on behalf of the Pacific Coast Branch.

Brief reports were presented by the secretary of the council on behalf of the following committees and commissions: Historical manuscripts commission, Public archives commission, Winsor prize committee, Adams prize committee, board of editors of the American Historical Review, board of advisory editors of the Historical Outlook, committee on bibliography, conference of historical societies, committee on the military history prize, committee on honorary and corresponding members, committee on the Historical Congress at Rio Janeiro, committee on policy.

Mr. Jameson reported for the committee on national archives and on London headquarters. Messrs. Learned and Schafer reported, respectively, for the committee on publications and the committee on history and education for citizenship in the schools.

It was voted that the public archives commission be suspended and that a special committee be appointed on the preparation of a primer of archives. The question of the future of the public archives commission was referred to the committee on policy for consideration and report.

A question having arisen as to the interpretation of the votes of the association respecting the conditions of the Justin Winsor prize and the Herbert Baxter Adams prize, it was voted that the competition for both prizes should be limited to essays submitted by the contestants.

It was voted that the standing committee on bibliography be suspended and that the question of its future be referred to the committee on policy for consideration and report; with the understanding that the present members of the committee should be continued as a special committee to cooperate with the American Library Association in the preparation of a manual of historical literature. (See council vote of Feb. 1, 1919.)

On the recommendation of the committee on publications it was voted that the chairman of the publication committee, in consultation with the secretary and the treasurer of the association, be authorized to dispose of all unbound copies of the prize essays on the best terms that can be made.

The chairman of the committee on publications having reported that he had been unable to find a suitable publisher for Mr. Nussbaum's prize essay of 1917 (see council vote of Feb. 1, 1919), the question of the obligations of the association in this matter was discussed at some length. The publication committee was thereupon requested, in the light of this discussion, to take up again with Mr. Nussbaum the question of the mode of publication.

Mr. Jameson, as chairman of the committee on London headquarters, made the following statement:

From what your committee has been able to learn from Mr. Biggar, treasurer of the London organization, from Prof. Fish, who for some months had charge of the British branch of the American University Union, and more recently from Prof. A. P. Newton, it does not appear that the room rented by the association in the building of the Royal Historical Society, at 22 Russell Square, has been used to any significant extent by American historical students in London. No doubt the number of such students will be greater hereafter, but, on the other hand, the American University Union, now established at 50 Russell Square, in quarters heretofore used by the American Y. M. C. A. for war work, and in a building which it shares with the Universities Bureau of the British Empire, will hereafter offer nearly all the same advantages which our room offered. It is true that that new establishment does not give students the privileges of the library of the Royal Historical Society, or such opportunities as they may have had at No. 22 Russell Square, for acquaintance with the members of that society and of the English Historical Association. But these latter opportunities were not extensive and at No. 50 students will have compensating advantages in the opportunity to meet a wider variety of American and of British students. The American University Union seems to be assured of continuance, if not of permanence.

Taking into consideration all these things, and also the budget of the American Historical Association, the committee concludes to recommend that the association give up its London headquarters and combine its interests with the others which are represented in London by the American University Union. After the first year, in which the institution was distinctly successful, the war prevented it from doing all the good we expected; but we content ourselves with believing that it has served a useful purpose as one of the contributory means that have helped toward establishing in London more complete arrangements for association of American and English academic interests.

The recommendation we have made to the council involves five steps:

1. Inasmuch as by the terms of our agreement with the Royal Historical Society, dated December 10, 1914, our tenacy is "from December 25, 1914, by the year, terminable by either party giving three months' notice in writing," it would be necessary to give immediate notice to the treasurer of the Royal Historical Society that we wish the agreement to come to an end.

2. We should make an appropriation to pay the rent on the next rent day after the council meeting, March 25, 1920, and, apparently, for three months more, on June 25, 1920. This would mean a payment of £16, and as £2 have already been advanced by the chairman of the committee for completion of the rent due on December 25, 1919, it is suggested that an appropriation that will yield £18, say $75, be made.

3. The furniture of the room should be disposed of. It is suggested that the treasurer in London, Mr. Biggar, be requested to turn over to the American University Union whatever articles of furniture it can use, and sell the rest.

4. Some disposition should be made of the books. Of these there now remain, apparently, only four volumes of guides to archives, published and presented by the department of historical research in the Carnegie Institution of Washington; the annual reports of the American Historical Association, 1903–1911; and some odd numbers of the American Historical Review. It is suggested that these might best be given to the library of the American University Union, which now consists chiefly of 400 or 500 volumes presented by the American Library Association, understood to relate mostly to American history and government.

5. Some message of thanks should be sent to those who have acted as officers of our London branch—Viscount Bryce, chairman; Mr. Hubert Hall, vice chairman; Prof. A. P. Newton, secretary; and Mr. H. P. Biggar, treasurer.

It was voted to approve the foregoing recommendations, with the understanding that the treasurer of the association would make such payments as might be required to meet the legal obligations of the association.

In accordance with the recommendation of the committee on honorary and corresponding members, it was voted that no action be taken on this subject at this time.

The statement made by Mr. Jameson for the committee which was appointed to act on the report of the special committee on American scientific and education interests in the Ottoman Empire was received and the committee discharged. (See council vote of Feb. 1, 1919.)

The secretary of the council reported a communication from Prof. E. P. Cheyney on the continuation of the work of the committee on bibliography of modern English history. It was voted that the work be resumed; that Prof. Cheyney be authorized to take such steps as might be appropriate for this purpose, and that he be requested to nominate his colleagues on the committee.

The session was interrupted at the noon hour for lunch, at which time the choice of a place of meeting for 1920 was informally discussed.

After the noon intermission the committee on appointments presented a partial report, which was approved. (See the list of committee assignments appended to these minutes.)

At 5.30 p. m. the council adjourned to meet the next day, December 28, at 3 p. m. at the University Club.

MINUTES OF THE MEETING OF THE EXECUTIVE COUNCIL OF THE AMERICAN HISTORICAL ASSOCIATION, HELD AT THE UNIVERSITY CLUB, CLEVELAND, OHIO, DECEMBER 28, 1919.

The meeting was called to order at 3 p. m. by President Thayer; other members present as on the previous day, with the addition of Mr. Charles Moore, treasurer.

On the recommendation of the secretary of the association the president, the secretary, and the treasurer of the association were authorized to institute legal proceedings for the protection of the public and of the association against certain so-called "historical societies;" provided that the above-mentioned officers, after full examination of the evidence on hand and after further consultation with legal counsel, deem such proceedings to be advisable.

On behalf of the secretary of the association Mr. Jameson presented the following proposed agreement with the Agricultural History Society, which was approved:

It is agreed:

I. That the Agricultural History Society shall hold its principal literary meeting at the same time and in the same city as selected by the American Historical Association.

II. The board of editors of the American Historical Review agree to carry a special rubric, "Agricultural History Society," in the section devoted to historical news whenever a sufficient number of appropriate items shall be furnished by the society.

III. It is further agreed that a maximum of 300 pages in the Annual Report of the American Historical Association be allotted to the Agricultural History Society, with the full autonomy to act in the choice of material for that report, subject to the approval of the committee on publications of the American Historical Association and of the proper officials of the Smithsonian Institution.

IV. Separate reprints of the section of the Annual Report devoted to the Agricultural History Society shall be furnished to the society at the cost of same to the American Historical Association.

V. That the American Historical Association shall allow the following representation of the Agricultural History Society:

1. The president of the Agricultural History Society, or a representative chosen by that official, may attend the meetings of the council of the American Historical Association, and discuss matters pertaining to the welfare of the Agricultural History Society, but will not be granted a vote in the council.

2. The chairman of the publications committee of the Agricultural History Society shall be ex officio a member of the committee on publications of the American Historical Association.

3. The secretary-treasurer of the Agricultural History Society shall be a member of the program committee of the American Historical Association, and shall assist in arranging for the program of the joint annual meeting.

VI. That the terms of this agreement shall be in force until January 1, 1921, but may extend for a definite or indefinite period by the mutual consent, at the annual business meetings in 1919, of the two organizations. (For action of the association, see minutes of the annual meeting of Dec. 30, 1919).

It was voted to recommend that the annual meeting of the association for 1920 be held in Washington.

It was voted that the customary meeting of the council at Thanksgiving time be omitted.

The treasurer of the association presented his annual report, which, in summary form, was as follows:

Statement of treasurer, Nov. 30, 1919.

RECEIPTS.

Annual dues	$6, 805. 73
Life membership fees	150. 00
Voluntary contributions paid with dues	1, 432. 00
Sale of publications	400. 87
Royalties	85. 72
Advance payments for directory	17. 00
Interest on investments	[2] 1, 729. 86
Interest on bank account	52. 60
Gift for London headquarters	140. 00
Miscellaneous	19. 02
	$10, 832. 80
Sale of American Exchange National Bank stock	4, 500. 00
Payment of mortgage	20, 000. 00
	24, 500. 00
Total receipts	35, 332. 80
Cash on hand Dec. 1, 1918	3, 253. 28
	38, 586. 08

EXPENDITURES.

Secretary and treasurer	$2, 008. 83
Executive council	264. 42
Committee on program	24. 00
Committee on publications	404. 42
American Historical Review	4, 206. 25
Historical manuscripts commission	100. 00
Adams prize committee	200. 00
Winsor prize committee	200. 00
Committee on history and education	103. 60
Writings on American history	200. 00
London headquarters	144. 40
Accounts payable Dec. 1, 1918	264. 07
	8, 119. 99
Liberty bonds purchased (par value $26,200)	24, 762. 80
Accrued interest on Liberty bonds to date of purchase	518. 57
Total expenditures	33, 401. 36
Cash on hand Nov. 30, 1919	5, 184. 72
	38, 586. 08

(Excess of net receipts over net disbursements, $2,712.81.)

ASSETS.

General:		
Bank balance	$5, 184. 72	
Liberty bonds (par value $29,450)	28, 012. 80	
Accrued interest on Liberty bonds	90. 05	
Cash in Central Trust Co. of New York (endowment fund)	188. 91	
		33, 476. 48
American Historical Review:		
Bank balance	967. 42	
Liberty bonds (par value, $1,200)	1, 131. 64	
Accrued interest on Liberty bonds	6. 38	
		2, 105. 44
		35, 581. 92

[2] This item includes $518.57 received from accrued interest on Liberty bonds.

Publications in stock, estimate	$7,280.00	
Furniture, office equipment, books, estimate	425.00	
		$7,705.00
		43,286.92

The treasurer, as chairman of the finance committee of the council, presented the following estimates of receipts and expenditures, which were approved as the budget for 1920:

RECEIPTS.

Annual dues	$6,800.00	
Sale of publications	200.00	
Royalties	75.00	
Interest	1,350.00	
Registration fees	125.00	
Miscellaneous	75.00	
		$8,625.00

EXPENDITURES.

Administration ($2,800):		
Secretary and treasurer	$2,500.00	
Pacific Coast branch	50.00	
Nominating committee	25.00	
Membership committee	150.00	
London headquarters	75.00	
Meetings and relations ($335):		
Program committee	$150.00	
Executive council		
Conference of historical societies	25.00	
American council of education	10.00	
American council of learned societies	125.00	
Rio Janeiro Congress	25.00	
Academia Americana		
Publications and prizes ($6,175):		
Publication committee	750.00	
American Historical Review	4,400.00	
Committee on bibliography	75.00	
Writings on American history	200.00	
Bibliography of modern English history	150.00	
Historical manuscript commission	150.00	
Public archives commission		
Adams prize	200.00	
Military history prize	250.00	
Special ($1,000):		
Committee on policy	150.00	
Committee on history and education	350.00	
Legal services	500.00	
		10,310.00
Net income		8,625.00
Deficit		1,685.00

It was voted to renew in 1920 the request made to members of the association in 1919 for a voluntary contribution of $1 each, in addition to the regular annual dues.

The proposed amendments to the constitution and by-laws of the association being under consideration, Mr. Burr moved the following resolution, which was adopted:

Resolved, That before considering the proposed amendment to the constitution and by-laws the council desires to express its deep regret that the two secretaries find it necessary to withdraw, and its high appreciation of their long and efficient service.

Its was voted to recommend to the association the following amendments to the constitution and by-laws:

For Article IV substitute the following:

Article IV. The officers shall be a president, two vice presidents, a secretary, a treasury, an assistant secretary-treasurer, and an editor.

The president, vice presidents, secretary, and treasurer shall be elected by ballot at each regular annual meeting in the manner provided by the by-laws.

The assistant secretary-treasurer and the editor shall be elected by the executive council. They shall perform such duties and receive such compensation as the council may determine.

For Article V, 1, substitute the following:

Article V. There shall be an executive council constituted as follows:
1. The president, the vice presidents, the secretary, and the treasurer.

To by-law IV add the following paragraph:

The council may provide for the payment of expenses incurred by the secretary, the assistant secretary-treasurer, and the editor in such travel as may be necessary to the transaction of the association's business.

It was voted to revive the committee on membership.

On recommendation of the special committee on the relations of the Historical Outlook with the American Historical Association the following votes were adopted:

1. That the present board of advisory editors be discontinued.
2. That a new board be created to be known as the board of editors of the Historical Outlook.
3. That the board consist for the year 1920 of five editors, appointed by the council, to serve for one year.
4. That the functions of the board shall be: (a) To cooperate with the managing editor, Dr. A. E. McKinley, in the securing of material for publication and in such other ways as may be found appropriate; (b) to report to the council at the annual meeting of 1920 such proposals respecting the future relations of the Historical Outlook with the association as may then appear desirable.

The committee on appointments was authorized to act for the council in filling such vacancies as had not already been provided for. The complete list of committee assignments is appended to these minutes.

It was voted to refer to the committee on the national archives certain communications presented by Messrs. R. M. Johnston and F. L. Paxson respecting the archives of the American Expeditionary Forces.

On motion of Prof. Burr the following memoir on the late H. Morse Stephens, former president of the association, was received and by a rising vote ordered to be spread upon the minutes of the council:

In the death of Prof. Henry Morse Stephens, on April 17, 1919, this association has lost one of those who during the past quarter century, have had largest part in its affairs. It was in 1894 that Cornell University called him across the sea to take the chair left vacant by the death of Herbert Tuttle. Of English family, educated in Scotland and at Oxford, a lecturer at Cambridge, known to historians by his writings on India, Portugal, the French Revolution, his experience was already wide, and not alone as scholar and teacher, but also as journalist and man of affairs. He came to America filled with projects for the organization and advance of historical scholarship. Connecting himself at once with this association he was a leader in the erection of the American Historical Review, gathered about him the younger leaders of historical work, and had much to do with the changes that broadened the policy of this association. And when in 1902 the University of California called him to the Pacific slope he did not leave the association behind. It was he who organized our Pacific Coast Branch and who remained a guiding spirit in its councils. Year by year he crossed the continent to our annual meetings, bringing always suggestion and stimulus. At last, in 1915, the expositions in honor of the Panama Canal made possible his long-cherished dream of inviting us to San Francisco, and there he presided at our sessions, as at those of the Panama Pacific Historical Congress, which was also his project and which, despite the war, he made a brilliant success. In Washington at

Christmastide he crowned his presidency with another notable address; and, still undaunted, he was in the following year again among us, though the journey cost a desperate illness. But his services to history at large were by no means confined to his work through this body. Throughout the country he brought as a lecturer inspiration to large audiences. Few teachers kindled so many to the lifelong service of history as did he by his perennial fascination for young men. Especially in California he built up a notable group of young historians; and he knew how to enlist the pride of the Coast in the provision of endowments for their research in the records of Spain and of Spanish America. To this wider mission of the teacher was even sacrificed much of the productiveness of his own pen.

Though his years had barely passed 60 his health had more than once suffered a break; but his remarkable vitality so rose to the emergencies brought by the war that during his last year he took upon him at Berkeley a new burden of executive duties. But the effort was perhaps too great. Returning by street-car from the burial of his old friend, Mrs. Hearst, the benefactress of the university, he was in conversation with a friend when almost momentaneously life merged into death. Few teachers have been so deeply or so widely mourned.

Adjourned, EVARTS B. GREENE,
Secretary of the Council.

APPOINTMENTS TO COMMITTEES, COMMISSIONS, AND BOARDS FOR 1920.

(The names of new members of standing committees are italicized.)

Historical manuscripts commission.—Justin H. Smith (chairman), *E. C. Barker,* Mrs. A. G. Draper, L. Esarey, G. Hunt, C. H. Lincoln.

Public archives commission.—Commission suspended for 1920.

Special committee on a primer of archives.—Victor H. Paltsits (chairman), W. G. Leland; these two to select one or more additional members.

Committee on the Justin Winsor prize.—F. L. Paxson (chairman), A. C. Cole, *C. H. Haring,* F. H. Hodder, *N. W. Stephenson.*

Committee on the Herbert Baxter Adams prize.—Conyers Read (chairman), *C. J. H. Hayes,* C. H. McIlwain, *Nellie Neilson,* Bernadotte Schmitt.

Editor American Historical Review (to serve six years from Jan. 1, 1920).—J. F. Jameson.

Committee on bibliography.—Committee suspended for 1920.

Special committee to cooperate with the American Library Association in the preparation of a manual of historical literature.—G. M. Dutcher, S. B. Fay,[1] A. H. Shearer,[1] H. R. Shipman.[1]

Committee on publications.—H. B. Learned (chairman); other members ex officio.

Secretary conference of historical societies.—J. C. Parish.

Committee on national archives.[4]—J. F. Jameson (chairman), Charles Moore, Lieut. Col. O. L. Spaulding.

Committee on membership.[4]—*T. J. Wertenbaker* (chairman), *Louise Brown, E. H. Byrne, A. C. Krey, F. E. Melvin, R. A. Newhall, Julia S. Orvis,[5] C. W. Ramsdell, J. G. Randall, A. P. Scott, J. J. Van Nostrand, jr., G. F. Zook.*

Board of editors Historical Outlook[4] (to serve in cooperation with A. E. McKinley, managing editor, for one year from Jan. 1, 1920).—*Edgar Dawson, L. M. Larson,* Lucy M. Salmon, St. George L. Sioussat, W. L. Westermann.

Committee on program, thirty-fifth annual meeting.—*C. J. H. Hayes* (chairman); other members to be selected by the council in consultation with the chairman.

---

[1] These members designated by the chairman in accordance with the council vote of Feb. 1, 1919.
[4] Members of this committee selected by the committee on appointments in accordance with the council vote.
[5] Declined appointment.

MINUTES OF THE MEETING OF THE EXECUTIVE COUNCIL OF THE AMERICAN HISTORICAL ASSOCIATION, HELD IN THE HOTEL HOLLENDEN, CLEVELAND, OHIO, DECEMBER 31, 1919.

The council met at 11 a. m. President Channing presided and Mr. Charles Moore acted as secretary pro tempore.

Pursuant to the vote of the association ratifying the constitution of the American Council of Learned Societies, Messrs. Jameson and Haskins were elected delegates to represent the American Historical Association in said council.

Mr. Allen R. Boyd was elected editor of the association. It was voted to define the duties of the editor as follows:

It shall be the duty of the editor under the direction of the committee on publications to—

(1) Collect, edit, and prepare for publication the annual report of the association.

(2) Transmit the report to the secretary of the Smithsonian Institution not later than July 1 of each year.

(3) Read the proofs of the report and cause them to be read by the various contributors.

(4) Cause suitable indexes to be made to the annual reports.

(5) Act as secretary of the committee on publications.

(6) Perform such other editorial services within reasonable limits as may be determined by the committee on publications.

Miss Patty W. Washington was elected assistant secretary-treasurer of the association. It was voted to define the duties of the assistant secretary-treasurer as follows:

It shall be the duty of the assistant secretary-treasurer—

(1) Under the direction of the secretary to keep the membership roll of the association; to correct the mailing list of the American Historical Review; to approve bills and vouchers that at present require to be approved by the secretary; to conduct the routine correspondence of the association; and in general to perform such duties as may be directed by the secretary.

(2) Under the direction of the treasurer to keep the books and accounts of the association, to collect the annual dues and other moneys payable to the treasurer, and in general to perform such duties as may be directed by the treasurer.

(3) The assistant secretary-treasurer shall be the custodian of the records of the association except as otherwise provided.

It was voted that the assistant secretary-treasurer be authorized to sign checks of the association and of the American Historical Review when countersigned by either the secretary or the treasurer of the association.

It was voted that the committee on local arrangements for the annual meeting of 1920, to be held in Washington, should consist of Hon. Thomas Nelson Page, chairman; Mr. H. B. Learned, secretary; and Mr. Charles Moore; and that these members be authorized to add to their number.

It was voted to appoint Mr. Carlton J. H. Hayes chairman of the committee on program for the annual meeting of 1920, with Mr. John C. Parish, secretary of the Conference of Historical Societies, and Mr. Lyman Carrier, secretary of the Agricultural History Society, as ex officio members; and it was voted to authorize and request the committee of the council on appointments, in consultation with Mr. J. F. Jameson, to make further appointments to the committee on program.

The resignation of Mr. Charles H. Haskins as a member of the board of editors of the American Historical Review was presented and accepted, Mr. Haskins having been elected second vice president of the association. Mr.

Dana C. Munro was elected a member of the board of editors to serve during the unexpired term of Mr. Haskins.

It was voted to authorize the treasurer to invest $3,000 of the association's funds in United States bonds.

Adjourned.

CHARLES MOORE,
Secretary pro tempore.

PROCEEDINGS OF THE EXECUTIVE COUNCIL ADOPTED BY CORRESPONDENCE WITH THE MEMBERS.

APPOINTMENTS TO COMMITTEES OF THE COUNCIL.

Committee on docket.—Edward Channing (chairman), John S. Bassett, W. E. Dodd, A. C. McLaughlin, J. T. Shotwell.

Committee on meetings and relations.—John S. Bassett (chairman), Charles H. Haskins, J. F. Jameson, G. M. Wrong, Ruth Putnam.

Committee on finance.—Charles Moore (chairman), John S. Bassett, Herbert E. Bolton, W. C. Ford, W. E. Lingelbach.

Committee on appointments.—Edward Channing (chairman), John S. Bassett, H. E. Bourne, W. L. Fleming, G. L. Burr.

Postal votes.

Upon canvass by the secretary of the committee on appointments it was unanimously voted to nominate Prof. Williston Walker to the board of editors of the American Historical Review for the term expiring in December, 1925, in place of Prof. Dana C. Munro, who was elected to the board by the council on December 31, 1919, but who declined to accept the election.

Upon nomination by the committee on appointments the executive council elected Prof. Williston Walker a member of the board of editors of the American Historical Review for the term of six years ending in December, 1925.

On motion of Mr. Moore, it was voted by the committee on finance that there be transferred from the appropriation for legal services the sum of $150 to be placed to the credit of the committee on policy in addition to its original appropriation of $150.

The secretary transmitted to the members of the committee on meetings and relations the following request from Prof. Morris R. Cohen, chairman of the research committee of the Peoples of America Society:

The Peoples of America Society is anxious to promote definite scientific knowledge on the questions of immigration and of the racial and social adjustments involved in the process of Americanization. We feel strongly that national policies in regard to these questions should be illumined by a greater amount of impartially ascertained knowledge than is now generally available; and we are, therefore, anxious to see the various scientific societies devote their energies to research in these problems. To this end we ask the American Historical Association to appoint a committee, to cooperate with similar committees appointed by the National Research Council and other scientific societies, to make a general survey of the sources of knowledge now available as to the problems of immigration and Americanization and to indicate the researches or investigations that might be undertaken.

The committee voted unanimously to recommend favorable action to the executive council.

The secretary transmitted to the members of the executive council the following recommendation from the committee on meetings and relations:

The committee on meetings and relations recommends that the council appoint two representatives to consult with representatives of the Peoples of America Society and the National Research Council in promoting investigations of race elements in American society. It is understood that the Peoples of America Society will assume the expenses of the investigation and that the arrangement shall continue subject to the approval of the council at its next regular meeeting.

The council voted that the recommendations of the committee on meetings and relations be adopted and that the committee on appointments be instructed to appoint a committee of two to cooperate with the Peoples of America Society.

On motion of Mr. Moore and Mr. Bassett, it was voted by the committee on finance that, commencing on July 1, 1920, the salary of the assistant secretary-treasurer be $1,800 per annum instead of $1,500.

APPENDIX.

ORGANIZATION OF THE AMERICAN COUNCIL OF LEARNED SOCIETIES.

Because of the leading part which the American Historical Association has taken in the organization of the American Council of Learned Societies, the following documents are printed in extenso:

American Historical Association, Washington.—American Academy of Arts and Sciences, Boston.

AUGUST 22, 1919.

DEAR SIR: The accompanying statement sets forth a plan, inaugurated in Paris last spring, for an international organization of the learned societies devoted to humanistic studies, parallel to the organization already effected in the field of the natural sciences. You will note that pursuant to action taken by a preliminary conference held in Paris in May a meeting of representatives of the various countries will be held in that city late in October for the purpose of effecting a definitive organization.

In order that the American societies may take part in this meeting it seems highly desirable to hold a conference of their officers or other representatives for the discussion of tentative plans which may enable them to have a full participation in the new international organization.

To that end the presidents and secretaries of the American Historical Association and the American Academy of Arts and Sciences, which were the only American societies represented at the May conference, take the liberty of suggesting that your society be represented at a conference to be held in Boston on Friday, September 19, at 11 a. m., in the building of the American Academy of Arts and Sciences at 28 Newbury Street. This conference must, of course, be quite informal, for it is realized that it will not be competent to take any binding action, and that officers or other representatives of societies who take part in it must in most cases do so on their own responsibility.

It is hoped that the discussion may lead to (1) the formulation of a tentative plan (to be presented in due time to the various bodies represented at the conference, and perhaps to others also), for the creation of some sort of an intersociety council or agency that will make it possible for the American associations to participate effectively in the proposed international organization; (2) the selection of two delegates to represent the United States at the October meeting in Paris; (3) the drafting of tentative instructions for the guidance of the delegates.

Prof. Charles H. Haskins, of Harvard University, who attended the Paris conference in May, will be present in Boston in order to supply full information respecting the proposed objects and activities of the international organization.

It is suggested that the objects of the conference will be facilitated if each society should be represented by its president and secretary and one other member.

This letter is sent to the secretaries of the societies included in the appended list, which is not, however, intended to be final, and additional copies of the letter and statement are inclosed for the convenience of the secretaries in communicating with the other officers of their respective societies. Further additional copies may be had upon request.

Please address all correspondence respecting the Boston conference to Waldo G. Leland, secretary of the American Historical Association, at Newton Lower Falls, Mass. (during August and September).

Very truly yours,

WILLIAM ROSCOE THAYER,
President of the American Historical Association.
THEODORE W. RICHARDS,
President of the American Academy of Arts and Sciences.
HARRY W. TYLER,
Secretary of the American Academy of Arts and Sciences.
WALDO G. LELAND,
Secretary of the American Historical Association.

American Philosophical Society.
American Academy of Arts and Sciences.
American Philosophical Association.
American Philological Association.
American Oriental Society.
Modern Language Association of America.
Archæological Institute of America.
American Historical Association.
American Antiquarian Society.
American Economic Association.
American Political Science Association.
American Society of International Law.
American Sociological Society.

UNION ACADÉMIQUE DE RECHERCHES ET DE PUBLICATIONS.

Proposed international organization of learned societies devoted to humanistic studies.

On March 24, 1919, Monsieur R. Cagnat, permanent secretary of the Académie des Inscriptions et Belles-Lettres, addressed a communication to the academies and learned societies of the allied and associated countries devoted to studies in archæology, philology, and history, inviting them to send delegates to a conference which was to be held in Paris in May, 1919, to consider a plan for organizing an "Interallied Academic Union."

In the project which accompanied the letter of Monsieur Cagnat reference was made to the dissolution, because of the war, of the International Association of Academies which had its headquarters in Berlin, and also to the organization in the fields of pure and applied science of a new international union, following conferences held in London and Paris late in 1918 upon the initiative of the Royal Society and the Académie des Sciences.

The objects of the union proposed by the Académie des Inscriptions et Belles-Lettres were set forth as follows :

(1) To establish, maintain, and strengthen among the scholars of the allied and associated States corporative and individual relations which shall be sustained, cordial, and efficacious, and which shall, by means of regular correspondence and exchange of communications and by the periodical holding of scientific congresses, make for the advancement of knowledge in the various fields of learning.

(2) To inaugurate, encourage, or direct those works of research and publication which shall be deemed most useful to the advancement of science and most to require and deserve collective effort.

As the result of the initiative thus taken by the Académie des Inscriptions et Belles-Lettres a preliminary conference was held in Paris on May 15 and 17 at the Bibliothéque Nationale, which was attended by the following :

Prof. Charles H. Haskins, of Harvard University, representing the American Historical Association and the American Academy of Arts and Sciences, and Prof. James T. Shotwell, of Columbia University, representing the American Historical Association.

MM. Pirenne and Bidez, representing the Belgian Académie Royale des Sciences, Lettres, et Arts.

MM. Senart and Homolle, representing the Académie des Inscriptions et Belles-Lettres, and MM. Rocquin and Boutroux, representing the Académie des Sciences Morales et Politiques, of France.

Senator Lanciani and MM. de Sanctis and Patetta, representing the royal Italian academies of The Lincei and of Turin.

Prince Soulzo, representing the Roumanian Academy.

M. Svoronos, unofficially representing Greece.

Mr. Anesaki, unofficially representing Japan.

Although the British Academy reserved its formal adhesion to the plan until it should have fuller information respecting it, the president of that body expressed his sympathy with the proposal, and the Archæological Institute of America, unable to be formally represented at the conference, likewise expressed unofficially its approval of the project in principle.

After full discussion the conference unanimously adopted a series of resolutions the substance of which is as follows:

I. In the present state of affairs resulting from the war it is desirable, for the purpose of international collaboration, to proceed to a new organization of the relations among academies and learned societies.

II. The purpose of this organization is the advancement by means of collective researches and publications, of studies in the fields of the philological, historical, moral, political, and social sciences.

III. The organization which is hereby constituted by the societies represented at this conference shall be called the Union Académique.

IV. The union is open to the learned societies of all the countries which are not excluded for an undetermined period because of the war (i. e., the enemy countries).

Admission shall be by three-fourths vote.

V. Each country shall be represented in the union by two delegates chosen by those societies of that country that are affiliated with the union.

VI. The assembled delegates shall constitute the executive committee. They shall consider and decide matters of general interest and especially the admission of new societies, plans of research and publication, and matters of finance.

They shall elect officers (un bureau) who shall preside at their various meetings, direct the general administration of the union, and be empowered to take necessary action between sessions and to convoke the committee.

The decisions of the committee shall be by majority vote except in the admission of new societies or the amendment of the by-laws.

Each country shall have two votes.

VII. The officers shall be elected for one year and shall be eligible for reelection, but not more than two times except after an interval of three years.

VIII. The permanent headquarters of the union shall be in Brussels, where there shall be established a secretariat, which, under the direction of the officers, shall conduct the current business and correspondence of the union, have the custody of its archives, and administer its finances.

The ordinary meetings of the executive committee shall be held in Brussels.

IX. The delegates shall meet in assembly as the executive committee at least once a year at a stated date.

X. Special meetings having the character of scientific congresses and celebrations to which the society belonging to the union shall be invited in a body may be held upon special invitation from an academy.

XI. The administrative expenses of the union shall be met from equal fixed annual contributions pledged by the participating societies.

The special expenses for research and publication shall be met either from funds secured or contributed by societies undertaking approved enterprises, or from funds or endowments at the disposal of the union.

XII. At least three months before the meeting of the executive committee projects which it is proposed to submit to that body should be laid before the societies belonging to the union in order that the delegates may receive instructions respecting them.

The proposers of any project should define it clearly, outline the general plan of work, estimate the expense, and indicate to what extent they themselves purpose to contribute to it, either scientifically or financially, and what degree of collaboration or aid they desire or are assured of. They may designate special agents for the presentation and discussion of their projects in the executive committee.

Any learned body which, with the assent of the committee, shall have assumed the support of any enterprise shall have full direction of it under the committee rendering an annual account of progress and expenditures.

XIII. The delegates present at the preliminary conference (May, 1919) shall be charged with communicating these resolutions and all other information to the societies which they represent. They shall also draw up a list of societies in countries (other than enemy) not represented in the preliminary conference, to which these resolutions should be communicated.

XIV. The delegates shall meet again in Paris in the second half of October next for the purpose of effecting, pursuant to their instruction from the academies and institutions which they represent and by virtue of full powers with which they will be provided, the definitive organization of the Union Académique. They shall likewise have power to submit to the vote of the committee the admission of the learned bodies which shall have decided to accept (qui auraient fait acte d'adhésion) the program of the Union, and to draw up in the order of importance the list of researches and publications which it may seem expedient to undertake in the various scientific fields.

With regard to the plan outlined above two questions present themselves to American scholars: (1) Is it desirable that America should be represented in an international organization such as the Union Académique? (2) How may such representation be best effected?

In the field of pure and applied science these questions have already been answered. The National Academy of Sciences was in a position not only to take an active part in organizing the union which resulted from the London and Paris conferences, but also, on its own initiative and authority, to represent the United States in the international group.

In the field of the humanistic studies, however, there is no single national body that would consider itself possessed of a mandate to represent American scholarship. There are, instead, a dozen or more national associations, each devoted to the cultivation of a single department of knowledge, which, although semipopular as to membership, are nevertheless governed in the interests of true scholarship and are properly entitled to be known as learned societies.

If America is to be represented at all in the Union Académique (as it is already represented in the scientific union) it must be through some joint action on the part of these associations. Without contemplating any close form of federation might it not be practicable to create some sort of intersociety council which should be thoroughly representative of the interests of the various associations and which should have power to act for them in such international matters as the selection and instruction of the two American delegates in the Union Académique?

Such a council, once established, would undoubtedly also prove of great utility in maintaining relations between the associations and in promoting cooperative undertakings, and in general would make for that solidarity of scholarship so essential to the advancement of learning.

Offices of the American Historical Association, Washington, August 22, 1919.

PROCEEDINGS OF THE CONFERENCE OF AMERICAN LEARNED SOCIETIES DEVOTED TO HUMANISTIC STUDIES, HELD IN BOSTON IN THE AMERICAN ACADEMY OF ARTS AND SCIENCES ON SEPTEMBER 19, 1919.

On August 22, 1919, the presidents and secretaries of the American Academy of Arts and Sciences and the American Historical Association invited 13 representative American learned societies devoted to humanistic studies to send delegates to a conference to be held in Boston on September 19. The purpose of the conference was to consider what action should be taken by American societies to enable them to take part effectively in the new international Union Académique which was organized in Paris in May.

The conference was held in the building of the American Academy of Arts and Sciences on September 19 and was attended by 20 delegates representing 10 societies as follows:

The American Philosophical Society: Prof. William B. Scott, of Princeton University, president.

The American Academy of Arts and Sciences: Prof. Theodore W. Richards, of Harvard University, president; Prof. Harry W. Tyler, of the Massachusetts Institute of Technology, corresponding secretary; Prof. Charles H. Haskins, of Harvard University.

The American Antiquarian Society: Mr. Waldo Lincoln, of Worcester, president; Mr. Clarence S. Brigham, of Worcester, librarian.

The American Oriental Society: Prof. James R. Jewett, of Harvard University, director; Prof. David G. Lyon, of Harvard University, director.

The American Philological Association: Represented unofficially by Prof. James C. Egbert, Prof. George M. Whicher, and Prof. George H..Chase.

The Archæological Institute of America: Prof. James C. Egbert, of Columbia University, president; Prof. George M. Whicher, of Hunter College, general secretary; Prof. George H. Chase, of Harvard University, member of the executive committee.

The Modern Language Association of America: Prof. Edward C. Armstrong, of Princeton University, president; Asst. Prof. William G. Howard, of Harvard University, secretary-treasurer; Prof. John Erskine, of Columbia University.

The American Historical Association: Dr. William Roscoe Thayer, of Cambridge, president; Mr. Waldo G. Leland, of the Carnegie Institution of Washington, secretary; Dr. J. Franklin Jameson, of the Carnegie Institution of Washington, member of the executive council.

The American Economic Association: Prof. Henry B. Gardner, of Brown University, president; Prof. Allyn A. Young, of Cornell University, secretary.

The American Philosophical Association: Prof. Mary W. Calkins, of Wellesley College, ex-president.

Three other societies had been invited to attend the conference, but were not represented at the meeting: The American Political Science Association, the American Sociological Society, and the American Society of International Law.

The conference was called to order by Prof. Theodore W. Richards, president of the American Academy of Arts and Sciences, who welcomed the delegates in the name of the academy and made brief remarks respecting the objects for which the conference had been called. He then asked for nominations for the permanent chairman and secretary of the conference.

Mr. William Roscoe Thayer was chosen permanent chairman, and Mr. Waldo G. Leland permanent secretary.

Mr. Thayer took the chair and directed that the secretary call the roll, which was done, the attendance being as indicated.

The chairman then called upon Prof. Charles H. Haskins, who had represented the American Academy of Arts and Sciences and the American Historical Association at the conference held in Paris in May to set forth the objects and scope of the Union Académique.

Prof. Haskins gave an account of the origin of the Union Académique and explained its purposes substantially as set forth in the circular which had already been distributed to the delegates. He pointed out that the organization of the union presupposed the existence in each country (as in England the British Academy) of a single body or group authoritatively representative of the humanistic studies. The United States, he said, was a striking example of a country having no national academy in this field, but having, instead, a number of strong voluntary societies, each devoted to a single field. He urged, therefore, that these societies should agree to form a group having some form of central organization which would enable the United tSates to take its appropriate part in the activities of the Union Académique. He cited the example of Italy, where the five independent academies have agreed to act as a unit in international matters.

During the general discussion which followed Prof. Haskins's remarks the following points were developed:

1. The encouragement of international congresses in different fields of learning would undoubtedly be one of the functions of the Union Académique.

2. The financial requirements of the Union Académique have not as yet been determined. The administrative expenses of the union are to be met by fixed annual contributions of equal amount from all countries represented in it. If an American union or council were to be formed it would pay this national contribution, assessing it in some equitable way among the societies belonging to it. The amount of the fee or contribution of each country would probably not exceed an amount which could be met by an assessment of 5 cents a member upon all the societies represented or invited to be represented in the present conference. The expenses for research and publication undertaken under the auspices of the Union Académique are to be met by voluntary contributions or from special funds or gifts, and no obligation not purely voluntary is incurred by any society with respect to this class of expenditure.

Further discussion brought forth a brief account of the organization of the International Research Council and of the National Research Councils upon which it is based, but it appeared that that form of organization, while well adapted to its particular purposes in the field of the sciences, can not serve as a model in the present case.

Upon motion by Prof. Whicher seconded by Prof. Scott, the following resolution was adopted:

Resolved, That it is the sense of this conference that American learned societies devoted to humanistic studies should participate as a group in the Union Académique.

The conference then proceeded to consider the appointment of two delegates to represent the United States in the session of the Union Académique to be held in Paris about October 15. The names of several American scholars known or thought to be in Europe were mentioned informally, whereupon it was voted that the chairman should appoint a committee of three to nominate the American delegates. Messrs. Haskins, Young, and Erskine were appointed such a committee.

Later in the session this committee reported the nomination of Prof. James T. Shotwell, of Columbia University, and Mr. William H. Buckler, of Baltimore, as American delegates to the October session of the Union Académique, and recommended that they be given power to fill vacancies in the delegation, should such occur.

The report of the committee was adopted.

The conference next took up the consideration of instructions for the American delegates and after discussion passed the following votes:

Voted, That all projects of research or publication which societies desire to have presented to the Union Académique at its October session in Paris shall be transmitted to the secretary of the conference not later than September 28 for forwarding to the American delegates.

Voted, That until the action of this conference shall have been ratified by the bodies represented and an organization of the societies for national representation in the Union Académique shall have been perfected, the delegates are instructed that they have no authority to commit the American societies to any particular project, but should confine themselves to a cordial indorsement of the general plan by those present at this conference, and that any projects submitted to the delegates should be regarded as the suggestions of individual scholars.

Voted, That it is the sense of those present at this conference that some form of bibliography of humanistic studies should be approved as an international undertaking.

Voted, That this conference desires to express its deep interest in the subject of explorations and researches in Western Asia, and hopes that a scheme of cooperation may be considered by the Union Académique.

After a recess for luncheon at the University Club the conference resumed its session at 3 o'clock.

The question for consideration by the conference was the organization of some sort of inter-society council or agency for the purposes developed during the discussions of the morning session.

The secretary of the conference presented a draft of a convention for establishing an American Council of Learned Societies, accompanied by a form of constitution for such a council, and it was voted that the conference adopt this draft as a basis of discussion.

The draft was then considered article by article and various amendments to it were adopted, after which the convention and constitution were adopted in the following form:

AMERICAN COUNCIL OF LEARNED SOCIETIES DEVOTED TO HUMANISTIC STUDIES.

By agreement among the societies signatory to this convention there is herewith established a body to be known as the American Council of Learned Societies devoted to Humanistic Studies, which shall be governed by the following constitution:

Article I.

This body shall be known as the American Council of Learned Societies devoted to Humanistic Studies.

Article II.

Sec. A. The council shall be composed of delegates of the national learned societies of the United States which are devoted to the advancement, by scientific methods, of the humanistic studies.

Sec. B. Each of the 13 societies herein named shall, upon ratification of this convention and constitution, be admitted to representation in the council: The American Philosophical Society, the American Academy of Arts and Sciences, the American Antiquarian Society, the American Oriental Society, the American Philological Association, the Archaeological Institute of America, the Modern Language Association of America, the American Historical Association, the American Economic Association, the American Philosophical Association, the American Political Science Association, the American Sociological Society, the American Society of International Law.

Sec. C. Other societies may be admitted to representation in the council by vote of three-fourths of all the delegates.

Article III.

Sec. A. Each society shall be represented in the council by two delegates, chosen in such manner as the society may determine.

Sec. B. The term of office of delegates shall be four years, but at the first election of delegates from each society a short term of two years shall be assigned to one of the delegates, and thereafter one delegate shall be chosen every two years.

Article IV.

The officers of the council shall consist of a chairman, a vice chairman, and a secretary-treasurer, who shall be chosen for such terms and in such manner as the council may determine, but no two officers shall be from the same society.

Article V.

The council shall determine its own rules of procedure and shall enact such by-laws, not inconsistent with this constitution, as it may deem desirable.

Article VI.

The council shall hold at least one meeting each year, which meeting shall be not less than two months prior to the stated annual meeting of the Union Académique.

Article VII.

The council shall choose such number of delegates to represent the United States in the Union Académique as may be prescribed by the statutes of the union, and shall prepare their instructions, and in general shall be the medium of communication between the union and the societies which are represented in the council.

Article VIII.

The council may upon its own initiative take measures to advance the general interests of the humanistic studies, and is especially charged with maintaining and strengthening relations among the societies which are represented in it.

Article IX.

Sec. A. In order to meet its own necessary administrative expenses and to pay the annual contribution of the United States to the administrative budget of the Union Académique the council shall, until otherwise provided, assess upon each society represented in it an annual contribution of not less than $25, nor more, except as the minimum contribution, than a sum equal to 5 cents for each member of the society.

Sec. B. The council may receive gifts and acquire property for the purposes indicated above.

Article X.

The council shall make a report to the societies each year setting forth in detail all the acts of the council and all receipts and expenditures of money.

Article XI.

Identical instructions from a majority of the societies which are represented in the council shall be binding upon it.

Article XII.

The council may be dissolved by a vote of two-thirds of the societies represented therein.

Article XIII.

Amendments to this constitution may be proposed by a vote of two-thirds of the council and shall take effect when ratified by a majority of the societies represented in the council.

Article XIV.

This convention and constitution shall be presented to the societies named in Article II, section B, and shall be put into effect when they shall have been ratified by any seven of them.

Following the adoption of the convention and constitution there was a brief discussion of an informal nature respecting the addition of other societies to the 13 named in the constitution, but no action was taken in the matter, and it appeared to be the general opinion that the question of additional societies should be left to the council when that body should have been organized.

It was voted that the secretary of the conference be authorized to transmit the proceedings of the conference to the societies named in the constitution of the council, as the unanimous action of the conference.

The conference adjourned at 4.45 p. m.

WILLIAM ROSCOE THAYER,
Chairman of the Conference.
WALDO G. LELAND,
Secretary of the Conference.

Delegates: William B. Scott, Theodore W. Richards, Harry W. Tyler, Charles H. Haskins, Waldo Lincoln, Clarence S. Brigham, James R. Jewett, David G. Lyon, James C. Egbert, George M. Whicher, George H. Chase, Edward C. Armstrong, William G. Howard, John Erskine, J. Franklin Jameson, Henry B. Gardner, Allyn A. Young, Mary W. Calkins.

DEFINITIVE STATUTES OF THE UNION ACADÉMIQUE INTERNATIONALE.

Adopted in Paris, October 18, 1919.

[Translation.]

I.

The learned bodies or groups of learned bodies belonging to the nations the names of which follow, and represented by delegates vested with full powers or duly qualified:

America.—American Philosophical Society, American Academy of Arts and Sciences, American Philosophical Association, American Philological Association, American Oriental Society, Modern Language Association of America, Archæological Institute of America, American Historical Association, American Antiquarian Society, American Economic Association.

Belgium.—Royal Academy of Sciences, Letters, and Fine Arts of Belgium.

Denmark.—Royal Academy of Sciences and Letters of Denmark.

France.—Academy of Inscriptions and Belles Lettres, Academy of Moral and Political Sciences.

Great Britain.—British Academy.

Greece.—Delegation of the Hellenic Government in place of the Academy of Athens, about to be created.

25066°—23——7

Holland.—Royal Academy of Sciences.
Italy.—National Academy of the Lincei of Rome, Royal Academy of Sciences
of Turin.
Japan.—Imperial Academy.
Poland.—Polish Academy of Sciences of Cracow.
Russia.—Russian Academy of Sciences—
consider that it is desirable to regulate by means of a new agreement the
cooperative relations among academies and learned bodies for the purposes of
international scientific collaboration.

II.

The purpose of this agreement is the cooperation in the advancement of
studies by means of collective researches and publications in the fields of the
sciences cultivated by the participating academies and scientific institutions:
philological, archæological, historical, moral, political, and social sciences.

III.

To this end the learned bodies and groups of learned bodies enumerated in
Article I resolve to form themselves into a scientific federation which bears
the name of Union Académique Internationale (U. A. I.).
By the word union they confirm the sentiments of friendly, trustful, equal,
and free fraternity which inspire them and the federation.
The word académique applies first and foremost to the learned bodies properly called academies and having a national character; it includes also, either
in default of academies or side by side with these latter and in agreement with
them, the scientific institutions, which may be considered as assimilated to
academies by reason of their national character, their scientific purposes, and
the nature and method of their work, and which in each of the countries
affiliated with the union have decided or shall decide to form a group and to
assure themselves a joint representation.

IV.

Each country, whatever the number of its academies or scientfic institutions
participating in the U. A. I., is represented by two delegates. These delegates
are appointed in each country by the learned bodies or group of learned bodies
affiliated with the union. The composition of these groups is left to the free
determination of each of the countries belonging to the U. A. I. on condition
that notice of it shall be communicated to the latter. Each of the national delegations as a unit is termed a member of the union.

V.

The learned bodies or groups of learned bodies of the countries not included
in the list in Article I should, if they desire membership in the U. A. I., indicate their wish either directly or by the medium of three members of the
U. A. I. A majority of three-fourths of all the votes of the U. A. I. is requisite
for the admission of new members. The ballot is secret and may be taken
directly or by correspondence.

VI.

The assembled delegates compose the committee of the union; they elect the
bureau of direction of the U. A. I.; they consider and decide all questions of
general interest, and especially the admission of new members, projects of collective research or publication, and the administration of the finances of the
U. A. I.
The decisions of the committee are given by an absolute majority of votes
except in the admission of new members and the amendment of the statutes,
in which cases a majority of three-fourths is required. (Arts. V, XIII.)
Each member (national delegation) has two votes. In case of the absence
for reason of one of the delegates the delegate present has a double vote.
Deliberations of the committee are valid only if more than one-half of the
members take part.

VII.

The bureau of the committee consists of the president, two vice presidents, a secretary, and two adjunct secretaries. It is elected for a period of three years; it is renewed by a rotation fixed by lot so that one president and one secretary retire each year.

The members of the bureau are eligible for reelection, but not immediately following the close of their term of office.

The same country may not be represented at any one time in the bureau by more than one of its delegates.

The bureau presides over the deliberations of the committee and sees to the general administration of the U. A. I. and to the advancement of its undertakings. During the intervals between sessions it is empowered to take such action as may be urgent, and if need be to summon a meeting of the committee.

VIII.

The Union Académique Internationale selects the city of Brussels for its permanent seat. There is established there through the Belgian delegation an administrative secretariat, which is charged, under the supervision of the bureau, with the transaction of current business, with the custody of the archives, and with the handling of the ordinary budget for administrative expenses (Art. XI); eventually it shall be charged with handling the funds which may come into the hands of the secretariat at Brussels through gifts, legacies, or endowments for the undertakings of the U. A. I. The French language is adopted as the official language of the U. A. I. for correspondence and for administrative documents.

IX

The delegates assemble at least once a year in Brussels in ordinary session. At each meeting they fix the date of the following meeting. They may be summoned in extra session by the bureau if the latter deems it necessary.

X.

Extraordinary meetings having the character of formal occasions, scientific or social, to which would be invited in a body the academies or assimilated institutions belonging to the U. A. I., may be held at any time upon invitation from one of the members of the union in any of the countries which belong to it.

XI.

The Union Académique Internationale possesses a budget which includes two chapters—the ordinary or administrative budget intended for the expenses of the secretariat in Brussels; the extraordinary or scientific budget intended for research and publications. The first is maintained by a contribution which is equal for all the members of the U. A. I. The second is provided as need may arise by the members of the union who shall have undertaken the initiative and assumed the charge of researches or publications approved by the union, either at the expense of their respective governments or their own bureaus of direction, or by means of resources at the disposition of the U. A. I. or of endowments of which the latter may take advantage. Inas much as the diversity of legislation with respect to gifts may oppose an obstacle to their being received directly by the U. A. I., it would appear expedient that in each country gifts should be made to the learned bodies concerned, with special assignment to the U. A. I., or that, to the same end, they should be assigned to the permanent secretariat in Brussels.

XII.

Projects of research or publication which it is proposed to submit to the committee should be communicated to the members of the U. A. I. at least four months before the meeting of the committee in order that the delegates may receive instructions and a definite mandate from the learned bodies or group of learned bodies which they represent.

Researches or publications may be initiated either by each of the members of the union, or by any of the learned bodies represented, or by the bureau of the union.

In all cases the proposers of an undertaking must present a precise definition of its subject, a statement of its purposes, a plan of work, and an estimate of expense. They must also indicate to what extent they themselves expect to contribute to its execution either scientifically or financially, and the collaboration or aid for which they ask or of which they are assured. They may designate special agents for the discussion of their proposal in the committee.

The learned body or bodies which shall have assumed, with the approval of the committee, the charge of a research or publication shall have the direction of it under the supervision of the committee; they shall organize the work, designate the place where it is to be carried on, select the collaborators, and bring them together when they deem it necessary.

If the proposal comes from the bureau, the committee, after having examined and approved it, determines upon the methods of execution. It names the special committees which are charged under its supervision with directing the researches or publications.

XIII.

Proposals for amendments to the statutes must be presented by three members of the union at least four months before the meeting of the committee.

The vote on these proposals takes place under the same conditions as the vote on the admission of new members (Arts. V, VI), by a majority of three-fourths.

Signed:

W. H. BUCKLER,
LOUIS H. GRAY,
       United States of America.
H. PIRENNE,
J. BIDEZ,
       Belgium.
J. L. HEIBERG,
OTTO JESPERSEN,
       Denmark.
EMILE SENART,
THEOPHILE HOMOLLE,
EM. BOUTROUX,
ARTHUR CHUQUET,
       France.
FREDERIC G. KENYON,
       Great Britain.
D. EGINITIS,
M. KEBEDGY,
       Greece.
C. VAN VOLLENHOVEN,
J. J. SALVERDA DE GRAVE,
       Holland.
LANCIANI,
G. DE SANCTIS,
F. PATETTA,
       Italy.
K. ONOZUKA,
J. TAKAKUSA,
       Japan.
CASIMIR MORAWSKI,
JEAN ROZWADOWSKI,
       Poland.
M. ROSTOVTZEFF,
       Russia.

REGISTER OF ATTENDANCE AT THE THIRTY-FOURTH ANNUAL MEETING OF THE AMERICAN HISTORICAL ASSOCIATION, CLEVE-LAND, OHIO.

A.

Abel, Annie Heloise.
Alvord, Clarence W.
Ambler, Charles H.
Ames, Herman V.
Anderson, Frank Maloy.
Andrews, Arthur Irving.
Appleton, W. W.
Attig, C. J.
Aydelotte, Frank.

B.

Barnes, Harry E.
Basye, Arthur H.
Belden, W. P.
Becker, Carl.
Bell, Herbert C.
Bemis, Samuel F.
Benjamin, Gilbert G.
Benton, Elbert J.
Betton, Rev. Francis S.
Beveridge, Albert J.
Bingham, Hiram.
Black, J. W.
Blakeslee, George H.
Boak, A. E. R.
Bogardus, Frank S.
Bolton, Herbert E.
Bond, Beverley W., jr.
Bonham, Milledge L., jr.
Boucher, Chauncey S.
Bourne, Henry E.
Bradley, Glenn D.
Brandt, Walther I.
Bretz, J. P.
Brown, Marshall S.
Brown, Samuel H.
Buell, Bertha G.
Burr, George L.
Byrne, Eugene H.

C.

Cahall, Raymond DuB.
Cameron, Janet G.
Carlton, Frank T.
Carrier, Lyman.
Carter, Clarence E.
Cathcart, Wallace H.
Chambers, Raymond.

Channing, Edward.
Chapman, Charles E.
Cheyney, E. P.
Christie, Francis A.
Clark, Arthur H.
Cole, Arthur C.
Cole, T. L.
Coleman, Christopher B.
Colgate, Lathrop.
Collier, Theodore.
Conger, John L.
Coulomb, Charles A.
Cox, Isaac J.
Crane, Verner W.
Crawford, C. C.
Crofts, F. S.
Cross, Arthur L.
Cruickshank, Ernest A.
Cumings, Mary M.
Custer, John S.

D.

Dargan, Marion, jr.
Davenport, Frances G.
Davies, George C.
Davis, Arthur K.
Dawson, Edgar.
Dietz, Frederick C.
Dodd, William E.
Donnan, Elizabeth.
Douglas, Charles H.
Dow, Earle W.
Downer, Edward I.
Dutcher, George M.

E.

Eddy, George W.
Edwards, Martha L.
Ellery, Eloise.
Elson, Henry W.
Esarey, Logan.

F.

Fairbanks, Elsie D.
Fay, Sidney B.
Fellows, George E.
Ferrin, Dana H.
Ferris, Eleanor.
Fish, Carl R.

Fisher, Edgar J.
Foote, Alice M.
Ford, Guy S.
Foster, Herbert D.
Frayer, William A.
Fuller, George N.
Fuller, Mary B.

G.

Garfield, James R.
Garrett, Mitchell B.
Gaskill, Gussie.
Gewehr, Wesley M.
Gibbons, Lois O.
Gillespie, James E.
Gipson, Lawrence H.
Godard, George S.
Goodwin, C. L.
Gras, Norman S. B.
Greene, Evarts B.
Gregg, Frank M.
Griffith, Elmer C.
Griffith, Mrs. Martha M.
Guilday, Rev. Peter.

H.

Hail, William J.
Hamilton, J. G. deRoul-hac.
Harding, Samuel B.
Hart, Albert B.
Haskins, Charles H.
Haworth, Paul L.
Hayden, Joseph R.
Hayes, Carlton J. H.
Hedger, George A.
Hershey, Amos S.
Hickey, Rev. Edward J.
Hickman, Emily.
Hicks, John D.
Higby, Chester P.
Hinsdale, Mary L.
Hinsdale, Mildred.
Hirsch, Arthur H.
Hockett, Homer C.
Hodder, F. H.
Hoover, Thomas N.
House, R. B.
Hubbard, H. A.

Hudson, Irby R.
Hughes, R. O.
Hunter, William C.
Hurst, Edith S.

I.

Inui, Kiyo Sue.

J.

Jackson, W. C.
James, Alfred P.
James, J. A.
Jameson, John Franklin.
Jernegan, Marcus W.
Jones, Guernsey.
Jones, M. Myvanroy.
Jones, Paul V. B.
Jones, Mrs. Ralph A.
Judson, Katharine B.

K.

Kellar, Herbert A.
Kellar, Mrs. Herbert A.
Kelsey, R. W.
Kerner, Robert J.
Kimball, Edith M.
King, Harold L.
Klingenhagen, Anna M.
Knaplund, Paul.
Knight, George W.
Knipfing, John R.
Knowlton, Daniel C.
Kohlmeier, Albert L.
Kull, Irving S.

L.

Landfield, Jerome.
Landrum, C. H.
Lapham, Martha.
Lapham, Ruth.
Larson, Laurence M.
Latourette, K. S.
Laughlin, S. B.
Layton, J. E.
Layton, Mrs. J. E.
Learned, H. Barrett.
Leebrick, K. C.
Libby, Walter.
Lindley, Harlow.
Lingelbach, William E.
Lingle, Thomas W.
Lord, Robert H.
Lowe, Walter I.
Lybyer, Albert H.

M.

McCann, Sister Mary
    Agnes.
MacDonald, William.
McFayden, Donald.
McGrane, Reginald C.
McLaren, W. W.
McMurry, Donald L.
McNeal, Edgar H.
Magoffin, Ralph V. D.
Malone, Carroll B.
Martin, A. E.
Martin, P. A.
Martin, Thomas P.
Martin, W. G.
Mendenhall, Kathleen.
Mereness, Newton D.
Merrill, Ethel L.
Middlebush, Frederick A.
Mitchell, James E.
Mitchell, Margaret J.
Moody, V. Alton.
Moon, Parker T.
Moore, Charles.
Moore, David R.
Moore, J. R. H.
Morgan, William T.
Myers, Clifford R.

N.

Newton, Arthur Percival.
Nicholas, Henry A.
Norwood, J. Nelson.
Notestein, Wallace.

O.

Oestreich, Rev. Thomas.
Oldfather, C. H.
Oliver, John W.
Olmstead, A. T.
Orbison, Inez.

P.

Page, Edward C.
Paine, Mrs. C. S.
Palmer, Herriott Clare.
Paltsits, Victor H.
Parish, John C.
Patterson, David L.
Paullin, C. O.
Pautz, William C.

Paxton, Frederic L.
Pearson, Henry G.
Pease, Theodore C.
Peck, Paul.
Pelzer, Louis.
Pence, Gwen J.
Perkins, Clarence.
Perrin, John W.
Phillips, Ulrich B.
Pierson, W. W.
Platner, S. B.
Pollard, Annie A.
Potter, Mary.
Priddy, Mrs. Bessie L.
Putnam, Mary B.

Q.

Quaife, M. M.

R.

Ramsdell, Charles W.
Randall, J. G.
Randall, Mrs. J. G.
Raney, William F.
Reeves, Jesse S.
Reilly, Drusilla M.
Reuter, Bertha A.
Riggs, Sara M.
Riker, T. W.
Risley, A. W.
Robertson, James A.
Robertson, James R.
Robertson, W. S.
Robinson, Edgar E.
Robinson, Morgan P.
Roseboom, Eugene H.
Russell, Elmer B.
Ryder, E. H.

S.

Salmon, Lucy M.
Schafer, Joseph.
Schlesinger, Arthur M.
Schmitt, Bernadotte E.
Scott, Mrs. George.
Severance, Frank H.
Shambaugh, Benjamin F.
Sharon, John A.
Shearer, Augustus H.
Sheldon, A. E.
Sheperd, W. J.
Shilling, D. C.

Shuart, Josephine M.
Siebert, Wilbur H.
Sioussat, Mrs. Albert.
Sioussat, St. George L.
Smith, Heman Hale.
Smith, Justin H.
Spaulding, Oliver L., jr.
Spencer, Henry R.
Stanclift, Henry C.
Steefel, Lawrence D.
Steele, Rev. James D.
Stephens, F. F.
Stephenson, Carl.
Stevens, Ernest N.
Stevens, Wayne E.
Stilwell, Lewis D.
Stine, O. C.
Stone, Mary H.
Storms, Albert B.
Sullivan, James.
Swain, Joseph Ward.
Sweet, William W.

T.

Takagi, Yasaka.
Tanner, Edwin P.
Thayer, William R.
Thompson, Frederic L.
Thorndike, Lynn.
Thuner, Edna.
Thwing, C. F.
Townsend, Andrew J.
Townsend, Prescott W.
Turner, E. R.
Turner, Morris K.

U.

Ulrick, Laura F.

V.

Vander Vilda, Alice.
Van Tyne, C. H.
Vaughn, Earnest V.

W.

Walsh, Annetta C.
Washburne, George A.
Webster, Homer J.
Westermann, William L.
Whiting, Williams.
Whyte, Alexander F.
Whyte, William M. E.
Wilde, Frederick E. J.
Wilson, Lucy L.
Wing, Herbert, jr.
Wittke, Carl.
Wood, George A.
Wood, Harlan N.
Woodburn, James A.
Wrench, Jesse E.
Wyckoff, Charles T.

Z.

Zéliqzon, Maurice.
Ziegler, Samuel H.
Zook, George F.

II. PROCEEDINGS OF THE FIFTEENTH ANNUAL MEETING OF THE PACIFIC COAST BRANCH OF THE AMERICAN HISTORICAL ASSOCIATION.

SAN FRANCISCO, CALIF., NOVEMBER 28–29, 1919.

Reported by WILLIAM A. MORRIS, *Secretary.*

The Fifteenth Annual Meeting of the Pacific Coast Branch of the
American Historical Association convened in San Francisco at 2.30
o'clock on Friday, November 28, 1919, after an intermission of two
years, occasioned by war conditions. The sessions were marked by
the high average of excellence of the papers presented and by the
decidedly representative character of the attendance. The annual
dinner, as well as all the sessions, was held at the Clift Hotel.

In calling to order the first session, the president, Mgr. Joseph M.
Gleason, referred to the fact that since the last meeting of the branch
affairs of great importance have transpired. Not only does the
period of these two years supply much matter for reflection and
much material for record, but it is marked by the loss of prominent
historical figures of the Pacific coast—Prof. Stephens, of the University of California; Prof. Cannon, of Stanford University; and
the historians, Bancroft, Hittell, and Eldredge.

The opening paper of the Friday afternoon session was read by
Prof. Payson J. Treat, of Stanford University, and was devoted to
" Japan's Leadership in Asia." Prof. Treat declared that the Japanese Empire is to-day the most powerful in Asia, and that this is
not due to its population, since in this respect it is behind China and
India. It is the most highly organized state—the state within which
industrial efficiency is greatest, the state that possesses the greatest
army and navy. All will probably agree that this is due to the
assimilation of western ideas and methods. But Japan, at first an
island empire, has no race antipathies, no language differences.
Feudalism trained its people to obey their masters. The restoration
of the empire in 1868 aroused intense patriotism.

The influence of Japan has not increased as consistently as her
power. The former was greatest after the Russian war. Even conservative mandarins admitted that Japan had mastered the secret of
national efficiency. Popular opposition to the partition of Bengal
in 1905 had great influence in Asia. At this time even the Persian
reformers found inspiration in Japan, and as far as the Dutch West
Indies and the Philippines there was much admiration for her

107

measures. She was respected and admired by all well-informe
Asiatics. To-day Japan is disliked by the Chinese and India
nationalists. She has tried to crush out national liberty in Kore
and has slighted China. She has proved too apt a pupil of the hate
aggressor.

Prof. Treat held that the qualities that won Japan her leadershi
will gain it again. It is necessary that she alter her ideas of leader
ship. She must recognize that the year 1914 marks a watershed,
great divide; that people can not be held in check by force; tha
service must come to the front.

At every point the forces of progress in Japan have had to com
bat the forces of conservatism. Prof. Treat asserted that the libera
leaders will turn from dreams of empire to constructive leadership.
In Japan brains rule to a high degree. When Japan shows she is
to be trusted and not feared, then she will rise. This will call for
the reassurance of China and a restoration of the national claims in
Korea. It will meet the opposition of conservatism. Prof. Treat
believes that Japanese statesmen will awaken to see that new lands
are not necessary to industrial development, as proved by the case
of Belgium. Japan aspires to be the Great Britain of Asia, and can
be only as she abandons the earlier policy of Great Britain.

Prof. Joseph V. Fuller, of the University of California, followed
with a paper entitled "A Prelude to the Austro-German Alliance:
The Russo-German Negotiations of 1876." Prof. Fuller asserted
that German complicity will not clear up the question of German
responsibility for the war. German relations with Austria were
shaped by the master hand of Bismarck, and as he shaped he brought
results in 1914.

By the late summer of 1876 Russia, convinced that no settlement of
the Bulgarian question by the consent of the powers was possible,
sought assurance from Germany. She asked whether Germany
could not hold Austria in check. Manteuffel returned to Livadia in
the Crimea with the assurance. Russia sought that it be put in
formal shape. Bismarck, angered with his attaché for transmitting
the request, took his time for a reply, asking that the question be
put in proper diplomatic form. In the meantime he told Prince
Hohenlohe that Germany could not see Austria crushed. The ambassador to Russia was told that he could not answer the question
specifically, since a third party was concerned. Russia had her
choice: Austria was to have her price for the liberation of Bulgaria,
or Russia was to face the combination against her.

Russia was to see more Slavic territory made over to the Haps-
burgs. Bismarck carried the thing through to the congress of
Vienna. He had underwritten the Austria foreign policy in the
Near East. The Austrian Government came to understand the ulti-

mate effect. Bismarck openly held out Great Britain as the real aggressor. Nothing could obscure his refusal to Russia and his support to Austria. Ultimately Germany must be confronted with the naked fact of this policy. Germany might continue to ride two horses, but Austria was never in doubt as to which Germany would cling when they broke apart. Germany went still farther in the dual alliance of 1879, which became the corner stone of the plan of a Middle Europe and developed into a community of interests.

Why could not the game of 1876 and 1908 hold again in 1914? German officials were caught in a plan of their own making. What could it profit to complain that the Austrian note to Serbia was too severe and was not communicated earlier? Von Tirpitz said that Germany knew the virtual terms of Austria's ultimatum on July 13. Bismarck signed a blank check upon which his empire was called to make payment in 1914.

The third paper of the afternoon was read by Prof. Roy Malcolm, of the University of Southern California, and was entitled "Some Historical Projects for a League of Nations." Prof. Malcolm held that the idea of such a league was no new one. It appears in the De Republica of Cicero. Very rarely has the project been a truly world-wide one. It is inherent in the idea of Islam. It was the dream of the Medieval Empire, although the line was drawn against the infidel. The idea of world supremacy of the empire inspired Dante, but his De Monarchia was an epilogue instead of a prophecy.

The paper presented the main features of the "Grand Design" of Henry IV, and then gave the views of William Penn, who in his essay on "The Present and Future Peace of Europe," held that all differences between sovereigns should be brought before a higher power, and that he who refused to bring questions to a decision or submit to this decision should be made to pay the expenses so incurred.

Two eighteenth-century plans were then outlined. That of the Abbe de La St. Pierre proposed a union of all sovereigns so far as possible, especially the Christian sovereigns, which was to employ its whole strength and care to punish the guilty. No sovereign was to take up arms but against him who should by three-fourths vote of the senate be deemed the enemy of all European society. He who refused to abide by the decision was to be deemed an enemy and forced to pay the expenses incurred by coercing him, and to lose permanently any territory taken from him in the process. Emanuel Kant believed conditions of permanent peace to demand that in each case the laws imposed should be based on self-rule. It was undesirable to make many into a single state. There was to be universal hospitality for members of any state in a foreign state.

The plan of William Ladd in 1840 based the enforcement of the will of the court on the good will of the litigants; that of James Lorimer suggested in 1884 an international body of two branches. Lorimer proposed that each State pay its deputies and fix their term of office. An international court was to sit. On the civil side judgment was to be by majority vote. No State might declare war independently. The power that did so was to be in the status of an international rebel.

In discussing the paper, President Gleason showed that one phase of Lorimer's plan was put into force by The Hague Conference three months before the war, Germany being one of the nine participating powers.

The closing paper, presented by Prof. R. G. Trotter, of Stanford University, dealt with " The Federalization of British North America." Prof. Trotter pointed out that not until the middle of the nineteenth century was it possible for discussion of union to become more than academic. In 1849 federation was proposed by the British American League as an antidote to a temporary Canadian agitation for annexation to the United States. Nine years later came the first sponsoring of the proposal by a party in power in the Province of Canada, but there was still general indifference.

In the early sixties internal and external affairs became increasingly critical and demanded a radical remedy. In the Province of Canada sectional and racial rivalry was producing constitutional deadlock. The problem of opening the great West to general trade and settlement and maintaining British sovereignty there demanded action. The American Civil War emphasized the weakness of the Provinces and increased British desire to have them more closely organized for self-defense. The Colonial Secretary, Newcastle, visiting the Provinces with the Prince of Wales in 1860, had become an enthusiast over the economic and political development of British North America. Another English enthusiast was the Duke's friend, Edward Watkin, who hoped to restore the fallen fortunes of the Grand Trunk Railway and build up British power. His work brought colonial leaders into closer contact, and a transfer in the control of the Hudson's Bay Co. increased the interest of an influential group of English capitalists in the unification of British America.

In 1864 political deadlock in Canada led to the great coalition. A Federal scheme was shaped in " Seventy-two resolutions." Borrowing certain Federal devices from American example, this frame of government was in the main built on British and colonial precedent and postulated a maintenance of the British connection. The Canadian Legislature asked for an act of the Imperial Government embodying the proposals, but in the Maritime Provinces local prejudices at first prevented acceptance. However, a favorable reaction soon set in, furthered by the British Government and stimulated by American economic hostility evidenced in the abrogation of reciprocity and by the menace of threatened Fenian invasion from the United States. In the winter of 1866–67, Canada, Nova Scotia, and New Brunswick sent delegates to London, where, on the basis of the Quebec scheme of 1864, a bill was drafted which was then enacted by Parliament. An opposition movement in the Maritime Provinces was ignored by the British Government and an offer from the new Dominion Government of better financial terms to the Provinces reconciled its chief leaders.

Federation was essentially the work of a few men, accepted by the people of the Provinces because of political crisis, economic pressure, and the fear of political and economic aggression from the United States, encouraged by the British Government in order to lessen its own burdens in defense and administration and to promote the consolidation and expansion of British economic as well as political interests in British North America. Federation made possible Canada's achievement of national autonomy as a partner in the British Commonwealth.

Before adjournment the president and the secretary both called to the attention of those present the advantages of membership in the American Historical Association, and the president announced the appointment of committees on nominations, auditing, and resolutions.

The annual dinner was held in the evening at 6.30, Prof. Herbert E. Bolton, of the University of California, presiding.

The president of the Pacific Coast Branch, Mgr. Gleason, took as the title of the annual address "Two World Conferences." Contrasting the present conference at Versailles with the Council of Constance, 500 years ago, he showed that both bodies were assembled to bring peace to Europe and to deal with social problems, the like of which Europe had not seen before. The great western schism by the beginning of the sixteenth century had disrupted Europe as never before. Europe had been virtually at war for 50 years. The peasantry was ground to the earth; morals had gone to the dogs. There was a realization that something must be done to save civilization. Mgr. Gleason also pointed out that the Emperor Sigismund, the strong man of the council, failed to carry out his plans.

The points of resemblance to the conference of Versailles as pointed out are, first, that the representatives consisted of both official and unofficial visitors. There were also experts at Constance, although only one ruler was in attendance. At Paris President Wilson was the only head of a state. When Sigismund came to Constance he took the reins in his own hands. So with President Wilson at Paris. At Constance there was a division of nations all under the thumb of a big four—Germany, France, England, and Italy—although later

Spain was also admitted. The Irish question was also brought up at Constance. At Constance the idealists from the University of Paris and elsewhere encountered a machine. The same selfishness and jealousy as at Paris were in evidence.

The opening address at the Saturday morning meeting, which began at 9.30 o'clock, was made by Prof. Herbert I. Priestley, of the University of California, who took as his subject " The Relations of the United States with Mexico since 1910."[1]

After designating the four periods into which Mexican history since 1910 falls—the rule of Diaz to 1911, the two years of Madero, the Huerta régime, 1913–14, and the rule of Carranza—Prof. Priestly spoke of the recent constitutional convention in Mexico and of its action affecting the oil interests of American citizens.

In conclusion he dealt with the question of possible American interference in Mexico, and said that only after complete pacification could real help be given to Mexico. We must be able to abjure territorial acquisition in compensation for loss of life and property. What is our proper course? Few things are sufficient to warrant actual war. National pride must not be evoked. Constructive statesmanship will be taxed to the utmost. Present conditions, however, may compel us to action against our better selves.

Prof. A. Harvey Collins, of Redlands University, followed with an account of " The Mormon Outpost of San Bernardino Valley." He showed that the settlement of San Bernardino Valley combined religious, territorial, and commercial motives. Brigham Young saw the whole California coast under the Latter Day Saints. In order to realize his dream, colonies of immigrants were founded here as outposts. The Pacific was the gateway through which foreign converts could be brought to Salt Lake City.

Prof. Collins devoted special attention to the Mormon Battalion of 500 Iowa Volunteers, formed during the Mexican War to aid in the conquest of California, under the command of Lieut. Col. Philip St. George Cook. They rendevouzed at Santa Fe, N. Mex., and the overland march was begun. On June 30, 1843, they arrived at San Diego, and after a rest of a few days the company was divided up. Those sent to Tehachapi became familiar with the climate of that region. A number of those who served in this battalion were impressed very favorably with the possibilities of farming on the Pacific coast and expressed a desire to form a colony there. President Brigham Young finally agreed. Capt. Jefferson Hunt and his two sons had been among the first to enlist in the Mormon Battalion. Being able to give definite information concerning San Bernardino Valley, he organized an expedition and led it through Cajon Pass into this valley. This colony settled on the Rancho de San Bernardino. The soil was very rich, and the people began to put in crops before the deed had passed to the new owners. Despite threatened Indian troubles the colonists by 1856 had became quite prosperous. The settlement was recalled by President Brigham Young in 1857, on account of trouble with the United States authorities. The complete evacuation of the valley was ordered. From 600 to 700 of the Latter Day Saints went back to Salt Lake City. In later years a number of these returned.

The concluding address of the morning was given by Prof. Levi Edgar Young, of the University of Utah. It was devoted to "Early Day Documents in Utah History," some of which were exhibited in facsimile.

Prof. Young spoke especially of the journal kept by David Pettigrew, chaplain of the Mormon Battalion, and of that of William Clayton, who was appointed historian of the command, with orders to study the flora and fauna and the types of Indians met; and of the journal of Robert Campbell, one of the secretaries of Brigham Young and territorial superintendent of schools in Utah. The memoirs of Harriet Young, wife of Lorenzo, the brother of Brigham Young, were also reviewed. Prof. Young suggested that the revelation of President Joseph Smith in the thirty's, in which he requested the brothers and sisters to keep a record of their experiences, probably explains the existence of so many Mormon journals. He also described the writings of Orson Pratt, a Dartmouth graduate and a philosophic writer, whose journal is in the possession of the Pratt family of Salt Lake; also the memoirs of his mother and her reference as a child of 11 to the Government expedition to Salt Lake, showing the Mormon fear of expulsion by the Federal authorities, and the determination to burn the city in case the troops should approach. Prof. Young spoke also of the archives in the State capital at Salt Lake and the records of the 19 city wards of Salt Lake City. Incidently he asserted his adherence to the view that the name Utah comes from the Piute language and means "on the heights," or possibly "land of plenty."

After a brief intermission the president called to order the business session.

The resolutions committee, consisting of C. E. Chapman, Joseph Schafer, A. Harvey Collins, and Percy A. Martin, reported the following resolution which was adopted:

Resolved by the members of the Pacific Coast Branch of the American Historical Association, That we deeply regret the irreparable loss we have been caused through the death of Henry Morse Stephens and Henry Lewin Cannon, and be it further resolved that the president of the branch be asked to appoint a member from the University of California and a member from Stanford University to draw up a suitable memorial to express our sorrow, copies of which should be furnished the Secretary and be spread on the records.

To serve upon this committee the president appointed Profs. Bolton and Treat. The special resolutions reported by the committee are the following:

Resolved, That in the death of Prof. H. Morse Stephens, Sather professor of history in the University of California, the Pacific Coast Branch of the American Historical Association lost its most distinguished member. A highly cultured gentleman of broad acquaintance, a widely read and versatile scholar, a distinguished specialist in portions of his field, a notable lecturer, and an inspiring teacher, he was withal a unique and outstanding personality in the world of historical scholarship. As one of the founders of the branch, a regular attendant at its sessions, and its best representative at the meetings of the parent association, of which he was president for a term, he contributed in superlative measure to the success of our organization.

Resolved, That the Pacific Coast Branch of the American Historical Association recognizes the great loss which it has sustained through the death of Henry Lewin Cannon on January 5, 1919. Prof. Cannon was a founder member of the branch, a faithful attendant at its meetings, a contributor to its programs, and a former officer. A thoroughly trained scholar, a careful investigator, and a suggestive teacher, he possessed qualities which had already won recognition and which would have assured a career of great usefulness. The members of the branch sincerely regret that they can no longer count upon his unselfish cooperation in advancing the work to which he had dedicated all his talents.

Further resolutions reported by the resolutions committee are the following:

Resolved, That in the death of Hubert Howe Bancroft the Pacific Coast of America has lost one of its most useful and uniquely picturesque pioneers. With enterprise unbounded and with audacious courage, he created the conditions which made possible the first scientific treatment of the history of one-half of our continent. His labors also endow the States and peoples of this coast with a priceless heritage of historical treasures, now placed at the disposal of scholars by the University of California. It is not our function to pass judgment, in detail, upon the histories produced under Mr. Bancroft's planning, management, and collaboration. But as heirs and beneficiaries in a special sense of the work which illustrates his enthusiastic devotion to a life ideal, it is fitting that this association should recognize the great debt which all workers in any portion of his field owe to Mr. Bancroft as writer, as publisher, and as collector of the far-famed Bancroft Library.

Resolved, That the members of the Pacific Coast Branch of the American Historical Association feel a deep loss in the passing away of Theodore H. Hittell, an honored and enthusiastic member, and one whose writings added so much to the historical literature of the Pacific slope.

Resolved by the members of the Pacific Coast Branch of the American Historical Association, That we deeply feel the loss from our number of Zoeth Skinner Eldredge, whose enthusiastic love of California, and whose many scholarly and interesting writings on the history of California have been an inspiration to us all and a lasting memorial to his name.

Resolutions were also adopted tendering to Archbishop Hanna, of San Francisco, and Bishop Cantwell, of Los Angeles, thanks for their letters agreeing to make all restorations of the California missions in accordance with the plans of the California Historical Commission, and tendering, thanks to the press of California for its generous efforts in promoting the restoration of the missions; also declaring it to be the sentiment of the branch that the paper by Prof. Treat, entitled " Japan's Leadership in Asia," and the paper by Prof. Priestley, entitled " The Relations of the United States with Mexico since 1910," are of such timeliness as to make their publication highly desirable; commending to the history teachers' session the desirability of expressing definite views in the form of resolutions on the course of study proposed by the committee on history and education for citizenship in the schools; and directing the secretary of the branch to write such letters and take such other appropriate action as may be necessary to carry out the foregoing resolutions.

The auditing committee, consisting of C. V. Gilliland, C. L. Goodwin, and A. M. Kline, reported that they had examined the accounts of the secretary treasurer and found them correct and in good order.

The nominating committee, P. J. Treat, H. E. Bolton, Roy Malcolm, Joseph Schafer, and L. E. Young, reported the nomination of the following to serve as officers for the ensuing year: President, Levi E. Young, University of Utah; vice president, Robert Glass Cleland, Occidental College; secretary treasurer, J. J. Van Nostrand, University of California. Members of the council in addition to the above: R. L. Ashley, Pasadena High School; A. M. Cleghorn, Lowell High School, San Francisco; E. E. Robinson, Stanford University; W. J. Trimble, University of Idaho. Upon motion the nominations were closed and the secretary instructed to cast the ballot for the above nominees, who were declared elected.

On behalf of the University of Southern California an invitation was extended to hold the next meeting of the branch in Los Angeles.

The president elect of the branch, L. E. Young, was chosen official delegate to attend the meeting of the council of the American Historical Association in Cleveland.

In his concluding remarks as president of the branch, Mgr. Gleason expressed personal gratification at the number in attendance upon the two sessions and at the character of the papers presented. In a brief review of the work of the branch for the last 15 years he spoke of the labors of the two large universities that have fostered a spirit of research, and of the two departments of history and political science working toward establishing a school of western historical scholarship. He spoke further in appreciation of the work of H. H. Bancroft in attempting to gather the original materials of history. Said he: " We are the legatees of him and of men like him, and we have the encouragement and the making of young men and women who are to be the historical writers of the future."

The teachers' session convened at 2 p. m., Prof. William A. Morris, presiding. The general question for consideration was history and education for citizenship in the schools. The session opened with an address by Prof. Joseph Schafer, chairman of the joint committee on history and education for citizenship in the schools, American Historical Association and the National Board for Historical Service, who spoke on the projected report of the committee on history and education for citizenship.

After calling attention to the fact that the committee had found California one of only three or four States in which there had been any considerable activity to reconstruct the history course in schools, he summarized the proposed report of the committee which divided the course of study into three parts—the elementary school course to the end of the sixth grade, the junior high school to the end of the ninth, and the senior high school to the end of the twelfth. He described the proposed elementary course as community history and American history and civics in elementary form. The junior high-school course consists of American history in its world setting, and in the ninth grade an inovation for which Prof. Schafer himself is responsible—a study of the activities of the American people in the present and historically along 10 great occupational lines.

In the third group we have the final study in high school which should consist of a group of courses enabling the student prepared to step out into civic life to make an intensive study of problems with which he will deal, as they find their orientation in the history of the country and the history of the world. This study will begin about the middle of the seventeenth century. If it can be done it would be advantageous to give a preliminary course covering world history from the beginning.

The portion of the course of study as proposed which has been most criticized is that for the first six grades. Here the committee took its suggestion from Prof. Henry Johnson. Mr. Johnson insists on two things as fundamental aims in history teaching: First, development of an attitude of mind toward society; second, the development of an attitude of mind toward historical material. What Mr. Johnson contends is that the two things mentioned can be secure through the teaching of history and not through the teaching o anything else in equal measure. Teaching children to read the news paper effectively would accomplish for citizenship results which hav never been accomplished. Our aim should be to afford childre some help by way of shaping their minds in getting at the truth tha is presented.

Prof. Shafer stated that it is his opinion these things can be done with very young students. A good many teachers have done them. Young children quickly pick up the elements of criticism. The idea of orderly evolution and change may not come by the end of the sixth grade. It may not necessarily come by the end of the college course, and many people go to their graves who do not yet sense the idea that human society has come to be what it is through an orderly process of change. When the child begins to reflect on things he will more readily get the idea than if his early training had been through the story of American history. By taking the history of the community from the beginning and then the history of the United States from the beginning, even if we turn the child out of school at the beginning of the seventh grade, when he reaches 15 or 16 he will look back over the system of facts and realize what it means.

Mr. William John Cooper, superintendent of schools in Piedmont, Calif., next presented a paper on the course for the first six grades. He said that undoubtedly Mr. Johnson's words would carry great weight, yet if he proposed to teach the newspaper it would be a good idea to teach by reading newspapers, and not something else. Other things should have weight. He doubted whether the orderly course in history would have results with all pupils. According to the Army tests the average drafted man brought before the examining boards could do work of no higher than the seventh grade. The committee should keep in mind that the group in the high schools is a selected group and not of average intelligence. The others drop out of school at the end of the sixth grade, when they have reached the level beyond which they can not do work. How much of orderly, systematic history can we put into this mixed group in the first six grades? At the expense of this orderly process of American history in which we come to 1600, 1816, or some other date, Mr. Cooper does not believe these are going to mean very much to the average child. Some may remember these facts, but the average child has no memory back of five years.

In laying out a course of history in the ordinary school we must remember that it will take a year and a half or two years for many to get through the first grade. It would be better to have a greater variety of material. In the fifth grade, or in some cases in the fourth grade, at the time of the presidential election the principles underlying elections can be taught. It is no use to wait until the eighth grade, when the students are not interested. A large number of topics should be outlined in the early grades as a suggestion to the students. Many people who work eight hours a day need some constructive suggestion for the use of leisure. If we can interest them in history so they will read it when they go out, they will learn more at that time than in school. Mr. Cooper would greatly enlarge this by alternative courses, making a much more extensive course. On the civic side the child will learn to be a good citizen by being a good citizen. We are getting away from citizenship as a book subject. Also, a division should be made between a course that could be used in the graded schools and one that could be used in the ungraded schools.

A paper on the course for the intermediate grades was presented by Miss Elsie M. Wood, of the San Jose High School. Some of the main ideas presented are the following: There will be a considerable body of students passing from the eighth grade to the ninth grade because of the intermediate schools. There is no reason why the course of study should not be the same for the eight to four plan. In the seventh grade, we should give the European background from the early seventeenth century to the constitutional period. In the eighth grade the constitutional period to the present time should be given. In the ninth grade we should give civics. In the seventh grade we have the early period of discovery. The beginnings of our land and liberty are central topics on which the work of the year turns. The distribution of topics has not been described, but more emphasis should be given to Massachusetts and Virginia social life and economic growth. In the eighth grade we have the development of natural resources, the westward movement, the growth of a national consciousness, the industries, and similar subjects. The Civil War is given in the first half year and the problems growing out of it in the second half year. In the ninth grade we try, first, to make the ideals of the American people part of the life of the student; second, to develop a constructive attitude in consideration of all problems which stimulate an interest to participate in community affairs; third, to present the subject as practically and concretely as possible. This is to be accomplished by research and the socialized recitation. Current topics should find a place here. We could carry our research rather widely, but not too deeply. The socialized recitation should be the best way to show the student his place in the community.

Mr. F. H. Clark, of the Lowell High School of San Francisco, in a paper on the course for the high school held that the needs of the growing child in the schools can not be overestimated. We in California have been inclined to go our own way. The committee of ten tended to fix standards in California when we were not ready for them and tended to cut off helpful experiments that were going on. This plan is essentially new in its aims. Mr. Clark believes the report will be received very favorably in California. Criticism would be largely wth the work of the first division. The high schools can not take a decisive attitude until the matter is perfected in the lower schools. If in the first six years the teachers can find their way to bring about results, an attitude of mind toward society, and an attitude of mind toward historical material, then the problem of the high school is solved. We can lay out any number of courses of history; if only the pupils can come to us with this previous training we will know what to do with them. The pupils come into the high school with a prejudice against history. The trouble is they have not had real history. As to the way in which the plan can be handled in the senior high school. The attitude in the California schools is that all academic subjects should come five times a week. This is largely due to the influence of the University of California which defines subjects in terms of units. There is an advantage in four periods instead of five. The student can take more subjects in the same time. A standardized course for the high school is not a problem for history teachers themselves, but for the whole school. Three years as a minimum requirement would mean that high schools would have to give up their plan of an elective system. This would not be possible in the upper years. One, two, three, or four recitations per week can be given. The difficulty is in providing conditions so that the student can get into a history course.

In the discussion which followed the reading of these papers Prof. Morris said that it is necessary for the child to have a knowledge of some history beyond that of his own country, and the question is whether this European history can be given satisfactorily in one year. Also, can United States history and civics be given well in one year?

Prof. Bolton then said that one of the difficulties we all seem to encounter is that boys and girls come into high school with a distaste for history. This is created by a course which is formalized and which follows the teacher's interest rather than the pupil's needs.

Miss Geraldine Hall spoke on citizenship, holding that we should try to treat better the content we have in training students for citizenship. It can be taught subjectively in every course in the curriculum. Teachers should be trained in good citizenship. We should not crowd too much content into a short space of time. A few problems well solved are better than many. History should not be treated as a descriptive but as a living science. Mr. E. E. Wood said that a great many students come into our high schools whose aim is vocational and who are not historically inclined. Those who go to high school for commercial and manual work will not have anything like three years to devote to history. American history and citizenship are necessary, and the course must be shorter than for the academic student. Citizenship must be taught in connection with vocations. A compulsory course one hour per week in the ninth grade and possibly in the tenth and eleventh grades should be considered.

Mgr. Gleason spoke of his experience with men in the military and naval camps, and favored the teaching of citizenship in ele-

mentary schools. The sore spot is that, as Prof. Bolton said, we have
so formalized our courses that the subject may become obnoxious to
the student. The high schools must take the law into their own
hands and put in four-hour courses instead of five. We should start
teaching citizenship to the little child. The environment can be
Americanized and the child will show a pride in living up to American standards. Through vitalization of the subject even a little
child can be aroused.

Prof. W. Scott Thomas, of the University of California, spoke
in approval of the plan outlined by Prof. Schafer. He said that
teaching words to little-folks is all that we have been doing. Some
get the work with less effort than others, and there are so many
different types of pupils that we can not say what the schools
should give. We must get away from the idea that all students in
all classes should have five hours per week.

At this point it was moved by Mr. Clark that the meeting indorse
the general plan offered by Mr. Schafer's committee for the first two
divisions of the course, and the outline for the senior high school
under conditions making it possible for all students to take the minimum course. The motion was carried.

Continuing the discussion Mr. Cooper asserted that in his opinion
the old committee of eight plan was better than this, and if this were
to supersede the older plans the influence would be bad for a while
at least; also he thought the course should be greatly enlarged.

Prof. Schafer then stated that he felt himself to be almost wholly
in harmony with the discussion by Superintendent Cooper. He
asked approval of the plan of the committee on education for citizenship in the schools, giving two hours per week in the second, third,
fourth, fifth, and sixth grades. This work may be given advantageously without disturbing the plan of the committee of eight.
Mild revisions may be made and alternative courses offered. In the
Washington meeting there was a strong sentiment in the committee for administering the lower-grade course according to this
earlier plan. If it is possible to teach arithmetic in an elementary
way it should not be impossible to teach history in an elementary
way. The committee intends to ask Mr. Johnson to prepare a
syllabus, for teachers must have something to work by, and there
must be a complete set of suggestions for selecting problems and
working them out. In reference to the senior high school and the
criticism of the plan by Mr. Clark, the speaker stated that the committee began with the idea that it might be possible to devise one,
two, or three hour courses. The suggestion was put to the teachers
and without exception they all said they must have five hours. The
resolution should be put to the committee on some other basis than
the five-hour plan.

III. JOINT CONFERENCE OF HISTORICAL SOCIETIES AND THE NATIONAL ASSOCIATION OF STATE WAR HISTORY ORGANIZATIONS.

JOINT CONFERENCE OF HISTORICAL SOCIETIES AND THE NATIONAL ASSOCIATION OF STATE WAR HISTORY ORGANIZATIONS.

The fifteenth annual conference of historical societies was held at Cleveland, Ohio, December 29, at 10 a. m., in the New Lounge of the Hollenden Hotel. The conference was a joint one with the National Association of State War History Organizations to discuss the general after-the-war questions.

The chairman, Dr. Thomas Lynch Montgomery, being unable to be present, Mr. W. H. Cathcart, director of the Western Reserve Historical Society, took the chair.

The first topic presented was "The Preservation of War Material," the discussion being opened by Frank H. Severence, of the Buffalo Historical Society. He said that to most workers in local historical societies the topic suggested two kinds of war material to be preserved; first, material which belongs to a library; second, museum material. War souvenirs and relics suitable for preservation in an historical museum needed only to be selected with judgment. Museums were prone to load themselves down with rubbish. Small institutions, naturally, found it difficult to secure valuable collections, but the sort of material that would go into a museum was so obvious that it did not appear necessary to dwell on the subject further in this connection.

The historical society in adding war material to its library should keep in view the special needs of its constituents and the special phase of war activities in which its home community was most interested. Taking an average institution which is not State aided, in an average city, the speaker suggested that its collections should be made on the following lines:

First and most important, as full a record as possible of the war service of all the men and women in the home community, whether in Army, Navy, Marine Service, Aviation, Medical Corps, Hospital Service, Red Cross, Y. M. C. A., K. of C., or other organizations. These records, based on the lists of the local draft boards, regimental muster rolls, and casualty lists as reported in the War Department Official Bulletin should be conveniently kept by a card system, classified according to service and indexed under each department with the name of the person whose card should bear his home address, his rank, and in the briefest form which would be clear, a summary of what his service had been. Such classification would naturally fall under the heads "killed," "wounded or gassed," "in prison or missing," "honors won," etc. The full official citation for honors should be part of the record.

Special classification should be made according to the special interest of the community. To illustrate: In Buffalo, an important point for airplane manufacture, with an aviation field, it had been found worth while to record aviation events which touch Buffalo or were shared by Buffalo men. Each community had something of particular interest which should be thus fully recorded. It had also been found useful to supplement the card records with loose-leaf scrapbooks, in which newspaper clippings were brought together in form easy for reference. In the speaker's work it had been found useful to preserve miscellaneous material under headings, "War records of Fort Porter" (a local post which was used as a convalescent hospital during the war), "Mine sweepers built at the Buffalo shipyards," "Home defense," "Profiteers," "Grocers disciplined and fined," "Church activities," "Erection of memorials," and other phases of the four years of war, not forgetting the various Liberty loans and the war service of civilians, some of whom, from the speaker's home community had been summoned by the Federal Government to important service abroad, and others to act on commissions at Washington as "dollar-a-year men." A brief card entry of subject, with reference to an available newspaper file for details, is the simplest and usually the most satisfactory guide for the inquirer.

Other lines of preservative work would naturally occur to the practical librarian; among them the collection of pictures and of posters for the various loans and fund-raising drives; recruiting posters of this and other countries; official proclamations; and, in general, all available material which in the judgment of the librarian would have an historical interest in days to come. The map collection should be as full as possible. The music of the war, including published songs, and the poetry which embodied the spirit of the time, might well be preserved; and also moving-picture films recording departure or return of troops, patriotic meetings, war-time decoration of streets and buildings, unveiling of memorials, etc. These films require care in handling and a specially constructed depository, but are historical records worthy of the librarian's attention.

Every historical society library, no matter how small, should have an official record of the part its home community bore in the war. In Buffalo the historical society had cooperated with the city in compiling material to be published by the city. It would supplement this in its own publications.

Unofficial material needs to be sifted. In cities where there are several public libraries, circulating and reference, duplication of much material may be avoided by an understanding between librarians.

Mr. Frank M. Gregg, of Cleveland, continued the discussion with special reference to posters. He said he had in mind in his collecting a source library. He felt that in this war, as in no other, with the exception of the French Revolution, " the nations "—that is, the peoples—had taken part. There was a formula of the statesmen which was applicable—" people, propaganda, public opinion." Gustave Le Bon had emphasized the difference between the psychology of the individual, which is based on reason, and collective psychology, which is mental contagion based on emotion. For examples, Mr. Gregg showed two illustrated posters, one a British poster of the flag, arousing faith, another, of Bolshevism, arousing fear. It was the effort of those who used posters to develop the collective contagion of the peoples by arousing these emotions. Mr. Gregg said he was not interested primarily in the technique of the posters and in the art, but in the emotional effect on the people and in the creation of public opinion. He had at one time collected ephemeral material of the Civil War and had found it difficult to secure such material after the time of its issuance had passed. So on the first day of this war he had cabled to the agents of the American Express Co. in all the European capitals to collect for him the ephemeral material and additional propaganda. As a result he had collected over 100,000 items, none of them books, but all of the kind that comes through one's mail day after day and is then thrown into the wastebasket. He had also secured over 10,000 post cards, 30 volumes of photographs, phonographic records, and all of the songs and Christmas cards touching on the war published in this country; in fact, all the material possible which was used to create public opinion. This will be the basis of the history of the war in the future, for it was a war of psychology rather than of troops.

With reference to the character of the posters, Mr. Gregg thought that the parliamentary posters of Great Britain were superior to any; and that the best was Abel Faire's " We'll get them." The next best posters were perhaps the Italian. America was late in entering the war and in developing the posters. Our artists used the mass of colors and complex composition, but some of their posters were extremely effective. The Russian posters delighted and pleased, especially those for the last Russian loan. The Germans showed their psychology in their posters, as in other things. They absolutely failed to recognize the psychology of their own people. The design and writing were such that it could not be read across the street.

The composition depended on mass colors. Germany was the only nation that used futurist drawings for posters, and most of them were very crude. This German work is, however, just beginning to come through. The proclamations, of which Mr. Gregg has 500, are only convincing proofs of the mental attitude of the Germans, and confirm on their own evidence the atrocities practiced in Belgium and France.

Mr. Cathcart spoke concerning the work of the Western Reserve Historical Society in collecting war material. At the opening of the war in 1914 he had felt that war collections were out of the line of the society, but when the United States entered the war he had thought it a duty to gather material as far as possible. He was fortunate in having the Palmer collection of Civil War material as a magnificent guide in the matter of collecting, as it illustrated the kind of material that would be difficult to secure 20 or 30 years later. Posters and broadsides which stared one in the streets at the time they were published had disappeared months ago. The Nation was unprepared, the people uneducated in liberal giving and not trained to participate in loans; hence the efforts made by the Federal reserve branches should be preserved, and likewise the material put out by the welfare organizations such as the Y. M. C. A. and the K. of C. The books, such as regimental histories would be of value, but they would come later. Mr. Cathcart had immediately put himself in touch with the governors of the Federal reserve banks and had received every item issued by the banks during the war. He had gathered all the American posters possible but had done very little with the foreign posters. The mounting of posters and the care of photographs is a tremendous task, but at present it is more important to collect and save. As for medals, he had arranged with the Treasury and Navy Departments to secure a replica, at the cost of manufacture, of all those issued. He finds that there is no way of stimulating the interest of school children so well as by this collection. As for the records of the local men, he had not found it necessary to do as the Buffalo Historical Society had done, for in Cleveland the strong city commission had made records of all participants, and had done this far better than the society would have been able to do it.

Dr. A. H. Shearer, of the Grosvenor Library of Buffalo, continued the discussion on posters. He referred to some of the large collections in public institutions, as at Clark University, Princeton, the New York Public Library, Library of Congress, and Harvard, and to the fact that each had been working out plans for the care and preservation of this material. A committee of the American Library Association had already made a preliminary report. In the matter of preservation there had been various experiments as to the mounting of material and the process to be followed.' In classification there seemed to be general agreement in favor of arrangement by broad subjects, such as recruiting, loans, and welfare organizations, according to countries. In cataloging, the use of first words as worked out by Princeton will perhaps prove the best, as it is not always possible to identify the artists or author. Where the posters are illustrated this plan is almost imperative, but in the case of proclamations the standard arrangement in cataloging will probably be followed. The value of posters is both artistic and historical. Speaking from a knowledge of French posters, and in particular of the Edward Micheal gift to the Grosvenor Library, of which some 350 are illustrated, he said that the work of artists formerly the most prominent had been brought together with the work of artists who had made their mark through the war posters. The history of the war will have to pay attention to the posters, and in examining them interesting facts will be discovered; for example, that these posters had to have the approval of the Government.

Mr. V. H. Paltsits, of the New York Public Library, said that the library had tried from the beginning to procure a copy of each poster issued in this country and had secured foreign posters from its representatives abroad. Twenty-five thousand people a month had visited the exhibit. This poster exhibit has been superseded by Signal Service photographs, to which more people had come, sometimes several thousand in one day. The collection of war books and pamphlets is the best in America. The poster exhibit was introduced by a selection of broadsides issued in America from the time of the Revolution.

Mr. George S. Goddard, of the Connecticut State Library, said that Connecticut had gone in quite early for the collection of war records. By a special act of the legislature the governor could take a census, and in February, 1917, this census had been taken, including also an industrial and agricultural and automobile survey. This was turned over to the State library, together with the files of the State council for defense and of the local war boards. These had been arranged in vertical files by separate classes and by towns. Each war bureau in the towns had kept personal records of each person in service in duplicate. Connecticut had probably four-fifths of these on cards. There was also a special blank of four pages on file at Hartford, containing on the first page a man's personal record before he entered the war; on the next two pages his military record, including his promotions, wounds, etc.; and on page 4 what he thought of the whole business before the war, in service, and since. These are filed under towns. Every county has a number in the hundreds; for example, 100 for Hartford County, and every town is arranged alphabetically; 101 is Avon, and 114 is Hart-

ford. A roll of honor is sent to each town as a certificate of all
its participants in the war. This roll becomes a table of contents of
all the persons in the files under the respective towns. The library
accepts gladly diaries and photographs of persons who have been
in service. It is also collecting records of civilian service. There
have been exhibits in the town halls and these have served to bring
in important material. The Connecticut Commandary of the Military Order of Foreign Wars has turned over all its collections.
From Capt. Brainerd, of Case, Lockwood & Brainerd, in Hartford,
has come to the library a remarkable collection of foreign posters,
all mounted on linen and in folders.

Dr. Albert E. McKinley, of the Pennsylvania War History Commission, was ill, but sent his paper, which was read by the secretary.
It properly follows at this point, although it was read later in the
program.

ARRANGEMENT AND CLASSIFICATION OF WAR HISTORY MATERIAL.

I. *Character of material received.*—Anything from a printed program to a
1,500-page typewritten report. Reports containing maps, and photographs of
all sizes. Posters from a few inches to many feet in length. Photographs
from cabinet size to one 30 by 40 inches, and many panoramic views. Printed
reports from a few pages to many volumes. Letters of every description,
bound reports of all sizes, thousands of cards of various sizes, honor rolls, etc.

II. *Arrangement.*—Various ways of arranging this material were examined,
and after careful thought it was decided to place all matter in folders in
filing cases, except posters, as it was believed that this method was cheaper
and would prove more satisfactory.

Many of the subjects are subdivided into the 67 counties in Pennsylvania.
Often there is only one report for each county, and this would take, if pamphlet boxes were adopted, 67 pamphlet boxes for every subject that was divided
into counties. A drawer of a filing cabinet will often contain 300 to 400
folders, each containing a small number of reports, at a cost for storage
many times less than if the pamphlet boxes were used, besides doing away
with the cost of expensive shelving and saving a great amount of space. Besides, loose papers in pamphlet boxes settle at the bottom and become crumpled,
and it is almost impossible to keep dust out of a pamphlet box.

If reports are larger than the folder, 9 by 11¾ inches, they are folded, unless
bound, in which case they are placed upon the top of the case holding the
drawer containing the subject, and a reference calling attention to this publication is placed in the folder.

Panoramic views are dissected into sections, 11 by 8½ inches, backed, and
filed in the folders.

Posters larger than the 9 by 11½ inches are placed in blue-print cases, the
drawers of which measure 32 by 42 inches.

III. *Classification.*—The main thing to consider in relation to classification
is the fact that our collections are not a finished product. It is preparatory
matter, from which the historian, or researcher, will write his papers and
print his books that must be given first consideration; and, furthermore, as
already stated under the heading "Arrangement," some of the classifications
that would be admirable were the material in bound form would be unworkable

in such a miscellaneous collection as is being sent in to war history commissions.

The numercial, alphabetical, and Dewey classifications were examined, and each deemed to have some objectionable features, and after a great deal of planning and study, the following classification was adopted as the practicable one for the class of material:

1. All material is placed in one of the 24 classes as follows:

1. Pre-war conditions.
2. Preparation for participation.
3. United States in war times.
4. United States administration in Pennsylvania.
5. Pennsylvania State Government in war times.
6. County and local governments in war times.
7. Military and naval participation.
8. Industries during the war.
9. Agriculture and food production.
10. Financing the war.
11. Transportation and communication in war times.
12. Commercial readjustments.
13. Social welfare and relief organizations.
14. Education as affected by the war.
15. Work of religious bodies during the war.
16. Labor and the crisis.
17. War work of the professions.
18. Public health under the conditions of war.
19. Women in the war.
20. Public sentiment before, during, and after the war.
21. Americanization.
22. Honor rolls, memorials, and parades.
23. Negroes in the war.
24. Reconstruction problems.

2. Under each class are the subjects, arranged alphabetically, which relate only to this particular class, while there are others which would be used in preparing material for one or more of the other classes.

Following each subject is a list of class numbers, showing the classes in which this subject should receive consideration. The particular class under which this subject is filed is given Roman numerals.

An asterisk in front, shows that the subject is subdivided into the counties of the State, and the # sign tells that these subjects are filed under this main class.

The following is a sample of a class, with the subjects filed under it, and the subjects related to it, but filed under other classes:

IX. *Agriculture and food production:*
 * Agriculture, 2, IX, 10, 13, 16, 19, 24.
 Automotive transportation, 8, 9, XI, 12, 16.
 * Banks and banking, 8, 9, X, 11, 13, 24.
 * Colleges and universities, 7, 9, 13, XIV, 17, 20, 24.
 * Commerce, 1, 9, 10, 11, XII, 16, 19, 24.
 * Conscription boards, 2, VII, 8, 9, 13, 17.
 * Dairy products, IX.
 * Farm implements and machinery, VII, 9.
 * Finance, 8, 9, X, 11, 12, 24.

25066°—23——9

* Flour and flour mills, IX.

* Food, IX.

* Food administration, IX.

* Fuel, VIII, 9, 11, 12, 16, 18.

Horses, IX.

Housing problem, 8, 9, 12, 13, 16, XVIII, 19, 24.

Labor and laboring classes, 1, 8, 9, 10, 11, 12, 13, XVI, 18, 19, 20, 24.

Leather, VIII, 9.

Liquor problem, 8, 9, 12, 13, 15, 16, 18, XX, 24.

Prices, 1, 8, 9, 11, 12, 19, 24. .

Profiteering, VIII, 9, 12, 16, 24.

Taxation, 1, 8, 9, X, 11, 12, 20, 24.

Tobacco, IX.

Transportation, 1, 8, 9, 10, XV, 12, 16, 24.

Wool, VIII, 9.

We have a list of subjects, and each report is assigned to one of these subjects. The number, or numbers, after the subject shows the classes under which the subject should be noted, and the Roman figure the class under which it is filed, as follows:

Subjects into which the material is classified.

NOTE.—Subjects marked with an asterisk are subdivided as follows: United States, Pennsylvania, Pennsylvania counties.

Advertising. (See Publicity.)

Agriculture, 2, IX, 10, 13, 16, 19, 24:

 Cattle.

 Corn.

 Domestic animals.

 Farm management.

 Fertilizers and manures.

 Grain.

 Oats. .

 Potatoes.

 School gardens. (See School gardens.)

 Vegetable.

 War gardens. (See War gardens.)

 Wheat.

Aircraft, VII, 8, 10, 17.

* Alien enemy property, 3, 8, 12, XX.

* Aliens, 3, 4, 7, 8, 13, 16, XX, 24.

* American Red Cross, 2, 7, XIII, 19.

* Arbitration, 8, 11, 12, XVI, 24.

Architects. (See Art, Architects.)

Artists. (See Art.)

Art, XVII; architects, sculptors.

Authors. (See Literature.)

Automobiles. (See Automotive transportation.)

Automotive transportation, 8, 9, XI, 12, 16.

Bakers and bakeries. (See Food—Bakeries and bakers.)

Banks and banking, 8, 9, X, 11, 13, 24, Federal Reserve Bank, X.

The same numbers mean the same class in every case.

IV. *Cataloguing.*—All reports, including illustrations, maps, etc., are catalogued under every subject in which they could be used and thoroughly cross indexed. All names of persons, especially inhabitants of the State, connected with committees, etc., are indexed upon cards.

War service records.—These are arranged alphabetically by county, town, and name and are used for Pennsylvania men who enlisted in the service of the United States and the Allies, and for Red Cross, K. of C., Y. M. C. A., etc., workers who were in active service.

A separate folder is given for each person, and in this folder is placed his war service blank, photograph, letter, newspaper clippings, or any other information relating to the particular individual.

Folders.—We use the folders divided into four positions. The tabs designate the following: First position, enlistment in Regular Army; second position, enlistment in National Guard; third position, enlistment in Naval Reserves, Navy, or Marine Corps; fourth position, enlistment in welfare workers in active service.

Rubber stamps.—We use the following stamps, and stamp on the outside of the folder any information of this character contained on the service blank: Allied Armies; American Library Association; Army nurse; citation; died of accident; died of disease; died from effects of gas; died of wounds; dishonorable discharge; gassed; home defense; killed; K. of C.; Liberty loan; loss of sight; lost at sea; Marine Corps; missing in action; National Army; National Guard; Naval Reserve; Navy; prisoner; Red Cross nurse; Red Cross worker; Regular Army; Salvation Army; shell shocked; Society of Friends; Students Army Training Corps; volunteer; War Camp Community Service; wounded; yeowomen; Y. M. C. A.; Young Men's Hebrew Association.

This enables us to select the various groups, without the necessity of reading the war service records, many of which are illegible.

This arrangement and classification of material and service records will enable us to give to the writers all material contained in our archives relating to one class, one subject, or one group of service records; and also, in cases where county histories are desired, all material relating to that particular county, without the necessity of going over thousands of files to pick out those subjects relating to some particular group, subject, or county, and with the least expenditure of time and money.

The second part of the program dealt with plans for publication of war material. The first speaker was Hon. Arthur Kyle Davis, of the Virginia War History Commission. His paper was as follows:

PUBLICATION OF WAR MATERIALS.

The matter of publication brings up at once the question of survival values. It is a matter that demands catholic view and some novelty of treatment. The old standards of value in war history have become antiquated and new survival values are emerging. Almost at the very outset there is need for a readjustment of our traditional scale and estimate both of absolute and relative values of war history material.

There is a new world of history, in which we have no guide, no blazed trail, no chart, no compass. It is a new world of history, because it is the history of a world in a new kind of war—a war of embittered nations with every nerve and fiber of the national life, even every filament of civilian life, alive and tingling with the vital currents of war activity. The historian has to do with the brand new and astounding fact that even the small-beer chronicles of industrial and civilian life have become an essential part of the story of the war. Banking and transportation, agriculture, and manufacture, even charity and religion, have become stated parts of a national war program.

The old modes of comparison, the old basis of pride, are broken down. Those gauges of patriotism and fighting spirit, the numbering of the hosts and the counting of the shekels, have been made obsolete by the new magic of the draft and quota. No State to-day may claim merit or plume itself unduly because it gave its quota of men or money. In fact, there is already something archaic in the reference in the current Scribner's to "the State which, with its population divided, boasts that in the Civil War it furnished more troops to either side than any other State." One may be perfectly sure that States will boast, but the boast must have a different basis. What we want to publish is the facts that give the best basis for State pride—facts that have best survival value.

This war was fought by the book of arithmetic, and an advanced book of arithmetic at that. The old and easy testing of efficiency by elemental methods of addition and subtraction is out of place in a war period where every national and State community and individual activity was conducted as a matter of course by methods of ratio and proportion. Since this uniform ratio and proportion was maintained in every part, nice discrimination is needed to choose that part of the record most worthy of preservation and of publication. Even the trained historian needs the proleptic mind for success in judging survival values in the history of this war. In the present uncertainty as to the relative value of military and civilian records, the only safe plan seems to be to gather all the facts of the many phases of these two aspects of the national life in war time.

So each State has set itself to the task of getting all the facts. We have put out a dragnet. We are searching the archives at Washington and we are seeking the scraps of history at every crossroad. We welcome with equal avidity the story of a division overseas or the story of a Red Cross drive at home. Food and fuel and morale and propaganda form history groups as authentic as munition making or shipbuilding and camps and cantonments. We include everything from war gardens to front line trenches, fearing to neglect any fact and fearing to magnify any specific set of facts. In this new history we are ignorant of survival values.

Almost each State commission must tell the full story of the reaction of the State to the stimulus of war. There the major reactions of the draft, training camp, the transport service, the S. O. S., the conduct of the troops at the front are told, but we must show also the minor reactions, the response of every filament of the embattled State as part of the Nation.

The publication of war material, then, calls for the publication of something of everything. The process of selection and the fixing of absolute relative limits for the publications will demand time and thought. On the one hand is the desire to have a seasoned history based on full records, and on the other hand is the desire to make a narrative sufficient and readable and complete before the present lively interest flags.

Virginia has faced this difficulty and has reached a decision on two basic questions. A definite plan for publication has been adopted.

On the 18th of November a resolution was passed that "in the publication of studies and narratives not less than 66 per cent of the total space (exclusive of the roster) be given to those men who actually bore arms or were in the auxiliary forces, and to those women who faced, in the field or in munition plants, the actual peril of life."

In view of the fact that the Virginia commission has more than a hundred local branches charged with the duty of collecting civilian as well as military data, this step is significant and interesting.

It was also resolved that "three volumes of approximately 600 pages octavo, each, be set tentatively as the published report of the commission," with the extensions to be made if necessary.

Thus it is planned to publish two volumes dealing with the military side to one volume dealing with the civilian aspect of war time, and it is planned to limit the present objective to three volumes or thereabouts. In other words, Virginia has come to a definite plan to publish a set of three (or perhaps more) volumes of readable matter of popular type, giving two-thirds of the space to military service.

These resolutions were passed after full debate and in the face of strong opposition. They seem to represent the opinion on the part of a majority that a condensed and readable narrative of the State's part in the actual warfare should be the present objective of the commission, together with the minor and even more condensed narratives of the auxiliary civilian activities.

As this is perhaps the first definite State plan for publication, it may be timely to outline more fully the status of the work in Virginia and to attempt to show the thought and purpose that form the basis of this action. The study of conditions in Virginia may be helpful in other States. There is no purpose to extol the plan, but simply to record the facts.

The first striking fact is that both of the steps taken—the condensation of the work into a few volumes and the stressing of the military side—seem to represent a reaction from the former action of the commission. While it is true that at the outset especial stress had been put on the collection of local records touching civilian as well as military matters, and that an indefinite plan for fifteen or more volumes had been mentioned in a general way, there can be little doubt that the recent action represented some impatience with a plan so vague and so broad; and also some impatience with the treatment of the local annals of civilian activities on the same basis as the military chronicles. The members of the body wanted something settled "here and now," as a professor of the university expressed it. Obviously it was felt that in deferring publication until full records should be available, valuable time and even more valuable enthusiasm would be lost. There was also the fear lest a ponderous collection of dry-as-dust chronicles might be the result of the labors of the body. The four points desired in the publication are (1) a war history, (2) a condensed history, (3) a readable story, (4) a history without delay. But this desire for a prompt, readable, succinct military history with civilian sidelights does not indicate that Virginia has called a halt in the collection and preservation of local material. On the contrary, the first of the series of resolutions mentioned urged the local branches in each city and county to collect "all possible source material." Nor was any essential feature of the plan changed.

Virginia is arranging a composite history under some 15 sections or topics. Each section or topic has a chairman and two associates charged with the duty of examining and editing the material collected by the local branches under his topic. If this plan is continued, as seems possible, the State will have a valuable series of source books collected and edited and preserved in local and central archives. Whether these source books will be published is not yet evident.

Thus the new plan of publication keeps the three essential features of the Virginia plan of collecting full military and civilian records through the local branches, of preserving these records in local and central archives, and of having this material treated by editorial groups under definite sections. The three volume history planned does not preclude the later publication of any number of source volumes that may be desired.

No appropriation has as yet been made for publication, nor has any appropriation been asked for this purpose. The legislature appropriated $10,000 for the work of the commission under its published plan to collect and edit the records of Virginia and Virginians in the war, and the money is being expended to this end.

Finally, it may be of interest to show in detail the outline of the projected history, given in memorandum recently submitted by the editorial committee, as follows:

Volume I.—Military.

	Pages.
The story of the draft, section 6	50
Virginia camps and cantonments, section 7	200
Navy and transport in Chesapeake Bay, section 5	50
Virginia soldiers and sailors overseas, section 2	200
Virginians of distinguished service, section 1	100
Total for volume 1	600

Volume II.—Military.

History of Virginia Organizations, section 6	200
War letters, diaries, and incidents, section 14	400
Total for volume 2	600

Volume III.—Semimilitary.

Pre-war conditions and activities, section 2	50
Virginia churches in war time, section 3	125
Virginia schools and colleges in war-time	125
Political contributions of Virginia, section 5	50
The Red Cross in Virginia, Section 12	50
War work and relief organizations, section 13	100
Financial contributions of Virginia, section 15	50
Post war conditions and activities, section 15	50
Total for volume 3	600

Volume IV.

Economc history of Virginia in wartime, section 8	300
History of Virginia communities in war time, section 9	300
Total for volume 4	60

Prof. Ben. F. Shambaugh, of the State Historical Society o Iowa, continued the discussion. He confined his remarks to th importance of the writing and publication of a contemporary histor of America's part in the World War. It is evident that the ma terials of this war will be collected and preserved, and that traine researchers will write and rewrite its history in the years that are to come. Is this enough? Or should there be compiled a contemporary history? Historians will doubtless answer that the writing of this war's history should be postponed for perhaps a generation; that the perspective of years is necessary to the highest success in such an undertaking. Admitting the truth of this answer, is there not also a place for a contemporary history written by trained historians? If there is to be adequate material for the writing of war history in succeeding generations, there should be prepared and published some reliable contemporary accounts. It is, perhaps, not far from the truth to say that if there are no contemporary histories of the war, one-fourth or one-third of the materials of war history will be lost forever. "Do it now" should be the motto of such agencies as war history commissions and State historical societies. The collectors of war history materials are doing excellent work, but the writers alone know what materials are indispensable when they actually come to write their narratives. Among the most valuable materials in the hands of historians in the future will be the contemporary accounts of the war compiled by trained research scholars and published by responsible historical agencies.

The conference of historical societies then took up the business of the conference. Mr. George S. Godard, of the Connecticut State library, was elected chairman. Mr. J. C. Parish, of the Iowa State Historical Society, was elected secretary. The committee appointed in 1907 to secure contributions and to supervise the work of making a calendar of the materials in the French archives relating to the Mississippi Valley could not present a formal report, so a statement was made by Dr. J. F. Jameson of the work done. Mr. Leland had supervised the work from 1908 to 1914 and had indicated the documents. The note taking, interrupted by the war, has been resumed and soon will be finished. The second stage, that of editing the material, is in process. The cost of completing the work, including the publication, will be greater than the amount raised. Only the process of note taking can be completed with the money collected. The editing has been done at the expense of the Carnegie Institution. This stage, it is confidently expected, will be finished during the present year.

It was moved and seconded that the committee be asked to present the status and plans for publication of this material at the next conference.

The National Association of State War History Organizations then went into business session, which was continued on Tuesday at 4 p. m.

Besides those mentioned, the following were also present: Gen. E. Cruikshank, of Ottawa; Prof. Harlow Lindley, of Indiana; Prof. C. W. Alvord, of Illinois; Arthur H. Clark, of Cleveland; Dr. N. D. Mereness, of Washington, D. C.; Dr. G. S. Fuller, of Michigan; Prof. H. E. Bourne, of Western Reserve; Morgan Robinson, of Richmond, Va.; Dr. James Sullivan, of New York; Prof. F. L. Paxson, of Wisconsin, Prof. Higbie, of West Virginia; Mr. Davies, of Cleveland; Prof. G. H. Blakeslee, of Clark University; Mr. Sharon, of Cleveland; and 44 others.

IV. AMERICAN HISTORICAL ACTIVITIES DURING THE WORLD WAR.

EDITED BY NEWTON D. MERENESS.

137

AMERICAN HISTORICAL ACTIVITIES DURING THE WORLD WAR.

INTRODUCTION.

A distinguished American educator, writing on the subject of scholarship during the World War, states that scholars in the human sciences "did not dominate the situation" as did scholars in the physical sciences; that they, "with distinguished exceptions, permitted the man in the street or the man in the editor's chair, or in Congress, or in the Cabinet, to proclaim his amateur pronouncement and to get away with it. The crises for the future," he warns, "will have to do with problems of human conduct rather than of the control of physical things; and as these crises come our scholars in human relations should be more ready to mobilize."[1]

The primary purpose of this survey of historical activities during the war has been the assembly of facts necessary to a stimulating comparison of actions and achievements in the field of history throughout the country, and particularly to draw more attention to the fact that in a crisis such as the recent one it may be even more important that historical scholarship should be mobilized for the winning of a war than for the doing of the things necessary to a history of that war.

Scholarship in the field of history is too unlike scholarship in the physical sciences for close comparison. But as for the measure of mobilization of history men in the late war, a brief summary discloses that shortly after the entry of the United States into the war the leaders of the historical profession established a National Board for Historical Service, primarily for the purpose of mobilizing historical scholarship for the education of the public with regard to the issues of the war; that a good measure of the more successful operations of the Committee on Public Information were under the direction of a historian; that a number of history teachers contributed to the war information series issued by that committee; that many were among its "four-minute" speakers. When the General Staff Committee on Education and Special Training began sending soldiers to colleges for vocational instruction and established the war aims course, two of the four inspectors of that work for the entire country were history men. Later 5 of the 12 division directors of the war issues course were history men. In the negotiation of a treaty of peace the services rendered by American historians were, perhaps, quite as effective as those rendered by the diplomatists.

---

[1] F. P. Keppel "Scholarship in War," Columbia University Quarterly, July, 1919.

In many of the States there was during the war a history committee of the council of defense, and in most of them there is now a war-records or a war-history commission for the collection and preservation of war records and for the preparation of a history of the States' participation in the war.

The reports by States, which comprise the greater portion of this paper, were, with few exceptions, furnished by directors or secretaries of these commissions in response to an appeal contained in the following letter:

> 1140 WOODWARD BUILDING,
> *Washington, D. C., January 23, 1920.*

WAYNE E. STEVENS, *Secretary,*
>   *War Records Section,*
>   *Illinois State Historical Library,*
>   *State Capitol, Springfield, Ill.*

DEAR DR. STEVENS: The National Board for Historical Service, at its last meeting in Washington, requested Mr. Leland, its secretary, to make arrangements for the preparation of an account of historical activities in the United States during the years 1917, 1918, and 1919, that were undertaken in consequence of the war, and for the publication of that account in the Annual Report of the American Historical Association.

Mr. Leland has asked me to assist in this matter, and in response I am seeking the necessary cooperation in every State in the Union. May I ask, then, that you be so good as to furnish us with the account for the State of Illinois? That there may be some measure of uniformity in the accounts from the several States I have prepared the following outline:

1. Historical research and the production of books for increasing the fund of historical knowledge regarding questions pertaining to the war.

2. The diffusion of historical information necessary to an enlightened public opinion regarding the issues of the war:

(a) By the contribution of articles for publication in newspapers and periodicals.

(b) By promoting the circulation of books and periodicals containing important historical information.

(c) By lectures.

(d) By teaching in schools and colleges.

3. Cooperation with the State council of defense, cooperation with the National Board for Historical Service, cooperation with the National Government in the prosecution of the war and in the negotiation of peace.

4. Preparation during the progress of the war of histories of the organization and operation of different branches of war service; for example, State and county food administrations.

5. The collection and preservation of war records.

6. Preparation for an early history of the State's participation in the war. Under this head it may be quite worth while in some States to contrast the so-called county history, produced primarily for the purpose of extracting the largest possible sum of money from the county, with the genuine county history prepared by a person with some historical training and for a much lower price.

The maximum space allotted in the report for the entire account, State and national, is about 200 pages.

Any suggestions from you for improving this outline will be most heartily appreciated. With keen interest in the subject and a justifiable measure of

State pride, who will say, that we can not make this project a large success for the National Board for Historical Service, for the American Historical Association, and for the historical interests of every State in the Union? Will it be convenient for you to have the account for your State prepared by the 1st of April?

In   Very truly, yours,

NEWTON D. MERENESS.

It will be seen that Nos. 1, 2, and 3 of the outline relate to contributions toward the winning of the war, and Nos. 4, 5, and 6 relate to the collection and preservation of a record of the struggle. On the latter head an appeal was also made to historical branches of the Federal Government and to a few sectarian organizations. The historical sketch of the National Board for Historical Service is by Mr. Leland, its secretary, and the director of this project for a survey of war-time historical activities.

From some States repeated appeals for a report have brought no response, and from others not all was reported that was desired. The majority, however, responded graciously and effectively, and the editor is under lasting obligations to all who have participated in this cooperative performance.

WAR DEPARTMENT.

By OLIVER L. SPAULDING, Lieutenant Colonel, General Staff, Chief Historical Branch.

For several years before the recent war interest in military history had been steadily increasing among officers of the Army, and its importance had come to be more fully realized than before. This interest was greatly stimulated by the establishment of well-planned historical courses at the service schools, but the evolution had not yet reached the stage of developing a special historical organ when the war began.

In the spring of 1918 this organ made its appearance in the form of the historical branch, war plans division, General Staff. This branch at once began its collection of historical documents and prepared to make use of them. It was fortunate in securing the services of several historians of standing, who joined it, serving under emergency commissions.

It was evident that nothing could be done for a long time on activities abroad, but a beginning was made with activities in the United States. Sections were formed to deal with diplomatic relations and with the economic and military mobilization of the country and for the collection and preservation of photographs. A detailed and careful analysis was made of the ground ultimately to be covered which resulted in an outline suitable for a very complete history of the participation of the United States in the war. This outline, of course, was never considered to be a finished product, but remained always subject to current revisions.

To fill the blank spaces left in this outline for operations, a member of the branch was detached and sent to France. He was placed on duty at general headquarters in the historical section, General Staff, American Expeditionary Forces, and established its archives. That section passed through many vicissitudes, but succeeded in collecting a large quantity of documents. It was finally designated as the custodian of all historical documents which had ceased to be "live files" in the office of origin.

In the spring of 1919, more officers having become available on account of the termination of hostilities, the general headquarters section was much enlarged and undertook a considerable amount of field work. The ground covered by the most important of the American operations was studied and record made of all evidence found there which might assist in later interpretation of documents. This evidence was put in the form of maps, sketches, photographs, and written field notes. This work was undertaken only just in time, for while evidence of this nature was still plentiful, it was rapidly disappearing. The clearing up of débris and the plowing of fields was progressing with great rapidity—a most encouraging indication of early rehabilitation of the country.

Meanwhile, a similar historical section had been established, independently, at headquarters of the Services of Supply, and had been very active in collecting material dealing with every phase of that intricate organization. Original documents were accumulated or located in the files where they originated, and special historical summaries were called for from all services.

After the armistice, when the peace conference assembled, a representative of the historical branch was sent to Paris to follow its proceedings. A large mass of material on the diplomatic situation was thus obtained.

In June, 1919, these activities abroad ceased. Representatives of each of the historical sections there were brought to Washington and placed on duty in the historical branch, which was then reorganized on a greatly reduced scale for work on a peace basis. Its functions were to preserve historical documents relating to the wars of the United States; to make these documents, or the information contained therein, accessible to agencies of the War Department and to students and investigators properly accredited; and to prepare historical monographs on military subjects of interest to the War Department. To these duties has recently been added supervision of historical work of all bureaus and services of the War Department.

The archives consist of two departments—one for written documents and one for photographs. The collection of written documents is not yet large, but is rapidly growing, and will become very important on the closing of general headquarters, American Expeditionary Forces, when all purely historical documents on file there will be added to it. It now includes all the original files of the branch dealing with activities at home; a considerable amount of diplomatic material; a valuable collection of papers of the services of supply in France; the files of the General Purchasing Board and of the American representative on the military board of allied supply in Paris; and a small collection of documents dealing with operations, including the field notes of the general headquarters historical section. The collection of photographs, both still and moving, is very large, including all official photographs of the Signal Corps illustrating the war with Germany and much private work; orders have recently been issued adding to it the Brady collection of Civil War photographs.

In connection with the archives a small bureau of information is maintained for answering inquiries on historical questions. These come in increasing numbers from agencies of the War Department and from outside inquirers. Lack of personnel prevents undertaking any considerable investigation, but when specific questions are asked an effort is made either to give the information or to indicate where and how it may be obtained. Facilities for research, somewhat limited as yet, are provided for properly accredited investigators.

Among the collecting activities of the archives, two are deserving of special mention here.

The connection between French and American units in operations was so close that it is impossible for us to form a picture of our own work without constant reference to French documents. Some of them are found in the files of the American units concerned, but by no means enough. Permission has therefore been secured from the French minister of war for a representative of the historical branch to work in the archives in Paris, and much valuable material is being secured in this way.

Strong efforts are also being made to secure personal narratives of participants in action. Superior commanders have been invited to contribute statements supplementing official reports and many are responding. To get the intimate detail of combat, a list of questions has been prepared and is being sent to selected subordinate officers and enlisted men. Their responses are coming in considerable numbers and are proving very interesting and valuable.

Relations have been established with the association of State historical bureaus. This will probably result in a marked growth of the demand for research facilities.

To make information really available, however, it is not sufficient to collect the documents. The files are accessible to few, and if they were more widely accessible the papers would be destroyed by constant handling. It is necessary, therefore, to print and distribute them.

For many reasons it would be desirable to arrange certain documents relating to the recent war on the plan of the records of the War of the Rebellion—that is, classified according to military operations. But this involves waiting until the documents for the entire series are in hand, which will not be for many years. A different plan of classification has been adopted which permits beginning at once with any documents that can be collected and filling in the series gradually.

The general classification is:

(A) Records of military operations overseas.
(B) Records of the services of supply overseas.
(C) Records of military activities in the United States.

Work has been commenced on class A. The detailed program is as follows:

Records of the World War.

Class A.—Records of military operations overseas.

Section I. General headquarters, American Expeditionary Forces, France.
Vol. 1. Commander in chief's office.
Vol. 2. Chief of Staff's office.
Vol. 3. First section, General Staff.
Vol. 4. Second section, General Staff.
Vol. 5. Third section, General Staff.
Vol. 6. Fourth section, General Staff.
Vol. 7. Fifth section, General Staff.
Vol. 8. Adjutant General's office.
Vol. 9. Judge Advocate General's office.
Vol. 10. Inspector General's office.
Vol. 11. Chief of Artillery's office.
Vol. 12. Chief of Infantry's office.
Vol. 13. Chief of Tank Corps' office.
Vol. 14. Chief of Air Service.

Section II. First Army.

Vol. 1. Field orders and annexes.
Vol. 2. Orders.
Vol. 3. Intelligence summaries.
Vol. 4. Operation reports.
Vol. 5. War diary.
Vol. 6. General orders.
Vol. 7. Correspondence and messages.

Section III. Second Army.

Vols. 1 to 7 as in Section II.

Section IV. Third Army.

Vols. 1 to 7 as in Section II.

Section V. First Corps.

Vol. 1. Field orders and annexes.
Vol. 2. Orders.
Vol. 3. Intelligence summaries.
Vol. 4. Operation reports.
Vol. 5. War diary.
Vol. 6. General orders.
Vol. 7. Correspondence and messages.

Section VI. Second Corps.

Vols. 1 to 7 as in Section V.

Section VII. Third Corps.

Vols. 1 to 7 as in Section V.
Sections VIII, IX, X, etc. One for each corps.

Section —. First Division.

Vol. 1. Field orders and annexes.
Vol. 2. Orders.
Vol. 3. Intelligence summaries.
Vol. 4. Operation reports.
Vol. 5. War diary.
Vol. 6. General orders.
Vol. 7. Correspondence and messages.

Will include the records of the brigades and regiments.

Sections ——. One for each combat division.

Section —. Miscellaneous units.

Vol. 1, part 1; vol. 2, part 2; vol. 3, part 3; etc., part 4 will include records of units which were assigned as Army or corps troops.

Class B.—Records of Services of Supply overseas.

Section I. Headquarters Services of Supply.

Vol. 1. Commanding general's office.
Vol. 2. Chief of Staff's office.
Vol. 3. First section, General Staff, Services of Supply.
Vol. 4. Second section, General Staff, Services of Supply.
Vol. 5. Fourth section, General Staff, Services of Supply.
Vol. 6. Adjutant General's Office, Services of Supply.
Vol. 7. Judge Advocate General's Office, Services of Supply.
Vol. 8. Provost Marshal General.
Vol. 9. Director General of Transportation.
Vol. 10. Director Motor Transport Corps.
Vol. 11. Chief Surgeon.
Vol. 12. Chief engineer .
Vol. 13. Chief of Chemical Warfare Service.
Vol. 14. Chief of Air Service.
Vol. 15. Chief Signal Officer.

Vol. 16. Chief Quartermaster Corps.
Vol. 17. Chief Ordnance officer.
Vol. 18. War Risk section.
Vol. 19. General purchasing agent.
Vol. 20. Renting, Requisition, and Claims Service.

Section II. Base section No. 1, Services of Supply.

Vol. 1, vol. 2, vol. 3, vol. 4, vol. 5, etc. Each section to correspond to the organization of the headquarters of the Services of Supply section.

Section III. Base section No. 2, Services of Supply.
Section IV. Base section No. 3, Services of Supply.
Section V. Base section No. 4, Services of Supply.
Section VI. Base section No. 5, Services of Supply.
Section VII. Base section No. 6, Services of Supply.
Section VIII. Base section No. 7, Services of Supply.
Section IX. Base section No. 8, Services of Supply.
Section X. Base section No. 9, Services of Supply.
Section XI. Intermediate section, Services of Supply.
Section XII. Advance section, Services of Supply.

Class C.—Records of military activities in the United States. To consist of the reports of the heads of departments and committees, together with the documents which were made public—e. g.:

Vol. 1. Secretary of War.
Vol. 2. Chief of Staff.
Vol. 3. Directors of General Staff Division.
Vol. 4. Adjutant General.
Vol. 5. Inspector General.
Vol. 6. Judge Advocate General.
Vol. 7. Quartermaster General.
Vol. 8. Director of finance.
Vol. 9. Surgeon General.
Vol. 10. Chief of Engineers.
Vol. 11. The Construction Division.
Vol. 12. Chief of Ordnance.
Vol. 13. Chief Signal Officer.
Vol. 14. Chief of Field Artillery.
Vol. 15. Chief of Coast Artillery.
Vol. 16. Director of military aeronautics.
Vol. 17. Bureau of Aircraft Production.
Vol. 18. Director of air service.
Vol. 19. Chemical warfare service.
Vol. 20. Chief Motor Transport Corps.
Vol. 21. Militia Bureau.
Vol. 22. Provost marshal general.
Vol. 23. The Council of National Defense.
Vol. 24. War Council.
Vol. 25. The Students' Army Training Corps.
Vol. 26. Commission on Training Camp Activities.
Vol. 27. Committee on Education and Special Training.
Vol. 28. War Credits Board.
Vol. 29. Claims Board, War Department.
Vol. 30. Real estate service.

A few of the papers of general headquarters were printed in France for limited distribution, but will ultimately be reprinted in this series. In selecting documents for publication efforts are being made to collect first those for which actual demand develops in the Army schools or elsewhere. Manuscript for five volumes has been sent to the Public Printer, as follows:

Section II. First Army.
Vol. 1. Field orders.
Vol. 3. Intelligence summaries.

Section VI. Second Army Corps.
Vol. 1. Field orders.
Vol. 3. Intelligence summaries.

Section IX. Fifth Army Corps.
Vol. 3. Intelligence summaries.

For the preparation of historical monographs the field is unlimited; as many officers and civilian writers as could be found could be kept busy for an indefinite period. It is only just beginning to be possible to undertake such work, and very few qualified officers are available. Relations have been established with the American Historical Association, and it is hoped that these may grow more intimate, so that historical workers in civil life may be led to take up military specialties.

In so far as the few officers of the branch are concerned it is necessary to limit the field; it still remains too broad. In the first place, work is being confined to the War with Germany. There is no present intention of preparing a complete "official account"; economic affairs must be omitted, except in so far as they may incidentally be drawn into question in connection with other investigations. This leaves, broadly speaking, three subdivisions of the work— mobilization and demobilization, includng all activities in the United States, operations abroad, and the services of supply abroad.

The detailed plan in so far as developed is given below. Where a title is given without special mark the monograph is contemplated or in preparation; a title in italics indicates a monograph completed and awaiting publication; a title in italics with a star indicates a published monograph.

Section I. Narrative History of Military Operations.

A. The major operations of the American Expeditionary Forces:
  1. "*Cambrai*"—*H. B. Monograph No. 5.*
  2. "Somme Defensive and Lys."
  3. "Aisne and Montdidier-Noyon."
  4. "Champagne-Marne and Aisne-Marne."
  4(a). "The Third Division on the Marne."
  5. "Somme Offensive, Oisne-Aisne, Ypres-Lys."
  5(a). "*Operations Second Corps in Somme Offensive.*"—*H. B. Monograph No. 10.*
  6. "St. Mihiel."
  7. "Meuse-Argonne."
  8. "*Blanc Mont (Meuse-Argonne-Champagne)*"—*H. B. Monograph No. 9.*
  9. "Vittorio-Veneto."
B. "Operations in North Russia, 1918–1919."
C. "Operations in Siberia, 1917–1920."
D. "Operations in Italy, 1917–1918."

Section II. Studies of Services of Supply.

A. " *Organization of Services of Supply, American Expeditionary Forces,*"— *H. B. Monograph No. 7.*

B. " *Replacement of Personnel, American Expeditionary Forces.*"—*H. B. Monograph No. 8.*

C. " Procurement of Supplies, American Expeditionary Forces."

D. " Initial Equipment and Supply, American Expeditionary Forces."

Section III. Special Tactical Studies.

*A. " *A survey of German Tactics, 1918.*"—*H. B. Monograph No. 1. W. D. Document No. 883, 1918.*

*B. " *A study in Troop Frontage.*"—*H. B. Monograph No. 4, W. D. Doc. No. 992, 1919.*

C. " *A study in Battle Formation.*"—*H. B. Monograph No. 6.*

Section IV. Military Activities in the United States.

*A. " *Economic Mobilization in the United States for the War of 1917.*"— *H. B. Monograph No. 2, W. D. Document No. 885, 1918.*

*B. " *A Handbook of Economic Agencies of the War of 1917.*"—*H. B. Monograph No. 3, W. D. Document No. 908, 1919.*

SECTION V. HISTORIES OF TROOP UNITS.

A. " Outline History of Divisions."

B. " Outline History of Regular Regiments."

The first and easiest work is to put into coherent shape the outline of each operation and of the service of each American unit and to make a general survey of the other fields—mobilization and the services of supply. This work, it will be seen, is well underway. The papers will be as short as practicable, but in sufficient detail to lead an investigator into any part of the subject which he may wish to study. Special attention will be given to citations of authority, and the aim will be to make the papers serve both as an accurate general statement and as an introduction to the documents.

Upon these will be based a series of monographs, each taking up some one particular feature of the basic papers and developing it. These, again, will serve, each in its own department, the same purpose as the general papers upon which they are based; they will bear the same relation to them, let us say, as the 1:20,000 map does to the 1:200,000. These should involve a considerable amount of critical study and should go somewhat deeply into the basic original documents. The purpose of each being limited, they can begin to use the magnifying glass; they can go beyond the operation report, perhaps, to the penciled message written in a shell hole.

These papers being so constructed as to serve as a further index to the documents, it is evident that the map scale may be again increased if desired. A smaller feature of any particular subject may be taken up and treated with greater elaboration of detail.

But historical work in the War Department is not limited to the work of the Historical Branch. While there is no other purely historical organization, many bureaus and services devote some attention to such work.

Shortly after the close of the war various services initiated steps toward the preparation of histories and reports dealing with their activities. When requests for authority to publish were received it was found impossible to grant these requests, as some services contemplated the most extensive publication, including all their activities, both at home and abroad, in the greatest detail, while others contemplated no publication at all. So the entire matter was referred to the Historical Branch, which was directed to make a survey of all historical work already published and contemplated by the services. This survey brought out the fact that there was a great divergence of views and intentions among the services as to what class of material should be published and as to the amount of publication. One service, for example, had accumulated a mass of material amounting to several hundred volumes, giving detailed data on their entire field of activities, beginning with procurement in the United States and Europe and ending with operations on the field of battle. Other services, on the other hand, while they had collected certain historical documents, did not desire any publications whatever other than their annual reports. Some services had not undertaken a collection of documents relating to their war activities. The survey indicated that if each service were authorized to go its own way in the matter of the publication of its history there would result a great deal of duplication as well as omission.

To meet this situation the Historical Branch was directed to prepare a general scheme to unify historical publications of the services, and it was also directed to assume supervision and control.

The general scheme, as approved, may be outlined as follows: Each chief of service was directed to appoint a suitable historical officer, who would represent his service in all matters of historical publication. Historical publications were divided broadly into two classes—those that treated of the activities of one service only and those that treated of two or more services. Papers of the first class are to be prepared by the proper historical officer, with the assistance of the Historical Branch, and those of the second class by the Historical Branch, assisted by the interested historical officers. Papers of a purely technical character require practically no supervision from the Historical Branch other than in matters relating to form and bibliography, while papers with a tactical or strategical bearing, or those dealing with general policy, would call for a very close coordination. A conference was held at the office of the Historical Branch of all service historical officers, where the general scheme was explained, and each historical officer was requested to submit to the Historical Branch a general outline of publication to meet the requirements of his particular service, such outline including all important activities of historical interest. These proposed outlines are now being received and are, when necessary, modified to fit into a general scheme for all War Department publications.

Particular attention is invited to the above plan as it constitutes the first step ever taken by the War Department to unify Government publications of a historical nature. While the plan provides a system by means of which a supervision is exercised over these historical papers, nevertheless, it by no means limits in any way or discourages the services; on the other hand, it will result in many valuable publications that otherwise would not be prepared. It is needless to say that these publications will conform to proper historical standards, and by no means the least value of this supervision will consist in the requirement that service publications shall be based in the future upon the best obtainable sources, and that such sources shall be indicated in the bibliography attached.

Somewhat akin to this work of War Department services is a custom now becoming established in the preparation of histories of troop units. The Historical Branch is preparing brief outlines, but many units desire to go into detail. When any unit seeks information from the War Department as to its own history, it is becoming the practice to refer it to the Historical Branch; in many cases a representative of the unit comes to Washington, where the Historical Branch furnishes him desk room and facilities for research, and gives advice and guidance as to method and form. In this way histories of several divisions and regiments are being prepared conforming to accepted historical standards.

APPENDIX.

SURVEY OF HISTORICAL WORK UNDER PREPARATION AND CONTEMPLATED BY VARIOUS SERVICES AND DEPARTMENTS OF THE WAR DEPARTMENT.

I. The following memo. was received by the Historical Branch, War Plans Division, on February 8, 1920:

FEBRUARY 6, 1920.

Memorandum for the Judge Advocate General.
Subject: Survey of historical work.

1. The chief of staff has directed a survey to be made at once of the historical work being done in each of the bureaus and services of the War Department. It has come to his knowledge that a considerable amount of work has been done in connection with the preparation of historical matter for the majority of the services. He desires that this work be unified, so that the completed histories will fit into some general scheme, and he has directed that the supervision and control shall be under the Historical Branch, War Plans Division.

2. An officer of the Historical Branch, War Plans Division, will accordingly call upon you with regard to this matter. I request that you afford him facilities for acquainting himself with the work already done and with the plans in prospect. As soon as this survey can be made the necessary conferences will be held in order to arrive at a basis for carrying on this very important task.

(Signed)   WM. LASSITER,
Colonel, General Staff,
Acting Director, W. P. D.

Copies to Historical Branch; Chief, Coast Artillery Corps; Chief, Militia Bureau; Chief, Signal Office; Chief, Chemical Warfare Service; Chief, Construction Division; Quartermaster General; Chief, Transportation Service; Chief of Ordnance; Director of Air Service; Chief, Motor Transport Corps; Chief of Engineers; Chief of Field Artillery; Surgeon General of the Army; Inspector General of the Army; Adjutant General of the Army.

II. Pursuant to this memo. an officer of this branch visited the services enumerated above. This officer had an interview with the chief of service when such was practicable. When this was not practicable he saw the second officer in charge; and in every case he interviewed the officer engaged in historical work and examined such historical data as were accessible.

III. The following is a result of this survey:

Coast Artillery.

1. No historical matter has been published, and no definite steps taken with a view toward publication, but it is the intention of this corps to prepare a history of Coast Artillery activities during the war. The material for such a publication is on file, but not collated.

2. No personnel engaged in historical work.

Militia Bureau.

1. No historical matter has been published and no definite steps taken with a view toward publication.

2. The bureau is considering the preparation of a document giving an account of the use of militia during the war in the capacity of "Home Guards," referring particularly to the guarding of important manufacturing plants, bridges, tunnels, etc., in case of national emergency.

3. No personnel engaged in historical work.

Signal Corps.

1. This corps is preparing a roster of the corps personnel of all grades and ranks (commissioned and enlisted) that took part in the late war. Not for publication.

2. There was prepared a history of the Signal Corps in the American Expeditionary Forces (operations and services of supply), consisting of over 2,000 typed pages, illustrated. This is not for publication.

3. A history of the Signal Corps in the United States during the war was prepared, but is not for publication.

4. The annual report of the Chief Signal Officer, 1919, which has been published and distributed, was based upon the above-mentioned histories.

5. No personnel available for historical work.

Chemical Warfare Service.

1. No historical matter published and no publication contemplated.

2. The attached Exhibit A, secured from the Chemical Warfare Service, gives a list of historical matter compiled, showing number of volumes and contents.

3. The following remarks pertain to the compilations enumerated on this exhibit:

(1) One volume, 300 pages, a résumé of Chemical Warfare Service activities in the United States, typed, temporarily bound, and indexed.

(2) Very brief, 10 pages.

(3) This compilation covers the subject technically.

(4) Fifty-nine volumes, temporarily bound, typed, indexed with maps and charts. Many documents attached to text.

(5) Eleven volumes, bound temporarily, typed, indexed, map charts and documents attached.

(6) Brief.

(7) Six parts, maps, charts, and index.

(8) Fifteen parts, typed, maps, and charts.

(9) A personal narrative, prepared by Gen. A. A. Fries, 70 pages, typed, temporarily bound and indexed.

(10) Ten parts, each 50 pages, typed, maps, and charts; copies of supporting documents attached.

(11) One part, 20 pages, maps, charts, and copies of supporting documents attached.

(12) One part, 30 pages, typed; supporting documents attached.

(13) Fifteen parts, 20 pages each, typed; maps and charts attached.

None of the above compilation should be published in their present form. They should constitute material upon which to prepare matter for publication. This is also the opinion of Gen. Sibert.

4. The Chemical Warfare Service has published in technical magazines various monographs of scientific interest.

5. No personnel employed in historical work.

Construction Division.

1. This division has compiled 556 temporarily bound volumes, typed and indexed, constituting a detailed history of the organization, functions, and operations of the division during the war, including a complete history of each construction project. It is 98 per cent complete. Exhibit B is a table of contents.

2. Based upon the above, there has been compiled 17 volumes, temporarily bound, 200 pages each, constituting a résumé. None of the above is for publication.

3. Seven clerks, no officers, are engaged in completing the first-named work.

Quartermaster Corps.

1. No historical matter published and none contemplated.

2. There has been compiled and filed a short history of every activity of this corps during the war. A short résumé of this has been compiled.

3. Exhibit G is a copy of a memorandum sent to every industrial firm in the United States that had business relations during the war with the corps. The replies received are filed and will constitute valuable data in an economic study of the war.

4. Personnel: Two clerks.

Transportation Service.

1. The annual reports of the Transportation Corps, 1918 and 1919, contain all the historical matter published.

2. A publication is under preparation in the Office of the Assistant Secretary of War, edited by Capt. R. F. Wilson, which will constitute a history of transportation service operations during the war. It is based upon the two annual reports referred to above, also upon additional data now being furnished by this service. The title of this work will be " The Road to France." It will probably be a publication similar to "America's Munitions."

3. Personnel: One officer, no clerks.

Ordnance Department.

1. A series of monographs have been published and are in process of publication relating to various ordnance material used during the war. The subjects are treated historically and technically. The entire series will comprise 35 publications, 27 of which are partly or wholly completed. These are issued as confidential documents for circulation within the Ordnance Department only. Exhibit D is a list of these monographs.

2. There is under preparation a history of each ordnance district. There were 13 districts, 12 in the United States and 1 in Canada. When completed this will probably be published in one volume of 300 pages. This will be a popular publication, showing what ordnance material was obtained in each district and from whom. It may be classed as economic rather than technical.

3. Material has been collected for a history of the Ordnance Department in the American Expeditionary Forces. This material has not yet been edited.

4. Personnel: Six clerks.

Air Service.

1. Data on Air Service history may be discussed under three headings: (a) Bureau of Aircraft Production; (b) Division of Military Aeronautics; (c) Air Service, American Expeditionary Forces.

(a) The text has been completed, but no steps taken toward printing. Many supporting documents collected; two volumes.

(b) The preparation of this work has not progressed very far. Supporting documents are being collected; two volumes.

(c) This work was compiled in France and consists of 269 volumes, including maps, charts, and supporting documents. One copy of this work is filed with general headquarters, American Expeditionary Forces, which copy contains many original reports of squadron and group commanders.

2. Personnel: One officer, 11 clerks.

Motor Transport Corps.

1. Two works on the history of the corps are in process of preparation—(a) history of the Motor Transport Corps in American Expeditionary Forces; (b) history of the Motor Transport Corps.

The work (a) consists of motor operations with troops at the front and motor operations in the Services of Supply. It will consist of 17 chapters, probably 600,000 words, including the appendix. The appendix will be approximately 65 per cent of the entire work; maps, charts, plans, photographs, and documents are included. All of the chapters have been completed except four which are now in the following state of completion (Feb. 16, 1920) : Chapter on supply, 60 per cent complete; chapter on repair, 15 per cent complete; chapter on literature of Motor Transport Corps, 95 per cent complete; chapter on conclusions, 20 per cent complete. Chapter 15 of this work is a bibliography.

The completed portion is typed and filed in folders. The text contains references to accompanying documents. The system of references should be improved.

The work has been read by Gen. Walker, who made certain corrections. Chapters on technical subject were reviewed by qualified technical officers, though this fact does not appear in the text. Chapters 1 to 16 may be classified as technical, in that they treat in considerable detail of Motor Transport Corps matters.

The work (b) is nearing completion. It will finally consist of two volumes of 2,000 pages in all.

A considerable portion of this work has already reached the printer, and first proof has been received for correction.

Of the entire work 60 per cent refers to American Expeditionary Forces' activities of the corps and 40 per cent to activities in the United States. The portion relating to American Expeditionary Forces' activities is based primarily upon the work (a). The work includes maps, charts, and photographs.

Col. Ireland, Motor Transport Corps, who is editing work (a), recommends that work (b) be completed at once, as it will be of considerable value to the corps, to the service schools, and to the motor-car industry.

Before publication this work should be examined to ascertain if references to supporting documents are complete.

2. Personnel: One officer, 2 clerks.

Corps of Engineers.

1. There was published, under date of July 8, 1919, but only recently distributed, a "Historical Report of the Chief Engineer, including all operations of the Engineer Department, American Expeditionary Forces, 1917–1919. There are 68 appendixes to this history, which were not published but are filed. They

consist of technical articles relating to particular Engineer activities, written by the officers who specialized upon the particular work. ;

2. There is on file a series of monthly reports on operations made by organizations (engineer) in the United States and American Expeditionary Forces, also voluminous reports on the engineer depot at Camp Humphries. The former consists of 36 temporarily bound volumes and the latter of 36 volumes. Both have maps and charts attached and are typed.

3. There was planned a final history of the Corps of Engineers, which was to consist of an account of the activities of each engineer organization. This work was never completed. The data to compile such a work is on file.

4. There is on file a series of "Reports of Individual Experience" of Engineer officers. These consist of personal narratives which all Engineer officers were asked to prepare. About 30 per cent of replies have been received.

5. A list of citations and awards, has been prepared.

6. There is a "research file," consisting of reports made by Engineer officers upon new methods of engineering observed either in the Allied or German armies.

7. This corps has a collection of photographs taken by Engineer personnel, classified according to geographical localities and by organizations. This collection has been fully indexed.

8. No personnel in historical work.

Field Artillery Corps.

1. No historical matter has been published and no such publication is anticipated.

2. There are being compiled data of artillery organizations that served with the American Expeditionary Forces.

3. There is a file devoted to historical material on the operations of the School of Fire and Artillery Officers' Training School.

4. Personnel: Two officers, one clerk.

Medical Corps.

1. No historical publications issued.

2. A work is under preparation, entitled "Medical and Surgical History of the World War." It was suggested by a similar work prepared after the Civil War. Various selected medical officers have been assigned subjects concerning which they have special knowledge. An editorial board is charged with the arrangement of the material. This work will include 15 volumes of about 500 pages each. Exhibit E attached gives the subject matter of the chapters. The first three chapters will relate to tactical and administrative subjects. Five volumes will probably be completed by June 30, 1920, and thereafter one volume every two months.

3. Personnel: Two officers, three clerks.

Inspector General.

1. No historical material yet published.

2. A history of the Inspector General's Department during the war is now being prepared. It will probably not exceed 75 pages.

3. No personnel engaged in historical work.

The Adjutant General.

1. No historical publication written.
2. There is under preparation a record showing the participation of organizations in engagements during the war.
3. It is contemplated to bring Heitman's Register of the Army up to date.
4. Data is being prepared showing losses during the war, classified according to organizations and States.
5. A card system has been established showing the strength of Regular organizations at the end of each month. This is based upon the monthly returns.
6. No personnel for historical work.

NAVY DEPARTMENT.

By Capt. DUDLEY W. KNOX, United States Navy, Officer in Charge of the Historical Section, Navy Department.

The fact that publication of the naval records of the Civil War is not yet complete, perhaps indicates an apathy within the Navy respecting the recording of its history. In any event, American participation in the Great War had progressed for more than a year before any definite steps were taken toward naval historical collection. Stimulated by the admirably organized British Historical Section of the War Cabinet, which, under the eminent naval historian, Sir Julian Corbett, had included the war activities of Navy, Army, and other governmental agencies since before 1914, Admiral Sims early recommended the formation of an American Naval Historical Section.

But it was not until June, 1918, that the Navy Department acted favorably upon Admiral Sims's recommendation, and even then only to the extent of forming an exceedingly small historical section in Washington, under the charge of Rear Admiral W. W. Kimball, retired. Notwithstanding repeated requests that the necessary personnel, including trained historians, be sent to London to undertake the collection of documents and data, Admiral Sims did not obtain the requisite authority to create an historical section of his staff until after the armistice was signed. On November 18, 1918, he received telegraphic instructions that, " owing to the signing of the armistice, it is considered too late to send an Historical Section abroad. Request that services of your staff be utilized as far as possible to collect data for naval history. * * *" Accordingly, a section was then created in London in charge of Capt. D. W. Knox, assisted by a number of other active and reserve officers, among whom was one historian, Lieut. T. B. Kittredge, United States Naval Reserve Force.

Since demobilization was impending, and was expected to include the abolition of headquarters in London, the work of the His-

torical Section abroad was limited necessarily to the selection, copying, arrangement, indexing, and filing of appropriate documents
from the voluminous and varied headquarters files. After preliminary study of French and British systems, it was decided to follow
the latter closely. Selections were limited to papers relating to the
operations of naval forces. All papers were arranged primarily by
geographical areas, and placed in chronological order within each
area. Subdivision by subjects, except for supplementary files, was
avoided when possible, since the British were most emphatic in stating that any attempt to collect and permanently bind records by
subjects was a mistake and would handicap historical writing
greatly. Necessarily some documents, such as reports covering a
long period of time, statistical data, etc., had to be filed by subjects;
but the geographical-chronological system was followed as closely as
practicable. This work occupied a large clerical force for about six
months, after which the historical collection was transferred to
Washington.

Meantime the Historical Section in the Navy Department, after
adopting the system of filing used in London, endeavored to collect
material through the various bureaus and offices of the department,
and the other naval organizations elsewhere, ashore and afloat. But
progress in this collection was exceedingly slow, owing to the handicap of very limited office force within the section, to the lack of
funds, and to the reluctance of many offices to part with their files.

In July, 1919, the Navy Library, which had previously had cognizance of naval historical records, was transferred to the Historical Section; and under the act of March, 1919, Congress first
appropriated money for the collection and classification of naval
data relating to the late war. These two events enabled the section
to make fair progress thereafter in its work, though funds, clerical
force, and office space were still inadequate, and these deficiencies
will probably prevent completion of the collection and filing of
material in a form suitable for use comprehensively by historians
for many years.

The historical archives are divided into three main branches—
pictorial, logistics, and operations. The former includes photographs, posters, maps, charts, etc. The scope of logistics is so vast
and the volume of documents so great that it would be physically
impossible for the Historical Section to handle them. The plan
has been adopted, therefore, of requesting each of the various logistic
offices and bureaus of the department to preserve its own documents
and to write the history of its own peculiar activities. Several
monographs of this nature have already been completed. Since
many logistic offices were abolished soon after the war, it will be
necessary for the section to undertake some work in connection with

logistic documents. But work in connection with the operation files—that is, the selection, arrangement, filing, and indexing of documents pertaining directly to the distribution, employment, and movements of ships and other naval combatant units—is expected to constitute the principal task of the section.

The operations material is divided into five classes: Telegrams, general correspondence, war diaries, docketed papers, and statistics; and in each of these the geographical chronological system of arrangement is followed as closely as practicable.

The intimate relation between the operations of the American and French Armies is paralleled by a similar relation between the operations of the American and British Navies. Much research work in the files of the British Admiralty may be necessary before American naval history covering the Great War can be written accurately and comprehensively; and the interdependence of the State, War, Navy, and other departments of the Government renders further reseach at home, outside of the Navy, indispensable.

General plan of files, Historical Section, Navy Department.

[Memorandum prepared by Lieut. (j. g.) P. B. Whelpley, U. S. N. R. F.]

In order to give a clear idea of the work undertaken, the following summary is drawn up as representing the work that has been done and the scope of the work projected:

I. *Records.*—The primary task is the selection, arrangement, and indexing of those papers in the Navy Department files which have historical significance. Only such papers shall be selected for the historical files as deal directly with the naval operations of the United States Naval Forces. All papers, letters, and telegrams relating to operations will be chosen for the collection, no matter whether the individual paper may seem of importance or not. The papers selected consist of several classes, each of which may be handled in a slightly different way. These classes are: (1) General correspondence and reports; (2) cables and telegrams; (3) war diaries; (4) documents and special reports; (5) statistical and related matters.

1. General correspondence and reports are filed in three ways—by areas, by subjects, and by dates.

(a) The area files are divided into six series, and letters are filed, in general, according to the date of the event referred to in the letter, if the matter dealt with is an active operation; or according to the date of the letter if the subject of the letter relates to plans, policies, or general discussions of some feature of the military situation.

(b) The subject files are divided into 19 groups, and are arranged as in the area files, chronologically, according to the date of the event to which reference is made.

(c) The chronological files are divided into two classes—(1) letters, and (2) cables and telegrams. These are not yet complete, but expansion is always possible by the copying of matter on hand in other files.

2. Cables and telegrams will be filed in three ways—chronologically, by areas, and by subjects. In the subject file, cables and telegrams are filed with letters and reports, but in the area and chronological files they are separate.

3. *War diaries.*—From these diaries there has been made up a special chrono-logical diary by days on cards. In addition to this card system the war diaries are being bound up intact and in such a way as seems most convenient for future reference.

4. *General files—Documents, reports, and special papers.*—In addition to the papers maintained in the historical chronological collection a file of documents and special reports of various kinds is being made. Those, for example, of in-telligence publications relating to war operation are being included in this de-partment of the collection and appropriately indexed. There is also included a complete set of such papers, as follows:

(*a*) Weekly reports of force commander, European waters, to Washington.
(*b*) Weekly reports from the detachment commanders.
(*c*) Daily information bulletins.
(*d*) Force instructions.
(*e*) Circular letters.
(*f*) Monthly roster of officers.
(*g*) Weekly staff memoranda, heads of sections.
(*h*) Admiralty daily reports of operations.
(*i*) French daily antisubmarine bulletin.
(*j*) Force commander's daily memorandum of admiralty conferences.

In addition to those named, there will be a number of others of a similar character.

5. *Statistical.*—Statistical and related matter is being collected and indexed thoroughly, and it is hoped that this class will form a useful part of the historical files.

II. *Indexes.*—The value of the historical collection will depend largely upon the completeness of the various indexes which shall be made. So far as it is possible to predict, these indexes should consist of the following:
(1) A cross-reference subject index; (2) a chronological index of events; (3) an alphabetical index of events; (4) a general index of cables and tele-grams.

1. For each series of papers there has been compiled a general cross-reference subject index. The headings under which subjects are indexed have been made a matter of careful study in order to insure uniformity and completeness in the indexing method. The matter has been arranged under several subject headings, and under appropriate subheadings so as to facilitate reference to all papers included in the collection relating to any subject on which infor-mation may be desired. This index is maintained on cards and includes ref-erences to all general correspondence, telegrams, war diaries, special reports, statistical data, and to any other matter, such as printed documents which may be included in the historical collection. In this way it should be suf-ficiently complete to permit one at a glance to determine exactly what informa-tion is available concerning any particular operation or event.

2. The chronological diary of naval events of the war prepared by Lieut. Whelpley is being enlarged both on paper and on cards, the former bound ac-cording to months, in temporary bindings.

3. The alphabetical index of events is the complement of the chronological diary, furnishing under names of persons, and vessels, and events, the same information given therein under dates. These together should constitute a quick reference to data pertaining to the Navy in the war.

4' The indexes of cables and telegrams sent from the Navy Department to London headquarters, and from the London headquarters to the Navy De-partment, have already been prepared.

UNITED STATES MARINE CORPS.

By Maj. Edwin N. McClellan, Officer in Charge, Historical Division, United States Marine Corps.

While the historical work of the United States Marine Corps began systematically on September 8, 1919, when the Historical Division of the corps was officially established under Maj. Edwin N. Mc-Clellan, considerable progress was made prior to that date.

Early in 1918 Maj. Theodore H. Low, in addition to his duties as the recruiting officer stationed in Washington, D. C., and with the assistance of the personnel of his recruiting office, voluntarily gathered certain historical material relating to the Marine Corps.

On February 28, 1919, Maj. Edwin N. McClellan was detached from Marine Corps headquarters and directed to proceed to France and report to the commanding general of the American Expeditionary Forces for assignment to duty as historical officer for the Marine Corps for the purpose of acquainting himself with all matters of historical interest to marines. Arriving at Chaumont, France, on March 13, 1919, Maj. McClellan received orders attaching him to the historical section, General Staff, general headquarters, American Expeditionary Forces.

Maj. McClellan divided his work into two general divisions: First, a study of all data on file at general headquarters, Second Division headquarters, Fourth Brigade of Marines headquarters, and included organizations of marines, and the records of the services of supply; and, second, a careful study of the ground in France, England, Scotland, Wales, Ireland, and Germany, where marines operated or were located. He was temporarily attached to the Fourth Brigade of Marines, Second Division, in Germany, from March 16 to 25, 1919, and June 21 to 27, 1919, engaged in this work. On various occasions he visited the marine battlefields in the Verdun sector, in the Marne salient, near Soissons, Marbache sector, St. Mihiel salient, Blanc Mont in the Champagne, and the Meuse-Argonne. He also visited the various points located in the services of supply where marines were serving or had served.

Maj. McClellan spent from May 19 to June 6, 1919, in visiting localities in the British Islands, such as Southampton and London, England; Rosyth, near Edinburgh, Scotland; Scapa Flow, Orkney Islands; Castletownbere, Bantry Bay, Ireland; and Cardiff, Wales, where marines had served either on board ship or ashore with the Navy.

On August 6, 1919, Maj. McClellan sailed from Brest and reported in Washington, D. C., August 20, 1919.

On August 23, 1919, the acting adjutant and inspector directed that the Historical Division of the adjutant and inspector's department be established and assigned Maj. McClellan to duty as official in charge.

On September 8, 1919, the major general commandant issued Marine Corps Orders, No. 53. This general order officially established the Historical Division with duties outlined as follows:

(a) To establish historical archives which shall be the depository for all material of a historical nature; that is, material from which administrative value has disappeared.

(b) To prepare a history of the United States Marine Corps for period of the World War.

(c) To revise and bring up to date the history of the United States Marine Corps.

Archives, including original documents and information from 1775 to the present date, were accordingly established and the work commenced on the preparation of a history for the World War. This work progressed so favorably that on November 26, 1919, a brief history called "The United States Marine Corps in the World War" was published preliminary to the final and detailed history of the United States Marine Corps during the World War in course of preparation. The first edition of this book, consisting of 50,000 copies having become exhausted, the major general commandant directed that a second edition of 100,000 copies, revised to as late a date as practicable, be prepared and published.

In addition to the above-mentioned history, the Historical Division has prepared and had published in various service magazines many articles referring to the history of the marines in the World War and in prior periods.

The work of revising and amplifying the present history of the United States Marine Corps is progressing steadily and within two years a history of the corps from 1775 to date will be published in several volumes.

STATE DEPARTMENT.

By GAILLARD HUNT.

In September, 1918, Secretary Lansing appointed Gaillard Hunt, special officer of the Department of State, to undertake the preparation of the State Department's history of the war. A small bureau was organized and the work has been continuously in progress since his appointment. The scope of the work is illustrated by the title "The history of the World War as shown by the records of the Department of State." While no printing has as yet been undertaken, several volumes of the work are ready for the printer. The plan contemplates a narrative account followed by the documents (all from the State Department's records) upon which the narrative is based. The work begins with the assassination of the Archduke Ferdinand, followed by the outbreak of hostilities in Europe; the repatriation and protection of American citizens at the beginning of the war; the custody of the interests of the belligerents by American diplomatic and consular officers; this Government's peace proposals; contraband of war and neutral rights; progress of the war, etc: How many volumes will be required for the completion of the work can not at this date be prognosticated.

THE NATIONAL BOARD FOR HISTORICAL SERVICE.

By WALDO G. LELAND.

ORIGINS AND ORGANIZATION.

1. The National Board for Historical Service was one of the organizations—the one most centrally located—which grew out of the desire and effort of historical scholars to render useful public service during the war. The idea of the board was evolved in the course of discussions by a small group in Washington during the first weeks of April, 1917, and was presented to a larger group in the form of an invitation from Dr. J. F. Jameson, director of the department of historical research in the Carnegie Institution, to attend a conference in Washington on April 28. The object of the conference was thus stated:

> The problem is one which has no doubt presented itself to the mind of every history man in the country. Many of them would doubtless be glad to spend a good deal of time in public service in war time, and most of all in service appropriate to their special acquirements, but are not in the way of hearing of useful tasks that they could undertake.
>
> Our thought is that if the questions involved could be immediately considered in a preliminary way, by an informal conference of a dozen members of the profession representing different regions of the country and different aspects of history—American, European, economic, diplomatic—an organization might be devised by which all this store of competence and patriotic good will, instead of running to waste or lying untouched, might be systematically drawn upon to meet actual needs, felt or unfelt, of the Government or the public.

The conference thus called was held in the offices of the department of historical research of the Carnegie Institution on April 28 and 29.[2] A docket has been drawn up which stated the problem of the conference to be as follows:

> (A) To provide a means for placing the historical scholarship of the country at the service of the Government.
>
> (B) To utilize historical scholarship for patriotic and educational ends, and to enable it to do its part in providing the general public with that fund of accurate knowledge which is an essential basis of intelligent opinion.

---

[2] The following were present during all or part of the conference: J. F. Jameson, who acted as chairman; W. G. Leland, who acted as secretary; Guy S. Ford, Frederic L. Paxson, Andrew C. McLaughlin, Henry E. Bourne, Frederick J. Turner, George M. Dutcher, Charles D. Hazen, Charles H. Hull, James T. Shotwell, Albert E. McKinley, Gaillard Hunt, John C. Fitzpatrick, H. Barrett Learned, Edmund C. Burnett, Victor Clark, Thomas W. Page, and Edward G. Lowry.

(C) To secure the interests of history and of historical students by promoting the intelligent collection and preservation of historical materials, and in other ways.

In the course of the ensuing discussion it soon became clear that historians in all parts of the country had had the problem, as presented to the conference, very much on their minds. The Mississippi Valley Historical Association, meeting two days before, had adopted resolutions urging that " means be taken by the Government of the United States to facilitate the sound historical instruction of the people of the United States to the end that a correct public opinion with full knowledge of the facts that have made for our freedom and democracy in the past may stand stubbornly in our struggle for the maintenance of those principles in the future." The department of history of the University of Wisconsin had drawn up, for discussion in the conference, a memorandum outlining the organization and functions of a " bureau of historical information " to be created under the Committee on Public Information, the general aim of which should be " to aid in the formation of a correct public opinion, to advise departments of Government needing historical data, to provide accurate data for writers and journalists, and to coordinate existing historical agencies." At Columbia University an organization of the faculty had already been effected and had commenced the publication of a series of " Columbia war pamphlets," the contents of which, however, were not confined to historical material. These examples but serve to illustrate the intense desire of historical scholars to find some way of rendering effective service of the nature for which their studies and special knowledge qualified them.

The conference devoted its attention principally to the consideration of the various kinds of service most needed and of the most effective means and organization for their performance. Each one present stated what he and his colleagues conceived to be most expedient in the region which he represented; Mr. Arthur Bullard presented the views of the Committee on Public Information as to the various ways in which its work could be furthered by historical scholars; Mr. Geoffrey Butler, of the British High Commission, who was present for a short time, explained what British scholars had been able to do along the lines under consideration, and Mr. Edward G. Lowry, experienced journalist and writer, made valuable suggestions as to practical methods of reaching the public. As the discussion progressed there appeared to be a striking agreement as to the needs which historical scholars might serve to satisfy. These were conceived of as, first, the education of public opinion with respect to the deep-lying causes and fundamental issues of the war and the reasons for American participation in it; second, the presentation of past national experience in so far as such experience might furnish useful lessons for application in the present emergency; third, the supply of technical services to the Government; and fourth, the assurance for the benefit of future historians of the preservation of the documentary and other material essential for recording the history of the present time.

As to the most effective methods of meeting these needs there was a variety of opinion. For the first two, chiefly educational in character, suggestions were made respecting the supply of material, largely in the form of popular historical articles, to the daily and periodical press, the publication of series of small pamphlets or even of books, the organization of lecture courses, and especially the provision of instruction in schools and colleges. It was also suggested that the compilation of reliable reading lists respecting the war for the use of public libraries would furnish a guidance much needed and sought for at the present moment.

For the third, the supply of technical service to the Government, it was clear that future developments would determine the nature of such services and the most appropriate methods of rendering them. Preliminary inquiries of the Council of National Defense, of the Bureau of Education, and of the Committee on Public Information made it appear that aid to the Government would probably take the form of cooperation with the last two. As to the fourth need to be met, the collection and preservation of material for use in future research, it was evident that this object would be accomplished indirectly through suggestions to existing organizations and institutions, such as libraries and historical societies and other agencies, and through watchfulness with respect to the archives of the Government—Federal, State, and local—especially the records of the various branches of war administration already created or likely to be developed in the future.

The form of organization best suited to render the services which have been indicated, most representative of the historical profession and most likely to inspire public confidence, was a matter that was long and earnestly discussed. Although the American Historical Association was represented in the conference by some of its officers and councilors, these had no authority to establish a war organization of any sort in the name of the association. Indeed, it was the feeling of some, perhaps of most present, that the nature of the situation required that each one taking part in the work of the new organization should do so as an individual scholar engaging no other responsibility than his own. It was felt that no group could represent the historical profession in any formal way, but only those members of it who sympathized with the purposes of the group and who accorded it their support. It was realized that the new organization must necessarily be informal and unofficial,

without authority except such as it might acquire through deserving
and gaining the support of historical scholars and the confidence of
the public. At the same time the possibility that the American Historical Association might think best to substitute some other form
of organization was not lost sight of and provision was made for
such an eventuality.

With these considerations in mind the following resolutions were
adopted:

As an emergency measure, to serve until action by the American Historical
Association, the undersigned, meeting in Washington upon invitation by the
Carnegie Institution of Washington through its department of historical re-
search, have adopted the following resolutions:

Resolved:

I. That there be formed a National Board for Historical Service.

II. That the headquarters of the board shall be in Washington, D. C.

III. That the purposes of the National Board for Historical Service shall be:

(*a*) To facilitate the coordination and development of historical activities
in the United States in such a way as to aid the Federal and the State Governments through direct personal service or through affiliation with their various
branches.

(*b*) To aid in supplying the public with trustworthy information of historical
or similar character through the various agencies of publication, through the
preparation of reading lists and bibliographies, through the collection of historical material, and through the giving of lectures and of systematic instruction, and in other ways.

(*c*) To aid, encourage, and organize State, regional, and local committees,
as well as special committees for the furtherance of the above ends, and to
cooperate with other agencies and organizations, especially in the general
field of social studies.

IV. That the board shall be composed of at least nine members who shall
select a chairman, vice chairman, secretary, and treasurer from their own number, and that the said board shall have power to add to its membership, to fill
vacancies, to appoint advisory and associate members, to organize affiliated
or subsidiary boards of committees, to receive and disburse moneys, and to
perform such other acts as may be necessary for the accomplishment of the
purposes herein stated.

V. That the board, until further action by itself in conformity with these
resolutions, shall be composed of the following: Victor S. Clark, of Washington;
Robert D. W. Connor, of Raleigh, N. C.; Carl Russell Fish, of Madison, Wis.;
Charles D. Hazen, of New York City; Charles H. Hull, of Ithaca, N. Y.;
Gaillard Hunt, of Washington; Waldo G. Leland, of Washington; James T.
Shotwell, of New York City; Frederick J. Turner, of Cambridge, Mass.

Adopted at Washington, D. C. April 29, 1917:

HENRY E. BOURNE.	H. BARRETT LEARNED.
EDMUND C. BURNETT.	WALDO G. LELAND.
VICTOR S. CLARK.	ALBERT E. MCKINLEY.
GEORGE M. DUTCHER.	ANDREW C. MCLAUGHLIN.
GUY S. FORD.	THOMAS WALKER PAGE.
CHARLES D. HAZEN.	FREDERIC L. PAXSON.
CHARLES H. HULL.	JAMES T. SHOTWELL.
GAILLARD HUNT.	FREDERICK J. TURNER.
J. FRANKLIN JAMESON.	

The first effort of the board thus created was directed to enlisting the support of the members of the historical profession, and at the same time to securing from these latter information respecting the state of public opinion and suggestions as to the kinds of service most needed. Accordingly the following circular letter was sent on May 1, 1917, to 165 historical scholars in all parts of the country, informing them of the organization of the board and of its purposes, and asking for information and suggestions:

Last Saturday, at the invitation of the Carnegie Institution, extended through its department of historical research, a score of students of history gathered in Washington and, after discussing what such men might do in the present emergency, elected a "National Board for Historical Service," with headquarters here. This is a voluntary and unofficial organization of individuals spontaneously formed in the hope that through it the store of competence and patriotic good will possessed by the history men of the country, instead of running in part to waste, or even lying untouched, may eventually be drawn upon to meet the needs of the public or of the Government. To that end the board, as a first step toward preparedness, both for continuing war and for eventual peace, takes occasion to solicit the cooperation of interested persons, and the present letter is to invite from you such advice and suggestions as you may care to contribute. The organization of subsidiary State or local committees to work under the direction of the board is not, so far as we are now informed, desirable, and it is understood that in cooperating with us for any of the foregoing purposes you will be acting, as we did, upon your individual responsibility, and that the function of the board will be, for the present, to serve as a coordinating body between voluntary workers in the common cause.

The generalness of this statement is sufficient indication that much remains to be done in determining the ends toward which, and not less in ascertaining the material devices and the personal means through which, such voluntary work may be performed.

But it appears that a survey of the situation and needs of the country in this respect, as they present themselves to the observation of history men in various regions, is one of the preliminary steps, and it is for cooperation in this that we first appeal to you.

Among the matters concerning which your opinion in as definite a form as possible is especially desired are:

(1) What is the attitude of people, or of various classes of people, in your region toward the participation of the United States in the war? Are our purposes understood? As understood, are they approved? Where approved, what can be done to keep popular attention fixed upon them, to the end that our national idealism shall not perish in the conflict, or yield to admiration of courage or of efficiency as ends in themselves? If our national purposes as understood in any degree fail of approval, by what argument, anywise historical in complexion, can they be so explained as to secure approval?

(2) How can such arguments or appeals be most effectually presented, by books or pamphlets, through the metropolitan or the local press, by speakers, or otherwise?

(3) What opportunities have you personally to procure the dissemination of appropriate matter, e. g., through your local press, through lectures to schools or to the general public, through libraries, or historical societies? Do you know any persons of historical knowledge and training in your region who have real

qualifications, either by experience in newspaper writing or in public speaking, for disseminating such information, and who could and would give time to doing it?

(4) Can you reach, or suggest some way of reaching, teachers before their vacations begin? Do you know of any summer schools, largely attended by teachers, the management of which would probably welcome lectures of such a character in case the board can suggest appropriate lecturers?

(5) In the conference many suggestions were made of subjects upon which useful articles might be prepared. The following may be instanced by way of example:

A. Historical aspects of war problems in the United States, e. g., raising and maintaining armies; exercise of war powers by the Federal Government; war taxation; economic adjustments; suppression of disorder; problems of transportation; supply and distribution of food, especially in the Confederate States; etc.

B. International and foreign problems, particularly those likely to influence American policy, e. g., Irish questions; conceptions of freedom of the seas; open door in China; enforcement of treaties; restatement of Monroe Doctrine; neutralization; American interests in Turkey; etc.

(6) Will you not make suggestions of other subjects, and possible writers?

(7) Have you knowledge of matter already in print (outside of such generally known material as would be noticed in the American Historical Review) that seems to be effective for such purposes? Where, specifically, may it be found?

(8) Do you know of any collections that are being made of local fugitive material illustrative of the war, especially of the attitude of sections of your community or region toward it? Are you in a position to encourage the making of such collections? Where and how?

(9) Do you know of any funds available for the actual and necessary expense of any parts of such an undertaking as has been suggested, either nationally or locally?

Will you not consult, especially as to regional needs and probable attitudes of mind, such of your colleagues or acquaintances as may be able to give useful advice on any of the points mentioned, or on any others pertinent to the general purposes of the board, and send the results, as promptly as practicable, to Waldo G. Leland, secretary, 1133 Woodward Building, Washington, D. C.?

The board will then endeavor to draw from the replies a statement of definite needs and possibilities, and will presently communicate with you again.

The response to this letter was most encouraging; not only did it indicate an almost unanimous approval of the purposes of the board and give promise of support and cooperation, but it furnished a large body of information relative to the state of mind of the country and the needs of the moment as well as a variety of practical and valuable suggestions.

Thus fortified the board was in a position to formulate the policy which was to guide it throughout its existence. This policy may be described briefly as follows: To maintain the nonofficial character of the board as a group of individual scholars each representing only himself; not to organize branches but to encourage or cooperate with regional or local groups having similar objects which might be created; to maintain a close contact with members of the historical profession in all parts of the country by informing them frequently of the work of the board and by proposing to them certain activities or calling upon them for services; not to express opinions or judgments as a board nor to attempt to establish standards of historical orthodoxy; not to publish pamphlets, articles, or books in the name of the board, but to leave to their authors full responsibility for all publications made under its auspices or pursuant to its suggestions; and, finally, to coöperate with or serve the Government in such ways as it might be called upon to do.

The activities of the board at once began to assume a varied character. It is not easy to classify them all, but most fall into one or another of the categories of research, publications, lectures, education, Government service, and preservation of war records. These categories are not mutually exclusive, for most research, for example, was undertaken in some form of Government service, and the publications and lectures were chiefly of an educational character; nor are they completely comprehensive, for there were numerous activities of a miscellaneous sort which can not be classified. They may serve, however, as a cadre for the following account of the board's work.

RESEARCH.

In the conferences which preceded the organization of the board and in the discussions which followed it was clear that there was a general feeling among historians that for the time being at least activities of research should be directed to matters having a bearing upon actual problems in order that accurate knowledge of the experience of the past might be invoked for such present guidance as it should afford. The resources of the board were not such as to enable it to carry out for itself any elaborate program of research; it was obliged, with few exceptions, to content itself with encouragement and suggestion. To this end a letter was composed and sent (May 11, 1917) to some 75 or more professors of history, most of whom had charge of graduate or research courses, in which the problem was thus presented:

European historians have long had the quickening, though at times dangerous, consciousness that their modern historical problems were instinct with life; that their topics for research involved sensitive international relations, were live wires connecting with stores of dynamite, were liable at any moment to pass from history into present action.

Are not American historians learning that some of the important facts in our democratic development are more intimately connected with present urgent choices of domestic policy and foreign relations than had been commonly appreciated?

Is it not possible that in research work during the present summer and winter, at least, we ought to make fuller use of our realization that out of history there are issues of life to-day?

Can we not give greater zest to our research work, both in seminary and as individuals by dealing with phases which are directly or indirectly connected with present problems? Shall we not feel better justified in following the scholar's calling if by our investigations we furnish material useful to Americans in determining their decisions in the great issues which now confront them and which will, in changing forms, confront them for a considerable future?

These are matters, not only of presenting the results of previous study and writing; they are matters for new and unforeseen adjustments of old to new; for research, and for research under the pressure of instant demand for information.

In the first place it is important to be able to furnish a background for news items. Our board is already in a position where we shall often have advance information as to what will be news in certain lines some time before the event. This advance information would give a student familiar with the field and bibliography of the suggested subject time to produce an article which, though not final, will yet possess an intimacy of touch and an orientation impossible to a reporter * * *.

In the second place there are certain aspects of history with which the public should be familiar, but the significance of which is apparent only to one with a long perspective. In such cases the historians of the country should take the initiative, not waiting for the press.

In his speech at the Gridiron Club dinner, in Washington, February 26, 1916, President Wilson showed how deeply he was influenced by the historical mode of approach to his problem. He said:

" You can never tell your direction except by long measurements. You can not establish a line by two posts; you have got to have three at least to know whether they are straight with anything, and the longer your line the more certain your measurement. There is only one way in which to determine how the future of the United States is going to be projected, and that is by looking backward and seeing which way the lines ran which led up to the present moment of power and of opportunity. There is no doubt about that."

The historical research and thought of the country should surely be concerned with this work of surveying American tendencies and ideals. It is important for us to know what, in the opinion of the profession, such subjects are, and to know whether they are being studied, and if so, where. If they are being neglected, we may be able to promote their study, and if they are being studied, we are in a position to bring the concentrated results before the public widely over the country.

The third function of research is one in connection with which the board can do little, but the leaders of research in the country by correspondence and intercourse may do much. It is obvious that the problem of world reconstruction will not cease to be vital to the next generation. Not in detail but in general, it is possible to foresee the kind of questions which it will ask of its historians. Ought not a good proportion of the young scholars in our seminaries be directed to interest themselves, whatever their fields, along lines which may contribute to the wise solution of these problems which will be the pivot of politics and legislation during their lives? An illustration may be made in the fact that the devotion and skill which have been given to a study of the Napoleonic wars, and even of our Civil War, have yet left almost untouched many subjects which throw most direct light upon the difficulties of to-day. Will it not be possible for us to do something—we all realize how little prophetic we are— to make this loss of experience as slight as it may be for the future?

As a first step will you not write the board any ideas you may have on the general subject and any contribution you may be prepared to make?

After we receive information, we shall be glad to communicate with you, noting whether certain topics seem to be in need of attention by historians. In case of subjects actually under study we shall be glad to be of use in giving a national currency to the concentrated historical results. Will you not convey the ideas of this letter to such of your colleagues as you think willing and able to assist in the work?

It is difficult to form an estimate of the results of this letter. In respect to furnishing the historical background for news items they were negligible, for the board never developed the close contact with journalism that it had expected in the early days of its existence to make. It is not probable, either, that the immediate course of seminar work in the universities was much affected; it is not easy to make sudden changes of direction and in any event most able-bodied members of the seminars were soon engaged in quite other lines of effort in the officers' training camps. Probably the letter stimulated individual research and production; certainly the war period was marked by a large output of historical publications, articles, and books having a bearing upon contemporary events and issues. A number of articles suggested by the board were published in the American Historical Review and elsewhere, and the board secured directly some 30 or more articles for the Historical Outlook, in addition to the documentary materials and the educational or pedagogical articles of a suggestive nature which it also contributed to the latter magazine. The board was undoubtedly a factor in creating the atmosphere which favored the production referred to; indeed, one of the most widely read books of the period was by a member of the board: " Alsace-Lorraine under German Rule," by Charles Downer Hazen.

The board took a more active part in the publication of bibliographical aids to research. A list of articles in periodicals relating to the war was prepared by Miss Harriette M. Dilla, who offered her services in the summer of 1917, and it was published in mimeographed form by the Library of Congress. Profs. G. M. Dutcher, A. H. Lybyer, and others compiled a " Selected bibliography of the war " which was printed in the Historical Outlook (then the History Teacher's Magazine) for April, 1918. An expansion of this bibliography, in which the board was much aided by Prof. Ella Lonn of Goucher College, was well advanced by the close of the war but was not completed. Members of the board assisted in preparing the bibliography compiled by Prof. T. W. Riker and published by the committee on special training and education of the War Department, (C. e. 17, Bibliography no. 1) for use in the war-issues course of the Students' Army Training Corps, and Dr. Leo F. Stock made a digest of the war legislation of the Sixty-fifth Congress and a calendar of the Executive orders relating to the war, the first of these compilations being published in the Historical Outlook for October, 1919. After the close of the war an elaborate bibliography of peace and reconstruction, prepared by Prof. Joseph Schafer, the vice chairman of the board, was published by the World Peace Foundation (League of Nations Series, II, special number).

The most important work of research carried on by the board or by its members was in cooperation with the so-called "House Inquiry" or "Peace Inquiry," the organization which under Col. Edward M. House gathered information respecting the problems which seemed likely to come up for consideration at the Peace Congress which would meet upon the conclusion of the war. The Inquiry had its own organization and the members of the board who belonged to it worked as individual scholars and not as representatives of the board, but it is worth noting that they were entrusted with some of the most important sections of the Inquiry's work. Thus Prof. J. T. Shotwell, the first chairman of the board, was an administrative officer of the Inquiry; Prof. Charles H. Haskins directed the investigation dealing with the problem areas of the Western Front, Belgium, Luxembourg, Alsace-Lorraine, etc., in which Prof. Wallace Notestein also took part; Prof. A. C. Coolidge conducted research in Russian and Polish matters, and Prof. Dana C. Munro was in charge of the investigations relating to the Near East.

But the board also conducted certain researches for the Inquiry in its corporate capacity. The most extensive of these investigations took the form of compiling a compendium of the diplomatic history of Europe, Asia, and Africa since 1870. This work, which was called for upon a month's notice, was directed by Professors Frank M. Anderson and Amos S. Hershey who secured the collaboration of 60 or more scholars. The result of this cooperation was published by the Department of State: Handbook for the diplomatic history of Europe, Asia, and Africa, 1870–1914 (Washington, 1918).

Another investigation called for by the Inquiry was into the nature and history of governments less than sovereign, which was conducted for the board by Profs. W. W. Willoughby and Charles G. Fenwick in cooperation with the Institute for Government Research.

PUBLICATIONS.

In early discussions as to possible activities of the board it had seemed that publication would take an important place. Comprehensive but somewhat vague plans were entertained for supplying material of various kinds to newspapers and periodicals, of establishing a series of pamphlets or small books; even of maintaining some sort of a periodical, but it was soon found that many difficulties, the nature of which may be readily imagined, opposed the execution of such ambitious projects. The members of the board did not have the experience in practical journalism which was essential to any atempt at feeding the columns of the daily press. Few members of the historical profession were in the habit of writing for newspaper publication or had acquired that style of literary expression which seems to be successful in American journalism. The two or three articles which the board furnished for rewriting and adaptation to newspaper use were so denatured in the process that there was little encouragement to continue the practice.

To a less extent the same difficulties surrounded the publication of magazine articles. It had been thought that the board might maintain a sort of reservoir of materials suitable for the popular or serious periodicals, and a tentative arrangement was even made with one of the standard monthlies whereby the board was to supply a certain number of pages of material for each issue, but the board had no more success as a literary agent than as a press agency, and wasted little time in fruitless experimentation.

It was realized from the beginning that the activities of the board along the lines mentioned, even if successful, must be largely supplemented by the individual and unorganized efforts of the members of the historical profession. Accordingly, the following letter of May 18, 1917, was sent to some 225 men and women, historians or teachers of history, in all parts of the country:

There has never been a period in American history when public opinion has needed such a broad foundation of unfamiliar fact. The crisis in which we are now, was brought upon the Nation by outside forces rather than by internal movements. The solution of the present situation moreover requires on the part of the people a large amount of fact with which they are unaccustomed to deal.

The historian knows that in determining the public opinion of the moment as well as that of to-morrow, which means so much for the future, the resources of human experience are bound to be drawn upon to a very great degree. He knows also how important it is that the facts furnished to the people shall be genuine and the interpretation of them made by experts rather than by quacks.

At no time in our history has the historian been so obviously called to the immediate service of the Nation; the formation of the National Board for Historical Service is an effort to provide a medium for the rendering of such service. The board, however, realizes that the major portion of the work must be done by the members of the profession acting in their own localities, where the influence of their personality is an established factor.

The correspondence which this board has already had with members of the historical profession in many parts of the country reveals an encouraging realization, on the part of historians, of their responsibilities and opportunities. We find that in many cases professors and teachers are giving special courses or series of lectures on the issues of the present moment; some are addressing public meetings, clubs, churches, or special gatherings; some are interesting themselves particularly in stimulating the teachers of the public schools, while many are writing special articles which appear in current magazines and newspapers.

It seems clear to us that the local press affords an important medium through which the historian may render a most useful service. By making the acquaintance of editors and reporters, by watching the columns of the local newspapers for statements that in the interest of truth should be controverted, by offering editorial material, by writing communications or special articles of historical character pertinent to immediate questions, and by furnishing the correct historical background for many items of current news the historian may exercise a salutary influence in his community.

It seems to us that this is a time when all the accumulated resources of reputation, information, and judgment belong to the Nation and should be put at the disposal of the public.

We shall be glad if you will keep us informed from time to time of your own and of other activities and especially if you will make such suggestions as may occur to you, in order that the board may serve the historical profession in general as a sort of clearing house of information.

The resources of the board did not allow it to embark upon any schemes of publication of its own. Plans for a series of pamphlets were much discussed but it was early determined, as a part of the board's policy not to publish or edit pamphlets or volumes. If the board had no publications of its own, however, it took an active part in preparing and editing the series of pamphlets issued by the committee on public information, an activity which will be described below as a part of the Government service which the board was called upon to render.

Furthermore, the board's relation with the Historical Outlook, the columns of which were placed at its disposal by the editor, Dr. Albert E. McKinley, and the publishers, the McKinley Publishing Co., of Philadelphia, was such as to make that periodical, for the time being, almost an organ of the board. The use which the board made of these facilities was chiefly in the conduct of its educational work and is described under that head. The single publication made by the board as such, the War Readings, prepared by Mrs. Dana C. Munro (Scribner), to a certain extent a deviation from its policy, was also educational in character.

During the last months of the board's existence the vice chairman was authorized to secure the publication, though not in the name of the board, of a volume of essays by different writers, entitled, "Democracy in Reconstruction."[3]

LECTURING.

In the field of lecturing the board formulated and carried out a more systematic program than in that of publications. It made a canvass of the historical profession in order to ascertain who of its

[3] F. A. Cleveland and Joseph Schafer, "Democracy and Reconstruction". (Boston, Houghton Mifflin, 1919). A volume of 23 essays grouped under the heads "Ideals of democracy," "After-war social problems," "After-war labor problems," "After-war transportation problems," "After-war political problems." The introductory essay is by Prof. Schafer, "The historical background of reconstruction in America.".

members were able to deliver lectures in the various summer schools, particularly in the schools most frequented by teachers, and suggested to the directors of these schools, through the Bureau of Education, that lectures on the issues of the war be made a feature of the summer program. The board also furnished the names of possible lecturers, and syllabi of lecturers for use when special lecturers were not available, and furnished the names of lecturers, on request, to such organizations as the community chautauquas, to churches, clubs, societies, etc.

In this connection should be mentioned the work of the New England Group for Historical Service, the organization of which grew out of suggestions by the board, and which cooperated most effectively with the latter.[4] This group not only delivered a series of lectures at Camp Devens under the auspices of the board, but also independently, a large number of lectures in the towns and summer resorts of New England.

The principal project of lecturing organized and carried out by the board was the delivery of 5 illustrated lectures in 22 of the major training camps.[5] These lectures were given under the auspices of the educational committee of the War Department's Commission on Training Camp Activities and with the material aid of the Y. M. C. A. and the Knights of Columbus. A large number of scholars took part in this work, which required in many cases an extended residence in camp. Each lecture was repeated a sufficient number of times to enable all men who wished to do so to hear it. The board provided the lantern slides, and by way of suggestion an outline of each lecture, the subjects of which were as follows: The warring countries and their geography; The growth of Germany and of German ambitions; The French Republic and what it stands for; The British Empire and what it stands for; How the war came about and how it developed; The American democracy and the war. In some cases the series was given by a single lecturer, in others by several, each one dealing with the subject with which he was most familiar. This activity of the board was organized and carried out by Dr. J. F. Jameson.

In the late spring of 1917 the board received a request from the University of London to provide a lecturer on American history for

---

[4] The New England Group for Historical Service was composed of the following, some of whom were also members of the national board: Arthur I. Andrews, secretary; H. J. Ahern, Warren A. Ault, S. P. R. Chadwick, Samuel L. Conner, A. C. Coolidge, Theodore F. Collier, Irving H. Countryman, Herbert D. Foster, Rollin M. Gallagher, A. H. Gilmer, Charles H. Haskins, Roy W. Hatch, J. L. Keegen, A. C. Lane, Charles R. Lingley, Leo S. McCollester, C. H. McIlwain, George S. Miller, Theodore Clarke Smith, Frederick L. Thompson, Mason W. Tyler.

[5] Camps Beauregard, Custer, Devens, Dix, Dodge, Doniphan, Fremont, Funston, Grant, Greene, Jackson, Lee, Lewis, Logan, McArthur, McClellan, Meade, Oglethorpe, Sheridan, Sherman, Taylor, Upton.

its summer session. This the board was unable to do on such short notice, but in the course of correspondence during which the original invitation was much broadened, it was decided that a lecturer should be sent to England to speak on American history and American participation in the war, before the universities of the United Kingdom and Ireland. For this mission the board, having secured from various sources [6] the requisite funds, selected Prof. Andrew C. McLaughlin, who sailed for England in April, 1918, accompanied by Mr. Charles Moore. Professor McLaughlin delivered lectures before the Universities of London, Oxford, Cambridge, Reading, Bristol, Birmingham, Sheffield, Leeds, Manchester, Liverpool, Newcastle, Nottingham, Exeter, Southampton, Bangor, Cardiff, Edinburgh, Glasgow, Aberdeen, and Dublin, his tour having been arranged by Prof. Arthur P. Newton, of Kings College, London. He also addressed the Royal Historical Society and gatherings of teachers of history in London, as well as a meeting of workingmen in Walsall.[7]

Another series of lectures arranged by the board was delivered by Prof. George M. Wrong, of the University of Toronto, who spoke on Canadian history and institutions before the summer schools of Harvard, Michigan, Indiana, Illinois, Chicago, Northwestern, and Wisconsin Universities in July and August, 1918.

EDUCATIONAL WORK.

No division of the board's work was more varied or more extensive in scope than that which dealt with education. Some of this work was carried on indirectly, some of it in cooperation with the Bureau of Education, and some of it by the board in its own name.

In May, 1917, the board furnished the Bureau of Education with the text of a letter to high-school principals, which had been composed by Prof. Guy Stanton Ford for use in Minnesota, urging that the approaching commencement exercises be directed "toward an elevated and enlightening discussion of the faith in popular government." This was distributed by the bureau as its "Civic Education Letter, 1917, No. 1." At the same time and in the same way a letter drawn up by the board was sent to all directors of summer schools (Bureau of Education, "Civic Education Letter, 1917, No. 2"), suggesting that lectures on the war be included in the school programs; this suggestion was followed up with correspondence and

---

[6] The contributors who made possible this mission were Messrs. Cass Gilbert, Thomas W. Lamont, Charles Altschul, J. M. Longyear, and G. S. Baker.

[7] Professor McLaughlin contributed an informal account of his mission to the Historical Outlook for December, 1918, under the title "Impressions of Britain in war time." His lectures have been published in book form, America and Britain (E. P. Dutton, 1919). Their subjects concerned America's entry into the war, British and American relations, the Monroe Doctrine, and the background of American federalism.

practical suggestions as to lecturers and subjects, an activity which has already been described.

: It was also through the Bureau of Education that the board inaugurated one of its most important undertakings, the publication of a series of suggestions respecting the teaching of history in the secondary schools, designed to show how the history courses might be made more profitable and more enlightening in view of contemporary events. These suggestions were prepared by four committees, each dealing with one of the fields of history which compose the high-school curriculum, ancient, general European, English, and American.[8] To serve as an introduction to the series the board prepared a pamphlet entitled " Opportunities for History teachers: the lessons of the Great War in the classroom," which was published by the Bureau of Education as its " Teachers' Leaflet No. 1, 1917," and distributed widely among teachers of history during the summer of 1917. In this pamphlet certain general suggestions were offered in an endeavor to point out the duties and responsibilities of the history teacher in the present emergency, the proper use of history in stimulating patriotism and especially in developing the sense of duty and of civic obligation, and to warn against the abuse of history and chauvinistic tendencies. Then followed more specific suggestions respecting the four fields of history which have been enumerated. This pamphlet was followed up by progressive suggestions and comment in each of these fields, which were published serially in the Historical Outlook (History Teachers' Magazine) from September, 1917, to May, 1918, and which were designed to accompany the four courses through the school year.

The preparation of a companion pamphlet of suggestions in history, civics, and geography for the use of teachers in the elementary schools was undertaken with the aid of Prof. J. M. Gambrill, but changing circumstances prevented its completion.

In the summer of 1918 a second pamphlet was prepared for the board containing an " Outline of an emergency course of instruction on the war," by Charles A. Coulomb, Arnold J. Gerson, and Albert E. McKinley. This was intended for use in both elementary and secondary schools and was published by the Bureau of Education as " Teachers' Leaflet, No. 4, 1918." [9] At the same time a short history

---

[8] These committees were as follows: Ancient history, R. V. D. Magoffin, chairman, J. H. Breasted, S. P. R. Chadwick, W. S. Davis, W. S. Ferguson, A. T. Olmstead, W. L. Westermann; medieval and modern European history, D. C. Munro, chairman, F. M. Anderson, Arthur I. Andrews, S. B. Harding, D. C. Knowlton, Margaret McGill; English history, A. L. Cross, chairman, Wayland J. Chase, E. P. Cheyney, Blanche E. Hazard, L. M. Larson, Wallace Notestein; American history, Evarts B. Greene, chairman, W. L. Fleming, R. A. Maurer, F. L. Paxson, T. C. Smith, James Sullivan, E. M. Violette.

[9] The authors of this pamphlet subsequently published a textbook based on their Outline School History of the Great War (American Book Co.).

of the war, adapted to the upper grades of the elementary schools, was written by Eva March Tappan, at the suggestion of the board, and published by Houghton Mifflin Co.: The Little Book of the War; while a selection of readings for school use was compiled for the board by Mrs. Dana C. Munro and edited by Prof. Robert C. Clark, of the University of Oregon. It was published by Charles Scribner's Sons under the title of " War Readings."

A French war reader for use in high-school and college classes was also compiled by the board, with the assistance of Prof. Charles A. Downer, who furnished the linguistic editing and vocabulary, the historical editing being done chiefly by Miss Esther M. Galbraith, but a series of untoward circumstances prevented its publication before the close of the war and it was abandoned. The introduction to the reader was, however, published in a translation by Professor Downer, in National School Service, the educational periodical of the Committee on Public Information, for December 15, 1918. This introduction was in the form of a charming address to American school children by the veteran French historian, educator, and academician, Ernest Lavisse, entitled " Why a Frenchman loves America," which was procured for the board by the French Mission.

Through the columns of the Historical Outlook the board published a number of aids to teachers in addition to the series of suggestions already noted. These took the form of special articles and particularly of " war supplements " containing documentary and other material. The first of these (January, 1918) was a " Topical Outline of the Great War," by Prof. Samuel B. Harding (also published as a pamphlet of the Committee on Public Information), which served as a most complete and valuable guide for the organization of courses, lectures, and readings. A companion supplement (March, 1918) was the " Selected Bibliography of the War," by Profs. G. M. Dutcher and A. H. Lybyer, already noted, while a geographical supplement (April, 1918), prepared by Professors Harding and William E. Lingelbach, furnished a small but exceedingly useful collection of war maps for school use. Other supplements contained documents and other illustrative material respecting the German occupation of Belgium, the war aims of Germany as regarded France, British views on reconstruction and historic peace congresses and. alliances, while two others were devoted to a bibliography of peace and reconstruction and to a digest of the war legislation of the Sixty-fifth Congress. One of the most important supplements (January, 1919) was a comprehensive review of the " Economic Mobilization of the United States," prepared by the Historical Branch of the General Staff under the direction of Maj. F. L. Paxson, a member of the board. The special articles took the form of discussions of specific problems such as the effect of the war on labor and capital, European neutrals and the peace conference, the Russian Revolution and the war, etc., and after the armistice there was contributed a series of narratives of personal experiences or accounts of special phases of war activity by various members of the historical profession.[10] Reprints of many of the contributions and entire copies of the Historical Outlook were purchased by the board in large quantities and distributed in response to requests for suggestions and information. In the second half of 1918, with the creation of the Students' Army Training Corps and the organization of the War Issues Course as a part of its curriculum, the cooperation of the board with the War Department's Committee on Education and Special Training became an important part of the former's educational work. This took the form of advising with respect to the War Issues Course, and particularly of aid in preparing a pamphlet of " Questions on the Issues of the War " (C. e. 21). This latter compilation, which was not in any sense a catechism, contained some 112 questions selected as most significant and representative from among several thousand queries actually presented in writing by men in military training. The questions were grouped under various heads and each group was accompanied by detailed references to easily accessible sources from which the information desired might be obtained. Also for use in the War Issues Course, Prof. A. E. McKinley brought together in a volume, " Collected Materials for the Study of the War," the war supplements of the Historical Outlook with some other material, and this collection of sources and aids was generally adopted to supplement the lectures and textbooks with which the course was conducted.

In the latter half of 1917, in order to stimulate teachers to prepare themselves for explaining the war to their classes, the board offered prizes for essays by teachers in the public schools on the subject " Why the United States is at war." This contest was organized in 15 States, the funds for the prizes being obtained chiefly through the

---

[10] This series was made up of the following articles: " The Food Administration : A test of American democracy," by E. S. Brown (May, 1919) ; " War tasks and accomplishments of the Shipping Board," by J. G. Randall (June, 1919) ; " With the First Division," by Lieut. R. A. Newhall (October, 1919) ; " The German press and the war," by Victor S. Clark (November, 1919) ; " Over there in Siberia," by Capt. L. B. Packard (December, 1919) ; " How American aviators were trained," by Col. Hiram Bingham (January, 1920) ; " Morale work in an Army camp," by Maj. R. V. B. Magoffin (February, 1920) ; " The committee on public information," by Prof. G. S. Ford (March, 1920) ; " The procurement of quartermaster's supplies during the World War," by Albert L. Scott (April, 1920) ; " Experiences of a Y. M. C. A. secretary in Russia," by T. P. Martin (May, 1920) ; " Intelligence work at First Army headquarters," by Capt. J. C. Parish (June, 1920) ; " Going over," by Ensign S. C. Clement (November, 1920).

generosity of various individuals.[11] In each State the competition was held in two groups, one comprising the teachers in the secondary schools, the other the teachers in the elementary schools, and in each group prizes aggregating $150 were offered, both first prizes being of $75. The winners of the first prizes competed in their respective groups for two national prizes offered by the board. Dr. Leo F. Stock had general charge of the content, and in each State a director was appointed who named the committees of award and attended to other details. Some 688 essays were offered in competition, North Carolina leading the other States with 94 competitors.[12]

The chief educational activity to which the board devoted the last months of its existence in 1919 was a fresh study of the whole program of historical instruction in the schools. The request to undertake this work came from the National Education Association through its commission on a national program for education, and the first step taken by the board was to secure the cooperation of the American Historical Association. The two organizations appointed a joint committee on history and education for citizenship in the schools,[13] the organization of which was completed in February, 1919. The committee held meetings and conferences in Washington, New York, and Chicago, and individual members of it were in constant contact with associations or other groups of history teachers in all sections of the country in order that the work of the committee might have the benefit of the best opinion and the widest experience. The program which the committee set for itself was formulated, as follows, in its " Preliminary statement " of March 15:

(a) Starting from the idea of education for citizenship, the committee will plan courses in history for the eight years of the common school and the four years of high school, taking account also of the "six-three-three" arrangement, where that is in vogue. In addition it will consider the special needs of the normal school, the vocational school, the rural school, and the distinctive Americanization programs.

(b) As its most urgent problem, the committee will study the question of the high-school history courses, and will prepare a report on a first year of history and a second year of history in the high school. These courses, to be given either in the first and second or the second and third years (this point

---

[11] The choice of States was determined by the ability of the board to secure funds, the donors specifying for which States their respective contributions were to be used. The contest was held in New Hampshire, Massachusetts, Rhode Island, Connecticut, New York, New Jersey, Virginia, North Carolina, Tennessee, Ohio, Indiana, Illinois, Wisconsin, and Minnesota. The donors were Charles Altschul, George L. Beer, W. A. Brice, Gen. J. S. Carr, Thomas Chadbourne, jr., Howell Cheyney, Paul Cravath, John Crosby, Samuel B. Harding, Dwight W. Morrow, Sigourney Stern, Cornelius J. Sullivan, and the North Carolina Historical Commission.

[12] The results of the competition and the names of the State directors and committees of award were announced in the Historical Outlook for April and May, 1918.

[13] The committee was composed as follows: Joseph Schafer, chairman; Daniel C. Knowlton, secretary; William C. Bagley, Frank S. Bogardus, Julian A. C. Chandler, Guy Stanton Ford, Samuel B. Harding, Andrew C. McLaughlin.

o be decided after further investigation), are to be (1) a course in modern istory and (2) a course in United States history.

(c) The committee accepts the report of the former Committee of Eight of he American Historical Association (The Study of History in the Elementary chools, New York, Scribners, 1909) as the basis of the common-school hisory work, but it expects to study this report with a view to adjusting its ecommendations to the new situation which will result from a recasting of he high-school work, and for the purpose of effecting other improvements hat may seem practicable. One suggested change is to strengthen and dignify he sixth-grade history, covering European backgrounds, in order to make it erve as an introduction to the modern history course in the high school as ell as to the American history course of the seventh and eighth grades. o that end the committee believes the sixth-grade work in history should e made a basis of promotion, as is the history of the upper two years.

(d) For controlling its procedure in the outlining of courses, the committee ill attempt to apply the principle that "every new step in history, instrucon should be a step forward in the subject." It will seek to eliminate dupliation by a careful selection of subject matter to be taught at each stage of the ork in history. It also contemplates setting up some effective standards for easuring results in history instruction.

(e) The committee are agreed that methods of teaching history should be onsidered in the forthcoming report, that specimen lessons should be preented, and that one of the guiding principles in methodology is the necessity f placing greater stress than formerly upon significant interpretative ideas as pposed to a multiplicity of unrelated facts.

The aims of the committee as set forth at the same time are also orth quoting in full both because of their high idealism and because f the clear conception which they reveal of the value of history as an ssential part of any program of education:

1. The supreme aim in the teaching of history and social science is to give ositive direction to the growth of those mental and moral qualities of chilren which, rightly developed, constitute the basis of the highest type of itizenship.

2. We gladly acknowledge that all sound training, through whatever feature f the school curriculum, contributes helpfully to this desired end; but we re nevertheless convinced that the historical training affects the result most irectly.

3. Historical training (a) frees the mind from the trammels of time and lace, substituting the idea of social development and change for the intinctive notion of a static social world, performing in this respect a service education analogous to that performed by biology for organic nature or by eology for inorganic nature. (b) It tends to produce openmindedness, which itigates native prejudice and permits truth to gain recognition. (c) It inuces patient inquiry for the purpose of disclosing the facts of a given situaon before passing judgment. (d) It gives some grasp upon the methods of westigation and the tests of accuracy. (e) It develops that form of judgent which deals with the shifting and conditional relations of men in society, upplementing the scientific judgment which arises from the study of animate nd inanimate nature and of mathematics. (f) It yields, or should yield, the igh moral and ethical concepts of loyalty to principles and to institutions by evealing the cost at which the elements of 'civilization' have been secured or us.

The work of the committee was actively carried on during the spring and summer of 1919, a tentative report being presented in the Historical Outlook for June of that year; and a further report was presented to the American Historical Association in December, 1919, and was published in the Historical Outlook for February, 1920. Upon the adjournment of the board on December 30, 1919, the committee was continued as a committee of the American Historical Association but its further history is not a part of this chronicle.[14]

The miscellaneous and minor activities of the board in the field of education were numerous. The board was represented by its chairman in the Emergency Council on Education which was organized under the National Research Council, and the chairman or members of the board took part in various educational conferences, such as those of the National Society for the Scientific Study of Education held at Atlantic City in February, 1918, and the Conference on International Relations in Education called by the United States Commissioner of Education, and addressed gatherings of teachers in different parts of the country. The board also carried on an extensive correspondence with educators and history teachers who wrote to it for suggestions, advice, or information. In these and in many other ways the board endeavored to serve the interests of history and of education and to advance the cause of reasoned and intelligent patriotism.

GOVERNMENT SERVICE.

Various services which the board performed for the Government have already been described, including the investigations undertaken for the Peace Inquiry, the service to the War Department in providing lectures in the camps and assistance in the organization of the War Issues Course, and the cooperation with the Bureau of Education in the publication of suggestions for teachers. The two principal forms of Government service, however, consisted of cooperation with the Committee on Public Information and the examination of the daily and periodical press of the enemy countries.

The Committee on Public Information was already at work before the establishment of the board, but its organization had not been completed. Partly as a result of suggestions from the board the committee created a division of civic and educational cooperation, of which Prof. Guy Stanton Ford was director, assisted later by Prof. Samuel B. Harding, both of whom were members of the board. The principal function of this division was the preparation of war

---

[14] Subsequent reports of the committee are printed in the Historical Outlook for March, April, May, June, 1920.

pamphlets of patriotic or informative character and their publication and distribution, a work in which the board cooperated to such an extent that it was to all intents and purposes an auxiliary of the division. The board advised with respect to the subject matter of proposed pamphlets, suggested writers, aided in the work of research which the nature of some of the publications made necessary, and served as a distributor of the pamphlets to teachers and students of history. The board procured for the division the material for certain pamphlets, as " The Great War: From Spectator to Participant," by Prof. A. C. McLaughlin, and " The Battle Line of Democracy," a collection of patriotic prose and verse of America and of the allied countries, compiled by Miss Elizabeth Donnan, and Miss Frances G. Davenport, and took an active part in the compilation of the War Encyclopedia. Members of the board wrote or compiled certain other of the pamphlets, notably " The Government of Germany," by Charles Downer Hazen; " American Interest in Popular Government Abroad," by Evarts B. Greene; " Conquest and Kultur," by Wallace Notestein, a compilation of quotations from German sources revealing the plans and purposes of pan-Germanism; and " German War Practices," by Dana C. Munro, dealing with the treatment of civilians and of conquered territory, based on a careful examination of German and neutral evidence and on the records of the Department of State. A special service rendered by the board was the critical examination of certain documents procured from Russia by Mr. Edgar Sisson, which seemed to establish the existence of a German-Bolshevik conspiracy. The authenticity of these documents having been questioned in some sections of the press the matter was referred by the committee to the board, which appointed a special committee of historical experts. The report of this committee, which pronounced in favor of the authenticity of the essential documents, though not of all, was published by the Committee on Public Information as " The German-Bolshevik Conspiracy (War Information Series No. 20)."[15]

The most important single undertaking of the board was the maintenance of an Enemy-Press Intelligence Service. In the spring of 1917 the Pictorial Service of the British High Commission procured for the board a regular supply of the more important German newspapers and periodicals. These were at first utilized by an experienced journalist, the late Gustav Pollak, who supplied the Committee on Public Information with translations of extracts suitable for use by the American press. When Doctor Pollak was obliged by reason of his health to give up this work a special Enemy Press

[15] A concise account of the work of the Committee on Public Information, by Prof. G. S. Ford, was published in the Historical Outlook for March, 1919.

Bureau was organized by the board upon direct request by the President,·and one of its members, Mr. Victor S. Clark, was made director of it. The work of this bureau rapidly assumed large proportions; additional newspapers and periodicals were procured some through the French Mission, some through the Belgian Information Service, and some through direct subscription in Holland and Switzerland, until the board was in current receipt of some 34 German and Austrian daily papers and about 50 periodicals, including carefully selected medical, agricultural, technical, scientific, political, and general journals.

This material was read by Doctor Clark, who dictated translations of summaries to a corps of stenographers. These summaries were typed in multiple and classified, and the various sets were distributed as they were produced. One set was transmitted to the State Department, two sets to the Military Intelligence section of the General Staff, one of which was sent to the General Staff of the American Expeditionary Force in France. A fourth set was sent to the Peace Inquiry, until it was transferred to Paris after the armistice. A fifth set was sent to the library of Princeton University in return for the services of a stenographer; and a sixth set was filed in the bureau. Special portions of the translated material were also transmitted to the Food Administration, the Public Health Service, the Federal Reserve Board, the Bureau of Education, and to other offices of the Government, and from time to time to certain periodicals when it was considered desirable to secure their publication in the United States. The State Department was occasionally furnished with copies of matters of unusual importance, as in the case of the German-Russian treaties.

The files of newspapers and periodicals were also used extensively by Government offices such as the War Trade Board, the Bureau of Labor Statistics, the Children's Bureau, and others in the course of special investigations by their own employees,[16] while the Committee on Public Information maintained a translator and typist in the bureau until the close of the war.

The work of the bureau was continued until July 1, 1919. The newspapers and periodicals were then disposed of in various ways, chiefly to the Library of Congress and to the Hoover collection of Stanford University; and the file of summaries was deposited in the Division of Manuscripts of the Library of Congress. These translations, numbering over 20,000 items, have been reproduced by photography for six subscribing libraries,[17] making available for re-

---

[16] For example, "The Food Situation in Europe," by Alfred Maylander, published by the Bureau of Labor Statistics, Bulletin No. 242, April, 1918.

[17] University of Illinois, University of Chicago, University of Michigan, University of Wisconsin, Vassar College, Pomona College.

search a large amount of carefully gathered information respecting economic, social, political, and intellectual conditions in the countries of the Central Powers.

COLLECTION AND PRESERVATION OF WAR RECORDS.

From the first days of its existence the board regarded as one of its most important duties the effort to encourage the collection and preservation of all material which would serve to record the mobilization of the military, economic, social, and intellectual forces of the country. It was realized that the emergency of war would necessitate a canvass of the Nation's resources, human and material, such as had never before been undertaken, and it was felt to be a matter of vital importance that the record of this canvass in all its details should be preserved. The efforts of historians of the present generation to reconstruct the social and economic history of the Civil War and the difficulties encountered by them in discovering and assembling the essential materials made them still more keenly aware of the necessity of immediate effort and activity with respect to contemporary records. Furthermore, agencies suitable for undertaking such activities, which were almost nonexistent in 1865, were now plentiful in the form of historical societies, State commissions of history, and libraries. Accordingly on May 10, 1917, a subcommittee of the board sent the following letter to all State historical commissions, to the more active historical societies, and to a large number of libraries, in all to some four or five hundred institutions and organizations.

The National Board for Historical Service is a voluntary and unofficial body, the principal object of which is to furnish a medium through which in the present crisis the historical scholarship of the country may render its appropriate and, we hope, effective service.

It seems clear to us that if the interests of the student of history are to be secured the various historical agencies of the country, and especially the historical societies and libraries, must bestir themselves to provide for the systematic and inclusive collection and the effective preservation of all kinds of material serving to record and illustrate present events.

Naturally such a problem presents itself in different ways to different agencies. The Library of Congress, the agent of the National Government, is endeavoring to collect all material of national importance; the State agency (historical society, department of history, historical commission, etc.) naturally seeks to preserve a record of State activities.

The amount of formal literature relating to the war is already of formidable extent, and only the largest institutions can hope to make any considerable collection of it.

There are, however, many kinds of material which are of the greatest value to the historian and which the library or society that interests itself in local matters can collect more effectively than can the larger institutions.

This material is such as illustrates the local state of mind—the local reactions, local events, etc. Such material includes the following:

1. Official documents, such as municipal ordnances, proclamations of mayors, notices of boards, etc.

2. Semiofficial documents: Resolutions of public meetings, of labor unions, of church societies, etc.

3. Public-service documents: Announcements, notices, orders, etc., issued by public-service corporations.

4. Fugitive printed material: Posters (recruiting and other); programs of concerts, meetings, fairs, etc., held for purposes connected with the war.

5. Economic material: Price lists, advertisements.

6. Propaganda material.

7. Clippings.

8. Pictorial material: Photographs of local events, of soldiers, and bodies of troops, etc.

9. Manuscript material: Letters, diaries, sermons, addresses, etc.

These categories are mentioned only by way of illustration. It is assumed that societies and libraries are as a matter of course acquiring such books and newspapers as they can.

It is a part of our plan, if the matter meets with general approval from those to whom this letter is addressed, to prepare a small pamphlet of information and suggestions respecting the collection of war material for permanent preservation.

Will you not cooperate with us to the extent of informing us as specifically and in as much detail as possible with respect to what your own society or library is doing or is planning to do along these lines?

We should also be glad to receive from you any constructive suggestions that may have occurred to you as a result of your experience.

For the board.

> GAILLARD HUNT,
> ROBERT D. W. CONNOR,
> WALDO G. LELAND,
> *Subcommittee.*

This letter brought a large number of replies which showed that many organizations, especially those officially connected with State governments had had the matter of record preservation seriously under consideration or had already engaged in systematic work to that end. From the replies there was also extracted much information which was of value to the board in its subsequent work but which was never compiled in the form of a pamphlet as had been suggested in the letter.

Three months later a similar action, but in a slightly different direction, was taken by the board when it learned of the organization, by certain State or county councils of defense, of special committees for the collection of war records, and accordingly sent the following letter of August 15, 1917, to the secretaries of all the State councils of defense:

The National Board for Historical Service is endeavoring to do two things: To make our past experience useful for the present, and to see to it that our present experience is preserved for the future. We believe that experience is the greatest human asset, and that its use and preservation are matters of the greatest public importance.

Would it not be within the range of the functions of your council to appoint a State committee on history?

The following quotation from a letter of the chairman of the history committee of the Council of Defense of Eau Claire County, Wis., gives an idea of the kind of work that may be done. Any Grand Army man must appreciate what it would have meant to him if this had been during the Civil War:

"It is the purpose of this committee to gather, preserve, index, and make available for public use a record of the sentiments and activities of organizations and individuals of the county in the present war.

"As regards the newspapers it is the intention to preserve in scrapbooks a complete series of the editorials and also the local news items bearing or connected with the war. All this material will be card indexed and this index will refer to the publication and issue from which each item is taken.

"Much attention will be given to the preservation, with proper data attached, of photographs and other pictures pertaining to the collections of organizations and individuals of the county in this war. Programs of patriotic gatherings and of all meetings in any way connected with the war. Also personal letters written by those in any branch of the military service will be gathered so far as possible. * * *

"A small credit was placed at our disposal by the county council of defense, and the committee had made up one hundred large scrapbook leaves * * *. This provides for every paper in the county except the one whose editor has not responded. * * *

"All material gathered will be handed over to our public library on completion of work."

Our board will be in a position to cooperate with such a committee. Without local assistance we will be able to do little.

As a result of the suggestion thus communicated a number of State councils appointed committees, or "State war history commissions," as they were more commonly termed, which were soon in active operation.

Meanwhile the board sent letters to certain nongovernmental war organizations calling attention to the probable value of their records for historical purposes and urging their careful preservation. Information was also secured with respect to the condition of governmental war records in Washington, and in some cases members of the board were called in consultation with respect to the classification and disposition of such material.

In order still further to focus attention upon the importance of the collection and preservation of war records the board proposed to the Public Archives Commission of the American Historical Association that the conference of archivists, which was to be held as a session of the annual meetings of the association in Philadelphia, in December, 1917, be devoted to a discussion of that subject. This suggestion was adopted and the secretary of the board and others

read papers respecting the value of certain groups of governmenta‘
archives and the status of State and local collections.[18]

During 1918, and especially after the armistice, many additiona‘
war history commissions were created, and a marked energy begar
to be displayed in most parts of the country in the collection of all
material that might serve to record the war activities of the various
States. With these bodies the board cooperated, in the summer and
fall of 1919, in the organization of the National Association of
State War History Organizations, the purpose of which was to further the work of the State bodies by exchange of information and
suggestions, and especially by the exploitation of the war archives of
the National Government for material of value to the States. The
connection of the board with this new association did not extend
beyond the aid in organizing it already referred to and placing at
its disposal all the information collected by the board with regard
to war records in Washington. Indeed, the association thus formed
practically took over from the board the function of encouragin
the collection and preservation of materials for the history of
the war.[19]

Thus, while the board's activity with respect to war records was
confined to encouragement, suggestion, and watchfulness, it had
nevertheless a very real part in starting an important movement
from which the history of the United States must receive an incal-
culable benefit.

PERSONNEL, PROCEDURE, FINANCES.

The membership of the board increased from 9 to 25 during the
32 months of its existence, most of the additions being of scholars
who came to Washington for longer or shorter periods of war work.
The complete personnel of the board was as follows:

Chairmen.—James T. Shotwell, April 29–November 9, 1917;
Evarts B. Greene, November 9, 1917–September 11, 1918; Dana C.
Munro, September 11, 1918–December 30, 1919.

Vice chairmen.—Charles H. Hull, April 29–November 9, 1917;
Dana C. Munro, November 9, 1917–September 11, 1918; Joseph
Schafer (executive officer), September 11, 1918–December 30, 1919.

---

[18] The proceedings of this conference are printed in the Annual Report of the American
Historical Association for 1917.

[19] An elaborate account of the work performed by the various State organizations was
contributed to the American Historical Review for October, 1919, by Franklin F. Holbrook, "The Collection of State War Service Records." The proceedings of the National
Association of State War Historical Organizations will be found in this report. A manuscript survey of war records in Washington prepared for the new association by Dr. Newton D. Mereness is in the Document Division of the Library of Congress; a more elaborate survey of the economic war records of the Government is in preparation by Waldo
G. Leland and Newton D. Mereness for the Carnegie Endowment for International Peace.

Secretary-treasurer.—Waldo G. Leland, April 29, 1917–December 30, 1919.

Members.—Carl Becker, Milledge L. Bonham, Victor S. Clark, Robert D. W. Connor, Archibald C. Coolidge, William E. Dodd, Carl Russell Fish, Guy S. Ford, Samuel B. Harding, Charles H. Haskins, Charles Downer Hazen, Charles H. Hull, Gaillard Hunt, J. Franklin Jameson, Henry Johnson, William E. Lingelbach, Charles Moore, Wallace Notestein, Frederic L. Paxson, Frederick J. Turner.

I To these should be added Dr. Leo F. Stock of the Carnegie Institution who, though not becoming a member of the board, served as its recorder and took an active part in its work.

Of the above, 6 were residents of Washington (Messrs. Clark, Hunt, Jameson, Leland, Moore, and Stock) and 12 resided there during all or part of the war (Messrs. Bonham, Fish, Ford, Greene, Harding, Hull, Munro, Notestein, Paxson, Schafer, Shotwell, and Turner); the other members were in Washington occasionally. There were also many other scholars in the capital during the war and from their counsel and active assistance the board profited much, as likewise from the advice, suggestions, and aid of many more whose duties lay elsewhere. In a very real sense the effective personnel of the board included a large section of the historical profession.

After its organization on April 29, 1917, the board held but few formal meetings, these being on May 7, May 31, and November 9–10, 1917, September 11, 1918, and December 30, 1919. During May and June, 1917, the members of the board who were in Washington held almost daily meetings of an informal character, of which, however, minutes were kept, and a general informal meeting was held in Philadelphia in December, 1917, during the annual meeting of the American Historical Association. The business of the board was transacted and its work directed by various committees. After November 9, 1917, an executive committee composed of the officers and of some of the members in Washington had the responsible direction of the board's activities and held frequent meetings; the executive committee was aided by four standing committees—on research, bibliography and records, education, and coöperation with other organizations and with the Government—and also by special committees appointed from time to time for temporary purposes. The period of full activity of the board extended from its organization until the end of 1918; during the first half of 1919 its work was confined chiefly to the educational survey and the Enemy Press Service, which have been described, and after July 1 its activities practically ceased.

The work of the board was supported chiefly by an appropriation from the Carnegie Institution, of Washington, made through its department of historical research. The department also provided offices, telephone and other service, and the assistance of the members of its staff, two of whom devoted practically all of their time to the board's work. Two officers of the board were made temporary associates of the department, thus enabling them to come to Washington for periods of service extending over several months. The Enemy Press Bureau derived its principal support from a direct appropriation by the Carnegie Institution and had its offices in the latter's Administration Building.

The funds which the board received from other sources than the Carnegie Institution were mainly in the form of gifts for special purposes, chiefly the British lecture mission and the prize essay competition, and of royalties from the sale of the War Reader. There were also certain miscellaneous receipts, the most considerable of which was from the sale of the German and Austrian newspapers and periodicals.

The final statement of the treasurer on December 26, 1919,[20] showed a balance of over a thousand dollars, with the prospect of certain additional receipts in the form of further royalties. After authorizing the treasurer to meet any outstanding liabilities, or such as might be incurred in closing up the affairs of the board, it was voted that the sum remaining in the treasury, together with future royalties, be given to the American Historical Association to constitute the Andrew D. White Fund, the income of which was to be employed in the support of such international undertakings as might be approved by the association's two representatives in the American Council of Learned Societies, of which it is a constituent member. The board also bequeathed to the association its committee on history and education for citizenship and the idea of a committee on service.

---

[20] *Final statement of receipts and expenditures, December 26, 1919.*

Receipts:

Department of historical research	$11, 558. 08
Other sources	7, 944. 17
	19, 502. 25

Expenditures:

Services	$2, 517. 82
Travel	1, 559. 57
Supplies	2, 216. 36
Bank charges	1. 00
Prizes	4, 670. 00
Historical Outlook	2, 006. 18
Committee on history and education for citizenship	1, 803. 90
Enemy Press Bureau	1, 752. 15
British lecture mission	1, 100. 00
Training camp lectures	510. 90
Services at Peace Inquiry	161. 39
War Reader	50. 00
French War Reader	47. 60
	18, 396. 87

Balance	1, 105. 38

It is impossible to estimate the permanent influence of the board and of its work. What it was able to do was only a small part of what was done by the historical profession as a whole, but the common experience demonstrated in convincing fashion that historical scholarship can serve effectively a multitude of needs and that historical scholars can contribute services of great value in time of emergency. Most important of all, however, was the fresh realization of the responsibility of the historian and of the teacher of history. It is through them that future generations will know and judge the period through which we have just lived. The conception which a people has of itself, of its principles of conduct and of its part in the affairs of the world, is the essential factor in determining its action at any given time, but this conception is itself determined chiefly by what it believes its past to have been and by the lessons which it draws from that past, and this belief and these lessons are shaped by the historian.

THE GENERAL WAR-TIME COMMISSION OF THE CHURCHES.

By Samuel McCrea Cavert, Associate Secretary, Federal Council of the Churches of Christ in America.

The General War-Time Commission of the Churches was organized September 20, 1917, by the Federal Council of the Churches of Christ in America, as the agency through which the Protestant churches of the country should cooperate in carrying on their work in behalf of the Army, the Navy, and the Nation during the war. During the five months preceding the organization of the General War-Time Commission preliminary activities had been carried on by the existing agencies of the Federal Council.

The first important historical record which the General War-Time Commission of the Churches has prepared appeared at the end of 1919 under the title, " War-Time Agencies of the Churches: Directory and Handbook," a volume of 337 pages, edited by Margaret Renton, office secretary of the General War-Time Commission of the Churches, and published by the commission. This volume is an account of the war activities of the various denominational and interdenominational agencies of the churches. It attempts to bring together the outstanding facts concerning the work which was done by the official authorized agencies of the churches for war service. It deals particularly with the agencies included in the constituency of the General War-Time Commission of the Churches, but, for purposes of completeness, a brief record of other religious bodies, such as the Jewish Welfare Board, the National Catholic War Council, the Committee on War Activities of the Knights of Columbus, and of the Christian Science War Activities, is given. Part I of the volume is a record of the work of the various denominational war agencies, giving in each case the personnel of the organization and of all its standing and special committees, and a summary of the lines of work which it carried on. The following organizations are thus treated:

The War Commission of the Northern Baptist Convention.

The War Council of the Home Mission Board of the Southern Baptist Convention.

The War Work Commission of the Christian Church.

The National Service Commission of the Congregational Churches.

The War Emergency Committee for the Disciples of Christ.

The Commission on National Service of the Evangelical Association.

The War Welfare Commission of the Evangelical Synod of North America.

The American Friends Service Committee.

The National Lutheran Commission for Soldiers' and Sailors' Welfare.

The Lutheran Church Board for Army and Navy, United States of America, of the Synod of Missouri, Ohio, and other States.

The War-Time Commission of the African Methodist Episcopal Church.

The National War Council of the Methodist Episcopal Church.

The War Work Commission of the Methodist Episcopal Church, South.

The War Work Commission of the Methodist Protestant Church.

The United States Service Commission of the Moravian Church.

The War Work Commission of the Cumberland Presbyterian Church.

The General War Work Council of the Presbyterian Church in the United States.

The National Service Commission of the Presbyterian Church in the United States of America.

The National Service Commission of the United Presbyterian Church.

The War Commission of the Episcopal Church.

The War-Time Commission of the Reformed Episcopal Church.

The Christian Reformed War Service Commission.

The War Service Commission of the Reformed Church in America.

The National Service Commission of the Reformed Church in the United States.

The War Work Council of the Unitarian Churches.

The War Commission of the United Brethren Church.

The War Service Commission of the United Evangelical Church.

Part II of the volume gives a similar record of the activities of the various interdenominational and cooperative agencies representing the Protestant churches in various lines of work. A summarized statement of each of the following organizations is given:

The Committee on War Work of the American Bible Society.

The Committee on War Literature of the American Sunday School Union.

The General War-Time Commission of the Churches.

The War Work of the other commissions of the Federal Council of the Churches of Christ in America.

The United Committee on War Temperance Activities in the Army and Navy.

The Home Missions Council.

The National Committee on the Churches and the Moral Aims of the War.

The War Service Department of the Salvation Army.

The Committee on the War and the Religious Outlook.

The National War Work Council of the Young Men's Christian Associations.

The Interdenominational Young People's Commission.

The War Work Council of the National Board of the Young Women's Christian Associations.

Special consideration is given to the work of the General War-Time Commission of the Churches as the inclusive organization made up of official representatives of practically all the existing Protestant agencies for war service. The work of its committees on Survey of the Field; on Army and Navy Chaplains; on Camp Neighborhoods; on Interchurch Buildings and War Production Communities; on the Welfare of Negro Troops; on Interchange of Preachers and Speakers between the Churches of America, Great Britain, and France; on the Employment of Returning Soldiers; on Social Hygiene; on Voluntary Chaplains; and other committees, is given in summarized form.

A supplement to the volume gives a complete list of the war-time publications of the various agencies of the Protestant Churches.

A further historical record is now in preparation—the Report of the General War-Time Commission of the Churches. This is to be a much more detailed history of the cooperative work of the churches through the General War-Time Commission of the Churches than is given in the War-Time Agencies of the Churches, described above. It will embody the official reports of its various committees, record all its more important actions and utterances, and present a general interpretation of the significance of the work which was done by the churches during the war. It will contain also appendixes giving statistical information concerning the number of regular chaplains

in the Army and Navy, voluntary chaplains, work done in war pro
duction communities and in the various other lines. The prepara
tion of the volume is in the hands of Rev. Gaylord S. White, formerly
associate secretary of the General War-time Commission.

The chief sources of data for this forthcoming record of the coop
erative work of the churches during the war are as follows:

The official record of the fortnightly meetings of the executive
committee of the General War-Time Commission of the Churches.

The official reports of the committees charged with responsibility
for various phases of work.

The data secured through the press-clipping service concerning
the work of the chaplains and the churches.

Extensive correspondence with chaplains, camp pastors, and other
workers in the camps.

Two comprehensive surveys of the religious forces at work in the
training camps, one prepared in November, 1917, the other in May,
1919.

The complete roster of the chaplains of the Army and Navy, together with their assignments and denominational affiliations.

The collection of war-time publications of the churches in the
library of the Union Theological Seminary.

It will be observed from this statement that no effort is being made
to secure a roster of all the members of the Protestant Churches who
served in the war. The aim is rather to chronicle the service which
was rendered by the authorized agencies of the churches.

NATIONAL CATHOLIC WAR COUNCIL

By the COMMITTEE ON HISTORICAL RECORDS.

Summary of the work which has been done by the committee on
historical records from its inception to April 1, 1920, and outline
of what remains to be accomplished. Broadly speaking, there were
three parts to the program:

I. A complete census of Catholic men in the service (Army, Navy, Marine
Corps).

II. *The foundation of national Catholic archives,* or a central depot where the
student of Catholic activity in the war would be enabled to find easily and
efficiently all the source material to be used for that purpose. This source
material, generally speaking, can be catalogued under three headings:

(a) Newspaper material: For this purpose a periodical department was instituted. Letters were sent out to all the Catholic papers, and immediately
the files of the Catholic press of the country began to grow.

(b) Private letters and diaries of those in the service.

(c) Books, published by every sort of organization on American cooperation
in the war, which would furnish materials for the Catholic historian.

III. *Cooperation.*—(a) Cooperation with the other national standing committees of the committee on special war activities. By this is meant that the

chairmen and secretaries of the other committees expected to be kept in constant touch with, all newspaper accounts dealing with their particular field of activity.

$_\nu$(b) Cooperation, with the Catholic press: It was hoped that the committee on historical records would be able to send out frequently, if not weekly, "releases" telling of the work done by individual Catholics in the service.

. (c) Cooperation with other agencies outside the committee on special war activities.

I. WHAT HAS BEEN ACCOMPLISHED.

A summary report of the work that has been done should contain a reply to the following general question: "How far has the committee succeeded in compiling and completing an accurate record of Catholic American activity during the Great War?"

Reports of the activities of the committee on historical records were made to the committee on special war activities, usually at monthly intervals, the first one being given on July 11, 1918. These reports show the following results:

(A) COMPLETION OF SERVICE LISTS.

In May, 1918, a general letter was sent to all pastors in the country, requesting a list of the men in the service. This was followed in August by a second general letter calling for the names of the men called in the second draft. The cooperation of the diocesan chanceries was secured in collecting the names. A card index of the parishes which reported was made up, the card for each parish containing the number of men in service in the various branches. After this analytical index was completed work was begun on a card index containing the service record of each Catholic who served. The results thus far in this whole work are as follows: Parishes reported, 4,815; total names reported, 243,349; individual service cards made, 58,310; itemized by dioceses in the following table:

Individual census cards written to April 1, 1920.

Baltimore	4,604	Scranton	3,338
Boston	24,173	Wichita	219
Chicago	3,548	Wheeling	1,875
Dubuque	060	Wilmington	128
Philadelphia	2,951	Winona	267
Altoona	3,307	Belmont	37
Erie	827	Alaska	34
Harrisburg	941	Ruthenian-Greek	36
Peoria	635		
Pittsburgh	10,788	Total	58,310

(B) COLLECTION OF HISTORICAL MATERIAL.

1. *Catholic newspapers.*—Files of 61 newspapers, printed in the English language and 19 in foreign languages, are collected in the periodical department. These files are more or less complete from the beginning of the war. A card index of all war material in 42 of the more prominent papers has been completed up to July 1, 1919.

2. *Catholic magazines.*—We have files of 43 American Catholic magazines, printed in English and 7 foreign-language magazines, together with 15 college publications.

3. *Episcopal pronouncements.*—A number of the heirarchy have sent us complete files of their pronouncements and addresses during the war. From many others we have received occasional papers of importance.

4. *Published reports of Catholic gatherings incidental to the war.*—We have gathered through the Knights of Columbus campaign committee and through the efforts of a number of interested indivduals newspaper clippings of detailed meetings held by Catholics throughout the country. These clippings approximate 10,000 in number. In addition to these we have on hand upwards of 1,000 memorial booklets recounting the various memorial gatherings held in various parts of the country.

5. *All other material.*—Our archives contain about 4,000 miscellaneous papers, such as letters of historical importance, diaries, reports of chaplains, photographs, etc. These have all been indexed analytically and filed for ready reference. Included in this material are the complete files of the war council's committee, which handled the drive for funds in connection with the committee or other war-service agencies.

(C) PROBLEMS OF COOPERATION.

The work of the other committees was soon found to be cognate to each other, but not of that distinctive historical bearing which necessitated prompt cooperation on the part of our committee. Had this cooperation been carried out in a systematic manner each one of the standing committees needing guidance or accounts of the work being done should have delegated one of its own staff as a searcher in their periodical department.

II. WHAT REMAINS TO BE ACCOMPLISHED.

(A) COMPLETION OF SERVICE LISTS.

It is estimated that fully 1,000,000 Catholic Americans served their country during the great war. As we already have the names of approximately 250,-000, it remains for us to gather in the records of 750,000 more. These names are to be secured from the 5,977 parishes which have not as yet sent in any report and from the 4,815 parishes which reported, since many of those lists were sent in before the full number was known. These remaining names should be collected in the following manner:

1. Letters should be sent to chancellors of all dioceses asking for any lists they may have on file and for assistance in securing cooperation of pastors in completing the census.

2. Letters will then be sent to every parish which has not reported, and follow-up letters will be sent out until the census is completed.

3. The reports received will be analyzed and indexed as heretofore, and individual census cards will be written. This means the making of 5,977 parish service cards and approximately 940,000 individual census cards.

4. After all the names are in our files they should be compared with the rosters in the adjutant general's office of each State, in order to secure a more complete and accurate record of the service of each man.

(B) COLLECTION OF HISTORICAL MATERIAL.

1. *Catholic newspapers.*—(a) The files must be completed by securing issues not yet received covering the period between 1914 and the present. Where these copies can not be secured from the publisher it will be necessary to inter-

est subscribers to send in the papers we need. This has been done already in several cases with good results.

(b) Some papers have never been received, and further efforts should be made to secure complete files for the period of the war.

(c) The card indexing of war material in all these papers must be completed. To do this it will be necessary, in addition to having some one to catalogue the English-language papers, to solicit the assistance of persons who can index the war items in French, German, Polish, Bohemian, and other foreign-language papers.

2. *Catholic magazines.*—Steps must be taken to complete the files of our magazines and to make up an index of the war articles in them.

3. *Episcopal pronouncements.*—It is believed that it will now be possible to secure sets of Episcopal pronouncements from each diocese. Those already received have been catalogued and additions to this file will be indexed upon receipt.

4. *Published reports of 'Catholic gatherings.*—While our newspapers and other files contain a great many such reports, a much larger number remain unrecorded in our archives, especially those reported in the public press. In order to complete our archives it will be necessary to have a report of every important Catholic gathering incidental to the war.

5. *All other material.*—While receipts of letters, diaries, photographs, etc., so far have been encouraging, this source of material has only been touched. Appeals must be made through the Catholic press and through pastors to make people realize the necessity of furnishing us with such material. In addition to our request for complete service lists, we should appeal to pastors to have their parishioners send us every bit of material of possible historical interest.

COOPERATION WITH OTHER COMMITTEES.

With the winding up of the other standing committees of the Committee on Special War Activities, we expect to secure for our archives the files of these committees, as the War Council archives should properly be in the custody of the Committee on Historical Records.

III. COMPOSITION OF THE HISTORY.

With all the necessary material in hand, properly analyzed and indexed, it will be possible to take up the work of actually writing a complete scientific history of Catholic American activity during the great war. The tentative outline for this comprehensive work is as follows:

I. Catholics in past American wars.

II. The Catholic Church during the period of American neutrality (August, 1914–April, 1917).

III. Catholics and the call to arms—the draft.

IV. Catholics in training schools and camps.

V. Catholic social, educational, recreational work in the camps.

VI. Catholics at the front—the Catholic honor roll.

VII. The organization of Catholic relief, national and local.

VIII. Catholic cooperation with national and State war administration.

IX. Catholics at home during the war—the fight behind the lines.

X. Catholics and the financing of the war: Liberty loans, war-saving stamps, contributions to welfare work, etc.

XI. Catholic contribution to allied relief—e. g., Belgium, etc.

XII. Catholic women and the war: (a) Catholics in the Red Cross and Army Nurse Corps; (b) sisterhoods; (c) other agencies of welfare at home and abroad.

XIII. Catholic students in the Students' Army Training Corps.

XIV. Effects of the war on Catholic life in America.

XV. Catholics at the close of the war.

Mr. Michael Williams, editor of the National Catholic War Council Bulletin, is now preparing a story of Catholic participation in the war, which will consist of about 400 pages of text and will be published September 1.[20] This book will outline in narrative form the record of American Catholic activity during the war in all its phases, and will be a companion volume to the recently published Knights of Columbus book.[21] While, of course, it will not be exhaustive, it will be as accurate as possible, and will furnish a very good starting point for the complete record which we hope to publish eventually.

THE COLLECTION OF JEWISH WAR RECORDS.

By JULIAN LAEVITT, Director Office of War Records, American Jewish Committee.

The establishment of a historical record of Jewish service in the war was undertaken in November, 1917, by the American Jewish Committee, acting in cooperation with the Jewish Welfare Board, the American Jewish Historical Society, the Jewish Publication Society, and other related organizations, under the immediate direction of Dr. Cyrus Adler.

The actual search for material was attended with problems of exceptional difficulty. As is well known, the official records of the Army and Navy were not accessible during the war; and even if they had been accessible they would have been of comparatively slight value in the initial stages of the undertaking, as they make no note of religious affiliations. Unofficial lists were not in existence. The Jews in the service came from every section, city, and village in the country, were scattered in every branch of the service, and in many cases were not affiliated with any known Jewish organizations or institutions. The combing out of their names involved, therefore, the organization of a systematic search among the men in the camps and at the front and among their friends and relatives at home. The Jewish Welfare Board assumed the first part of the task, instructing its workers in America and overseas to forward all information of a statistical character gathered by or known to them, including religious censuses taken by the board or by their agencies, furlough records for Jewish holidays, and individual registration cards signed by the Jewish soldiers in the welfare huts. The office of Jewish war records, on the other hand, concentrated upon the families and friends of the soldiers and sailors in the United States. To this end it enlisted the cooperation of all religious, fraternal,

---

[20] American Catholics in the War. New York, 1921.
[21] The Knights of Columbus in Peace and War. New Haven, Conn., 1920.

industrial, and labor organizations throughout the country, distributing among them several million registration cards calling for information as to name of soldier; home and service address; age, nativity, branch of service, rank, regiment, company; date of induction, or discharge, whether volunteered or drafted; in what actions engaged, and whether wounded, cited, or promoted.

In addition the office instituted a press-clipping service for the collection of data as to all reports of enlistments, service-flag dedications, honor rolls, and all other possible sources of information. All Army orders and assignments, casualty lists, the records of local draft boards, Red Cross lists, and similar sources were thoroughly searched and followed up for possible clues.

From all these sources there were collected more than 500,000 records, which were carefully collated, and, after duplicates were eliminated, copied in triplicate, and filed in three separate catalogues—one arranged alphabetically and so devised as to bring together automatically all variant forms of names which are especially liable to misplacements because of common errors in reporting, copying, or transliterating; another catalogue arranged by branches of the service, with officers and honor men "signaled"; and a third arranged by States, cities, and towns.

At present the collection covers about 150,000 records of individual soldiers, sailors, and marines, freed of all duplications; about 25,000 press clippings systematically arranged; numerous photographs; letters and documents of historical value; and about 8,000 questionnaires (holographic, with few exceptions) embodying the following information as to commissioned officers, casualties, and citations:

1. Name in full.
2. Present service or business address.
3. Legal residence.
4. Date and place of birth.
5. Birthplace of parents.
6. Education.
7. Brief summary of civilian career before joining service.
8. Full name and highest rank.
9. Arm of service.
10. Branch.
11. Method of entrance into service.
12. Date of entrance into service.
13. Rank or rating upon entrance into service and first organization, unit, station, or ship.
14. Date of leaving service. (If still in service, so state.)
15. Highest rank or rating and last organization, unit, station, or ship.

16. Promotions or official recommendations for promotion received, with dates thereof.

17. Length of time spent overseas or afloat, counting toward service chevrons.

18. Duties and general location of organization, unit, or ship.

19. Participated in the following actions.

20. Honors, medals, citations, official expressions of appreciation or thanks, etc.

21. Casualty. (Circumstantial details as to nature of casualty, time and place, name of hospital, etc.)

22. Summary of service record in form of chronological statement of official movements and duties. (Wherever possible, send photographs, diaries, copies of official citations, etc.)

As the process of gathering and verifying the data is still underway, it is as yet impossible to furnish definitive figures bearing upon the record of American Jews in the war. Certain preliminary findings have, however, been published in the first and second reports of this office, which may be had upon application to the American Jewish committee, 31 Union Square, New York City.

THE NATIONAL ASSOCIATION OF STATE WAR HISTORY ORGANIZATIONS.

Responding to the call of Dr. James Sullivan, State historian of New York, representatives of the war history organizations of 16 States met in Washington, D. C., in September, 1919, to discuss problems confronting them in the collection and compilation of the records of the participation of their respective States in the World War, and in particular to determine the most effective and economical means of procuring information from the national archives. The immediate outcome of the deliberations was the establishment of the National Association of State War History Organizations with the following constitution:

I. The name of this organization shall be the National Association of State War History Organizations.

II. The headquarters of the association shall be located at Washington, D. C.

III. The purpose of the association shall be to facilitate the gathering of historical materials relating to the participation of the several States in the World War from the archives of the United States Government and other central depositories, and to provide for the exchange of publications and information among the members.

IV. The membership of the association shall be limited to any official organization or agency in each State or Territory of the Union empowered to collect material pertaining to the World War.

V. The officers of the association shall be a president, a vice president, and a secretary-treasurer, no two of whom shall be from the same State or Territory. The duties of these officers shall be those usually appertaining to their respective offices.

VI. The executive committee shall consist of the officers of the association and two additional members elected by the association. Meetings of the executive committee shall be held on call of the president, or upon the written request of any three members of the committee. This committee shall be empowered to make provision for carrying out the purposes of this association.

VII. The annual meeting shall be held in April of each year in the city of Washington. Special meetings may be called by the executive committee, and shall be called upon the written request of 10 members.

VIII. The officers and two elective members of the executive committee shall be chosen each year at the annual meeting.

IX. A quorum for a meeting of the association shall consist of a majority of the members of the association. A quorum for a meeting of the executive committee shall be three.

X. This association shall come into existence as soon as 10 official organizations have joined. There shall be an annual membership fee of $200 for each member of this association, payable in advance. The funds of this association shall be expended at the direction of the executive committee, subject to any specific instructions of the association.

Dr. Newton D. Mereness, director of research of the association in Washington, has made a preliminary survey of the records in the national depositories which may be considered of value to State war history organizations. The report of this survey, with three appendixes, is a document of 126 typewritten pages. A more detailed study of the records of the Food Administration, the Shipping Board, and of the hearings before the House and Senate committees, is well underway. The number of inquiries coming to the Washington office is growing steadily and attention to a request from some one State has often been a means of acquiring information of value to other States. There is also being assembled in the Washington office a small collection of documents, any one of which may, upon application, be loaned to a member of the association.

THE AMERICAN LEGION.

By EBEN PUTNAM, National Historian.

Such activities of the American Legion as might be classed as "along historical lines" have been to the present time chiefly cooperation with organizations established for the purpose of collecting and preserving data relating to the World War. The American Legion is the largest organization of its kind in the world, and its activities are manifold. It is essentially an organization of young men, men from every walk in life, individually holding varying

ideas with regard to matters generally, but unanimous in their love
for their country. It is therefore not to be wondered at that the
organization along with its welfare committees, and the usual activities of an organization of veterans of the military and naval service,
has developed plans for increasing the interest every veteran should
have in his country's history and his community and for inculcat-
ing American ideas in the mind and heart of the alien resident
with us.

The former is handled through the department and post historians,
the latter through the Americanization committees of the national
and departmental organizations.

Nearly every department and nearly every post of the American
Legion has provided for the office of historian, and nearly every one
of these has filled that office by election. The constitution of the
national organization did not provide for such an officer, and when
the need arose for a national official who might aid in coordinating
the efforts of the department historians, the executive officers of the
legion selected the historian of the Massachusetts department to act
as national historian.[22]

The legion historians are primarily concerned in preserving data
pertaining to the history of their respective units; that is, the department or post. The post historian is particularly concerned in collecting data concerning the members of the post, especially their
service in the war.

Most of these department and post officers have had no training
in historical work and have had to be instructed with regard to the
manner in which they should perform their duties. It has been the
policy of the national organization to urge the local legion historians
to cooperate with whatever agency was in existence for preserving
data relating to the war. In many instances this policy has been
carried out with considerable success. Town war-history committees,
State and county war-history organizations, local libraries, and
historical societies have benefited by the help given by the legion
organizations. As time passes and as the various posts become more
stable in their membership the cooperation between the legion posts
and local historical organizations will increase.

The American Legion is as yet a young organization. Its policies
along lines of historical work have yet to be established. So far it
has assisted in the collection of the records, service and family, of
its members; the collection of data concerning the relatives of men

---

[22] At the second national convention the constitution of the American Legion was
amended to provide for a " National Historian " elected by the National Executive Committee, which body prescribes his duties. Eben Putnam was chosen to the office thus
established.

who died in the service; the compilation of a complete report of all persons who died in the service; the collection of materials for museum exhibits (loaned by legion members or others upon the recommendation of the legion); and the sponsoring of movements for the erection of proper war memorials.

The work which it has been suggested might be done by department and post historians is best learned by the annexed bulletins, the first intended for department, the second for post historians. In many cases the recipient of these bulletins has adopted the suggestions with enthusiasm and has succeeded in accomplishing a substantial beginning.

As this note will doubtless reach the hands of secretaries and other officers of historical societies throughout the country, it is hoped that they will appreciate the fact that the American Legion is willing to help in the great task of collecting data for the history of the part taken by towns and other communities in the war and will inform themselves of the address of the post historians in their vicinity and obtain their cooperation in this work. Under proper guidance great assistance can doubtless be obtained from the legion posts.

APPENDIX.

The American Legion, National Headquarters, Meridian Life Building, Indianapolis, Ind.—Bulletin.

JUNE 11, 1920.

Organization No. 50.

Subject: Department historian, duties of.

1. The duties of the department historian should bring him in touch with national headquarters, post officials, and with Federal, State, and local organizations concerned in collecting data pertaining to the war, its preservation and utilization.

2. These duties naturally divide themselves under the following heads: Annalist, necrologist, archivist, librarian, cabinet keeper.

(A) Annalist: The department historian is an annalist, inasmuch as he makes a report yearly of an historical nature. These yearly reports over a number of years, the annals of the department, should be an inspiration and guide to the historian who in years to come will write the history of the department. The yearly report should summarize (a) department activities; (b) post activities.

(B) Necrologist: As necrologist, the department historian should preserve obituary notices of department officials, important members of the legion who have died within the department, and of officers of posts who died in office. He should have a complete list of all members of the legion who have died within the department, with statement of their service and what can be ascertained concerning their life and their immediate family.

(C) Archivist and librarian: The department historian should have charge of all printed and manuscript materials, dealing with the World War, or any other subjects, which come into possession of the department headquarters. All department records not in current use should pass into his charge. Records of dormant or defunct posts should be turned over to the care of the department historian. He should be consulted by posts planning to make collections pertaining to the war, and with regard to selection of depositories, should posts determine to part with any collections.

(D) Cabinet keeper: All articles other than printed or written narratives and books, such as relics, souvenirs, things of curious and interesting nature, such as naturally would find a place of rest in a museum, which come into possession of the department headquarters should pass to the care of the department historian. A collection of this nature would form in time a museum. The term cabinet keeper is used in the sense of curator.

3. It is essential that the department historian should communicate with post historians as occasion demands. He should have knowledge of local conditions existing wherever a post is situated, in order that he may be in a position to advise the post historian regarding the best method of carrying on his work. To this end information should be sought of local post officials, to discover whether there exist local organizations which could cooperate with the post.

4. The department historian should be informed concerning the existence and activities of organizations which are gathering information concerning the war. He should cooperate with State commissions, historical societies, and libraries engaged in this work. He should see that proper recognition is extended to him as representing the American Legion in the department, so that the American Legion, representing ex-service men and women, will be consulted with regard to the work these bodies carry on.

5. Whatever publications of a nature affecting the legion in the department are issued by public authority should be filed with the department historian. He should endeavor to obtain copies of all publications issued within the department which relate to participation in the war, preparation for war, and resulting effects. The collection of such material should be carried on in no narrow spirit, rather too much than too little.

6. The department historian should report at stated intervals to the national adjutant. These reports should cover:

(a) Principal features of his work as department historian since last report, and development of work formerly reported as in progress.

(b) What laws or legislative acts concern the collection and preservation of data concerning the part the State has taken in the war, what changes may have been made or are in contemplation, with remarks pertinent to the subject.

(c) What commissions are in existence, or contemplated, dealing with matters which should come under his observation, and what is being accomplished by these commissions.

7. The annual report of the department historian should be in print, and copies distributed to national headquarters, the various department historians, all posts within the department, and such libraries and other places of deposit as may desire them. In case the annual report is not printed, duplicate copies should be filed at national headquarters.

8. Attention is directed to a bulletin entitled " Notes on historical work " submitted to national headquarters by the Minnesota Historical Society, copies

of which may be had upon application to the organization division, national headquarters, and which every department historian is requested to procure and place on file.

9. In order that department historians may familiarize themselves with some of the activities of State war record commissions, they are advised that by application to Prof. A. E. McKinley, secretary of the National Association of State War History Organizations, 1300 Locust Street, Philadelphia, Pa., information may be obtained concerning matters of interest. Also, that a summary of the proceedings and publications of the various units eligible to membership in the above association was printed in the October, 1919, American Historical Review (address Woodward Building, Washington, D. C.), under the title, "The collection of State war service records." Membership in the American Historical Association is suggested as an aid to keeping in touch with historical conditions throughout the country.

10. National headquarters of the American Legion has been very ably assisted in preparing the outlines of all historical work by Eben Putnam, department historian of Massachusetts. Mr. Putnam will very gladly give any assistance desired. Address any requests to him at Wellesley Farms, Mass.

LEMUEL BOLLES,
National Adjutant.

The American Legion, National Headquarters, Meridian Life Building, Indianapolis, Ind.—Bulletin.

JULY 19, 1920.

Organization No. 54.
Subject: Post historian, duties of.

1. The post historian should be selected for his interest, his methodical habit, his intelligence, and tactfulness. These are fundamental requirements for the position, which is one of no light duties and responsibilities. Faithfulness in the face of repeated discouragements will be found to be an essential qualification, but eventually the work accomplished by the post historian will be found to be not only of importance but increasing interest and value.

2. The post historian can well bear in mind the words of the department historian of Iowa, "the patriotic duty of the hour is the collection and preservation of the historical materials relating to the World War." Ten years from now the work of the historian will be more appreciated than it is to-day.

3. The work of historian can be best performed in small to medium sized posts. Large posts should make provision to distribute the work of post historian among several members, appointing committees to assist the historian, each member to have charge of certain sections. As post historians serve without pay, have duties which if properly performed must interfere largely with their leisure hours, too much can not be expected of them.

4. The duties of the post historian affords a wide field of activity. There should be close and effective cooperation between the adjutant and historian; the work of one supplements that of the other.

5. The average community will quickly respond to well-directed efforts of the post historian; his work will interest people in the post and will help the post and the community as well. Do not fail to realize that if valued letters and other materials are loaned or given to the post for preservation there is created an obligation which is sacred and which should be lived up to. Here the post

historian is responsible, for he should, as a rule, have charge of collection of materials of historical nature.

6. Some of the duties of the post historians:

(*a*) Obtain from each member as complete as possible a statement of his or her participation in the war. It is advisable not to confine the work to members only. Complete records of every person eligible to membership should be secured. Interest the families of the men and women who served, and through their help much valuable information and material can be collected.

(*b*) Get information regarding the family affiliation of members, also sufficient facts concerning their life before and since the war to enable a brief but satisfactory biographical notice to be prepared should the occasion arise. Eventually it may be desired to publish a post history, in which case, unless attention is given these matters as members are received, needed information will be lacking.

(*c*) Obtain copies of letters, extracts from diaries, written while in the service, copies of orders affecting any post member relating to decorations, citations, etc.

(*d*) Obtain information regarding those who died in the service, who if living would be eligible to membership. An honor roll containing the names of those who died in the service should be in every post headquarters. Permission might well be sought of their next of kin to enroll their names as charter members.

(*e*) Cooperate with the local historical society, the local library if such organizations exist. If they have done nothing along the lines of collecting data concerning the town's part in the war, try to stimulate and develop a proper interest in your work, and obtain their cooperation. Seek information from the county or State historical society, or from the war records commission, if one is appointed in your State. Representatives of such organizations will be very glad to help advance your work.

(*f*) Keep informed regarding the activities of the post, especially of matters which should be mentioned in the annual report of the historian. Do not depend upon the formal records of the adjutant; file everything which is printed concerning the post.

(*g*) Keep in touch with the department historian; be prompt to answer inquiries; be prepared to make your annual report to the department historian when called upon before the annual department convention.

7. National headquarters has compiled a form for the use of post historians in gathering the individual records, and sample copies may be obtained upon request.

8. The above suggestions were compiled by our acting national historian, Eben Putnam, of Wellesley Farms, Mass., and approved by national headquarters.

LEMUEL BOLLES,
National Adjutant.

ARIZONA.

By H. A. HUBBARD, of the Department of History, University of Arizona.

The various departments of the University of Arizona cooperated in a course of lectures to the student body, and an outline of the entire course was prepared by these departments under the direction of Miss Frances Perry, head of the department of English composition.

A number of the members of the faculty gave lectures in Tucson and other towns of the State on the historical background of the war.

The Arizona Historical and Archæological Society has made an effort to have all the newspapers of the State bound and filed, so that this record may be permanently preserved. A meeting has been called to attempt to secure the cooperation of various organizations in preserving a record of their work.

ARKANSAS.

By DALLAS T. HERNDON, Secretary of the Arkansas Historical Commission, from his report January, 1919, to the Board of Trustees.

Now that the Great War is over, even though it be but a few days ago that the guns ceased firing, it would seem to be not a day too early to begin maturing and executing plans for salvaging the history of Arkansas's part in the greatest of all wars "for right against might—for justice, freedom, and peace." Indeed, to have waited until after the war was won, even though it had been but the day after peace; to begin saving material for the history of the mighty efforts and achievements daily in process about us now all but two years since, would have been in our present circumstance, it seems, nothing short of criminal negligence.

The particular circumstance here to which reference is had—that circumstance which has made it not only possible but also a duty, at least implied, to store up day by day as the war went on the essential facts of Arkansas history actually in the act of unfolding—is the fact that the State maintains a department of public archives and history under the form and title of the Arkansas History Commission. In peace as in war, in times of stress or in times of easy-going contentment, the business of the commission is clearly set down in words to this effect: Keep always reaching out hands in every direction, guided by discriminating eyes, firmly grasping and eagerly gathering in such information as will in aftertime reveal the essential facts of the history of all those sundry activities in flux and vital to the material and spiritual development of the State as a whole.

For a view of the whole mass of matter saved thus far as seemingly material to the history of the State in the war, I doubt if I can possibly define it better at a single stroke than I did in a letter of date as early as August, 1917, addressed the State council of defense. Says that letter in part:

Nearly everything of any particular significance in the way of information concerning the status or movement of the Arkansas National Guard organizations since the day this commission first began its work, a not inconsiderable fund of information revealed in dispatches relating to the mobilization and tour of service of the Arkansas National Guard on the Mexican border last year (1916), as well, and even more especially, nearly everything, I believe, of any importance that has been and is being done or said in Arkansas by way of preparation for war since the declaration against Germany—we have made it our business and mean to continue systematically to treasure up day by day in the public archives of this commission agreeable to what I esteem the very best practical method for getting at the facts of history contained in the daily news and sundry contemporary reports.

If, on the other hand, now one turn with me to the card catalogue of this material; if one but scan only hastily the principal subjects which appear at the top of each card in the file, and take no account for the moment of all the other more searching details set out in the index outline obviously suggestive of nearly everything of any bearing at all upon the war where in any manner it has touched Arkansas, here it is—a copy of the subjects so presented in the order of one's a, b, c's:

War, the Great—In Arkansas: Aliens; Army; Aviation; Banks; Boards of commerce; Cantonments; Casualties; Censorship; Children; Churches; Civil War veterans; Council of Defense; Court-martials; Daylight saving; Declaration of war; Decorations; Deserters; Discharges; Discipline; Disloyalty; District boards; Draft; Exemption boards; Farmers; Flag, the; Food Administration; Food conservation; Food preparedness; Foreign born; Fort Roots; Four Minute Men; French Orphans; Fuel Administration; Fuel conservation; Give-a-bushel; Health; Heroism; Home Guards; Hospitality; Hospitals; Industry; Insignia; Insurance; Jews; K. of C.; Labor; Legislature; Letters; Liberty loans; Libraries; Liquor; Loyalty; Medical Corps; Members of Congress; Military bands; Mining; National airs; National Guard; Navy; Navy League; Negroes; Newspapers; Patriotism; Peace; Post Office; Prisoners of; Profiteering; Promotions; Questionnaires; Reconstruction; Recreation; Red Cross; Relics; Salvation Army; Sanitation; Schools; Schools of officers; Service flags; Slackers; South, the; Sports; Taxation; Thrift; Transportation; Tuberculosis; Unfit, the; Universal service; Vice commission; Volunteers; Valor honored; Weather; Woman's service; Woman suffragists; Y. M. C. A.

Again, if one were actually in quest of information about any one of these all but a hundred subjects which appear in the aforesaid outline of general topics, as, let us say, for example, the Red Cross, then the choice of material even now at one's disposal would comprise the following articles, and many more besides:

Red Cross: Parade in Little Rock; Tour State; Pulaski County Society organized; Story of growth; State must do its part; Drive by counties; Why it should be helped; Train to tour State; Pulaski County over top in financial campaign; To raise $5,000 in Argenta; One thousand members march in parade; State gives $664,000; Fund exhausted; Hospital unit T mobilized; State's quota of subscriptions; State's quota of members, 325,000; Campaign manager prays; Headquarters opened at Hotel Marion; In time of disaster; Mass meeting; State's work for, praised; Raising funds for; State's quota oversubscribed; Organize for Christmas drive; and Pulaski County; State surpasses quota; Organize for selling seals of; State oversubscribes quota; Making Christmas drive; Carry bundles and help; Campaign for pure milk; Made Navy garments; Workers hold rally, etc.

With reference to the matter of starting a World War museum in connection with our State history museum work, I quote the following from the same report:

It has long since occurred to me that, at the proper time, measures should be taken to procure for the history museum of the State an impressive collection of memorials commemorative of the deeds and experiences of Arkansas soldiers in camp and on the battlefields of France. The spirit, if not indeed the letter of the law to which our State museum owes its existence, seems ample in the sweep and compass of its aims, to warrant us in proceeding forthwith to negotiate plans, to the end that the commission be, in the fullness of time, fitted out handsomely with suitable exhibits of the war. Agreeable to that view of the provision of law which makes it "the duty of the commission to collect and preserve memorials of the Mexican and Civil Wars," and otherwise "to build up a museum at the capitol," I have written several letters to friends in France who, I thought, might possibly be in a position to help us forward such a plan. The following letter, for example, written and posted November 12, the day after peace was announced, purposes the minimum of what, it seems, the commission ought to vouchsafe upon this head:

"Now that the war is over—Little Rock celebrated the peace only yesterday, and such a spontaneous manifestation of happiness I never expect to see again—I venture to hope the stress upon you has somewhat relaxed. Moreover, the times now seem ripe for laying out certain plans as regards the work of the history commission, which I believe you can and will gladly help us perfect. Whence I presume to write you at this juncture.

"Arkansas will want and must have a 'War Museum' for the benefit of those of us now living and those to come after, in order that we may thus be enabled to visualize something of the grim realities of this greatest, no doubt, of all wars. We have the place to equip such a museum, and I am just now getting up our biennial budget of recommendations to the legislature, which meets, as you know, in January. I trust the commission may think proper to urge an appropriation to be used in acquiring the necessary collection of memorials. Wherefore, I am writing to know if you can not at once procure and send me a collection of material such as you may think proper, said collection to be set aside, marked permanently, as your personal contribution. I know of no one better qualified than yourself to make a suitable collection. If you can do this thing I believe it will be a service never to be forgotten; assuredly I shall not forget it. I wish you might start a large box moving this way at the earliest possible moment. I shall hope to hear from you very shortly."

Agreeable to the plans set out above, we have received and catalogued nearly a thousand relics of the various battlefields in France
where Arkansas soldiers and other Americans participated in the
Great War. The following introduction to the catalogue of the
aforesaid souvenirs of the Great War is taken from my last annual
report, submitted to the board of trustees on the 17th of this January:

The exhibits in this quarter of the Arkansas History Commission are catalogued below by sections in the order of display, the first cabinet being designated cabinet A. Each item listed is accompanied by significant descriptive
matter, which has been carefully selected and briefly phrased from informal
memoranda furnished the director of the department by Mr. Gulley, who, at
the instance and request of the history commission, made the collection while
in France in the employment of the overseas postal service of the American
Expeditionary Forces. It was and is the aim of the commission, as vouchsafed
by the measures taken in season to procure this, an initial collection, to
make forthwith a beginning in the matter of collecting memorials of the World
War, which collection is here distinctly set apart as a World War museum.
Such a museum, to which it is hoped may be added hereafter from time to
time other more significant donations touching the part which Arkansas played
in the war, will stand, in some small degree, as a fitting reminder through the
years to come of the spirit of patriotism which the citizenship of Arkansas
evinced at home in loyal self-denial and in deeds of valor on the field of battle
in an hour when the mettle of every man's loyalty to the Nation was tried in
the fire of a national peril.

The history men of Arkansas took charge of the war aims course,
which was given to the Students' Army Training Corps. They were
also active in the drives for the sale of Liberty bonds and for the
collection of funds for the Red Cross and other war agencies.

CALIFORNIA.

By GENEVIEVE AMBROSE, Secretary, War History Department, California Historical Survey Commission.

The formal preparation, during the progress of the war, of histories of the organization and operation of different branches of war
service began when the war history committee of the State council
of defense was organized in March, 1918, at which time circulars
were sent to every war agency advising them of the importance of
preserving the records of California's part in the war; and later, in
August, 1918, there was sent to every war agency in the State a request for a comprehensive report of its activities. Many of the war
agencies, such as the State food administration and the Red Cross,
etc., diverted a part of their staffs to the preparation of the historical records, and other war agencies requested their several departments to furnish complete reports of their particular fields of work.

In some cases the official annual reports of the organization and operation of the war agencies served as excellent historical records. It has been discovered recently that in a few instances the preservation of the war history started prior to the organization of the State war history committee. This is true of a few of the California exemption boards. One local board in particular, realizing the importance of the preservation of war records, began by having one of the local papers photograph each group of men as they were called by the board. This plan was carried on up to the signing of the armistice on November 11, 1918, in order to secure a complete gallery of all the men inducted into service.

The war history committee of the State council of defense, the members of which were appointed by the director of the State defense body in 1918, was the first central State agency to undertake the collection and preservation of the California war records. The plan of organization called for the formation, under the direction of the executive secretary of the State committee, of a county war history committee in each county in the State. Nominations for the members and chairmen of the county committees were usually made by the chairman of the county division of the State council of defense to the executive secretary of the State war history committee, and by him submitted to the director of the State council of defense, who then made the formal appointments. No set form of organization was prescribed, so that each county committee was created as best fitted the conditions of that particular county. It was aimed to have on each county committee representatives of the various war agencies, librarians, editors, history teachers, and other persons who might seem best qualified to render assistance. The work outlined by the State war history committee for its county committees was of a twofold character: First, they were expected to prepare reports or contemporaneous histories dealing with local war activities, and to gather and compile such other statistical information as might relate to the part taken by their respective counties in the great conflict. Second, they were expected to assemble and preserve newspaper clippings, war programs, war addresses, photographs, manuscripts, documents, posters, and fleeting war history material of every character. Special attention was directed to obtaining biographical sketches and photographs of all men in our country's service.

Upon organization, which occurred before the termination of hostilities seemed likely, the county committee was expected to prepare an exhaustive and detailed history of the county's participation in the war to date, with quarterly reports in the future. To insure

25066°—23——14

uniformity, a general form of report was arranged, in which were set forth the various war activities upon which a detailed report from each county committee was desired, among which were Red Cross; liberty loan, war-saving stamp, and thrift drives; food administration; four-minute men; women's organizations; legal aid committee; Americanization committee; war community council; farm labor committee; public service reserve; medical and dental aid; Boy Scouts; soldiers' welfare; rehabilitation of returned soldiers; public health, etc. On each county committee one person was designated as historian and was made responsible for compiling the full report for the county. The suggestion was made by the State war history committee that the county historian should parcel out the work to representatives of the war agencies, and that after the reports of the various war activities had been assembled the full report should then be forwarded to the State war history committee. The State committee prescribed a set of uniform rules regarding the reports and records, such as preserving the source material from which various reports were compiled, using a uniform-size page for the reports, making duplicate copies of each report, noting whether or not the records of the organization considered in the report were kept in a full and accurate manner, and whether or not there was danger of their being lost to future historians. The State war history committee laid great stress upon the importance of collecting biographical sketches and photographs of all men in the service, and suggested the cooperation of the local newspapers in every community to make this collection complete.

On January 31, 1919, the State council of defense formally went out of existence, at which time its various committees lost their legal status. However, the executive chairman of the State council of defense, on the date of the council's disbandment, recommended that certain of its committees, among which was the war history committee, be continued until provision could be made for their support by other existing agencies. The work of the war history committee was therefore continued and largely supported by the State board of control, where it was located until July, 1919. The California Historical Survey Commission, whose secretary was appointed executive secretary of the war history committee, also devoted a portion of its funds to the maintenance of the war history work. During the interim between January and July the State legislature met and enacted a law which placed the work of compiling the war records under the jurisdiction of the California Historical Survey Commission, where it was duly transferred from the State board of control on August 1, 1919, and placed under the direction of the war history department of the historical survey commission.

The plans for carrying on the work which were made by the war history committee of the State council of defense have been followed in the main by the war history department. With the development of the work, however, it has been necessary to make a few changes. For instance, the war history department advocates the enlargement of the county committee to include representatives of the following organizations: Local exemption boards; local posts of the American Legion; local press; boards of trade or chambers of commerce; board of supervisors; women's clubs (women especially active in war work); librarians (county and city); district attorney. In addition to this list the county committee have been urged to secure the cooperation of local historians and historical societies, and also representatives of educational institutions and of the various civilian war activities. The county chairmen have been asked to make the nomination of the members whom they wish to add to their committees to the secretary of the war history department, who submits the same to Gov. William D. Stephens, by whom formal appointments are made. The county committees are urgently requested by the war history department to collect all records and reports in duplicate, so that one set may be retained in the county archives and the other set forwarded to the war history department for lasting preservation in the State archives.

Specific plans for the publication of the material which is collected are now underway, and the proposal has been made that each county publish its own war history, since much of the material that will be of vital interest to the counties can not be included in the State résumé of the particular county's war activities. It has been suggested, therefore, that a bill be introduced at the next session of the State legislature that will provide for State cooperation with the counties in the publication of their histories to the extent of perhaps one-third the cost of said publication. The majority of counties favor this plan for the county publication and feel that the preservation of the military records and the war activities of the citizens of each county will be, in future years, a matter of tremendous interest to every person in the county.

The procedure of the county committees, after their organization along the lines above mentioned, is much the same as that outlined by the war history committee of the State council of defense. For example, the war history department recommends that each member of the county committee be assigned the task of collecting or supervising the collection of material pertaining to one or more of the following 14 main divisions of the war history as set forth in the "Sug-

gested Outline for a State or County War History," which has just
been issued:

1. Period before America's entrance in war.
2. Military, naval, and aviation activities.
3. Agriculture and the food supply.
4. Industry and labor.
5. Commerce, transportation, and communication.
6. War finance and revenue.
7. Social, welfare, and relief agencies and work.
8. Education.
9. Religion in the war.
10. Professional men and women in war work.
11. Women in the war.
12. War legislation and administration of government.
13. Public opinion and the war.
14. Post-war period.

The suggestion has been made that the member so assigned to the
one or more particular subjects may wish to associate with himself
others who are interested in or have valuable information of the particular phase of the war history, in which event he should be named
the chairman of a subcommittee composed of those whom he wishes
to call upon for cooperation in his work. The suggestion has been
made also by the war history department that subcommittees of the
main county committee be organized in each township or other political subdivision.

COLORADO.

By C. C. ECKHARDT, Department of History, University of Colorado.

Although Colorado was as remote from the scenes of the World
War and suffered as little physically as any region in the country,
there was a lively interest in the war long before America entered the
great conflict, and once the Nation had determined to do its part in the
titanic struggle there were many in the State that felt not merely the
need of doing what they could to give the public information as to
the causes and meaning of the war, but also to collect and preserve
records of Colorado's part in prosecuting the war.

Prof. M. F. Libby, of the department of philosophy of the University of Colorado, wrote a syllabus, "War Points for Americans,
a brief statement of our position regarding the war," which was published by the National Security League.

Prof. C. C. Eckhardt, of the history department of the University
of Colorado, wrote articles on "The Alsace-Lorraine Question,"
"The North Slesvig or Dano-German Question," and "The Old Internationalism and the New League of Nations," which appeared in the
Scientific Monthly for May, 1918, and January and May, 1919.

The various libraries of the State posted lists of books and articles in the war, and through the extension division and the library of the University of Colorado many hundreds of books and articles were sent to all parts of the State to individuals, clubs, and schools.

Many members of the faculties of Denver University, Colorado College, State Teachers' College, the Colorado Agricultural College, and the University of Colorado gave numerous addresses on the war and its origin. Prof. M. F. Libby, of the University of Colorado, made an extensive tour in the Southern States giving lectures on the war under the auspices of the National Security League.

In 1918 members of the history department of the University of Colorado gave courses on the war: Prof. T. M. Marshall, "The United States and the War"; Dr. Donald McFayden, "The Diplomatic Background of the War"; and Prof. Libby, of the philosophy department of the same institution, gave a course on the war, and after the armistice, a course on "The World Outlook."

The University of Colorado cooperated with the State council of defense in gathering war records, part of the funds for which being supplied by the State council of defense.

The University of Colorado gathered war records of all men and women in the service, records of its own graduates as well as all others. In spite of the persistent efforts of Prof. James F. Willard, head of the history department, and the faithful cooperation of many others throughout the State, this work is by no means complete. In the southern part of the State, when the Mexicans were asked to fill out these war record blanks, they were quite suspicious, and in some cases refused to comply with the request, fearing that they were filling out some kind of registration blank for a new military draft. One school superintendent in a number of cases took the sheriff of the county along to aid in securing the desired information and signature. But even with these heroic measures. the records are not complete for that district. Elsewhere our friends report that it is very difficult to get responses from the war veterans or their families. It seems much easier to fight for victory than to fill out blanks that tell about it.

The most extensive and comprehensive undertaking was the collection of newspaper clippings on war activities throughout the State. Over a hundred newspapers from all parts of Colorado were sent gratis to the history department of the State University. Here, under the direction of Prof. James F. Willard, a class read the papers, made clippings, and classified them as to general State activities, activities of the various counties, the subheadings being as follows: Red Cross, food and fuel consumption, war gardens, Knights of Columbus, Y. M. C. A., Liberty loan, Women's Council of Defense, etc. Great quantities of information were thus preserved, but owing to a lack of funds the work could not be complete.

The State historical society collected copies of all draft lists, and these are on file in Denver at the society's headquarters, as are also the complete records of the Four-Minute Men of some parts of the State. The society also sent out questionnaires to men and women in the service, these being distributed through the efforts of the Daughters of the American Revolution, the Women's Council of Defense, and the American Legion. The society also sent out civilian questionnaires. The society has been making an energetic drive to secure photographs of the men, war pictures and trophies, letters and diaries, and anything else connected with the war.

The records of the State council of defense and the Women's Council of Defense are preserved with the State historical society. Duplicates of most of these records are also deposited at the University of Colorado.

In many counties vigorous efforts were made to keep a record of the men in the service, El Paso, Gunnison, Boulder, and others really succeeding, while in the remainder of the counties the records are incomplete.

GEORGIA.

By LUCIAN LAMAR KNIGHT, State Historian.

The department of archives and history, State of Georgia, was created less than two years ago in the midst of the great World War, and while trying to keep an observant eye on the international horizon the State historian and director of the department was also charged with the responsibility of assembling together in one place all of the scattered archives of the State capitol for permanent preservation, safe custody, and classification.

In conjunction with the State council of defense, which organization has now ceased to exist, the department has compiled a roster of all who have made the supreme sacrifice, whether engaged in service on land or water, or in the air, from the State of Georgia. It has also compiled a complete list of Georgia casualties, including every Georgia soldier, sailor, or marine who was wounded in the service of the United States.

It has been the purpose, only partly carried out, however, to gather together all information concerning the effect of the war on Georgia's social, financial, educational, economic, and religious condition; the State's attitude toward the war; local activities, etc.

No attempt has been made to compile a roster of all the Georgia troops enlisted, because such an effort would only parallel, with poor success, the activities of the United States Government along this line, which, under an act of Congress, will no doubt be thorough and can be secured by the various States on application.

, However, the department is trying to secure a complete list of all Georgia boys who, prior to the declaration of war by the United States, enlisted under foreign flags.

ILLINOIS.

By WAYNE E. STEVENS, Secretary War History Section, Illinois State Historical Library.

Historical activities in the State of Illinois, which were undertaken as a consequence of the World War, may be conveniently considered from two points of view—(1) as a contribution toward the winning of the war and the arranging of a lasting peace; (2) as a means of preserving for posterity a record of the struggle itself. In many specific instances these two phases of historical activity necessarily coincided, but the distinction is a convenient one and has been observed in the preparation of this survey.

The most valuable contribution of historians to the winning of the war was unquestionably the molding of public opinion through the dissemination of information concerning war aims, both from the lecture platform and through the medium of the press. In Illinois the lead was taken by the colleges and universities, and immediately upon the outbreak of war systematic publicity campaigns were organized. At the University of Illinois a war committee was authorized in December, 1917, the purpose of which was to spread information concerning the war, not only among members of the university, but throughout the State. Divisional committees were appointed as follows: Publication of leaflets and pamphlets, publicity, talks and lectures at the university, and lectures throughout the State. Shortly after the outbreak of hostilities a committee on publicity was organized at the University of Chicago, which was later divided into subcommittees on speakers and publications. It need scarcely be said that the members of the departments of history, as well as those of the closely related departments of political science and economics, were active in the work of these committees.

Pamphlets were published, the purpose of which was to set forth clearly, and with a strict regard for accuracy, the issues of the conflict. Two series of pamphlets may be mentioned, the "University of Chicago War Papers"[23] and the "University of Illinois War Leaflets." The first series, for example, included such titles as "The Threat of German World Politics," "Americans and the World Crisis," "Sixteen Causes of War," and "England and America." Many of these pamphlets were published in large editions and distributed widely throughout the State.

[23] See "The University Press and the War," in University Record, January, 1919, p. 106.

Illinois educational institutions also rendered an extremely valuable service through organized public speaking. Shortly after the
outbreak of war, a speaking campaign was opened at the University
of Chicago by a series of lectures on "Why We are at War."[24] At
the University of Illinois, a series of lectures on war subjects was
given by members of the department of history, which was later supplemented by addresses arranged by the committee on talks and lectures. There were also occasional lectures on historical topics connected with the war by visitors at the University, while faculty
members spoke from time to time in various parts of the State. At
the same institution there was a committee on extension lectures,
which arranged for a series of talks to the soldiers at Camp Grant
by members of the departments of history, economics, and political
science. Among the subjects of these talks were "The Geographical
Background of the War," "The British Empire and What It Stands
For," and "Germany and Her Ambitions." Prof. James W. Garner,
of the department of political science at the University of Illinois,
also delivered a number of lectures before American soldiers in
France. Professors of history wrote bulletins for the use of Liberty
loan workers, while they themselves often spoke in behalf of the
various war drives. They rendered particularly valuable service
by contributing articles on war subjects to newspapers, as well as certain of the more popular magazines. The University of Chicago
committee on publicity arranged at an early date for the publication
of articles in the leading Chicago dailies, while it was arranged
that some of this material should be handled by news syndicates. In
this connection it should be stated that from April to October, 1918,
the work of the Committee on Public Information in Italy was directed by Prof. Charles E. Merriam, of the department of political
science of the University of Chicago.

One of the most obvious methods of educating the public with reference to war aims was through the adaptation of courses in the public schools, colleges, and universities, as well as by the organization
of new courses. In the very nature of the case, the principal burden
of this task fell upon the teachers of history. An enumeration of
even a relatively small number of such courses is impossible. There
were general courses dealing with the origin and backgrounds of the
war while there were others dealing with more specific aspects of the
struggle, which were given by specialists in certain phases of European history. The University of Chicago, for example, offered a
course on "The Background of the Great War" which is fairly typical. Political, social, and economic conditions among the European

[24] For an account of war lectures delivered under the auspices of the University of
Chicago, together with lists of lectures and subjects, see University Record, January,
April, and October, 1918, pp. 54, 105, and 239.

belligerents were considered, while special emphasis was placed upon the traditional attitude of the United States toward European affairs, together with the causes and influences leading up to our participation in the war. Departments of political science offered new courses in diplomacy and foreign relations which were adapted to current war issues and were essentially historical in character. Mention must not be omitted of the war issues course, which was given at various institutions in connection with the Students' Army Training Corps. The extremely large enrollment in this course often taxed to the utmost the resources of the departments of history, and it became necessary to obtain assistance from other departments. At the University of Illinois a committee on the war issues course was established, which became in large measure responsible for the general task of disseminating information concerning the war and related subjects. Prof. Evarts B. Greene, head of the department of history of the University of Illinois, as chairman of the National Board for Historical Service, cooperated with the Committee on Education and Special Training of the War Department in planning this course.

There were two national war agencies, the function of which was to assist in the formation of an enlightened public opinion—the Committee on Public Information and the National Board for Historical Service. It was also the purpose of the Committee on Public Information to follow closely and keep itself informed concerning the state of public opinion throughout the country. The attitude of the large German-speaking element of the population was of special concern, particularly in the case of a State like Illinois, where there is a relatively large German population. For a period of several months Prof. Laurence M. Larson, of the department of history of the University of Illinois, read some 20 daily and weekly German-American newspapers published in the State, summarizing and reporting upon their contents to the Committee on Public Information. One of the most valuable publications of the Committee on Public Information was the War Cyclopedia, many of the articles in which were contributed by members of the departments of history and political science of the universities of the State. At the request of the committee, Prof. W. S. Robertson, of the department of history of the University of Illinois, who was in South America during a part of the war, made certain investigations concerning Latin America and the war and the relations between Latin American Republics and the United States.

The second agency which assisted in the formation of public opinion was the National Board for Historical Service. Prof. Evarts B. Greene, of the University of Illinois, was chairman of the board from November, 1917, to September, 1918, and in this capacity cooperated with the Committee on Public Information, the Committee on Education and Special Training of the War Department, the various allied commissions, and organizations of similar character. On behalf of the National Board for Historical Service, Prof. Greene organized certain historical investigations for the use of the House "Inquiry." Prof. William E. Dodd, of the department of history of the University of Chicago, was also a member of the board.

During the war it came to be recognized that it was of the first importance that there should be the most complete accord between the United States and the associated powers. Such an accord could only be based upon a mutual understanding between the nations at war with Germany of their ideals and purposes. The historian, by reason of his cosmopolitan outlook and his familiarity with the ideals and institutions of nations other than his own, was especially qualified to assist in bringing about such an understanding. It was the privilege of Prof. A. C. McLaughlin, head of the department of history of the University of Chicago, to be instrumental in furthering friendly and cordial relations between the United States and Great Britain. Prof. McLaughlin was sent on a mission to England by the National Board for Historical Service, where he lectured extensively in the spring of 1918. The intimate knowledge of conditions in England acquired during his visit abroad enabled him, upon his return to the United States, to inform the public through the medium of lectures and published articles of the ideals for which the two nations had been jointly striving during the war. One tangible result of Prof. McLaughlin's visit was the publication after his return to the United States of a volume entitled "Britain and America," New York and London, 1919.

Because of skill in research and wide knowledge of world affairs, acquired in many instances through years of study, the services of the historian were invaluable in the gathering of data upon the basis of which the peace settlement was formulated. In 1917 Col. Edward M. House instituted his "Inquiry into the terms of peace" and gathered about him a group of experts for the purpose of collecting the necessary information. Prof. Albert Howe Lybyer, of the department of history of the University of Illinois, an authority on the Balkans and Near East, joined the House "Inquiry" in August, 1918. Prof. Laurence M. Larson carried on certain investigations relating to Slesvig, Finland, Spitzbergen, and other problems of Scandinavian interest which were expected to arise at the peace conference.

The American Commission to Negotiate Peace was organized shortly after the armistice and attached thereto were numerous experts, from whose number were selected the American members of the committees, commissions, and councils that were created by the peace conference. Prof. Lybyer, who had already been associated with the House "Inquiry," was also attached to the Commission to

Negotiate Peace, serving as assistant in the Balkan division of experts from December, 1918, to April 1, 1919. On the latter date he became general technical advisor to the King-Crane Commission on Mandates in Turkey, and visited Syria, Palestine, and Constantinople. Prof. Pitman B. Potter, at present of the University of Illinois, prepared for the commission two studies, entitled "Peace Proposals, December 12, 1916, to November 11, 1918," and "Autonomy and Federation within Empire."

After the armistice the University of Illinois began the publication of a series of pamphlets on problems involved in the international settlement, in which work the department of history took the lead.

In the foregoing discussion attention has been directed largely to the services rendered by professional historians and other persons in related departments of academic life. Their work is of unusual interest in a survey of this character because of the special qualifications which they possessed for the work described, by reason of their ability to ascertain facts derived from long practice in research; their ability to interpret facts, acquired through the process of sifting and analyzing historical data; and by reason of the fund of historical information already at their disposal, accumulated through years of study. There were numberless other persons and agencies, in Illinois as elsewhere, which did extremely valuable work along similar lines, but space does not permit a discussion of their activities.

Having considered briefly the service which historical training contributed to the winning of the war, something should be said concerning the agencies in Illinois which have been active in preserving a record of the events of the war and in collecting and preserving the materials which must be used by future historians. First of all will be considered historical studies which have already appeared or the publication of which is planned in the near future; and, secondly, progress made in the collection and preservation of war records in Illinois.

Few general historical studies relating to the State in the war have appeared as yet, owing to the comparatively short period of time which has elapsed since the cessation of hostilities. In Bogart and Mathews, The Modern Commonwealth, 1893–1918 (Vol. V, Centennial History of Illinois) is a chapter by Prof. Arthur C. Cole, entitled "Illinois and the Great War." Though of necessity very brief, this chapter constitutes by far the best summary of the history of Illinois in the war which has appeared. Several projects for publication are known to be underway. An official history of the State's participation in the war is planned, to consist of several volumes, some of which will be devoted to a narrative of events, while others will include selected documentary material. The publication of this history may not be expected for some two or three years, but in the meantime the necessary material is being collected. A work entitled "Illinois in the World War," a commercial project which has been undertaken by the State Publication Society, is expected to appear shortly. It will consist for the most part of accounts of various State war activities written by the persons who directed them. Thus it will in reality constitute a source, or a collection of sources, rather than a real history in the form of a connected narrative.

Certain studies of the war in its more general aspects have been made from time to time by Illinois writers. A volume by Prof. William E. Dood, entitled "Woodrow Wilson and His Work," has been published by Doubleday, Page & Co. Prof. James W. Garner has written a treatise on "International Law and the World War" in two volumes, which at the time of writing this article was in the press of Longmans, Green & Co. This study, while it belongs properly within the field of political science, will necessarily contain a large amount of historical material. The same may be said of Prof. John A. Fairlie's "British War Administration," which has appeared as a volume of the Preliminary Economic Studies of the War, published by the Carnegie Endowment for International Peace.

Several military histories have been published, relating to units made up in whole or for the most part of Illinois troops. There is now being edited for the press a history of the Thirty-third Division, by Col. Frederic L. Huidekoper, division adjutant. Besides a narrative account of the organization of the division, which was composed of Illinois National Guard troops and its operations in France, there will be a volume of appendixes containing official orders, memoranda, and other documentary material. There will also be a volume of official operation maps. This history, which is being published at the expense of the State, is a scholarly work in every sense of the term, and will not only be of interest to the general reader, but of value to the student of military science. An account of one of the units of the Thirty-Third Division has already been published in a work entitled "The 131st U. S. Infantry (1st Inf., Ill.. N. G.) in the World War." The general narrative is by Col. Joseph B. Sanborn, commanding the regiment, while the conduct of operations is described by Capt. George N. Malstrom. A splendid pictorial record of the Thirty-third Division is contained in a volume entitled "Thirty-third Division Across No-Man's Land," Kankakee, 1919. A history of the Eighty-sixth Division, which was formed at Camp Grant and contained a large number of Illinois men, has been compiled by members of the Eighty-sixth Division Association and is now in the press of the State Publication

Society. A very comprehensive and semiofficial narrative is contained in the volume entitled "Great Lakes Naval Training Station, A History," by Francis Buzzell, Boston, 1919. The author was historian of the ninth, tenth, and eleventh naval districts.

Of great interest, though of rather unequal value, are the "official" histories and final reports of the various war activities carried on within the State. Noteworthy among these publications is the "Final Report of the State Council of Defense of Illinois." Besides giving a general description of the work of the council, the report summarizes the activities and achievements of the various subcommittees, while there is an appendix which contains a large amount of exceedingly useful material in the form of texts of statutes, resolutions, reports, etc. Supplementing this report is the "Final Report of the Woman's Committee of the State Council of Defense of Illinois and the Woman's Committee of the Council of National Defense, Illinois Division," a volume of 316 pages. "The Web," by Emerson Hough, of Chicago, is the story of the American Protective League. Besides a general description of the origin and work of the league, the volume includes a more detailed account of its activities in the larger cities, including Chicago. Mr. George R. Jones, State chairman of the Four-Minute Men, has published a useful little volume entitled "History of the Four-Minute Men of Chicago." Many of the welfare organizations are planning to preserve a record of their activities in permanent form.

A history of the war activities of the Young Men's Christian Association throughout the central department, which includes Illinois, is being compiled under the auspices of the National War Work Council.

The military edition of the Columbian and Western Catholic, October 17, 1919, contains a series of articles describing with considerable fullness the work of the Knights of Columbus in Illinois. The various establishments of the War Camp Community Service in Illinois have compiled separate reports describing their work. Of special interest are the reports covering the work of the organization in Chicago and Rockford.

No official history of the Red Cross in Illinois has been prepared, nor has any general report of its work been compiled covering the central division, of which Illinois is a part. At the request of the director of the central division, however, nearly all of the county chapters have prepared brief histories of their war activities. These histories, as a rule, vary in length from 1,000 to 5,000 words, and a few have been published.

A number of educational institutions have undertaken to preserve a record of their war service. Schools, colleges, and universities have included much data of this sort in their catalogues, bulletins, annuals, alumni publications, etc. At Northwestern University a history of the various war activities connected with the institution is in manuscript and will soon be ready for the press. The University of Illinois has designated a committee, including two members of the department of history, to undertake the preparation of a record of the university in the war. The collection of material has been going forward for several weeks, and the committee is formulating plans for publication. A similar committee has been appointed at the University of Chicago. The University Record, October, 1917–January, 1919, inclusive, contains a series of articles edited by Dr. David A. Robertson, which constitute a very good general summary of the war service of the institution. At the Western Illinois State Normal School a manuscript is ready for the press which includes the names of students and alumni of the institution who were in uniform, together with a brief record of each man's service. The projected volume will also include a summary of the contributions of the school to civilian war activities.

The libraries of the State rendered inestimable service by acting as distributing centers for information of all sorts relating to the war. Mr. P. L. Windsor, of the University of Illinois library, has undertaken a State-wide survey of this phase of the work of the libraries, the result of which it is hoped to publish at some future date.

The county war history is a popular form of expression of interest in local war achievements, and in a large number of the 102 counties of Illinois such projects are underway. In many instances these histories are in the nature of commercial enterprises, while in other counties the work has been undertaken by public-spirited citizens of the locality with no idea of personal profit. The commercial publication as a general rule is characterized by expensive printing and ornate binding, though the content is usually less valuable than in the case of the second class of county histories mentioned above. Most of these "histories" conform pretty closely to a standard type. They include the names and sometimes fairly complete service records of persons who were in the Army, Navy, and Marine Corps. There is usually a brief sketch of each of the various civilian war agencies within the county. In these sketches the names of personnel and statistics of work accomplished, funds raised, etc., usually predominate.

The preservation of the original records relating to Illinois in the war is perhaps of more immediate importance than the writing of history, for it is upon material of this sort that the future historian must depend. The war records section of the Illinois State Historical Library is the agency which is organizing the work throughout the State. A war history committee was appointed under the State council of defense and a movement initiated looking to the preservation by the various counties of the State of original war records. The organization of the State council of defense was disbanded soon after the armistice, however, the result being that very little was accomplished. In July, 1919, the general assembly appropriated the sum of $20,000 for the following biennium, to be used by the Illinois State Historical Library for the purpose of collecting and preserving data relating to the State in the war. A war records section was organized, responsible to the library board of trustees, a secretary was appointed, and the gathering of material was commenced.

The work of the war records section consists of two separate, though closely related, phases (1) the gathering and preserving of material relating to the State as a whole, and (2) the organization of local war history committees, the duty of which is to perform a similar service for the counties in which they are located. General records and data pertaining to the participation of Illinois in the war are being assembled at Springfield, where they will constitute a permanent war records collection, which will be housed ultimately in the Centennial Building now being erected adjacent to the State capitol. A detailed description of this material will be unnecessary as it resembles very closely that which is being gathered in other States. Particular emphasis is being placed upon original records, in the form of correspondence, minutes of proceedings, memoranda, reports, etc., of State war activities. The headquarters of these State agencies have been carefully canvassed, and in some instances the war records section has been made the depository of a part or all of their working files covering the period of the war. Copies of county Red Cross chapter histories are being obtained for the war records collection while reports from local food and fuel administrators, as well as the chairmen of other county war activities, are being gathered. Ephemeral material in the form of pamphlets, circulars, bulletins, and publicity matter of all sorts is being collected. The section also has a growing collection of posters and photographs. A survey of Illinois manufactures during the war has been undertaken. A memorandum has been sent to several hundred concerns in the State, requesting data concerning their commercial and industrial problems during the war, and a large number of valuable reports have been received. The collection of soldiers' letters and diaries will also be emphasized.

Immediately upon its establishment the war records section began the task of organizing the various counties of the State to insure the preservation of local material. War records committees were organized in certain counties, while elsewhere other agencies, already in existence, were persuaded to undertake the task. In this connection the libraries of the State, particularly those located at the various county seats, have been very useful. The sort of material which the counties are being asked to collect is similar in character to that which is being gathered by the State, save for its more local interest and value. Special effort is being made to insure the preservation of the records of local committees which comprised the community war administrative machinery. In some counties the material gathered is being placed in the courthouse, while in others it is being placed in the library at the county seat for safe keeping. Some county committees have published war histories, while others are planning to do so. As has been stated it is planned ultimately to publish an official history of Illinois in the war; and in the collection of material, both State and local, this end is being kept constantly in view.

The libraries of the State, acting independently, and upon their own initiative, have done extremely valuable work in the collection of general material relating to the war. This is especially true of the libraries of our educational institutions, which in planning their collections have kept in mind the needs of future research students. In many instances their activities have extended to the gathering of European material, as well as that pertaining to the United States. The University Record, October, 1918, page 237, contains a good description of the activity of the University of Chicago library in collecting historical material.

INDIANA.

By JOHN W. OLIVER, Director War History Records, Indiana Historical Commission.

One of the first steps taken in Indiana to acquaint the people at large with the many issues involved in the World War was the publication of a war-service Textbook. Immediately following the organization of the State council of defense in May, 1917, the members realized the need of carrying home to every family in Indiana a thorough understanding of the causes of the war and the great issues at stake. The best medium through which this informatio could be diffused was a textbook—one that could be read and understood by school children as well as adults. Acting upon the suggestion of the State council of defense, Gov. James P. Goodrich authorized the publication of such a volume. The State board of education was requested to edit and publish the volume, and in January, 1918, it was ready for distribution.

The volume, numbering 151 pages, contains two of President Wilson's messages—the one read to Congress on April 2, 1917, and the message read at the opening of Congress, December 3, 1917;

addresses by Gov. James P. Goodrich, and Ex-Gov. Samuel M. Ralston; a discussion of State councils of defense by George Ade; an article on the meaning of war by Louis Howland; and several other articles devoted to some phase of the World War. Numerous war poems are also included in the volume. Several thousand copies of this volume were distributed throughout the State, and it became a great factor in bringing home to the people the real meaning of war.

In an effort to enlighten the public regarding the many issues of the war, a great work was done both by individuals and by organizations. A pamphlet entitled " The Soul of the German Empire," published in 1915 by William M. Cochran, Indianapolis, was one of the first to appear calling attention to the character of the nation that was later to become our enemy. Two other pamphlets written by an Indiana man, that were circulated throughout the country before the United States entered the war, were " Germans in America " and "America's Debt to England," by Lucius B. Swift, Indianapolis, 1916. This latter paper was read at the annual meeting of the American Historical Association at Cincinnati, 1916. The Quarterly Bulletin, issued by the Indiana State Library, June, 1917 (vol. XII, No. 2), was devoted entirely to a bibliography on war publications. A selected list of books dealing with war finance, military science, education and the war, universal military service, relief work in the war, food supply, women and the war, and other kindred subjects, was distributed throughout the State in the summer of 1917. "War Readings, a bibliographical reference to war items from current literature, 1917," by Katherine Merrill Graydon, professor of English in Butler College, Indianapolis, furnished a most valuable guide for the war material in magazines and periodicals.

The schools, colleges, and universities of Indiana carried on a systematic war-educational campaign by means of lectures, war courses, and assigned readings in order to reach the thousands of students enrolled in these institutions. Indiana University led the way by offering a special course on the World War and its causes during the summer school for 1917. The course was also offered during the regular sessions of 1917–18, and again during the summer term of 1918. In the fall term of 1918, a course on war aims was offered for the students enrolled in the Students' Army Training Corps. Several articles relating to the war were written by different members of the faculty, and were printed in each issue of the Alumni Quarterly. The chief contributors were Profs. James A. Woodburn, Samuel B. Harding, A. L. Kohlmeier, and James C. McDonald.

At Depauw University, Greencastle, a special series of lectures relating to the World War was provided for by the Mendenhall

Foundation. Dr. John R. Mott gave six lectures; Dr. John Kelman, of Edinburgh, Scotland, gave several; and President W. H. P. Faunce, of Brown University, gave several addresses on the war. All of these have since been published by the Abingdon Press, of New York City. In addition to this special series of lectures a course on the causes of the war and the "war aims course" were given by the department of history. Prof. W. W. Sweet, head of the history department, published a series of brief articles relating to the war in the Indianapolis News.

Special courses relating to the World War were also given by Purdue University; University of Notre Dame; the two Indiana State Normal Schools, Terre Haute and Muncie; Butler College, Indianapolis; Earlham College, Richmond; Wabash College, Crawfordsville; Hanover College, Hanover; Tri-State College, Angola; Franklin College, Franklin; Vincennes University, Vincennes; Central Normal College, Danville; and Indiana Central University, Indianapolis. In addition to the special courses on the war, given in each case by the department of history, the faculty members in each institution gave a series of lectures during the convocation periods, and on other special occasions. Several articles relating to war subjects were contributed by the faculty members to the local school papers and magazines. In each of the institutions mentioned the libraries arranged a special collection of ready reference books, pamphlets, and periodicals, containing war material, which the students were urged to read. Several of the college libraries circulated their collection of war material and assisted local clubs and societies in making a study of the war.

The most important contribution made by the historical profession in Indiana during the session of the Peace Conference was a series of articles on the League of Nations, prepared by Prof. James A. Woodburn, of Indiana University, and published in the Indianapolis Star during the month of April, 1919.

Special mention should also be made of the war services rendered by another Indiana historian, Prof. F. S. Bogardus, of the Terre Haute Normal School. He was one of the first men called into service by the War Department, early in 1918, to formulate the war issues course used by all colleges and universities that enrolled men for vocational and technical training. The same course was later used by the Students' Army Training Corps institutions. Prof. Bogardus had charge of the central district, covering 13 States in all, extending from West Virginia to Colorado.

During the progress of the war no steps were taken on the part of the State looking toward the publication of any special histories on war organizations or particular units.

With respect to the collection and preservation of war records, the Indiana State Library took the lead in April, 1917, in urging upon all local libraries and historical societies the importance of selecting and preserving all material relating to the war activities in Indiana. Special attention was called to the value of preserving complete files of all local newspapers. Early in 1918 a bulletin was issued by the Indiana State Library calling upon the different counties to take steps toward building up a collection of local war records. A few months later a second bulletin, issued jointly by the State library and State council of defense, was sent to all county councils of defense, urging them to prepare a final report covering the work of their organizations.

Immediately following the signing of the armistice, Gov. Goodrich called together the members of the Indiana Historical Commission and suggested that this organization take steps at once to collect and compile the official war history of the State. The expenses incurred for the work were paid out of the governor's emergency contingent fund until the legislature convened, when an appropriation of $20,000 was voted for this special work. The historical commission opened headquarters in the statehouse, and proceeded at once to organize local war-history committees in each county in the State. Two bulletins were issued setting forth an outline of the work that was to be covered in building up a State war-history collection.

The counties were urged to make their own local collections of records complete in every detail, and to include a report covering every organization that had helped toward the winning of the war. Also the counties have been urged to prepare their histories for publication at the earliest possible date. At this writing (Apr. 1, 1920) eight counties have published their war histories, and more than half of the counties in the State have their material assembled.

The scope of the work carried on by the historical commission covers every organization in the State that engaged in war work. Reports of the State council of defense, the history of the five Liberty loan drives, the fuel and food administrations, the numerous war-relief organizations, and all other phases of war work are to be included in the collection of war records.

[6] Three of the five volumes which the historical commission expects to publish are now under way, and it is expected that they will be in the press within the next few months. The first of these will be the gold star memorial volume. It will include the name and a brief biographical sketch of every man in Indiana who lost his life in the World War; also the pictures of as many men as can be obtained will be included in this volume. The second volume will be given over to the history of the State council of defense and the activities of the State conscription board. The third volume will con-

tain the history of the five Liberty loan drives and the war savings and war thrift stamp campaigns. Further publications will have to be deferred until an additional appropriation is made.

IOWA.

This report was prepared under the auspices of the State Historical Society.

Historical activities in the State of Iowa during the years 1917, 1918, and 1919, undertaken in consequence of the World War, were largely confined to the schools, including the higher State and private educational institutions, and to certain State institutions which were particularly interested in the dissemination of historical knowledge regarding the war or in the preservation of historical materials.

Along the lines of historical research and publication of war material, the State University of Iowa issued in January, 1919, a Syllabus on the Issues of the War, prepared by the collaboration of members of the university staff in connection with the war issues course for the Students' Army Training Corps. Through its extension division the university also issued various bulletins bearing upon historical aspects of the war. Among these may be named one on "German Submarine Warfare Against the United States, 1915–1917," by Louis Pelzer, and one on the "Monroe Doctrine and the War," by Harry G. Plum. Bulletin No. 40 published in August, 1918, is a bibliography of war materials prepared for use by the Iowa Patriotic League in the high schools of Iowa. It is supplemented by Bulletin No. 48, which brings the bibliography down to May, 1919.

The State Historical Society of Iowa during the period 1917–1919 issued 24 numbers in a series of booklets entitled "Iowa and War." Although many of these numbers dealt with earlier wars in which Iowa had a part, the following titles will indicate the scope of the material relating to the World War: "Iowa War Proclamation," "An Iowa Flag," "The First Three Liberty Loans in Iowa," "Social Work at Fort Dodge," "Organized Speaking in Iowa During the War," "The History of Iowa's Part in the World War," "A Tentative Outline for a County War History," "A Tentative Outline for a State War History," "The Writing of War History in Iowa."

The State Historical Society also published in 1919 a bulletin of information entitled "Collection and Preservation of the Materials of War History—A Patriotic Service for Public Libraries, Local Historical Societies, and Local Historians."

The diffusion of historical information through newspapers and periodicals was considerable in amount, though not the result of a great deal of organized effort from within the State. The newspapers drew much material from the publications of the National Committee on Public Information. A reversal of this service is typified in the contribution to the Historical Outlook (a publication of nation-wide circulation) of an historical outline under the title "United States and the World War" by Harry G. Plum, of the State University of Iowa.

The libraries of the State made every effort possible to secure and make accessible to the public books and periodicals containing important historical information. Lectures concerning the issues of the war were provided by the higher educational institutions, the public schools, and by numerous other agencies. With the cooperation of the State council of defense, a bureau of speakers for Iowa was organized, which coordinated the public speaking in the State, particularly in connection with the campaigns for funds for welfare organizations, for Liberty loans and for other war purposes. The diffusion of historical information through this agency was very considerable.

In the schools and colleges teachers naturally emphasized the historical phases of the World War. In most of the colleges courses on the issues of the war were given and had large enrollments. A valuable adjunct to the teaching of history in the high schools was the work of the extension division of the State University of Iowa, in organizing in August, 1918, the Iowa Patriotic League, which enrolled high schools and high-school students in the study of the great problems of the day, especially those problems brought out by the war and reconstruction.

Cooperation with the State council of defense was close in all efforts which had historical connections; as, for example, the organization of the bureau of speakers and the Iowa Patriotic League, and in the diffusion of war information through the printed word. Cooperation with the National Board for Historical Service and with the National Government in the prosecution of the war and in the negotiation of peace was of a general nature only.

During the progress of the war the State Historical Society of Iowa drew up and published in the Iowa and War Series tentative outline plans for the writing of histories of the various war activities of the State. In accordance with these plans the society began the preparation of volumes on the Food Administration in Iowa, The Red Cross in Iowa, Welfare Campaigns in Iowa, and other similar subjects. A short sketch of "The Fuel Problems in Iowa during the World War" has been published by the fuel administrator for the State, Mr. Charles Webster.

The collection and preservation of war records has been carried on in the counties through the county historical societies, public libraries, and other agencies, and for the State at large by three principal organizations. The general assembly of Iowa provided for the organization of an Iowa war roster commission and granted an appropriation of $20,000 for the preparation and publication of a roster of Iowa soldiers, sailors, and marines in the recent Mexican border service and in the World War. The active part of this commission is the adjutant general of the State, for whose office Col. Frank E. Lyman, cooperating with the War Department, is now engaged in the compilation of the war records of Iowa men.

The historical department at Des Moines has been, during and since the war, actively engaged in gathering information, through questionnaires and other means, concerning Iowa soldiers. A large body of material has been secured and placed upon cards and a considerable collection of photographs of soldiers has been made. A special effort has been made to secure data in regard to casualties among troops from the various Iowa counties.

A somewhat different system of collection has been adopted by the State Historical Society of Iowa. Although efforts have not been neglected to collect material of a general nature and along all lines of war activities, the collection along individual lines has been pushed. For example, assignments of special topics for research and writing have been made in various fields, and the individual who is to write upon a given subject is given the task, and afforded every aid possible therein, of collecting the material bearing upon his subject. The material thus gathered, though not covering so wide a field, is more intelligently selected and lends itself immediately for publication purposes. A considerable body of war material has been collected in this way for use and for preservation.

The preparation of histories of Iowa's part in the war has already made considerable headway, although as yet comparatively little has been published. In a number of the counties of the State "honor rolls" have been published. These are, for the most part, collections of photographs of men in the service from the county, together with a brief statement of each man's service record. These is usually little or no other content, the purpose of the publication being commercial rather than historical. A few publications are appearing in which reading matter predominates, and it is expected that the number will steadily increase. In many counties histories of a more promising character are being prepared. A county historical society has been organized in one county with this purpose in view, and it is hoped that the existing county historical societies will take an active part in seeing that the history of the part taken by the county is written with regard to future historical value rather than present financial value. A history of the Eighty-eighth Division, recently published, is typical of the attempt to record the history of combat organizations recruited in whole or in part from the State.

The roster which is being compiled by the Iowa war roster commission will be accompanied with a certain amount of historical
matter of a general nature, and will constitute a most valuable
addition to the war history of the State.

The most comprehensive plan for the writing of Iowa's part in
the World War is that of the State Historical Society of Iowa.   In a
series entitled "Iowa Chronicles of the World War" the society is
planning to issue volumes covering all phases of the war activities
of the State both at home and overseas.   These volumes will be
assigned to historically trained men and will be the result of careful
research.   One volume is already completed and several others are
nearing completion.

KANSAS.

This report was prepared from a letter by F. H. HODDER, Department of History and Political Science, University of Kansas.

The history men of the University of Kansas were sufficiently
active during the war.   Mr. Hodder organized 50 sections of the
war aims course, taught two of them, and lectured at Camp Funston.
Mr. Patterson was one of a committee of three that administered
all the educational work of the Students' Army Training Corps.   He
also taught two sections of the war aims course.   Mr. Moore was in
Washington working, first for the War Trade Board and later in
the Department of State.   Mr. Melvin gave all the lectures for seven
sections of the vocational group.   Mr. Davis was engaged in Red
Cross work on the firing line in France.   Mr. Crawford and Mr.
Chubb did double duty in teaching.   The instructors in other educational institutions were, in all probability, equally active.

KENTUCKY.

By FRED P. CALDWELL, State Historian for Kentucky Council of Defense.

There was not, during the years 1917, 1918, and 1919, nor is there
at this time a Historical Commission in Kentucky.   The only war
history work that has been done is that which is being done under
the direction and supervision of the Kentucky Council of Defense.
That body was created by the Kentucky Legislature in March, 1918.
While the purpose of the council was "to assist the State and Federal Governments during the contiuance of war," it was felt that
this statement of the purposes of the council was broad enough to
include the diffusion of historical information, and the gathering
and preserving of historical material.

From the date of its creation the Kentucky Council of Defense cooperated with the Council of National Defense and the Committee
on Public Information in the diffusion of historical information

necessary to an enlightened public opinion regarding the issues of the war, this being done by procuring the publication in newspapers and periodicals of articles furnished for that purpose, and also by promoting the circulation of books and periodicals containing important historical matter. Books and pamphlets furnished by the Committee on Public Information were widely distributed for the use of speakers. Many speakers of national and international fame were brought to the State by the State council of defense with the cooperation of the Council of National Defense and the Committee on Public Information, Sir Frederick E. Smith (now Lord Birkenhead), then attorney general of Great Britain and now lord chancellor, being among the number. The week of September 25 to 30 was set apart by the publicity committee of the State council of defense as patriotic week, and during that period 898 different patriotic meetings were held in the State under the direction of Dr. H. H. Cherry, chairman of that committee, the total number of meetings held under the direction of that committee during the war being more than 3,000. Prizes were awarded in the schools and colleges for essays and speeches on patriotic subjects, and in other ways the young people of the State were enlightened as to the issues of the war. The Kentucky Council of Defense, the food administration, the fuel administration, the American Red Cross, and other war agencies cooperated with the Federal Government in many and varied ways in the prosecution of the war.

Realizing that much valuable material relating to the part which Kentucky was playing in the war would be lost unless promptly collected and preserved, the State council, in September, 1918, took active steps to collect and preserve historical records. It appointed a "State historian," and caused local historians to be appointed in each of the 120 counties in the State. The county historians in turn appointed assistants in the various parts of their counties, and thus the work was begun.

The historical work not having been finished on March 15, 1920, when the State council of defense passed out of existence, the Kentucky Legislature continued it in existence as the Kentucky Council of Defense for two years longer—that is, until March 15, 1922—for the sole purpose of completing and preserving Kentucky's war history.

When the work was first taken up by the council there were few precedents to guide it. It was necessary to formulate a plan of its own, and to prepare forms and blanks. It was determined that two main branches of work would be done—first, to collect in the central office records of State-wide interest, and, second, to collect in each county records of special interest to the people of the county.

First, as to the county records. The plan adopted for the county records called for three separate lines of work; first, making individual records on "war record sheets" of all soldiers, sailors, marines, chaplains, nurses, aviators, and others from Kentucky who were in the service during the war; second, making records of the work done by the county councils of defense, Red Cross, Liberty loan committees, war savings stamps committees, Y. M. C. A., Y. M. H. A., Knights of Columbus, Jewish Welfare Board, women's clubs, War Camp Community Service, Salvation Army, Boy Scouts, Boys' Working Reserve, food and fuel administrators, War Mothers, Four-Minute Men, churches, schools, and all other organizations which did war work; third, collecting and preserving other war data and records of historical interest.

In June, 1919, the council of defense conducted a State-wide "historical drive," the purpose of which was to arouse public interest in the collection and preservation of historical material. In this drive the newspapers of the State were of great help. They published for several weeks lists of the men who died or were wounded in the service, citations of men who had won special honors, sketches of Kentucky's ranking officers, reports of work done by local organizations, and articles prepared by the local historians relating to the county's war history.

In several counties the local historians prepared the material for, and the papers printed, "historical" and "memorial" editions. In this way a great deal of material of permanent historical value was preserved. These special editions contained fairly complete records of the part which the various counties played in the war, both through their armed forces and their civilian war workers. Some of the papers published photographs of the men who had given their lives, and photographs of the principal civilian workers. The historical drive was an unqualified success, and through the publicity which it created the local historians were able to collect a great deal of valuable material.

By the use of "war-record blanks," which were sent to each county, it was proposed to secure the following information as to each person in the service: Name, rank, address, nearest relative, date and place of entrance into the service, branch in which he served, promotions, casualties, date of discharge, etc. While many of the counties have had war-record blanks filled for practically all of the men in the service, there are still many counties in which only a small number of blanks have been filled, and some in which no records of any kind have been made. To remedy this condition it is the purpose of the council, during the next two years, to send to each county a copy of the "statement of service" of each soldier and sailor from that county. This can be done by copying the

"statements of service" when they are sent to the adjutant genera
of Kentucky by the adjutant general of the United States.

When the county records are completed they should contain state
ments of service of all soldiers and sailors who lived in that county
reports of war work of civilian organizations, records of the me
who died or were wounded, copies of the citations of the men wh
won special honors, photographs, addresses, and newspaper and othe
articles of historical value. The records will be bound in permanen
form and placed in the archives of the county.

It will thus be seen that the main purpose of the council is to hel
each county make for itself a permanent record of its war activitie
It is believed that such records, using each county as a unit, will b
of far greater value than would be the gathering of a great mas
of material at one central depository. No plans have been made a
yet for the publication of any material. No doubt many of th
counties will at some time in the future publish their county wa
histories.

Most of the material to be collected and preserved in the centra
office of the council will be records of State-wide interest. Some rec
ords collected and to be collected include the following: Records o
Kentuckians who lost their lives in the service; records of th
wounded; list of Kentuckians who won special honors, with copie
of official citations and newspaper clippings with reference to suc
honors; reports of State-wide work of Kentucky Council of Defense
Liberty loan campaigns, war savings stamp campaigns, food and
fuel administrators, Red Cross, Y. M. C. A., Y. M. H. A., Knight
of Columbus, Jewish Welfare Board, women's clubs, schools
churches, Four-Minute Men, selective service department, and othe
war work agencies; histories of overseas divisions in which Ken
tucky men served; naval activities; transport service; rosters o
Kentucky men in each division; rosters of Kentucky men at officers
training camps; Students' Army Training Corps; roster of Ken
tucky National Guard; histories of Camp Taylor, Camp Knox, and
Fort Thomas; statements of services of Kentucky physicians, nurses
chaplains, and Army welfare workers in the war zone.

From this statement it will be seen that it is proposed to make
the war history of each county in the State complete in itself, and
collect at the central office war literature and records of State-wide
interest.

LOUISIANA.

By M. J. WHITE, Department of History, The Tulane University of Louisiana.

Louisiana has not been particularly active in the collection and
publication of war history material, but from present indications

the legislature, which assembles at Baton Rouge this month (May, 1920), will make an appropriation for the purpose.

The State council for defense undertook an important work when it made arrangements for compiling a record of every soldier, sailor, marine, volunteer, and member of the National Guard of the State who was in Federal service. A war record director has been appointed for each of the 64 parishes, a house-to-house canvass undertaken for the purpose of securing the necessary data, and the records are to be preserved in leather-bound volumes. A copy of the record for each parish is to be placed on file at the parish courthouse, and a complete record for Louisiana will be kept in the State files at the capitol.

Since the first of the year two pamphlets dealing with war activities in Louisiana have been published. "Louisiana in the War," by Herman J. Seiferth, published and sold by the Times-Picayune, of New Orleans, consists in the main of short reports by chairmen or members of the various committees and boards that made up the State war organization. Isoline Rodd Kendall (Mrs. John S. Kendall) has written "A Brief History of Woman's Committee, Council of National Defense, New Orleans Division."

In the public parks of New Orleans and in many of the cities and towns of Louisiana memorial groves of live-oak trees have been set out; memorial tablets have been placed in public buildings all over the State; libraries have collected war books and pamphlets and war posters; and the Louisiana State Museum, at New Orleans, has brought together a considerable collection of valuable war relics.

At the present time $300,000 is being raised by public subscription, portions of this sum being allotted to each of the parishes, for a State memorial, to be placed upon the grounds of the State university at Baton Rouge, in memory of Louisianians who lost their lives in the war.

Prof. William Woodward, of the Newcomb School of Art, Tulane University, has, upon his own initiative, and at his own expense, painted the portraits of several Louisiana men and women who served their country in Europe. He has hopes that his pictures may become the nucleus of a State collection to record the late war.

MAINE.

By ORREN C. HORMELL, Department of History, Bowdoin College.

The historically trained men and women of Maine at the outbreak of the war were among the first to devote themselves to the prosecution of the war either in the active military service or in those lines of domestic service for which their training had best prepared them. Those in the historical profession in Maine who were so unfortunate as to be excluded from active military or naval service contributed in no small measure toward making the prosecution of the war successful. Members of the department of history and government in all four Maine colleges (Bates, Bowdoin, Colby, and the University of Maine) gave public lectures upon historical and political subjects which would aid the citizen to understand the issues of the war and win their undivided support for a vigorous prosecution of the war. During the life of the Students' Army Training Corps the departments of history and government of the four Maine colleges were turned over almost entirely to the teaching of war subjects. At Bates College the war issues course was given by Prof. R. R. N. Gould; at Bowdoin, Prof. O. C. Hormell was the director of the course and Prof. Daniel Stanwood of the department gave some of the lectures. At Colby, Prof. William Black had charge of the course; while at the University of Maine Prof. Caroline Colvin and Asst. Prof. Albert A. Whitmore shared in the conducting of the course.

Prof. O. C. Hormell, of Bowdoin, and Prof. Stewart Macdonald, of Colby, gave a course in military law in their respective colleges.

From March until June of 1919 Prof. O. C. Hormell, of Bowdoin, as a member of the Army Education Corps of the American Expeditionary Forces taught civics at the American University at Beaune, Côte d'Or, France, and lectured on political subjects at several American Expeditionary Forces posts in France.

The most noteworthy work done in consequence of their historical training, by historically trained men in Maine, during the war, was by Prof. (Capt.) Herbert C. Bell and Prof. (Capt.) Thomas Van Cleve, of the department of history at Bowdoin College. When it was discovered by general headquarters in December, 1917, that Capt. Bell was a trained historian, he was assigned the task of submitting daily, to the commander in chief, confidential reports on the political developments in the various belligerent countries. Soon afterwards he was made editor of the Press Review. In May, 1918, Capt. Bell was detailed to write the confidential cables which were sent regularly twice a day by the commander in chief to the Secretary of War. After the armistice he was sent to London to investigate all known schemes for a league of nations, and to prepare copies for Gen. Bliss of the Peace Commission. During December (1918), and January (1919), he submitted three reports—(a) a collection of schemes, (b) a critical abstract of the schemes presented, and (c) a proposed constitution for the league based upon the abstract. In this work he was ably assisted by Lieut. Lawrence Crosby (Bangor, Me.), who had received his historical and legal training at Bowdoin and Oxford.

Prof. (Capt.) Van Cleve, September, 1918, was made a member of a special department maintained at general headquarters for studying the political conditions in the allied and enemy countries. He was put in charge of the "enemy sections" and prepared several articles each week on Germany and Austria-Hungary. The articles, especially after the armistice, dealt with such questions as German morale, activities of the political parties, revolutionary movements, the financial and economic situation, workingmen's and soldiers' councils, the new German constitution, etc. The articles prepared by Prof. Van Cleve appeared in the "Press Review, Second Section, General Staff, General Headquarters, American Expeditionary Force."

State and local war materials were quite generally preserved throughout the State. Through the offices of the adjutant general, State librarian, and committee of public safety, records have been kept of the various war activities within the State, much of which will be published by the State in due time. Much data concerning the local participation in the war have been preserved by the Maine Historical Society Library, Evelyn L. Gilmore, librarian; Bangor Public Library, Charles A. Flagg (now deceased), librarian; Portland Public Library, Alice C. Furbish, librarian; and by the libraries of the four Maine colleges.

Rev. Edwin Carey Whittemore, a trained historian, of Waterville, collected data on, and is now preparing a history of, the war records of Waterville and Winslow.

MARYLAND.

By KARL SINGEWALD, Maryland War Records Commission.

Patriotic Education.—The work of patriotic education was carried on actively and effectively in Maryland, especially by the educational committees of the Maryland Council of Defense and of the women's section, and by the four-minute men. The committees cooperated with the Government to the fullest extent in distributing the literature issued by the Committee on Public Information and other Government agencies, and conducted public meetings continually throughout the State.

Dr. John H. Latane, professor of American history, and Dr. A. O. Lovejoy, professor of philosophy, of Johns Hopkins University, were notably active in patriotic speaking and in directing the educational campaign. Dr. Lovejoy prepared a pamphlet, "What are we fighting about?" which was printed by the Maryland Council of Defense. This pamphlet went through five editions, and attained a considerable circulation even outside of the State of Maryland.

The history department of Goucher College devoted its efforts largely along war lines. A series of eight public lectures upon the Origin of the Great War was delivered by Asst. Prof. Katharine J. Gallagher. The department cooperated with the National Board of Historical Research in furnishing bibliographies upon special issues of the war. Asst. Prof. Mary W. Williams prepared a bibliography of the war for the History Teachers' Magazine in 1918. Dr. Ella Lonn prepared a syllabus for general courses on patriotic education. This syllabus was published as "What Uncle Sam and Maryland do for you," under the auspices of the Americanization committee of the women's civic league of Baltimore. All members of the department were active in patriotic speaking and instruction.

Mention should be made also of the book, America's Case Against Germany, by a Marylander, Dr. Lindsay Rogers, adjunct professor of political science, University of Virginia, an excellent study of the events leading up to our entrance into the war in the light of international law.

War records.—The State of Maryland has made adequate provision for compiling its war records in a very comprehensive and thorough way. The Maryland Council of Defense, after the armistice, created a historical division for this important undertaking. The legislature, at its recent session, passed an act creating a war records commission of five members to take up and carry on the work of the historical division.

The undertaking of the historical division includes: (1) records of all Marylanders who served in the military and naval forces of the United States or of the Allies in the war, and letters, diaries, etc.; (2) records of military units composed largely of Marylanders; (3) records of military establishments in Maryland during the war; (4) records of Marylanders who rendered noteworthy service in relation to the war in a civilian capacity, in Government positions, in welfare or relief work, in finance or industry, etc.; (5) records of nonmilitary war agencies and activities, in Maryland; (6) records of Maryland war industries; (7) war exhibits—photographs, posters, publications, etc.

Historical committees were organized in the counties of the State. These committees are serving gratuitously, and in many of the counties are doing excellent work. Altogether the compilation of the historical records is progressing very satisfactorily.

The report of the Maryland Council of Defense to the Governor and General Assembly of Maryland, a printed volume of 330 pages, covers fully the history of the council and of the many war activities conducted with its support. The appendix is an important collection of documentary material—laws, reports, and other papers.

PROGRAM FOR WAR RECORDS.

1. *Military Records (individual).*—Over 60,000 Marylanders were in the service. The commission is endeavoring to obtain the war service record of every such Marylander, on a form prepared for this purpose. It is meant to include Army, Navy and Marine Corps, and also services transferred to the military forces during the war—Public Health Service, Coast Guard, Lighthouse Service and Coast and Geodetic Survey personnel, etc. It is desired also to include those who served in the forces of the Allies, whether before or after the entrance of the United States into the war.

In addition to the formal war service records, the commission urgently requests photographs, copies of citations and commendations, clippings, letters, narratives, diaries, etc. Such material is of very great interest and value for the historical collection.

Marylanders include not only those who entered the service from Maryland, but also those who formerly lived here. Whenever, for any reason, the form cannot be filled out by the one who was in the service, it should be done by a member of the family.

2. *Military Units.*—It is extremely important to gather as full records as possible of the military units in which Marylanders served, and of ships and naval stations. The records desired include histories, rosters, especially of Maryland men (with addresses), copies of official orders and other records, narratives, diaries, unit newspapers, photographs, insignia, trophies, souvenirs, etc.; also records of activities of auxiliary organizations of the various units.

3. *Military Establishments in Maryland.*—Maryland, on account of favorable location, received a large share of the big Army and Navy establishments required by the war—notably Camp Meade, Camp Holabird, Aberdeen proving ground, Edgewood Arsenal, Curtis Bay ordnance depot, zone supply and port storage office, General Hospital No. 2 at Fort McHenry, General Hospital No. 7 at Evergreen, Jr., United States Naval Academy, Indianhead naval proving ground, section 1 of Fifth Naval District, Naval Overseas Transportation Service, and a score of other camps, posts, and offices.

Official histories and records of personnel are being received, of course, but it is greatly desired to obtain also all possible records, including historical statements or narratives by Marylanders stationed at such establishments, copies of camp or post newspapers, other publications, clippings, photographs, souvenirs, etc.

4. *Civilian records (individual).*—A form of war service record somewhat similar to the military form is being used for record of civilians connected with the Army or Navy or in the war work of the welfare organizations, and of those who rendered service of special importance or had experiences of unusual interest in any capacity in relation to the war—in government position, in finance or industry, in patriotic, welfare or relief agency, etc. It is desired to include services prior to the entrance of the United States into the war, and also reconstruction activities.

5. *Civilian war agencies and activities.*—There were a number of war agencies that stood out conspicuously: the Maryland Council of Defense; such United States Government agencies as the Selective Service Boards (military in function), Food Administration, Fuel Administration, Shipping Board, Railroad Administration, Liberty loan, war savings; the Red Cross; welfare organizations operating under the Commission on Training Camp Activities, including

the Y. M. C. A., Y. W. C. A., K. of C., J. W. B., Salvation Army, A. L. A., and W. C. C. S.

The compilation of war records, however, is not limited to these especially conspicuous agencies It is important to secure adaquate records of every agency and activity in Maryland in relation to the war: United States Government offices and activities; State, county, and local governing bodies and officers; patriotic, welfare, and relief organizations; financial institutions and business houses; commercial, agricultural, and labor organizations; professional associations; churches, schools, fraternal organizations; public meetings, celebrations or other notable events, etc. Broadly, it may be stated that a historical report is desired from every organization that did anything worthy of record in relation to the war.

The records desired include history of war activities, including record of personnel; clippings; forms, publications, posters; photographs and other exhibits, etc. The war records commission, moreover, is the proper depository for the files and records, e. g., minute books, correspondence, etc., of agencies of a temporary character.

6. *War industries.*—The contribution of Maryland's industries to the winning of the war was very large, notably in shipbuilding and munitions, but also in a great many other lines. The war records commission urgently requests a historical report from every Maryland manufacturer, producer, dealer, or contractor on production, supply, or construction work for war purposes.

7. *Newspaper files and clippings.*—Newspaper files for the period of the war constitute very important historical records. Since it is impossible in many cases to obtain complete files, it will be helpful if anyone who has copies preserved of Maryland newspapers of date between July 1, 1914, and October 1, 1919, will contribute them. Clippings also of items of war interest are valuable.

8. *War literature, etc.*—It is desired to collect all literature—books, pamphlets, addresses, sermons, poetry—produced by Marylanders, or related to events in Maryland in connection with the war. Also, similarly, music, drawings, paintings, cartoons, etc.

Note.—For the sake of uniformity, all reports, papers, etc., as far as possible, should be on letter size paper (8½ by 11).

MICHIGAN.

By CHARLES LANDRUM, Special Historian of the Michigan War Preparedness Board.

In no war has there been so full a realization of the importance of events and relationships as in the late World War. Along with the development of the destructive branches of the military, there have been evolved constructive agencies that were to outlast the war activities of the Governments and contribute much toward the solution of reconstruction problems which now confront the Nation. Important among these agencies is the historical interest shown during the war by which the contemporary activities, both civil and military, are being chronicled and carefully preserved for the use of the future historian. In the State of Michigan the importance of this historical interest was early recognized and provision made for the collection, classification and preservation of such documentary and ephemeral material, as would make it possible to transmit to the coming generations a complete and accurate account of the State's civil and military activities in the war.

During the period of the World War prior to America's entrance, sufficient time elapsed to permit a thorough consideration of the issues at stake in the great struggle. Viewing our participation in the war as a remote possibility, students directed their energies and efforts along almost purely historical lines. These lines of investigation almost invariably lead through the labyrinthian windings of the diplomatic relations involved in the evolution of the Triple Alliance and that of the Entente, together with a more or less superficial study of the unification of Germany and the development of the military system of Prussia with its counterpart in the respective nations involved in the war. Students and scholars used this purely historical background as a setting for comparisons between the Prussian and American systems of government.

With the end of American neutrality and our entrance into the struggle appear such articles as "The University of Michigan in the War," by Robert Mark Wenby and by Arthur Lyon Cross; "Michigan in the Great War," by Col. Roy C. Vandercook; "History of Camp Custer," by Lieut. George H. Maines; "History of the Thirty-Second Division," by Lieut. Col. August H. Gansser; and many others bearing on aspects of the relation of Michigan to the war; while the book entitled "Democracy and the Great War," by George Newman Fuller, secretary of the Michigan Historical Commission, put out by the State department of public instruction for use in the schools throughout the State and largely used in the Students' Army Training Corps, in a very concise and able manner dealt with the national phase of the subject. These and many other creditable productions had for their motive, for the most part, the clarification of the issues of the war with a view to deepening spiritual convictions and thus making the State more efficient as a unit in the war machine.

The collection and preservation of the official records and other historical data relating to the war has largely devolved upon the public libraries of the State, which have become the depositories for all agencies engaged in this phase of the work. The State board of library commissioners made plans for the performance of this service, and all the libraries of the State have assisted in its execution. In such libraries as the Detroit Public Library, State Library, the libraries of the University of Michigan and the colleges of the State, Grand Rapids Public Library, Saginaw Public Library, Kalamazoo Public Library, the Houghton Public Library, and many others, are preserved complete files of the newspapers and magazines of

Michigan, as well as the documentary and more ephemeral material relating to the war. These collections are increasing daily in volume, and only the lack of facilities properly to care for this material will embarrass the librarians who have voluntarily assumed the responsibility for this work.

The popular lecture proved to be a valuable means of enlightening the public in regard to the causes of the war and in maintaining a spirit of devotion, service, and sacrifice, which was so apparent throughout the entire period of the war. The efforts of the university, the colleges, the pulpit, the four-minute men, the Chautauqua and lyceum bureau, and the Open Forum were especially commendable. Prominent among the platform orators were Prof. Claude H. Van Tyne, in the National Security League, and Caroline Bartlett Crane, head of the women's work in the State, and many others, who gave their time and talent in an effort to foster and sustain a spirit of cooperation and unity.

In the World War the colleges played a more important rôle than in any previous war—a result of the tremendous growth and expansion of the colleges and universities in the last half century. Not only did the alumni and students furnish the leaders in the preparation for and prosecution of the war, but the colleges themselves become nuclei from which radiated the influences necessary to sustain the war spirit and in which were carried on the scientific activities essential to the successful prosecution of a modern war. Thus, during the war, the university and the colleges of Michigan were transformed from a peace basis to a war basis, and the curricula revised to meet the exigencies of the time, by the introduction of courses on causes of the war, food conservation and substitutes, nursing, military training, naval engineering, etc. So complete was the transformation that by the close of 1918, when the Students' Army Training Corps had been introduced, the university and colleges presented the appearance of armed camps rather than institutions of learning.

This transformation of the higher institutions was inevitably reflected in the high schools and graded systems. By legislative enactment, military training was made compulsory in high schools where classes of 20 or more made application for that subject. Such organizations as the Junior Red Cross and the Boys' Working Reserve were all-inclusive of the public-school system, and demand for instruction made it necessary that the State department of public instruction supply a special course of lessons upon the great war, thus disseminating much historical information throughout the State and rendering public opinion more enlightened and resolved. By such methods public opinion was thoroughly aroused and sentiment so crystallized around the "win the war" effort that the State readily responded to every call made upon it in the struggle.

The most important agency, both as regards the prosecution of the war and the collection, compilation, and preservation of historical material relating to the war, has been the Michigan War Preparedness Board, created by legislative enactment April 18, 1917, with the duty of assuming general control and management of all war operations within the State. By this act the war preparedness board was to consist of Gov. Albert E. Sleeper, chairman; Attorney General Alex. A. Groesbeck; Auditor General Oramel B. Fuller; State Treasurer Samuel Odell; Secretary of State Coleman C. Vaughan; and Superintendent of Public Instruction Thomas E. Johnson (successor to Fred L. Keeler, deceased). '

Diversified and engrossing as were the duties of this board, yet it found time to provide for the historical interests of the State. Provision was made for the collection of war records of the soldiers and sailors from their respective counties and for collecting and preserving the records of civilian activities relating to the war. Through the cooperation and courtesy of the Michigan Historical Commission and the Michigan Pioneer and Historical Society, the services of their joint secretary, Dr. George Newman Fuller, were secured by the war board to take charge of collecting the material and of publishing a history of Michigan in the Great War.

Coeval with the activities of the war preparedness board the Michigan Historical Commission had been organizing the work of collecting and preserving the material relating to the war, both ephemeral and documentary. The Michigan History Magazine, published quarterly by the commission, had special articles giving publicity to the drive for historical material, and a carefully prepared bulletin (No. 10) containing a detailed plan for collecting material in the various counties, together with an outline for county histories, was widely distributed throughout the State.

The method of collecting the material has been to organize the county as a unit, enlisting the cooperation of the local historical societies and various social and patriotic organizations, such as the women's clubs, the Daughters of the American Revolution, the Grand Army of the Republic, together with the schools and libraries, and, where possible, the lodges, churches, and business men's organizations. The material is brought to a central depository in the county, usually a public library at the county seat, where it is classified and filed for preservation. In this way the spirit of local interest and pride has been made productive along historical lines and much material that would otherwise be lost has been saved from destruction and made available for the future historian of the war.

MINNESOTA.

By WILLIAM STEARNS DAVIS, Department of History, University of Minnesota
and FRANKLIN F. HOLBROOK, Secretary of the Minnesota War Records Commission.

When America entered the World War it is probable that only
in two or three States of the Union were there larger elements which
misdoubted the need of belligerent action, and which for varying
motives preached " neutrality," than were present in Minnesota.
This was not entirely due to the existence of a large German population. The State was remote from any possible scene of hostilities; the chief economic interests centered around agriculture, and
international problems, dangers, and duties were very vague in the
minds of many entirely patriotic citizens. The moment, therefore,
that Congress declared war, and indeed for some months earlier,
as it became clearer that we must participate in the European struggle, the obligation of social science teachers in the colleges and universities of the State was plain—to assist in teaching their fellow
citizens the awful seriousness of the world crisis and the unavoid-
ability of our playing a manly part in it.

Thus, in the faculties of the private institutions, Prof. John D.
Hicks, of Hamline University, published numerous articles on war
issues, gave patriotic lectures and conducted with success the Students' Army Training Corps war aims courses in his institution.
Similar important services were rendered by Prof. Henry D. Funk,
of Macalester College; and Prof. James Howard Robinson, of Carleton College, was on the board of lectureship for the National Security League and conducted the Students' Army Training Corps
war aims work at Northfield, while his assistant, Mr. Henry R.
Mueller, was privileged to render active military service in France
during the war period.

At the University of Minnesota very soon after the declaration
of war a conference was held of the active members of the history
and political science departments, at which it was agreed to undertake systematically a campaign of patriotic education throughout
the State. The keynote of the conference was that it was criminal
to ask citizens to make heavy economic sacrifices, and, very possibly,
themselves to fight and die, unless every possible means were taken
to convince them of the justice and necessity of our joining in the
struggle. It was arranged to prepare an annotated edition of President Wilson's War Message, explaining all the historical and diplomatic allusions in a form capable of very general circulation.
The manuscript of this annotated edition was ready in April from
the pens of Profs. C. D. Allin and William Anderson, of the po-

litical science department, and William Stearns Davis, of the history department; but before it could be printed locally it was taken by the Federal Committee on Public Information at Washington. By them it was published officially as the first in their much circulated War Information Series under the title "The War Message and the Facts Behind It," the alterations and additions to the original draft being very few.

This publication was merely the forerunner of a number of patriotic, informational documents prepared by members of the State university faculty. In May, 1917, Dean Guy S. Ford, of the graduate school, was summoned to Washington as director of the civic and educational division of the Committee on Public Information. He remained at this important post for the duration of the war. It is not too much to say that he was responsible for an extremely large fraction of all the undeniable successes which the committee achieved, and that he was never associated with any of those discussions which arose around some by-products of that well-known organization. The departure of Dean Ford was the beginning of an exodus from the university faculty, which sometimes made the prosecution of the prosaic but indispensable historical teaching work something of a problem.

At the request of the Minnesota State Public Safety Commission a popular handbook was prepared, mainly by the social science departments, in June, 1917—"Facts About the War"—a brochure of some 60 pages, containing brief concrete articles calculated to supply patriotic speakers with handy, specific information on such matters as "Submarine aggressions," "Conscription v. the volunteer system," "The Pan-German dream," "The Belgian deportations," etc. The pamphlet was in such request that it was soon reprinted, and a good many of the articles were also reprinted in their own speaker's handbook, issued by the South Carolina State Council of Defense.

In the fall of 1917 Prof. A. C. Krey, of the department of history, went to Washington and devoted considerable time rendering effective service in the preparation of the pamphlet, "German War Practices," which was issued under the editorship of Dr. Dana C. Munro, of Princeton, by the Committee on Public Information, and which ranked among the most effective documents issued during that time of ardor.

Prof. Wallace Notestein, of the department of history, in collaboration with his colleague, Dr. Elmer Stoll, of the English department, about the same time, published through the same committee, first, an annotated edition of "The President's Flag Day Oration (June 14, 1917)," and then a fairly elaborate volume, "Conquest and

Kultur: Aims of the Germans in Their Own Words." In the fir[
pamphlet they had the assistance of Profs. William Anderson ar[
A. C. Krey; in the second that of Profs. Anderson and Mason W[
Tyler, also two or three other scholars in sister institutions. Th[
last-named compilation, prepared with learning and scrupulo[
accuracy, was widely reprinted in the newspapers of the country.

Prof. Notestein was then given leave of absence from the Unive[
sity of Minnesota for the duration of the war. He worked mainly c[
Col. House's "Inquiry" of experts to prepare data against th[
negotiation of peace, dealing chiefly with the problem of Alsac[
Lorraine; subsequently he went to Paris in 1919 and occupied a di[
tinguished position on the American Commission to Negotiate Peac[
as "chief of the German section." Prof. Mason W. Tyler als[
conducted investigations and prepared reports for the House "I[
quiry," his field being the Balkans and the Adriatic.

While these gentlemen were serving the cause away from th[
campus the "common task" went on for their less fortunate co[
leagues, handling a student body, which, if it somewhat lost i[
numbers, still remained large and replete with exacting problem[
The history department was administered in the absence of Dea[
Ford, by Prof. A. B. White; and in September, 1918, he unde[
took the arduous duty of director and organizer for the "war aims[
work of the Students' Army Training Corps, when suddenly son[
4,000 students, many of them with exceedingly fragmentary notior[
of human annals, had to be put through an adequate course i[
what amounted to the history of Europe for the past 40 year[
Thanks to Dr. White a sufficient corps of instructors were assen[
bled, library facilities mobilized, and a very disjointed body c[
student soldiers set at systematic problems. The Students' Arm[
Training Corps in this university showed the vicissitudes of th[
same undertaking in other institutions, but it is right to assert c[
the "war aims" work that it genuinely gave to the pupils a grea[
deal; that many of them left the university with clear notions c[
scientific history, as well as a mass of patriotic propaganda; and th[
the success of the "war aims" course was attested by the fact th[
after the Students' Army Training Corps was disbanded man[
students who had attended by compulsion while in khaki cheerfull[
elected history when they continued their studies by free choice.

Nearly all the other members of the history and political scienc[
groups found opportunities for something more than the classroor[
routine. Profs. C. D. Allin and William Anderson, of the politic[
science department, gave numerous patriotic addresses and taugh[
Students' Army Training Corps classes in "war aims." Pro[
Jeremiah Young, of the same department, besides similar service, d[
rected and organized special courses of study in European problem[

especially available for teacher's institutes, in several States of the Northwest. He also acted as district inspector in the Students' Army Training Corps.

In the history department Prof. L. B. Shippee taught several sections in the "war aims" work and contributed to the handbook on diplomatic history published by the Government under the chief direction of Prof. Frank M. Anderson, of Dartmouth College. Prof. Mason W. Tyler cooperated in these same forms of work. In addition he assisted the Committee on Public Information in the preparation of several of its pamphlets, and did not a little to assemble material on many significant diplomatic subjects for Col. House's "Inquiry" and Prof. F. M. Anderson's handbook on foreign relations before mentioned. Prof. Solon J. Buck, besides his large services through the Minnesota Historical Society, elsewhere referred to, gave public addresses and taught a class in "war aims" during the Students' Army Training Corps epoch. Prof. N. S. B. Gras was instructor in a similar course; and prior to his coming to Minnesota, in the fall of 1918, he had been research assistant in the War Trade Board at Washington, busied chiefly with the details of American trade with Italy and the British Empire.

Finally may be mentioned the work of Prof. William S. Davis, who, in addition to teaching in the Students' Army Training Corps work, wrote, in collaboration with Profs. William Anderson and Mason W. Tyler, already named, "The Roots of the War—a Nontechnical History of Europe, 1870–1914." This book was published in May, 1918, by the Century Co., at the suggestion of the Committee of Public Information. It enjoyed considerable circulation in civilian reading circles and military libraries, and was adopted by about 50 colleges and universities as their textbook in the Students' Army Training Corps.

From the very beginning of American participation in the war the Minnesota Historical Society has been active in the collection of local war history material, but for some time the burden of this work has rested upon a separate, though closely affiliated, agency—the Minnesota War Records Commission.

This commission was created provisionally, at the suggestion and with the cooperation of the historical society, by the Minnesota Commission of Public Safety in October, 1918, and was established by law the following April. Its primary object is to collect and preserve, in State and county war records, collections, all available material relating to Minnesota's part in the war. The commission acts through its immediate representatives, which include a field agent; through voluntary county war records committees, which have been organized in all parts of the States; and with the cooperation of other State departments and organizations, including the American

Legion. The work of the central body is financed by the State at the rate of $5,000 a year during the present biennium, 1919–1921, while the county committees draw their support from county boards and other local governing bodies, which are specially authorized by law to appropriate funds for local war record purposes in amounts ranging from $250 for villages and $1,000 for counties to $5,000 for cities of the first class.

One of the commission's aims is to compile and collect records of the individual services of all Minnesota soldiers, sailors, marines, Army welfare workers, and leaders in civilian war work, and to duplicate these records so far as possible in the State and county collections. For this purpose use is made of a series of appropriate blank forms, or questionnaires. The usual means are taken to reach members of the various groups under canvass, but in the case of the largest group, the service men, the commission has enjoyed an exceptional advantage. In the fall of 1919 the legislature granted a cash bonus to these men and created a body known as the soldiers' bonus board to raise and distribute the funds allowed for this purpose. At the suggestion of the war records commission the board included the commission's military service record form among the blanks which every applicant for the State bonus is required to fill out. As a result the commission has received through the bonus board upward of 80,000 completed service records, and there is every prospect that the arrangement will result in the recording of rather complete data on the careers of most Minnesota men in the service. In addition to such formal statements of service, the commission seeks, and in many instances has obtained, from service men and others supplementary material, such as photographs, letters, citations, and other personal records. From a number of individuals prominent in different lines of activity the commission has obtained, through personal solicitation, private collections of material which is valuable not only for its personal associations, but also for its contributions to various phases of the history of State and national participation in the war.

Other material acquired for the State collection relates to the history of organized or group activities conducted on a State-wide basis or otherwise of interest to the State as a whole. Books and printed matter assembled by the commission and the historical society include histories of military units, county war histories, files of local newspapers and of camp and overseas publications, and numerous collections of the printed and other miscellany which formed a part of the working paraphernalia of every prominent war organization. Another class of material secured consists of unpublished reports and narrative accounts covering the work of leading State and local war agencies, including Minnesota county chapters of the American Red Cross, State and local branches of the Food Administration, the University of Minnesota, and the State branch of the Fuel Administration. In the course of the personal canvass which has yielded much of the foregoing material, special efforts have been made to secure the custody of the headquarters files of official correspondence and papers of the various war agencies active in the State. Considerable bodies of such records have already been received from the Minnesota branches of national agencies, such as the United States Employment Service, Woman's Committee of the National Council of Defense, Y. M. C. A. War Council, Jewish Welfare Board, American Library Association, and War Camp Community Service; from State agencies, such as the department of home economics of the State agricultural college and the Americanization committee of the Minnesota Commission of Public Safety; from local agencies, such as councils of home defense, Liberty loan committees, recruiting agents, and Boy Scouts; and negotiations for other similar bodies of original records are in progress. To the collection of battlefield relics, motion-picture films, photographs, posters, and other mementoes of the war period assembled in the historical museum, the commission has been able to make notable additions.

The county committees of the commission are asked to collect the war records of their several communities in accordance with suggestions outlined in bulletins entitled "A State-wide Movement for the Collection and Preservation of Minnesota's War Records" and "County War History: Prospectus and Guide to the Collection of Material," the latter being issued in mimeographed form. The work of the committees is directed for the most part at long range through the medium of these bulletins and of circular letters and correspondence, though State workers have had personal conferences, either at State headquarters or in their home communities, with some 25 of the local leaders. Widely varying degrees of interest and efficiency are shown by the local organizations, but it may be stated that, taken as a whole, the committees are accumulating considerable material of value, and that committees here and there throughout the State will undoubtedly see the work through. A number of the committees in rural counties have obtained from their county boards the legal maximum of $1,000 and the city of St. Paul has granted to its county committee the sum of $5,000. These committees and others which have secured smaller sums have their own letterheads, printed circulars, and blank forms, and a number employ paid secretaries or clerks. Ten committees have decided, upon their own motion, not only to gather the counties' war records, but to prepare and publish county war histories. One of the most active committees, reporting in November, 1919, had compiled complete lists of service men, Gold Star men, Red

Cross nurses, and others in war service from the county; secured service records and photographs from about 75 per cent of these men and women; collected group photographs of all draft contingents National Guard companies, and local war-work committees; made transcripts of practically all of the records of the local draft board (except questionnaires) before the originals were sent to Washington; and assembled more or less complete files of reports and original records representing the activities of practically all the leading local war agencies. All the committees are encouraged to build up collections of material for preservation in the counties, and to send in for the State collection such duplicate material as can readily be secured or provided.

When the State commission was established as a statutory body it was directed not only to collect material but also "to provide for the preparation and publication, as a permanent memorial record, of a comprehensive documentary and narrative history of the part played by the State in the World War, including conditions and events within the State relating to or affected by the war; and also for the preparation and publication of a condensed narrative of Minnesota's part in the war, suitable for distribution to the soldiers and sailors from the State in recognition of their services to the Commonwealth." A tentative plan for the proposed comprehensive history, previously submitted in a bulletin entitled "Minnesota's Part in the War; Shall it be Adequately Recorded?" contemplated a 10-volume work, consisting of three volumes giving brief individual mention of all service men and leading civilian war workers of the State; one volume containing biographical sketches and portraits of the men who lost their lives in the service; three volumes of important, typical, and interesting documents of the period; and three volumes presenting in a series of historical narratives the story of the State's war service in all its various phases. But the realization of this, or of any other plan of publication which the commission may adopt, awaits the granting of more adequate funds by the legislature. In the meantime the commission is devoting its energies to the more immediately important task of collecting material.

MISSISSIPPI.

The following letter was received from the director of the Department of Archives and History:

JACKSON, MISS., *March 8, 1920.*

Mr. NEWTON D. MERENESS,
  Washington, D. C.

MY DEAR MR. MERENESS: I am in receipt of your appeal to the various historical agencies to join you in a cooperative plan for the preparation of an account of historical activities in the United States during the recent war. At present all available funds in this department are used in local historical work for the collection and classification of materials relating to the war. We wish, first, to get all our local material collected and in shape before going further.

Regretting that we are not in a position to join you, and with kind regard, I am,

Sincerely, yours,

DUNBAR ROWLAND.

MISSOURI.

By FLOYD C. SHOEMAKER, Secretary of the State Historical Society of Missouri.

Historical research for increasing the fund of historical knowledge regarding questions pertaining to the war was confined to magazine and newspaper articles, if exception is made of the voluminous literature published by State institutions, boards, and organizations of a purely utilitarian character, and if further exception is made in the case of all research that is nonhistorical. By strict criticism exception might also be well taken in the case even of newspapers, but such a criticism could hardly apply to some of the journalistic productions. The Missouri Historical Review, published by the State Historical Society of Missouri, carried a series of articles, beginning in April, 1917, on "Missouri and the War." This series was not concluded until July, 1919. The articles were written in a popular style, but were based upon historical research. They summarized the questions pertaining to the war as far as they concerned Missouri, and summarized the activities of Missouri in connection with these questions.

A large percentage of public-spirited and educated citizens of Missouri contributed articles for publication in newspapers and periodicals for the diffusion of historical information necessary to enlighten public opinion regarding the issues of the war. These contributions were, however, not necessarily more extensive or valuable than those which appeared in the newspapers and periodicals of other States. It was part of the patriotic spirit of the times to perform this service. The result was thousands of contributed articles of this character.

The circulation of books and periodicals containing historical information was largely under the control and direction of the Missouri Library Commission at Jefferson City, acting through the public libraries of the State. The most important agencies were the university library and the large public libraries in St. Louis, Kansas City, and St. Joseph. Special mention should also be made regarding this character of work of the five State teachers' college libraries and also the denominational college libraries.

Lectures on historical subjects were either under the control and direction of patriotic organizations or educational institutions. Of the latter, special mention should be made of the University of Missouri and the five State teachers' colleges.

Cooperation between the State council of defense and the State Historical Society of Missouri was very close. It resulted in the former body placing all of its correspondence and records, both public and private, on deposit with the historical society.

War histories under preparation during the war relating to the organization and operation of different branches of war service were confined to reports of State boards having direct connection with such service, such as the Report of the Missouri Council of Defense for 1917, 1918, and 1919, published by the State of Missouri in 1919, and the proposed report of Adjutant General Harvey C. Clark, State of Missouri, on the complete roster of Missouri men in service.

The collection and preservation of war records have been undertaken by two agencies, the adjutant general's office in Jefferson City and the State Historical Society of Missouri, Columbia. The former has confined its activities to soldier records, enlisting in this work citizens in each of the counties of the State and in the city of St. Louis, and enlisting also the services of the Missouri Historical Society. The State Historical Society of Missouri has confined its activities to the collection and preservation of the published reports of volunteer organizations, ephemeral war literature, such as posters, circulars, etc., records of Missouri casualties, embracing personal histories of each casualty, the records of the State council of defense, and copies of reports of State-wide volunteer war organizations.

There is no work in preparation covering the history of the State's participation in the war. This matter has, to a large extent, been met by the articles which appeared in the Missouri Historical Review during the progress of the war. A number of county histories, however, have been produced, or are in process of compilation. Some of these are commercialized projects; others are genuine county war histories.

MONTANA.

By PAUL C. PHILLIPS, of the Department of History and Political Science, University of Montana.

Historical activities in Montana in connection with the war amount to practically nothing. There was no historical research. With regard to the diffusion of historical information necessary to enlighten public opinion there were about the usual number of articles appearing in newspapers. Most of the articles, however, were syndicate matter and unsigned. I personally wrote several articles while I was in Washington, and these were published in a number of Montana newspapers. The libraries furnished a good many books regarding the war, and a number of people took correspondence courses on subjects relating to the war. The university extension department offered a number of lectures on such topics as "The Nations of the War," throughout the State, while the war was going on. The university offered in the summer time a special course on the historical background of the war and the war itself. The course on the historical background of the war was very similar to the course on war issues offered to the Students' Army Training Corps. Nothing has been done to collect and preserve a record of the war.

NEBRASKA.

Information supplied by the Secretary, of the Nebraska State Historical Society.

The secretary of the Nebraska State Historical Society was overseas during the war, acting in the capacity of a war correspondent. He brought home files of European newspapers, pamphlets, war handbills and posters, and museum material. The society has received the records of the State council of defense and is still collecting manuscript and other material for future book publications. Several county histories have already appeared, and two or three of them are of real merit. An appropriation of $7,000 for war-record and war-history work was made by one branch of the legislature in 1919, but was cut out in conference committee.

NEVADA.

By JEANNE WIER, Secretary of the Nevada Historical Society.

1. Historical research and the production of books for increasing the fund of historical knowledge regarding questions pertaining to the war: No publication of books; some research work conducted by Nevada Historical Society.

2. The diffusion of historical information necessary to an enlightened public opinion regarding the issues of the war:

(a) By the contribution of articles for publication in newspapers and periodicals: "Why America is in the war," by President Walter E. Clark, University of Nevada; "Who is it that rules Germany," by Charles W. Spencer, professor of political science, University of Nevada; "What Germany wants," by Jeanne Elizabeth Wier, professor of history, University of Nevada. All of the above were printed in the Reno Evening Gazette, March 11 to April 1, 1918.

(b) By promoting the circulation of books and periodicals containing important historical information: Library of the Nevada Historical Society containing war literature was open to the public. The department of history in the University of Nevada constantly cited its students to such articles.

(c) By lectures: A series of lectures was given by members of the university faculty at the Reno high school. Prof. Romanzo Adams spoke on the economic causes of the war on March 27, 1918.

(*d*) By teaching in schools and colleges: The history department
in cooperation with the economics department at the University of
Nevada gave a three-hour course on war history, for one semester,
to the Students' Army Training Corps. Dr. Romanzo Adams, of
the economics department, gave one-third of the lectures, and Asst.
Professor Feemster, of the history department, gave the remainder.
Prof. R. C. Thompson and Prof. Jeanne Elizabeth Wier assisted
with the quiz sections, and were to have delivered the later lectures
of the course had it not been discontinued with the first semester.

. 3. Cooperation with the State council of defense, etc. The Nevada
Historical Society acted as the historical division of the council of
defense.

4. Preparation during the war of histories of the organization
and operation of different branches of war service: Nothing completed though beginnings were made.

. 5. Collection and preservation of war records: Nevada Historical
Society has gathered much material.

6. Preparation for an early history of State's participation in the
War: The Nevada Legislature of 1919 appropriated $5,000 for col-
lecting and writing its war history, and $2,000 for the printing of
the same. Work assigned to secretary of the Nevada Historical
Society, Jeanne Elizabeth Wier.

NEW HAMPSHIRE.

This report was prepared from a letter by RICHARD WELLINGTON HUSBAND,
associate dean, Dartmouth College.

In August, 1917, Mr. R. W. Husband was appointed State war historian by the New Hampshire Committee on Public Safety. His duties
were twofold: first, to write a narrative of the activities during the
war period of the committee on public safety and of its eighteen subcommittees; second, to compile the service record of all persons of New
Hampshire who were in the military or naval forces of the United
States and its allies. The first part of the task is completed and
ready for the press; the second is nearing completion. New Hampshire had approximately 23,000 persons in the service, and Mr. Husband has succeeded so far in securing the service record of over
20,000 of them. All material for this record has been collected by
voluntary workers in each town and city of the State. During the
war Mr. Husband, on various occasions, published articles in the
newspapers and elsewhere giving some account of New Hampshire's
progress in meeting its obligations at the close of the war. He published an article in the Granite Monthly on "The Wartime Temper
of the State."

The history of the New Hampshire Food Administration has been written by James W. Tucker and Prof. Richard Whorisky, and is an excellent record of what was done by Huntley N. Spaulding, Federal food administrator for New Hampshire, and his associates.

Prof. Frank M. Anderson, of Dartmouth College, was commissioned to prepare a thoroughgoing account of diplomatic relations of the United States from about the year 1870. He accompanied the Peace Commission to Paris as expert advisor in American diplomatic relations.

The New Hampshire Historical Society, acting upon the recommendation of the State war historian, has voted to apply to the State government for an appropriation necessary to secure possession of all documents still existing in the State which tell of the various war activities.

NEW MEXICO.

By LANSING B. BLOOM, Secretary of the State Historical Service.

The State Historical Service of New Mexico, consisting of a board of three members, was organized in August, 1917, for the purpose of gathering and compiling the war records of the State. A secretary, under salary, took charge of the office October 1, and quarters were furnished by the State museum.

In 18 of the 26 counties representative men and women accepted positions as "county historians" and some of them have given very effective help to the historical service. In other counties cooperation has been given by units of the Red Cross home service and the American Legion and by various individuals.

It was decided that the historical service should secure, among other data, the records of the men in military service, and accordingly one of the first tasks undertaken was to card-index every man who entered service from New Mexico. So far as possible this was done from official sources of information, but the data thus secured were a relatively small part of the information gradually gathered and entered on the records of these men. Some sixty daily and weekly papers of the State supplied their issues to the historical service during the war-period; everything of historical value was blue-penciled, and the papers were filed chronologically for preservation and for reference as needed. The great mass of data on all lines of civilian activities during the war has not yet been digested, but before the papers were filed every item on the men in miltary service was entered on the proper index card. As a result the usual experience is that, when a former officer or enlisted man asks to see his record in the archives, he is surprised at the completeness and correctness of the information already entered.

These military records have been further supplemented, however, by a special record-blank, printed in the fall of 1919 and sent out to every man in the index. Of these about 25 per cent have been returned undelivered, which corresponds favorably with the reported 33 per cent which the Federal authorities have been unable to reach at their home addresses. Some 4,500 have been filled out and sent back, accompanied by unmounted pictures, and these have been filed individually in fireproof cases. Original letters and copies and miscellaneous papers are placed in their respective files. Many of the men have not yet sent in their records, but forms are continually coming in, and it is hoped with the cooperation of local agencies ultimately to have this part of the records very complete.

As soon as casualties were reported, correspondence was taken up with relatives or friends. Of the 456 who died in service, or directly from disabilities incurred in service, pictures of 398 and complete records of nearly all are in the archives, and the rest are being obtained gradually, though in some cases with great difficulty and after long search. Copies of the pictures, in uniform size and with names in gummed lettering, are being placed in fixed frames under glass on the walls of the memorial room in the old palace of the governors, and similar copies accompanied by biographical sketches will complete the "Book of Gold," which lies on the table. Still other copies have been sent to the relatives, as well as more than 300 enlargements furnished at cost. This photographic record alone represents an outlay in labor and materials of approximately $2,000, or an average of $5 for each man of whom a picture has been secured. Three large tablets placed on the walls of the memorial room show, in six long columns, the names and home addresses of all who died in service; and a framed map, indicating the counties in outline, shows by gold stars the total that died from each county. In glass cases are displayed a valuable aggregation of war souvenirs, including both loans and gifts to the State museum. The number of these is steadily growing, as men who served turn in documents, histories of units, souvenirs, and curios which they brought back from the front.

The value of the State's war archives has already been demonstrated repeatedly, and a few instances may be cited. Last summer the father of one who died in service lost all his possessions by fire, including all records relating to his son; but he received from the historical service a transcript of the data in the archives and a copy of the picture which he had first loaned. Relatives of a Santa Fe county man who died after discharge lost the papers necessary to secure the bonus due them, and the War Department could not locate his record. He was found indexed in the State office and his identity established. Lists and information have been supplied to various units of the Red Cross home service, and of the American Legion, to the Federal Office for Vocational Training, to State and county offices in connection with tax exemption.

Similar indexes and records of civilians and their part in the war might be built up, if an adequate office force and the necessary funds were provided, by digesting the great mass of material already in the archives and by gathering in the records now scattered all over the State.

In January, 1919, a preliminary history of New Mexico in the Great War was prepared in manuscript, with illustrations, but a combination of circumstances prevented its intended publication. Four chapters, however, appear in the 1919 Blue Book.

The historical service, having been left without funds in January, 1920, was formally transferred to the State museum in April of that year.

NEW YORK.

The information in this report was furnished by JAMES SULLIVAN, State Historian and Director of the Division of Archives and History.

Several members of the University of the State of New York delivered lectures in various cities and villages of the State, sometimes under the auspices of the local historical or patriotic societies, and at other times as agents of the Committee on Public Information or in behalf of the Liberty loans, to make clear to the people the issues at stake. The people chosen for this work were naturally those from the history field, as it was a work which came in their particular bailiwick.

The Division of Archives and History, along with the State library, did a considerable amount in the matter of making selections of books to be distributed to the libraries throughout the State on subjects pertaining to the World War. It also undertook to distribute to historical societies and others the numerous pamphlets which were sent to it by the Committee on Public Information. Exhibitions were given in the State library at Albany and also in local libraries of this kind of material. Special shelves were set aside in the high school and other libraries of the State, and pamphlets relating to the war placed thereon.

By means of the University Bulletin, which is issued to all of the schools of New York State twice a month, lists of books and material of a patriotic nature were got together by the division of archives and history and placed in the hands of the teachers for the purpose of encouraging them to convey to their pupils the full information with reference to the objects for which the war was being fought.

The division cooperated with the State council of defense, and the head of it, at the request of the adjutant general and the governor, made a tour in certain sections of the State during what was known as "Wake-up America week." The division also cooperated with the same body and with the Department of Justice of the United States in making certain translations of correspondence and other papers which were taken from aliens and others.

Within a few days after the declaration of war on the part of the United States circular letters were sent out from the division to the 110 historical societies of the State; to all of the 750 libraries; to the corresponding number of school libraries; to patriotic societies, such as the Daughters of the American Revolution and the Sons of the American Revolution; to chambers of commerce; to certain individuals; and to town, county, village, and city clerks, urging upon them the extreme desirability of starting a collection of all kinds of material listed under categories similar to those indicated by the National Board for Historical Service. A correspondence was also carried on with the chairmen of the county councils of defense, subordinate branches of the State council of defense, along similar lines. Many of those appealed to undertook this work with a considerable degree of enthusiasm, but very many were so pressed with other duties of the war service that very little was done. The Y. M. C. A. and Red Cross were petitioned to have accounts prepared of their work in New York State. Some of this is still underway. The material which has been gathered has in some cases been transmitted to the State library for classification and preservation, and in other cases the local library, particularly when it is in a fireproof building, has retained the local material.

The Senate and the Assembly of the State passed a resolution in April, 1919, calling upon the division to prepare a history of New York State's participation in the World War. To assist in the collection of this material the Legislature also passed a law calling for the appointments of local historians in each political unit of the State. About 50 per cent of these have so far been duly chosen and have been set to work to gather material of interest for this history. In some localities the political division has already published the results of these investigations; the city of Buffalo may be cited as an example. In some counties—Chautauqua for example—there has been undertaken a history of the county's participation in the World War by a commercial publishing company. Similarly in some cities commercial agencies have undertaken this work; namely, in Albany.

Paragraphs 1198 and 1199 of the act are as follows:

A local historian shall be appointed, as provided in this section, for each city, town, or village, except a city of over 1,000,000 inhabitants. Such local historian shall be appointed as follows: For a city, by the mayor; for a town, by the supervisor; for a village, by the president of the board of trustees. Such historian shall serve without compensation, unless the governing board of the city, town, or village for which he or she was appointed, shall otherwise provide. In a city having a board of estimate and apportionment a resolution or ordinance establishing compensation or salary for such historian shall not take effect without the concurrence of such board. The local authorities of the city, town, or village for which such historian is appointed may provide the historian with sufficient space in a safe, vault, or other fireproof structure for the preservation of materials collected.

It shall be the duty of each local historian, appointed as provided in the last section, in cooperation with the State historian, to collect and preserve material relating to the history of the political subdivision for which he or she is appointed, and to file such material in fireproof safes or vaults in the city, town, or village offices. Such historian shall examine into the condition, classification, and safety from fire of the public records of the pubic offices of such city, town, or village, and shall call to the attention of the local authorities and the State historian any material of local historic value which should be acquired for preservation. He or she shall make an annual report, in the month of January to the local appointing officer or officers and to the State historian of the work which has been accomplished during the preceding year. He or she shall, upon retirement or removal from office, turn over to the local city, town, or village authorities, or to his successor in office, if one has been then appointed, all materials gathered during his or her incumbancy and all correspondence relating thereto. The State historian, at regular intervals, not less than once a year, shall indicate to the local historians the general lines along which local history material is to be collected.

So far as this State is concerned there seems to be a disposition to turn to the historians for expert guidance along the lines indicated in the questionnaire. The historical and patriotic societies of the State, under the urging by the division, seemed to feel that it was their particular duty to see that the historian undertook the work of conducting the publicity in such a fashion as to make the population a unit in its opinion about the conduct of the war. Though this was but a natural line of activity, too much tribute can not be paid to the work of these bodies in placing before the public the facts that made the people whole-hearted in their support of the Government.

NORTH CAROLINA.

By ROBERT BURTON HOUSE, Collector of war records, North Carolina Historical Commission.

During the years 1917, 1918, and 1919 history exerted a vital, practical force in North Carolina, resulting in a more intelligent and effective effort to win the war by the people of the State and in a renewed and deepened appreciation of history. The study, teaching, and writing of history, and the preservation of historical material manifest a renewed and varied activity to-day because of the service rendered by history during these years.

History served both to form opinion for war and to conduct th
war. Even while it was yet a European struggle the war force
itself more and more insistently on the people of North Carolin
as a problem on which to inform themselves and take sides. Neu
trality of opinion rapidly became impossible. History, both pas
and contemporary, formed the subject matter of their consideratio
during this period of forming opinions. The entry of the Unite
States into the struggle found the people enthusiastically in suppor
of this action, but unready for it. History then became the guide t
organization and action. Historians not only furnished historica
information to the people of the State as a guide to action, but als
themselves, in many instances, directed action as executives. By
teaching, writing, speaking, and doing specific pieces of war work
they put both history and historians squarely into the war.

Naturally, therefore, history retains to-day in large measure the
interest, importance, and support which it gained during the years
of the war. A larger proportion of the people of North Carolina
study history now than before the war. More fields of historic in
terest are being explored now than before the war; and institutions
both for teaching and for preserving history receive increased
support.

Enthusiastic support by them of the war as a national undertak
ing engendered in the people a desire to know more about America
as a nation, about American national ideals in particular; for the
utter repudiation of opposing national ideals brought out a positive
assertion of our own. Study of American national ideals led nat
urally to consideration of the national ideals of the whole race of
English-speaking peoples. Citizens of the State, both in the schools
and colleges, and outside of them, formed clubs to study and per
petuate American and British national ideals and traditions.

To furnish materials for this study two books appeared through
the research and industry of four professors in the University of
North Carolina: American Ideals, by Norman Foerster and W. W.
Pierson (Boston, Houghton, Mifflin & Co., 1917), and The Great
Tradition, by Edwin Greenlaw and J. H. Hanford (Chicago, Scott,
1919). American Ideals brings together in one volume the great
expressions of American national ideals from the earliest times to
the present. The Great Tradition includes within one volume the
national ideals of all English-speaking people from the earliest
times to the present. Supplementing these books and giving addi
tional vital information, the following books appeared from the
pens of North Carolinians or in North Carolina: The Nation at
War, A. B. Scherer (New York, Doran, 1918); Our War with Ger
many, J. S. Bassett (New York, Knopf, 1919); The Navy and the
Nation, War Time Addresses, Josephus Daniels (New York, Doran,

1919); Builders of Democracy, Edwin Greenlaw (Chicago, Scott, 1918); and Bulletin No. 25 of the North Carolina Historical Commission (Raleigh, Edwards & Broughton, 1919), a series of papers on Anglo-American relations designed to be read at Raleigh at the Tercentenary of Sir Walter Raleigh in 1918. The celebration of the tercentenary was prevented by the influenza epidemic, however.

Because of the rural nature of North Carolina, and the consequent isolation of families and sections from the currents of enthusiasm and information so strong in more urban States, the newspaper, the church, the school, the public speaker, and the library were vital factors in disseminating information and forming opinion. Through these agencies historians exerted their greatest influence. There is not a paper, a church, a school, or a college in North Carolina that did not radiate their influence. The speakers' bureau for the Liberty loans, publicity for chapters of the Red Cross, and other forms of publicity service, were directed by Mr. R. D. W. Connor, secretary of the North Carolina Historical Commission. All the colleges of the State sent professors out to speak on the war. The University of North Carolina, through its Bureau of Extension, gave a war information service of nation-wide usefulness. By extension study centers, group lectures, correspondence courses, single lectures, readers' service through the library, and a series of war information leaflets, it reached every corner of the State with vital information. The service rendered by the other colleges of the State was of a nature similar to that of the University of North Carolina, but not so extensive. Every library in the State had to expand its service to meet the unprecedented demands for material on the war. All of the college libraries sent out packets of books and pamphlets upon request.

The formal teaching of history in those colleges maintaining a Students' Army Training Corps suffered a slump, however, in 1918. The Students' Army Training Corps courses forced academic students to revise their regular courses, and because history was one of the easiest subjects to defer till normal times, in practically all the colleges of the State, history was deferred in favor of military science. This slump in the usual courses was compensated for in some degree by the large attendance on the war issues and war aims courses of the Students' Army Training Corps. Moreover, all academic classes expanded in some way to include an interpretation of the war. One popular method was by keeping a bulletin board of information. Since the war, however, history seems to be regaining its attendance with interest. All of the leading institutions of North Carolina have modified their American and modern European history courses to interpret the war. And in addition they offer courses in contemporary American history, inter-American relations, new diplomacy, origins of the Triple Alliance, American foreign policy, causes and outcome of the World War. There is also manifested an increasing interest in Hispanic-American history.

The full power of this historical service was therefore behind the State council of defense and all the war-work organizations. Dr. D. H. Hill, himself a historian, turned from his work of years (the preparation of a history of North Carolina in the Civil War) to direct the North Carolina Council of Defense. Not only did the historians in the State throw their influence behind the great financial drives, but contributed largely to them personally both in money and in direction. Practically all the colleges of the State were 100 per cent contributors to war finance and war charity. Practically all of them sent several members of their faculties into whole-time war work.

The concentration of the people of the State on action prevented any great concentration on preparing histories of this action. In fact, the war-savings stamps committee was the only organization to prepare and publish a history of its activities. However, the council of defense, food administration, fuel administration, and draft executives preserved completely their records. Likewise all the colleges of the State preserved records of their students, faculties, and alumni who were in the service. The State College for Women also collected and published information on the contributions of North Carolina women to the war.

The North Carolina Historical Commission exerted a powerful influence in preserving all forms of war records. Its secretary, Mr. R. D. W. Connor, directed the historical committee of the council of defense. This committee organized assistants in a majority of the counties of the State, and even by the conclusion of the war had preserved a fairly representative collection of war records.

The work of the North Carolina Historical Commission in preserving war records was given support by the general assembly of 1919, when they authorized and directed the historical commission to employ a person not only to continue collecting war records, but to prepare from them a History of North Carolina in the Great World War.[25] The work of collecting data for this history is now actively progressing.

NORTH DAKOTA.

By O. G. LIBBY, President of the North Dakota War History Commission.

The War History Commission of North Dakota was appointed by Gov. Frazier in 1918. At the session of the Legislature in 1920 the State made a small appropriation to assist the Commission in its

---

[25] Chapter 144, Public Laws, 1919, secs. 3–5.

work. A plan has been devised by Adj. General Fraser for securing the service record of every man in the Army or Navy from North Dakota.

The commission has secured the cooperation of most of the county superintendents in collecting war material. A small pamphlet has been prepared which will be mailed to a selected list of citizens who will be asked to aid in the collection and compilation of the materials for a State history of the war.

OHIO.

By C. B. GALBREATH, Secretary of the Ohio State Archæological and Historical Society.

, No definite information is at hand regarding the contributions by the history men and women of Ohio toward the winning of the World War. The people of Ohio were, however, active in seeking and disseminating information that would lead to a clearer understanding of the issues of the war. Clippings from newspapers and periodicals in the files of the Ohio State Archæological and Historical Society show that almost every section of the State contributed something toward the enlightenment of the community in which they circulated on the causes and issues of the great conflict.

The library interests of the State early saw the opportunity for service that came with our entrance into the war, and promptly took action to supply books, newspapers, and periodicals to the various camps and cantonments in Ohio. Before the soldiers arrived at Camp Sherman a small working library had been established on the site of that cantonment, through the cooperation of the Ohio State Library and the public library at Chillicothe, and a system of operating it had been carefully worked out by J. Howard Dice, library organizer of Ohio; Burton E. Stevenson, librarian of the public library of Chillicothe; and Miss Edwina Glenn, former librarian of one of the branch libraries in Brooklyn, N. Y., and daughter of Maj. Gen. Glenn in command at Camp Sherman. Later Mr. Dice entered the military service and returned from France in July, 1919. Mr. Stevenson continued in charge of the work at Camp Sherman for a time, and because of the excellent record that he made here was later sent to France as the representative of the American Library Association to take charge of the work near the scene of military operations. Excellent work was done also at other military posts in Ohio, and the soldiers in training in this State, as well as those temporarily within its borders on their way to cantonments in other States or points of debarkation on the coast, were liberally supplied with reading matter.

There was much public speaking. In this way every school district of the State was reached. There were addresses by the Four-Minute Men under direction of the national organization and voluntary lectures by practically every man and woman in the State able and willing to speak on the war. There were, of course, numerous addresses by distinguished speakers from other States and other nations, and patriotic appeals in the Liberty loan, war chest, and, other campaigns. The State-supported universities and normal schools were centers of great activity and enthusiasm in everything pertaining to the war.

In February, 1918, Gov. Cox appointed the Historical Commission of Ohio. This action was purely voluntary on the part of the governor, as there was no legislation providing specifically for this action. It had the hearty support, however, of a number of citizens, who realized the importance of the work that such an organization might perform. The commission was appointed as the official agency of the State for the collection and preservation of records and materials pertaining to Ohio's part in the present war. The following were designated as members of the commission: Elbert J. Benton, Western Reserve University; John E. Bradford, Miami University; Glenn D. Bradley, Toledo University; Isaac J. Cox, University of Cincinnati; George A. Cribbs, Mount Union College; Elizabeth Crowther, Western College for Women; Martha L. Edwards, Lake Erie College; George C. Enders, Defiance College; K. S. Latourette, Granville; Thomas N. Hoover, Ohio University; Walter D. Niswander, Ohio Northern University; William F. Peirce, president of Kenyon College; Benjamin F. Prince, Wittenberg College; Emilius O. Randall, secretary Ohio State Archaeological and Historical Society; A. S. Root, Oberlin College; Arthur M. Schlesinger, Ohio State University; Charles Snavely, Otterbein College; Richard T. Stevenson, Ohio Wesleyan University; John I. Stewart, Muskingum College; Elizabeth A. Thompson, Municipal University of Akron; Mary A. Young, Oxford College for Women; Rev. Francis W. Howard, Holy Rosary Church, Columbus, secretary general of the Catholic Educational Association of the United States.

The purpose of the commission, as specifically stated, was to collect and preserve records and materials pertaining to the World War. Prof. Arthur M. Schlesinger, of the Ohio State University, was chairman of the commission. His report, bearing date of October 25, 1918, is here given:

The commission proceeded at once to effect a cooperative arrangement with the Ohio State Archaeological and Historical Society, according to which the headquarters of the commission were established at the society's building, the facilities of the building were placed at the disposal of the commission, and an agreement was reached, with the consent of the governor's office, that the collections of the commission should be lodged in the library of the society. The Ohio State University also cooperated with the commission to the extent of releasing the chairman from one-half of his teaching duties during the second semester of the year 1917–18 and of assisting in providing office supplies. At the outset the commission decided that it would endeavor to build up a great centralized collection of war records of all kinds, civilian and military, which would represent the activities of the people of the State with reference to the present war. To explain the scope of the proposed collection a bulletin was published for free distribution to every interested person. Pursuant to the purpose agreed upon, the work of the commission during the seven months of its existence has consisted of two phases:

1. The appointment of chairman of county branches of the historical commission. Up to the present time 63 county chairmen have been appointed, besides a special representative in Camp Sherman. It is the business of each county chairman to collect the documents, reports, and other records which show how the war has affected the life of his community in all its aspects. This material he is directed to send to the central office when a sufficient amount had been accumulated.

2. The collecting of material: A vast amount of Ohio's war records has already been collected and tentatively classified. A detailed enumeration would be out of place here; but perhaps it may be in order to submit a brief characterization of the general classes of material.

(a) Pictorial material: The pictorial records of the present war are unique as compared with those of any other war in which the United States has been engaged. The commission has collected 240 large paper posters and an even greater number of lithographs, representing the many phases of activity of the Federal and local governments and of the nonofficial war service agencies. When proper supplies are obtained for the purpose, all the posters will be mounted on cloth to insure permanent preservation. At the present time 63 of them have been so cared for. The R. E. Wagner Co., official photographers at Camp Sherman, have presented the commission with a large collection of exceptionally fine panoramic views of the camp while the Eighty-Third Division was there. The commission has acquired two sets of motion picture films, one being the six reel film entitled "The Remaking of a Nation." This film, which is more than a mile in length, was presented to Maj. Gen. Edwin F. Glenn and depicts a draftee's life at Camp Sherman from the time of his first arrival until he is turned out a finished product. Another item of interest is an autographed photograph of our war President, Woodrow Wilson.

(b) Printed material: The printed records of Ohio's part in the war are of many kinds and only a few classes can be mentioned here. The commission is receiving 139 newspapers representing most of the counties in the State. The newspapers of certain of the leading counties are being bound up, and those from the rural counties are being clipped for all references to local war activities and the clippings placed in scientifically planned scrapbooks. In addition to newspapers of the ordinary kind the commission has made a special effort to gather camp newspapers and magazines printed in camps and elsewhere wherever Ohio soldiers are to be found in large numbers. Besides possessing one of the few absolutely complete files of the Camp Sherman News, the commission has files of two other papers from Camp Sherman, four papers from Camp Sheridan, three from Wright Field, the Ohio Rainbow Reveille printed "somewhere in France," and other papers of a similar character.

The many war service instrumentalities which have sprung into existence to meet the needs created by the war have also been responsible for a large crop of printed periodicals and mimeographed publicity matter. As an ex-

ample of such printed periodicals the commission has files of the Ohio Foo
Bulletin, the Lake Division News, and the Central Liberty Loan Committo
Bulletin (Cleveland). With reference to publicity material the commissio
has established points of contact with practically every governmental or no
governmental war agency in operation in Ohio and is receiving regularly a
literature prepared for the use of newspapers, as well as other publicatiou
issued.

In order to have a record of how the war has affected the religious an
industrial life of the people the commission is receiving a fairly complete lis
of the religious periodicals of Ohio and also a representative list of chambe
of commerce publications, labor newspapers, agricultural periodicals, trac
papers, and house (industrial corporation) organs. The collection of the con
mission contains much other printed material of a varied character whic
reflects religious and economic activities within the State in their relationshi
to the war.

The racial contributions of Ohio to the war are represented by collection
of German, Slavonic, Rumanian, and Negro newspapers. Under the superv
sion of Mr. Carl Wittke, of the Ohio State University, all references to Ger
man-American activities and opinions in connection with the war have bee
clipped and mounted in scrapbooks; and it is not too much to say that thi
series of books will hold a unique value for future students of history. On
product of the activity of the commission, along this line has been the gif
by Mrs. Bertha H. Krauss, Maj. Gustav Hirsch, and Mr. Ralph Hirsch, o
Columbus, of 260 bound volumes of the Express and Westbote, covering th
important historical period from 1843 down to the present time. Through th
agency of the Federal authorities in the State the commission has obtained a
number of interesting examples of antiwar propaganda used in Ohio.

(c) Written records: The commission has the substantial nucleus of a col
lection of soldiers' letters and diaries, the most important acquisition being a
collection of several hundred letters received by Prof. Wendell Paddock, o
the Ohio State University, from former students in many branches of th
service. The commission also possesses a number of patriotic addresses in
written or typed form, and also some accounts written by public officials o
their activity in war service; such as, for instance, the account of the fue
crisis in Ohio during the winter of 1917–1918, written by Mr. E. D. Leach
former assistant State fuel administrator.

(d) Emblematical material: This portion of the collection consists of badge
and buttons representative of the many branches of war service carried or
in the State, of medals presented by counties and municipalities for patrioti
service, and of banners and flags symbolic of wartime celebrations or patrioti
achievement.

(e) Relics: The commission has made little progress in the collection of
relics of the European battle fields, believing that this is a function which
can be better performed by the curator of the Museum. However, the commission has encouraged the collection of relics and expects to cooperate in every
way with the curator in this work.

However tedious the foregoing enumeration may have seemed, I desire to
state again that it is merely suggestive of the work performed and is in no
sense a complete statement of it. Surely enough has been said to suggest the
vast possibilities of the work in which the historical commission is engaged and
the solemn responsibility which rests upon the State of Ohio to collect war
records which will show our American boys overseas that their splendid work
is being appreciated now and being commemorated for all time to come. Ohio
has neglected this work in the case of former wars; she is one of the foremost

States in this work now and will have no excuse for not carrying it through properly.

Those of you who are skillful in reading between lines have already guessed that such progress as the historical commission has already made would have been impossible without the material assistance and wise counsel given to the commission through the good offices of the secretary of the Ohio State Archæological and Historical Society, Dr. E. O. Randall. Such financial aid was indispensable in view of the fact that the historical commission was created between sessions of the general assembly. To Dr. Randall, the commission and the interests represented by the commission can not be too grateful. However, it should be evident that the historical commission can not properly accomplish the purposes for which it was created without funds of its own; and as an affiliated branch of the Ohio State Archæological and Historical Society, I believe that the society will wish to see that generous provision is made by the general assembly for the performance of this work.

In 1919 Prof. Schlesinger resigned to accept a position at the head of the department of American history in the University of Iowa. In his absence the work was taken up by W. Ferrand Felch. On August 26, 1919, Mr. Felch made a report to the Ohio State Archæological and Historical Society which is summarized as follows:

The writer of this statement of the condition of the archives of the Historical Commission of Ohio has been in the office as executive secretary of the commission for only two short months, and can not, therefore, give anything more than a cursory and insufficient report of the work.

Owing to the retirement of Dr. Arthur M. Schlesinger, the duties thereof have devolved upon the acting chairman, Dr. E. O. Randall, from whom a full report can be expected at the end of the year.

The historical commission was appointed by Gov. James M. Cox in February, 1918. The members designated to conduct its work were, in the main, the leading historical professors of all the colleges and universities of the State. This commission has since been augmented by the appointment of a series of county chairmen, acting under the instructions of the State chairman, to gather all available material in the counties that might otherwise be thrown away.

The complete and satisfactory history of any county's participation in the war can be printed only after it has been edited or largely compiled from the archives of the State commission.

It was my first impression, and Dr. Schlesinger's that the archæological museum will become in time the Mecca for county historians, or, as he phrased it, a " laboratory " for scientific historical research, experiment, synthesis, and exploitation—forever.

We are still receiving papers from 67 of the 88 Ohio counties, in many cases two or three papers from a county, making about 150 papers in all. Scrapbooks are being formed steadily, by daily accretion. Ten are on the shelves; 16 are ready for the bindery, and 10 more partially filled out to the requisite average of 200 pages to a volume. We receive a goodly number of German newspapers, which are read and edited for our scrapbook collection by Prof. Wittke, of the historical department of the university, who is also the representative in the business of accumulating the data for this commission in Franklin County. We have also a number of Slavonic newspapers, Rumanian, Bohemian, Polish, and other languages, published in Ohio—at Cleveland, Cincinnati, and Youngstown principally; and we are still receiving, also, all forms of blanks, press releases, printed and regulated forms, from the United States Government and State bureaus of governmental activity, which are yet in use.

It appears from the report of Mr. Felch that 21 counties of Ohio are not represented in the material collected and preserved in the Ohio State Archaeological and Historical Society. It is the purpose of the secretary of the society at an early date to make an effort to collect newspapers and newspaper accounts relating to the war from each of these 21 counties. This will be much more difficult now than it would have been 2 years ago, but not so difficult as it will be 8 or 10 years hence; and the matter is of such importance that effort and expense should not be spared to make the newspaper record for the State complete.

Prof. Carl Wittke, instructor in American history, of Ohio State University, has critically examined the collection of German papers and clippings made from the same by himself for the commission, and has published an interesting monograph entitled "Ohio's German-Language Press and the Peace Negotiations" in the January, 1920, number of the Ohio Archaeological and Historical Quarterly. It has also been issued in separate form. In this connection it is proper to note that Prof. Schlesinger has contributed an excellent article to the Mississippi Valley Historical Review, December, 1919, entitled "The Khaki Journalists, 1917–1919."

A few histories of military units from Ohio have already been published. Some of these are a credit to the authors, while others are a little like certain county histories, projected not so much for the purpose of faithfully portraying the service of the military organization as for extracting money from soldiers and their civilian friends. Some historian, or organization of historians, could probably at this time render a substantial service by preparing a statement in circular or pamphlet form, designed to guide those writing, or contemplating the preparation of histories of the various military organizations that participated in the World War.

At present there is a project underway for the preparation of a history of the Thirty-seventh Division, made up almost entirely of Ohio soldiers, by coöperation of the Ohio State Archaeological and Historical Society and a committee on history appointed by representatives of the division. A similar plan is suggested for a history of the Eighty-third Division, which was organized and trained at Camp Sherman. It is too early to make any definite predictions in regard to the outcome of these plans, but the prospect is promising.

The historical commission is taking up and hopes soon to press with vigor a systematic collection of narratives from Ohio soldiers who rendered distinguished service in the war. Two instances will illustrate: A small number of Ohio men were with the little handful of American engineers under Gen. Carey when his " scratch " army halted the advance of the great German drive before the gates of Amiens. At least two of these Ohioans were killed and a surviving comrade is writing for the society an account of this action as he saw it. A number of Ohio soldiers were with the first troops that marched through London, August 15, 1917. Some of these will give their impressions of this historic march. They were the first foreign troops that had marched through that city since the days of William the Conqueror in 1066.

.RHODE ISLAND.

By ST. GEORGE L. SIOUSSAT, Brown University, with the cooperation of H. W. CHAPIN, Librarian, Rhode Island Historical Society, and H. O. BRIGHAM, State Librarian.

I. Historical research and the production of books for increasing the fund of historical knowledge regarding questions pertaining to the war.

Answer. No special lines of historical research, and there have been no books pertaining to the war, except as hereinafter noted.

Prof. Theodore Collier, of Brown University, prepared and published in Paris (1919) "A New World in the Making: Constructive Studies in the Issues of the War, for the use of the soldiers of the American Expeditionary Forces"

Prof. St. George L. Sioussat, of Brown University, contributed to the "War Cyclopedia," published by the Committee on Public Information.

II. The diffusion of historical information necessary to an enlightened public opinion regarding the issues of the war: (a) By the contribution of articles for publication in newspapers and periodicals; (b) by promoting the circulation of books and periodicals containing important historical information; (c) by lectures; (d) by teaching in schools and colleges.

(a) There appears to be no record of organized effort directed toward the end indicated. Prof. St. George L. Sioussat, of Brown University, contributed to the History Teacher's Magazine for October, 1917, a brief article, " English Foundations of American Institutional Life."

(b) No such activities recorded, except that collections of books on the war and its historical phases were made at the Providence Public Library, Brown University, and the Providence Atheneum.

(c) In addition to lectures which might incidentally have an historical bearing, which were given under the authority of the colleges, the chamber of commerce, the Y. M. C. A., the Bureau of Public Information, and other such agencies, definitely organized lectures upon the causes of the war and the relation to it of the United States were given at some of the training camps of the Army, the Navy, and the Merchant Marine, in and near Boston, by Prof. Sioussat, in connection with the work of the New England group for historical service. Prof. Collier gave lectures of similar character in Rhode Island and later in Y. M. C. A. service overseas devoted much time to lectures to the men in the American Expeditionary Force.

(d) The course upon the issues of the war, planned by a committee under the authority of the United States War Department, was given at the Rhode Island State College, in the summer of 1918, to the Training Detachment, Mechanics' Unit, by President Howard Edwards; also, in connection with the Student Army Training Corps, this course was given from October to December, 1918, by President Edwards and Prof. Churchill.

In Brown University the war issues course was given, in the summer, by J. M. Gathany. In the first third of the college year 1918–1919, in connection with the Students' Army Training Corps, the management of the course upon the issues of the war was placed in the care of a committee consisting of Prof. H. B. Gardner, W. G. Everett, and St. George L. Sioussat. The lectures in the course were given by Prof. Sioussat, with a final lecture by President W. H. P. Faunce; and a number of quiz sections were conducted by Profs. Harkness, Gardner, Fowler, Benedict, Griffith, and Drs. Hansen and Bratcher, in cooperation with Prof. Sioussat.

III. Cooperation with the State council of defense, cooperation with the National Board for Historical Service, cooperation with the National Government in the prosecution of the war and in the negotiation of peace.

Apparently no such service is recorded as rendered by men devoted to the historical profession, other than the service overseas of Prof. Collier and the war-camp lectures of Prof. Sioussat, to which reference is made elsewhere. In 1919 Dr. K. K. Smith, assistant professor of Greek literature and history in Brown University, spent several months in Greece in Y. M. C. A. work.

IV. Preparation during the progress of the war of histories of the organization and operation of different branches of war service; for example, State and county food administrations.

Answer. S. Ashley Gibson, city editor of the Providence Journal, has prepared, at the request of Gov. R. Livingston Beeckman, a brief history of the State council of defense in relation to the war, with short sketches of the different branches of war activities. In addition, the following sketches exist in manuscript: Herbert O. Brigham, "History of the Food Administration"; J. Taylor Wilson, "History of the Food Administration"; Mrs. Albert D. Mead, "History of the Woman's Committee."

Of material already in print may be cited the Yearbooks of the Providence Chamber of Commerce for 1917 and 1918-19, in which are included reports of the committee of one hundred of the chamber of commerce and the war council of the Providence Chamber of Commerce. These are very informal.

A selective service manual was issued by the director of selective service. There may be noted also the publication entitled "Roll of Honor, Ward Eight," compiled under the direction of the executive committee of the Eighth Ward Republican Club.

Statements of the service of the officers and students of Brown University and of the Rhode Island State College are included in the printed annual reports of the presidents of the respective institutions. These reports contain also an interesting record of the changes in the organization of the work of these institutions which were brought about to meet war conditions.

Rhode Island State College has published a brochure, "Rhode Island State College to Her Sons, 1917–1919." This contains an honor roll of "Our hallowed dead," and a list of "Our living heroes."

Brown University has published "Brown University in the War: A Report of the War Records Committee" (Providence, May, 1919). This comprises the "Brown Honor Roll: Biographical Sketches of Forty-two Brown Men who died in Military or Naval Service"; a "Directory of Military Service," which is intended to give the names of all men in all branches of service, and an article, "Brown University in the War," by Prof. J. Q. Dealey. Other publications of Brown University are a leaflet, "Brown in the War" (August, 1918); "Information in Regard to the Military and Naval Courses to be Offered during the Academic Year 1918–19 at Brown University" (September, 1918); "Bulletin of Brown University, Reorganization of the Curriculum for the Period of the War" (October, 1918).

Commendably full accounts of the activities of the National Society of the Colonial Dames in the State of Rhode Island and Providence Plantations are found in the annual year books of the society (1915–16, 1917, 1918, 1919). Besides supporting many phases of Red Cross and other relief work and the various drives, the society in 1917 prepared and presented to the President of the United States a protest against the German deportations in Belgium, and in 1919 contributed to the Red Cross a motor ambulance with kitchen trailer.

In the annual reports of the Rhode Island Hospital is summarized the work of one of the chief agencies of Rhode Island's contribution to the medical side of the war, both as to personnel and in the performance of services. Especially to be noted is the record of the organization of naval base unit No. 4, organized in connection with this hospital. The Halifax disaster was the occasion for the organ ization of an emergency relief corps.

The Sons of the American Revolution, other societies, churche and civic bodies have taken part in exercises of a character partl historical, in connection with national holidays, school celebration Americanization courses, etc. These events could be traced by th clippings elsewhere mentioned, but no systematic attempt to compi a general record appears to have been made.

V. The collection and preservation of war records.

Answer. The service records have been transferred to the custod of the War Department at Washington. The soldiers' and sailor information bureau have maintained a card file of questionnaire and the soldiers' bonus board have now in preparation a card recor based upon the statements made in discharge papers. Secondar war records have been kept as follows: Photographs and illustrativ material were collected by the soldiers' and sailors' informatio bureau and transferred to the custody of the State librarian. Mo ing-picture films illustrating certain phases of the local activitie have been deposited in the Rhode Island Historical Society. Paper of the Americanization committee have also been deposited with th society. The Rhode Island Historical Society has confined its post collection entirely to those issued in Rhode Island, of which the have been a limited number.

During the war the Rhode Island Historical Society clipped a the items in the Providence Journal dealing with the part played b Rhode Island and Rhode Islanders in the Great War, including th activities in Rhode Island and beyond its borders. These clipping have been mounted chronologically in a series of scrapbooks.

The Rhode Island Historical Society also began to make extrac of historical material which was contained in letters from boys the front. These extracts were typewritten, arranged by subject and mounted in scrapbooks. Owing to the vast amount of lette this work was by no means exhausted, and has been discontinued o account of lack of funds.

The soldiers' and sailors' information bureau, operated by th director of the draft, maintained a clipping file, which was place in the custody of the State librarian.

On the day the United States declared war the Rhode Island Hi torical Society issued an illustrated broadside containing a pictu of the Hessian sword captured by Americans on Rhode Island i 1778. This sword was placed on exhibit in the portrait gallery of th society during the war and labeled "A Trophy Captured from th Germans by Americans in 1778." The other side of the case was le vacant, with a card stating that the space was reserved for trophi captured from the Germans in the present war. Later this was filled with such trophies.

VI. Preparation for an early history of the State's participation in the war. Under this head it may be quite worth while in some States to contrast the so-called county history, produced primarily for the purpose of extracting the largest possible sum of money from the county, with the genuine county history prepared by a person with some historical training and for a much lower price:

Answer. There has already been published " Battery A, One hundred and third Field Artillery in France" (an organization largely composed of Rhode Island men). Similar publications are in compilation by Battery B and Battery C, One hundred and third Field Artillery.

There are no plans for an early history of the State's participation in the war except as stated above.

" The Providence Journal Almanac " for the years 1918, 1919, and 1920 has numerous articles concerning the activities of Rhode Island war relief organizations, State's welcome to returned service men, Rhode Island honor men in the World War; also list of events local to Rhode Island.

SOUTH CAROLINA.

This report was prepared from a letter by A. S. SALLEY, Jr., Secretary, Historical Commission of South Carolina.

The history men of South Carolina seem to have nothing to report regarding their contributions toward the winning of the war. There was no special war program for teaching history in the schools and colleges. There was also no collecting of records during the war, there being no one to collect, no money to use for that purpose, and no place in which to keep the records if they had been collected. It is reported as not known whether the council of defense saved its records or not. " Those who did things," we are told, " seemed to think it would never be necessary to tell anybody what was accomplished." However, in 1919 the general assembly appropriated $500,000 for the erection of a building as a memorial chapel to South Carolina soldiers in the war. This building is to house the historical department of the State, which is expected to gather materials relating to South Carolina's part in the war.

SOUTH DAKOTA.

Contributions by the history men of South Dakota toward the winning of the war consisted mainly of addresses and the war-aims course to the Students' Army Training Corps. The legislature has provided for a State historical commission, to consist of the gov-

ernor, adjutant general, and three members to be appointed by t[
governor. The adjutant general is to have personal supervision [
the work; a historian, appointed by the commission, is to ha[
charge of the details. An enumeration of all service men is to [
made by assessors on blanks provided by the adjutant gener[
County superintendents of schools and the teachers of the Sta[
have also been asked to assist in this matter. The department [
history has in preparation reports of activities of several w[
agencies. A number of county histories have been published [
private enterprise and others are in preparation.

TENNESSEE.

This report was prepared from a letter by JOHN TROTWOOD MOORE, Director [
the Department of Library, Archives, and History, State of Tennessee.

The Department of Library, Archives, and History is actively e[
gaged in collecting the individual records of Tennessee soldie[
sailors, airmen, and marines in the World War. For this purpo[
the State is thoroughly organized in each of the 96 counties. The[
is a county mother chairman, with subchairmen in each civil distri[
collecting individual records, original letters, and trophies. T[
records are to be housed in a memorial hall, for the erection of whi[
the legislature has appropriated the sum of $2,000,000.

For the publication of war history there is the Tennessee Hi[
torical Committee of 25 members appointed by the governor. Th[
are now actively at work under various subheads collecting a[
publishing all of Tennessee's war history from the organization [
the State to the present time. A few volumes have already be[
published.

TEXAS.

By MILTON R. GUTSCH, Director, Texas War Records, University of Texas[

The declaration of war against Germany and the passage of t[
draft law caused so much confusion in the organization of the high[
institutions of learning in the State of Texas that relatively litt[
time could be devoted to research and production in the field [
causes of the conflict. Nevertheless, a great deal was accomplish[
in the diffusion of historical information relating to the war issu[
for the purpose of instructing the public and establishing an enligh[
ened public opinion. Articles were prepared by the faculties of t[
University of Texas and the Agricultural and Mechanical Colle[
of Texas for publication by the State press. The Texas Histo[
Teachers' Bulletin of May 15, 1918, published by the history sta[
of the University of Texas, contained a 75-page summary of t[
causes and events of the war prepared by Professor Duncalf. T[

 summary was entitled "A War Text for Texas Schools." It made no pretense of being either a thorough or final treatment of the war. Its purpose was to gather in concise form the more significant phases of the war so that they would be easily taught in the Texas schools. In the preface the author emphasizes the responsibility of the teachers in the development of wholesome public opinion. He says:

A heavy responsibility rests upon all history teachers in our present crisis, or their instruction will have great influence upon the opinions of their pupils. Amid the bitterness and hatred that war develops it becomes increasingly necessary for as many people as possible to keep clearly in mind the main issues of his conflict. Disloyalty and intrigue are abroad, and Americans should one and all so understand our part in this war that no doubt or faint heartedness can turn us aside from what we have undertaken to do.

This war text consists of eight chapters. The first, " Conditions at the Outbreak of the War," is divided into the following: "America," "The Rivalry of European Nations," " Prussia," " The German Contitution," "Why Germany has not Become Democratic," "Germany's Demand for a place in the Sun," " Germany's Justification of the War," " The Growth of Large Armaments," and " Efforts to Limit the Preparation for War." The second chapter discusses the "Historical Background of the War," " The Franco-Prussian War," "The Triple Alliance," "The Dual Alliance," " Change in English Policy," " The Anglo-French Entente," " The Morocco Question," "The Rise of the Balkan States," " The Development of German Interests in the East," "Austrian Annexation of Bosina and Herzegovina," " The Balkan Wars," " Germany and Russia," and " Germany and England." Chapter 3, on the "Austro-Serbian Controversy," emphasizes "Austrian Hostility toward Serbia," "The Menace of Pan Slavism to the Dual Monarch," " The Assassination at Serajevo," and the " Austrian Ultimatum." Chapter 4 discusses the "Efforts to Avert War and Their Failure," " Russia's Position," "Sir Edward Grey's Proposals," " Germany's Attitude," and " Mobilization." Chapter 5 on "How the War Began," the more important topical headings are " Great Britain not Prepared for War," "England Anxious to Preserve Peace," " The Neutrality of Belgium and Luxemburg," " German Demands upon Belgium," " England Enters the War," and " Other Countries Enter the War." Chapter 6 on " The Progress of the War," discusses the " Methods of Warfare," and contains a chronological summary of the military progress of the war. Chapter 7 takes up the question of " How the United States Entered the War;" and Chapter 8 is a summary of " The Issues Involved," with the following divisions: " German Militarism Must be Crushed," " No Hope for Peace from the German People," "The Principle of Nationality," " What Allied Victory Will mean," "A League to Enforce Peace."

This text book was used in many of the Texas schools and a secol edition was necessary.

The Texas History Teachers' Bulletin, issued quarterly and se free of charge to every history teacher in the State of Texas, pu lished regularly selected bibliographies on the war. It also ma an effort to ascertain what was being done in the high schools the State in the teachings of the war, and to make known the resul of this investigation to the history teachers of the State. On Apl 8, 1918, a questionnaire submitting the following questions was se to every high school in the State of Texas:

1. Is any attention being given to the study of the present conflict in t history classroom? If so, how much?

2. What effect, in general, has the war had upon (a) the content of each the several history courses in your curriculum; and (b) upon the method instruction?

3. What effect, if any, has the war had upon the students' knowledge of (geography, (b) government, (c) ecnomics? Do the students know the locati of the most important States involved in the war and their geographic rel tions? Are they sufficiently interested in the struggle to observe voluntari the shifting battle lines?

4. What methods, if any, are followed in the study of the war?

5. What attention, if any, is given to (a) the causes of the entrance of t United States of America into the war, (b) the part which America ought play, (c) the aims of the United States?

The answers received to this questionnaire showed a wholesom interest in the study of the war throughout the State. On tl average one-sixth of the time allotted to history was consumed in tl study of the war, its causes, events, and objects. Parallels and col trasts were made use of in each of the courses. Contemporary per odicals, bulletin boards, pictures, lantern slides, lectures, class di cussions, and war maps were used in the instruction. The teache were unanimous in stating that the war acted as a stimulant to tl study of geography, economics, and government. The responsibilit of the teacher in teaching good citizenship was emphasized by all.

With reference to the circulation of books and periodicals col taining important historical information relating to the war, tl extension loan library of the University of Texas made the followir report for the year 1918:

Number of libraries loaned on war subjects, April, 1917, to Novembe 1918, 1,113.

Estimated number of people who used libraries, 5,500.

Most popular subjects, with the number of libraries loaned on each: Milita training, 161; Red Cross, 54; women and the war, 37; school entertainmen (patriotic), 35; patriotism, 34; United States and the war, 32; thrift, 3 causes of the war, 30; results of the war, 29; Russia and the War, 29; war, 2 food conservation, 28; conscription, 24; democracy, 24; Government contr of railroads, 24.

Purposes for which libraries were used:
} School work—
}(   ) Supplementary reading.
   Theme writing.
   .   Debates.
,)(School entertainments.
nClub work.
· Campaigns to raise money for the Red Cross, Liberty loans, and United
   war work.
For the information of individuals who desired to inform themselves on
   war topics.

Professors Barker, Bantel, Duncalf, Henderson, Hendrix, Penick,
;iker, Royster, and others of the State university, delivered a series
f lectures to the several classes of soldiers stationed at Camp Mabry.
. number of the faculty also assisted in the dissemination of war in-
ormation by serving as members of the four-minute speakers' organi-
ation.

The department of extension of the University of Texas cooper-
ted with the Texas State Council of Defense through the inter-
:holastic league, the division of home economics, and the division.
f information. A book entitled "Patriotic Selections," edited by
)r. E. D. Shurter, chairman of the Interscholastic League, and paid
)r by the State council of defense, was presented to every school
elonging to the league. In presenting this book to the schools
)r. Shurter had this to say:

Let all the speakers in the declamation contests remember this, that you
·e commissioned by our Government to deliver to Texas audiences the patriotic
essages from our leaders that are contained in this book; that whether you
in in a particular contest or not you are performing a patriotic service that is
ficially recognized by our State council of defense; and, above all, that you
·e doing your part in helping America to win a World War which involves
)t only the freedom of our own country, but the freedom of republican govern-
ent everywhere.

It is estimated that the boys and girls belonging to the Inter-
:holastic League delivered patriotic selections from this book to
exas audiences aggregating 200,000 people in the various local,
)unty, district, and State contests of the league. The division of
ome economics of the department of extension in cooperation with.
ie State council of defense published bulletins for free distribu-
on giving war-time recipes. In its annual report in 1918 the divi-
on of information, department of extension, University of Texas,
ad this to say:

The publicity committee of the Texas State Council of Defense has recognized ·
iis division of the university department of extension as the depository for .
:sual instruction material used in its work, and has placed here $1,000 worth .
{ equipment to be circulated throughout the State. This equipment con-
sts of 10 steropticons, fitted not only with high-power mazda lamps, but also ·

with high-power acetylene gas lamps, so that they can be taken into any rura church or school and operated with a Prest-o-lite gas tank, such as can be ob tained from a garage, and 2,000 lantern slides, which are to be divided int sets of about 50 each, and sent out with appropriate lecture material. M Riker, of the school of history, is preparing a number of sets of slides wit lecture material that will also circulate under the auspices of the Texas Stat council of defense. The first set deals with Germany's dream of empire, an traces the development of the German Empire from the little Duchy of Brader burg to its present "Mittel-Europa" form.

Besides the equipment provided by the State council of defens for the spread of war information, this division itself purchased great many lantern slides on such subjects as "Destroyed Art i Belgium and France," "The Story of the Flag," "The Bell and th Flag," and "America and Destiny." It also cooperated with th United States Food Administration in circulating lantern slides deal ing with food problems of the war.

All freshmen and sophomores in both the University of Texas an the Agricultural and Mechanical College of Texas were required t take the course on "War aims and issues." Uniformity in subjec matter and instruction at the University of Texas was obtained b means of a syllabus prepared by the department of history. Th history department in every possible way cooperated with the Na tional Board for Historical Service.

A great deal of progress has been made in the collection and classi fication for permanent preservation of the war records of the State o Texas. This work is being done by the Texas war records collec tion, an organization created by the board of regents of the Univer sity of Texas, October 22, 1918, under the supervision of Dr. Milto R. Gutsch, adjunct professor of history in the University of Texas At that time an appropriation of $7,500 for the collection of Texas records and of $5,000 for the collection of general war records wa made. The organization consists of the director and the central ad ministrative staff, the county and community war records organiza tions, and the auxiliary agencies. The chairman of the county wa records committee in each county is appointed by the director upo the recommendation of prominent citizens. The chairman then ap points his own committee. The Daughters of the Confederacy, the Daughters of the American Revolution, and the Federation o Women's Clubs are assisting in the collection of the county wa records of the State.

The objects of the organization are: (1) The collection of all ma terial relating to the contributions of Texas in men and resources to the winning of the war; (2) The classification of such material and (3) its preservation. The materials to be collected are: (a) Gen eral material, both American and foreign; (b) State materials; (c) county and community records.

(a) The general records consist of books relating to the war and reconstruction, about 1,800 to date; pamphlets, numbering about 1,600 acquired without cost to the university, circular letters having been sent to every organization or individual in this country known to have published any such material; a collection of posters and broadsides, consisting of approximately 1,500 different designs; 15,000 official United States war photographs; war and reconstruction files of several representative newspapers from Great Britain, France, Italy, Germany, Austria, Australia, Canada, Mexico, Argentina, Brazil, and Chile; maps from the National Geographic Society, the Carta D'Italia, Rand McNally maps, the Kenyon war maps, and others; mementos, consisting of a small collection of tags, buttons, etc.

(b) State records now in the archives of the Texas war records collection are the council of defense; Liberty loan; food administration; State draft board, consisting of complete lists of men inducted into the service of the United States and classified by counties; Red Cross; Jewish Welfare Board; War Camp Community Service; war speakers' bureau; Boy Scouts, a portion of the Armenian and other relief organization records; a large number of camp photographs; and records from the United States Employment Bureau.

State records now being compiled for the university are war savings stamps and certificates of indebtedness; Y. M. C. A.; Y. W. C. A.; Knights of Columbus; Salvation Army; State government records; war industries records; and county and community records, including military and naval service records, records of the several war service organizations, and records of local conditions, most of which are to be collected by means of questionnaires by the county war records committees.

Nothing as yet has been done regarding the preparation of a complete history of the State's participation in the war. A number of local organization histories, however, have appeared. Among these the most important are "The History of the Nineteenth Division," and "Kelly Field and the Great World War." Other histories that have appeared are "Houston's Part in the World War," "Anderson County War History," "Leon County Boys in the World War," "Final Report of the Texas State Council of Defense," and a number of histories of county chapters of the American Red Cross.

UTAH.

By A. L. NEFF, Department of History, University of Utah.

Often in history an inland State has displayed marked disinclination to comprehend its duties as measured in terms of the whole. The remoteness of Utah from menace of attack and invasion might lead one to suppose that it was more or less oblivious to national and international dangers. Quite the reverse was the situation. The quota assigned to Utah in the first Liberty loan was oversubscribed 42 per cent; the second 62 per cent; while the State finished fifth in the Nation and second in the twelfth federal reserve district in the third loan. Indeed every financial call was promptly and fully met. The State's record along lines of food production and conservation was truly enviable, while its man power went forth willingly to fight for the principles of democracy. Results of such character and magnitude indicate keen appreciation of international values and intense patriotism for America and the principles for which it stands.

The contribution of university men toward the creation of the splendid war spirit in Utah was considerable. The people looked to the institutions for higher learning, particularly to the department of history and political science for guidance in the interpretation of the issues of the hour. Courses were offered on "the causes of the war," "American ideas and ideals," and "issues of the war" for resident, extension, and correspondent students. Communications to the press from the pen of history men exerted influence in yet other fields. The State council of defense published a series of bulletins setting forth our war aims prepared by the staff of the University of Utah. Profs. George E. Fellows and Levi Edgar Young performe valuable service as platform speakers. Dr. John A. Widtsoe, president of the University of Utah, and Dr. E. G. Peterson, president o the Utah Agricultural College, were members of the State council for defense and gave unstintingly of their expert knowledge especially along lines of food production.

Dr. George Thomas, head of the department of economics, was the efficient director and organizer for the Students' Army Training Corps, which was becoming a promising feature of the University of Utah when the war closed. Similar activities were underway at the agricultural college and the Brigham Young University.

Compilations were prepared and published by the State council of defense during the war, and a comprehensive report of its activities gotten out on the termination of its war functions.

The collection and preservation of war materials and records is now the especial duty of the Utah Historical Society. The council of defense had begun the collection of war data, having appointed a war historian for that purpose; but the legislature which convened the winter of 1918–1919 designated the Utah Historical Society as the proper depository for all historical material. Furthermore, this legislature authorized the society to prepare a history of Utah's participation in the World War and appropriated the sum of $5,000 for this purpose, the construction of which is now actively underway under the direction of Dr. A. L. Neff, assistant professor of history in the University of Utah.

VIRGINIA.

By Arthur Kyle Davis, Chairman of the Virginia War History Commission.

The historical activities in the State of Virginia, in consequence of the Great War and in order to preserve source material for the future historian, included active work on the part of organizations and individuals.

In the war period there were formed throughout Virginia a number of local groups organized for the specific purpose of securing and preserving the full records of the several military organizations that went from the State. As examples of such associations may be mentioned the Richmond Blues' Association and the Richmond Howitzers' Association, composed largely of the relatives and friends of those organizations and formed for the double purpose of ministering to the needs of the members and of preserving the story and experiences of the unit as a whole and of the individual members.

In most of the counties of Virginia a similar work was undertaken with reference to the volunteers and drafted men represented in the service flag of each county. This work of helpfulness and of authentic recording of history was largely undertaken in the counties through some patriotic local society already in existence. The first specific impetus to this work was probably given by Sussex County, where the first county service flag was unveiled with proper ceremonies under the auspices of the Daughters of the Confederacy. This flag contained about one thousand stars, one or two of them being gold stars, and the address on "The Virginia Symmachy," made on this occasion by Mr. Arthur Kyle Davis, of Petersburg, contained the germ of the plan later adopted in the work of the Virginia War History Commission.

Most of the patriotic organizations of Virginia, such as the Colonial Dames, D. A. R., U. D. C., the S. A. R., as well as the social welfare organizations, such as the Y. M. C. A., the Elks and others, made active effort to secure the true records and experiences of their members in the service in addition to coöperating in all the patriotic undertakings of the time.

The plan of the service flag probably reached its fullest development in the case of the churches of all denominations. Throughout Virginia these service flags were displayed in the churches and in many cases the lists of the men in service were posted in the vestibules of the churches. In addition to this, many of the churches located near the camp areas kept records of their activities in connection with soldier welfare, while the various branches of the Red Cross throughout Virginia, both in the cities and in the counties, kept accounts of their relief work.

The Virginia schools and colleges kept the records of their members in military service and civilian service, as it was recognized from the beginning that the war record of each institution would be subjected to the jealous scrutiny of the members and alumni in the future. In many cases definite clipping bureaus were kept by the institutions with this end in view, so that a mass of material for the history of the participation in service and war work were secured during the war itself.

The newspapers of Virginia threw open their columns to all interesting war material and thousands of soldiers' letters and stories of courage and gallantry were published side by side with the daily record of military and civilian activities of war time.

In many of the counties patriotic individuals undertook the compilation and sometimes the publication of the records of the county soldiers. One of the earliest of these publications was the pamphlet issued by one of the contributors to the Richmond Times Dispatch, notably, the "Book of Honor," giving the story of all the Virginia soldiers that fell in war time. An example of work of this sort is "The Final Roster," a bound book of about 250 pages containing the story of the war work of Nottoway County and giving the service records of all the men from that county. This book was edited by Mr. W. W. Cobb, captain of infantry, United States Army. As a further example of such patriotic work may be mentioned a collection of material touching the history of Bath County, made and preserved by Dr. J. T. McAllister, which is being prepared by him for the files of the Virginia War History Commission and which he is now putting in shape for a definite history of Bath County in the war. Another notable instance of the collection of material for preservation is that of the city of Hopewell. Dr. Helen Love Bossieux collected a great mass of material which is now being used by her and her associates in the preparation of a history of that unique community.

The University of Virginia and Hampden-Sidney College were among the institutions that first put into print the definite records of their alumni in the World War. Through the Alumni Bulletin, a monthly publication, the University of Virginia collected historical data touching its alumni throughout the whole period of the war, and the work of preparing and compiling a definite account of the participation of the students and alumni was early under way. Hampden-Sidney College was perhaps first in publishing a full record of its activities in the Hampden-Sidney Bulletin. We hardly need explain that other colleges and institutions of the State did similar work in the collection of historical material touching their own men and women.

As another type of work in war history may be mentioned such contributions as that of Miss Genoa Swecker, entitled "Rockingham County's Contribution to the World War," published in the Normal Bulletin of October, 1919. This 10-page résumé of Rockingham County's activities is in the nature of a summary, rather than a detailed statement, but it will form the basis of a fuller treatise and shows the care with which the local records are being preserved.

The records of the State council of defense were carefully kept and from them the story of this great branch of war history is now being compiled for the war history commission by the secretary of the council, Col. Charles R. Keiley, who has placed scores of volumes of correspondence and publications of the State council of defense in the files of the Virginia War History Commission. This is, perhaps, the most important single gift that the commission has yet received.

The office of the adjutant general of Virginia, Gen. Jo. Lane Stern, has been one of the major agencies for the preservation of every available bit of historical material. General Stern, fully realizing Virginia's lack of records of the Civil War period, has been most efficient in securing and preserving material of permanent value for the Virginia records.

Individual soldiers of Virginia, both privates and officers, have been wise enough to keep the records of their experiences and impressions, sometimes in diaries and sometimes in printed books. Col. Ashby Williams, of Roanoke, has published a valuable and interesting record in "Experiences of the World War," a book of some 200 pages; and Col. Jennings C. Wise has produced several publications of real value, including his "History of the Eightieth Division." Among the diaries may be mentioned that of Capt. Lucien Cocke, of Roanoke, which has for some time been among the files of the Virginia War History Commission.

By teaching in the schools and colleges, by lectures, by circulation of periodicals, and by the contribution of articles in newspapers and magazines Virginia men and women endeavored to bring the issues and the facts before the people of the State.

The results of all war-history activities are being brought to a common center through the work of the Virginia War History Commission, a body of 18 members appointed by Governor Davis in January, 1919, and now working through 122 local branches throughout the State. Definite plans for the publication of a State history in 4 volumes of 600 pages each are well under way and valuable source material touching civilian and war activities is being stored both in the central archives in Richmond and in local archives throughout the cities and counties of the State.

The publications of the war history commission include seven issues of the Virginia War History Commission's News Letter and three pamphlets; No. 1, "Plans and Personnel of the Virginia War History Commission"; No. 2, "Virginia's War History"; and No. 3, "Virginia in the War."

The progress of this work of the commission may be summed up in a quotation from page 10 of "Virginia's War History":

The commission has to its credit at least 10 matters of great pith and moment that deserve the name of action, as follows:

1. *Virginia plan of history.*—The Virginia Commission originated and published the first specific and comprehensive plan by sections for a State history.

2. *Associate group of editors.*—It secured for its important task the patriotic cooperation of a large and distinguished group of associates.

3. *State plan of local branches.*—It organized throughout the State local branches or committees of three in every city and county.

4. *Booklets and news letters.*—It has published and distributed to the members one pamphlet on the general plan, one on community history, and seven News Letters.

5. *Outlines and questionnaires.*—It has prepared and furnished to the local branches outlines and questionnaires covering the varied phases of State activities.

6. *Monthly and quarterly meetings.*—Monthly meetings have been held for reports and discussion with inspirational meetings and addresses each quarter.

7. *Field agents and stated drives.*—Four field agents for the counties and one for the cities are now at work, and six special drives for data are under way.

8. *Military and civilian records.*—A goodly percentage of service records and many reports of civilian activities have been secured and are on file.

9. *Central and local archives.*—The commission has established central archives in Richmond and local archives in every city and county of the State.

10. *Appeal to all Virginians.*—Through the press, through letters and circulars, and through many addresses constant appeal is being made to all Virginians.

WASHINGTON.

This report was prepared from a letter by EDMOND S. MEANY, Department of History, University of Washington.

The members of the history department in the University of Washington were active in patriotic work throughout the war. Dr. Ralph H. Lutz, assistant professor of European history, was a lieutenant in the Intelligence Department with the American Army in France.

On that portion of the campus bordering on Lakes Union and Washington the Government maintained a naval training camp, the numbers rising from 300 to 2,000. Lectures were in demand there.

A trip of three hours reached Camp Lewis, one of the Government's larger cantonments. Through the Y. M. C. A. and the Knights of Columbus regular courses of lectures were given by the members of the history department.

When the National Board for Historical Service undertook to give six illustrated lectures before all the troops in training, early in 1918, the department took over the work for Camp Lewis and purchased an independent set of slides for that purpose. In giving the lectures the members of the department were assisted by Prof. Walter S. Davis of the College of Puget Sound, Tacoma; Mr. O. B. Sperlin, of the Stadium High School, Tacoma; and Mr. S. E. Fleming, of the Franklin High School, Seattle. J. N. Bowman, associate professor of European history, University of Washington, was especially successful in this and similar work at Camp Lewis. He subsequently left the University and is still engaged in the Government's placement work among returned soldiers and sailors.

Various communities of the State and leaders of Liberty bond selling drives made much use of the history men of the university. Oliver H. Richardson, professor of European history, was especially active with community lectures.

Prof. Edmond S. Meany supervised the war aims course for the Students' Army Training Corps. Those giving the lectures were Prof. Oliver H. Richardson, Prof. Richard F. Scholz, Associate Prof. Edmond McMahon, of the history department, and Dean Stephen I. Miller, Jr., of the College of Business Administration.

One of the younger men, Victor J. Farrar, research assistant in Northwestern history, served 18 months as sergeant first class with Base Hospital 50, in France.

When the appeal came from the National Board for Historical Service to organize the State for the preservation of historical records of the war, it was decided to organize Washington into county units. This work, under the direction of Professor Meany, was completed and the reports show that most of the 39 counties were successful in accumulating materials for deposit in the most central library of each.

WEST VIRGINIA.

By OLIVER PERRY CHITWOOD, Department of History and Political Science, West Virginia University.

West Virginia did not provide for a war history commission, and consequently very little has been done throughout the State in collecting records. The legislature made provision for the county clerks to secure the war records of the men from their counties, but, apparently, few of them made any effort to carry out the provision. Mr. W. W. Smith, of Huntington, compiled a record for Cabell County, which has been published and is a very creditable piece of work. A similar record for Ohio County has been compiled.

Mr. Clifford R. Myers, State historian and archivist, has been energetically collecting relics and papers of the war. However, he is considerably handicapped in this work, owing to the fact that the restricted quarters of the department of archives and history at Charleston do not afford ample housing space for all the relics and documents that he can collect. The library of West Virginia University has also kept complete files of Government publications and pamphlets, and the publications of the American Association for International Conciliation, the National Security League, and other patriotic organizations.

The adjutant general's office has received from the war department a card index record of all the men in the service who gave West Virginia as their place of residence, which is now being prepared for publication. Gov. Cornwell has had printed a complete record of the draft. It includes the name, place, and serial number of each man. The old National Guard records are in the adjutant general's office. From these a fairly complete record of the West Virginians who took part in the war can be compiled. Of course in cases where the man enlisted in another State and gave his place of enlistment as his residence, the record will credit him to the place of enlistment. We may lose many men in that way, yet at the same time some will be gained.

The war gave a great impetus to historical instruction in West Virginia. A great many of the addresses and short speeches made in connection with the various patriotic drives were more or less historical in character. These addresses were made by professors in the university and denominational colleges, teachers and superintendents in the normal and high schools, lawyers, and public-spirited men representing all trades and professions. These speeches were delivered at high school commencements, educational and religious meetings, and on practically all public occasions. These addresses were generally if not always in the nature of propaganda; but despite this fact a good deal of sound historical information was spread abroad through these agencies. Of the agencies of this character, the most effective was the organization of the Four Minute Men. These speakers were heard in every motion-picture theater and every schoolhouse in the State.

So far as I know, few books dealing with the war have been written by West Virginians. The best account of the part played by West Virginia in the war is found in the "West Virginia Legislative Handbook and Manual and Official Register for 1918 and 1919," prepared by John T. Harris. In the edition for 1918 there are 70 pages devoted to West Virginia's activities in the war. This includes a short but valuable account of West Virginia's share in the conflict prepared by the late Wilson M. Foulk, former State historian and archivist; an honor roll giving the names of West Virginians who were killed or died in action, as well as all who were missing, taken prisoners, or wounded; and an account, more detailed, of all of the various war and charity organizations. These latter accounts were prepared by the chairmen or other prominent members of those organizations and are quite valuable. They give lists of names and important statistics. They are, however, incomplete. The Handbook for 1919 devotes 20 chapters to war activities. It discusses more completely subjects treated in the 1918 edition and also contains much new material.

One other book might be mentioned—" The Immediate Causes of the Great War," by Oliver Perry Chitwood, professor of European history, West Virginia University, 1917. Revised and enlarged 1918, T. Y. Crowell Co., New York. This work gives a brief survey of the events of recent European history that preceded and led up to the outbreak in 1914; a fuller account of the diplomatic negotiations of the twelve days; and the reasons for America's entrance into the conflict.

While West Virginians were too busy to write many books during the war, there were some important historical articles published by them. Three of the professors of the department of history of the State University published in the West Virginia School Journal and Educator historical articles dealing with some phases of the war. But probably the most important articles written during the war were those published by Dr. J. M. Callahan, head of the department of history and dean of the college of arts and sciences of the university. He wrote a series of five articles for the Foreign Press Bureau of the Committee on Public Information for publication in the Latin American press. The object of these articles was to show to the South American peoples the bases of our foreign policy, to allay any feeling that they might have against the United States, and to create a better feeling that would lead to a closer coöperation in the war and foreign relations. Several of the articles prepared by Dean Callahan for the " Encyclopedia Americana " (new edition) also had a bearing on the war. Of these, special mention should be made of one published about 1918 giving a survey of our diplomatic relations with Germany. Dean Callahan also gave a series of lectures on problems of international law and international relations at the University of Colorado in the summer of 1918.

A course in current European history was given each semester during the war in nearly all of the high schools, West Virginia Wesleyan College, Davis-Elkins College, Bethany College, the various normal schools, and the university. In the university this was a popular course open to freshmen, both men and women. War history was required of all students in Davis-Elkins College. This course was also well attended in West Virginia Wesleyan College, the average attendance for the year being about 50. The current history or war-history course usually dealt with the current events of the war and the more important facts in recent European history that constituted the background of the war. Besides, every course in history was linked up with the war so far as possible.

In addition to the above-mentioned courses, offered to all students, the war-issues course was, of course, given to all Students' Army Training Corps students. The institutions at which these students were enrolled were West Virginia Wesleyan College, Davis-Elkins College, and the university. In these, instruction was give as far as practicable in accordance with the suggestions and directions issued by the War Department. There were two classes of these students—the vocational (section B) and the regular college students (section A). About 931 of the former class were stationed at West Virginia University in the summer and autumn of 1918. They were lectured to once a week for a period of about 8 weeks for one class and 12 weeks for another. These lectures were given by instructors in the department of history of the university. They dealt with the political and economic conditions of Europe just prior to 1914 and their relation to the outbreak of the war; gave a brief survey of some of the leading events that created the enmities and paved the way for the great struggle; and outlined briefly the diplomatic negotiations that immediately preceded the outbreak.

Students of section B were divided into two classes—those who had not had elementary courses in English composition and those who had. To the former a course of three hours per week, called war English, was given by the departments of English and history. One period was devoted to lectures on history and quizzes on assigned historical readings; the other two periods were given over to English composition. The subject material for the themes was taken from the lectures and assigned readings in history. The second class were required to take three hours a week in war issues. This course was under the entire charge of the history department. It dealt with the historical background of the war, the diplomatic alinements of the European powers, the indirect and direct causes of the war, etc. The results accomplished for both classes of students were, however, very unsatisfactory, owing to the precedence accorded military training.

WISCONSIN.

From the reports of the executive committee of the State Historical Society of Wisconsin for the years 1918 and 1919.

1918. From the beginning of the war in Europe in the summer of 1914 the several departments of the society's working staff have labored to the limit of their ingenuity and ability to collect for permanent preservation the records concerning the war that were being currently produced and, for the most part, currently consigned to oblivion. When the United States entered the arena of warfare it became obvious that some special administrative machinery must be devised if the work of collection of war materials was to be continued on anything like an adequate scale. Accordingly the matter was brought to the attention of the State council of defense, and early in the year 1918 Chairman Swenson responded to the representations that had been made on the subject by appointing a war history commission of the State council (composed of M. M. Quaife, chairman, Madison; Wm. W. Bartlett, Eau Claire; Carl Russell Fish, Madison; J. H. A. Lacher, Waukesha; W. N. Parker, Madison; A. H. Sanford, La Crosse, and Capt. H. A. Whipple, Waterloo), charged with the general duty of seeing that the records of Wisconsin's participation in the great war were gathered for permanent preservation.

In view of the nature of this task, and further of the identity of personnel as between the war history commission and the society (the superintendent being the chairman of the commission and all its members but one being prominently identified with the historical society) it was taken for granted that the society would cooperate to every reasonable extent with the commission in the prosecution of its work. The plan of operations adopted by the commission contemplated the organization of war history committees in the several counties of the State, each of which should undertake to collect the personal and other records of the county's participation in the war, the courthouse or some centrally located library being made the depository of the collection. To initiate and direct the county organizations the services of Dr. Oliver, of the society's research staff, were loaned to the commission for a period of several months, together with such stenographic and other assistance as was needed.

The work of organization was pursued with vigor and enthusiasm by Dr. Oliver during the spring and early summer, with results, on the whole, highly gratifying to the commission. Unfortunately for its further prosecution, however, Dr. Oliver resigned in August to enter the Army, and became henceforth a maker rather than a collector of war records. To the present time (Oct. 24) no successor has been provided, the work of central supervision being carried on as far as practicable by the superintendent from the society's office in Madison. Arrangements have been made, meanwhile, to have Mr. A. O. Barton, of Madison, take up the work beginning November 1. Under his supervision it is expected the results of the good beginning made in the early months of the commission's activities will be conserved and further extended. With a view to prosecuting

25066°—23——19

the collection of historical records and war museum objects abroad as well as at home, the commission has invoked the approval and support of the State council of defense and of the governor that funds and authority necessary for the sending of an agent abroad may be provided. At the time of making this report the hearty support of the State council and of the governor have been enlisted for the project. Unless the Federal authorities shall withhold consent it seems probable, therefore, that the mission will be undertaken.

Another war drive, in the prosecution of which the historical society is intimately interested, may receive appropriate mention here. The field of European history is assigned, by mutual agreement, to the university library. Because of its character that library does not cultivate any particular field intensively, as does the historical library the relatively limited one marked out for it. Hence, if there was to be assembled at Madison a thoroughgoing collection of materials pertaining to the great war on other than its American side, some special provision for its upbuilding was required. Such provision was made by the university early in the year. A special appropriation of $5,000 annually was made for the development of a war collection and Dr. A. C. Tilton, formerly of the historical library staff, but in more recent years of the New York Public Library and the Library of Congress, was engaged as curator. Through the special committee of the university (of which the superintendent of the society was made a member) the combined resources of the several departments of the university and of the historical society are coordinated under Dr. Tilton's oversight, with a view to providing on the European side of the war a collection of historical materials comparable to that which the society is developing in the American field.

1919. The preceding report told the story down to the latter part of October, 1918, of the organization and work of the war history committee of the State council of defense of which the superintendent was chairman, and the funds and direction of which were supplied by the State Historical Society. From November 1, 1918, to August 1 of the present year Mr. A. O. Barton, of Madison, was employed by the society in the capacity of director of the war history committee. This work he carried on with enthusiasm and success, and on laying it down was able to render the gratifying report which we present below. Since the historical society had taken up this work as the most appropriate agency for meeting a war emergency, it was felt that the legislature of 1919 should indicate its approval of the work by making regular and adequate provision for its continuance, lacking which, the work would necessarily be terminated. Accordingly the chairman of the war history committee drafted a bill providing for a Wisconsin War History Commission, which with important modifications was enacted into law. The law creates a nonsalaried war history commission of six members (the governor, the adjutant general, the superintendent of this society, and three citizens appointed by the governor) to which the duty of collecting the materials and compiling a history of Wisconsin's part in the World War is intrusted. For this work an appropriation of $10,000 annually is made, and in addition a special appropriation of $25,000 for the purpose of publishing an official history of the Thirty-second Division. This commission organized in mid-October, Gen. Charles King, of Milwaukee, being made chairman and John G. Gregory, of Milwaukee, secretary. To it, therefore, the further direction of the war history drive is committed. We can not refrain, in concluding, from publicly thanking the hundreds of individuals, some of whose names appear below, for the unpaid and public-spirited cooperation they afforded, and in large part are still affording, the war history committee (henceforth the new war history commission) in securing the contemporary records of Wisconsin's part in the World War. A most gratifying spectacle of popular participation on an extensive scale in the altruistic work of saving our historical records for the instruction and benefit of posterity has been afforded. The report of Mr. Barton upon the status of the work, when he laid it down, follows:

The war history work may be said to be in a satisfactory condition in the great majority of counties. While a number of counties have reported that they have nearly completed their records, none have entirely ceased work and the greater number are still some distance from their goal. This is due largely to the fact that many of the State's troops have but recently returned or are still abroad.

It is gratifying to note that in most of the counties having the larger cities, such as Superior, Racine, Sheboygan, Fond du Lac, Kenosha, Green Bay, La Crosse, Janesville, Appleton, Eau Claire, Manitowoc, and Stevens Point, the work fell into capable and interested hands. In all these counties excellent results have been obtained. Perhaps the larger counties with the best records are Sheboygan, Fond du Lac, Eau Claire, Outagamie, Racine, Kenosha, and Brown; among the smaller Adams, Clark, Waukesha, Taylor, Dunn, Crawford, Waushara, and Green Lake show the best reports. In the two largest counties, Milwaukee and Winnebago, the progress has been less; however, in both these counties the war mothers have come forward with substantial aid of much promise. A half dozen counties have little to show as yet. Among these are Juneau, Dodge, Iowa, Oconto, and Waupaca. Juneau and Iowa will probably receive good attention soon. Some county councils of defense made appropriations for the history work; others gave neither funds nor encouragement. The correspondence files will give further light on the status of the individual counties.

In a number of counties war histories and albums are in course of publication, chiefly by outside concerns. Among such counties may be mentioned Brown, Columbia, Burnett, Dunn, Door, Iowa, Crawford, Polk, Rusk, St. Croix, Oneida, Marquette, Waushara, and Green Lake. It is also probable that histories will be written by local historians in the counties of Kenosha, Green,

Racine, Lafayette, Trempealeau, and Ozaukee. The historians, acting or prospective, are: Brown, Chicago publishers; Door, H. R. Holand, Ephraim; Columbia, J. E. Jones, former editor, Portage; Marquette, C. H. Barry, editor, Montello; Waushara and Green Lake, R. S. Starks, editor, Berlin; Crawford, Lyman Howe, editor, Prairie du Chien; Polk, editor, Luck Enterprise, Luck; Rusk, D. W. Maloney, editor, Ladysmith; Burnett, E. Huth, editor, Grantsburg; Iowa, Granville Trace, editor, Dodgeville; St. Croix, F. A. R. Van Meter, editor, New Richmond; Dunn, M. C. Douglass, editor, Menomonie; Kenosha, Miss Cathie McNamara, Kenosha; Racine, E. W. Leach, Racine; Green, C. H. Dietz, teacher, Monroe; Lafayette, P. H. Conley, Darlington; Trempealeau, Judge H. A. Anderson, Whitehall; Ozaukee, Rev. T. A. Boerner, Port Washington, Oneida.

Your retiring director visited 50 of the 71 counties and met the chairman of a number of others. The counties not visited were chiefly those in the far northern part of the State or such as seemed so well organized as to need less attention.

Several hundred pictures have been received from a number of counties, including Washington, Sauk, Dane, Trempealeau, Milwaukee, Jefferson, Dunn, Eau Claire, and Green; more are promised from other counties. These should be filed. Final reports from several State activities have been received, including council of defense, fuel administration, county agents, physicians, naval enlistments for the State, etc.

In a number of counties the war mothers have enlisted to collect the military biographies, letters, and pictures; they are now at work in Dane, Milwaukee, Winnebago, Langlade, Jefferson, Polk, and perhaps other counties.

WYOMING.

By Dorothy Hale, Assistant State Historian.

Inasmuch as the Wyoming Historical Department was not created until February, 1919, and the State historian did not take up her activities until March of that year, there are not many of the points as outlined in which the department took active part. During the past year a history of the Sixty-sixth Field Artillery Brigade was published and a copy of the same donated to the files of the department. The One hundred and forty-eighth Field Artillery was a part of this brigade and the artillery was partly made up of the Third Wyoming Infantry. Thus it records the war history of many Wyoming men.

The Wyoming Historical Department is making every effort possible to secure the records of her men. Prior to the organization of the department the war history committee of the Wyoming State council of national defense began collecting the war records of the men of Wyoming. A chairman was appointed in each county, who in turn appointed committeemen for the various localities. In addition to this the war history committee began the collection of official blanks, instructions, and orders relating to such matters as the draft, Liberty loans and food administration; the records of semiofficial or unofficial war agencies; posters, programs, badges, etc.; all pamphlets issued by national, State, and local agencies to disseminate general information; local military statistics, such as muster rolls, draft records, etc.; photographic material illustrating war activities; price lists, advertisements, or any other material throwing light on the economic or industrial effects of the war; data showing the changes of our educational programs and institutions to meet the emergency; records of honor families having three, four, or five sons in the war; record lists of Wyoming men who were decorated or commended for bravery; records of Wyoming men and women who served with the Red Cross, Y. M. C. A., or other war relief agencies; newspapers files, letters, and diaries of soldiers and sailors or of war workers; all correspondence of war relief societies; and relics which can be displayed in war museums. It desired also to secure a complete and detailed history of each county's participation in each of the war's activities.

Upon its organization the historical department took over this work. At the present time it has nearly completed an alphabetical card index, by counties, of the 13,000 men who served in the late war. Plans are underway to make a complete alphabetical record of the men and a record of all casualties. The records now on file are not as complete and as accurate as desired, but until funds are appropriated which will enable more clerical aid and permit us to get into closer touch with the counties this cannot be accomplished. The State library has a complete file of the Trench and Camp, the publication at Camp Lewis, the cantonment to which the Wyoming drafted men were sent.

No definite steps have been taken to prepare a history other than to gather the material above mentioned and obtain the pictures of the men and the Wyoming organizations in the late war.

In the report of the publicity department of the State council for national defense, the following statement is made:

Weekly news letters were sent to the 75 State newspapers and 40 to publicity departments of other State councils and offices at Washington. Stories were sent out urging war gardens and extensive publicity was given on all drives and organization activities with gratifying results. The report closes in saying: "Without the publicity which the press has generously given to all the departments of war work, the wonderful results which Wyoming has achieved would not have been possible."

Throughout the work of the Four-Minute Men splendid cooperation was received from the Wyoming State Council for National Defense and the expenses of the State Director's office were handled by them. At no time did the State have less than 22 chairmen and the maximum number was 27, while 200 men lent their aid in making addresses.

V. ROMAN POLICY IN ARMENIA AND TRANSCAUCASIA AND ITS SIGNIFICANCE.

By DAVID MAGIE,
Princeton University.

ROMAN POLICY IN ARMENIA AND TRANSCAUCASIA AND ITS SIGNIFICANCE

By DAVID MAGIE
Princeton University

ROMAN POLICY IN ARMENIA AND TRANSCAUCASIA, AND ITS SIGNIFICANCE.

By David Magie.

The relations between Rome and the kingdom of Armenia had their origin in the defeat administered by the Scipio brothers to Antiochus the Great in the battle of Magnesia. In the ensuing break-up of the western portion of the Seleucid Empire the satraps of the districts comprising the high table-land of Armenia and the valley of the river Aras made submission to the Romans and received from them the title of King.[1]

Artaxias, thus constituted king of the eastern section, enlarged his kingdom by the annexation of the surrounding districts, until it embraced most of the Armenian table-land. His capital was Artaxata, near the modern Erivan, where the Aras Valley broadens out into the plain which modern Armenians hold to be the cradle of the human race.

It was, however, Artaxias's descendant, Tigranes the Great, who caused Rome to tighten her hold on Armenia. As a result of his imperialistic ambitions and his alliance with his father-in-law, Mithradates of Pontus, he came into conflict with the Romans. After a crushing defeat at the hands of Pompey he was forced to admit a Roman garrison into Artaxata and to make submission to the Roman general, placing his crown in Pompey's hands, to receive it again from him as the gift of Rome. From this time on Armenia was, by turns, a vassal kingdom under a scion of the house of Artaxias or a Romanized princeling from some petty kingdom of western Asia, a Roman client state under a younger son or brother of the King of Parthia, a province of the Empire, and again a Roman protectorate ruled by a Parthian.

A relationship, moreover, not very dissimilar, was developed between Rome and the kingdoms northeast of Armenia—Iberia, corresponding to the region about the modern Tiflis, and Albania, including the basin of the lower Kur as far as the Caspian Sea. These districts also were overrun by Pompey. He defeated their kings, forced them to give hostages and sue for peace,[2] and displayed their

---

[1] Strab. XI., pp. 528, 531f.

[2] Plutarch, Pomp., 34–36; Dio XXXVII, 2–5.

names in his triumphal procession in the list of the monarchs whom he had conquered.[3] For a time, at any rate, he held the strongholds of Armastica and Seusamora near Tiflis, which command not only the valley of the Kur but also the Pass of Dariel.[4]

The policy of Pompey was continued by Antony. Artavasdes, the son and successor of Tigranes, was ordered to furnish troops for Antony's Parthian campaign in 36, and P. Canidius Crassus occupied once more the strongholds south of the Caucasus and forced the kings of Iberia and Albania to become so-called allies of Rome.[5]

With the accession of Artavasdes's son, Artaxes, begins the long series of Roman and Parthian intrigues that play so great a part in the story of Roman policy in Armenia. Renouncing all allegiance to Rome, Artaxes formed an alliance with the Parthian monarch, Phraates, and ruled Armenia under Parthian suzerainty. Roman intrigue, however, was not inactive. Phraates was persuaded to abandon Rome's rebellious vassal, and the pro-Roman faction in Armenia was impelled to murder Artaxes and send a deputation to Augustus, requesting that Artaxes's brother, Tigranes, then a captive in Rome, be sent to rule in the kingdom of his ancestors.[6]

Tigranes, accordingly, was crowned king at Artaxata in 20 B. C. The act of coronation was performed by Tiberius Claudius Nero, stepson of Augustus, and Roman troops were present at the ceremony.[7]

So Roman suzerainty over Armenia was established, and at Rome coins were struck bearing the legend *Armenia Capta.*[8]

The reign of Augustus shows a series of determined, and sometimes almost desperate, attempts to retain this suzerainty. A succession of petty princes, first from the Armenian royal house, then, when this became extinct, from the neighboring principalities of Media Atropatene and Cappadocia were proclaimed kings of Armenia by the grace of Rome. Meanwhile the Parthian monarchs spared no effort to stir up trouble for the Roman vassal and to annex Armenia to the Parthian Empire. The ceremony of investiture performed by Tiberius in 20 B. C. was repeated by Gaius, the grandson of Augustus, in 1 A. D., acting as the special representative of the Roman Emperor. But toward the end of Augustus's reign the Roman claimant was driven from Armenia, and all the efforts to establish a Roman vassal king seemed to have been made in vain.

In Transcaucasia, on the other hand, the diplomacy of Augustus produced better results. The alliances that had been imposed by

---

[3] Appian. Mithradatica, 107.
[4] Strab. XI, p. 501; Dio XXXVII, 1.
[5] Strab. XI, p. 501; Plutarch, Anton, 34; Dio XLIX, 24.
[6] Mon. Ancyranum, V, 24; Tacitus, Annals, II, 3; Dio LIV, 9.
[7] Mon. Ancyr., V, 24–28; Suetonius, Tib., 9; Tacitus, Ann. II, 3; Dio LIV, 9.
[8] Eckhel, Doctrina Numorum, VI, p. 98.

Canidius Crassus upon the princes of Iberia and Albania were perpetuated, and these monarchs were included by Augustus in the list of those who sought his friendship.[9]

The policy of holding Armenia in vassalage was continued with more success by Tiberius. Zeno, a prince of Pontus, was crowned by Germanicus at Artaxata as vassal king of Armenia,[10] and after his death, about 35 A. D., the kingdom was conferred on Mithradates, brother of Rome's ally, the King of Iberia.[11] During the reign of Zeno the Parthians had made no move against Armenia, but at his death Artabanus III of Parthia seized the kingdom and proclaimed as king, first, his oldest son Arsaces; then, after his assassination by Mithradates, a younger son, Orodes.[12] Finally, however, he was forced to recognize Mithradates as king, Armenia again became a vassal state of Rome, and a Roman garrison was quartered near Artaxata.[13]

Rome's suzerainty, however, did not last for long. Mithradates was overthrown by his nephew,[14] and the Parthian monarch, Vologaeses I claimed Armenia for his brother Tiridates. The result was a war with Rome. The government of Nero despatched Domitius Corbulo to Armenia. The table-land was invaded and Artaxata captured. Another Romanized princeling, one Tigranes, was established as king and the Roman garrison returned to Gorneae.[15] The new claimant, however, did not remain in his kingdom for long. Vologaeses, roused by an unprovoked attack on the part of Tigranes, again proclaimed his brother Tiridates king of Armenia.[16] Corbulo, evidently not deeming Tigranes worth the price of a Parthian war, entered into a series of negotiations looking to a diplomatic solution of the Armenian question. After many delays and in spite of a defeat administered by Vologaeses to Corbulo's colleague Paetus, governor of Cappadocia, it was finally arranged that Tiridates the Parthian should be king of Armenia, but as the vassal of Rome. As the result of this agreement Tiridates laid down his crown before the statue of Nero in the Roman camp and journeyed to Rome to receive it again from the Emperor himself.[17]

So the policy of Augustus was replaced by a new solution of the Armenia question—a compromise between Roman and Parthian. A Parthian prince ruled in Artaxata, but as Rome's vassal, and only

[9] Mon. Ancyr., V, 53.
[10] Tacitus, Ann., II, 56; Strab., XII, p. 556.
[11] Tacitus, Ann., VI, 32–33; Dio LVIII, 26.
[12] Tacitus, Ann., VI, 33; Dio LVIII, 26; Josephus, Ant. Jud., XVIII, 2. 4.
[13] In the fortress of Gorneae; Tacitus, Ann., XII, 45; cf. Strab., XI, p. 529. It was doubtless on the Garni River, a tributary of the Aras.
[14] Tacitus, Ann., XII, 44–49.
[15] Tacitus, Ann., XIII, 6–8, 39–41; XIV, 23–26; Dio LXI, 16.
[16] Tacitus, Ann., XV, 1–2; Dio LXII, 20.
[17] Tacitus, Ann., XV, 24–31; Dio LXII, 22–23.

after recognition by the Roman Emperor. This policy was maintained by the Flavian Emperors, who thus kept a peaceful hold on Armenia. Iberia, too, they held in control by a garrison at Armastica.[18]

Not until toward the end of Trajan's reign was there any change of policy. Then, in answer to an attempt on the part of the Parthian monarch to set up a king in Armenia in opposition to Rome, Trajan declared war, invaded the table-land, ordered the Parthian claimant to leave the country, and declared Armenia a Roman province.

This policy of outright annexation was reversed by Hadrian. Once more Armenia received a Parthian as king, but under the supremacy of Rome, and the compromise begun by Corbulo under Nero was continued through the second century. Even the war waged by Lucius Verus and his generals against the Parthians, in which Armenia was overrun by both Roman and Parthian and Artaxata destroyed, did not ultimately change the policy of Rome. A Roman garrison was maintained at the new capital, Valarshapat (now Etchmiadzin),[19] built by a Roman general to replace the destroyed Artaxata. Roman garrisons, too, were stationed at the eastern end of the Black Sea, and the kings of Iberia and Albania were kept in a position of dependence.

Amid the various changes in the policy pursued by Rome in Armenia, one principle stands out clearly: Armenia must be under Roman control and its king might rule only by the grace of Rome. In Transcaucasia a similar principle was followed. The King of Iberia was kept in close relationship, termed an alliance, but actually a position of dependence and even vassalage. A Roman garrison was maintained in the Plain of Erivan; and in Iberia Rome held the fortress of Armastica, commanding both the valley of the Kur and the Pass of Dariel.

The question is inevitable: Why this insistence on the control of these regions—the table-land of Armenia and the valleys of the Aras and the Kur? Why dispatch so many generals and so many armies to maintain this supremacy?

The reason is not to be found in the natural wealth of the country. Alexander, indeed, was told of gold mines in the Armenian mountains.[20] But he was unsuccessful in his quest of the precious metal, and there is no evidence that any later search was made. The copper deposits in the mountains between the valley of the Aras and the basin of the lower Kur seem to have been altogether unknown in antiquity. And, though the plains of Armenia are rich and fertile,

---

[18] According to an inscription found there of 75 A. D.; see C. I. L., III, 6052, and Cagnat, Inscr. Graec. ad Res Rom. pert. III, 133.
[19] C. I. L., III, 6052.
[20] Strab., XI, p. 529.

no attempt was made to use them as a grain-producing area for the Roman world.

( ) Nor was the aim of the Romans merely the maintenance of prestige in the East. It was not the method of Rome to squander resources of men and money merely for the maintenance of prestige, as the conservative policy on the Rhine and Danube frontiers sufficiently attests.

(b) Nor, on the other hand, was the reason one of military necessity. Mommsen, it is true, finds an explanation in the statement that Armenia "was by its position, in a military point of view, a sally port for each of the great powers (Rome and Parthia) into the territory of the other,"[21] and this theory has found wide acceptance. It does not, however, accord with practice. Of all the Roman attacks on the Parthians or the Persian Sassanids, two only were conducted by the route leading across the Armenian plateau and thence by the Aras into Persian Azerbaidjan—that of Antony in 36 B. C., and that of Severus Alexander in 232 A. D.; and both of these were utter failures. All other invading Roman armies advanced against Ctesiphon by way of northern Mesopotamia. On the other hand, the Parthians never entered Roman territory by way of the Armenian plateau and the upper Euphrates, but always by the routes south of Malatia and the great gorge. Clearly, Armenia was little used as a "sally port."

(c) It is perhaps not without significance that Trajan, after the acquisition of the new provinces of Mesopotamia, Assyria, and Babylonia, established customhouses on the Euphrates and the Tigris.[22] It is perhaps not an unsafe assumption that a similar customhouse was maintained on the Aras at the bridge near Artaxata. However this may be, this bridge was a thoroughfare, the importance of which was indeed great. To the west of it extended the important highway leading across the table-land of Armenia to Erzerum and Ilidja on the upper Euphrates, thence to Satala on the upper Kelkit Irmak, and so northward to Trebizond or westward to Asia Minor. This was the road that Corbulo used in order to send to his armies supplies from the Black Sea,[23] and this was the route by which Trajan invaded Armenia in 114.[24] Southeastward from Artaxata the great highway led down the valley of Aras, the route of the modern railway.[25] One branch followed the course of the river to the Caspian, another went to Ecbatana-Hamadan, whence led the caravan road through the Caspian Gates to India and China.[26]

[21] Provinces of the Roman Empire, II, p. 37.
[22] Fronto, Princ. Hist., p. 209 N, cited by Mommsen, Provinces, II, p. 75.
[23] Tac. Ann., XIII, 39.1.
[24] Dio-Xiphil., LXVIII, 18–19.
[25] Tab. Peuting, Sec. X ; Miller, K. Itineraria Rom., p. 654f.
[26] Tab. Peuting, Sec. XI ; Miller, K. Itin. Rom., pp. 781f and 792f.

Between Ecbatana and the western world only two routes were
possible, for the Hakkiari and Zagros Mountains are an effective barrier between the Iranian plateau and the basin of the Tigris. Of
these, one led over the Zagros Pass back of Khanikin and along
the upper course of the Diala River.[26*] This was the route of Alexander. The other was the road along the Aras and through Armenia. The former must remain under Parthian control, for none
but a Trajan or a Severus tried to hold the Tigris basin. The latter
on the other hand, would be controlled by the power that held Artaxata and the table-land to the west. The commercial and financial
advantages of the control of the Plain of Erivan and of the Armenian plateau are evident.

This highway, however, the Romans could never hope to possess.
So long as the Parthians held Ecbatana, they could divert traffic to
the Khanikin route and away from the road which led to Artaxata.
Iberia, on the other hand, afforded another means of communication
with the East, a trade route undisturbed by Parthian or Persian. As
early as the beginning of the third century B. C., Patrocles, acting
under orders from Antiochus I, explored the Caspian Sea and reported the existence of an important trade route leading from northern India to the River Oxus, down the river by ship, and so into the
Caspian Sea, either through a channel of the Oxus flowing into the
Caspian, or from the river to the sea by some overland route.[27]

Wares were then shipped across the Caspian and up the Kur to the
head of navigation. From this point they were carried via Tiflis and
Armastica to the Black Sea.[28] This route was investigated also by
Pompey, the originator of the policy of Roman control of Armenia
and Iberia. His exploring party maintained that in seven days a
caravan could travel from India to a point on a navigable tributary
of the Oxus. From here wares could be sent by ship to the Caspian
and thence up the Kur to a point distant only five days' journey from
the Black Sea.[29]

The control of Iberia, therefore, assured the control of the western
end of the trade route which led from the Black Sea through Transcaucasia to the mouth of the Kur, thence by way of the Caspian to
the upper Oxus. From the valley of the upper Oxus, a road led
via Merv across the Paropamisus Range to Herat,[30] corresponding

[26*] Tab. Peuting, Sec. X; Miller, K. Itin. Rom., p. 791f.

[27] The ancient writers seem to have believed that the Oxus flowed into the Caspian,
and until recently a depression between the lower course of the river and the Caspian
Sea was regarded as the old bed of the Oxus. Now, however, it is more generally believed that the Caspian in antiquity extended much farther eastward than at present, and
it is not impossible that the Oxus emptied into the eastern extension. For a summary of
the question see P. Kropotkin, Geogr. Journal, XII (1898), p. 306–310.

[28] Strab. XI, p. 509; cf. Pliny, N. H., VI, 58.

[29] Pliny, N. H., VI, 52.

[30] Tab. Peuting, Sec. XI; Miller, K. Itin. Rom., p. 794f.

presumably to the modern route. The short cut to India, however, led from the Oxus across the range of the Hindu Kush, probably by the Khawak Pass,[31] to Alexandria in the Hindu Kush, situated, according to Pliny,[32] 50 miles from Ortospana, the modern Kabul. Ortospana was the junction of the roads leading from Herat, from Bactra, and from India.[33] From Alexandria in the Hindu Kush and from Ortospana, well-defined routes led to the basin of the Indus.[34]

The Plain of the Oxus was also the starting point of the trade route to China, over which passed the caravans that brought silk to the western world.[35] In the first century B. C. Bactra became a great silk market. The caravan routes from central China converged at Kashgar in the northeastern corner of Chinese Turkestan. From here the China trade crossed the mountains of Pamir past the Lithinos Pyrgos, mentioned by Ammianus Marcellinus,[36] and thence via Faizabad to the Oxus.

Thus the Oxus valley was a great trade thoroughfare; its means of approach to the western world was by the way of the Caspian and Transcaucasia, and with the possession of the isthmus between the Caspian and the Black Seas the control of this route came into the hands of Rome. Accordingly, the policy of maintaining Roman supremacy in Armenia and Transcaucasia was dictated, not by military, but by economic and commercial considerations.

During the nineteenth century the control of the land routes to India was acquired by Russia. Beginning in 1801 with the annexation of the vassal kingdom of Georgia, she extended her Transcaucasian domain at the expense of Persia and Turkey, until, in 1829, she acquired Poti, on the Black Sea, and her frontier had been extended southward and eastward to the Aras and the mouth of the Kur.[37] The control of the great isthmus was completed by the acquisition of Batum in 1878. Finally, in 1907, the famous Anglo-Russian agreement secured to Russia the control of all northern Persia with the route from Teheran to the Afghan border. Railways followed in the wake of Russian expansion. The line from Tiflis to Alexandropol was continued past Erivan and down the valley of the Aras to Djulfa on the frontier of Persia, and about 1914 it was carried on to Tabriz, whence it was to proceed to Teheran.

---

[31] This seems to have been the pass used by Alexander on his northward journey. See Arrian, Anab. Alex., III, 28–29.

[32] Nat. Hist., VI, 61.

[33] Strabo XI, p. 514, and XVII, p. 723.

[34] See Ritter, Erdkunde II, p. 14f.

[35] Herrmann, A. Die alten Seidenstrassen zwischen China und Syrien, Berlin, 1910, p. 5f.

[36] XXIII, 6, 60.

[37] Quadflieg, F. Russische Expansionspolitik, 1774–1914, Berlin, 1914, p. 112f.

Meanwhile, however, another route to India was planned by Russia. This was nothing less than the old caravan route by way of the Caspian and the Oxus plain to the Hindu Kush Range and thence to Kabul and India.

In 1869 Krasnovodsk, on the Caspian, was fortified. This was followed by the conquest in 1881 of the western part of the present Province of Transcaspia, and by the annexation of Merv in 1884. Thus Russian domination was extended to the Oxus. Here also the railway followed annexation. The Transcaspian line was begun in 1880; in 1886 it was extended to Merv, and in 1895 a branch line was constructed from Merv to Kushka, on the Afghan frontier.[38]

British Russophobes have regarded the construction of this line as an important part of a Russian advance upon India.[39] They have pointed to the ease of invasion which its proximity affords, and have shown that with the aid of the Batum-Baku line, troops could be conveyed from Odessa to Merv in four or five days, and that the terminal station of Kushka is only about 75 miles distant from Herat. However this may be, the possession of Transcaspia assured to Russia the control of the northern routes into India. The road from Kushka leads to Herat and thence to Kabul to the east, or Kandahar to the southeast,[40] while another way is available from Tchardjui, where the railway crosses the Oxus, up the river by boat to Kilif, and thence by way of Balkh (ancient Bactra) across the Hindu Kush to Kabul,[41] closely approximating the ancient trade route. From Kabul to Peshawar in the Punjab the distance is only 172 miles.

The recent Anglo-Persian treaty seemed to advance British control westward from Herat to the Aras and the border of Armenia and to ensure an approach to India through northern Persia. This approach can be connected with the western world by two routes—the one, the Zagros Pass, leading from Hamadan through Khanikin to the Tigris basin and the Bagdad Railway; the other, the way through Armenia, either to the Black Sea at Batum or Trebizond, or across the table-land into Anatolia and Constantinople.

The conquest of Mesopotamia seems to have assured to Great Britain the control of the Zagros approach, but the future status of Armenia is still undecided. The power that controls it will control, even as the Romans did, a highway of great economic and strategic importance and a position of advantage in the Near East.

---

[38] The distance by rail from Krasnovodsk to Kushka is 753 miles; Baedeker, Russia, 1914, p. 512.

[39] Curzon, Russia in Central Asia, London, 1889, p. 267f.

[40] Herat to Kabul, 500 miles; Herat to Kandahar, 389 miles; see Curzon, p. 418.

[41] Kilif to Kabul via Balkh, 380 miles; Curzon, p. 418.

VI. THE EPEIROS–ALBANIA BOUNDARY DISPUTE IN ANCIENT TIMES.

By HERBERT WING,

Dickinson College.

25066°—23——20

THE EPEIROS-ALBANIA BOUNDARY DISPUTE IN ANCIENT TIMES.

By HERBERT WING.

The modern State of Albania[1] lies along the eastern shore of the Adriatic directly opposite the "heel" of Italy.[2] The larger part of the country is included between the fortieth and the forty-second parallels of north latitude and between the nineteenth and twenty-first meridians of longitude east of Greenwich. Thus situated, it occupies a district known in ancient times variously as South Illyricum, West Macedonia, and Praevalis. Its southern boundary, as delimited by the international commission in .1913–14, follows in general the northern rim of the Kalama Basin (ancient Thyamis) from a point opposite Corfu northeastward across the Viosa (ancient Aoos) to the Boion Range, and thence north toward Lake Ochrida (ancient Lychnis).[3]

South of Albania is the Greek province, Epeiros, until recently a part of the vilayet of Jannina.[4] This district derives its name from the Greek word for "mainland" or "continent." That in ancient times it was used vaguely is shown by the fact that it sometimes included Akarnania to the south and sometimes was extended northward to the Skumbi River (ancient Genousos).[5] The limits usually fixed by ancient writers—for example, Pliny the Elder[6]— are the Glossa Promontory and the Gulf of Arta. The eastern and northeastern frontiers were, as we shall see, uncertain, although Pindos formed the boundary toward Thessaly.[7]

Between Epeiros as it is now constituted and a line drawn nearly straight from Cape Glossa to Lake Ochrida is a region inhabited

---

[1] Albania was established as an independent state in 1913. See Nationalism and War in the Near East (by a diplomatist). Carnegie Endowment for International Peace, Division of Economics and History (Oxford, 1915), pp. 340–6; L. Stoddard and G. Frank, Stakes of the War (N. Y., 1918), pp. 209–218; W. M. Sloane, The Balkans, a Laboratory of History (N. Y., 1914), passim; N. Forbes, A. J. Toynbee, D. Mitrany, D. G. Hogarth, The Balkans (Oxford, 1915), passim; J. A. R. Marriott, The Eastern Question (Oxford, 1918), passim; D. G. Hogarth, The Nearer East (N. Y., 1902), passim.

[2] Hence its importance in Italian diplomacy. The Straits of Otranto are only 45 or 50 miles broad, or approximately twice those at Gibraltar.

[3] Dotation Carnegie pour la Paix Internationale, Enquête dans les Balkans (Paris, 1914), map on p. 198.

[4] C. Bursian, Geographie von Griechenland, 2 vols. (Leipzig, 1862), I, 9–40; W. M. Leake, Travels in Northern Greece, 4 vols. (London, 1835), passim.

[5] Approximately the line of the Egnatian Way. Strabo, VII, ch. 7, 4; cf. ch. 5.

[6] Pliny, Natural History, IV, 1.

[7] F. W. Putzger, Historische Schul-Atlas (Leipzig, 1901), pl. VI.

chiefly by Albanians of the Liab and Chiam tribes.[8] It contains
the towns of Delvinon, Argyrokastron, Tepeleni, Moskopolis, and
Koritsa. This district, approximately ancient Chaonia, Atintania
and Paravaia, and part of the country of the Illyrian tribes, Enche
leai and Dassaretai,[9] the modern Greeks call Northern Epeiros; and
they ask its surrender on the grounds that its culture and religion
are Greek; that its population, although Albanian in speech, is
Greek in race and political adherence; and that the region itself
is historically a part of Hellas.[10]

Our problem is to ascertain where the northern line of Epeiros
was drawn in ancient times, and whether there was a recognized
racial or cultural difference in the tribes north and south of that
line whom we may conveniently name Illyrians and Epeirotes. We
must further try to discover whether the Epeirotes were considered
by the Greeks as belonging to the Hellenic race.

With the exception of " wintry Dodona," which Homer mentions,[11]
the whole region north of the Gulf of Arta to the River Save is
scarcely mentioned in extant Greek literature before the age of
Pericles. Herodotos apparently considered the Nekyomanteion on
the Acheron and Dodona near Lake Jannina to be Greek, at least
in language.[12] A century later Aristotle expressed the belief that
Epeiros was the original home of the Greeks.[13] Thucydides, on the
other hand, plainly asserted that the Chaonians, Atintanians, Thesprotians, Molossians, Paravaians, and Orestians were barbarian
tribes in the service of the Spartan general Knemos operating in
Akarnania in 429 B. C.[14] This statement was not made definite
by indicating to what branch of the barbarians these tribes belonged,
as Thucydides had done in the case of the Taulantians, an Illyrian
tribe dwelling near Durazzo (ancient Epidamnos or Dyrrhachium).[15]
This omission may or may not be significant. The tribes mentioned
included practically all of Albania-Epeiros south of a line running
from Cape Glossa to Mount Grammos in the Boion Range, or pos-

[8] M. E. Durham, The Burden of the Balkans (London, 1905), p. 281. Cf. G. Soteri-
ades, An Ethnological Map Illustrating Hellenism in the Balkan Peninsula and Asia
Minor (London, 1918) ; E. Venizelos, Greece before the Peace Congress of 1919 (N. Y.,
1919), pp. 2–3.

[9] Longman's Classical Atlas, pl. XIII.

[10] Venizelos, op. cit., pp. 2–5.

[11] Iliad, II, 750; XVI, 233.

[12] Herodotus, II, 56; V, 92; cf. VII, 176; I, 56; VIII, 43.

[13] Aristotle, Meteorologia, I, 353a (cited in G. Busolt, Griechische Geschichte [Gotha,
1893–], I, 198, note.)

[14] The Chaonians lived on the slopes of the Keraunian Mountains (Pliny, Nat. Hist.,
IV, 1; Strabo, VII, 7, 5). The Atintanians occupied the upper basin of the Viosa
(Strabo, VII, 7, 8; cf. Appian, Illyrian Wars, II, 7). The Thesprotians included south-
western Epeiros (Pliny, IV, 1; Strabo, VII, 7), the valley of the Acheron. The Molos-
sians held the upper Arachthos and the plain of Jannina (Bursian, Geographie von
Griechenland, I, 9ff.) The Paravaians and Orestians were situated on the slopes of the
Boion Range (Strabo, VII, 7, passim). The specific reference in Thucydides is II, 80.

[15] Thuc., I, 24.

sibly even farther east to Lake Kastoria and the Nercka Platina (ancient Bora). If their association was more than accidental it would point to the existence of an Epeiros which included one-third to one-half of the area claimed by the Greeks, but which was considered as essentially non-Greek in race. This latter element is not decisive, both because of the disagreement among ancient writers and because of our uncertainty as to whether Thucydides determined race by language or by culture. A somewhat parallel case is that of the Macedonians. The evidence down to the fourth century is, on the whole, adverse to the historical claims of the Greeks not only to Northern Epeiros but also to Epeiros south and east of the Kalama Basin. It, however, tends to indicate a racial solidarity among the tribes south of the Glossa-Grammos line and a difference between them and the Illyrian peoples farther north.

The process of Hellenization of the Epeirote tribes, already noticed by Thucydides in the case of Amphilochian Argos,[16] continued in obscurity during the next three centuries. The heir to the throne of the Chaonians was sent to Athens to be educated.[17] An Epeirote king, Alexander, was counted a Greek when he invaded Italy. Pyrrhus was held without dispute to be a Greek.[18] The kingdom which he established won general recognition as a Greek people.[19] The Illyrians were considered distinct from the Epeirotes.[20] The boundaries of Epeiros at this time are not clearly discernible; but from a demand of Pyrrhus on the Macedonians that Tymphaia and Paravaia be given to him.[21] we may infer that the northeast limit was Mounts Lingon and Amyros (approximately the Mitsikeli Range), and that Epeiros, therefore, did not include Konitsa or the district of Koritsa.[22] If Plutarch can be trusted, the Epeirotes had by the time of Pyrrhus attained a fair degree of national spirit.[23]

After the tragic death of Pyrrhus at Argos,[24] and the rule of some minor kings, the Epeirotes, in 234 B. C., abolished royalty and organized their state on the mode of the federal leagues in Aitolia

[16] Thuc., II, 68.
[17] Justinus, XVII, 3, 11; Cf. Bury, Greece, p. 614.
[18] Pausanias, Description of Greece, I, 11: 7.
[19] Their dialect belonged to the northwest branch of Greek. Cf. P. Giles, Manual of Comparative Philology (London, 1895), p. 472, and J. Beloch, Griechische Geschichte (Strassburg, 1893–), I, 38.
[20] Plutarch, Pyrrhus.
[21] Ibid.
[22] This triangular strip of land between the lines drawn from Cape Glossa to Mount Grammos, and from Mount Grammos to Lake Ochrida, and from Lake Ochrida to Cape Glossa, was inhabited in antiquity by the Cheledonii, Encheleai, and the Dassaretai, all of whom were in ancient times considered Illyrian. Besides these, the Atintanians, in the upper Viosa Basin, were sometimes considered Epeirotes (Pliny, Nat. Hist. IV, 1, 1), and sometimes as Illyrians (Appian, Illyrian Wars, II, 7).
[23] They act in concert and are spoken of under the general name Epeirotes instead of by their several tribes (Plut. Pyrrhus, passim).
[24] Pausanias, I, 13, 8; Plut., Pyrrhus.

and Achaia.[25] This step was followed by Illyrian attacks on Epeirote, Akarnanian, and Aitolian cities.[26] Phoinike, a strongly fortified and powerful city in the territory of the Chaonians, was taken and sacked.[27] The Epeirotes who fled from the attack took refuge among the Atintanians who lived along the Viosa.[28] The victorious Illyrians, recalled by their queen, Teuta, to repel an invasion of the Dardanians, gave back to the Epeirotes the captured freemen and their city for a fixed ransom, and returned to Illyricum, part by sea and part by the land route through Antigoneia (modern Tepeleni).[29] The relieving force of Aitolians and Achaians, which had its position at Halikranon near modern Delvinon,[30] made no attempt to molest the freebooters as they passed.

It is obvious from this account that in 230 B. C. the northern boundary of Epeiros must have included Chaonia and possibly Atintania; or, in modern terms, the frontier ran about due east from Cape Glossa through Tepeleni and the Viosa. The northeastern boundary can not be determined.

Then Teuta angered the Romans by capturing Italian ships and refusing satisfaction to the Roman ambassadors sent to demand guarantees for the future.[31] The Roman consul, Cn. Fulvius, with 200 ships, was sent to compel obedience. Although he arrived too late at Corcyra to prevent its capture by the Illyrians, he managed to persuade Demetrios of Pharos, the commander, to put the city into his hands and guide the Romans in their subsequent campaign against Teuta. This succeeded admirably. The Atintanes and Partheni surrendered unconditionally, the Ardiaians (possibly Bordaians) were subdued. Corcyra, Apollonia, and Epidamnos were taken under Roman protection. Teuta fled to Rhizon on the Bocche di Chattaro,[32] and made a treaty of peace the following year by which the Illyrians agreed not to sail beyond Alessio [33] with more than two galleys both unarmed.[34] This provision, if strictly obeyed, would protect the Greek cities in Albania and the regions farther south from Illyrian raids. The Illyrians in Albania were taken under a kind of protectorate. The Atintanians were made practically Roman subjects,[35] the first east of the Adriatic. Again the boundary ran along the Griva Mountains and the southern edge of the Viosa Basin. The northeastern boundary can vaguely be discovered from

[25] J. P. Mahaffy, Alexander's Empire (N. Y., 1887), p. 170.
[26] Polybius, II, 2–4.
[27] Polybius, II, 5.
[28] Polybius, II, 5.
[29] Polybius, II, 6; see also Leake, Travels in Northern Greece, map at end of vol. I.
[30] Polybius, II, 6.
[31] Polybius, I, 8–10.
[32] Polybius, II, 11.
[33] Anc. Lissos.
[34] Polybius, II, 12.
[35] Polybius, III, 16.

;he campaign which Philip V of Macedon waged in 217 B. C. against
;he Dassaretans an Illyrian tribe living south of Lake Ochrida in
;he present district of Koritsa.[36] This region was outside of the
;imits of Epeiros as then constituted.

I[l] 215 B. C. a treaty of alliance was concluded between Philip V
;nd Hannibal. It contained this article among others, sworn to by
;he Carthaginians:

And when the gods have given us victory in our war with the Romans and
;heir allies, if Hannibal shall deem it right t● make terms with the Romans,
;hese terms shall include the same friendship with you (i. e., Philip V and
;he Macedonians) made on these conditions: (1) the Romans not to be al-
;owed to make war on you (i. e., Philip V); (2) not to have power over Corcyra,
;pollonia, Epidamnos, Pharos, Dimale, Partheni, nor Atintania; (3) to restore
;o Dametrios of Pharos all those of his friends now in the dominion of Rome.[37]

This unwilling testimony points to the de facto existence of a
;rovince in present Albania between the Arsoen[38] and the Viosa
;ivers. The omission of Epeiros from the treaty indicates a
;eparate state south of the Roman sphere of influence. Philip's at-
;ack on Lissos in 213 B. C. brought the Illyrian tribes of North
;lbania under his control,[39] and prepared the way for the later
;rganization of Albania as a part of the Roman province of
;acedonia.[40]

The son of Philip, Perseus, won the support of the Illyrians and
;f the Epeirotes with disastrous results to both. Genthios, the
;llyrian king, who had possessed himself of Lissos during the weak-
;ess of Philip after Cynoscephalae, and who had attacked the Roman
;art of Illyricum (i. e., central Albania), was captured.[41] The
;llyrians, like the Macedonians, suffered a division of their terri-
;ory.[42] The people of Scutari, together with the Dassaretans and
;elepitani and other Illyrian tribes unnamed, but doubtless includ-
;ng the Atintanians, Eordaians, and Partheni, paid tribute to Rome.
;hus practically all of Albania north of the Viosa was under Roman
;ontrol. The second division of Illyricum included Montenegro
;nd southern Dalmatia; the third, Istria and northern Dalmatia.[43]
;t is again worth while to note that the Dassaretan territory around
;oritsa was counted as Illyrian and not as Epeirote.

Seventy Epeirote towns, chiefly in Molossis, were sacked by the
;roops of Aemilius Paulus; 150,000 persons were sold into slavery.[44]

---

[36] Polybius, V, 108.
[37] Polybius, VII, 9 (Shuckburgh's translation).
[38] Anc. Palamnos.
[39] Polybius, VIII, 15–16.
[40] See below; also Putzger, Hist. Schul-Atlas, pl. 12 (inset).
[41] Appian: Illyrian Wars II, 9; Polybius, XXVII–XXX, passim, esp. XXVII, 15; XXIX,
—4; XXX, 3, 14; Livy, XLIV, 30–32.
[42] Livy, XLV, 26.
[43] Livy, XLV, 26.
[44] Polybius, XXX, 16; Livy, XLV, 34.

From this blow the Epeirotes never fully recovered.[45] The country remained semi-independent until the war in Macedon in 146 B. C., when it was joined to Macedon and Albania as the Province of Macedon.[46]

Thereafter the history of Epeiros and of Albania follows the history of Rome. Administrative exigencies might cause the two districts to be united to Macedon or separated; but the line of cleavage was largely political and not so much racial or linguistic. The same influences that spread Roman law throughout the Mediterranean world, and Greek language and culture throughout the region east of the Adriatic, blotted out the distinctions between Albanian and Epeirote until the incursions of barbarian tribes and the decay of civilization, with interruption of communication, led to the development of new distinctions of race and language. But that story is the task of the historian of the Middle Ages.

I shall briefly mention the chief oscillations of the northern boundary of Epeiros between the time of Mummius (146 B. C.) and that of Irene (ca. 800 A. D.). Under Augustus, Epeiros and Albania were still ruled by the Roman proconsul of Macedonia.[47] The boundary between them, according to Bury[48] was the Viosa River. Pliny the Elder marks the limit as the Arkokéraunian promontory just south of the Viosa.[49] Strabo includes among the Epeirote the Atintanians, the Tymphaians, and the Orestians,[50] although he admits these peoples were mingled with Illyrian nations.

Trajan reorganized the empire. Under him Epeiros was made an independent province with Akarnania added. Albania was still joined to Macedon. The line was at the Viosa; but Epeiros included Atintania and Paravaia.[51]

Diocletian split up the older provinces of Macedonia and Achaia into six or seven—namely, Macedonia, Thessaly, Achaia, Praevalitana, Epirus Nova, Epirus Vetus, and Crete. These belonged to the diocese of Moesia and the prefecture of Illyricum.[52] Praevalitana was the present Albania; Epirus Vetus was the region south of the Griva Range; Epirus Nova comprised the territory of the Viosa Basin.[53] This diocese under the name of Macedonia went to the share

[45] Th. Mommsen, Roman Provinces (N. Y., 1886), I, 277.
[46] Ptolemy, III; H. F. Pelham, Outlines of Roman History (N. Y., 1893), pp. 152, 154; cf. J. Marquardt, Roemische Staatsverwaltung (Leipzig, 1873), I, 164; W. W. How and H. D. Leigh, History of Rome to the Death of Caesar (London, 1896), p. 282.
[47] Mommsen, Rom. Prov., I, 277.
[48] J. B. Bury, Roman Empire (N. Y., n. d.), pp. 97, 103; cf. map opposite p. 82.
[49] Pliny, Nat. Hist., IV, 1.
[50] Strabo, VII, ch. VII, 8.
[51] G. S. Goodspeed, A History of the Ancient World (N. Y., 1912), p. 476; Pelham, op. cit., p. 310.
[52] W. Arnold, Roman Provincial Administration (London, 1906), p. 195.
[53] Caesar, Civil War, edited by C. E. Moberly (Oxford, 1880), map opposite p. 72.

of Arkadios, when, in 395 'A. D., the empire of Theodosios was divided.[54]

The raids of barbarians became more disastrous.[55] With the coming of the Slavs, the Albanians and other suppressed peoples of the Balkan Peninsula became aggressive and encroached on the Hellenic population. This movement Finlay puts in the time of Heraklios.[56] The area of Greek civilization was restricted to the district south of a line running from Durazzo to Constantinople. Practically all north of that was given up to the invaders, and much of the inland country south of the line was seized by the Slavs. In the anarchy that followed all significance of the Epeiros frontier was lost, since Epeiros, with the exception of Jannina fell a prey to Albanian and Slav;[57] then to Bulgarian and Turk.[58] In this condition it remained until in our own days the armies of George I recovered Southern Epeiros and those of Constantine occupied Northern Epeiros.[59]

To sum up: Epeiros in ancient times was more fully Hellenized than was the region north of the Viosa. Its northern boundary was usually drawn from Cape Glossa along the Griva Mountains toward Argyrokastron, and thence east toward Konitsa; but sometimes it ran from the Gulf of Valona, through Tepeleni to Mount Grammos. At no time during the ancient period does it seem to have included Koritsa and the district around Moskopolis.

---

[54] D. C. Munro, History of the Middle Ages (N. Y., 1902), map before ch. 1.

[55] E. Gibbon, Decline and Fall of the Roman Empire, passim.

[56] G. Finlay, Greece Under the Romans (N. Y., n. d.), p. 329; id., Byzantine Empire (N. Y., n. d.), passim.

[57] S. B. Harding, New Mediaeval and Modern History (N. Y., 1918), pp. 28–29.

[58] J. H. Robinson, History of Western Europe (Boston, 1903), map on p. 152 (1000 A. D.).

[59] Forbes and others, Balkans, p. 241; Marriott, Eastern Question, pp. 457, 472.

VII. PETER OF ABANO: A MEDIEVAL SCIENTIST.

LYNN THORNDIKE,
Western Reserve University.

PETER OF ABANO: A MEDIEVAL SCIENTIST.

By Lynn Thorndike.

Peter of Abano, or Peter of Padua, as he is often called, from the larger city near which he was born and where he did much of his teaching, one of the most influential men of learning during the last years of the thirteenth and the opening years of the fourteenth century, of whose writings in medicine, philosophy, and astronomy many are extant and most of these in printed editions, has never been adequately or accurately discussed in English. In our language there have been merely brief notices of, or incidental references to him, in histories of science and medicine, or of the Inquisition and of rationalism in Europe. Such passages and parallel ones in foreign languages often give dates of his life or death incorrectly (as distinguished a scholar as Steinschneider, for example, gives the year of his birth as 1253 or 1246), or do injustice to his opinions, or represent him as a victim of the Inquisition and an example of the hostility of the medieval church to science, to an extent which the sources do not justify.

In the time now at our disposal it will hardly be possible to do more than briefly indicate Peter's general position in the history of science and then discuss the sources for, and chief known events of, his life, with some allusion to his writings.

Peter of Abano was not one of the earliest medieval men of science. Indeed, he may be regarded as one of the last representatives of the Latin revival of mathematical and natural science which seems, like the general medieval revival of civilization, to have started in the tenth and eleventh centuries and to have reached its height in the twelfth, thirteenth, and early fourteenth centuries. Coming thus, in a sense, at the close of a period or movement in the history of science, Peter not unnaturally occupied himself especially in supplementing, correcting, and reconciling the work of his predecessors. Some works that had been unsatisfactorily translated he retranslated. Such important works of Aristotle, Galen, and others, as he could find that had not yet been translated, he translated from Greek into Latin. He added to the medical work of Mesuë the Younger. And in his Conciliator, a tome of enormous bulk, he endeavored to reconcile and harmonize the conflicting opinions of the medical men and philosophers who had gone before him.

Pico della Mirandola at the close of the fifteenth century made a trenchant criticism of Peter's erudition, when he characterized him as "a man fitted by nature to collect rather than to digest." But this judgment was also too severe, for Peter was not a mere compiler, but something of an experimental astronomer as well as a painstaking and critical translator, a voluminous commentator on Aristotle, and a great medical authority. In the Conciliator he makes several references to his personal astronomical observations and to other treaties which he has composed upon astronomical topics. Some of these are extant in print or in manuscript, including the preface and first six Differentiae of the Lucidator which paralleled in the fields of astronomy and astrology his Conciliator in the field of medicine. Peter was as keenly interested in astrology as in astronomy, and was a firm believer in astrological medicine. But that pseudo science was a universal failing of his time, and even in Pico della Mirandola's day it was not merely "the less learned" who were "wont to admire" Peter "most when he lies most." Peter, however, had faith in the power of words as well as in the stars, and twice, in the Conciliator, states, in all seriousness, that he had made progress in science by means of a prayer to God made under a certain constellation.

Peter has often been called a disciple of Averoës and the founder of Averroism in Italy, but as far as I have examined his works I have found little to substantiate this. Peter did not foresee the achievements of modern chemistry, for he declared that it was impossible ever to find the quantities and weights of the constituent elements in objects. Such despair was, however, not surprising in view of the old Greek theory of four elements under which medieval scientists were still trying to work.

Peter's own writings, in which there are a number of personal statements and citations from his works, are the most reliable source for the events of his life. His will was published by dal Verci in 1789, and documents relating to his call to the new university at Treviso are reported both by dal Verci and Tiraboschi. Thomas, of Strasburg, prior general of the Augustinian Friars from 1345 to 1357, states one posthumous fact concerning Peter as an eyewitness, while later in the fourteenth century Benvenuto of Imola, in his Commentary on the Divine comedy, tells an anecdote about Peter's deathbed which sounds apocryphal. Rather legendary, too, seem some of the statements made about the middle of the fifteenth century, in the work on the great citizens of Padua in the past, which was composed by Michael Savonarola, the noted physician and medical writer, and grandfather of the famous friar who tried to reform Florence. But he adds new information concerning Peter's life, and seems to have had access to documents which we no longer possess, as well as to local tradition. He states that he treasures in his possession the original manuscript of Abano's chief work, the Conciliator, in Peter's own handwriting, and he mentions having read with great pleasure an abundance of letters by which the people of Padua recalled Peter to their midst from Paris. Savonarola's account is also important because of his sympathy with Peter's views, and appreciation of his learning. Scardeone, who wrote in the sixteenth century On the Antiquity of the City of Padua, can hardly be regarded as so good an authority as Savonarola, but he makes one or two new assertions concerning Peter's life.

In the seventeenth century Gabriel Naudé has something to say of Peter in his Apology for Great Men who have been falsely Suspected of Magic, published in 1625, but incorrectly places Peter's death in 1306; while Tomasini, in 1630, gives 1316 as the date and includes a portrait of Peter of Abano in his Eulogies of Illustrious Men adorned with Pictures. I have not had access to Duchastel's account of Peter in his Lives of Illustrious Physicians, published at Antwerp in 1618, nor to Goulin's A Historical and Critical Notice on the life of Abano, printed in 1715, but have used an article with a similar title by Count Gian-Maria Mazzuchelli, published in 1741, and a monograph by Colle which first appeared in 1823. Colle's article was reprinted with variations the next year. A monograph by Ronzoni appeared in 1878, and in 1884 Gloria adduced new source material in his Monuments of the University of Padua. Sante Ferrari discussed his contributions to biology in a pamphlet published in 1900, when it was stated that he would soon publish a volume upon Peter, but this expectation does not seem to have been realized. Meanwhile, in 1912, appeared an article by B. Nardi on The Theory of the Soul and the Generation of Forms according to Peter of Abano, and in 1916 Antonio Favaro wrote on Pietro d'Abano ed suo Lucidator astrologiae.

Peter's own statements in his chief work, the Conciliator, show that he wrote it in 1303, after having worked it over in classroom lectures and discussions for 10 years previously, and that he was 53 years of age at that time. In other words, he was born in 1250. On one point at least of Peter's biography we have more precise and scientific detail than is customary in the lives of the great men of the past, for he confides to us exactly how long a time elapsed before his birth, 9 months and 14 days, as he had learned by astrological scrutiny and from his "most capable mother." From Peter's will and from Scardeone we learn that his father was a public notary and that Peter himself had one son named Beneventus.

At some time of unknown date Peter was in Sardinia, where he says he saw a case of poisoning from "Pharoah's fig"; and in Constantinople where he discovered a volume of the Problems of Aristotle, which he translated into Latin for the first time. It was probably there, too, that he saw a Greek version of Dioscorides arranged alphabetically—his own edition of Dioscorides, however, follows another text—and secured the works of Galen and other treatises which Savonarola says he translated from Greek into Latin. Peter is also said to have visited Spain, England, and Scotland, but I have as yet found no proof of this.

There is more than one indication that Peter enjoyed papal patronage and protection, just as Arnald of Villanova, a medical contemporary of his, was papal physician to Clement V, at Avignon, and wrote treatises for that pontiff. Colle, however, doubted the story that Peter was court physician to Honorius IV (1285–1287) and charged him one hundred florins a day, on the ground that Peter would be too young at that time, and for the better reason that the chronicler Filippo Villani tells the same tale of a Florentine doctor. Peter's treatise on poisons is addressed in some manuscripts to Pope John XXII who was not elected until August 7, 1316—a date later than that usually set for Peter's death. But there is no very good reason for thinking Peter dead by 1316. It is true that he made his will in May, 1315, but that does not prove that he died soon after, for, to illustrate again by the life of Arnald of Villanova, Arnald made his will, which has come down to us, in 1305, but did not die until about 1312. Peter's citation, in his work on poisons, of some work by Avenzoar, which was translated for a pope whose name is abbreviated to "Bo," can only refer to Boniface VIII, pope from 1294 to 1303, and so indicates that Peter did address his work on poisons to John XXII and that perhaps he succeeded to the place which Arnald of Villanova, dead by 1312, had occupied in the favor of Clement V, John's predecessor. As we shall see presently from Peter's own words, Boniface VIII was probably the pope who had earlier protected him from certain persecutors. It is again interesting to note that Arnald of Villanova was rescued by the same pope, in 1300, from the theological faculty at Paris, who had detained him in France because of his book predicting the coming of Antichrist.

Much of Abano's life was spent at the University of Paris, where, Savonarola says, he was regarded as a second Aristotle, and called "the great Lombard." There he wrote his work on Physiognomy, which he dedicated to the man who was captain general of Mantua from 1292 to 1299. In 1293 Peter found astrological writings of the Jew, Abraham ben Ezra, who had flourished at Toledo in the twelfth century, defectively translated from Hebrew to French, and therefore published a more correct Latin rendition of his own, adding treatises that had not been included in the previous translation. He talked with the famous oriental traveler, Marco Polo, at some time between the latter's return to Venice, in 1295, and the completion of

ıe Conciliator, in 1303, in which he cites Marco's statements to him
ıncerning tropical countries near the Equator. Some, at least, of
eter's translations of Galen had already been executed, since they
·e referred to by him in the Conciliator, and others are found in
anuscripts dated 1304 and 1305. Savonarola states that Peter com-
ıeted the Conciliator and began the composition of his commen-
ıry on the Problems of Aristotle at Paris, and this is confirmed
ſ the Explicit of the latter work, which states that Peter wrote
ırt of it at Paris and finished it at Padua in 1310. One of several
anuscripts of the work now in the Bibliothèque Nationale at Paris
dated 1310 and is perhaps the autograph.

Colle estimated that Peter was recalled to Padua about 1306. Grab-
ann in his recent researches concerning the thirteenth century
anslations of Aristotle, has called attention to a translation of the
istory of Animals made from the Greek in 1260, which Peter of
baṇo purchased in 1309 from Francesco of Mantua for seven Vene-
an soldi. Peter's own work on the motion of the eighth sphere is
ıted 1310 in a Vatican manuscript of it of the fourteenth or fifteenth
ıntury, but, as he cites it in the Conciliator, this date must be in-
ırrect, or the text a revised and later one. In August, 1314, Peter's
ıme headed the list of three names to be balloted upon for the newly
tablished chair of medicine at Treviso, but either he was not elected
· refused the appointment, since Peter of Suzara was finally ap-
ıinted. A bequest in his will made in May, 1315, seems to indicate
at he did not expect to teach any longer in Padua. The only ques-
ɔn is, therefore, whether he died immediately or lived on and taught
Treviso. One manuscript of his work on poisons not only is ad-
·essed to Pope John XXII, but represents Peter as acting dean of
e University of Montpellier at that time, which would be 1316
· some later date. If this be true, we should have one more resem-
ance between the careers of Peter and Arnald of Villanova, whom
ılls of Pope Clement V twice mention as having " once long ruled "
Montpellier.

The statement has often been made that Peter of Abano was
ought to trial before the Inquisition on charges of heresy, magic,
astrology, and that he was only saved from a worse fate by dying
fore the trial was over. Indeed, often two trials are mentioned—
e in 1306 and another at the time of his death in 1315 or 1316. Let
see what evidence there is on these points.

In the Conciliator, written in 1303, we find a germane statement
Peter himself at the close of a chapter in which he has discussed
·e determination of periods in history and the rise of new prophets
d religions, by the course of the stars, and the connection of seven
gelic intelligences with the seven planets. After this somewhat

bold but for that time scarcely novel indulgence in astrology, Pete
concludes:

So much then has been said as can be comprehended by reason concernir
this matter according to the skill of the world's scholars, in no way derogatir
from divine wisdom in what has been written above, but rather in all poin
confirming it, since it alone is truth and life. In this matter, however, son
mischief makers, unwilling or rather unable to hear, for a long time ha\
freely vexed me, from whose hands at last the said truth has laudably snatche
me and mine, with the intervention, too, of an apostolic mandate.

Peter, in other words, has gotten the better of his would-be de
tractors or persecutors, and the pope, presumably Boniface VII
has issued an injunction in his behalf. But this can not refer to
trial in 1306 or 1315, since it was written in or before 1303. In fac
it need not have reference to a trial, or to the Inquisition, at all. I
does, however, show that Peter's astrology had aroused considerabl
opposition, presumably at Paris.

It should be added that in a number of passages in his work
Peter recognizes that the Peripatetic, or Aristotelian philosophy, an
Christian dogma do not agree, and, while carefully stating and pe
haps secretly agreeing with the philosophical argument, gives h
adhesion, at least outwardly, to the orthodox faith. He divides h
Conciliator into three parts in honor of the Trinity; he employ
such devout phrases as "Si deo placet" and "Deo gratias" in h
Addition to Mesuë, and he argues that trust in God is of avail in th
art of medicine. In his last will and testament, as drawn up in 131
he makes profession of firm faith in the Trinity, Creed, and Articl
of Faith, and declares that he believes "in all respects just as Hol
Mother Church believes and teaches" and that he will remain i
this belief until his last breath. "And if it should be found that h
has ever said anything contrary to the Faith, he said it not becaus
he believed it, but probably for purposes of disputation."

It was probably on the basis of such facts as these just stated the
Benvenuto of Imola sixty or seventy years later elaborated h
anecdote of Peter's deathbed. About to die, he told the student
friends and fellow physicians who stood about his bed, that he ha
devoted his life especially to three noble sciences, of which one mad
him subtle, and that was philosophy; the second made him rich, an
that was medicine; the third made him a liar, and that was astrolog

Thomas of Strasburg, however, who, as we have said, was pri
general of the Augustinians from 1345 to 1357, has another tale t
tell in his Commentary upon the Sentences. He calls Peter of Abar
a heretic, although a most capable physician, one who derided th
miracles by which Christ and the saints raised the dead by arguin
that men afflicted with a certain disease often fall into a trance fc
three complete revolutions of the sky. And when asked if Lazaru

vas not in the tomb for four days he would say that it was for only
hree full days, since the first and fourth days were incomplete.
Thomas does not distinctly state that Peter ventured to deny the
esurrection of Christ, but concludes his incidental allusion to Peter
y saying: "But in this his iniquity he was deceived and received
he reward of his error. For I was present when in the city of
Padua his bones were burned for these and his other errors." The
nference which has been made from this brief statement is that at
ome time after Peter's death he was condemned by the Inquisition
nd his body disinterred and burned. Of this more presently.
'erhaps one further parallel in the career of Arnold of Villanova
nay be remarked, for five years after his death an inquisitor at
Tarragona pronounced some passages in his works to be heretical.
But be it further noted that Thomas does not say that Peter was on
rial before his death, nor does he charge Peter with magic or as-
rology. Indeed, in other passages of his own Commentary on
he Sentences, he displays a considerable faith in astrology himself,
sserting that the sky itself has a real action on inferior objects. He
ffirms, it is true, that the human will is free and that the stars can
ot act upon it directly; but he admits that they may exert an indi-
ect influence owing to the radical union within us of sense appetite
nd intellectual appetite.

A century later Michael Savonarola supplements with further de-
ail the general impression of an opposition between Peter and at
east a certain party in the church which we have already received.
Ie tells us that Peter's great knowledge of astronomy enabled him to
nake predictions so accurate that men thought he resorted to magic,
nd that the present tradition among the citizens of Padua is that
e was an adept in magic. "Moreover," adds Savonarola, who
pparently has a favorable opinion at least of natural magic, "this
elps round out his teaching, nor is it contrary to his other sciences,
ut makes the man the more illustrious." This reputation for magic,
owever, led the Dominican inquisitor to denounce Peter as a heretic
t Paris and try to lead him to prison and the flames. "But he was
eld in so great veneration by royal majesty and the entire uni-
ersity that means were not supplied the inquisitor to take him."
avonarola goes on to say that, when Peter learned of this, he in-
uced the king and university to call a council of doctors of Holy
cripture whom he convinced by forty-five arguments that not he but
he Dominicans were heretics. "And after sentence had been so
iven," continues Savonarola, "if the story is to be believed, it was
rought about that the Dominicans were driven from Paris as here-
cs and exiles and were unable to reside there for 32 years." But, of
ourse, we do not credit this story of the expulsion of the Dominicans,
hich is not recorded elsewhere, and therefore Savonarola's entire

account is open to suspicion. He goes on to say, however, that the case was then appealed to Rome and that by intervention of the Pope peace was at last made between the Dominicans and Peter, and that in his testament, "which is held in great veneration by many Paduans," Peter directed that his body should be buried in the church of the Dominicans as a sign to God and the world that he had kept the peace with them. "But," concludes Savonarola, "the Dominican inquisitor, full of venom and breaking the truce to which he had sworn—an action the more detestable in a clergyman—in the dead of the night opened the sepulchre, burned the body, and gave the ashes to the wind. O unspeakable crime!" Thus Savonarola says nothing to indicate that Peter was being tried by the Inquisition at the time of his death. All that he says goes to prove the contrary.

As we recede still farther from Peter of Abano's own time to Scardeone's sixteenth century account, still more specific details accumulate. Scardeone states that a rival physician, Peter of Reggio, jealous of Abano's science and fame, reported him to the Inquisition as a heretic and necromancer; and that the Inquisition twice instituted proceedings against him; namely, in 1306 when three illustrious men whom Scardeone names were his patrons and he was acquitted, and in 1315 when he died during the trial and was buried in the church of St. Anthony. Even Scardeone says nothing to suggest that Peter's death was due to torture or that he was tortured. The Inquisition proceeded, however, to condemn him upon the basis of his writings; but meanwhile his friends had removed and hidden his body, and the inquisitors had to be content with burning him in effigy. "This," coolly continues Scardeone, "is why Thomas of Strasburg wrote that he saw the bones of Peter of Abano burned in the square at Padua." Thus Scardeone not merely makes new assertions based on no one knows what, but contradicts the statements of Savonarola, who lived nearer to the event, and of Thomas, an eye witness. It is on Scardeone's account, nevertheless, that most modern allusions to Peter of Abano and his fate seem based. And he is apparently the first writer to state that Peter died while under trial by the Inquisition. Another story, which is not even in Scardeone, is that Peter's housekeeper Marietta kept his body hidden and afterwards buried it in the church of St. Peter at Padua.

One more point bearing upon the question of Peter's relations with the Inquisition is the inscription upon a statue of him at Padua which Naudé has recorded. It read: "Peter of Abano and Padua, most learned in philosophy and medicine, and on that account winner of the name of Conciliator; in astrology indeed so skilful that he incurred suspicion of magic, and, falsely accused of heresy, was acquitted." Thus only one trial is mentioned and nothing said of any condemnation. But unfortunately Naudé does not give the date of the inscription.

There is not time to mention other legends that grew up about Peter's name, and other works that, correctly or incorrectly, have come down to us under his name.[1] But before closing I should like to give a few specimens of the questions discussed in his noted work, the Conciliator.

11. Is the number of the elements four or otherwise?

14. Has air weight in its own sphere?

23. Is the brain of hot or moist complexion?

28. Is manhood hotter than childhood or youth?

30. Does blood alone nourish?

42. Is the flesh or the heart the organ of touch?

52. Does the marrow nourish the bones?

57. Is vital virtue something different from natural and animal virtue?

66. Is spring temperate?

67. Is life possible south of the Equator? (Peter answers, Yes.)

69. Is the white of the egg hot and the yolk cold?

70. (Supplement.) Is wine good for children?

72. Is there a mean between health and sickness?

77. Is pain felt?

79. Is a small head a better sign than a large one?

80. Are the arteries dilated when the heart is, and constricted also when it is?

81. Is there attraction exercised when the arteries dilate and a loosening when they are constricted?

83. Is musical consonance found in the pulse?

101. Can a worm be generated in the belly?

103. (Supplement.) Is death more likely to occur by day or night?

110. (Supplement.) Are eggs beneficial in fevers?

114. Does the air alter us more than food or drink does?

115. Is life shortened more in autumn than other seasons?

118. (Supplement.) Should one take exercise before or after meals?

119. Should heavy food be taken before light?

120. Should one eat once, twice, or several times a day?

121. Should dinner be at noon or night?

122. Should one drink on top of fruit?

123. Should one sleep on the right or left side?

135. Does confidence of the patient in the doctor assist the cure?

153. Is every cure by contrary?

[1] A fuller account of his life, works, science, and superstition, together with detailed references to the source material, will be given in my History of Magic and Experimental Science, Chapter LXX.

154. Should treatment begin with strong or weak medicine?

157. Does sleep help the cure?

171. Is cold water good in fevers?

182. (Supplement.) Can fever coincide with apoplexy?

183. Is paralysis of the right side harder to cure than that of th left?

193. Can consumption be cured?

194. Does milk agree with consumptives?

204. Is a narcotic good for colic?

206. Is blood letting from the left hand a proper treatment fo gout in the right foot?

VIII. ABSTRACT OF COMMISSIONS AND INSTRUCTIONS TO COLONIAL GOVERNORS IN AMERICA: 1740.

By ARTHUR H. BASYE.
Dartmouth College.

327

ABSTRACT OF COMMISSIONS AND INSTRUCTIONS TO COLONIAL GOVERNORS IN AMERICA: 1740.

By Arthur H. Basye.

The following entry appears in the Journal of the Board of Trade and Plantations under date of February 22, 1738:

"The Board having had several general instructions under their consideration, have ordered that an exact transcript be made of all such instructions as are general in their nature and applicable to all His Majesty's governments in America without distinction.

"That the said general instructions be digested under the several heads to which they belong respectively, such as Council, Assembly, Courts of Judicature, Granting of Lands, etc.

"That there likewise be a distinct transcript made of all such local instructions as are applicable to any particular colony or colonies."[1]

No further mention of this matter occurs in the journals; no document such as is here described is to be found among the papers of the Board in the Public Record Office. In the Newcastle collection in the British Museum, however, there is a volume bearing the date of 1740 which was obviously prepared as an "office handy book" for the use of the Board of Trade and which, in general, conforms to this order of 1738. Its title is, "Abstract of the Commissions and Instructions formerly and at this time given to the governors of His Majesty's Plantations in America with References to the Books and Papers showing the Alterations that have been made therein, as also Observations on the most remarkable Occurrences in each Government especially before the Establishment of the Office in 1696".[2] This volume also includes "copy book" forms of the proper methods of addressing formal communications to members of the Privy Council, to other high officials, and to the colonial governors, whose official and technically correct titles varied from colony to colony; there is, in addition, a list of the members of the Board from 1696 to 1749, showing for each the term of service, the reason for withdrawal—i. e., death, resignation, dismissal—and the line of succes-

---

[1] C. O. 391 : 47, pp. 24–25.
[2] British Museum, Additional Manuscripts, 30372.

sion.[3] It is, therefore, a convenient book of reference; as such it would be as useful to the Secretary of State as to the Board of Trade, and it is not difficult to understand why this document, along with many others of a like public nature, came into the hands of the Duke of Newcastle.

The value of the abstracts of the commissions and instructions is self-evident to all those who have attempted to trace the development of the colonial governorship; it is unfortunate that the whole of the colonial period is not covered, but with the aid of these summaries the task of collating the later commissions and instructions is made a comparatively simple one.

No editorial changes have been made except the change of omitting the rather complicated system of cross references to the papers of the Board. These references are, naturally, in the old office form and are of little or no value to one who has not direct access to the documents.

ARTHUR HERBERT BASYE.

[3] For further description see Andrews, Davenport, Guide to the Manuscripts Materials for the History of the United States to 1783, in the British Museum, in Minor London Archives, and in the Libraries of Oxford and Cambridge, p. 121.

Folio 2b

When the several clauses began or were altered.	Abstract of the Governors Commissions.
1660/1. Jamaica.	Revocation of the former Commission & the new Gov.ᵗ appointed who is to act according to his Commiss.ⁿ & such Instructions as he shall receive under the Sign Manual, or by Order in Council. To take the State Oaths himself & administer them to the Council.
1672. Barbados. } Leeward Isl.ᵈ 1686. }	Power to suspend Councillors & L.ᵗ Gov.ʳˢ in the Leew.ᵈ Islands, & Dep.ᵗʸ Gov.ʳˢ in y.ᵉ Islands dependent on Barbados.
1685. Virginia.	To send Accounts of all Vacancies in Council to the King. A Quorum of each Council to be ⎱3 in⎰ S.ᵒ Carolina. N.ᵒ Carolina. Virginia. New Jersey. New York. New Hampshire. ⎱5 in⎰ Barbados. Leeward Islands. Jamaica. Bahamas. Bermuda.
1673. Barbados. 1626. Virginia. 1660/1. Jamaica.	May fill up Vacancies in the Council to 7 but no higher. .... 9 in Virginia only. To call Assemblies (according to the Laws or Usage of the Place) according to the usage of other Colonies.
1680. Jamaica is the first precedent of Instructions for passing Laws as they now stand in the Commissions for all Governors, vid. Commission to Col. Dungan for New York 1683. vid. Commission to ditto to make all Laws with Consent of Council only 1685. Ibid.	Assembly Men must take the State Oaths, before they Act. Governor with Advice & Consent of the Council & Assembly may make Laws agreeable & not repugnant to English Laws. Laws must be sent within 3 months, for the Kings Approbation or Disallowance. Laws disallowed by the Crown shall be deemed void. Governor to have a Negative Voice in passing of all Laws. He may adjourn, prorogue & dissolve Assemblies. He shall keep and use the publick Seal.
1660/1. Jamaica.	He may administer or cause to be administered the State Oaths to all he thinks fit.
Ibid.	With Advice & Consent of Council he may erect Courts of Judicature and cause Oaths to be administered to Judges &c.
Ibid.	To appoint Judges, Comm.ʳˢ of Oyer & Terminer; Justices of the Peace &c.
Ibid.	May reprieve for Treason & Murder, all other Offences he may pardon.
1679. Virginia.	Power to collate Parsons to Beneficies.
1660/1. Jamaica.	May establish a Militia, pursue Enemies & put 'em to death, & execute Martial Law. With Advice & Consent of the Council may erect & demolish Forts, Castles &c.
1663. Barbados.	May make Cap.ⁿˢ, Lieuts. &c. of Ships of War, with power to execute Martial Law.
1684. Jamaica. 1685. Jamaica.	Gov.ʳˢ not to meddle with Offences committed at Sea on board the Kings Ships. But Officers or Sailors belonging to the Kings Ships he may punish for Offences on shore.
1679. Virginia.	All publick money to be issued by the Gov.ʳˢ Warrant, with Advice & Consent of Council.
1660/1. Jamaica.	To grant Lands with like Advice & Consent, reserving Quit Rents &c under publick Seal. And with same Advice & Consent to appoint Fairs, Marts & Markets, Ports, Harbours &c. All Officers, Civil & Military & all other Inhabitants to be aiding and assisting to the Governor & to the Commander in chief for the time being, who is to enjoy the same power as the Governor himself.
1625. Virginia. first Rule for Devolution of Government. 1680. Barbados. 1707. Virginia. 1674. Jamaica. 1702. New York.	If there is no Lieut. Governor, then the Governm.ᵗ in case of Death or absence of the Governor, is to devolve on the President of the Council. Governors to continue only during the Kings Pleasure. | an Exception to this Rule in the Leew.ᵈ Islands in 1731. vide Ent. K., fol. 108. | See a Deputy upon this Point between Estrida & Phipps of St. Kitsin 1728. Leeward Island, bun. T. 13, 14, 15, 16.
1691. New England. altered in Relation to Rhode Island in 1730.	The Gov.ᵗ of New York has Power to command the Militia in Connecticut. Gov.ᵗ of the Massachusetts the same Power in Rhode Island in time of war.
1697. New England.*	Gov.ʳˢ of the Massachusetts & New Hampshire have an implicit Power to suspend Patent Officers, all other Governors have that Power in their Instructions.

Folio 3.

When the several Powers were granted.	Observations on Powers and Restrictions formerly inserted in Governors Commissions & Instructions.
1680. Barbados.	The Governors had Power to appoint Deputy Governors in the dependent Islands, and Councillors, but those Councillors were not to be Judges.
Ibid.	S.ʳ John Witham was appointed President of the Council, tho' not eldest. Rule for Devolution of Governm.ᵗ established, then on the Council in gen.ˡ
1625. Virginia. } 1673. Barbados. }	In the Leeward Islands on the Lieu.ᵗ Gen.ˡ, then on Lieu.ᵗ Gov.ʳ of Nevis and last on the President of the Council of Nevis. .... (altered in 1732 as it now stands).
	Governors of Leeward Islands have Deputy Gov.ʳˢ in the Virgin Islands tho' no Power by their Commissions to appoint them.
	Governors formerly had a Power by their Com.ⁿˢ to suspend Cap.ⁿˢ of men of war. (revoked in 1702.)
1702.	Governors had Power for that Purpose given them by the L.ᵈ H. Admiral. Quite taken away in 1707. Jamaica. G. 348.
1692.	The Gov.ʳ of New York had Power to govern Pennsylvania also, but upon Mr. Penn's Petition and Submission in 1694, that Commission was revoked. Pennsylvania entries fol. 26, 51, 63.
1660. Jamaica.	In case of the Governors Death the Council were impowered to elect a new one.
Ibid.	Form of a Writ for electing Assembly Men directed by the Crown.
1661/2. Ibid.	Lord Windsor instructed to encourage Commerce with the Spaniards, and to force a Trade with them, if necessary.
1677. Jamaica.	Lord Vaughan was directed to suffer Spaniards to buy Blacks in Jamaica.
1687. D.º	The Duke of Albemarl was allowed to confer the Honour of Knighthood.
1684. D.º	Spaniards to be admitted to Trade to Jamaica by the Kings Letter, The Opinion of the Commiss.ʳˢ of the Customs thereon.
1704. Trade. C.	British Ships allowed to trade with the Spanish West Indies in time of War.
1660. Jamaica.	Governor to have 12 Councillors, Secretary to be one, & 11 elected by the
ib.	People, the Lieu.ᵗ Governor and Major were afterwards added to the Council.
ib.	Governor impowered to grant Commiss.ⁿˢ to Persons to find out new Trades.
1665. ib.	Governor has Power to erect Courts of Admiralty.
Jamaica.	An Order about Vice Admiralty Jurisdiction.
1674. Jamaica.	Power to erect Custom houses & Officers relating thereto.
1678. Ibid.	Governor impowered to Lease Mines out for 21 years.
Do. Do.	No Law to be passed that shall apply Fines or Forfutures [forfeitures?] to the Publick.
1680. Ibid.	Governor privately instructed to get a Revenue settled.
1686. New York.	King James allowed the Governor of New York to issue publick money without the advice of Council, and ordered all Laws relating to the Franchises and Liberties of the People to be deliver'd void, but commanded him to continue all the Laws for raising of Taxes in full Force, and impowered him to pass Laws with Advice of Council without an Assembly.
1667. Barbados.	Lord Willoughby was instructed to permit Spaniards to import at Barbados, Pearls, Gold, Silver, &c, and export thence Goods carried thither in English Bottoms. (vide Barbados, Bun. T. 240, 241).
1685. Jamaica. } Journal, Vol. 5. }	This Trade further extended.
1663. Barbados.	The Governor allowed to choose his own 12 Councillors, and change 'em at Pleasure.
ib.	And with their Advice, without an Assembly, to make Laws, but not to take Peoples Right away.
ib.	A Power to erect Courts to try Causes in Marine Affairs for 7 years only.

Folio 3b

When the several Powers were granted.	Observations on Powers and Restrictions formerly inserted in Governors Commissions & Instructions.
1663. Barbados..	Power of Martial Law exceeding great in making Articles of War.
1666. Do.	Governors allowed to accept of Presents from the Assemblies.
Do. Do.	Governors impowered to impress Merchant Ships.
1673. Do. Do.	Work Houses to be erected for employing the Poor. (1721. Barbados. When discontinued.)
1679. Virginia.	The King ordered that no suspended Councilor should be allowed to sit in the Assembly.
1638. Do.	Assemblies to be called yearly, and the Councilors & 10 Servants each, to be exempt from all Publick Charges, except to War, Parsons, Churches &c.
Do.	Hemp, Flax, Naval Stores & Silk Productions to be encouraged.
1662. Do.	The Governor to imitate New England in building Towns upon Rivers.
1676. Do.	The Governor and five Councillors to try all Treasons, Murders &cᵃ.
1679. Do.	Lord Culpepper had a Commission to be Governor during Life, with a Power to lease out Royal Mines for 21 years reserving to the Crown 1/10th of the Ore.
	And in Case of his and the Lieut. Governor's Death or Absence. the Council were to Assume the Government but to do nothing without Consent of the Major and Secretary.
ib.	He was forbid to call Assemblies without the Kings Leave.
	He was to have all Draughts of Bills approved here before passed, Except to raise money upon Emergencies.
1687. Bermuda.	Governor to secure one half of all Treasure fisht out of the Sea for the King.
695. Leeward Isds.	Colo. Codrington was impowered to supply vacant Commissions in Colo. Holts Rigiment.
16 Plans. Genˡ. } 1682/3. Barbados. }	Captains of Men of War, not to carry Merchants Goods on the Kings Ships.
16885. New England.	Colo. Dudley appointed Temporary Governor wᵗʰ a very remarkable Commᵃ.
16866. ib.	Sr. Edmund Andros appointed Governor, with Power to make Laws and raise
Do.	Taxes by advice of Council without Assembly. To have the same Power
Do.	over New York, New Jersey, Connecticut & Rhode Island.
1691. Do.	Governor of Massachusetts empowered to appoint an Attorney General.
	Queens Mandamus to the Governor about prosecutions for Witchcraft, and about Persons possessed with Divils & casting 'em out.
1696. Plansᵃ. Genˡ.	Governors with Advice of Council impowered to impress Seamen.
1683 and } Virginia. 1685 }	Governor to get a Law passed to impower him & the Council to levy Money on Emergencies without an assembly.
1686. New England	The enacting Stile of Laws to be by the Governor and Council only.
Plans. Genˡ. } Bermudas. }	Governors Allowance for Transportation to their Governments.
1679. New England.	The first Civil Government in New Hampshire by a Presid.ᵗ & Council, very different from all other Governments.
1682/3. Leew.ᵈ Islds.	Governor to pass Laws to Oblige Malefactors to serve 7 years.
1729/30. New Engl.	} The Commission for the Government of New Hampshire was altered as to a
1741. New Hampshire.	} Recital of its Boundaries, in 1729, and again in 1741.

Folio 4.

| | It has always been usual for the Crown to give Rank to new Councillors according as they stand recommended by the Lords of Trade, and it was so determined in Council upon a Memorial of Governor Clinton's relating to the Appointment of John Moore whose warrant bore date prior to the Commission of M[ess]ʳˢ Warren & Murray who had been recommended to his Majesty prior to John Moore. vid. Order of Council 23 July 1745. |

America. Abstract of

Copied from British Museum,

References when began or altered.	Abstract of the General Instructions.
	Governors to repair to their Govern⟨ᵗˢ⟩ & call the Council as herein named ......
1661. Jamaica. 1673/4. Do. 1672. Barbados. 1677. Jamaica.	To publish his Commission, take the State Oaths & Administer the same to ye Council. To communicate each of his Instructions to the Council, wherein their Advice is required.
1660. Jamaica.	To allow Freedom of Debate and Vote in Council. .... Governors on the Continent not to act with a less Quorum than five Councillors, unless upon Emergencies, when a greater number cannot be had.
1683. Virginia. 1684. Barbados.	To send the Names & Characters of 12 Persons fit to supply Vacancies in the Councillors.
	6 in the Leeward Islands & Bermuda only.
1672. Barbados. 1673/4. Jamaica. 1681. Virginia.	In case of Vacancies Govᵗ may fill up the Council to 7 and no more............, 9 in Virginia only.
	In the Massachusetts the Councillors are appointed yearly by the Assembly & the Governor is to send their Name and Characters.
1698. Virginia. 1727. Virginia.	In Virginia Councillors not to be protected from Suits at Law, but to obey Summons.
1672. Barbados. 1673/4. Jamaica.	Qualifications required for Councillors, Judges, Justices, & other Chief Officers.
1672. Barbados. 1717. Jamaica. Barbados.	Rules for suspending of Councillors & Lᵗ Govᵗˢ also in the Leeward Islands...
1686. Leeward Island.	Capⁿ Genˡ in the Leeward Islands may supply the Vacancy of a Lᵗ Govᵗ till further Order.
1681/2. Virginia.	Councillors not to be absent above ⎰12 months with the Govᵗˢ Leave⎱ on ⎰2 years without the King's Leave⎱ Penalty of losing their Places.
1707. Planⁱ Genˡ	Councillors residing in yᵉ Govᵗ & not attending after Admonition to be suspended.
1733. Planⁱ Genˡ	Surveyors Genˡ of the Customs to be Councillors extra. [ordinary]? in their respective Districts.
1676. Virginia. 1685. Do.	Rules for electing Assembly Men..
Then in the Commission.	
1729. Roger's Instructions Bahama.	The Governor may appoint a Clerk to the Assembly in the Bahamas only......
1702. New Jersey 1709. Provided for by an Act.	Place for the Assembly's meeting & Qualifications of yᵉ Members & Electors..
1676. Virginia. 1692. New Hampshire.	To reduce the Assembly Men's pay with Caution.........................
1713. Planⁱ Genˡ Jamaica.	The Persons of Assembly Men only protected during the Session..............
1730. Sᵒ Carolina.	
1720. Carolina. 1730.	Speaker of Assembly not to be chose even protempore, withᵗ the Governors Approbation.

the General Instructions.

Additional MS. 30372.

Number of each Articles to												Memoranda.
Barbados.	Leeward Islands.	Jamaica.	Bahamas.	Bermuda.	S° Carolina.	N° Carolina.	Virginia.	New York.	New Jersey.	Massachusets.	New Hampshire.	
1	1,2,3,4 & 5.	1	1	1	1	1	1	1	1	1	1	in 1733 the Words time being were added to the Lieutenant Gen! & Lieut. Governor of the Leeward Islands.
2	6	2	2	2	2	2	2	2	2	2	2	
3	7	3	3	3	3	3	3	3	3	3	3	
4	8	4	{The Commiss^ns limit the Quorum to 5 in the Islands.}		4	4	4	4	4	4	4	
					5	5	5	5	5	....	5	Jamaica old Instructions ordered all the Councillors to be summon'd each meeting, which order ought to be revived it being complained of at New York that the Governor only summon'd 5 at a time, which 5 he chose occasionally out of the 12.
5	9	5	5	5	6	6	6	6	6	5	6	
6	10	6	6	6	7	7	7	7	7	....	7	
....	....	....	....	....	....	....	....	....	....	....	....	
7	11	7	7	7	8	8	9	8	8	6	8	
8	12	8	8	8	9	9	10	9	9	....	9	
....	13	....	....	....	....	....	....	....	....	....	....	
9	14	9	9	9	10	10	11	10	10	....	10	
10	5	10	10	10	11	11	12	11	11	....	11	
....	....	....	....	....	....	....	....	....	....	....	....	
....	....	....	11	11	12	12	13	....	....	....	12	
....	....	....	12	....	....	....	....	....	....	....	....	This was first in New Hampshire Entries fol. 57. The Govr of the Leew^d Islands removed the Clerk of the Assembly of St Xtophers. Leew^d Islands L. fol 22.
....	....	....	....	....	....	....	....	....	....	12 & 13	....	
....	....	....	....	....	13	13	....	....	....	....	13	{This Article is remedied in New Hampshire by an Act passed there in 1732.
....	....	18	13	....	14	14	....	....	....	....	....	
20	....	....	....	....	....	....	....	....	....	....	....	

Folio 5ᵇ

References when began or altered.	Abstract of the General Instructions.
1728. Barbados. 1717. Jamaica. 1730. S? Carolina.	Assembly not to adjourn themselves more than de die in diem with! Govᵗˢ leave Councillors shall be allowed to amend money Bills..................................... Assembly Men in no Case to have greater Privileges than Commoners of G! Britain.
1670. Jamaica. 1679 1685 } Virginia 1684. Barbados.	Stile of enacting Laws and Rules for passing them.............................
1670. 1680. } Jamaica 1682 Barbados.	Rules for passing of Money Bills...
1674. Jamaica 1680 1732 } Barbados. 1679. Virginia 1730. South Carolina	No money to be levied without being accountable to the Treasury here........ To alter the Method of Poll Tax & lay an Impost on Liquors................. Arrears of Quit Rents to be forgiven, provided they pay for the future, and Fees also in N? Carolina, and Salaries to be paid in Proclamation Money.
1680. Barbados. 1717. Jamaica. Do.	Directions for passing Acts for Imposts on Liquors & raising of Supplies of Govᵗ. No Treasurer or Commissioner for receiving publick money to be appointed by the Assemblys. Councillors to be joined with Assembly men in corrisponding wᵗʰ the Agents..
1674 1718 } Barbados. 1674. Jamaica 1697. Plan! Gen! 1727. New York	Limitation of Laws reviving repealed Laws, & repealing Laws in being........
1720. Plan! Gen! 1721. Barbados 1730. S? Carolina 1740. Plan! Gen! 1706. Barbados. 1717. Virginia 1718. Plan! Gen! 1724. Jamaica. 1724. New York.	Passing Acts for issuing Bills of Credit & laying out Townships in S? Carolina.. For inforceing the Act relating to foreign Coins passing in the Plantations..... Acts of extraordinary Nature, or that effect the Trade Shipping &c of G! Britain
1708. New York. 1734. Jamaica. }	Rules for passing private Acts altered in 1721. Barbados I. fol. 143 & 1723 Plan! Gen! F. fol. 8.
1673. Jamaica 1716. Plan! Gen! }	To send Copies of all Laws fairly abstracted in the Margins...................
1707 1708 } New York.	All such Copies to have Dates, & the Governors Observations thereon.........
1714. Leewᵈ Islds. 1730. S? Carolina }	To revise the Laws and send a compleat Body of them.......................
1679. Papers of English and Alien Plan! no. 122.	Secretary of the Government to furnish Copies of Laws & Journals of Councils..

1679. Jamaica.
   Leewᵈ Islands.
   Virginia.
	Clerk of the Assembly to furnish Copies of all Votes of Assembly..............

| Number of each Article to. | | | | | | | | | | | | Memoranda. |
Barbados.	Leeward Islands.	Jamaica.	Bahamas.	Bermuda.	S? Carolina.	N? Carolina.	Virginia.	New York.	New Jersey.	Massachusets.	New Hampshire.	
20	....	15	14	....	13	14	14	....	....	....	....	
....	....	16	....	....	13	14	....	....	....	....	....	
....	....	....	....	....	13	14	....	....	....	....	....	
11	16	11	15	12	14	15	15	12	14	7	14	
12	17	12	16	13	15	16	16	13	15	8	15	
13	18	13	17	14	16	17	17	14	16	9	16	
....	....	....	....	....	....	18	....	....	....	....	....	In 1731, an Act was passed in pursuance of this Instruction (The said Act is no. 86). 1688 Orders about granting Lands & Quit Rents N? Carolina Propriety book fol. 29.
14	19	14 17	18	15	17	19	18	15	17	10	17	Quære, if this should not be general to all Governments.
....	....	19	....	....	....	....	....	....	....	....	....	
15	20	20	19	16	18 19	20	20	16	18	11	18	
16	21	21	20	17	....	21	21	17	19	12 15	19	
17	....	....	....	....	....	....	....	18	....	13	20	
18	22	22	21	18	20	22	22	19	20	14 16	22 23	
19	23	23	22	19	21	23	23	20	21	17	24	Fines & Recoveries passed in England, cannot affect the Plantations. (Plans. Gen! Bundle M., no. 21.)
21	24	24	23	20	22	25	24	21	22	18	25	An Act was passed for all the Leeward Islds in 1705 to suply this defect.
22	25	25	24	21	23	26	25	22	23	19	26	
....	26	....	....	....	100	24	....	....	....	....	....	
23	27	26	25	22	24	27	26	23	24	20	27	
24	28	27	26	23	25	28	27	24	25	21	28	

Folio 6ᵇ

References when began or altered.	Abstract of the General Instructions.
1717. Jamaica.	About supporting the Soldiers in Jamaica.................................
1683. Virginia. 1702. Barbados. 1703. Dº 1709. New Jersey. Planᵗ Genˡ 1727. New Jersey. 1728, 1729, 1730. New land.	No Gifts. Presents nor Grants to be made excepting House rent in some Governments. to Governors or others but to the King.
1697. New England. Barbados. 1729. Planᵗ Genˡ	Governors Salaries settled, & Additional Salaries alowed to some Govrs...... Fishing for Whales to be free to all his Majesty's Subjects...................
1679. Virginia. 1691. Dº 1698. Dº 1727. Dº	All Tobacco shipped in Virginia to pay Virginia Duties & Naval Officers to be sworn to do justly in regard to the Duty of 2ᵈ per hogshead on Tobacco and to give an Account of their Behaviour to the Treasury and Plantation Office.
1679. 1683. } Virginia.	About finishing and repairing the Governor's House..........................
1729. Govᵗ Rogers's Instructions Act.	All money levied to be lodged in the Publick Treasury....................
1686. 1689. } Bermuda.	Several things to be proposed to the Assembly of Bermuda..................
1729/30. New England.	Several irregular Proceedings of the Assembly to be redressed................
—— Jamaica. 1680. Planᵗ Genˡ 1682. Barbados. 1688. Virginia. 1695. Barbados.	Governors not to come to Europe without Leave but Southern Govrs may go Northward for recovery of health.
1707. Leewᵈ Islds.	Governor of Leeward Islands to reside at Antigua & Visit the other Islands often.
1618. Barbados. 1707. Planᵗ Genˡ 1721. Barbados. 1682. Barbados. 1698. Planᵗ Genˡ Dº New York.	Devolution of Government & Restraint of the Presidents Power when he Commands. Devolution of Government in Pennsylvania Proprieties F. fol. 147. When Lᵗ Govrs or Presidents command, they are to have half yᵉ Govrs Salary & Perquisites.
1679. Virginia. 1680. K. James allowed it to be done without the Advice of Council 1702. Minutes of Council. Massachusetts Bay 1703. Dº	All publick Money to be issued by the Govrs Warrant with Advice & Consent of the Council; But the Assembly may examine Accounts of Money raised by them.
1680. Barbados.	To hold frequent Courts of Exchequer in order to recover the Rights of the Crown.
1681/2. Virginia. 1689. Bermuda. 1727. New York. 1782. Jamaica Act.	Governors not to remit Fines of above £10 without the King's Leave; Nor dispose of Forfeitures or Escheats, without securing the Produce for the Crown.
1730. Sº Carolina.	The Boundaries of North & South Carolina settled & settling Townships on the Frontiers of Sº Carolina & New Hampshire Purrysburgh included.
Virginia. 1689. Jamaica. 1698. Virginia. 1788. New York. 1717. Jamaica. 1727. Virginia. 1702. Jamaica Act.	Rules for granting of Land, and reserving of Quit Rents.....................

Number of each Articles to												Memoranda.
Barbados.	Leeward Islands.	Jamaica.	Bahamas.	Bermuda.	S° Carolina.	N° Carolina.	Virginia.	New York.	New Jersey.	Massachusetts.	New Hampshire.	
....	....	28 29	....	....	....	....		....	....	....	....	
25	29	30	27	24	26	29	33	25	26 27	22 23	29	
26	30	31	28	25 27 26	27 28	30 31	35	26 27 28	27 28	23 24	29 30	
....	....	....	....	....	....	....	28 29 30 31 32	....	....	....	....	
....	....	....	....	....	....	....	34	....	....	....	....	
....	....	....	29	....	....	....	....	....	....	....	....	
....	....	....	....	28	....	....	....	....	....	....	....	
....	....	....	....	....	....	....	....	....	....	27	....	
27	31	32	30	29	29	32	36	29	29	25	31	
...	32	....	....	....	....	....	....	....	....	....	....	
28	33	33	31	30	30	33	37	30	30	26	32	
29	34	34	32	31	31	34	38	31	31	28	33	See Disputes upon this Art^le New England. I. fol 58 in 1717 & Jamaica bundle V. no 12. in 1709 New York Ent. H. fol 130 & 368.
30	35	35	33	32	32	35	39	32	32	....	34	
...	36	....	....	33	33	36	40	33	33	....	35	
31 32	37 38	36 37	34	34 35	34 35	37 38	41 42	34 35	34 35	29	36 37	Q. if this Art. does not contradict positive Laws in some of the Plantations; & if Barbados & Leew^d Islands are not the best worded.
..	....	....	....	....	36 104 106 102 103 109	101	....	....	....	....	38	
..	....	38 39	....	....	98 101	39 40 41	43 44 45 46 47	36 37 38	....	....	39 40	In 1737/8 The Gov^t of Jamaica was instructed to grant Regulations.

Folio 7.?

References when began or altered.	Abstract of the General Instructions.
1661/2. Jamaica 1686. Leew'd Islands.	Directions for keeping a Proportion of White Servants & Encouragem! for them.
1673. Barbados. 1673/4. Jamaica 1693. Barbados.	Not to displace Judges, Justices &c without good Cause, nor to grant Commissions but with the Advice & Consent of Council & not for a limitted time.
1681/2. Virginia 1685. Jamaica. 1727. Virginia	Not to erect new nor dissolve old Courts, without the Kings express Licence.
1708 New Jersey 1711. Leew'd Islands.	To erect a Court for the Tryal of Small Causes.....................
1730. S? Carolina.	To enquire into Grants of Offices from the late Proprietors. ....
	Who shall preside in the Court of Chancery in Antigua. ....
1678 Jamaica 1703. Plant Gen! 1730. Massachusets	To send an Account of all Courts, Officers and Offices, & the Charges attending them.
1661/2. Barbados. 1663/4 Jamaica 1698. Virginia.	To regulate all Salaries & Fees, & cause Tables thereof to be sett up where payable.
1684. Barbados. 1700 D? 1700 Plant Gen! 1700. D?	To prevent delays & undue Proceedings & cause Justice to be done in all Courts.
1709. Barbados.	To get Salaries settled on Judges, & Fees on their Clerks & Marshals..........
1679 1698. Virginia.	About adjourning of Courts and entering of Orders in the Journals of ye Courts..
1729. New England.	Governor not to take higher Fees for Registring Ships, than as usual..........
1702. Barbados. 1707. Virginia. 1729. Bahama. 1730. Carolina.	Habeas Corpus to be allowed in the manner herein prescribed................
1673. Barbados. Jamaica	Qualification for Jurors to be established by Acts............................
1663. 1673. Jamaica 1712. Creaghs Case. Jam? 1679. Virginia.	No Man's Life &c. to be taken away, but by known Laws nor any sent as Prisoners to G. Britain without Proofs of their Crimes transmitted with them.
	To pass Laws to prevent inhuman Severities, to Servants or Slaves..........
Ib. 1673. Barbados.	All Writs shall be issued in the Kings' name............
	To keep the Prisons and Court Houses in good Repair.

	Barbados.	Leew'd Islands.	Jamaica.	Bahama.	Bermuda.	So & No Carolina.	Virginia.	N. York.	N. Jersey.	N. Hampshire.

References	Abstract	Barbados.	Leew'd Islands.	Jamaica.		
1679. Virginia. 1680. Journal. vol. 3. 1681 Virginia 1684 Barbados.	To admit Appeals from Inferior Courts to ye Gov? & Council if above					
1700. D? 17.. D?	And from thence to the Crown if for above the Sum of ..	300	500	200		
1717 Jamaica. 1718 Barbados. 1726. Plant Gen! 1727. Jamaica.	And to the Crown also in Cases of Fines, if for above ye sum of	50 100 100 100 50 100 100	300	200		

	So & No Carolina.	Virginia.	N. York.	N. Jersey.	N. Hampshire.
(Fines)	300 200 300 100 100				

Number of each Article to												Memoranda.
Barbados.	Leeward Islands.	Jamaica.	Bahamas.	Bermudas.	So Carolina	No Carolina	Virginia	New York.	New Jersey.	Massachusets	New Hampshire	
33	39	41	35	36	37	42	48	39	36	....	43	
34	40	42	36	37	38	43	49	40	37	....	44	
....	....	....	....	....	....	....	....	....	....	38	....	
....	....	....	....	....	45	....	....	....	....	....	....	
....	41	....	....	....	....	....	....	....	....	....	....	
35	42	43	....	38	39	44	50	41	39	30	45	
36	43	44	37	39	40	46	51	42	40	31	46	
37	44	45	....	40	41	47	52	43	41	....	47	
38	....	....	....	....	....	....	....	....	....	....	....	
....	....	....	....	....	42	48	53	....	....	....	....	
....	....	....	....	....	....	....	....	....	....	32	....	
40 to 49	....	....	40 41	....	43 to 52	49 to 58	54 to 63	....	....			This ought to be left out of So Carolina, an Act being passed for that purpose in 1712.
....	45	46	....	....	53	60	....	44	....	....	....	An Act is passed in No Carolina for this Purpose, Vide Barrington Collecr foll. 399.
39 40	46	47 48	38	41	54	59	64	45	42 43	33	48	
41	47	....	39	42	55	61	65	46	44	34	....	Laws passed for this in Barbados, Jamaica, Virginia, & New Hampshr
50	48	49	42	43	56	62	66	47	45	35	49	
51	49	....	48	....	57	63	67	....	....	36	50	
52	50	50	44	44	58	64	68	48	46	....	51	In Bermuda, consult the confirm'd Laws. Printed Acts. fol 35. 69 &c.
52	51	50	44	45	59	65	68	48	47	....	52	
53	52	51	45	46	60	66	69	49	48	....	53	

Folio 8?

References when began or altered.	Abstract of the General Instructions.
1672. Barbados. 1679. 1685. }Virginia. 1717. Jamaica. 1718. Barbados.	Rules for suspending Patent Officers or their Deputies, & to protect them in their Rights.
1698. Virginia.	To examine into an old Complaint about y? Secretary's Office & Admiralty Fees
1699. Plan? Gen?	Governors to encourage the Officers of Admiralty & Customs (& of the 4½ per C? in ye Charibbee Islands).
1721. Barbados. 1733. Plan? Gen?	Custom House Officers not to serve on Juries Parochial Officers or militia.... Surveyors Gen? of the Customs to be Councillors extra- [ordinary]? in y? respective Plan?
1727. Proprieties.} Virginia. }	Governors in the Absence of the Surveyors Gen? may supply Vacancies in y? Customs.
1729/30. New England.	{Governors to put in Force the Acts for Encouraging Naval Stores & for the { Preservation of the Woods, & to assist the Surveyor Gen? of the Woods.
1701. New York. 1686. New York.	To send Missionaries among the five Nations of Indians........................ To administer or cause to be administered the State Oaths to all Persons he thinks fit.
1702. New Jersey.	Quakers Affirmation may serve in New Jersey even to Qualifie Assem? Men..
1673. Jamaica.	To permit Liberty of Conscience to all People (except Papists) if they offend not y? Government.
1639. Virginia. 1661. Barbados. 1677. Journal vol. 2. 1686. New York. 1717. Jamaica. 1718. Barbados. 1721. Plan? Gen? 1727. D? 1662. Virginia.	Directions about the Service of God, Parson's Glebes, Vestry, Schoolmasters, Bishop of London's Jurisdiction, Licencies for Marriages, Probates of Wills, Tables of Marriages, Punishm? of Vice, Encouragem? of Virtue & Conversion of Negroes.
1730. South Carolina.	To use all the Indians well, see Justice done & peace kept especially with y? Cherokees.
1673. Barbados. 1680. S? Rich? Duttons. Inst. art 32, 33.	To enquire into Offices granted by the late Lords Proprietors................. To send an Account of the Number of Planters & Inhabitants, & of their Increase. To Cause Registers to be kept & sent over of Births, Burials, Marriages &c....
1661/2. Jamaica. 1666. Barbados. 1679. Virginia. 1698. D? 1702. New Jersey.	To establish a Militia, but not to put in force the Law Martial without the Advice & Consent of Council, and appoint good Officers on the Frontiers.
1680. Barbados. 1696. Plan? Gen? 1699. D? D?	To settle Military Discipline for such Soldiers as are sent from hence..........
1715. New England.	{Governor of the Massachusets not to meddle with the Militia in Rhode Island { in time of Peace except in Case of Apparent Danger.
1638.}Virginia. 1679.} 1686. New York. 1722. New Jersey. 1727. Virginia.	To incourage Trade and Alliances with the Indians........................

Number of each Article to												Memoranda.
Barbados.	Leeward Islands.	Jamaica.	Bahamas.	Bermuda.	St. Carolina.	No. Carolina.	Virginia.	New York.	New Jersey.	Massachusets.	New Hampshire.	
54	53	52		47	61	67	70	50	49			
							{ 71 / 75 }					
55	54					68						
56	55	53 / 54	46	48	62	69	72 / 73	51	50	37	54	
57	56	55	47	49	63	70	74	52	51	38	55	
										39	{ 41 / 42 / 56 }	
								54				
58	57	56	48	50	64	71	76	53	52	40	57	
								53				This should be left out. An Act being pass'd for that Purpose in 1727.
59	58	57	49	51	65	72	77	55	55	41	58	
60 to 66	59 to 66	58 to 64	50 to 58	52 to 59	66 to 76	73 to 82	78 to 87	56 to 65	56 to 62	42 & 43	59 & 60	
					{ 108 / 110 / 107 }	77	83					
67	67	65	59	60	77	84	88	66	63	44	61	
68	68	66	60	61	78	85	89	67	64	45	62	
69	69	67	61	62	79	{ 86 / 87 }	91 / 92 / 94	68 / 69 / 70	65 / 66 / 67	46 / 47 / 48	63 / 64 / 65	
70	70		62	63		88	93	71	72	49	66	An Act of Jamaica in 1681 gave great Power to the Gov.r in this Case; but two other Acts passed there in 1734 & 1735 have restrained that Power.
										50		
							{ 96 / 97 }	73		51	76	All the Gov.ts have Laws sufficiently provided for this.

Folio 9?

References when began or altered.	Abstract of the General Instructions.
1696. Plant Genl Jamaica. 1702. Do. 1696. Do. 1717. Do. 1701. Plant Genl 1703. Journal H. 1711. Plant Genl	To execute Powers of Vice Admiralty according to his Commission for that purpose may grant Commissions to Privateers according to the Term granted in Great Britain, but not against States in Amity with his Majty all Privateers to were Colours as herein described.
1673. Jamaica. 1704. Plant Genl 1702. New York.	To send an Account of the State of Defence of his Government with an Inventory of Stores of War in the Forts, &c., and what have spent, decayed &c... To Collect Powder, Duty upon Shipping trading to his Governments.......... To build Storehouses for the keeping of Arms and other publick Stores........
1661. Jamaica. 1670. Do. 1701. Barbados.	To survey, repair & fortify Landing Places, Ports, Harbours &c...............
1686. Bermuda.	To take care of Forts, keep good Watch, & provide for Invalids, regulate Militia.
1661. J...... Barbados. 1702. Leewd Islands.	The King declares he has ordered the 4½ per Ct to be applied to build Forts....
1661. Jamaica. 1661. Barbados. 1673. Jamaica.	To send a Map describing the Governmt Forts, Harbours & Plantations...... To send an Account of the Strength of his Neighbours, be they Indians or others.
1673. Jamaica. Barbados.	To assist other of the English Plantations, when in distress....................
	Gen. Oglethorpe to Command the Forces in South Carolina...................
1673. 1684. Barbados. 1702. 1694. Leeward Islands.	To prevent Foreigners settling on Sta Lucia, Dominico, St Vincents, Tobago, and to encourage the Natives of those or any adjacent Islands but not to encourage Planting in any of the Islands except Barbados, and to remove the French from Sta Lucia, And to assert the King's Right to all the Virgin Islands.
1685. 1686. Bermuda.	All Ships to anchor, load & unload in Castle Harbour in Bermuda............
1708. New York.	To encourage the Exportation of Naval Stores to this Kingdom, to preserve Mast Trees, and other Ship Timber, and to prevent burning the Woods....
1660. Jamaica. 1732. Plant Genl	Not to suffer the engrossing of Commodities, but to incourage Trade & give Account of Laws made, Manufactures sett up &ct that may affect the Trade of G. Britain...
1670. Jamaica. 1672. Barbados. 1721. Do.	To encourage Merchants, & others who shall bring Trade, especially African Trade...
1672. Barbados. 1673. Jamaica. 1704. Plant Genl	To take care that Payment for Negroes be duly made to Agreement...........
1700. Plant Genl	To enquire into an old Complaint of the too frequent Adjournmt of Courts......
1689. 1692. New York. 1700.	For Defence of the Northern Frontiers of New York...........................

Number of each Articles to												Memoranda.
Barbados.	Leeward Islands.	Jamaica.	Bahamas.	Bermuda.	Sᵒ Carolina.	Nᵒ Carolina.	Virginia.	New York.	New Jersey.	Massachusets.	New Hampshire.	
71	76	71	62	64	80	89	98	74	71	52	67	
&	78	72		65		90			72			
72	79	73	63	66		91	99	75	73	53	68	
	77		64	67		92			74			
						93						
73	80	74	65	68	81	94	100	76	75	54	69	
74						96			77		70	
75	81	75	66	69		95	101	78	76	55	71	
76	82	76	67	70	82	97	102			56	72	
				71								There is a Law passed in Bermuda, that sufficiently provides for it.
	83											
									79			
84	84	77	70	72	85	100	45	82	80	57	74	
77	85	78	68		83	98	103	83		58		
78	86	79	69		83	99	104		77	59	73	
					84							
96												
97												
98												
99												
100	87											
				73								
								{84 85 86}				
79	88	80	71	74	86	102	95	87	81	60	75	
80	89	81	72	75	87	103	105	88	82	61	76	
81	90	81	73	76	87	104	106					
	91	82		77	88							
								{79 80 81}	73			

Folio 10ᵇ

References when began or altered.	Abstract of the General Instructions.
1727. 1731. } Jamaica.	Not to pass Acts laying Duties on Felons or Slaves imported...............
1672. } Barbados. } 1673. } Jamaica. }	To send half yearly Accounts of Negroes imported.........................
1686. Bermuda.	To enquire about publick Lands to continue to the publick Officers their Allow- ance of Land Slaves. To Enquire after Slaves belonging to the late Compᵞ.......................

1703. } Planᵗ Genˡ
1704. }
1727. Jamaica.
1686. New York.
1717. Barbados.
1728. Planᵗ Genˡ
1717.   Do.   Do.
	All Publick money to be paid into the Treasury, All Officers to Account....
	To prevent { Intelligence to Enemies by Letters from the Plantations to G.
	                 Britain.
	               { Trade & Correspondence wᵗʰ Enemies in Time of War.........
	Treaty of Neutrality with the French to be observed.....................

1687. Jamaica. } 1700. Barbados. } 1727. Jamaica. } 1686. Jamaica. 1727. Planᵗ Genˡ 1728. An Act passed this year. }	In trying Pirates the Acts for suppression of Piracy, are to be observed...... To assist the Receiver Genˡ of Admiralty Dues.........................
1673. Barbados. 1684. Virginia. 1691. New England. 1715. New England.	To erect Fairs & Markets in the four Principal Towns..................... Lord Baltimore's Pretensions to the Lands on Potomack River............. To appoint an Attorney Genˡ & suffer none other to Act................. To take care that the Acts for Preservation of the Woods be complied with, and in granting of Lands, that it be for the Improvement of the Province.......
1702. New Jersey.	To get a Law passed to confirm the Proprietors Titles................... And none but the Proprietors or their Agents to purchase Lands of the Indians. To assist the Proprietors Surveyors & Agents who take the State Oaths &cᵉ..
1729. New England. 1661. Jamaica. 1673. Do. } 1673. Do.	Boundaries between the Massachusetts Bay & New Hampshire settled....... To send an Account of the Wants & Defects of their Governments &c........ To take care of the Govᵗ in all extra [ordinary (?)]. Cases, with the Advice of Council, but not to Declare war without the King's Leave, except against Indians.. To Corrispond with the Secretary of State & Commissʳˢ for Trade............

Number of each Article to												Memoranda.
Barbados.	Leeward Islands.	Jamaica.	Bahamas.	Bermuda.	S° Carolina.	N° Carolina.	Virginia.	New York.	New Jersey.	Massachusetts.	New Hampshire.	
82	92	83 84 85	73	....	....	105	109	....	....	....	....	
83	93	86	74	78	89	106	110	89	93	....	....	
....	....	....	....	79 to 83	....	....	....	....	....	....	....	All obsolete. See Bermuda. A. fol. 14 & 235 & B. K. n°. {125 131 132}
85	94	87	75	84	90	107	111	90	84	62	77	
86	95	88	76	85	91	108	112	91	85	63	78	
87	96	89	77	86	92	109	113	92	86	64	79	to be omitted during the War.
88	97	90	78	87	93	110	114	93	....	65	80	
89	98	91	79	88	94	111	115	94	87	66	81	
90	....	....	....	....	....	....	....	....	....	....	....	
....	....	....	....	....	....	....	116	....	....	67	....	
....	....	....	....	....	....	....	....	....	....	68	82	
....	....	....	....	....	....	....	....	....	....	69	....	This should be left out, the Gov? having no power to grant Lands.
....	....	....	....	....	....	....	....	....	89	....	....	
....	....	....	....	....	....	....	....	....	90	....	....	
....	....	....	....	....	....	....	....	....	91	72	85	
91	99	92	80	89	95	112	117	95	88	70	83	
92	100	93	81	90	96	113	118	96	92	71	84	
93	101	94	82	91	97	114	119	97	93	73	86	

Folio 12ᵇ.

References when begun or altered.	Abstract of the Instructions relating to the Acts of Trade and Navigation.
All these Instructions were prepared & altered by the Commissrᵃ of the Customs in 1685. 1685. Planᵗ Genᶜ 1686 Bermuda. 1697. Planᵗ Genᶜ Proprieties A. 1700. Bermuda. 1708. New York. 1717. Jamaica. 1721. Barbados. 1727. Proprieties. 1737. Planᵗ Genᶜ	To take care that all Acts relating to Trade & Navigation be duly observed.. All Naval Officers are to give Security to the Commissioners of the Customs... No Ships but British, own'd & manned by Natives, shall trade in yᵉ Plantations. And such Ships shall give Security to carry enumerated Goods to G. Britain or yᵉ Plantations. Rules to prevent Counterfeit Certificates of having given Security or discharg'd ladings. Payment of Duties shall not excuse bringing enumerated Goods to G. B. or Plantᵉ To send an Account of the Trade (as per Scheme annext) to the Treasury, this Office &c. No European Goods to be imported into the Plantᵉ, but what are shipped in Great Britain.
1729. Plans. Genᶜ 1737. Doᵒ Doᵒ	Rules to prevent forged Cocquets and Contraband Trade...................... No Laws to be allowed of in the Plantᵉ contrary to the Acts of Trade.......... Governors to assist the Officers of the Admiralty & Customs.................... Govrᵗ to assist the Collectors of 6ᵈ per month out of Seamen's Wages;......... And the Collectors of the Customs in relation to the Act for securing the Sugar Colonies. In all Prosecutions for illegal Trade, the Jurors shall be natives................. All places of Trust shall be in the Hands of Natives........................... Governors to supply Vacancies in Courts of Justice, with Persons of known Loyalty. Govrᵗ shall correspond with Commissrᵃ of the Customs & advise them of all Frauds. If any Person shall offer to sell Land to Aliens the Govr is to give the King notice of it.

1687 Virginia.
1692. Maryland.
1701 Planᵗ Genᶜ
    Doᵒ
    Doᵒ
	Rules for registring Ships to prevent foreign Ships trading under British Names.
	To prevent the Exportation of Wool, or woollen Manufactures of the Plantations
	To prevent Frauds in the Importation of Bulk Tobacco......................
	Officers of the Customs to be allowed the Liberty of appealing to the Crown...
	And the same Liberty of pleading the Genᶜ Issue &c. as in Great Britain......
	Fees on such Trials payable by the Officers to be moderated, & the Officers assisted.

1717. Jamaica.	Custom house Officers not to be obliged to serve on Juries, Parish Offices, Militia &c.
1727. Virginia Doᵒ Proprieties. 1726. Planᵗ Genᶜ	Governors in the Absence of the Surveyor Genᶜ may supply Vacancies in yᵉ Customs. In all Appeals to the Crown, Execution shall be stopt, unless Security be given &c.
1721. Trade. 1692 Bermuda. 1697 Planᵗ Genᶜ 1699. Virginia	To prevent Clandestine Trade to the East Indies, Madagascar &c............ Negligent Governors to lose their Places & forfeit £1000 & Proprietors their Charters.

to the Acts of Trade & Navigation.

No. of each Article to			Memoranda.
Islands.	Continent.	Proprieties	
1	1	1	Upon a Complaint of Mr Brown, Judge of the Admiralty in Pennsylvania in 1730, several Reports were made thereon & an Instruction proposed to be sent to all the Govrs to prevent Instructions from the Common Law Courts against the Judgements or Decrees of the Admiralty Court.
2	2	2	But Mr Brown dying the Affair dropt, & has not been revived, tho' of great Consequence to the Trade of this Kingdom 1730. Plans. Genl .... & Proprieties H.[etc].
3	3	3	
4	4	4	
5	5	5	
6	6	6	
7	7	7	
8	8	8	N. B. The Article in the Genl Instructions to the King's Governors against passing Laws which may affect the Trade & Shipping of Great Britain, ought to be put in the Bonds & Instructions to Proprietary Government.
9	9	9	
10	10	10	
11	11	11	
12	12	13	
13	13	15	
14	14	12	
15	15	14	
16	16	......	
17	17	16	
18	18	17	
19	19	18	
20	20	19	
......	21	20	
......	......	21	
......	......	22	
......	......	23	
......	......	24	
......	......	25	
......	......	26	
21	22	27	
22	23	28	

IX. LINCOLN AND THE PROGRESS OF NATIONALITY IN THE NORTH.

By N. W. STEPHENSON,
College of Charleston, S. C.

LINCOLN AND THE PROGRESS OF NATIONALITY IN THE NORTH.

By N. W. STEPHENSON.

Browning's famous line, "We know in art how fashions end", applies also to the pursuit of history. What it was fashionable to do, and to refrain from doing, a generation ago, seems to-day as curious as hoop skirts. A capital illustration may be found in the life of Charles Francis Adams by his gifted and now lamented son. The younger Adams does not mention his father's anxieties over the purchase in England of munitions. Anything that involved slavery or secession appeared to Charles Francis II momentous. But it did not seem to him worth while, in a brief memoir, to tell his countrymen how the elder Adams, staggered by the emptiness of his country's arsenals, perceiving that it was life or death to secure, or fail to secure, munitions abroad, pledged the credit of the United States without warrant from Washington. The memoir ignores the dispatch of June 7, 1861,[1] in which Adams says:

> Aware of the degree to which I exceed my authority by taking such a step, nothing but a conviction of the need in which the country stands of such assistance * * * has induced me to overcome my scruples.

And yet this dispatch was actually in print when the memoir was published. To be sure, it was buried deep in that incomparable hodgepodge, the official records of the Union and Confederate armies. Conceivably, no copy exists among the Adams papers. But that it was unknown to the author of the memoir is surely not conceivable. Our only explanation of his silence is the transitoriness of fashion. Slavery and secession were for the mental drawing-room those days; munitions of war were to be classed with the butcher's bill, metaphorically speaking, and left to the insignificance of the pantry.

There is another illustration of the caprice of fashion that I can not refrain from mentioning. In Mr. Rhodes's history—so large minded, so far removed from the ordinary faults of American historical writing—munitions, if I am not in error, are alluded to just once, and then casually in a quotation from Stanton. Slavery and secession fill the horizon, or are temporarily displaced in the reader's imagination by the armies with banners. On the one hand, constitutional problems; on the other, the armed conflict of heroes, "in proud battalia ranged"; these, in the fashion of hoop-skirt days,

---

[1] Official Records of the Union and Confederate Armies, Series III, Vol. I, 293.

25066°—23——23   353

are the things to take seriously. Not yet had it become the prop
thing to ask where the heroes got their arms. You will search i
vain through the acute pages of Mr. Rhodes for even the shado
cast from a great distance, of that first real episode of the Civil Wa
the commercial duel in Europe to control the munitions market. N
suggestion of the furious bidding against each other of norther
agents and southern agents; no word of the frantic rounding u
of the whole marketable stock of arms, ammunition, and supplie
until, one might almost say, both groups of agents knew where w
located every available musket, every available bolt of army cloth,
England, France, Belgium, and the Germanies. . Of the desperate co
duct of this commercial duel, this campaign on which all the splend
of the battle depended, Mr. Rhodes has nothing to say. The thre
ministers who did the work for the North—Adams at London, Da
ton at Paris, Sanford at Brussels—are known to him as diplomat
but are strangers to him as commercial agents. That indefatigab
special agent, George L. Schuyler, who, with his heroic appetite f
munitions, ranged Europe seeking what he might devour, has n
even got his name into the Rhodes index. Nor have Baring Bro
whom we might call, in the fashion of a later day, the English branc
of the United States Treasury. So far as Mr. Rhodes is concerne
no one would ever guess that Sanford in November, 1861, had ser
home that jubilant dispatch which, for its varied implications, i
testimony to commercial battle past and to victory within sight, i
presage of the final northern triumph on the field of battle, its i
direct forecast of the eventual southern tragedy, is without a riv
among the state papers of that fateful hour.[2] Who in these la
days of the World War could resist the impulse to quote from
momentous a document, so curiously neglected:

"I have now in my hands," Sanford writes to Seward, "complet
control of the principal rebel contracts on the continent—viz: 206,00
yards of cloth ready for delivery; already commencing to mov
forward to Havre; gray, but can be dyed blue in 20 days; 100,00
yards, deliverable from 15th of December to 26th of January, ligh
blue army cloth same as ours; 100,000 blankets; 40,000 guns to
shipped in 10 days; 20,000 sabre bayonets to be delivered in six week
* * *. As Mr. George P. Smith has come out about cloth, I a
telegraphing for him all over Europe, and if he does not reach m
by to-morrow morning my option for buying up these contracts wi
have expired, and it will be too late. If we can carry out the who
operation it will be the greatest victory yet over the enemy. Th
winter clothing for 100,000 men taken out of their hands, when the
can not replace it, would almost compensate for Bull Run."

---

[2] O. R. Ser. III, Vol. I, p. 631. See also Ordnance Report, June, 1862, in O. R., Ser. I
Vol. II, p. 85, rifles purchased in Europe, 726, 705.

I have cited this topic of munitions, not in the illusion that it was fresh knowledge, but simply because it focussed sharply the comarative bloodlessness of a point of view that is passing. Further-ore, it typifies a recent tendency to insist that Lincoln's difficulties ave never been adequately portrayed; that even now we do not appreciate their magnitude. Especially, that we do not appreciate his ifficulties at home.

What, then, of the opposition to Lincoln within the North? What lation, if any, has it to the general subject of the development of merican nationality?

To be specific, what was the real inspiration of, for example, ose extensive secret societies which all through the war seem al-ays on the verge of a rebellion in the Middle West, which fought incoln so bitterly at the polls? In 1864, the chief of these, the ons of Liberty, claimed a membership of a million.[3] The Govern-ient Secret Service, in its elaborate report on this society, cuts the embership in half.[4] Even thus, here is something which ought to ave been formidable. But its formidableness is a problem of that itter-day phase of historical analysis which we are beginning to bel, perhaps unnecessarily, the psychological. That is to say, a half illion men consciously inspired by an abstract political idea, taking course, because of that idea, in opposition to the majority of their eighbors—here is a phenomenon which is utterly bewildering unless e assume in its membership a high degree both of character and rains. That there were instances in the anti-Lincoln societies of en who fit this assumption, some of us know from personal experi-ice. Among my own friends of the preceding generation is a trained ientist, a character of fine metal and a mind as clear as day, who ined during the war the Mighty Order of Minutemen, because, ough a northerner, not desiring his State to secede, he was a theo-tical secessionist, an antinationalist, who looked upon a sectional umph as portending the destruction of the Commonwealth of hio. But was this man, with his clear-cut conscious motive, a pe of them all? The elder history, reasoning unaware from con-ous motive as the one source of political action, assumes that he s. Two or three things stand in the way of that conclusion. rst of all, the bulk of the Sons of Liberty lacked character. Their dge ought to have been the white feather. Though they seem have intrigued with the Confederacy, and pretty certainly formed rt of the inspiration of Morgan's raid through Indiana and Ohio, y were very careful, when their mood of dreamy speculation had ught them in sight of danger, to make haste to establish an alibi. t for them the courage of the real enthusiast. Particularly was

---

O. R., Ser. II, Vol. VII, p. 935.
Ibid.

this made plain in 1864. Their plot to stampede the Chicago con
vention and rush the Northwest out of the Union, which, thoug
so near to opera bouffe, imposed on the Confederates in Canad
and led them to send officers in disguise to Chicago; that plot col
lapsed because, when the time came, not a Son of Liberty would pr
his head in the lion's mouth. Indeed, their appropriate name woul
have been the " Order of the White Feather."

Finding them to be so completely wanting in the stuff of characte
we are not surprised to find them also wanting in mental qualit
They doted upon that vile form of rhetoric which for certain typ
of visionary will always be the fulmination of Jupiter. What
revelation both of character and intellect is this appalling rhetor
taken from the ritual of another of these societies of the pusillan
mous, the American Knights:

I do further solemnly promise and swear that I will ever cherish the sublin
lessons which the sacred emblems of our order suggest, and will so far as in n
lies impart those lessons to the people of the earth, where the mystic aco
falls from its parent bough, in whose visible firmanent Orion, Arcturus, and tl
Pleiades ride in their cold resplendent glories, where the Southern Cross dazzl
the eyes of degraded humanity with its coruscations of golden light,' etc.

Are we to take seriously the idea that men of such vague mentalit
as is indicated by the swearing of this farcical oath stood for an
thing intellectual? If these men of the white feather were an in
pediment to nationalism, if they stood for something that nationalis
has had to overcome, is it fair to confuse them with my cultivate
friend, in whom gabble about the Pleiades and Arcturus is inconcei
able; or with the actual secessionists, those who flung themselv
against the front of destiny; sword in hand? Surely, the more v
study the event the more we tend toward this conclusion: An in
pediment to nationalism these men were; but their psychology ar
that of the real secessionists were widely different. And it is wor
remembering that there was a corresponding group in the Co
federacy with the same impracticable ideas, the same joy in decade
rhetoric, the same lack of genuine imagination, the same passion f
riding the off-horse. The type was common to America. It wou
have obstructed the formation of a southern nation quite as wilful
as it aimed to obstruct the northern. And is not the type famili
still? Here is a problem of temperament, of psychological histor
not of constitutional. In this place, with a paper limited to
minutes, the short cut to one's conclusion is all that is possible. B
is it a dizzying transition to skip the intervening steps and land up
the conclusion that the orders of the white feather help us to und

---

' This wording is found in Foulke's Life of Morton, Vol. II, p. 390. It differs sligh
from the wording in O. R., Ser. II, Vol. II, p. 294, where a supposedly complete rit
is given. See also same volume, O. R., pp. 228–239.

tand the dreaming pacifists of our own day? Can we not imagine certain distinguished gentlemen, and some even more distinguished ladies, taking the oath of the Pleiades in perfect seriousness?

Let us go to the other extreme, turn our eyes upon another group of Americans, also an impediment to nationalism, but who had clearer views of life, whose tongues were in their cheeks. You know what I mean when I mention the Boston Board of Trade. You remember those two documents which figure to-day in damning juxtaposition in Volume 122 of the Official Records,[6]—that pathetic report of the quartermaster general describing the "troops before the enemy * * * compelled to do picket duty in the late cold nights without overcoats, or even coats, wearing only the thin summer flannel blouses," and along with this report, the formal protest of the committee of the Boston Board of Trade against the purchase in Europe of clothing for the Army. Even the profiteering of the World War can not beat that! Of course to-day everybody knows what was back of it all. The new-born woolen industry was demanding its chance. Even if the war had to stand still the wool growers and the wool manufacturers must have their fling—and all in the name of patriotism, all to take care of American business. They had their fling. While the Nation groaned under its taxes, profits in wool rose to 40 per cent. But there were no more devoted nationalists, so far as words went, than these ruthless profiteers, who held up the Washington Government for their own exclusive benefit. Well might Lincoln say, "Few things are so troublesome to the Government as the fierceness with which the profits in trading are sought."[7]

Is it not plain that we may attribute to the northern opposition quite other motives than those of the secessionists and yet perceive in them great obstacles to nationality? We have got in the habit of saying that North and South had been developing upon different lines during 40 years before the war, but have we followed out all the ramifications of that idea? Have we given enough consideration to the fact—obvious, it seems to me—that while the North had passed into a second stage on the road to nationalization it was still far from the ultimate stage? Though the smaller territorial units had lost their hold upon men's imagination, though an economic community had been established, there was not yet established, when the first gun was fired in 1861, the power to effect a complete, uniform, national reaction. A wave of passion is not necessarily an expression of nationality. The fury that swept the North in 1861 deserves more analytical study than has sometimes been ac-

---

[6] O. R., Ser. III, Vol. I, pp. 583–586.
[7] Complete Works of Abraham Lincoln, Nicolay and Hay, enlarged edition, Vol. IX, p. 10. (June 29, 1863.)

corded it. That, at the back of it, something in the way of a national spirit had arrived is past the question. But it was still an
unsolidified sense of nationality that was cut across and broken up
by disintegrating tendencies—tendencies which were producing
temperamental units, class units, highly dangerous to the whole;
and there was still lacking that profound spiritual cohesion which
transforms a horde into a nation. To Americans in the mass, in
1861, in 1864, we might apply Meredith's famous line, "Their sense
is with their senses all mixed in." And nationality is a spiritual, not
a sensual, thing.

How entirely this applies to some of the most devoted antiseces-
sionists of that day. It is one clew to the pacifist wing of the aboli-
tionists and to such gentle dreamers as the poet Whittier. It fits
perfectly the great but disordered genius of Wendell Phillips. Take
his terrible orations against Lincoln. As political thunder they can
not be rated too high, but as revelations of character—I will not be
so rash as to suppose I can improve upon Meredith—"their sense is
with their senses all mixed in."

Then, too, there is that strange assemblage of dreamers—known
to-day by the name of this very city—the Cleveland convention,
which put up Fremont as a candidate against Lincoln in 1864, to
which Phillips wrote a letter that now his admirers would like to
bury in oblivion. And I need not remind you there was no secession talk at the Cleveland convention. It stands for another obstacle to nationality, different from the moral quicksand of the
secret societies, different also from the antisocial predatory consciousness of the profiteers. To sum up in one neat phrase what lay
behind it were difficult. I will take the better part of valor and
not attempt to do so. Nor will I undertake to say whether all the
exaggerations of individualism which flourished in America in those
troublous times—not only this Cleveland convention, but such other
groups as the one led by Horace Greeley which was always ready
to follow him on a tangent—whether all these, at bottom, had the
same psychology. You observe I am dodging any discussion of the
Democratic Party of those days. The subject is too complex to be
treated incidentally. But, at least, one may say in passing, that
whatever else it contained it had members who, like Phillips, like
Greeley, stood for emotional individualism gone mad—the illegiti-
mate modern descendants of fifth monarchy men.

And all this is but a way of saying that the North, though it had
broken down men's loyalty to the smaller territorial units, the States,
was still struggling with the task of creating a pervasive larger
loyalty to replace the one that had been lost. The truth is, the
political and economic molds in which northern life had been contained were broken up between 1830 and 1860, but the imaginative

1olds, which are so much more intimate than the political ones, were
ot broken up. To reconstruct certain of these molds, to make pos-
ible a new fusion of their contents, to establish a new channel for
political imagination, was the great task in the development of
American nationality not yet complete in 1861.

In the accomplishment of that task the colossal central figure is,
f course, Lincoln. Therefore, his views on his own rôle, on the
unction of his office, are so intensely interesting. What, then, was
Lincoln's conception of that community, not fully realized in his own
ay, which he calls in his messages our National Union? How did
e expect the people of this Union, weltering as they were in diver-
ity, to arise out of their confusions one nation? As an expression
f their nationalism, how did he conceive his own high office?

It is a great misfortune that Lincoln has not left us a general
tatement of his views on any of these points. What lay back of
is actions, what in time he might have formulated, we must infer,
s best we can, from certain crucial events and from a relatively
mall number of utterances. But a few things are plain: First, his
onception of the permanent form of our National Union was a
ederal one. If there is any belief of his that can be proved beyond
peradventure from his own words it is his acceptance of the group
f States as the fixed term in our political science. Lincoln was
ot a Hamiltonian. He did not hesitate to declare "that the main-
enance inviolate of the rights of the States and especially the right
f each State to control its domestic institutions according to its own
udgment exclusively, is essential to that balance of powers on which
he perfection and endurance of our political fabric depend." [8]

Secondly, Lincoln conceived our National Union as preeminently
people's government. This, in spite of our literary fondness for
he last sentence of the Gettysburg address, is too often forgotten.
Whether we like it or not, we must see Lincoln as a statesman of
he masses. Thus he conceived himself. With startling explicit-
ess—for when was Lincoln not explicit?—he committed himself to
he belief that the mass, the laborers, were the part of the Nation
ntitled to the greatest share of its benefits. In his speech at Cin-
innati, February 13, 1861, he said, "the workingmen are the basis
f all governments." [9] This frank utterance was expanded in the
1essage to Congress, in December, 1861. That message was quoted
nd affirmed in his reply, in 1864, to certain New York working-
1en who had elected him an honorary member of their order. He
sed, both in the message and the letter to the workingmen, these
7ords: "Labor is prior to, and independent of, capital. Capital

---

[8] Ibid., Vol. VI, p. 88.
[9] Ibid., Vol. VI, p. 119.

is only the fruit of labor, and could never have existed if labor had not first existed. Labor is the superior of capital and deserves much the higher consideration."[10] It is most significant that the two speeches made to passing soldiers in August, 1864, contain nothing upon either slavery or secession as such. Their theme is democratic opportunity. In the speech of August 18, he says:

We have, as all will agree, a free government, where every man has a right to be equal to every other man. * * * There is involved in this struggle the question whether your children and my children shall enjoy the privileges we have enjoyed. I say this in order to impress upon you, if you are not already so impressed, that no small matter should divert us from our great purpose.[11]

In the speech of August 22:

I happen temporarily to occupy the White House. I am a living witness that any one of your children may look to come here as my father's child has.[12]

But while insisting on these radical utterances of Lincoln one must immediately qualify them by the limitations imposed by related utterances. Though Lincoln excluded aristocracy from his political vision—real artistocracy—he also excluded the political science of fairyland. In the republic of Lincoln's dream neither the Marquis of Lansdowne nor Prof. Scott Nearing would find a place to cease from troubling. For neither of these is there any consolation in Lincoln's views when displayed in their entirety. Isolated sentences might appear to attach him to either extreme. His own harmonizing of the extremes is in another passage of his letter to the New York workingmen:

The strongest bond of human sympathy, outside the family relation, should be one uniting all working people of all nations and tongues and kindreds. Nor should this lead to a war upon property or the owners of property. Property is the fruit of labor; property is desirable, is a positive good to the world. That some should be rich shows that others may become rich, and hence is just encouragement to industry and enterprise. Let not him who is houseless pull down the house of another, but let him work diligently and build one for himself, thus by example insuring that his own shall be safe from violence when built.[13]

The third main feature of Lincoln's conception of the National Union is more elusive. It is involved in his attitude toward the source and mode of political authority. He asserts the practical dictum that the majority must govern. You may say that in doing so he is conventional. Lord Charnwood in his admirable biography, so refreshingly free from the faults of certain earlier books, implies as much. I think a case could be made against the point, but it can not be made in parenthesis. However, the heart of the matter

[10] Ibid., Vol. X, pp. 51–52.
[11] Ibid., Vol. X, p. 199.
[12] Ibid., Vol. X, p. 202.
[13] Ibid., Vol. X, p. 53.

lies deeper. Lincoln was not a friend of the plebiscite or of the referendum; on the contrary, he was a staunch believer in representative government in the strict sense. Why have the champions of stable authority forgotten Lincoln's challenge to the country when refusing to yield to the clamor over military arrests? Asserting the right of the President to assume in emergency vast authority, he concludes that "if he uses the power justly, the * * * people will probably justify him; if he abuses it, he is in their hands to be dealt with by all the modes they have reserved to themselves in the Constitution."[14] Elsewhere he asks, "Must a government of necessity be too strong for the liberties of its own people, or too weak to maintain its own existence?"[15] Time forbids me, in this connection, to attempt to extract the true historical significance of his undeniable assumptions of arbitrary power. Enough, that in his own mind, whether rightly or wrongly, they lay outside this question; that they were to him part of the general right to wage war. Setting aside for to-day the case of Vallandigham and all the rest, what is more to the point is Lincoln's refusal in various matters not involving his military authority to make any attempt to find out the popular will; likewise his frequent disregard of the nearest approach he had to a plebiscite—the opinion of the majority of the House of Representatives. And let the blind admirers of Lincoln remember that in some of the disagreements between himself and Congress—as for example the Mexican issue—it is not proved past doubting that Lincoln was right and Congress wrong. What should hold one here is not Lincoln's wisdom, or lack of wisdom, but the boldness with which he planted himself on the idea of delegated authority. He refused to be the mere spokesman of the people. He was in his own mind their representative, on whom, for a time, certain powers had been bestowed. For that time these powers were his. Horribly reactionary, the Bolshevik would say. In a way, yes. So reactionary, in a way, that there does not exist, probably, as a summary of Lincoln's basal attitude toward his own electorate, a better statement of fundamental theory than that immortal letter to the electors of Bristol signed by Edmund Burke.

There is a fourth main feature of Lincoln's conception: It has been pointed out that most American reasoning about nationality is in terms of people. On this fact is grounded, I am told, a distinction between the poetry inspired in America by the World War and that of England. The American poets attach their loyalty to the group of people, their countrymen. The British poets, while having that, have also something more—a sense of the soil, a loyalty

[14] Ibid., Vol. IX, p. 4.
[15] Ibid., Vol. VI, p. 304.

to the very earth, our mother. Lincoln in his vision of nationality had outstripped his time and had the British point of view.

"A nation," he asserts, "may be said to consist of its territory, its people, and its laws. The territory is the only part that is of certain durability. 'One generation passeth away and another cometh, but the earth abideth forever.' It is of the first importance to duly consider and estimate this ever-enduring part."[16] These words are taken from the annual message of December, 1862. They are attended by a discussion of geographical predestination, as revealed by the map of the United States, which any professor of history, however self-important, might hold worthy of his genius.

It is not permissible for me to trespass longer upon your patience! So large is the subject, so intricate the psychology of that day, so profound Lincoln's creative relation to his time, that inevitably in all our minds his career is now being reconsidered; old values are fading away, new values are asserting themselves. The subject becomes almost boundless. In it the central fact seems now to be this: Lincoln's deepest significance was as a statesman of successful 'democracy; incidental to this he was a statesman of nationalism, laboring for cohesion in a people that were precipitating, as a chemist would say, the sense of nationality, but in whose general consciousness the precipitation was not complete.

To sum up, Lincoln encountered in the North, especially in Ohio and Indiana, something in the way of a survival of true States' rights ideas. The measure of this political force will never be known. To risk a mere dictum, the more I study it, the more it appears to shrink in quantity. The conviction grows that the economic community established in the North between 1830 and 1860 had given a death blow to geographical sectionalism. No Northern State in 1861 remained genuinely self-conscious.

However, an economic community and a true psychological community, are vastly different things. Lincoln, conceiving our Federal Union as an elaborately articulated but also an entirely interdependent community, psychologically one, had to contend, at home, with the sharply separatist impulses of four groups of people, each too conscious of its own standard type to be fully conscious of the Nation as a whole. To label them, there were the rhetorical visionaries represented by the Golden Circle; the fanatics represented by Greeley; the parasites, represented then as now by the profiteers; the labor group, whose activity was obscure and can not be typified by any one familiar figure.

You may object that I am indicating types which are perpetual, that are always to be reckoned with. True. It is not the presence

[16] Ibid., Vol. VIII, p. 110.

of these types that gave Lincoln's problem its significant cast. It is, first, the intensity of their limitations which rendered them unimaginative, incapable of forming ideas larger than their personal experience; second, their lack of an inherited body of ideas not limited by the traditions of their group, that stood to them as a bequest of something loftier and more authoritative than the group— the Nation. To what extent this group provincialism of Lincoln's day has been overcome is a crucial question not germane to the present topic. The historical importance of group provincialism is not to be overstated. When the leading types in a community are so limited mentally that they are overconscious of the bond uniting all specimens of the type, when they are so deficient in imagination that for them the world outside their group is a world of shadows, these types create inner communities within the apparent community and the whole has not yet achieved genuine nationality.

X. THE STRATEGY OF CONCENTRATION OF THE CONFEDERATE FORCES IN THE MISSISSIPPI VALLEY IN THE SPRING OF 1862.

By ALFRED P. JAMES,

University of Pittsburgh.

THE STRATEGY OF CONCENTRATION OF THE CONFEDERATE FORCES IN THE MISSISSIPPI VALLEY IN THE SPRING OF 1862.

By Alfred P. James.

Concentration in warfare, at least in practice, is not at all a recent idea. On the contrary, it is practically as old as recorded military history. In fact, nearly 5,000 years ago, in the neighborhood of the Persian Gulf, a Sumerian city king had organized his infantry in phalanx formation,[1] or, in other words, had adopted the idea of concentration in tactics. Less remote ancients—Persians, Greeks, Carthaginians, and Romans—made frequent use of both the tactics and strategy of concentration. Even the so-called Dark Ages furnish many examples of application of what, in the course of time, had become not only the practice but the principle of concentration in warfare. It is not necessary to be specific, for the facts are everywhere accessible, and only tedium would result from any attempt to trace with the greatest brevity the application of this principle throughout the centuries. However, it is necessary in this paper to give a moment's consideration to the Corsican child of destiny—Napoleon Bonaparte—whose influence has vitally affected all later warfare and all later military theory. The strategy and tactics of concentration were the foundation of the military successes of this remarkable man, whom an Oxford tutor of mine, in a private conversation, described as "the sole outstanding personality of the first half of the nineteenth century." As we know, Napoleon obtained his ideas of strategy and tactics, partly at least, from profound study of the past. In early manhood he pored over the campaigns of Alexander the Great and Julius Caesar. He read eagerly and carefully Plutarch's Lives and Caesar's Gallic Wars. Of modern masters of military art he made a particular study of Marlborough and Frederick the Great. Inevitably he found striking examples of the application of this principle of concentration and he profited by his studies.

The location of his artillery at a vital central spot on the 13 Vendemiare illustrates Napoleon's early use of the principle of concentration. Concentration, in either strategy or tactics or in both, characterizes the majority of his campaigns. It is seen in Italy in 1797 and in 1800; along the Danube in 1805 and 1809; in Prussia in

---

[1] J. H. Breasted, Ancient Times, p. 120.

1806; in Russia in 1812; and, above all, in France in the memorable campaign of 1813–14. It is true that at times Napoleon violated the principle of concentration. The failure to withdraw his garrisons from the German fortresses in 1813 can be cited by way of example. But on the whole he was an exponent of the principle of concentration. At his fall he left behind not only the example of his campaigns and battles but written exposition of his maxims of war.

One of the most significant exhibits in the Confederate Museum in Richmond, Va., is a small volume entitled "Napoleon's Maxims of War," which on the death of Stonewall Jackson was found in his haversack. Jackson, the greatest of the strategists in the Confederate Army, was essentially Napoleonic in his warfare.

"Concentrate to fight; unity of command is necessary to success; time is everything." [2] Such are the maxims of Napoleon. I believe that few campaigns in history are more valuable as a study of the application and validity of these maxims than that of the Confederate armies in the Mississippi Valley in the first half of the year 1862.

For political and economic reasons of great validity, which President Davis saw very clearly, and the recognition of which involved him in serious quarrels with some of his generals, the Confederate forces in the winter of 1861–62 were scattered across southern Kentucky and northern Tennessee. Polk was at Columbus, Ky., on the Mississippi; insignificant forces were at Forts Henry and Donaldson on the Tennessee and Cumberland Rivers. Albert Sidney Johnston, commander of the department, was stationed at Bowling Green, Ky., watching Buell. Small and scattered Confederate forces were in east Tennessee and southwest Kentucky.

Facing the Confederates were greatly superior numbers. Halleck, in the spring of 1862, commanded in the West, according to his own estimate, about 270,000 men. [3] Against these it is doubtful if the Confederates could have opposed much more than a third of this number, even when various forces in Arkansas, along the Mississippi, at Mobile and Pensacola, and along the Atlantic coast as far north as the North Carolina-Virginia frontier, are included.

In the Confederate line in southern Kentucky and northern Tennessee there was a weak but vital spot. This was where the Cumberland and Tennessee Rivers opened up a waterway to Nashville and as far south as Alabama. In the preceding autumn forts had been begun at the point where the rivers approach each other. The importance of the point was well understood, by some at least. Gideon Pillow, on December 11, 1861, had written to W. W. Mackall, assistant adjutant general to Albert Sidney Johnston, warning him that

he enemy would ignore Columbus, Ky., and make a heavy attack
ipon Fort Henry.[4]

It was at this weak but vital spot that Grant broke through in the
niddle of February. The loss of Forts Henry and Donaldson forced
he Confederates to fall back all along the line. Albert Sidney
Johnston for a time was overwhelmed by the disaster and by the
insparing criticism which fell upon his head. At the time, he was
most severely criticized for the loss and abandonment of Kentucky
nd central Tennessee. The very bitterness of this in 1862 is evi-
lence of the strength of the considerations which led him to accept
he policy of territorial defense. Critics of a later date have largely
lwelt upon his violation of the principle of concentration. That his
trategy was of the highest type certainly can not be maintained.
Ie probably erred in a timely and proper valuation of the vital spot
n the Confederate line of defense. Roman,[5] the biographer of Beauregard, credits him with a sound opinion on this matter early in
February, 1862; but it was too late then to prevent a calamity. He
lso made a poor selection of men to defend this vital spot, even
hough it be admitted that his choice was very limited.

After the event, concentration appeared to all as the only avail-
ble policy. Roman, of course, gives Beauregard credit for the ear-
iest advocacy of concentration in the Mississippi Valley. I am not
onvinced from the official records that anyone in particular was
argely responsible for the origin of this suggestion, which would
aturally occur, in time, to everyone. Bragg, from Mobile, wrote
o the Government on February 15, urging concentration in Ken-
ucky.[6] Benjamin in reply, on February 18, claimed this as the pro-
osed policy of the administration, saying: " We had had in con-
emplation the necessity of abandoning the seaboard in order to de-
end the Tennessee line." [7] In a letter to R. E. Lee, on February 24,
Benjamin wrote: " The railroad line from Memphis to Richmond
ust be defended at all hazards." [8] Even Albert Sydney Johnston
n his report on the evacuation of Nashville, dated February 25,
dvanced the idea of concentration in the assertion of his intention
f going to Mississippi by way of Decatur.[9]

But, discounting Roman's narrative, as one inevitably will, the
ase of G. T. Beauregard seems worthy of special consideration.
cting on general orders issued late in January, Beauregard had
eft Virginia for a command in the Mississippi Valley. Having
rrived at Bowling Green, Ky., on February 4, he was, after some
onferences, assigned to command at Columbus, Ky. By reason

[4] O. R., Ser. I, Vol. VII, p. 758.
[5] Roman, Military Operations of Beauregard, Vol. I, pp. 214–215.
[6] O. R., Ser. I, Vol. VI, p. 826.
[7] O. R., Ser. I, Vol. VI, p. 828.
[8] O. R., Ser. I, Vol. VI, p. 398.
[9] O. R., Ser. I, Vol. VII, p. 427.

of his rank of general, which had been awarded for his work at
Manassas, he was second in command in the West under Albert Sidney Johnston.

Of all the Confederate commanders Beauregard was the clearest
theoretical advocate of the strategy of concentration. Previous to
the first battle of Manassas he had formulated strategical ideas of
concentration which were presented to President Davis and which,
though not adopted until it was evident what the enemy would do,
had led to the junction of the forces of Joseph E. Johnston, Beauregard, and Holmes, which later made victory possible. The quarrel
about this matter which later arose between Beauregard and Davis
may be ignored here.

Beauregard's correspondence throughout the war is full of the
theory of concentration. By way of example, in a letter to Dabney
F. Maury, in June, 1863,[10] he wrote:

The true motto of every general should be, "United we stand, divided we
fall," and the essence of the art of war is to concentrate on the proper point
at the right time.

On his transfer to the Mississippi Valley Beauregard followed
consistently his theory of concentration. From the records much
credit must be given him in connection with the organization leading up to the battle of Shiloh or Pittsburg Landing. When, by
reason of the fall of Forts Henry and Donaldson, Albert Sidney
Johnston, his superior, fell back from Bowling Green, Ky., to
Nashville, Tenn., and from Nashville through Murfreesboro to Shel-
byville, Beauregard drew back Polk and Pillow from Columbus,
Ky., urged upon Van Dorn in northwest Arkansas the necessity
of bringing his forces across the Mississippi,[11] made strong appeals
to the governors and citizens of the threatened States,[12] and impressed upon Albert Sidney Johnston the vital necessity of concentration at Corinth.[13] At this time Beauregard suffered greatly from
a severe affection of the throat, brought on by exposure in northern
Virginia in the preceding autumn and winter. His activity, in this
state of his health, was really remarkable, if we can judge by the
extent of his correspondence.

If ever the strategy of concentration was employed to a remarkable extent in warfare it was done by Johnston and Beauregard in
the Mississippi Valley between the middle of February and the first
of April, 1862. Van Dorn and Price were summoned from northwest Arkansas, Bragg was called up from Mobile and Pensacola, and
Mansfield Lovell was persuaded to send most of his forces from New
Orleans. The available seasoned troops of the Confederacy were

[10] O. R., Ser. I, Vol. XXVIII, pt. II, p. 160.
[11] O. R., Ser. I, Vol. VIII, p. 771.
[12] O. R., Ser. I, Vol. VII, p. 000.
[13] O. R., Ser. I, Vol. VII, p. 896.

;radually concentrated at Corinth. By strenuous effort about 0,000 men were assembled by April 1. Grant's failure to make a apid counter-concentration gave the Confederates the chance of uccess.

"Concentrate to fight"; "unity of command is necessary to suc- ess"; "time is everything." The Confederates had carried out plendidly the first of these maxims of Napoleon. On the two latter hey fell down.

It was expected to march from Corinth to Shiloh in time to open he battle at dawn on April 5; but severe rains made the roads luddy, the quartermaster's department was poorly equipped for ich an emergency, and the staff work was faulty. On one occasion ours were lost at a crossroads while one corps crossed the route of nother. Time, which in this particular case was truly everything, as irretrievably lost. It was not until the dawn of April 6 that ohnston, having moved about 20 miles from Corinth to Shiloh hurch, was ready to fall upon the five isolated divisions left by rant upon the west side of the Tennessee River. The battle which ollowed was the first really great battle upon the continent. No ich large bodies of men had before grappled upon American soil. t was an undreamed-of experience for commanders and men alike.

I shall not go into details concerning the struggle, but the tempta- on to quote a sentence in Beauregard's report is too strong: "Like n Alpine avalanche our troops moved forward, despite the deter- ined resistance of the enemy, until after 6 p. m.," wrote Beauregard.[14] he phrase, "until after 6 p. m.," is important in throwing light on he old but intensely interesting problem of the failure of the Con- ederates to push home their attack on the evening of April 6. The eport[15] of Maj. R. T. Harvey, Second Arkansas Infantry, "We then etired, it being 6 p. m.," confirms Beauregard's statement. In no her report is there a definite statement as to the hour. As a reason or his failure to continue the battle after this hour, Beauregard ave the exhaustion of his men after 12 hours of fighting without ood, when already jaded by the muddy march from Corinth.[16] ome gave the fire of the gunboats as a reason. This from a careful udy of the war I am inclined to discount. In the language of the eport of Col. George Maney, who faced this fire from the gunboats a that day, it was "more noisy than destructive."[17] His statement fortified by a letter of W. H. C. Whiting, one of the ablest engineers the Confederate Army, to a newspaper in regard to a similar casion in Virginia waters. Direct gunfire by gunboats upon in- ntry he held to be alarming but not very dangerous. For the

[14] O. R., Ser. I, Vol. X, pt. I, p. 386.
[15] O. R., Ser. I, Vol. X, pt. I, p. 577.
[16] O. R., Ser. I, Vol. X, pt. I. p. 387.
[17] O. R., Ser. I, Vol. X, pt. I, p. 455.

failure of the Confederates to advance farther I have seen given as a reason the reorganization of a portion of Grant's artillery and infantry upon a final line of defense. Really, if one cause must be cited above all others, it was the accidental loss of unity and continuity of command through the unforeseen death of Albert Sidney Johnston. The second maxim of Napoleon, above quoted, was not maintained, though destiny was at least partially responsible for its miscarriage.

On the night of April 6 fresh troops under Buell came up to join the forces of the Union Army. Grant did heroic work in the reorganization of his line on the west banks of the river. Outnumbered and defeated, Beauregard fell back toward Corinth on the afternoon of April 7. Here he was joined by Van Dorn, who had crossed the Mississippi at Memphis, but who did not join the concentration in time to engage in the decisive battle of the campaign. Along the Charleston and Memphis Railroad, which passed through Corinth, Beauregard threw up fortifications to defend this highly important center. For nearly two months the Confederate and Union armies faced each other in this region. Finally, when Halleck had raised his forces at this point to 100,000 men, and was at last ready to besiege Corinth, Beauregard, on the advice of his subordinates,[18] withdrew to Tupelo, Miss., about 40 miles to the south. The unsanitary conditions of the encampment, poor water, and much sickness were given as reasons for this retirement.[19]

This retreat to Tupelo marked the end of the Confederate campaign of the first half of 1862. Halleck did not pursue. A summer interlude in this unhealthy region resulted, to be followed by Grant's Mississippi campaign and Bragg's remarkable movement into Tennessee and Kentucky.

In the failure at Shiloh the whole purpose of the earlier concentration of the Confederate forces was defeated.

Now come up for consideration the concomitant aspects of the concentration so thoroughly carried out in this campaign. A long paper would be required for an adequate discussion of these. Political, economic, and military affairs were alike affected, and, as usual in warfare, these affairs were inextricably commingled. Only a partial consideration of them is possible. Much must be omitted and great gaps left in the treatment.

Across the Mississippi River, in Missouri and Arkansas, important results followed the concentration at Corinth. The seasoned troops needed for the defence of this valuable source of supplies for the Confederacy were drawn away under Van Dorn and Price. Not until nearly a year later was a mere remnant of these returned to the

---

18 O. R., Ser. I, Vol. X, pt. I, p. 762.
19 O. R., Ser. I, Vol. X, pt. II, p. 545.

trans-Mississippi department, under Price,[20] whose main interest was in Missouri and whose wishes to be returned to the west bank of the Mississippi were for a long time overridden. Missouri and northern Arkansas were thus lost to the Confederacy. Had it not been for the hills and the east and west rivers of Arkansas, which made north and south communications difficult, it is probable that all Arkansas would have been overrun. As it was, southern Arkansas, by reason of droughts and the predominance of the cotton crop, was of little value to the Confederacy during the war.

Elsewhere the story is much the same. On the withdrawal from the bluffs at Columbus, Ky., in February, the Confederate forces closing the Mississippi from the north, fell back down the river to Madrid Bend, New Madrid, and Island No. 10, places of greatly inferior strength. Neither the ability of the commanders[21] nor the character of the forces placed at those points seems to have been fortunate. The best of everything was concentrated at Corinth. In March and April these places were easily captured by Pope with the assistance of the fleet of gunboats. On March 14 Pope wrote Halleck from near New Madrid: " To my utter amazement the enemy hurriedly evacuated the place last night, leaving everything."[22] On April 8 he was able to announce:

Everything is ours. Few, if any, of the enemy escaped. Three generals, 3,000 prisoners, an immense quantity of ammunition and supplies, 100 pieces of siege and several batteries of field artillery, great numbers of small arms, tents, wagons, horses, etc., have fallen into our hands. We have not lost a man in crossing the river or in pursuing and capturing the enemy."

From these points the Confederates fell back nearer to Memphis and fortified Fort Pillow, the last place of any strength above Memphis. This point was held as long as Beauregard remained at Corinth. When early in June Beauregard drew back to Tupelo, Fort Pillow and Memphis fell into the possession of the Union forces. The Mississippi River was opened up as far as the neighborhood of Vicksburg. The railroad line from Memphis to Richmond, which Benjamin wanted defended "at all hazards," was permanently cut by the loss of these places.

At the lower end of the Mississippi River equally important events occurred. For the concentration at Corinth, Lovell had sent off his available seasoned troops. A result was that his defensive forces were dangerously weakened. Just at this time an armament under Farragut and Butler attacked the defenses of New Orleans. Mismanagement, particularly in the restoration of the boom which had been swept away by floods, and the divided command of land and naval defenses, were a partial cause of the disaster which followed,

[20] O. R., Ser. I, Vol. XXII, pt. II, p. 791, Feb. 27, 1863.
[21] O. R., Ser. I, Vol. VIII, p. 138.
[22] O. R., Ser. I, Vol. VIII, p. 613.

but the insufficiency of numbers and the character of the defender proved fatal. In his official report Lovell, with some self-control remarked:

> I will here state that every Confederate soldier in New Orleans, with th exception of one company, had been ordered to Corinth to join Gen. Beau regard in March, and the city was only garrisoned by about 3,000 90-day troop called out by the governor at my request, of whom about 1,200 had musket and the remainder shotguns of an indifferent description.[23]

For the loss of New Orleans Lovell was later tried by a military court. The finding of the court substantiated this statement o Lovell in the following language:

> His ability to hold that line against such an attack was greatly impaired by the withdrawal from him by his superior authority of nearly all his effective troops.[24]

In the light of these statements is it too much, therefore, to say that the loss of New Orleans was part of the price paid for the concentration at Corinth? If so, it was a dear price for the success actually attained, for New Orleans, once lost, was never recovered and it served as a base for the attempt to complete the opening of the Mississippi River from the south the following winter and year. By its fall another route connecting the Confederacy was cut, and a most favorable place for blockade running lost to the South.

In conclusion, concentration is unquestionably a sound tenet of military strategy. But, whatever the merit of concentration in the abstract, does not the history of this campaign show that it has very definite limitations? Counter considerations of great importance certainly existed in the Confederacy in the first half of 1862. A natural objection to this interpretation of the campaign is that the obvious alternative of scattered defense along territorial lines was still worse. But this obvious alternative was not the only solution. Concentration must have certain definite concomitants. Complete and continuous unity of command and intense activity must go with the strategy of concentration. "Time is everything." Rapidity of movement should characterize the concentration and the blow of the forces thus concentrated; and to use an expression very popular at the present time, the blow must be followed through. When the blow fails, as it did in this case, the counter considerations at once are sacrificed or endangered.

Concentration within limits and when necessary, and the utilization to full advantage of interior lines, in conjunction with audacity, activity, and aggressiveness, would seem to have been the best strategy for the Confederacy, not only in this campaign, but throughout the war between the States.

---

[23] O. R., Ser. I, Vol. VI, p. 513.
[24] O. R., Ser. I, Vol. VI, p. 641.

XI. POSSIBILITIES OF INTENSIVE RESEARCH IN AGRICULTURAL HISTORY.

By R. W. KELSEY,
Haverford College, Pa.

POSSIBILITIES OF INTENSIVE RESEARCH IN AGRICULTURAL HISTORY.

By R. W. Kelsey.

I. INTRODUCTION.

This paper proposes a brief inquiry into the intensive as contrasted with the extensive study of agricultural history.

Extensive study in this field has long been in evidence. Outstanding facts in various periods, or important movements and conditions covering a considerable area or epoch, are a commonplace in American history. Examples in point are the influence of the plantation system in the South, the effect of the new harvesting implements in the wheat area, the reaction of the farming community to various forms of the cheap money propaganda. Just now we have before our eyes the possibility of a fundamental transformation of farming conditions through the general introduction of the automobile and the tractor into the economy of rural life. Such influences, movements, and changes are writ large, and he that runs may read. It is probable, however, that many very important influences of agriculture upon the main currents of American life can not be discovered until a goodly amount of intensive research in various fields of agricultural history has been accomplished. A very slight contribution to such results is here made as the outcome of some tentative excursions into the history of agriculture in early Pennsylvania.

II. METHOD.

So many students of history are now entering this field of study that some exchange of ideas on method should be helpful.

The present writer has adopted a combined system of small note slips and large sheets. Short notes are taken in full on the small slips. The large sheets carry the fuller material. The matter on the larger sheets is, however, indexed on the smaller slips. Thus the file of small slips, arranged by topics, and in chronological order within each topic, is at all times a complete compendium of the ma-

terial gathered to date. The notes thus far taken have fallen within
12 main topics, as follows:

I. Soils.
II. Tools.
III. Crops.
IV. Live stock.
V. Farm practice: Methods and results.
VI. Farm industries and business.
VII. Manners and customs.
VIII. Population.
IX. Farmers and the Government.
X. Farmers' organizations.
XI. Epochal events.
XII. Miscellaneous.

Most of these general topics have fallen into subtopics as the note
taking proceeded.

Topic VII on manners and customs has, for example, developed
the following subtopics: (a) General; (b) Home, social life, amuse-
ments, temperance; (c) Churches and schools; (d) Roads, bridges,
travel, taverns; (e) Neighborhood industries; (f) Hunting and fishing; (g) Indian relations; (h) Labor and wages; (i) farm buildings.

Most of the topics have not developed so many subtopics as this
one, but the 12 main divisions indicated above have brought forth
thus far 72 rubrics altogether, making an average of six subtopics
for every topic.

III. Materials.

(a) secondary works.

Secondary material on the history of agriculture in Pennsylvania
is conspicuous by its absence. In the many general histories that
have been written there is almost nothing on this subject. In the
special histories of counties and towns, of sects, or racial elements
there is surprisingly little. The greatest exception to the rule is
found in the publications of the Pennsylvania German Society.
Agriculture has been a fundamental occupation in all ages of human
history. Throughout the colonial period in Pennsylvania a very
large majority of the inhabitants were engaged in it exclusively.
Yet in the histories of Pennsylvania this great phase of life is passed
over in almost complete silence.

(b) printed sources.

When the historian's hand is set to the source materials the story
is very different.

The laws of Pennsylvania alone open a great mine of information.
As early as 1683 a fine of £5 was levied for allowing a stallion less

than 13½ hands high to run at large.[1] Perhaps this and later enactments of a similar nature account in part for the great size and strength of Pennsylvania horses, as noted by so many travelers in the later period.

The food control act of our late war had an early precedent in Pennsylvania history. As early as 1693 a law was passed requiring every baker to have a distinct mark on his bread. The size and weight of loaves were also regulated and the price fixed in accordance with the price of wheat per bushel.[2] These and many similar regulations bore directly, or indirectly, upon the development of agriculture.

The Pennsylvania Archives and the Records of the Council contain a great amount of miscellaneous material, ranging from regulative laws to discussions about the Hessian fly.

The volume by Albert Cook Myers in Dr. Jameson's series of Original Narratives contains reprints of great value on the subject in hand. The amount that can be included in such a volume is of course quite limited, but in this case it is so carefully selected as to be of great value in itself and to suggest the type of material to be sought after in further study.

The earliest newspapers contain little material other than current prices of farm products in the Philadelphia market. In 1729 the Pennsylvania Gazette decided to encourage its country readers by reprinting an article on hemp from Chambers's Universal Dictionary.[3] This ambitious effort surely did not increase subscribers, for the policy was at once discontinued. After the Revolutionary War, under the impulse of the Philosophical Society and the Agricultural Society, the papers contain many articles on fertilizers, tillage, crop rotations, and general farm practice.

A most important division of the printed source material is of course that of early travel. Happily there were several travelers in Pennsylvania who were especially interested in agriculture, and they have left a mass of interesting and valuable data on many phases of farm life and methods. Brissot de Warville, Crèvecoeur, Lincklaen, Mellish, Rochefoucauld-Liancourt, and Schoepf are examples in point.

What better material could historian desire than the following from Schoepf, in 1783:

Hereabouts (in southern Bucks County) there is a seeding plough in use and highly regarded, which is known as the Bucks County plough. Elsewhere the wheat is seeded on fallow broken but once, and then the seed ploughed

---

[1] Charter to William Penn and Laws of the Province of Pennsylvania passed between 682 and 1700, p. 164; see also pp. 167, 288.
[2] Charter to William Penn and Laws of the Province of Pennsylvania passed between 682 and 1700, p. 230.
[3] Pennsylvania Gazette, Oct. 9, 1729, p. 1.

in. The allowance is one-half to one bushel of seed to an acre, according as the wheat is old or new, if new a half bushel is sufficient. They commonly expect, from three-fourths of a bushel seed on unmanured land, 10–15 bushels yield, but in other parts of Pennsylvania, about Reading and in the Tulpe hocken Valley, the yield is 25–30 bushels. A four-horse wagon hauls 40–50 bushels of wheat to the city, the price at this time being one Spanish dollar a bushel, or 7 shillings 6 pence Pennsylvania current. What with the quantity of land many farmers own, they can not work the whole of it properly, and therefore many acres lie fallow 5–6–7 years together. The usual practice is to plant maize the first year; the second year wheat is sown along with English grass seeds; and after the wheat is off, the field is pastured for four or five years. At other times they sow buckwheat (one-half bushel to the acre) after wheat, or it may be turnips.[4]

Here in one paragraph is poured forth information on seeding implements and methods, amount of seed per acre, amount of yield in various places, transport of crops to market, prices received, various forms of money and its comparative value, fallow practice on the farm, and rotation of crops. While such a paragraph is above the average in works of travel, it is by no means unique.

Finally, under the heading of printed sources, must be mentioned American Husbandry (1775) in two volumes, and the Memoirs of the Philadelphia Society for Promoting Agriculture, 1808, 1811, 1814. These volumes are a mine of information, most of which is not to be found elsewhere.

(c) MANUSCRIPT SOURCES.

In the far-flung domain of manuscripts the material is so limitless that the merest intimation of its extent and variety can be given at this early stage of the quest.

In the Library of Congress, the State Library of Pennsylvania, and the Library of the Historical Society of Pennsylvania in Philadelphia are great stores of material, including the almost untouched shelf loads of transcripts from English archives.

A morsel from the last-named collection is William Penn's testimony to the board of trade, in 1700, on the workings of the intercolonial trade laws. One such law prohibited the sale and transport of wool from one colony to another. Consequently a farmer would sell his entire flock of sheep to a merchant across the border. The sheep would then be driven over, shorn of their wool, and sold back immediately to the original owner at a price formerly agreed upon.[5] So the Pennsylvania farmer dealt as cleverly with the English trade laws as did the merchant of New England.

A great increase in the production of tobacco in Pennsylvania may be discovered in a study of the same sources. In 1699 Col. Quary,

---

[4] Schoepf, Travels in the Confederation, 1783–1784, I, 130.
[5] Board of Trade Papers, Proprieties, VI, Dec. 8 and 13, 1700 (Hist. Soc. of Penna.).

admiralty judge in Pennsylvania, wrote to the board of trade as follows:

The greate price yt tobacco yealds here encouredges the Country to plant more than ever [;] itt hath beene sold here this year for above thirty Shillings pr. [c. ?] lb.

A few months later he remarked to the board of trade, on the industry of Pennsylvania farmers, and continued:

They have improved tilledge to that degree that they have made Bread flower and Beer a drug in all the Markets in the West Indies, so that finding that Trade overdone they resolve to goe on wth the planting of Tobacco in the three upper Countys where never any was planted yet.

With these clues as to the increase of tobacco culture at this period it is not surprising to find William Penn writing in December, 1700:

We shall this year advance from 1500 Hogsh^{ds} to 3 or 4000 of tobacco.[6]

Some idea of the extent of such sources may be gained from the statement that the Penn manuscripts are in 190 large volumes, the Logan in 73 volumes, the Pemberton in 70, and the Norris in 75. All of these furnish valuable material on agricultural history, and many other sets not yet examined contain from 20 to 100 volumes each.

Aside from these outstanding collections there are, of course, miscellaneous papers, almost limitless in number, kind, and location. Such papers are in the libraries mentioned above, in other libraries of Pennsylvania and adjoining States, and in collections of local historical societies all over Pennsylvania. There are the land and probate records in every county. There is also, of course, much untouched material in various local archives in Great Britain and continental countries. The present writer is now making some search of libraries and private collections in western Germany to locate letters and diaries written by early emigrants to Pennsylvania. The Department of Historical Research of the Carnegie Institution is having a survey made of materials for American history in the West Indian archives, and some report on this work is to be made by Prof. Bell at one of the sessions of this conference. The same department of the Carnegie Institution is preparing a compendium of entries bearing upon American history, in the catalogues of foreign manuscript collections. All such compilations are sure to uncover material concerning early agricultural history in Pennsylvania and elsewhere.

One example may be cited of the discoveries of entirely new material that will come on occasion if a subject of this kind is pursued intensively. Some months ago a little pocket journal was found in the Library of Congress. It was written in a very small, almost

---

[5] For above letters of Quary and Penn, see Board of Trade Papers, Proprieties, III; 267; V, 257; VI, Dec. 8 and 13, 1700 (Hist. Soc. of Penna.).

microscopic hand, much of it nearly illegible. It had been purchased from a Paris dealer and had lain in the library for nearly a score of years, untranslated and practically untouched. Although it was entirely anonymous a careful study of internal evidence proved it to be a journal kept by Theophile Cazenove, in a journey from New York City across Jersey into central Pennsylvania and back to Philadelphia, in 1794. Cazenove was at that period the general agent of the Holland Land Co. in America, and so his prime interest was in farming lands. As a consequence his journal is a mine of information on the agricultural conditions of that day. He tells in the utmost detail of crops, live stock, seeding and tillage methods, rotations, transportation and sale of crops, labor conditions, wages, and prices, and above all the social conditions of country life.

A touch of Cazenove's pen may not be out of place on this paper. While passing through Maxatawny township, Bucks County, Pa., he wrote:

Generally an acre of land produces 20 bushels of wheat, 25 bushels of barley, 25 to 30 bushels of buckwheat, 1¼ to 2 tons of hay each cutting, 1½ to 2 tons of clover, two cuttings, and then turn the cattle in; a little corn [raised]. Plowing is done with horses, but the custom of plowing with oxen is gaining more and more.

They generally sow wheat. The Hessian fly is very detrimental to them. For fertilizer manure is used. Plaster of Paris is very good for clover the first two years, but they find out that it uses up the land.

A good 300-acre farm is offered for sale near here; fair house, very good barn, near the river; 60 acres meadow, 230 tillable, 10 woods; excellent land, for 4,000 pounds cash.

A glimpse of the social life of Lancaster and vicinity is given in the following paragraph:

During the fair, which lasts for three days in June, and while court is held (which is once every three months) all the county farmers and their children come to Lancaster, and then everything is good cheer. All the young farmers and their wives must have pleasure, as they have none the rest of the year; people say that nothing is more interesting than their loud joy and the big kisses exchanged everywhere by the sweethearts who fill the streets. So the young people have a chance to see each other and marriages follow, while the fathers get drunk in the taverns.

The thrift of the German farmers showed its seamy side to this aristocratic traveler, as witness the following:

In the Downingtown Inn, Chester County, where I spent the night, there were that same evening 14 Lancaster farmers; each one was driving a big 4-horse wagon, with 12 barrels of flour, to Philadelphia. I found them in a room next to the kitchen, all lying on the floor in a circle, their feet to the fire, each one on one or two bags of oats which they have with them to feed the horses on the way. They were covered with poor blankets; no caps, and all dressed. This lodging did not cost them anything, the innkeeper gave them this shelter to be able to sell them the small quantity of liquor they buy. In this group there were farmers known to be worth from 6,000 pounds to 8,000 pounds in good land, and in money lent on mortgage upon good lands.[t]

III. RESULTS.

These pages have touched very lightly and inadequately upon some of the possibilities, in method and materials, of the intensive study of localized agricultural history.

The results of such study might ultimately appear in various forms. Specialized articles could be written on the history of any important phase of farm practice. New light could be thrown upon many critical periods of political history, showing the reaction of the farming community to and upon the events of the time. Social histories could be written, compassing the whole round of country life, economic, social, educational, and religious. Finally, the general history of a State or a section could be rewritten, filling in that important background of rural life, so fundamentally important to the picture, yet so largely omitted in almost every history.

These are some of the possibilities of intensive research in agricultural history, as pursued in a restricted field of time or place. Such studies must be the scaffolding for the more extensive surveys and generalizations that will ultimately build the story of country life into the growing structure of American history. The intensive study should not be called more important than the extensive. They are mutually supplementary, not competitive in their nature. The intensive study is different in kind, essential in its place, and alluring to a degree.

---

[t] Cazenove, Relation d'un voyage dans l'Amérique du Nord, 1794, pp. 21, 47, 61. In Manuscript Division, Library of Congress.

XII. SOME FEATURES OF TOBACCO HISTORY.

By GEORGE K. HOLMES,

Bureau of Agricultural Economics,
United States Department of Agriculture.

25066°—23——25

SOME FEATURES OF TOBACCO HISTORY.

By GEORGE K. HOLMES.

The purpose of this paper is not to give a history of tobacco, for hat would be impossible within a short time limit, but the purpose s partly to correct some popular misunderstandings, partly to supply ome interesting features not generally known, and partly to indi-ate very briefly some lines of an historical narrative.

USED BY INDIANS.

At the time of the discovery of America, the custom of smoking obacco, of chewing it, and of snuff taking—that is, of using it in ome way—was diffused over the greater part of this vast conti-ent between the southern part of South America and the boreal egions of North America. The Indians of the West Indies and f South America smoked cigars and cigarettes and took snuff, ex-ept in the district of La Plata, Uruguay and Paraguay, where no orm of tobacco was used until the Spaniards introduced it. From the sthmus of Panama and the West Indies to southern Canada and o California, smoking was practiced by the Indians, and circum-tances show that this was of ancient origin.

Why did the Indians use tobacco? It will not do to interpret a ustom of another people and of ancient times in terms of our-elves and of our own times. It is a false picture to think of the ndian as smoking his after-dinner pipe, or cigar, or cigarette, or as iting off a chew of navy plug as he paused in the cultivation of his orn. The tobacco plant was indigenous to America and the Indian ıust have used it before he raised it in his garden, and this he was oing when the white people first saw him.

The primary service of tobacco to the Indians was of a religious ature. Before the Spaniards came it was not used as a habit nor or the sake of sociability. Rather, it was related to the unseen orld. To the Indians of what is now the United States, the to-acco plant had a sacred character; it was almost invariably used n solemn occasions, accompanied by suitable invocations to dreaded pirits. It was ceremonially used to aid in disease or distress, to vard off danger, to bring good fortune, generally to assist one in eed, and to allay fear.

387

The planting of medicine tobacco was one of the oldest cere monies of the Crows, consisting, among other observances, of a sol emn march, a foot race among the young men, the planting of seed the building of a hedge of green branches around the seed bed, a visit to the sweat house, followed by a bath and a solemn smoke all ending with a feast.

In Virginia, tobacco was believed to be a special gift from the realm of the departed. The leaves were arranged in a circle, from the center of which adoration was offered to the sun, accompanied by eccentric gestures and contortions of the body, by dancing, stamp ings, and uplifting of the hands and by fixed starings toward the sky. The object was to propitiate an evil intelligence. When crushed into powder, tobacco was sowed to the wind when a drought prevailed or when a tempest was blowing on the water; or it was sprinkled over the weirs when fishes began their annual migration from the sea. It was tossed into the air, as an offering of reward to a spirit, after an escape from some unusual danger, or when the warriors returned to town after a successful war, or hunting expe dition, or long journey in which they had been exposed to many perils and hardships.

DISSEMINATION BY SPANIARDS.

Medicine was related to religion in the affairs of primitive man It was observed by the Spaniards who early came to the West Indies and to the mainland of America that tobacco was used by the Indians for medicinal purposes and to prevent a feeling of fatigue. His torically this is a matter of subsequent great importance, because it was the cause of the rapid spread of the cultivation and use of tobacco throughout the world. Tobacco was first observed by Europeans within present knowledge, in 1492 in the West Indies. The subse quent sequence of events in the introduction of tobacco to Europe is uncertain and the record is contradictory. It is said that the Span iards began the cultivation of tobacco in the West Indies before 1535 and shortly after made the tobacco of the Island of Trinidad famous in Europe. Soon they developed production on a large scale in the West Indies, Venezuela, and Brazil.

My assumption is that tobacco was going from Spanish plantations to Spain and Portugal for use there before a few noted men got them selves into the historical record as introducers of the plant. One item of record is that a famous physician, Francisco Fernandes, who was sent to Mexico by Philip II of Spain in 1558, was the first to bring the plant to notice in Europe with the specimens that he took. In 1560, Jean Nicot, French ambassador to Lisbon, found tobacco seed here, which he sent to Paris. The popular belief is that Sir Walter Raleigh was the man who first took tobacco to England, but the writers of history have no good excuse for making this error. Apparently Sir John Hawkins was the first to take tobacco to England, in 1565, and it is of record that tobacco was growing in that country about 1570. Yet one of our historical authorities states that in 1586 tobacco and pipes were first brought to England by Sir Francis Drake. Evidently there is a great deal of error in tobacco history as it is written.

It is well to bear in mind that social history is made mostly by the masses of the people and little by historical figureheads; and I would suggest that the conflicting statements concerning the first transfer of tobacco to Europe be ignored and that the responsibility for this be placed on the Spanish sailors and sea captains who early came to the West Indies and whose names are unsung by history. The fact that Spaniards were cultivating tobacco in the West Indies before 1535, and apparently on a commercial scale soon after, indicates that they were finding a market for it in Spain about that time.

FIRST USED BY WHITES AS A MEDICINE.

There is much in this subject of tobacco that pertains to psychology. Why did Europeans begin to use tobacco? Certainly not because they believed that it put them favorably in touch with the spirits of evil. The misery of the first sickness in acquiring the use of tobacco by smoking—and this was the first use in Europe—would seem to have been a formidable obstacle to taking the first step.

From the beginning in the sixteenth century, or perhaps at the end of the fifteenth century, and for an indefinite and variable later time, tobacco was smoked by Europeans mainly because of the wonderful properties attributed to the smoke. It was supposed, and the belief was derived from the Indians, that the smoke not only cured disease but was a prophylactic as well. Moreover, it prevented the pangs of hunger and fatigue. The visitation of the plague encouraged the use of tobacco enormously. It was for a long time prescribed as a medicine by physicians in Spain, France, and England.

There is or has been until recently a last remnant of the belief in the curative power of tobacco in the United States. I have seen a countryman take a chew of tobacco from his mouth and apply it to a wound with the expectation that the healing would be hastened.

In the meantime tobacco was going to other countries. It was introduced into Turkey at the beginning of the seventeenth century, and the Persians soon received it from Turkey. It reached far-off China still earlier, before the end of the sixteenth century.

During the first 50 years after tobacco began to be used in England, smoking spread with extraordinary rapidity to all classes of society—peers, squires, parsons, and peasants. Soon, smoking entered another phase of its history. It began to withdraw from the domain of medicine and to become fashionable. Sir Walter Raleigh's true place in tobacco history is that he was responsible for its common use in smoking for pleasure. Long before his death in 1618, smoking had become fashionable.

A social pipe, the same pipe, was passed from person to person around the dinner table. There was smoking at the theater. In 1620, the London Society of Tobacco Pipe Makers was incorporated, with the motto, "Let brotherly love continue." Much was written in favor of tobacco. Marston wrote in 1607,

> Musicke, tobacco, sacke, and sleepe
> The tide of sorrow backward keep.

Edmund Spenser, in the Faerie Queen, calls tobacco, "The sóveraine weede, divine tobacco."

A French traveler who was in London in 1633 wrote that the English were naturally lazy and spent half their time in smoking. The habit was not confined to London, but had extended to the country and into Scotland. Smoking was a particular feature of the Lord Mayor's show in London in 1672. Then, as before, pipes and tobacco were a usual provision for city feasts.

That immortal smoker, Raleigh, had many distinguished followers. John Milton was a smoker, even after he was blind. I have heard smokers say that they do not like to smoke in the dark—they want to see the smoke. At any rate, Milton smoked after he became blind. Sir Isaac Newton smoked immoderately. Thomas Hobbes and Isaac Walton were smokers, and each lived to be 90 years old.

But tobacco had many enemies. Besides King James I, who wrote the Counterblaste to Tobbacco, there was Dekkar, the dramatist, who refers to tobacco as "thou beggarly monarch of Indians, and setter-up of rotten-lunged chimney sweepers." Burton, of the Anatomy of Melancholy, believed in tobacco as a medicine, but denounced the common smoking "by most men, which take it as tinkers do ale," as "a plague, a mischief, a violent purger of goods, lands, health—hellish, devilish, and damned tobacco, the ruin and overthrow of body and soul."

In the latter decades of the sixteenth century smoking became less fashionable and general. Yet, in Queen Anne's time smoking was still common although decadent. Then followed a long period when smoking was under the social ban in England. In the eighteenth

:entury it was confined largely to the middle and humbler classes, o use an English expression; but there were numerous exceptions. Country parsons smoked, and their parishioners, from squire to aborer.

SNUFFING FOLLOWS.

Looking backward from the present time, it would seem as though smoking had a most improbable and absurd successor in fashionable London and later in England. Who could guess, without knowing the historical fact, that it was tobacco snuff? The original users of snuff were the Indians of South America and of the countries northward to Mexico. From them Spaniards acquired the habit and in consequence became the first snuff makers of Europe. The Dutch, English, and Scotch extended the industry, as they in turn became users of snuff.

It is said that by 1759 snuff taking had apparently occupied the place of pipe smoking in the fashion of London. In a satirical poem of the time, one of the verses asserts that—

> Coxcombs prefer the tickling sting of snuff.

The populace, however, was still on the side of smoking. Dr. Johnson said in 1773:

> To be sure, it is a shocking thing, blowing smoke out of our mouths into other people's mouths, eyes, and noses, and having the same thing done to us; yet, I can not account why a thing which requires so little exertion and yet preserves the mind from total vacuity, should have gone out.

Dr. Johnson and all his company took snuff, as every one did in the fashionable world, and a great many outside of the charmed circle, although on the outside pipes were still in full blast.

In the first two or three decades of the nineteenth century, smoking reached its nadir in England. The snuffbox was all powerful. The Prince Regent was devoted to snuff and had "a cellar of snuff" which after his death in 1830 was sold for 400 pounds. The oldest method of taking snuff in England was to scrape it with a rasp from a root of the tobacco plant; the powder was placed on the back of the hand and snuffed up into the nose. This is why a coarse kind of snuff made from the darker and ranker tobacco leaves has been called rappeé, a corrupted spelling and pronunciation of a French word meaning rasped. The rasp was carried in a waistcoat pocket and soon became a luxurious implement of carved ivory, bejeweled and ornamented.

But the habit of using snuff reached its peak in Great Britain and then followed a long period of decline, ending in desuetude by the end of the nineteenth century, when the snuffbox disappeared from the mantlepiece of the clubs.

Next enters the vogue of the cigar in England. The Spaniards first saw Indians smoking cigars in the West Indies and in turn became smokers and makers of cigars themselves. Cigars and cigar making were introduced into Spain and by one channel and another a few cigars reached England from time to time. But until the early years of the nineteenth century, cigars were almost unknown in England. By 1830, they were freely, if privately, smoked. Why this new custom?

Bear in mind that pipe smoking had by no means become extinct in Great Britain, but it was mostly confined to what English writers like to call the humbler classes, with some survival in classes above. That country sent many soldiers to the Peninsular War in Spain and Portugal, and many came back, and when they returned they brought with them cigars and the habit of smoking them. Then followed the acquiring of the habit of cigar smoking by those classes that had early been pipe smokers and later snuff takers.

Cigar smoking grew rapidly in England. Sir Walter Scott smoked cigars and so did Byron. Byron's poem, The Island, is known to-day only because it contains his apostrophe to tobacco. Thackeray was another cigar smoker. Others, however, detested cigar smoking. The Duke of Wellington was annoyed by the increase of cigar smoking among the officers of the army, and in the early forties he issued a general order against smoking in mess rooms and against smoking by officers of junior rank. Queen Victoria and the Prince Consort detested tobacco and it was taboo wherever court was.

Since the Peninsular War, the pipe and the cigar have gone hand in hand in Great Britain, with a tendency in later years of the pipe to return to its respectability; and in the more recent years the cigarette has become very prominent. You will remember that Tennyson was a pipe smoker of strenuous performance and that he was a guest at Shadwell Rectory when he wrote In Memoriam. When he began its composition, his pipe created such a smudge in the rectory that he was removed by his host, very politely, of course, to a workshop in the garden, and that was the birthplace of this immortal poem, on account of the poet's pipe.

So far, I have purposely remained out of the Thirteen Colonies, partly because there is a deal of important tobacco history before the first tobacco export from Jamestown, partly because English history throws necessary light on the early tobacco production and the tobacco habits of this country; and partly also to avoid the appear-ince of making Jamestown the creator of the smoking habit in England. That is an impression that one gets from a little reading of colonial history.

Our national tobacco history begins at the Jamestown settlement. The Virginia plant rarely exceeded a yard in height. It had a small yellow flower, like that of henbane, and had short, thick leaves, weak in flavor but biting to the tongue. The West Indian plant was 9 to 12 feet high. The Jamestown settlers followed the Indian custom of planting tobacco seed as they did corn, and did not transplant from a seed bed. Later the practice of transplanting was suggested by the old English practice with regard to vegetables. The Indians removed suckers to give the leaves greater size, and pulled the leaves from the standing stalks and dried them by fire or sun. For 150 years the colonists dried the leaves by hanging them in barns exposed to the free circulation of air. The Indians ceased to plant tobacco as soon as their white neighbors began to cultivate it on an extensive scale, and obtained their tobacco from the whites by exchange.

John Rolfe raised the first tobacco at Jamestown in 1612, and by 1618 the export of tobacco to England amounted to 20,000 pounds in that year. Rolfe's object was to obtain goods from England in exchange for tobacco. Already some sassafras had been exported. Tobacco at once became the chief export because it returned more for the labor required for its production than anything else. England was urging the raising of wheat for export, but this was uneconomical for the colonists as compared with tobacco.

It has been asserted by critical writers that, without export tobacco, the first settlement of Virginia would have been a failure. This seems to me to be an exaggeration by those who have looked at the subject through a pinhole. Certainly the Jamestown people did not eat tobacco, although I have seen tobacco chewers who seemed to be eating it, and, since other colonies survived without early tobacco exports or other exports that had any such prominence as tobacco did in Virginia, it is not logical to suppose that Jamestown would have been abandoned in want of tobacco. If the statement had been made that the corn of the Indians saved the colonists from starvation and made the colony permanent it would have been nearer the mark. Tobacco exports were exchanged mostly for textiles, clothing, and metal and leather goods. So readily were these obtained by raising tobacco that it is reported that Jamestown was more than once near starvation because tobacco was raised too much to the exclusion of foods.

It is not my intention to repeat the familiar story of the service of tobacco as money in early Virginia, but I venture to offer a few words of comment. Our school histories and, indeed, our larger histories are likely to create the impression that there was some inherent and exclusive virtue in tobacco that qualified it to perform duty as money. This, of course, is thoroughly erroneous. Tobacco, in the trade between Virginia and England, was readily exchangeable in England for any and all of the things that the colonists bought; hence to them it had one of the attributes of money, or exchangeability, but it did not possess the other attributes of money. The fact of ready exchangeability, joined to the fact of export, created a situation for tobacco in Virginia in which it could serve as money in a limited way. At a time when real money was scarce a clergyman or a laborer willingly took his pay in tobacco, because he knew that he could take it to the nearest merchant and receive from him goods or credit in exchange; for the merchant knew that he could send the tobacco to England by the next ship and receive therefor its equivalent in goods. There have been numerous other instances throughout the ages, and in other parts of the world, of limited money service by commodities. Among them are cattle, wheat, corn, rye, tea, furs, rice in Carolina, sugar in the West Indies, and dried codfish in Newfoundland.

BEGINNINGS IN THE STATES.

The culture of tobacco in New England began at the time of the various settlements, but was opposed by many of the Puritans, so that the crop did not develop to any great extent for many years. As early as 1640, the Connecticut colony made a law restricting the use of tobacco to that grown in the colony, with penalty of 5 shillings for every pound of money expended for imported tobacco unless license had been obtained from a court. This was to stimulate home production, and yet in 1646–47 a law was enacted forbidding every person under 20 years old and every other person who had not become a tobacco user, to use any tobacco without certificate from a physician that it would be beneficial to him. Nor should tobacco be used publicly in the streets, with penalty of 6 pence. Somewhat similar prohibitions existed, or had existed, locally in England, so that this was not legislation that was the first of its kind. Massachusetts Bay had similar restrictive legislation. There was a diversity of opinion in New England with regard to tobacco. John Eliot, the preacher and missionary among the Indians, denounced tobacco, but the pastor of the first church of Charlestown "was always seen with a pipe in his mouth."

So important had tobacco become to the Connecticut colony by 1753, that an official inspection was established for export tobacco for securing sound, well-ripened, and well-cured tobacco. The export tobacco was for cigars and until 1800 was bought by local merchants and shipped mostly to the West Indies.

Statements may be found with regard to the first year when tobacco was raised by the whites in some of the States, but such statements are to be accepted with caution. It may be supposed that the first settlers lost no time in cultivating this plant.

In Maryland, it is supposed that the first white man to raise tobacco was a Virginian who migrated to Kent Island in the eastern edge of the Chesapeake Bay opposite Baltimore in 1631. Penn's colonists early engaged in tobacco raising; as early as 1689, or only seven years after the Proprietor came from England, 14 cargoes of tobacco were exported by them to that country. Tobacco was raised by the first French or Spanish settlers of Illinois, Missouri, and Louisiana, and by the first settlers of Tennessee. In Missouri, it did not become a staple crop until 1822 or 1823. Having been introduced into Louisiana by the Western Co., a considerable quantity of tobacco was produced by 1718. In 1752, its culture was encouraged by the French royal governor, who took the whole crop at 7 cents a pound, and the Spanish colonial government gave the same sort of encouragement in 1776.

The earliest information for Kentucky is that in 1785 General Wilkinson, of Lexington, contracted with the Spanish governor in Louisiana to deliver several boatloads of tobacco in New Orleans. Probably some of this tobacco was grown on the Ohio River and in Kentucky as well as in Spanish settlements on the Mississippi River.

By 1810, tobacco had become a great staple crop in Tennessee. Florida's beginning, it is said, was not until 1829. It is incredible that tobacco was not raised in New York until 1845 in Onondaga County near Rochester, and yet that is the assertion of the historians. It is pertinent to inquire what the Dutch settlers in the Hudson and Mohawk Valleys were doing for more than 200 years before 1845. We don't need to depend on that learned historian, Knickerbocker, for tales of the Dutchmen's devotion to their pipes.

THE WORLD'S TOBACCO.

This amazing plant, the use of which has penetrated every part of the world, has also become diffused throughout the world as a crop. The pioneer and first settler raised tobacco with his first food crops. While it is not possible to ascertain how much tobacco is produced in the entire world, it is possible to do so for many countries and thus account for most of the world's production. For countries for which estimates were available, the total of 1900 was 2,201,000,000 pounds. The world crop touched 2,834,000,000 pounds in 1910 and fell to 2,254,000,000 pounds in 1914 and 2,153,000,000 pounds in 1915. About one-half of the world's tobacco crop, as nearly as can be ascertained, was produced by the United States in 1915. The fraction previous to 1909 was hardly one-third back to 1900, before which year the world's crop has not been compiled. By 1915 the United States and its possessions produced more than one-half of the world's crop of tobacco, and in 1914 and 1913 about an even one-half.

While tobacco production is found in many countries, only a few of them produce a surplus, above their own consumption, of sufficient proportions to be noticeable. The average yearly exports of tobacco in the world's trade grew from 755,000,000 pounds in 1904–1908 to 924,000,000 pounds in 1909–1913, of which latter quantity the share of the United States was over 41 per cent. In the latter period, the Sumatra leaf of the Dutch East Indies supplied 18 per cent of the world's tobacco exports; 6.5 per cent went from Brazil, 5 per cent from Turkey, 4 per cent from Cuba, 3 per cent each from British India and the Philippine Islands, and 2.5 per cent each from Algeria, Russia, and Santo Domingo.

While tobacco has been moving out of the countries as a surplus of production, it has not only been entering countries having a deficient production, but also countries having a surplus, as an exchange of one variety for another. Before disturbance of the world's trade by the war, the world's tobacco imports, which were mostly ascertainable, increased from the yearly average of 717,000,000 pounds in 1904–1908 to 844,000,000 pounds in 1909–1913. Germany was the chief tobacco importer among the nations, and received 22 per cent of the world's total in the former period and 20 per cent in the latter. The United Kingdom received 12 and 14 per cent, respectively, in the two periods; France, 9 and 8 per cent; and other countries each less than 8 per cent.

PROGRESS IN THE UNITED STATES.

Tobacco's insignificant beginning in John Rolfe's garden in 1612 has had magnificent results in this country. You will remember that by 1618, 20,000 pounds were sent to England. The export of tobacco from Virginia doubled the next year, and in three years from 1618 it trebled. A half million pounds measured the export in 1627, about 1,500,000 pounds in 1639, about 23,750,000 pounds in 1664—presumably from Maryland as well as Virginia—and with an irregular upward movement the quantity exceeded 107,000,000 pounds in 1770. Exports were small, but did not cease, during the Revolution, after which they rapidly rose to 101,000,000 pounds in 1790 when the estimated production was 130,000,000 pounds.

The first United States census of agriculture, for 1839, found a crop of more than 219,000,000 pounds of tobacco, but in 1849 it was under 200,000,000 pounds. By 1859 it had more than doubled the crop of 1849 and reached 434,000,000 pounds, followed by reduction to 263,000,000 pounds in 1869 in consequence of the Civil War. After that year, production advanced to 868,000,000 pounds in 1899, to 1,056,000,000 pounds in 1909, and to 1,508,000,000 pounds in 1920, the largest crop ever raised in this or any other country.

Virginia led in tobacco production in 1839, with 34 per cent, or more than one-third of the national total. The Civil War placed Kentucky in the lead, and by 1869 that State produced 40 per cent of the whole crop. This lead has been held to the present time, with an average of about 35 per cent. By 1899 Virginia had fallen behind North Carolina also, when the latter State produced 15 per cent of the total crop, but North Carolina did not continuously hold second place until recent years.

Tobacco production per capita apparently declined from 11.1 pounds in the period 1839–1844 to $7._4$ pounds in the decade following the Civil War. The information is not as dependable as is desired, but at least the indication was a declining ratio of production to population. The tendency of the ratio was reversed after 1865–1874, and by 1895–1904 the ratio was 9.3 pounds, followed by 10 pounds in 1905–1914. The yearly ratios of 1915–1920 ranged from 10.6 to 14.1 pounds.

Tobacco is rated as a crop of considerable importance from a national point of view, and of high importance within the limits of some of the States, and yet the area occupied by it is a very insignificant fraction of farm and of crop area. The census for 1909 found 1,294,911 acres devoted to tobacco, and this area was only 0.41 per cent of the total crop area, and 0.15 per cent of the farm area.

Fundamental to agriculture is the yield per acre. In the case of tobacco, 10-year averages have been adopted, when possible, to smooth out yearly variations. During 1865–1874, the national average yield per acre was 722.3 pounds, and it fell to 719.9 pounds in the following 10 years, and to 714.4 pounds in 1885–1894. Thereafter the gain has been marked, and the average of 768.8 pounds during 1895–1904 was followed by 827.5 pounds during 1905–1914. During 1915–1920 the yearly yield per acre ranged from 730.8 to 873.7 pounds.

The average yield of tobacco per acre per 1,000,000 of the population was 18.5 pounds in the decade 1865–1874; it fell to 14.4 pounds in the next decade, to 11.5 pounds in 1885–1894, to 10.1 pounds in 1895–1904, and to 9.1 pounds in 1905–1914, and the yearly averages for 1915–1920 range from 6.9 to 8.3 pounds. The inference is plain that the yield of the soil in tobacco has declined for half a century in its ratio to population.

In pre-war years, the United Kingdom received more than one-third of the tobacco exported from this country, and about one-tenth went each to France, Germany, and Italy. Over 6 per cent went to the Netherlands, 5 per cent to Spain, 4 per cent each to Australia and Canada, 3 per cent to Belgium, and 2 per cent to China. Of course, the war very much disturbed these percentages.

The exported fraction of the crop has been a diminishing one. For 1790 the fraction was 78 per cent; for 1845–1854, 67.2 per cent; for 1875–1884, 53.9 per cent, from which the decline was steady to 40.6 per cent in 1905–1914. The percentage was 43 for 1915, 38.1 for 1916, 26 for 1917, 47.5 for 1918, and 49 per cent for 1919, no allowance being made for the carry over.

Tobacco varies greatly in its characteristics as they appear to smokers; and fancy, perhaps created by habit, gives preference to one or another of the many varieties and subvarieties of the plant produced throughout the world. For this reason the United States, the greatest tobacco producing and greatest tobacco exporting country in the world, also imported tobacco enough to make it the fifth in order among the tobacco-importing countries of the world before the World War.

The fragrant leaf of Cuba is by far the chief tobacco imported into the United States. Before the recent war it was 45 per cent of the total leaf-tobacco imports, but the fraction greatly declined during the war and in the year beginning with July, 1917, it was only 19 per cent, and in 1919, 25 per cent. In pre-war times, 12 per cent of this country's tobacco imports came from Turkey in Asia and 10 per cent from Turkey in Europe, or 22 per cent from that Empire. The war extinguished the direct trade movement, but apparently tobacco imports from Greece, which were normally little more than 1 per cent, took up this movement, with the result that tobacco imports from that country grew to 17 per cent of the total in 1917. Next in order below was Sumatra's thin leaf, with 11 per cent of the total tobacco imports into the United States before the war.

By the 10-year periods, tobacco imports were equal to 2.2 per cent of the crop of this country in 1865–1874, followed by irregular increase to 3.2 per cent in 1895–1904 and to 4.9 per cent in 1905–1914.

It has already been made apparent that the United States has always been a surplus country as a net result of the inward and outward movements of tobacco in foreign trade. From the small beginning at Jamestown, the national tobacco surplus grew to be 36,000,000 pounds in 100 years, 80,000,000 pounds in 200 years, and 326,000,000 pounds in 300 years, or, rather, in the normal years before the World War. Most of this tobacco has been unmanufactured when exported. The national net surplus of tobacco, as a fraction of the production, persistently declined from the Civil War to the present time; the decline being from 74 per cent of the crop in 1865–1874 to 34 per cent for the five years 1915–1919.

The computed per capita consumption of tobacco in this country has been steadily gaining since 1865–1874. Before that time, back to 1839, it seems to have been about 3.3 pounds. Following the Civil War, the computed average is as low as 2 pounds, and this was followed by a climbing movement that reached 6.4 pounds in 1905–1914 and 8 pounds during the following four years—8 pounds for every man, woman, child, and baby.

Relationships exist among several per capita ratios. Tobacco production per capita is increasing because tobacco acreage is increasing faster than population. Production per acre per capita is decreasing; fertility improvement is not keeping up with human multiplication and immigration. The excess of the tobacco exports per capita is declining. The result of all these movements is an increasing per capita consumption of domestic tobacco that is absorbing a larger and larger fraction of the per capita production.

USES IN THE UNITED STATES.

Pipe smoking was brought to the Thirteen Colonies by the first settlers; and they observed the Indians smoking pipes. The Indians had smoked tobacco in pipes for so many centuries that there is no evidence when they began. The primitive pipe in what is now southwestern United States seems to have been a hollow reed stem or a section of cane, later made of other materials in the form of a tube, probably straight. In North America, many forms of the Indian pipe have been found, varying from a straight tube to a curved one, to cones joined at the apexes, to bowl and stem joined at an angle, at a right angle, and even at an acute angle. Pipes were made by Indians from baked clay, wood, bone, metal, or stone, or a combination of these materials. Pipes, such as some of us now use, were originally shaped by Europeans.

In Great Britain only clay pipes were used until 1859, when the brier-root pipe appeared, made from the root of the white heath. The name is a perversion of the French name. This country has added to the variety the corncob pipe, now Missouri's famous product. The tube or double cone is an implement of great antiquity elsewhere than the American Continent, and was used upon occasion for smoking substances other than tobacco for the curative properties supposed to be in the smoke.

The cigar seems to have reached the white people of this country in a devious way. Columbus found the Indians smoking it, and it

seems to have come to this country by way of Spain and England.
Quite similarly the domestic turkey, the potato, and some varieties of
the bean, all originating somewhere in America, reached us through
Europe. It is said that the first commercial cigars made in this country
were made in the houses of the early tobacco growers in the Connecticut
Valley and sold in New York and other towns. Cigar factories were
established at East Windsor and Suffield, Conn., about 1810, and
some of the tobacco used by them was from Cuba and Brazil. The
cigars were peddled in wagons throughout the country. In 1825 a
tobacco warehouse was erected at Warehouse Point, Conn., and cigar
tobacco was packed there and shipped to New York in bales of about
100 pounds.

Since 1895 the Commissioner of Internal Revenue has ascertained
and published the quantities of leaf tobacco used in this country
in the manufacture of cigars, cigarettes, and "tobacco and snuff,"
the tobacco of the last class being chewing and smoking tobacco.
After converting these three classes into percentages of the total
leaf tobacco used by manufacturers, it appears that the fraction for
cigars increased from 25 per cent in the calendar year 1896 to 30
per cent in 1907, when the advance was arrested. From 1908 to 1914
the percentage ranged from 27 to 29, and a rapid decline followed during the World War to 26.5 per cent in 1915 and 1916, and to 25 per cent
in 1919. In 11 years the fraction of the leaf tobacco used for cigars
declined from 30 to 25 per cent.

By the time that this country had recovered from the industrial
depression of 1893–1897, the production and consumption of tobacco products had become fairly normal. The Commissioner of
Internal Revenue reports that the average yearly number of large
cigars made in 1899–1901 was about 5,500,000,000 and that the number had increased to the yearly average of 7,200,000,000 for 1916–
1918, or 30 per cent. Corresponding figures for small cigars, including cheroots, are 669,500,000 made in the average of 1899–1901 and
900,100,000 in the average of 1916–1918, an increase of 35 per cent.
Exports of cigars and cheroots reached the number of about 2,400,000
in the year ending with June, 1917, 15,000,000 in 1918, 33,000,000 in
1919, and 67,000,000 in 1920.

More than one-half of the leaf tobacco annually used by manufacturers during 1896–1918 became chewing and smoking tobacco
and snuff, but the fraction has been a declining one. From about
70 per cent of the total in the earlier years, it fell to 61 per cent by
1915, followed by a rapid fall to 46 per cent in 1919, or less than one-
half of the leaf tobacco used by manufacturers.

In weight, smoking tobacco by far leads every other product.
For 1899–1901, the average was 105,400,000 pounds, and in 1918–1
the quantity had grown to 240,000,000 pounds, a gain of 12

er cent. Plug tobacco is next in weight below smoking tobacco, nd averaged 170,700,000 pounds in 1899–1901 and 158,000,000 ounds in 1918–19.

Tobacco chewing seems to have been reserved to become a great ational habit first and only in the United States. The chewing abit appears to have been very sparingly followed in any other ountry. Prof. McGuire, of Washington, says that there is some vidence that tobacco was chewed in Central America when first isited by Europeans. De Candolle ventures the statement that obacco chewing was practiced by the Indians throughout the greater art of America. I can not help but doubt this statement. The Iandbook of American Indians of the Bureau of American Ethnolgy does not mention tobacco chewing by Indians.

Sailors were the first white tobacco chewers. Tobacco history vas made, not so much by the officers of the poop deck, who got heir names into print, as by the unknown men in the forecastle. Although English sailors chewed tobacco in the ports of England, he chewing habit made no headway among the landsmen of that ountry, nor did it obtain a footing in any country save the Thireen Colonies. In this country, the people were living in the midst f a great national habit, with which all had become so familiar hat they were hardly conscious of its existence, when Dickens gave he country a great national jolt by reporting what he saw, in Martin Chuzzlewit. I have the impression that chewing has long been delining, especially so in recent years.

Snuff taking in the nose, as we already know, was a gentleman's abit in England early in the nineteenth century and, in declining egree, long after. From England it was brought to this country nd flourished for many years. As far as I have been able to learn, he habit is all but extinct. I last saw a snuff box in use in western Iassachusetts 35 years ago. When I came to Washington 30 years go I heard the tale that a snuff box was maintained in the Senate Chamber for common use at public expense, but I have not verified he statement. A woman doing clerical work in one of the offices of Vashington takes snuff in her nose, and this is the only instance rithin my knowledge.

Women have long used snuff in this country by " dipping," and the abit at one time permeated all social grades, but not all parts of the ountry. One end of a small stick of wood, say 3 inches long and bout as thick as a lead pencil, was chewed until the fibers became eparated from one another, and this brushlike end was dipped in nuff and held in the mouth between the teeth and the cheek. This as usually done at home and when free from observation by guests nd strangers, but not always. About 25 years ago I saw a white woman enter a railroad car at Woodstock, Va., with a snuff stick protruding from her mouth, and she sat in the car without removing it. She was probably from the adjacent mountains. In those mountains in 1920 I saw women with a snuff stick.

I have often inquired of men, and women, too, who have traveled much throughout the United States, or resided in various parts, whether they had seen or heard of snuff taking in the nose or of snuff dipping in recent years, and hardly a person whom I have questioned has been able to say that these uses of snuff have been seen or heard of.

The average production of 15,300,000 pounds of snuff, in 1899–1901, grew to 34,900,000 pounds as the average of 1916–1919, a gain of 127 per cent, a conspicuous fact for such a product. It is not exported.

What is done with this great quantity of snuff? For the purpose of this paper, I wrote to the secretary of the Tobacco Merchants' Association of the United States, and from him I have a long-sought explanation. He informs me that about 98 per cent of the snuff used in this country is used somewhat as chewing tobacco is used, and that the same results are obtained without the necessity of chewing it. This use of snuff is common among the negroes of Washington. The processing of tobacco in the manufacture of snuff eliminates much of its acidity and bitterness; therefore less sweetening is required to make it a pleasant, agreeable " chew." The smaller the quantity of sweetening in the tobacco, the less saliva is created and the less spitting necessary. "While it is difficult to estimate how much is used for snuffing," the secretary of the association writes, " we place it at less than 2 per cent, and would not be surprised if it were not more than 1 per cent."

The most outstanding fact in the tobacco industry is the production of small cigarettes. The average number made in 1899–1901 was 3,200,000,000, and a number that reaches a billion seems large; but in 1916–1918 the average production of small cigarettes was 35,800,000,000, a gain of more than 1,000 per cent in 17 years. In 1918 the number rose to 47,900,000,000, and in 1919 to 53,000,000,000. It is true that billions of these cigarettes were exported in the war years, the number for the year ending with June, 1917, being about 6,500,000,000; for 1918 about 9,100,000,000; for 1919 about 13,600,000,000; and for 1920 about 17,500,000,000. Still the number remaining for domestic consumption averaged about 28,400,000,000 per year in the four years, 1917–1920 and the consumption by the military and naval forces of the United States, wherever situated, is almost entirely treated as " domestic." In 1918, 34,500,000,000 cigarettes were consumed in this country; and in 1919 nearly 36,000,000,000.

The weight of leaf tobacco used for cigarettes has been known as far back as 1896. About that time 5 per cent of all leaf tobacco used by manufacturers was converted into cigarettes, but years of decline followed to only 3 per cent in 1905. Thereafter the upward movement was strong. It reached 4 per cent in 1908, 10 per cent in 1913, 20 per cent in 1917, and 30 per cent in 1919, or more than the leaf tobacco used for cigars. Within a very few years the cigar has been losing its vogue relatively and the little cigarette has been overwhelmingly advancing.

The cigarette started with the Indians and it was given to the Spaniards in the West Indies; it soon acquired much popularity among the Spaniards everywhere and this popularity has been held to this day. The early Indian cigarette was rolled in tobacco leaf, and in Mexico a dry corn husk was used by the Aztecs. I have bought corn-husk cigarettes from the Mexican Indian women who made them in New Mexico. Eventually the Spaniards used a paper covering, the rolling still being done by hand. The cigarette spread throughout Europe, with eventual popularity. It was comparatively a cheap smoke when taxes made tobacco costly; it was a short smoke under circumstances in which a pipe or cigar would have been impossible or a waste; and it fitted into temperaments and states of mind incompatible with the deliberation and serenity of a pipe or a cigar.

At the exposition of 1876 at Philadelphia a new machine was making cigarettes wrapped in paper, and doing the work rapidly and automatically. Soon thereafter the future of the cigarette radically changed, and it became the "coffin nail" of millions and hundreds of millions of devotees throughout the world. Demand for cigarettes was enormously increased by the World War, and evidence of this is not confined to the United States. It comes also from Great Britain and the Continent. In five years the consumption of cigarettes nearly doubled in Great Britain. As many as 4,920,000,000 cigarettes were sold in France in 1919, an increase of 31 per cent in six years.

TOBACCO DECEPTIONS.

In the early days of smoking in England, smoking tobacco was adulterated by the use of cheaper materials to increase its weight. My supposition is that this was the origin of the use of licorice, molasses, and other things found to-day in some smoking and some chewing tobacco. New smokers and new chewers learn to like them in combination with tobacco. These adulterants are mostly responsible for the offensive odor of pipes.

One of the deceptions of the tobacco manufacturer and of the dealer in this country is in the use of the word "Habana." Among the well-informed tobacco men a cigar made wholly of Cuban tobacco is a "clear Habana," and one made of the Habana variety raised in the United States is called simply an "Habana." But many ignorant retailers and most of the public at large are deceived into believing that "Habana" tobacco is Cubán tobacco.

Another widespread deception has appeared in recent years, and that depends on the use of the word "Egyptian" in connection with cigarettes. In the first place there is no Egyptian tobacco. The plant is not raised in Egypt. But perhaps the use of the word may be defended by saying that the cigarettes were made in Egypt. It is true that Turkish tobacco is imported into Egypt and there made into cigarettes, some of which are exported. In a recent Egyptian foreign trade report it is observed that only about 3,000,000 pounds of tobacco were imported into that country in each of the years 1918 and 1919. About 244,000,000 cigarettes were exported to all countries in 1918 and 344,000,000 in 1919. These are minute numbers in cigarette consumption. The foreign trade report of the United States states that in 1918 only 875,000 cigarettes were imported from Egypt and in 1919 only 450,000. Young women could be mentioned, all cigarette smokers, each of whom would smoke one-thirtieth of these cigarettes in the regular performance of her daily "stunt." If the cigarettes imported into this country from England are all made in Egypt, still the imports would be only twice the very small record. So that is all of the truth that there is in the Egyptian cigarette in this country.

TOBACCO SIGNS.

The wooden figure of an Indian offering cigars was everywhere seen in front of retail tobacco shops in this country less than half a century ago. Tobacco-shop figures of Indians, negroes, Scotchmen, Dutchmen, and now and then a figure of Mr. Punch were everywhere in evidence, and then, presto, they had disappeared.

The origin of these figures is of some interest. When Sir Walter Raleigh had made pipe smoking popular in England, there was an enormous number of shops in London where tobacco was sold. It was sold by apothecaries very naturally, because it was a medicinal plant at that time. Grocers and chandlers in general sold it, and keepers of inns and alehouses. Buildings were not numbered in those days and businesses were known as being conducted at the sign of the Cat and the Fiddle, and so on, the object being sometimes a picture and again a wooden figure. The Black Boy was the first wooden figure used by a tobacco dealer, a figure previously and also subsequently used in other business. It is mentioned as a tobacco sign by Ben Jonson in Bartholomew Fair in 1614. It was known that negroes in the West Indies cultivated tobacco for the

English market. After a while, the wooden figure of an Indian appeared, resulting from the false belief that Indians produced export tobacco. This sign was readily adopted in this country because it was known that the whites learned to use tobacco from the Indians.

Other significant early tobacconists' signs were a figure of Sir Walter Raleigh, of the Virginian, the Three Tobacco Pipes, the Wooden Midshipman, the Jolly Sailor, a Scotchman holding a snuff-box—this derived from the fact that the Scotch at that time were famed as snuff takers and as snuff makers. The Dutch were great smokers and hence a Dutchman was for a long time a common figure. In the eighteenth century in England a frequent sign was three figures—a Scotchman, a Dutchman, and a sailor, explained by this rhyme:

> We three are engaged in one cause,
> I snuffs, I smokes, and I chaws.

You observe that the sailor was the chewer.

WOMEN AS TOBACCO USERS.

Something must be said concerning the use of tobacco by women. Indian women did not use tobacco—they seem to have had no power to restrain the spirits of evil; but white women have used tobacco from early times. Soon after Spanish men began to smoke, Spanish women smoked cigarettes with hardly an exception, in all grades of society. Among women of other continental European countries, pipe smoking has always been uncommon, and cigar smoking and snuff taking too.

In England, a few women smoked very soon after the introduction of tobacco. Tradition has it that Queen Elizabeth once smoked with unpleasant results when Sir Walter Raleigh offered her a pipe. In some parts of England there was general pipe smoking by women of "the humbler classes" in the seventeenth century, and this fact continued to Victorian days. It was not until the sixties of the nineteenth century that cigarette smoking began to creep into feminine circles in England, and since that time this habit has advanced slowly until the World War. This war caused an extraordinary spread of cigarette smoking among women in England. The newspapers are saying that they learned to smoke during the war and that they were able to buy cigarettes because so many of them became wage earners.

It is well known that cigarette smoking by women has long been common in many of the continental countries.

In the United States, too, women have their tobacco history. Some of them were pipe smokers in colonial times, and many of these seem to have been of the humbler sort, as an Englishman would say. This habit seems now to be confined mostly to the southern Appalachians.

Cigar smoking never gained a foothold among women of this country, nor of any other country.

Snuff taking, by snuffing into the nose, was practiced by women in this country to some extent in snuff-taking days and, according to the extent of my information, mostly in the North Atlantic States. This habit seems to have become almost extinct among women.

Snuff dipping was long very prevalent in the South among white women of all social grades and among negro women. The small remnant of this habit that is left seems to be confined to the southern mountains. I have not found any one who lived or traveled in the South who has lately seen a snuff stick or heard of its recent use, even among the negroes, outside of the mountains. While, strictly speaking, this is not tobacco chewing, it is closely allied to it. I have been unable to learn of any real chewing of tobacco in this country by women at any time, nor in any other country. Yet there is to-day, certainly among negro women and possibly among some of the white women of the Appalachian Mountains, a habit derived from snuff dipping, and that is the holding in the cheek of a little snuff. Within my knowledge, this habit exists among the negro women of Washington.

In all but one of the various uses of tobacco, white women of this country and of Europe have participated in great or small degree and have recoiled or retreated until they have all but fully, if not fully, abandoned these uses. But everywhere they have been conquered or are in process of being conquered by King Cigarette.

Why has the cigarette been victorious over women? It is a fact that the cigarette is a toy smoke and is not the more formidable undertaking that a cigar or a pipe is. But this does not fully explain. A woman is usually a miserable coward in the presence of convention, and hence in modern times, at least, she began to smoke cigarettes in secret, or with companions under cover. It was known that women in Europe smoked cigarettes. Women in "the smart set" got a notion that it was "smart" and a little naughty to be known as daring to smoke cigarettes; and then followed imitation, not only in that social clique but outside. Imitation is the great propagator of habits and customs.

Neither sex can make itself repulsive to the other. That is forbidden by the nature of our being. Has the use of tobacco by women made them repulsive to men? Tobacco chewing seems to have been regarded as taboo without a trial. The snuff stick was never used in the presence of men, except in the mountains of the South by the "poor whites" and by the negroes. Although this custom flourished for a while under its various conditions, it has become almost extinct.

It certainly became less and less respectable, as times changed, and hence it became also more and more repulsive to the other sex.

Snuffing by women must always have been repulsive. I shall ever remember, as a childhood observation, an old woman living near my grandfather's farm whose nostrils and upper lip were covered and discolored with snuff.

Pipe smoking, it is reported, is spreading in London and in England among women who are not of "the humbler classes." Little of the custom remains in this country, and that little in the Appalachians. I doubt that any man, elsewhere, would like to see his wife, or sweetheart, or any woman, smoke a pipe. And yet circumstances alter cases. In one of my rambles in the Alleghany Mountains in West Virginia I was kept for a cold night in November at a log house in the wilderness. After supper the housewife proceeded with her work with the end of a snuff stick in her cheek. Her mother, a woman of 70 or more, took a blackened clay pipe from the mantel above the fireplace and was about to fill it with shag, when I offered her my bag of tobacco. This she accepted and we sat before the log fire and smoked together and exchanged information until 9 o'clock struck the end of the day. A pipe in the mouth of a woman of that age, at that place, and at that time, did not seem at all repulsive to me.

No man would want to see a woman walk along F Street smoking a cigar, nor a cigarette, either. He would not like to see her smoke a cigar anywhere. But he can become accustomed to the cigarette smoking of women, and has become accustomed to it in certain places and times. It seems to be a matter of repetition of experience to establish familiarity, especially in the younger years of a man's life. The cigarette, unlike the cigar and the pipe, can blend with the daintiness of woman, and it has not been repulsive to man to see her smoke according to the custom of the country and where he has always seen it smoked.

A conservative, like myself, does not want to see the custom established in his own home, and yet somewhere else he can see women smoking cigarettes and not feel any antipathy. It seems to be a matter of generality of custom and frequency of seeing it in practice. Horses that were at first disposed to jump the roadside fence at sight of an automobile eventually paid no attention to it, so I expect that women will continue to smoke cigarettes in this country, that more women will adopt the habit, and that the screen of secrecy, the little that is left, will continue to be removed. Perhaps it will be a vogue that will have its day and then be embalmed in history, and perhaps not. Women of Spanish descent have been smoking cigarettes for 400 years.

XIII. NOTES ON THE AGRICULTURAL HISTORY OF MAIZE.

By G. N. COLLINS,
Bureau of Plant Industry,
United States Department of Agriculture.

NOTES ON THE AGRICULTURAL HISTORY OF MAIZE.[1]

By G. N. COLLINS.

The history of a subject is not infrequently introduced by a brief review of what there may be of prehistoric evidence. This prehistoric evidence is usually limited to the legends and archeological remains that have been left by primitive man before a written language was adopted. In the history of a cultivated plant there often is prehistoric evidence that goes back to a still earlier period. Properly interrogated, the plant itself may disclose much of its early history, which in the case of maize probably goes back to the beginnings of agriculture on the American Continent. This early evidence is naturally somewhat elusive and is open to more than one interpretation, but should not on this account be disregarded.

One bit of prehistoric evidence contributed by the maize plant itself is that maize is of American origin. Although for many years disputed, this statement may now be made with assurance. So long as the argument was confined to archeological and philological fields there was room for a reasonable doubt, although the disputants seldom admitted as much; but with the recognition of the close relationship between maize and the native American grass, *Euchlaena mexicana*, together with the complete absence of maize relatives from the Old World, the contention for an Old World origin became untenable.

Although of American origin, there are some reasons for believing that maize may have reached Asia before the time of Columbus. At one time the balance of evidence appeared in favor of this view. But a rather extensive examination of the pre-Columbian Chinese literature, made by Dr. W. T. Swingle, has failed to disclose any certain reference to maize. This, together with the evidence presented by Doctor Laufer,[2] leaves the burden of evidence in favor of a post-Columbian introduction. The question should still be left open; but in any case the introduction of maize into the Old

[1] Paper read before the Agricultural History Society, May 12, 1919, with slight additions.
[2] Laufer, B., The Introduction of Maize into Eastern Asia, Congres International des Americanists, 15th Session, Quebec, 1907.

411

World must have been long after its domestication, and it is only
necessary here to insist that this question shall not obscure the fac
that maize must have been domesticated in America.

Before attempting to trace the early history of maize it will b
well to consider the different theories that have been advanced re
garding the manner of its origin or domestication.

Viewed in relation to natural wild species, maize is a monstrosity
In any of its known forms it is quite incapable of maintaining it
self without the aid of man. This fact alone removes practicall
all hope of discovering the wild prototype of maize. To be wil
this plant would have to be very unlike maize.

Instead of possessing adaptations for distribution, the seeds ar
persistent on a closely packed spike and are further protected agains
dispersion by being surrounded by a series of long bracts or husks
The young plants are unable to compete successfully with othe
vegetation. Neither is maize particularly resistant to drought, alkali, cold, or excessive moisture.

All of the other cereals under favorable conditions may escape
from cultivation and persist for a time unaided, but there are no
records of escaped maize. These facts must be kept in mind in
attempting to trace the domestication of maize.

Three general theories of the domestication of maize have been
advanced. Briefly stated, these are as follows:

(1) The cultivated forms of maize are descended from pod corn,
or *Zea tunicata*, which it has been claimed is a wild plant in Paraguay.

(2) Maize has been derived by gradual evolution from some plant
related to teosinte (*Euchlaena mexicana* Schrad), a native Mexican
grass.

(3) Maize is the result of a hybrid between teosinte and some
other species of grass.

To these might be added a fourth method, which, so far as I know,
has never been advocated, but which seems worthy of consideration,
viz, that maize originated as a mutation or sport from teosinte or
some ancestor of teosinte.

POD CORN AS THE PROGENITOR OF MAIZE.

The early accounts of maize abound in references to pod corn as
a wild or primitive type of maize. The distinguishing feature of
podded maize is that, in addition to the husks which cover the ear,
each individual grain is completely inclosed by the glumes. Pod
corn was first reported by August de Saint-Hilaire in a letter addressed to the president of the French Academy of Sciences and

published in 1829.[3] The specimen presented by Saint-Hilaire consisted of a part of an ear received by him from the Abbé Larranhaga of Montevideo. It was accompanied by the statement from the abbé that this variety was cultivated by the Guaycuru Indians. This statement of Larranhaga's was questioned by Saint-Hilaire, who claimed that the Guaycurus were a wild, nonagricultural tribe. When, however, the podded ear was shown to a young Guarany Indian of Paraguay, who had accompanied Saint-Hilaire to France, this Indian recognized the specimen as from his country and said that it grew in the humid forests. Without apparent warrant, the word " wild " has crept into this quotation until there are now many statements to the effect that maize, especially podded maize, has been found growing wild in Paraguay.

That pod corn is cultivated by the Guaycuru Indians of Paraguay is further attested by Azara. This author, after describing two normal varieties, says:

As I have not had occasion to see frequently the variety of corn called " abatý-guaicurú," I presume that it is not believed to be separate from the others in quality. It is nevertheless peculiar. In effect, whereas the ear is exactly like those of the preceding varieties and has the same husks (envelopes), each grain is enveloped in minute leaves which resemble completely the large ones which envelop the whole ear.[4]

There is thus little doubt that pod corn is considered a variety in Paraguay, but there is no reason for believing that it exists as a wild plant there or anywhere else. Pod corn, as we know it, would be quite incapable of maintaining itself without cultivation. Furthermore, pod corn is known to have arisen more than once by mutation from nonpodded varieties. The long glumes of pod corn are distinctly an ancestral character, nearly all grasses having the seeds inclosed in glumes after the manner of pod corn; and although pod corn may not be considered as an ancestor of maize, the fact that it exhibits ancestral characters makes it a matter of great interest to know more of the part which it plays in the agriculture of the Indians of Paraguay.

---

[3] Annales des Sciences Naturelles, Vol. 16, (1829), p. 143.
[4] Azara, F., Voyages dans L'Amérique Méridionale, Vol. I, (1809), p. 146–148. The same author describes a fourth variety of corn which, if it is maize, as the author assumes, should be of great interest. He describes it as follows: " I do not remember the name given to the fourth variety of which the stalk, much more slender, is terminated—not by an ear, but like millet, with a kind of whip with second lashes (' Discipline à plusieurs cordes ') of which each is covered with seeds exactly like those of maize but smaller. I also am ignorant as to the particular use to which this may be applied. I know only that in boiling in fat or oil the seeds of this inflorescence burst open without separating, which results in a splendid boquet that could be worn at night by a lady in her hair without one recognizing what it is. I have often eaten these popped grains and found them very good."

The only other reference to pod corn as a cultivated variety that has been found is that of Parker[5] who lists pod corn as one of the varieties grown by the Iroquois in New York, the Indian name for it signifying original corn. The characters of pod corn have figured to some extent in genetic studies, but so far as we can learn pod corn has never been established as a true variety; that is, it will not come true to seed, but continues to produce a certain percentage of plants with normal ears.

TEOSINTE AND THE ORIGIN OF MAIZE.

In discussing the other theories of the origin of maize, it will be necessary to make frequent references to teosinte, the closest wild relative of maize. This plant is a tall grass unknown in the wild state outside of Mexico. It has much of the general appearance of maize. The chief difference in habit is that instead of having a single stalk or a strong central stalk surrounded by a few slender branches or suckers, the teosinte plant commonly produces numerous stalks of the same size. The tassel or staminate inflorescence is also more profusely branched and lacks the characteristic central spike of maize. There are many other minor differences but after all, teosinte is much like maize, except in its pistillate inflorescence, or the part corresponding to the ear of maize. Instead of the thick ear bearing many rows of naked seeds, the seeds of teosinte are borne on a much-branched inflorescence, the individual seeds being loosely attached to one another like strings of triangular beads. The seeds instead of being naked are deeply embedded in segments of the rachis which fall apart, each segment with its inclosed seed. In spite of these profound differences maize and teosinte hybridize freely. In fact maize is as easily and completely fertilized with teosinte pollen as it is with maize pollen. This perfect fertility between two distinct genera seems the more remarkable when it is realized that perhaps nowhere else with other plants or animals has it been possible to obtain fertile hybrids between two forms separated by such profound morphological differences.

The many resemblances between maize and teosinte, together with the fact that the two forms interbreed with perfect freedom, makes it certain that whatever the origin of maize it must be intimately associated with teosinte or some near relative of that plant. Very little is known regarding the part played by teosinte in the economy of the natives of Mexico. It is planted by the peons of Mexico as a fodder plant, but there is nothing to show that it has ever been used as human food.

---

[5] Parker, A. C., Iroquois Uses of Maize and Other Food Plants. University of the State of New York, Edu. Dept. Bul. No. 482, Albany, N. Y., 1910.

The idea that maize originated from some extinct ancestor of teosinte as a result of selection operating on small variations, while more plausible than the pod corn hypothesis, seems very unlikely.

Any plant closely resembling teosinte would seem very poorly adapted to human use The seeds are small and each seed is tightly inclosed in a horny and inedible segment of the rachis from which it can be removed only by crushing or grinding. The fragments of the rachis would be of practically the same density as the seed, and it is doubtful if the two could be separated by winnowing. Of the seeds of grasses used as human food, the nearest approach to teosinte is the seed of Coix, or Job's tears. The seeds of this plant, like those of teosinte, are inclosed in a hard covering. But in the varieties of Coix used for human food, the hardened envelope is brittle, and can easily be removed from the seed without crushing the latter. It would seem that the prototype of maize must have been at least edible in its wild and unimproved form, and this may scarcely be said of teosinte. There are hosts of wild grasses that have never been domesticated, any one of which would seem more promising material for the primitive plant breeder than teosinte.

HYBRID ORIGIN OF MAIZE.

To the writer it seems more reasonable to believe that the qualities adapting teosinte to the uses of man resulted from accidental hybridization with another species instead of being developed through selection from such an unpromising beginning.

The theory of a hybrid origin seems to reconcile the evidence that maize is undoubtedly closely related to teosinte with the equally clear evidence that many of the characters and tendencies of maize are entirely foreign to teosinte or the group of grasses to which it belongs. To argue this point would lead to a detailed discussion of morphology and genetics already presented elsewhere, that would be out of place.[6]

From studies of the comparative morphology of maize and teosinte and hybrids between these two species, it is believed that this unknown ancestor of maize must have belonged to the Andropogoneae, a tribe closely related to the Maydeae, in which maize and teosinte are placed. From the standpoint of human utilization this plant

[6] Collins, G. N., Origin of Maize, Jour. of Wash. Acad. of Sci., Vol. II, No. 21, Dec. 19, 1912.

Collins, G. N., Structure of the Maize Ear as indicated in Zea-Euchlaena Hybrids, Jour. of Agri. Research, Vol. XVII, No. 3, June 16, 1919.

See also Harshberger, J. W., Maize, a Botanical and Economic Study. Philadelphia, 1893 (cont. from Bot. Lab. Univ. of Penna., Vol. I, No. 2) ; Harshberger, J. W., Fertile Crosses of Teosinte and Maize, Garden & Forest, Vol. 9, (1896), pp. 522–523 ; Weatherwax, Paul, The Evolution of Maize, Bull. Torrey Club, Vol. 45, (1918), pp. 309–342 ; Kempton, J. H., The Ancestry of Maize, Jour. of the Wash. Acad. of Sci., Vol. IX, No. 1, Jan. 4, 1919.

must have differed from teosinte in having naked or nearly naked seeds borne on a rigid rachis. I am still hopeful that remains of this ancient food plant will be brought to light as a result of ethnological investigations.

FOSSIL MAIZE.

The earliest tangible evidence of the existence of maize is a fossil ear from Peru recently described by Dr. F. H. Knowlton, of the Geological Survey.[7] The specimen is undoubtedly an ear of maize and Doctor Knowlton is positive that it is an undoubted fossil whose age must be measured in thousands of years.

The specimen was not found in place, and there is nothing in its history, beyond the fact that it came from Peru, to indicate where it was first discovered. The bare fact of its existence, however, is highly significant, for if Doctor Knowlton is not entirely misled regarding the age of the fossil it is perhaps the earliest record of man's existence on the American Continent. If the beginning of maize culture meant merely the growing and harvesting of a wild plant, the discovery of the fossil remains of such a plant would not call for special comment; but, as stated above, maize could hardly have existed as a wild plant in anything even remotely resembling its present form. We must, therefore, think not only of primitive Americans as cultivating maize at the time when this fossil was formed, but we must realize also that the important changes necessary to produce or domesticate maize from wild forms must have taken place in still earlier times.

The fossil specimen is so much like existing Peruvian varieties that it throws little light on the botanical origin of maize. It shows, however, that all the important steps in the domestication and improvement of maize had been taken before this specimen became fossilized, and makes what we have accomplished in 400 years look discouragingly small. Some consolation may be derived, however, from the proof, which this fossil ear affords, of the very long time during which the Indians themselves effected little or no improvement.

Next in point of time is the evidence from the prehistoric graves of Peru and Bolivia. In these graves were found ears of maize wonderfully preserved through desiccation. With the actual ears are replicas of ears wrought in clay and used to adorn ceremonial vessels. In some of these the ear is so faithfully reproduced as to lead to the belief that they must have been formed in molds in which actual ears were used as models. These specimens show no characteristics not found in existing types, and some might even be classed

---

[7] Jour. of Wash. Acad. Sci., Vol. 9, No. 5, (Mar. 4, 1919), pp. 134–136.

as belonging to present-day Peruvian or Bolivian varieties. Yet none of the examples of prehistoric maize from South America that I have seen are approximated by existing varieties in Central America, Mexico, or the United States. The specimens, therefore, afford no evidence that maize was introduced into South America from the north. It should be noted that the most striking South American type, the large-seeded maize of Cuzco, is not represented in the prehistoric series.

Ears found in the prehistoric cliff dwellings of our Southwest are similar to the types grown in that general region. In like manner charred ears from the Indian mounds of Ohio are not unlike the varieties of soft corn grown by the Indians of the Middle West. More recently maize has been found in the cysts of the basket makers by Kidder and Guernsey [8] and in the pre-Pueblo remains of southern Colorado by Judd. I take it these represent the earliest evidence of maize within the borders of the United States, yet aside from their color, which is unlike anything known in North American varieties, they possess no characters that would differentiate them from varieties grown by the Papago, Zuñi, and Hopi Indians. Even their yellowish brown color, which resembles that of certain Bolivian varieties, may have resulted from a disintegration of the common blue aleurone and be due to their great age. Thus all prehistoric evidence indicates that the geographic distribution of types as we now find them has obtained for a very long time.

In the intensive genetic studies to which maize has been subjected in recent years many minor abnormalities, or mutations, have come to light. One of these new Mendelian characters causes the seeds to split open or pop before the ears are harvested. We had just succeeded in isolating this character into a pure strain and were experiencing the satisfaction of having discovered something new, even though it was worthless, when through the kindness of Doctor Judd, of the Bureau of Ethnology, we were permitted to examine this series of prehistoric maize ears, which he had unearthed from the pre-Pueblo ruins of Colorado. The specimens were beautifully preserved and two of the ears were perfect examples of our new Mendelian character.

None of the human remains found in America by archeologists can show records of antiquity comparable with those of the Old World. If archeologists, however, would consider cultivated plants as artifacts they might wish to revise their findings, for the plants themselves indicate that the origin of the native food plants of America may be as ancient as those of Europe, Asia, and Africa.

---

[8] Kidder, A. V., and Guernsey, S. J., Archaeological Explorations in Northeastern Arizona. Bul. 65, Bureau of American Ethnology, (1919).

Before quitting the discussion of prehistoric maize, I wish to state my belief that in maize, the New World has given man the oldest cereal. This may appear as another instance of an enthusiast claiming great antiquity for his specialty, but before the claim is dismissed as altogether absurd, I wish to recall attention to some of the features that distinguish maize from the other cereals:

(1) Maize is the only cereal so profoundly modified that its wild prototype is unknown.

(2) Maize is the only cereal completely dependent on man for existence.

(3) Maize is the only cereal known in a fossilized condition.

(4) No other cereal compares with maize in the great diversity of its forms.

If the changes brought about since the time of the oldest prehistoric specimens that have yet been found are any criterion, the time necessary to develop from a common ancestor, the diversity that now exists must be measured geologically and not by centuries.

In all our wealth of highly developed maize varieties there is little that was not already represented in the Indian varieties at the time of the discovery. These in turn seem to have changed very little from the types represented in the earliest archeological and fossil remains.

If, with a base line several thousands of years in length, we fail to get a measurable parallax on the development of maize, it would appear to the biologist that the initial steps in the domestication of maize must have been made at a time more remote than that set by most anthropologists as the time of man's advent on the American Continent.

MAIZE AT THE TIME OF THE DISCOVERY OF AMERICA.

Before taking up the post-Columbian history of maize it may be well to review briefly the more striking similarities and differences of the types of maize that were being grown in the different parts of the American Continent.

The primary classification of maize proposed by Sturtevant is based entirely on seed characters: In dividing the varieties into flint, dent, pop, soft, and sweet, Sturtevant gave expression to differences already recognized by agriculturists. To this series the waxy maize of China has since been added. Sturtevant's class of tunicate or pod corn may be disregarded here since this class is not based on a seed character and is now recognized as a mutation that may appear in any of the other classes.

Many writers on maize assume that this classification, based on the texture of the seed, is fundamental and natural, with certain ear and plant characters associated with each class. This is not true. Seed texture is no more fundamental than ear and plant characters. The shape of the seed, the number of the rows, or the habit of the plant might be used with equal propriety as a basis for arranging the varieties into types. There is, furthermore, little or no agreement in the results obtained by the use of these different criteria, and none of them give results that correspond with the geographical distribution of varieties. Flint varieties are found throughout the entire range of the species, as are eight-rowed varieties and varieties with long and slender ears. It is, therefore, futile to attempt to define the range of flint, dent, soft, or sweet varieties as such.

Certain combinations of characters, however, are peculiar to certain regions. The wide-seeded, eight-rowed, flint varieties with slender stalks and numerous suckers are practically confined to the northern and eastern parts of the United States. Varieties differing from these only by the substitution of soft for the flint type of seeds are common among the Indian tribes of the Missouri Valley and south to the Mexican border. Many-rowed, round-seeded, soft, and slightly dented varieties are common in the Southwest. Many-rowed, round-seeded, flint varieties with large culms and few suckers are found throughout the lowland Tropics. Ten and 12-rowed soft varieties with long pointed seed are characteristic of the highlands of Bolivia. Eight-rowed varieties so common in the United States are practically absent in Mexico, but appear again in the large soft-seeded Cuzco varieties of Peru.

Amid this great diversity and extreme freedom of recombinations, it is difficult to form any general views of relationship and probable migrations. But since it is becoming increasingly difficult to unravel the mixtures resulting from the interchange of seed, it may be permissible to hazard a few guesses and question some of the existing theories. It has been suggested that maize in the eastern part of the United States came from the West Indies. The varieties found in those regions afford no evidence in support of this view. The New England flints appear most closely related to the eight-rowed soft varieties of the Missouri Valley. This relationship may indicate that the New England flints were derived from the soft type of the Middle West or that the eight-rowed soft varieties have resulted from a mixing of the New England flints and the more southern soft varieties.

Neither can the West Indies be considered as a center of distribution to the west, since in passing down the Mississippi and around the Gulf to Florida and the West Indies the importance of maize decreases rather than increases, as one would expect were the West Indies to be considered as a source.

EARLY ACCOUNTS OF MAIZE.

The first definite date in the history of maize is November 5, 1492. On this day maize was first brought to the attention of Columbus. Apparently maize had not been met with in the smaller islands or on the coast of Cuba, and was first encountered by two Spaniards sent by Columbus to the interior of Cuba to learn something of what the country produced. They left the coast on October 28 and returned on November 5. One is rather disappointed at the apparent lack of interest which this novel plant created. After mentioning a kind of root, probably cassava, and a species of beans it is remarked that some of the ground was sown with "a sort of grain they call maiz, which was well tasted, bak'd, dry'd, and made into flour." [9]

The earliest printed reference to maize which I have found is in the Decades of Peter Martyr,[10] said to have been first printed in 1511. The reference as it appears in Eden's translation, 1555, is as follows:

They make also an other kynde of breade of a certayne pulse called *Panicum* muche lyke unto wheate, whereof is great plentie in the dukedome of Mylane, Spayne, and Granatum. But that of this countrey is longer by a spanne, somewhat sharpe towards the ende, and as bygge as a mannes arme in the brawne; The graynes whereof are sette in a maruelous order and are in fourme somewhat lyke a pease. While they be soure and unripe, they are white; but when they are ripe they be very blacke. When they are broken, they be whyter than snowe. This kynde of grayne, they call *Maizium*.

The accurate observation regarding the late stage at which the color of the seed develops, stamps the description as truthful, but unless the early explorers were much less muscular than has been supposed we are compelled to believe that the size of the ear was somewhat exaggerated.

To canvass the works of Columbus, and those in which he is cited as authority, for references to maize, would of itself be an undertaking of some magnitude, and it has not been attempted. Columbus refers to the plant as growing in Cuba, Santo Domingo, Trinidad, and the mainland of South America, but in view of the numerous descriptions of plants and animals given by Columbus, the significant fact would seem to be that he made such slight and infrequent reference to this plant, which must have appealed to a European as a striking novelty. It seems clear that the principal food plant in this part of the world was cassava, with maize occupying a

---

[9] Churchill's Voyages, Vol. 11, (London, 1732), p. 533.

[10] The Decades of the Newe Worlde or West India. Written in the Latine tonnge by Peter Martyr of Angleria, and translated into Englysshe by Rycharde Eden. (London, 1555). In Arber, Edward. The first three English Books on America (Birmingham, 1885), p. 67.

secondary position. Thus Dr. Chanca,[11] who accompanied Columbus on his second voyage and who wrote from Haiti in 1494, makes no mention of maize, although the food of the natives is described in some detail.

MAIZE AND THE EARLY COLONISTS.

With both the Jamestown and the Plymouth colonies, starvation was averted by virtue of maize, and in both settlements the colonists learned from the natives how to grow this new food plant.

The Puritans appear to have been the more apt pupils and to have made more intimate contacts with the natives. It would also appear that the agriculture of the New England Indians was of a more advanced type than that of the Indians of Virginia. At any rate our agricultural practices seem to have been derived from New England rather than from Virginia. We are told in Mourt's Relation how the first party landing on Cape Cod under the leadership of Miles Standish found fields where maize had grown, this being in November. A little farther they found newly made mounds of earth. In one of these which they opened they found—

a little old basket, full of fair Indian corn; and digged further, and found a fine great new basket, full of very fair corn of this year, with some six and thirty goodly ears of corn, some yellow, and some red, and others mixed with blue, which was a very goodly sight.[12]

With the maize they found a large kettle, and the eagerness with which this maize was appropriated is indicated by the following:

* * * We were in suspense what to do with it and the kettle; and at length, after much consultation, we concluded to take the kettle, and as much of the corn as we could carry away with us; and when our shallop came, if we could find any of the people, and come to parley with them, we would give them the kettle again, and satisfy them for their corn. So we took all the ears, and put a good deal of the loose corn in the kettle, for two men to bring away on a staff. Besides, they that could put any into their pockets, filled the same. The rest, we buried again; for we were so laden with armor that we could carry no more * * *

After securing the first prize, they later returned for more. The same account on page 141 says:

* * * This done, we marched to the place where we had the corn formerly, which place we called Cornhill; and digged and found the rest, of which we were very glad. We also digged in a place a little further off, and found a bottle of oil. We went to another place, which we had seen before; and digged and found more corn, viz., two or three baskets full of Indian wheat, and a bag of beans, with a good many of fair wheat[13] ears. Whilst some of us

[11] The Letters of Dr. Diego Alvarez Chanca. Translated by A. M. Fernandez de Ybarra. Smithsonian Miscellaneous Collections, Vol. 48, part 4, (1907).

[12] Young, A., Chronicles of the Pilgrim Fathers of the Colony of Plymouth, from 1602 to 1625. (Boston, 1841), p. 133.

[13] The reference to "Indian wheat" doubtless applies to maize.

were digging up this some others found another heap of corn, which they digged up also; so as we had in all about ten bushels, which will serve us sufficiently for seed. And sure it was God's good providence that we found this corn, for else we know not how we should have done; for we knew not how we should find or meet with any of the Indians except it be to do us a mischief

MAIZE CULTURES OF THE INDIANS.

The early colonists came well supplied with seeds of European crops, yet at both Jamestown and Plymouth they were able to become self-supporting only by promptly adopting maize and following the Indian method of cultivation, a method of cultivation radically different from anything known to the colonists.

Maize is usually thought of as differing from the principal European crops by being intertilled, but is this the most important difference? The Indians grew their crop without the aid of animals and relied on hoeing to suppress the competition of weeds. This method was practicable only with plants large enough to be given individual attention. Wheat must be treated en masse, as it were, but a maize plant may be given individual consideration. Was it not the large size of the individual plant, obviating the necessity of plowing, that really distinguished American from European agriculture? Maize, cassava, and the potato, the three great food plants contributed by America, are all grown as individual plants, while few of the important European annuals can be so treated.

It is difficult to understand how the colonists expected to produce wheat and other small grains without the aid of draft animals, yet the Plymouth colonists did not have cattle until 1624. Edward Winslow,[14] writing in 1621, says:

I never in my life remember a more seasonable year than we have here enjoyed; and if we have once but kine, horses, and sheep, I make no question but men might live as contented here as in any part of the world.

It was Winslow himself who first introduced cattle, in 1624.[15]

Indian agriculture is commonly thought of as having been of a very temporary character, the tribes, except in the Southwest, being

[14] Young, Alexander, Chronicles of the Pilgrim Fathers (Boston, 1841), p. 233.

[15] It would appear that to Bradford and Winslow we owe practically all of the detailed information regarding the early days of the Plymouth colony. The most complete account of the first landing is found in Mourt's Relation which in Young's Chronicles is credited to Bradford and Winslow. Certainly this part of William Bradford's history agrees very closely with Mourt's Relation, though many passages are omitted. There are, however, numerous minor changes in the language and in a few instances additions. Mourt's Relation was first published in 1622 and reprinted without omission in Young's Chronicles of the Pilgrim Fathers of the Colony of Plymouth in 1841. Although parts of William Bradford's manuscript were used by early writers, no part of it was published, as such, until a portion found by Young in Plymouth was published in 1841. By a happy series of accidents the complete manuscript was subsequently discovered in London and published by Dean in the collections of the Massachusetts Historical Society, Vol. III of the Fourth Series, (1856).

nomadic. The early accounts indicate, however, that nomadic tribes living by the chase were the exception rather than the rule, and that permanent agriculture existed in nearly all parts of the United States. G. F. Will, a student of maize culture among the Mandan Indians, makes the pertinent remark that Indian agriculture declined with the advent of the horse, which made the buffalo a much larger contributor of food.[16]

Unlike the primitive tribes of the American Tropics, who abandon a field after growing one crop, the fields in which maize was grown by the more northern tribes were used year after year. This practice had evidently continued in some localities until the fertility of the soil became impaired and the use of artificial fertilizers had been adopted.

When the first white settlers reached America they found maize being grown over practically the same range of territory as that in which it is now cultivated.

All the recognized seed types of maize, with the exception of the comparatively unimportant waxy maize recently discovered in China, were being grown by the American Indians at the time of the discovery. It may even be said that in the four and a quarter centuries during which the white race has been growing maize almost nothing has been produced that can not be duplicated among the cultures of the aborigines. The most highly developed varieties of the flint, flour, pop, and sweet types are little if any superior to individual types in native cultures, the chief advance having been toward uniformity. The dent varieties of the West and South represent the widest departure from the Indian types. No variety of maize now grown by the Indians, and not under the suspicion of having been secured from the white man, approximates the more highly developed dent varieties.

There is, however, direct evidence that the Indians of Virginia had originally a variety of maize of a pronounced dent type. In Beverley's History of Virginia four sorts of Indian corn are described, two early and two late varieties. Of the late variety he says:

The late Ripe Corn is diversify'd by the Shape of the Grain only, without any Respect to the accidental Differences in Color, some being blue, some red, some yellow, some white, and some streak'd. That therefore which makes the Distinction, is the Plumpness or Shrivelling of the Grain; the one looks as smooth and as full as the early ripe Corn, and this they call Flint-Corn; the other has a larger Grain, and looks shrivell'd, with a Dent on the Back of the Grain as if it had never come to Perfection; and this they call She-Corn.[17]

[16] Atkinson, Alfred, and Wilson, M. L., Corn in Montana, Mont. Agri. Exp. Sta. Bul. 107, (1915), p. 36.

[17] Beverley, Robert, History of Virginia, (London, 1722), pp. 126–127. I am indebted to Mr. Lyman Carrier for this reference.

This description would appear to establish the fact that true dent varieties were grown by the Indians, but since they have not been preserved it is impossible to judge of their quality or exact nature.

Although possessed of all of the seed types we now recognize, the seed types, with the exception of the sweet varieties, were not distinguished by the Indians as such. Their varietal names usually apply to more minute subdivisions, frequently referring to the color of the seed.

It is interesting to note that sweet corn, which genetic investigations indicate to be of comparatively recent origin, is the youngest of the seven corn sisters in the Zuñi mythology.[18]

Although widely distributed among the Indians, sweet varieties seem not to have been especially prized for eating in the green state. Will and Hyde say: "The upper Missouri Indians rarely picked the true sweet corn while green, but permitted it to ripen."[19] The Papago Indians, who possess a rather extensive series of varieties, told me the same. Their sweet variety was considered a fine sort for making meal, but was not especially prized as green corn.

Unfortunately, the Spaniards were not such apt pupils of the Indians as were the settlers of Virginia and New England, and it is from the eastern tribes, representing only the outer fringe of aboriginal maize culture, that we have derived our varieties and agricultural practices.

Had the Spaniards made such intimate contacts with the Indians of Mexico and of the Southwest as did the Puritans with the Indians of New England, our knowledge of maize culture would have proceeded much more rapidly. In Mexico and the southwestern part of the United States maize culture was highly developed. The specialization of types adapted to different environmental conditions, discrimination in the use of varieties for food, and agricultural practices were all much more highly developed than in the East. Much of the knowledge possessed by these primitive cultivators, as well as valuable types, have doubtless been lost, and it is only in recent years that we have regained in some measure the attitude of our forefathers by realizing that the Indians' long acquaintance with maize has produced results worthy of our serious consideration.

It is a commonplace remark that maize is the gift of the Indian. But the extent to which the details of agricultural practices have been copied from the Indian has never been fully appreciated. Perhaps copied is not the right word, for in more than one instance a

---

[18] Cushing, F. H., Zuñi Breadstuff, The Millstone, Vol. IX, No. 1, (Indianapolis, June, 1884), p. 3.

[19] Will, G. F., and Hyde, G. E., Corn Among the Indians of the Upper Missouri, (Saint Louis, 1917), p. 117.

new practice has been adopted without knowing that the same ground had been traversed long before by the Indian.

From their Indian friend, Squanto, the Plymouth colonists learned among other things that they should catch fish with which to fertilize the ground. We learn from a letter written by Edwin Winslow, dated December 11, 1621, that the colonists had planted some 20 acres to maize the preceding season, all manured with fish. Regarding this use of fish, Morton says:

> There is a fish, by some called shads, by some allizes, that at the spring of the year pass up the rivers to spawn in the ponds; and are taken in such multitudes in every river that hath a pond at the end, that the inhabitants dung their ground with them. You may see in one township a hundred acres together set with these fish, every acre taking a thousand of them; and an acre thus dressed will produce and yield so much corn as three acres without fish.[20]

The growing of maize as individual plants instead of by the European system of broadcasting or growing in rows has already been referred to. The number of seeds planted in a hill has not been changed from the practice of the Indians. The importance of regulating the number of seed in accordance with the distance between the hills and the fertility of the soil was also appreciated by the Indians.

Even the separation of the seeds in the hill that has only recently been advocated [21] was practiced by the Indians of Virginia, and was described in 1585 by Hariot in the following words:

> * * * beginning in one corner of the plot, with a pecker, they make a hole, wherein they put foure graines with that care they touch not one another, (about an inch asunder)[22]

Flint says:

> The custom of hilling corn was derived from the Indians, who planted it so, and even occupied the same hills or mounds year after year successively, raising three clusters of stalks on each large hill, and scraping fresh soil upon them, so that they remain to our day. The similar cultivation now even sometimes followed is called planting in Indian Hills.[23]

We have since abandoned the Indian practice of hilling maize as less advantageous than flat culture. It is just possible, however, that we have to some extent missed the point. The large permanent

[20] Young, Alexander, Chronicles of the Pilgrim Fathers of the Colony of Plymouth, from 1602. (Boston, 1841), p. 231, footnote.

[21] Hartley, C. P., A More Profitable Corn-Planting Method, U. S. Dept. of Agriculture, Farmers' Bulletin 400, May 27, 1910.

[22] Hariot, Thomas, Narrative of the First English Plantations of Virginia, (London, 1590), pp. 23–24.

[23] Flint, C. L., Agriculture of Massachusetts, (1859), p. 84, Sixth Ann. Report, Mass. Board of Agriculture.

hills used by the Indians would not be subject to most of the objections to the temporary hill system and may have decided advantages, especially where maize was grown without plowing.

Dr. W. E. Safford has called my attention to the Indian practice of preserving green corn by packing it in pits from which the air was excluded. Thus the silo, which is frequently pointed out as the most important advance in the utilization of maize, was definitely foreshadowed by Indian practice.

Although Indian varieties are usually much mixed there is abundant evidence that they appreciated the importance of pure cultures. Will is authority for the statement that the Mandans kept no less than 13 varieties of maize pure by means of isolated plantings.

Among the Navajo Indians there is a very distinct variety that shows through breeding experiments that it is uncontaminated by other sorts. Inquiry among the Navajos developed the fact that this variety was in the custody of one Indian, Lone Cedar Tree, who received the variety from his father. A peculiar color pattern which has recently figured in genetic literature is derived entirely from this variety and owes its preservation in a pure state to this one Indian.

In addition to the isolation of particular strains by the Indians, which in recent years at least is largely for ceremonial reasons, choice of the best appearing ears for seed was a general practice, especially among the more agricultural tribes.

The various colors exhibited in the seeds of maize and which play such an important part in the maize ceremonies of the Indians were in some tribes kept pure by assigning each of the colors to an individual who was charged with maintaining the stock by planting selected seed in isolated localities. The Indians, however, did not make the mistake committed by our early maize breeders of applying a system of close breeding. Maize is a cross-pollinated species, and rapidly deteriorates when self-pollinated. The converse of this deterioration, that is, the additional vigor obtained by crossing distinct strains, was foreshadowed in the Indian practice of deliberately planting seeds of different colors in the same hill. It is not to be understood that the Indians maintained pure strains, took advantage of the vigor that follows crossing, practiced seed selection, and performed the many agricultural practices which have since been laboriously developed by the white man, for any such reasons as are now assigned. The Indian nearly always has a reason for what he does, but it seems never to have been what we now believe to be the true reason. That he adopted so many methods and practices for which justification has since been found should be looked upon as the result of the working of a kind of natural or unconscious selection.

As·with more civilized agriculturalists, he was sometimes governed more by the logic of his theory than by practical results. Thus the Zuñi Indians went to great trouble to distribute the spores of corn smut in their fields. In thus spreading a serious disease, they were possessed by the theory that the spores of corn smut were the fertilizing agent of corn. It seems not impossible that they dimly sensed the function of pollen, and confused this with the spores of smut. On the other hand they may have been unconsciously impressed with the fact that a smutted corn plant is frequently larger and more vigorous than its disease-free neighbors.

In utilizing the great diversity of types in the preparation of different kinds of food, we are still far behind the Indians. We have but two kinds of corn meal, yellow, and white. The Indians carried the specialization much further. In Mexico especially, particular varieties are preferred for almost every dish or method of preparation.

With such a wealth of diversity it is difficult to understand why we have limited our discrimination to such an unimportant and ephemeral character as endosperm color.

The colonists who at first adopted maize to avoid starvation soon learned to prize it even in comparison with the longer-known cereals. After two or three generations, it came to be recognized as a national food, pined for by Americans forced to reside abroad. After a long residence in France, deprived of this native food, Joel Barlow was so moved by the kindness of his host in providing a dish of corn-meal mush, that he became inspired to write his epic, The Hasty Pudding.[24] Many were impelled by a missionary spirit to enlighten their cousins in the Old World regarding the virtues of this new food. Prominent in this work were Henry Coleman and Dr. John Bartlett. The latter in a letter addressed to Lord Ashburton presented the case as follows:

First. That the laboring classes and the poor of Great Britain require a cheaper article of food than wheaten bread.

Second. That although wheat contains a larger portion of gluten, or the nutritive ingredient, bulk is necessary, not only to satisfy the craving of hunger, but to promote digestion by the " stimulus of distension," which bulk alone can give.

Third. That the craving of hunger being removed or alleviated by the quantity taken, the mind is more at ease; the mental irritability consequent upon hunger is assuaged, and man goes to his labor with cheerfulness and vivacity, becoming a more peaceful citizen and perhaps a better man.[25]

---

[24] Barlow, Joel, The Hasty Pudding, Harper's New Monthly Magazine, (July, 1856), pp. 145–160.

[25] Browne, D. J., American Institute Report, 1846 (Albany, 1847), p. 419.

A somewhat less utilitarian appeal is made by Elihu Burritt, better known as the "learned blacksmith," who made a pedestrian tour of Europe spreading the gospel of maize. In one of his letters he says:

I have just got out " An Olive Leaf, from the Housewives of America to the Housewives of Great Britain and Ireland, or Recipes for making Various Articles of Food, of Indian Corn Meal " containing all the recipes I received before leaving home from our kind female friends in different parts of the Union—heaven bless them! I have had 2,000 of these Olive Leaves struck off, and intended in the first place, to send a copy to every newspaper in the realm. I shall have a thousand, all of which I shall put in the hands of those I meet on the road. I have resolved to make it a condition upon which only I consent to be any man's guest, that his wife shall serve up a johnny-cake for breakfast, or an Indian pudding for dinner. I was invited yesterday to a tea party which comes off to-night, where about thirty persons are to be present. I accepted the invitation with the johnny-cake clause, which was readily agreed to by all parties. So to-night the virtues of corn meal will be tested by some of the very best livers in Birmingham.[26]

If we may believe Thomas Carlyle, the efforts of the "learned blacksmith" were not of an intensely practical nature. Carlyle, in writing to Emerson, refers to him as follows:

Elihu Burritt had a string of recipes that went through all newspapers three years ago; but never sang there oracle of longer ears than that,—totally destitute of practical significance to any creature here.[27]

Carlyle had been experimenting with Indian meal, and, finding it "nigh uneatable," appealed to Emerson for help and for direction as to how to prepare it. Emerson rose to the occasion, and in a letter acknowledging the receipt of a shipment of corn from Emerson, Carlyle says:

Still more interesting is the barrel of genuine Corn ears,—Indian Cobs of edible grain, from the Barn of Emerson himself! It came all safe and right, according to your charitable program; without cost or trouble to us of any kind; not without curious interest and satisfaction! The recipes contained in the precedent letter, duly weighed by the competent jury of housewives (at least by my own Wife and Lady Ashburton), were judged to be of decided promise, reasonable-looking to every one of them, and now that the stuff itself is come, I am happy to assure you that it forms a new epoch for us all in the Maize department; we find the grain *sweet*, among the sweetest, with a touch even of the taste of nuts in it, and confess with contrition that properly we have never tasted Indian corn before.

It is really a small contribution towards World-History, this small act of yours and ours; there is no doubt to me, now that I taste the real grain, but all Europe will henceforth have to rely more and more upon your Western Valleys and this article. How beautiful to think of lean tough Yankee settlers,

---

26 American Institute Report (1846), pp. 420 to 421.

27 Carlyle-Emerson Correspondence, edited by Charles Eliot Norton, Vol. II (Boston, 1883), p. 170.

tough as gutta-percha, with most *occult* unsubduable fire in their belly, steering over the Western Mountains, to annihilate the jungle, and bring bacon and corn out of it for the Posterity of Adam! The Pigs in about a year eat up all the rattlesnakes for miles round; a most judicious function on the part of the Pigs. Behind the Pigs comes Jonathan with his all-conquering plowshare,— glory to him, too! Oh, if we were not a set of Cant-ridden blockheads, there is no *Myth* of Athene or Herakles equal to this *fact:*—which I suppose *will* find its real "Poets" some day or other; when once the Greek, Semitic, and multifarious other Cobwebs are swept away a little [28]

Time has shown that Carlyle was rather too optimistic. Europe has never learned to appreciate maize as an article of diet. Had there been successors to Burritt, Barlow, Carlyle, and Emerson, we might have avoided the crisis that arose during the war when it was necessary to resort to heroic measures to produce wheat to keep Europe from starvation, because Europe was unfamiliar with maize.

---

[28] Op. cit., pp. 175–177.

XIV. THE EARLIEST AMERICAN BOOK ON KITCHEN GARDENING.

By MARJORIE FLEMING WARNER,

Bureau of Plant Industry,
United States Department of Agriculture.

431

THE EARLIEST AMERICAN BOOK ON KITCHEN GARDENING.[1]

By MARJORIE FLEMING WARNER.

In his introduction to the bibliography of American horticultural literature in the Standard Cyclopedia of Horticulture, L. H. Bailey has pointed out that the literature of gardening, as such, was very little developed in this country previous to the nineteenth century, though several gardeners' calendars, one of which is credited to the year 1752, are supposed to have been issued, mostly with local almanacs. Few of these calendars can now be identified, and very few, in all probability, are now extant, so it may never be known to what degree they have enriched the experimental knowledge of gardening in America. One of them, however, which is still in existence though chiefly known in its nineteenth-century editions, has been regarded as the earliest and possibly only original horticultural work of the eighteenth century: Robert Squibb's The Gardener's Kalendar for South-Carolina, Georgia, and North-Carolina (Charleston, 1787). Although in calendar form this is a work of considerable extent, and is said to have played an important part in the development of the art of gardening in the vicinity of Charleston; but beside this, and probably antedating it by at least 15 or 20 years, there is an equally important manual for the description and culture of garden vegetables. While the "Treatise on gardening, by a citizen of Virginia," as reprinted in the second edition of Gardiner and Hepburn's American Gardener (Georgetown, D. C., 1818), is the earliest form of the work now in existence, it has recently been shown by Alfred J. Morrison in the William and Mary College Quarterly[2] that it had previously been published at Richmond as early as 1793 or 1794, and there had apparently been yet earlier printings. The work is ascribed to John Randolph, jr. (1727–1784), the last King's attorney

[1] The credit for the rediscovery of the main facts in regard to authorship belongs to Mr. A. J. Morrison; my own study of the work, extending through some half dozen years, has been directed more particularly to defining the period in which it was written, its relation to other literature, and possible influence on the gardening tradition of its time.
[2] A Treatise on Gardening by a Citizen of Williamsburg. William and Mary College Quarterly, Vol. 25, (October, 1916), p. 138–139; also The Gardener of Williamsburg, Vol. 25, (January, 1917), pp. 166–167.

of Virginia, who, though a native Virginian, was one of the loyalis
who went to England at the outset of the Revolution, dying the
in 1784.

I have long and vainly tried to discover the date of the origin
issue of this book, which seems to have left no contemporary trace
but the evidence for Randolph's authorship, taken all together,
conclusive.

I. Thomas Jefferson, who was a contemporary of the attorne
and on intimate terms with him, could hardly have referred to an
one else of the name when he credited the book to " John Randolph
as he did in more than one instance. In the Catalogue of th
Library of the United States (Washington, 1815), which was the li
arranged by himself of the books which the Government bough
from Jefferson in 1814, we find on page 31 " A Treatise on garde
ing by John Randolph." No date is assigned, but it must hav
been the same copy which appears in the Library of Congres
catalogue of 1840, page 129, as "Randolph, John: Treatise o
gardening. 16s. Richmond, 1793." As the fire of December, 185
destroyed the agricultural portion of the Library of Congress, thi
copy is of course no longer in existence. The work is likewis
credited to John Randolph in the manuscript catalogue of Jef
ferson's library which is preserved at the Massachusetts Historica
Society, and it appears to have been highly valued by Jefferson
as he included it among titles recommended for an agricultura
library, March 3, 1817 [3], and there was another copy, not neces
sarily the same edition, among Jefferson's books which were sol
at auction after his death, in February, 1829, but the entry in th
auctioneer's catalogue [4] gives no data in regard to the work, thoug
it suggests the relation between this book and that of Gardiner and
Hepburn as follows: " 274. Hepburn's American Gardener; 27£
Randolph's Treatise on Gardening; 276. Hepburn and Randolph.

II. In the American Gardener (Georgetown, 1818), page 268
there is a note by the editor, presumably Joseph Milligan, of George
town, who published this edition, stating that " The annexed littl
Treatise was written many years ago, by a learned and eminen
citizen of Virginia * * * who printed it for the use of hi
friends, by whom it has been long and highly prized for the usefu
information it conveys * * * The residence of the author, and
his garden, from which he drew his observations, were in Williams
burg, Virginia." If, as seems probable, this note was based on

[3] American Farmer, Vol. 2, (1820), p. 94.
[4] A catalogue of the extensive and valuable library of the late President Jefferson * * * to be sold at auction, at the Long Room, Pennsylvania Avenue, Washing
ton City, by Nathaniel P. Poor. Washington, 1829.

)ersonal knowledge, it gives strong support to the theory of Ran-
lolph's authorship.

III. A positive statement of the author's identity is made by
[dmund Ruffin in the Farmers' Register for 1839 [5] : " The author was
'ohn Randolph, of Williamsburg, attorney general under the colon-
al government." Ruffin calls it "the oldest Virginian work on
ultivation, of any kind," but says that its date " is not shown by
nything in the oldest edition which we have seen, which is as
ate as 1794." He reprints the entire work " in its original form,
vhich was without the name of the author." Ruffin's statement
arries great weight, as he was in a position to know at first hand,
n 1839, many facts with regard to Virginia history and agriculture,
vhich have been lost to memory in the four-score intervening years.

IV. The Massachusetts Horticultural Society has a copy of the
American Gardener (1818), with the following note on page 269:
'This treatise is by John Randolph, of Williamsburg, father of
[dmund Randolph, Secretary of State during the administration
f General Washington [6]." This is without date or signature, but
vhile it is possible that it may have been written later, and perhaps
)ased upon some other statement such as Ruffin's, the handwriting
nay be that of General Dearborn, in which case there is a strong
)robability that it is even earlier than Ruffin's, and founded upon
[uite as definite personal knowledge. Henry Alexander Scammell
)earborn (1783–1851) was the son of Gen. Henry Dearborn
[1751–1829), who was Secretary of War in Jefferson's Cabinet, and,
lthough the father was from Maine, the son entered the College
f William and Mary at Williamsburg in 1801, graduating there in
803, and afterwards studied law in Virginia with William Wirt.
His interest in agricultural matters must have begun rather early,
s we find him in 1816 publishing a translation of a French work on
lye plants by Lasteyrie du Saillant, and thenceforth he was con-
inually writing, speaking, and organizing in the interests of agri-
ulture and gardening, being one of the prime movers and the first
)resident of the Massachusetts Horticultural Society. He was
reatly interested in building up its library, and although it is not
ertain that the annotated copy of the American Gardener was his
[ift, it must have been the very one which was listed in the original
atalogue published by him as chairman of the library committee
n the New England Farmer in 1831. Nothing is more plausible
han that the work of Randolph, perhaps in the form known to
efferson, supposed to have been printed about 1793, may have been

[5] Randolph's Treatise on Gardening. Farmers' Register, Vol. 7, (January, 1839), pp.
1–54.
[6] Standard Cyclopedia of Horticulture, ed. by L. H. Bailey, Vol. 3, (1915), p. 1579,
ketch of David Hepburn, by Wilhelm Miller.

in use in Williamsburg while Dearborn was a student there, thus furnishing the original basis for this note, though it is also conceivable that the information may have come by way of Jefferson.

V. In 1826 the Treatise on Gardening was reprinted at Richmond by Collins & Co. with the title: "Randolph's Culinary Gardener enlarged and adapted to the present state of our climate, by an experienced gardener, a native of Virginia." The latter probably refers to the numerous additions by "M.," whom I have not been able to identify, and although the book is credited to "Mr. Randolph," it gives no hint of his identity, or to the date of the original issue, save the intimation that it must have been considerably previous to 1826. This reprint was advertised in the Richmond Enquirer, February 16, 1826, at the price of 50 cents per copy.

Besides the proofs of Randolph's authorship, it may be well to dispose of one or two obviously impossible attributions.

I. In printing a catalogue card for Gardiner and Hepburn's American Gardener, the Library of Congress originally indicated an added entry for the Treatise on Gardening under John Taylor (1750–1824), a rather reasonable assumption, as the latter's famous "Arator" essays were first published in 1813 under the soubriquet of "A Citizen of Virginia," but quite inconsistent with the previously quoted statement of the editor, in regard to the author's residence and garden in Williamsburg, which throws out Colonel Taylor, of Caroline. In this connection, moreover, it would have been quite as natural to credit the work to another writer who posed as a "Citizen of Virginia," i. e., Filippo Mazzei, a Florentine who was actually carrying on practical experiments in agriculture near Williamsburg at about the time the Treatise on Gardening was written, and whose "Recherches Historiques sur les États Unis de l'Amérique Septentrionale * * * par un Citoyen de Virginie" was published at Paris in 1788. However, apart from the fact that Mazzei could never have achieved the easy English of the Treatise, we can be sure that Jefferson, who knew both men intimately, would never have attributed his work to Randolph.

II. J. W. Randolph, the publisher and bookseller of Richmond, who had an extensive knowledge of Virginiana, on more than one occasion advertised for sale a copy of the Culinary Gardener of 1826 under the name of Sir John Randolph (1693–1737), the father of John Randolph, jr., but this possibility is excluded by the fact that the book contains quotations from another work which was not published before 1752.

Inasmuch as the Treatise is based, so far as the account of the vegetables is concerned, upon Miller's Gardener's Dictionary, it is most fortunate for our purposes that its author used an edition [7] which in many respects is different from those which preceded or followed it. Certain statements in the Virginian work have been compared with 13 editions of Miller, and while some are to be found in earlier or later issues, it is only in the sixth folio of 1752, or its abridgement, published in 1754, that we can identify them all. One point of absolute difference is the date for sowing cauliflowers, quoted from Miller as the " 10th or 12th of August." So far as I can discover, every edition prior to 1752 specifies that seed should be sown on the 10th of August, while in the seventh folio, published in 1759, Miller says " about the twenty-first of August," having previously explained that he has " in this edition, altered the days to the New Style "; and we find that the alternative dates " 10th or 12th " appear only in the 1752 and 1754 editions. Again we find the " Citizen of Virginia " quoting Miller in regard to the Portugal or pocket melon, which " has been called by the name of King Charles' melon, because he used to carry one in his pocket, and also Dormer's melon, because brought from Portugal by a general of that name." Neither of these names occurs in any edition of Miller before the sixth folio, and while the " Dormer melon " is again mentioned in the seventh, the other name does not appear after the fourth abridgment in 1754. Granting then, the theory that our book was the work of John Randolph, jr., we must assume that it was written between 1752, the date of Miller's sixth folio, and 1775, when Randolph left Virginia. Certain bits of internal evidence, moreover, suggest a further limitation of this period. The " Col. Ludwell " who gave the author seed of Aleppo lettuce, must have been Philip Ludwell, of Green Spring (1716–1767), third of that name and last of the Virginia Ludwells, who died in England in 1767, but had returned hither probably as early as 1761 or 1762, so that the exchange of garden seeds, which was fresh in Randolph's mind, must have been before that date. On the other hand, the author uses the past tense throughout his description of the method of " Col. Turner of King George, who was eminent for cauliflowers," suggesting that this was probably written after that gentleman's death. The allusion is undoubtedly to Thomas Turner, who died in 1758, and who is mentioned by Washington in his diary, January 14, 1760, when on his way to Port Royal he passed " the plantation late Col° Turners." Another bit of internal evidence which furnishes material for thought is the names of garden peas in the Treatise, which differ considerably from

[7] Miller, Philip, The Gardener's Dictionary, 6th edition, London, 1752, F°. Also same, abridged from the last folio edition, by the author, 4th edition, London, 1754, 3 v., 8°.

those in Miller's Dictionary but resemble those of an advertisemer
of garden seeds in the Virginia Gazette in the springs of 1767 an
1768. I have examined a quantity of material, both contemporar
and later publications, without finding any trace of the original ed
tion of this book; but from the evidence submitted I venture th
theory that it could hardly have been written previous to 1760 an
probably not later than 1770, when Randolph, then in his early fortie
would have had sufficient practical experience to test and pass upo
the precepts of Philip Miller's Gardeners' Dictionary. We have no
the slightest clue to the form of the original publication, which ma
either have been printed on some local press in a very limited edi
tion for circulation among friends of the author, or possibly issue
as a supplement to the Virginia Gazette. I have wondered if th
abbreviation " p. f." which follows the title in the manuscript cata
logue of Jefferson's library previously referred to might not hav
signified "pamphlet folio." This would have been appropriate i
it had been printed in the Gazette, as was some other matter o
economic interest, like the essays on the cultivation of the vine, by
Robert Bolling, jr., which are still extant, and a paper on the fly
weevil by Col. Landon Carter, of Sabine Hall, which according to
his statement in a similar paper in the first volume of the Transactions of the American Philosophical Society, had been printed "in
cur gazettes," but even then, in 1768, was impossible to get hold of. It
may be noted that while they regarded imported books with respect,
the colonists seem to have been remarkably careless about preserving
the product of their own presses; and whether as a tiny separate
booklet or a large ungainly sheet, neither Carter's nor Randolph's work
would have had much chance of survival; and the latter, at any rate,
is not to be found in the most extensive file known—which is nevertheless far from complete—of the Virginia Gazette.

One feature of Randolph's work should be specially noted; whereas all the other early American gardening books, Squibb, McMahon,
Gardiner and Hepburn, and the Practical Gardener, published by
Fielding Lucas at Baltimore in 1819, are in the calendar form, showing what operations are to be performed " monethly throughout the
year," Randolph takes up the subject from the point of view of the
plants cultivated, which in the editions known to me are arranged,
not under their Latin names, as in the Gardener's Dictionary, but in
an alphabetical order of English common names, though the latter
are usually followed by their Latin or Greek derivations, apparently
taken direct from Miller's work.

The most important thing about the book, apart from the problem
of its authorship, is that while many of the agricultural writings of
that period were mere compilations from previous works, this little

volume [8] bears frequent testimony to the author's personal observation and, experience. Randolph's reliance on Miller's Dictionary is much in evidence, but it does not prevent him from forming and expressing his individual opinion; witness his remarks (p. 67) on the 'netted wrought melon," which Miller "does not esteem, though I have found them very delicious in this country." Again he says (p. 67):

There is a rough knotty melon called the Diarbekr, from a Province belonging to the Turkish Empire, in Asia which is reckoned the most exquisite of all melons, which have been brought to great perfection here, and which are not taken notice of by Miller, probably because it has been brought into England since the publication of his dictionary, unless it is the Zatta.

Unhappily I have been unable to trace the introduction of the Diarbekr melon into either English or American gardens, or to identify it with the Zatte, apparently a very old name. We often find Randolph quoting Miller in comparison with his own experience, or, for information outside the range of his personal knowledge, as (p. 76) Miller's opinion in regard to the identity of the Ciboule and Welch onion, and (p. 79) the probability that the Chives and the Shallot are not distinct species.

The difference in climate between London and Virginia is noted by him, as (p. 35):

Miller says that for spring cauliflowers the seed should be sown on the 10th or 12th of August, but in Virginia, the 12th day of September is the proper time, which is much the same as in England, allowing for the difference of climate, the ratio of which ought to be a month sooner in the spring, and the same later in the fall; our summer months being intensely hot in this place.[9]

On the other hand, Randolph observes (p. 94) that the severity of the Virginia winters is too great to permit growing radishes out of doors, as practiced by the gardeners about London.

Nor were Randolph's observations strictly limited to his own garden, as indicated by his allusion (p. 37) to the method of "Col. Turner of King George, who was eminent for cauliflowers," though it had apparently succeeded with him also. He tried the Aleppo lettuce

[8] The page references which follow have been made from the Culinary Gardener (1826), which while in some respects the least satisfactory, is the only edition in separate form; the alphabetical arrangement, moreover, makes it easy to identify any reference either in Gardiner and Hepburn's American Gardener (1818), or in the Farmers' Register Vol. 7, (1839), pp. 41–54.

[9] Jefferson, in his Notes on Virginia, says that Williamsburg is in the hottest part of the State. The interest shown by the early Virginians in meteorological conditions is quite remarkable, and some of the available data must be important. For the vicinity of Williamsburg there are not only observations made by Jefferson during the years 1772–1775, but there is a calendar of the weather for the year 1759, made by Lieut. Gov. Francis Fauquier (1704–1768), which is appended to Andrew Burnaby's Travels Through the Middle Settlements of North America (London, 1775).

which Colonel Ludwell had given him (p. 66), "but it did not please me so well as the other more common sorts." Under the turnip, of which he quaintly remarks that it " will not apple kindly "[10] after the middle of August, he states (p. 106) that "Lord Townsend (sic) sowed an acre in drills and worked it with the plough," etc., referring to " Turnip "Townshend (Charles, second Viscount Townshend, 1674–1738), who, on his retirement from political life in 1730, experimented with the cultivation of turnips on a large scale at his estate of Raynham, in Norfolk. Though the source of his information on Townshend's experiments was undoubtedly Miller's Dictionary, it seems that Randolph's reading was not entirely confined to that work, as he quotes (p. 18) Bradley's opinion that an asparagus bed, if properly managed, ought to last for 20 years[11] as compared with Miller's, that it should be good for 10 or 12.

Randolph in general throws little light on the varieties of vegetables in use in his time, but under peas (pp. 83–85) he mentions several of the old names, "Charlton Hotspur, Reading Hotspur, and Master Hotspur" (all given in Miller's Dictionary)—which he says are "very little differing from one another"—the "Rouncivals, the Spanish Marollo Peas and the Marrow Fat, or Dutch Admiral "; while farther on he states that "the Ormonds are the Hotspur." One can not but wonder if he bought his garden seeds from " William Wills, Chirurgeon in Richmond Town, and John Donlevy in Petersburg," who advertised in the Virginia Gazette of March 26 and April 2, 1767: "Fresh imported from London and Bristol * * * Pease: Golden Hotspur, Early Charlton, Early Ormond, Marrowfat, Sugar Blues, Blue Rounceval, Dutch Admiral, Nonpareil do., Spanish Morattoes, Large Saletine." The next year their advertisement in the Gazettes of March 10 and 17, 1768, was varied chiefly in its spelling: "Early Golden Hotspur, Early Charlton, Ormeret Hotspur, Large Blue and White Rouncevals, Spanish Morotoes, Large Marrowfats, Nonpareils, Bunch, Sugar Blues, Dutch Admirals, Sallatine," etc.

Mr. Morrison found this little book lacking in local color, which is of course due to its thoroughly practical, not to say prosaic, character, which leaves little room for " atmosphere " or those bits of local history dear to the heart of the antiquarian; it aimed to be, and succeeded as a practical manual of vegetable gardening for the author's

[10] This use of the term " apple," meaning to fill out, is used with reference to the turnip by Miller and other writers of the period.
[11] Bradley, Richard, New Improvements of Planting and Gardening, [1st ed.] Vol. 3 (London, 1718), p. 144. Same in 6th edition, (London, 1731), p. 292.

)wn locality and period, but leaves us entirely ignorant of his per-
ionality.

It is practically impossible, moreover, to reconstruct anything of
hat personality from other sources. Those who have attempted it,
ike Conway and Miss Katherine Wormeley, Randolph's great-grand-
laughter, who cherished a few family traditions, have only suc-
:eeded in presenting generalities, while the actual documents relate
)nly to his legal or political career, his activities (most obnoxious to
nany of his countrymen) in connection with the "writs of assist-
ince," and his opposition to Patrick Henry's resolutions on the stamp
ict, or occasionally an opinion on a land title or other legal matter.
Wirt in his Life of Patrick Henry stresses the idea that Randolph
vas the most brilliant lawyer of Virginia in his time, undoubtedly
vith the object of throwing into high relief the peculiar genius of
Henry, who in many respects excelled him. Then one finds a few
·ecords indicating the conspicuous position of Randolph and his
:amily in Virginia society, as when Col. Landon Carter, of Sabine
Hall, notes in his diary (Nov. 21, 1770), that "Col. John Randolph
& his Lady & daughters dined here on Monday," or Washington's
liary (Aug. 4, 1774) records during a stay in Williamsburg: "Dined
it the Attorney's & spent the evening at my own Lodgings." The
ictual records of John Randolph's life are meager. The son of Sir
John Randolph, who is said to have been the only native American
·ver knighted, he was born in Williamsburg in 1727 (according to
;ome in 1728). He was graduated from the College of William and
Mary, and went to England to study law, being admitted to Middle
Temple April 18, 1745, and called to the bar February 9, 1749. He
·eturned to Williamsburg to practice, and, like his father, Sir John,
ind his son Edmund, who was Attorney General in Washington's
idministration, he was an able lawyer, and in 1766 was appointed
:o the post of King's attorney for Virginia, which had been held by
iis father and his elder brother Peyton. Unlike that brother, who
vas a conspicuous patriot, John Randolph was a staunch loyalist,
ind leaving Virginia in August of 1775, took his wife and daughters
:o England, where he spent the remainder of his life in poverty and
obscurity. He died in Brompton January 31, 1784, but his wish to
)e buried in his native Virginia was fulfilled and his remains were
)rought back and placed beside those of his father and brother Pey-
:on beneath the college chapel of William and Mary. His daughter
Ariana, who performed this filial service, was the wife of James
Wormeley, also a Virginia loyalist, a descendant of Ralph Wormeley,
if Rosegill; and their son Ralph Randolph Wormeley afterwards
)ecame a Rear Admiral in the Royal Navy.

History is silent as to John Randolph's interest in gardening or
his work as an author,[12] although he is mentioned as a man of literary tastes; and it is somewhere stated that he inherited the fine
library collected by his father, to which he probably made large
additions. A number of his books came into the hands of his friend,
Thomas Jefferson, and there is good reason to suppose that a list [13]
of about 300 works in some 670 volumes, which was advertised for
sale in the Virginia Gazette of November 25, the very day on which
the effects of the attorney general were to be sold at auction by his
trustees,[14] must have been part of his library. While this list includes
Miller's Gardeners' Kalendar and Bradley on Husbandry and Gardening, it does not comprise any edition of Miller's Dictionary, which
may, however, have passed already into the hands of others; there
seems to be no evidence that Jefferson ever owned a copy of this work.
Even though the original issue of the little book which John Randolph is said to have " printed for the use of his friends " may never
come to light, there remains the thrilling possibility that some newly
discovered copy of the Gardeners' Dictionary may sometime reveal
the original observations which he made upon his Williamsburg
garden a century and a half ago.

---

[12] He is also credited with the authorship of two other books, no more definitely if as
well proven as that of the Treatise on Gardening. One is the Considerations on the
Present State of Virginia, a rare political tract printed in 1774, and reprinted in 1919
with notes by E. G. Swem, as one of C. F. Heartman's Historical Series; while the other
is the famous Letters from General Washington to Several of His Friends in the Year
1776 (London, J. Bew, 1777), which has been many times reprinted; and there is a
specially good edition in 1889, with a full bibliography and discussion of the authorship
by W. C. Ford. I have examined both works with more or less care, but fail to find any
evidences of a common literary style.

[13] Virginia Gazette, No. 1268, Nov. 25, 1775; reprinted in William and Mary College
Quarterly, Vol. 15, (October, 1906), pp. 101–113.

[14] Virginia Gazette, No. 1266, Nov. 11, 1775.

XV. AN EARLY AGRICULTURAL PERIODICAL.

By MARY G. LACY,

Librarian, Bureau of Markets,
United States Department of Agriculture.

AN EARLY AGRICULTURAL PERIODICAL.

By Mary G. Lacy.

The Annals of Agriculture, edited by that sagacious observer, Arthur Young, is doubtless thought of by many people as the first appearance of agriculture in the field of English periodicals. In the preface to volume one of the annals, however, the editor says:

The idea of a periodical publication as a general channel for information relative to Agriculture, is at least a century old. Houghton, in King James the Second's reign, published a paper for this purpose twice a week, and continued it with little interruption to the beginning of Queen Anne's.

This statement from so eminent a writer as Arthur Young induced a careful examination of Mr. Houghton's husbandry and trade—an examination yielding delight upon every page, from the preface by Richard Bradley, the well-known professor of botany in the University of Cambridge, to the "Epitome of the 19 volumes. A farewell," with which the work closed.

This modest little periodical, issued twice a week during a part of its career and once a week for the remainder, was "esteemed as valuable as choice manuscripts" in 1727, when the scarcity of these papers and the reputation which they had gained made it advisable to republish them. Richard Bradley collected a set of the single papers of which he said that there were probably "not in all our English libraries ten complete sets" and was instrumental in having them reprinted in book form. In 1728 there was a second reprinting, without change. Richard Bradley's preface to the second printing of this pioneer among agricultural periodicals is entitled "An introductory discourse to Mr. Houghton's Husbandry." It provides eight pages of sound agricultural doctrine as well as delightful reading. After a few pages devoted to advice as to fertilizers, the advantage of draining wet fields, and directions as to the best methods of doing so, the author says:

But it is not only by rich manure or labour that an estate may be enriched; it may be done another way, viz, by examining the soil and its depth in every field; and likewise by having a due regard to the situation; and then to assort

445

to every soil such sorts of plants as are naturally the produce of such soils, or will best thrive upon them. But this has been constantly overlooked by our English farmers, who generally imagine that ground is not good unless it will produce good corn or good grass; but give me leave to expostulate with them a little. Have we not grains and plants enough that will turn to as good profit as corn or grass, and much more, too?

And a page further:

And then again, if lands are dry, there are plants, which one can cultivate on them, which will turn to good account; as for instance some of the French grasses, which our author [Houghton] gives many instructions about; but the best of them all is the Lucern which one may cut three or four times a year, and will last a long time; so that there is no ground however poor or unprofitable it may be thought to be but will produce something beneficial to the farmer with no more than common trouble. * * * Nor can I find it necessary to let any land lie fallow, since I have observance that every different plant draws a different nourishment; then by shifting the sorts one may have a continued succession of crops without exhausting the strength of the soil, or losing of time. * * *

From this able presentation of the theory of rotation of crops, Bradley passes on to a statement recognizing the relation of markets to the value of crops and of land.

But there is one thing more which ought to be considered in the improvement of land; and that is, to judge what will be most acceptable at the neighbouring markets; or what convenience of carriage there may be had for things of the greatest burden. For tho' we may have good crops that would be valuable at one place, they may not have worth at another; or, if they will fetch the same price in every market, yet the difficulty in carriage to one place more than another, will make an alteration in the farmer's profit, as may be very easily calculated; and then it appears that two pieces of ground in different places that are equally good, and bring crops of the same goodness, yet if the markets do not equally demand them, one piece is worse than another.

This "Introductory discourse to Mr. Houghton's Husbandry, by R. Bradley " is placed in the front of what we are led by the binder's title to consider volume one of the " Collection for improvement of Husbandry and Trade." The date of the first paper in this volume is March 30, 1692, whereas the first paper in volume 4, according to the binder, is dated September 8, 1681. The heading or title of this issue of September 8, 1681 is " A collection of letters for the improvement of Husbandry and Trade," the date of the latest communication in the volume being November 14, 1683. It appears probable, therefore, that these " letters " dating from 1681–1683 are the forerunners of the regular issue of the " collection " which began in 1692 and ran through September 24, 1703. That nine-year gap between the two series presents an interesting field of study for the bibliophile. We will not attempt to enter it here, however, but will confine ourselves to the actual contents of the reprinted volumes as they have come down to us.

In the earliest, or "letters" volume, 1681–1683, there is an interesting opening statement by John Houghton himself which he calls a "Preface by way of a letter to J. B. D. D., S. R. S." in which he speaks of the revival of the "committee for agriculture" of the Royal Society of which he had the "honour to be a member" and states that his design is to—

* * * publish such papers as shall cause his kingdom to be so well husbandry'd as to exceed not only the United Provinces but also what on another occasion you were pleased to stile the garden of the world, Barbadoes. And feeling what the husbandman is concerned for, is the *materia prima* of all trade, and that the finding of a vent for his commodities is as necessary to his end, as it is to know the ways of tilling, planting, sowing, etc. * * * therefore I design not only to give instructions for that end, but also the best accounts I can meet with, how they [fruits, corn, grain, pulse, etc.] may be advantageously parted with which will necessitate me often to treat of such things as more strictly come under the second head of my title, viz. trade."

On the succeeding page there is the following:

A catalogue of the books in the library of the Royal Society, relating to agriculture.

Worthy Sir, It will I think by all be granted that the art of *agriculture* hath not been a little improved by the use of books, and more it may, were it well known what are written of the subject: at present I will give you a list of what I find in the catalogue of our library, and hereafter of what I meet with elsewhere.

Adriana (Presbyter) Carmina de Venatione.
Apitius Gaelius de re Coquinaria. lib. X.
Aristotelis Historia Animalium.
Baptiste Jo. Ferrarii de florum Cultura.
Di Bonardo Richezze del'Agricoltura.
Cato (M.) de re Rustica.
Columella (L) de Cultu Hortorum Carmine Script.
Di Crescentio (Pietro) Agricoltura.
Forest Laws, by Jo. Manwood.
Herbarium Ling. Germ.
Hortorum Cultura, per Lucium (Jun.) Columellan.
Macer (Philoseph.) de natr. & virtut. Herbar.
More (Sir Tho.) Utopia.
Oppiana de Ventione piscium.
De Ro. Piscibus.
De Animal. Industria (per Sym. Grynaeum)
Di Tatti (Giov.) Agricoltura.
Terentius M. Varro Agricultura.
Tobae Aldimi descripto Planter in Horto Farnesiano.
Herbarium (Antiq.) Anglice scriptum. M. S.
Junii Mod. Columel. rei rustic M. S.
Herbarum nomina & Vires (Carm. Hexametro) M. S.
Johannis de loco Frumentario pars secunda. M. S.
Evelyn (Jo.) Sylva.
Bacon (Sr. Fr.) Sylva Sylvarium.
Evelyn (Jo.) of Gardens.
Cotton (Ch.) Planters Manual.

Evelyn (Jo.) Philosophical Discourse of Earth.
Hughes (Will.) Complete Vineyard.

Icones and descriptiones {Sicilae / Melitae / Galliae & / Italiae} per Paul. Boccon.
Plantarium

M. Malpighius de Bombyce.
Johnson de Animalibus.
Christoph. Merret Pinax verum Nat. Britannicar.
Anatomy of Vegetables, by N. Grew M. D.
Two Herbals.

These are what I have chiefly taken notice of; the author adds naively, I
is possible among so many books (upwards of three thousand) I may have
overlooked some, but I think none that are material.

It is obviously impossible within the bounds of a single paper to
fully analyze the contents of these four remarkable volumes. We can
only hope like a good showman to point out some of the most enticing
of the contents so that the reader's curiosity may be whetted to examine for himself what must, for lack of space, remain undisplayed.

Dr. Robert Plot, Oxford professor of chemistry, secretary of the
Royal Society, keeper of the Ashmolean Museum, and author of the
Natural History of Oxfordshire, was a frequent contributor and was
always interesting. In a contribution dated November 24, 1681, he
deplores the lack of interest shown by one locality in the crops or
practices of another and adds:

> Much less are the grains of one county known in another, witness the sort
> of wheat called red-stalked wheat, sown plentifully about Oxford, which though
> endued with the excellent quality of seldom or never smutting, a conveniency
> which best pleases the chapman of any, yet either hath not been heard of, or
> is wholly neglected in most other counties. Nor less ignorant is the husband-
> man of long-cone wheat, notwithstanding its not being subject to lodging or
> being eaten by birds, and its constant freedom from that epidemical (I had
> almost said also incurable) disease of corn, commonly called the mildew, three
> inconveniences sometimes so fatal that by one, two or all of them he loses his
> crop; whereas, had he known these grains and would have taken the pains to
> procure, and have used them, how free might he have been from all of these
> inconveniences, wherever his grounds had been liable to them.

There follow similar observations about a little-known barley
that has—

> Many times been sown and returned to the barn again in two months' time
> * * * whence it plainly appears that could you make yourself the
> happy instrument of communicating such notices as these to all the
> parishes in England and so effectually as to get them put in practice, for
> that is the greatest work (though one would think indeed men should make
> but weak oppositions against their own emoluments) you would (for ought I
> know) deserve as much of the publick as the founder of Christ's-hospital, and
> all its benefactors, and receive the acclamations and applauses of all great
> men as the result of so great an achievement.

The same spirit of wonder at the failure of husbandmen to profit by the experience of others is voiced by Adam Martindale, of Cheshire, in a letter dated May 18, 1682, about improving land by marl. He says in part:

> I labour under great discouragements, in reference to that little which I know, from the conceited surley humours of people that will not be beaten out of their old roads, by the most powerful discourses bottomed upon reason, and backed by the experience of wise and faithful persons. To what else can it be ascribed, that the speaking trumpet (so notably fitted for the criers in great courts, and proclaimers of things in tumultous markets) should find little more entertainment than to be ridiculed in plays? Or (to come nearer the matter) what else can be the reason why the great advantage got by our neighbours in Staffordshire or Worcestershire by sowing of clover, can scarce prevail with any of us in Cheshire or our neighbors in Lancashire, to sow an handful upon the very same sort of land? Nor the vast incomes by marling land in Lancashire and Cheshire, tempt our neighbors of other counties before mentioned, to make a little search for that great natural improver marle.

After a full, though conservative statement as to the sorts of land likely to be improved by the application of marl, the writer proceeds to tell of the profits that may accrue from its use and adds:

> I wonder that the gentlemen of Staffordshire of our intimate acquaintance, that have so much land fit, (of mine own knowledge) for this purpose, should so far neglect their own advantage as not to send for skilful searchers for marle out of our county, which if succeeding, would be incomparably above their liming for durableness, and perhaps in some places far less costly. I am confident that I saw marle there at a brook side, and little doubt, but by search of skilful persons, a good quantity might be found; but how much, how good, or how conveniently it lies, cannot be resolved without search, neither there nor here. He that will not run such a poor hazard as that, is not worthy of so much gain.

There are other contributions from Mr. Martindale, of Cheshire, in this same volume on the manner of getting the marl out, the different kinds of it, the kind of lands which usually abound in it, the method of using it, etc.

John Evelyn, in his day a recognized authority on landscape gardening and best known to us as the author of Sylva and Pomona, appears often; sometimes as a contributor and sometimes as the author of a work under discussion. Under date of January 16, 1682, he makes a nine-page contribution entitled—

> An account of bread from the learned John Evelyn, Esq.; entitled Panificium or the several manners of making Bread in France where by universal consent the best bread in the world is eaten.

This article contains a number of recipes for bread and numerous sage observations, such as:

> The whiter the flower, the less goodness in taste.
> Some make bread (as about Rouen in Normandy) without at all sifting the bran, as it comes from the mill; this at first eating seems to be rough and harsh, but by custom it is both pleasant, and wholesome and very strengthening.

This Collection of Letters for the Improvement of Husbandry an Trade, as the 1681–83 volume is called, contains many observation and contributions which indicate that the author interpreted " hus bandry' and trade " very broadly. A few of these we will mention b title.

An essay to prove that it is better to have Ireland rich and prosperous tha poor and thin.

Some considerations upon the proposals approved on by the city of Londo for subscriptions upon lives wherein are some observations and conjectures upo the East-Indian Company and bankers.

This last is a life-insurance scheme with the death probabilitie carefully worked out by 10-year periods. This volume also contain lists of goods imported and exported with quantities and dates; als the number of outgoing and incoming ships with destination an port of departure carefully given.

There is an account of a new method of plowing with careful draw ings so that the " wayfaring man though a fool, can not err therein. There are " Directions in the making of colonies for Bees, by a new invented model of Hive, to improve them, whereby without killing may be enjoyed the fruit of their labour."

This entire volume four of "letters," 1681–1683, can not, however be considered in the accurate meaning of the term a periodical, as th communications were issued irregularly and without apparent plan The three volumes which are introduced by the Bradley preface however, can unquestionably be considered a periodical. They bega on Wednesday, March 30, 1692, and were issued once a week o Wednesdays through the rest of the year. There was issued also beginning Saturday, April 30, a paper each Saturday, extracted from the customhouse bills, which gave the name and quantity o goods imported and exported " in order that trade may be better understood and the whole Kingdom made one trading city." Thes Saturday papers were numbered consecutively with the Wednesday papers, so that through June 25, 1692, Husbandry and Trade Im proved was issued twice a week. Occasionally more than one numbe was published on the date of issue. Thus, Nos. 19 and 21 each i dated June 11, 1692. No. 23 is dated June 25, 1692; and No. 24, Jan uary 20, 1693. The author explains this hiatus as being the result o pecuniary difficulties; " but now having a contribution of a guinea a year from some gentlemen and expecting it from more, I go on, and shall sell them for a penny each." Houghton does not give the names of the " gentlemen " who believed enough in the value of his undertaking to give him a guinea apiece, but we can guess them pretty well from the signatures to the "testification" dated November 11,

691, which was included in the first issue of the modest little peri-
dical. It was as follows:

NOVEMBER 11, 1691.

*These are to testify our knowledge of the approved abilities and industry
f* Mr. JOHN HOUGHTON, *citizen of* LONDON, *and fellow of the* ROYAL
OCIETY *there, in the discovery and collection of* matters *worthy observation,
nd more particularly such as relate to the* improvement *of* HUSBANDRY *and*
RADE. *Towards his furtherance wherein, and in his laudable inclination
lready experienc'd, and now further design'd, to the communicating the effects
iereof to the* publick; *we do hereby most willingly give him this* testimony
' our *knowledge and esteem, in order to the recommending him to the* notice,
ssistance, and *encouragement of all gentlemen and others, desirous of pro-
oting the endeavours of a person so qualify'd and dispos'd to the service of
ls country.*

obert Southwell.	Nehemiah Grew.
homas Meres.	Edward Tyson.
)hn Hopkins.	Frederick Slare.
eter Pett.	Robert Pitt.
nthony Deane.	Hans Sloane.
)hn Evelyn.	Hugh Chamberlen.
homas Henshaw.	William Hewer.
braham Hill.	Henry Whistler.
imuel Pepys.	Alexander Pitfield.
)hn Creed.	Richard Wailer.
homas Gale.	Edward Haynes.
)hn Scott.	Thomas Langham.
obert Plot.	Francis Lodwick.
aniel Coxe.	Edmund Hally.

These things, consider'd, such like may be expected, at least *once a* week,
om

England's *hearty well-wisher,*
JOHN HOUGHTON, F. R. S.
WEDNESDAY.

It is very significant of their breadth of vision that such men as
amuel Pepys, the brilliant diarist; Edmund Halley, the astrono-
er, at that time secretary of the Royal Society; Hans Sloane,
under of the Botanic Garden, whose collections formed the nucleus
: the British Museum—that such men as these should recognize
ie fundamental importance of agriculture to England's best in-
rests.

The list contains the names of various officers of the Royal So-
ety, John Hopkins, at one time its president; Abraham Hill, treas-
er; Robert Plot, Edmund Halley, and Nehemiah Grew, secre-
ries.

Varied interests also are represented. Anthony Deane was a ship-
uilder and a great friend of Pepys; Thomas Henshaw was a charter
ember of the Royal Society, and a scholar, having written a history
: China; John Creed was deputy treasurer of the Fleet, Thomas

Gale was dean of York and a biblical scholar of note; John Sco
was probably the canon of St. Pauls, although, as there were sever
John Scotts living, one can not be sure which one he was; Dan
Coxe, Hugh Chamberlen, Robert Pitt, Frederick Slare, and Edwa
Tyson were physicians, the latter having written several monograp
on animals. Nehemiah Grew was a vegetable physiologist, and b
some considered the first observer of sex in plants. His work w
recognized by Linnaeus who named a genus after him. Edmu
Halley, besides being an astronomer, is thought to have originat
by his suggestion Newton's Principia, which he introduced to t
Royal Society.

The papers abound in sage observations as well as sound dc
trine on agricultural matters, as, for instance, when Houghto
remarks at the end of a comprehensive argument on the advanta
of inclosures over commons: "The ground is never weary of doi
good, if well fed and well worked."

Houghton's observations on the potato are especially interestin
as the field cultivation of the plant began about the time Hought
wrote, or from 1680 to 1690. He said in number 386, December 1
1699:

"*Potatoe* is a *bacciferous* herb, with *esculent* roots, bearing winged leaves a
a *bell* flower.

This I have been inform'd was brought first out of *Virginia* by *Sir Wal*
Raleigh, and he stopping at *Ireland*, some was planted there, where it thriv
very well to good purpose; for in their succeeding wars, when all the co
above-ground was destroyed, this supported them; for the soldiers, unless th
had dug up all the ground where they grew, and almost sifted it, could n
extirpate them; from thence they were brought to *Lancashire*, where they a
very numerous and now they begin to spread all the kingdom over.

They are a pleasant food boil'd or roasted, and eaten with butter and sug

There is a sort brought from *Spain* that are of a longer form, and are mo
luscious, than ours; they are much set by, and are sold for six pence or eig
pence the pound.

Whether these differ more than what is caused by the different soils th
grow in, I know not.

They are easily increased by cutting the root in several pieces; for each pie
will grow. They require a good fat garden mold, but will grow tolerably in ar
Surely in some places it may be worth while to plant abundance, if it we
only to feed their cattle and poultry. I believe the more husbandries we ha
the better."

It is utterly impossible, however, to give an accurate idea of t
mingled quaintness and sagacity of these papers without an und
amount of quotation, and it seems best to reproduce Houghton
"Epitome of the 19 volumes.[1] A farewell," with which be brin

---

[1] Houghton refers to his work by volume numbers but the separate issues have c
secutive numbers only.

he work to a close, rather than to make quotations at random. This epitome " is dated September 24, 1703, and gives a very fair sumary of the contents of the volumes, but with the exception of the st three paragraphs, lacks entirely the zest and vigor of the papers hemselves. It is as follows:

In my first volume is the nature of *earth, water, air* and *fire*, with their ffects and reasons for many of their operations: In my second, *natural his-ory*, with the *taxes, acres, houses*, etc. in each county of *England* and *Wales*, ith notes particularly of *Yorkshire* and *Derbyshire:* In my third the doctrine f *fermentation*, history of cyder and clay: In my fourth, a continuation of *lay*, and all its uses I could learn, with the history of *wheat:* In my fifth, the istory of *joint-stocks* and *kine:* In my sixth, I went on about kine, showing the se and manufacture of most parts, the doctrine of *nutrition, circulation* of the lood, with reasons of its ascent, and manner of growing of *bones* and other arts: In my seventh, I have carried on the history of *kine* in discourses upon *lood, butter, cheese, cows, cream, dung, milk, urine, whey*, and other particurs: In my eighth, is an account of the ships that came from abroad to *London* rom *new year's day*, 1694 to the same day 1695, with the number from each rince's territories, and of all the goods imported that year, mentioned in the lls of entry, with the quantities from each place, and all together.

Upon these I have made some notes *natural* and *political*, as the advantages f a *coalition* with *Scotland*, the true case of *free-trade, a regulated company* nd a *joint-stock* with an easy and certain method for mending the roads, etc. n my ninth, are histories of imported *stones, glass, salt*, and a farther account f roads: In my tenth, a farther account of *salt*, the history of *nitre, gun-owder, profits* of the *Indian* trade, history of *vitriol, copperas, brimstone, oker, tt* and *coal:* In my eleventh, are the farther histories of *coal*, also of *arsenick, ipis, haematities* and the 7 metals, with a description of all things I could learn ere made from them, with some discourses about *air, alkali, colours, exchange*, re, the manner of fluxing with *mercury, money, poison, trade, pumps*, and *ood.* In my twelfth, I have given a division of plants, the history of *mush-ooms, wheat, rye, barley, oats, canes*, and *sugar*, with all the historical and olitical notes relating to them I could think proper; as the *quantum* of *beer* nd *ale* that paid excise in divers years, the quantity of malt brought from *Jare* by water in a year, with a discourse about navigable rivers, and making hem so: the difference about water and land carriage, with the quantities of *ugar* and other things imported. In my thirteenth, I have given the history f *saffron, onions, tuberose, asarum, ros solis, gentian, aloe*, with the manner of mbalming and managing the dead in many countries; the history of *kelp, ladder, spurry, rhabarb, buckwheat, hemp*, and *flax:* As also the history of *nen, thread, tape, lace, twine, dying, printing, maps, pictures, oil-cloth, buck-ams, pasteboard, playing-cards, rags, paper-hangings*, the *printer's office* with he life of *Bleau*, &c. In my fourteenth, is the history of *hops, weld* or *wood, nnise, turnips, carrots, parsnips, caraway-seeds, pellitory* of Spain, *polymoun-ain, dittany, teasel, coloquintida, scammony, tobacco, birthwort, potato*, and he *vine;* with a proposal how to enrich *England* and employ the poor. In my fteenth, is the history of *jessamine, capers, pomgranates, oranges, lemons, lumbs, prunellos, prunes, olives*, with a proposal to preserve health in hot lantations; also of the *turpentine* and *fir-tree, mastich, clove, nutmeg cina-won, bey, yew, holly, juniper, sassafras, walnut, almond, hazel, chestnut, beach, acao* or *chocolate*, and *coffee.* In my sixteenth, is the history of *cotton* and the *oak*, and all things I could think useful to say of it; particularly demonstrative arguments for the destruction of *wood* and the proposal how we shall never want naval stores. In my seventeenth, is the history of *alder, cedar, cypress, elm, ash, maple, birch, aspen, poplar, abele, willow, lime-tree,* and *guaiacum* or *lignum vitae.* In my eighteenth, is a history of *bees, silkworms, oysters, fish,* as *whales, sturgeon, codfish, mackerel, herrings, sprats, pilchards, anchoveys, turbets, salmons:* Also an account of the *fishing-trade,* with proposals how to improve it both at home and abroad. In my nineteenth, is a history of *birds,* viz. *eagles, hawks* and *falconry, woodcocks,* with a conjecture how birds fly over sea. The *estrich,* with the manner of taking fowl in the *Islands* of *Feroe, Hirta,* and *Stacka Donna,* with the strange and difficult manner of climbing rocks by those inhabitants: and having also gone thro' the principal histories of the *mineral, vegetable* and *animal* kingdoms, except *beasts,* of which I have only given the history of *kine,* but that I have done very largely, and designed to have carried on this twentieth volume with the histories of the *horse, sheep, goat, stag, hog, coney, castor, dog,* &c and then have given over.

But truly, since (beside my trade as an *apothecary,* wherein I have always been and still am diligent) I have fallen to the selling of *coffee, tea* and *chocolate* in some considerable degree, I cannot without great Inconvenience to my private affairs, which must not be neglected, spare time to carry on this history so well as I would do; and besides considering what the antients have done in this affair, as also the moderns, viz. Mr. *Ray, Blundevill, Markam, Solleysel,* in his *Compleate Horseman,* and divers others, I refer it to some that has more leisure and skill; altho' I have endeavoured to make it the best account of *trade* upon the best and most sure foot that ever has yet been published, and I could hear of. And all this I have done for the benefit of my country; not doubting but if those in authority will consider, and apply what I have writ for *England's* advantage, It may quickly be made the richest and happiest nation the sun sees.

But if these things are not, or will not be understood, I'll no ways fret myself, well knowing that I fare as well as a great many *persons,* whose *charms* are not heard, tho' they *charm* ever so wisely.

I most humbly and heartily thank all sorts of my assistants, and shall testify my respects to them whenever I have opportunity; and I must particularly say, for a great many of the *Royal Society,* that they have been genteel, kind, and ready to *communicate* most knowledges I have asked them, in their power; without which, I own, I could not have carried on a great deal of what I have written.

Thus I take leave of these papers, wishing that *knowledge* may cover the *earth* as the *water* covers the sea, which is the hearty prayer of the World's well wisher,

JOHN HOUGHTON, F. R. S.

INDEX.

Compiled by H. S. Parsons, Library of Congress.

ANNUAL REPORT

OF THE

ERICAN HISTORICAL ASSOCIATION

FOR

THE YEAR 1920

IN ONE VOLUME
AND A SUPPLEMENTAL VOLUME

WASHINGTON
GOVERNMENT PRINTING OFFICE
1925

LETTER OF SUBMITTAL

he Congress of the United States:

accordance with the act of incorporation of the American His-
al Association, approved January 4, 1889, I have the honor to
it to Congress the annual report of the association for the year
. I have the honor to be,

Very respectfully, your obedient servant,

CHARLES D. WALCOTT, *Secretary.*

3

ACT OF INCORPORATION

; it enacted by the Senate and House of Representatives of the 'ed States of America in Congress assembled, That Andrew D. te, of Ithaca, in the State of New York; George Bancroft, of hington, in the District of Columbia; Justin Winsor, of Cambridge, ae State of Massachusetts; William F. Poole, of Chicago, in the e of Illinois; Herbert B. Adams, of Baltimore, in the State of yland; Clarence W. Bowen, of Brooklyn, in the State of New x, their associates and successors, are hereby created, in the rict of Columbia, a body corporate and politic by the name of the rican Historical Association, for the promotion of historical ies, the collection and preservation of historical manuscripts, and :indred purposes in the interest of American history and of his- in America. Said association is authorized to hold real and onal estate in the District of Columbia so far only as may be ssary to its lawful ends to an amount not exceeding $500,000, to ot a constitution, and make by-laws not inconsistent with law. association shall have its principal office at Washington, in the rict of Columbia, and may hold its annual meetings in such places ae said incorporators shall determine. Said association shall re- annually to the Secretary of the Smithsonian Institution con- ing its proceedings and the condition of historical study in rica. Said secretary shall communicate to Congress the whole uch report, or such portions thereof as he shall see fit. The Re- s of the Smithsonian Institution are authorized to permit said ciation to deposit its collections, manuscripts, books, pamphlets, other material for history in the Smithsonian Institution or in National Museum at their discretion, upon such conditions and ar such rules as they shall prescribe.

Approved, January 4, 1889.]

5

LETTER OF TRANSMITTAL

AMERICAN HISTORICAL ASSOCIATION,
Washington, D. C., June 30, 1921.

ʀ: As provided by law, we have the honor to submit herewith
Annual Report of the American Historical Association for the
1920. This report includes the usual statement, in detail, of the
eedings of the association during the year 1920 and certain
ortant papers read at the annual meeting in December. A sup-
lental volume contains a bibliography of writings on American
ory during the year 1920, compiled by Miss Grace Gardner
in.

Very respectfully yours,

H. BARRETT LEARNED,
Chairman of the Committee on Publications.
ALLEN R. BOYD, *Editor.*

ɔ the SECRETARY OF THE SMITHSONIAN INSTITUTION,
Washington, D. C.

7

CONTENTS

CONSTITUTION

I

The name of this society shall be the American Historical Association.

II

Its object shall be the promotion of historical studies.

III

Any person approved by the executive council may become a member by paying
, and after the first year may continue a member by paying an annual fee of $3.
ι payment of $50 any person may become a life member, exempt from fees. Per-
ıs not resident in the United States may be elected as honorary or corresponding
ɪmbers and be exempt from the payment of fees.

IV

The officers shall be a president, two vice presidents, a secretary, a treasurer, an
istant secretary-treasurer, and an editor.
The president, vice presidents, secretary, and treasurer shall be elected by ballot
each regular annual meeting in the manner provided in the by-laws.
The assistant secretary-treasurer and the editor shall be elected by the executive
ʋncil. They shall perform such duties and receive such compensation as the
ıncil may determine.

V

There shall be an executive council, constituted as follows:
ɪ. The president, the vice presidents, the secretary, and the treasurer.
ʔ. Elected members, eight in number, to be chosen annually in the same manner
the officers of the association.
ʒ. The former presidents; but a former president shall be entitled to vote for the
ee years succeeding the expiration of his term as president, and no longer.

VI

The executive council shall conduct the business, manage the property, and care
the general interests of the association. In the exercise of its proper functions,
ɪ council may appoint such committees, commissions, and boards as it may deem
ɪessary. The council shall make a full report of its activities to the annual meet-
: of the association. The association may by vote at any annual meeting instruct
ɪ executive council to discontinue or enter upon any activity, and may take such
er action in directing the affairs of the association as it may deem necessary and
ɪper.

VII

ʔhis constitution may be amended at any annual meeting, notice of such amend-
nt having been given at the previous annual meeting or the proposed amendment
ɪing received the approval of the executive council.

BY-LAWS

I

The officers provided for by the constitution shall have the duties and perform the functions customarily attached to their respective offices with such others as may from time to time be prescribed.

II

A nomination committee of five members shall be chosen at each annual business meeting in the manner hereafter provided for the election of officers of the association. At such convenient time prior to the 15th of September as it may determine, it shall invite every member to express to it his preference regarding every office to be filled by election at the ensuing annual business meeting and regarding the composition of the new nominating committee then to be chosen. It shall publish and mail to each member at least one month prior to the annual business meeting such nominations as it may determine upon for each elective office and for the next nominating committee. It shall prepare for use at the annual business meeting an official ballot containing, as candidates for each office or committee membership to be filled thereat, the names of its nominees and also the names of any other nominees which may be proposed to the chairman of the committee in writing by 20 or more members of the association at least one day before the annual business meeting, but such nominations by petition shall not be presented until after the committee shall have reported its nominations to the association, as provided for in the present by-law. The official ballot shall also provide under each office a blank space for voting for such further nominees as any member may present from the floor at the time of the election.

III

The annual election of officers and the choice of a nominating committee for the ensuing year shall be conducted by the use of an official ballot prepared as described in by-law II.

IV

The association authorizes the payment of traveling expenses incurred by the voting members of the council attending one meeting of that body a year, this meeting to be other than that held in connection with the annual meeting of the association.

The council may provide for the payment of expenses incurred by the secretary, the assistant secretary-treasurer, and the editor in such travel as may be necessary to the transaction of the association's business.

12

AMERICAN HISTORICAL ASSOCIATION

anized at Saratoga, N. Y., September 10, 1884. Incorporated by Congress, January 4, 1889.

WILLIAM MILLIGAN SLOANE, Ph. D., L. H. D., LL. D.
Columbia University

WILLIAM ARCHIBALD DUNNING, Ph. D., LL. D.
Columbia University

ANDREW C. McLAUGHLIN, A. M., LL. B., LL. D.
University of Chicago

GEORGE LINCOLN BURR, LL. D., Litt. D.
Cornell University

WORTHINGTON C. FORD, A. M.
Massachusetts Historical Society

WILLIAM ROSCOE THAYER, LL. D., Litt. D., L. H. D.
Cambridge

EDWARD CHANNING, Ph. D.
Harvard University

(Elected Councilors)

JAMES T. SHOTWELL, Ph. D.
Columbia University

RUTH PUTNAM, B. Litt.
Washington

ARTHUR L. CROSS, Ph. D.
University of Michigan

SIDNEY B. FAY, Ph. D.
Smith College

CARL RUSSELL FISH, Ph. D.
University of Wisconsin

CARLTON J. H. HAYES, Ph. D.
Columbia University

FREDERIC L. PAXSON, Ph. D.
University of Wisconsin

ST. GEORGE L. SIOUSSAT, Ph. D.
University of Pennsylvania

PACIFIC COAST BRANCH

TERMS OF OFFICE

(Deceased officers are marked thus: †)

---

†ANDREW DICKSON WHITE, L. H. D., LL. D., D. C. L., 1884–1885.
†GEORGE BANCROFT, LL. D., 1885–1886.
†JUSTIN WINSOR, LL. D., 1886–1887.
†WILLIAM FREDERICK POOLE, LL. D., 1887–1888.
†CHARLES KENDALL ADAMS, LL. D., 1888–1889.
†JOHN JAY, LL. D., 1889–1890.
†WILLIAM WIRT HENRY, LL. D., 1890–1891.
†JAMES BURRILL ANGELL, LL. D., 1891–1893.
†HENRY ADAMS, LL. D., 1893–1894.
†GEORGE FRISBIE HOAR, LL. D., 1895.
†RICHARD SALTER STORRS, D. D., LL. D., 1896.
†JAMES SCHOULER, LL. D., 1897.
†GEORGE PARK FISHER, D. D., LL. D., 1898.
 JAMES FORD RHODES, LL. D., D. LITT., 1899.
†EDWARD EGGLESTON, L. H. D., 1900.
†CHARLES FRANCIS ADAMS, LL. D., 1901.
†ALFRED THAYER MAHAN, D. C. L., LL. D., 1902.
†HENRY CHARLES LEA, LL. D., 1903.
†GOLDWIN SMITH, D. C. L., LL. D., 1904.
 JOHN BACH McMASTER, PH. D., LITT. D., LL. D., 1905.
 SIMEON E. BALDWIN, LL. D., 1906.
 J. FRANKLIN JAMESON, PH. D., LL. D., LITT. D., 1907.
 GEORGE BURTON ADAMS, PH. D., LITT. D., 1908
 ALBERT BUSHNELL HART, PH. D., LL. D., LITT. D., 1909.
 FREDERICK JACKSON TURNER, PH. D., LL. D., LITT. D., 1910.
 WILLIAM MILLIGAN SLOANE, PH. D., L. H. D., LL. D., 1911
†THEODORE ROOSEVELT, LL. D., D. C. L., 1912.
 WILLIAM ARCHIBALD DUNNING, PH. D., LL. D., 1913.
 ANDREW C. McLAUGHLIN, A. M., LL. B., LL. D., 1914
†H. MORSE STEPHENS, M. A., LITT. D., 1915.
 GEORGE LINCOLN BURR, LL. D., LITT. D., 1916.
 WORTHINGTON C. FORD, A. M., 1917.
 WILLIAM ROSCOE THAYER, LL. D., LITT. D., L. H. D., 1918–1919.
 EDWARD CHANNING, PH. D., 1920.

†JUSTIN WINSOR, LL. D., 1884–1886.
†CHARLES KENDALL ADAMS, LL. D., 1884–1888.
†WILLIAM FREDERICK POOLE, LL. D., 1886–1887.
†JOHN JAY, LL. D., 1887–1889.
†WILLIAM WIRT HENRY, LL. D., 1888–1890.
†JAMES BURRILL ANGELL, LL. D., 1889–1891.
†HENRY ADAMS, LL D., 1890–1893.
†EDWARD GAY MASON, A. M., 1891–1894.
†GEORGE FRISBIE HOAR, LL. D., 1894.
†RICHARD SALTER STORRS, D. D., LL. D., 1895.
†JAMES SCHOULER, LL. D., 1895–1896.
†GEORGE PARK FISHER, D. D., LL. D., 1896–1897.
 JAMES FORD RHODES, LL. D., D. LITT., 1897–1898.
†EDWARD EGGLESTON, L. H. D., 1898–1899.
†MOSES COIT TYLER, L. H. D., LL. D., 1899–1900.

†CHARLES FRANCIS ADAMS, LL. D., 1900.
†HERBERT BAXTER ADAMS, PH. D., LL. D., 1901.
†ALFRED THAYER MAHAN, D. C. L., LL. D., 1901.
†HENRY CHARLES LEA, LL. D., 1902.
†GOLDWIN SMITH, D. C. L., LL. D., 1902-1903.
†EDWARD McCRADY, LL. D., 1903.
JOHN BACH McMASTER, PH. D., LITT. D., LL. D., 1904.
SIMEON E. BALDWIN, LL. D., 1904-1905.
J. FRANKLIN JAMESON, PH. D., LL. D., LITT. D., 1905-1906.
GEORGE BURTON ADAMS, PH. D., LITT. D., 1906-1907.
ALBERT BUSHNELL HART, PH. D., LL. D., LITT. D., 1907-1908.
FREDERICK JACKSON TURNER, PH. D., LL. D., LITT. D., 1908-1909.
WILLIAM MILLIGAN SLOANE, PH. D., L. H. D., LL. D., 1909-1910.
†THEODORE ROOSEVELT, LL. D., D. C. L., 1910-1911.
WILLIAM ARCHIBALD DUNNING, PH. D., LL. D., 1911-1912.
ANDREW C. McLAUGHLIN, A. M., LL. B., LL. D., 1912-1913.
†H. MORSE STEPHENS, M. A., LITT. D., 1913-1914.
GEORGE LINCOLN BURR, LL. D., 1914-1915.
WORTHINGTON C. FORD, A. M., 1915-1916.
WILLIAM ROSCOE THAYER, LL. D., LITT. D., L. H. D., 1916-1917.
EDWARD CHANNING, PH. D., 1917-1919
JEAN JULES JUSSERAND, F. B. A., 1918-1920.

SECRETARIES

†HERBERT BAXTER ADAMS, PH. D., LL. D., 1884-1900.
†A. HOWARD CLARK, A. M., 1889-1908.
CHARLES HOMER HASKINS, PH. D., 1900-1913.
WALDO GIFFORD LELAND, A. M., 1908-1919.
EVARTS BOUTELL GREENE, PH. D., 1914-1919.
JOHN SPENCER BASSETT, PH. D., 1919-

TREASURERS

CLARENCE WINTHROP BOWEN, PH. D., 1884-1917.
CHARLES MOORE, PH. D., 1917-

CURATOR

A. HOWARD CLARK, A. M., 1889-1918.

EXECUTIVE COUNCIL

WILLIAM BABCOCK WEEDEN, A. M., 1884-1886.
CHARLES DEANE, LL. D., 1884-1887.
MOSES COIT TYLER, L. H. D., LL. D., 1884-1885.
EPHRAIM EMERTON, PH. D., 1884-1885.
FRANKLIN BOWDITCH DEXTER, A. M., LITT. D., 1885-1887.
WILLIAM FRANCIS ALLEN, A. M., 1885-1887.
WILLIAM WIRT HENRY, LL. D., 1886-1888.
RUTHERFORD BIRCHARD HAYES, LL. D., 1887-1888.
JOHN W. BURGESS, PH. D., LL. D., 1887-1891.
ARTHUR MARTIN WHEELER, A. M., LL. D., 1887-1889.
GEORGE PARK FISHER, D. D., LL. D., 1888-1891.
GEORGE BROWN GOODE, LL. D., 1889-1896.
JOHN GEORGE BOURINOT, C. M. G., D. C. L., LL. D., 1889-1894.
JOHN BACH McMASTER, PH. D., LITT. D., LL. D., 1891-1894.
GEORGE BURTON ADAMS, PH. D., LITT. D., 1891-1897; 1898-1901.
THEODORE ROOSEVELT, LL. D., D. C. L., 1894-1895.
JABEZ LAMAR MONROE CURRY, LL. D., 1894-1895.
H. MORSE STEPHENS, M. A., LITT. D., 1895-1899.
FREDERICK JACKSON TURNER, PH. D., LL. D., LITT. D., 1895-1899; 1901-1904.
EDWARD MINOR GALLAUDET, PH. D., LL. D., 1896-1897.
MELVILLE WESTON FULLER, LL. D., 1897-1900.
ALBERT BUSHNELL HART, PH. D., LITT. D., 1897-1900.
ANDREW C. McLAUGHLIN, A. M., LL. B., LL. D., 1898-1901; 1903-1906.
WILLIAM ARCHIBALD DUNNING, PH. D., LL. D., 1899-1902.
PETER WHITE, A. M., 1899-1902.

97244°—25——2

18   AMERICAN HISTORICAL ASSOCIATION

J. FRANKLIN JAMESON, Ph. D., LL. D., Litt. D., 1900–1903.
A. LAWRENCE LOWELL, Ph. D., LL. D., 1900–1903.
HERBERT PUTNAM, Litt. D., LL. D., 1901–1904.
GEORGE LINCOLN BURR, LL. D., 1902–1905.
EDWARD POTTS CHEYNEY, LL. D., 1902–1905
†EDWARD G. BOURNE, Ph. D., 1903–1906.
†GEORGE P. GARRISON, Ph. D., 1904–1907.
†REUBEN GOLD THWAITES, LL. D., 1904–1907.
CHARLES McLEAN ANDREWS, Ph. D., L. H. D., 1905–1908.
JAMES HARVEY ROBINSON, Ph. D., 1905–1908.
WORTHINGTON CHAUNCEY FORD, A. M., 1906–1909.
WILLIAM MacDONALD, Ph. D., LL. D., 1906–1909.
MAX FARRAND, Ph. D., 1907–1910.
FRANK HEYWOOD HODDER, Ph. M., 1907–1910.
EVARTS BOUTELL GREENE, Ph. D., 1908–1911.
CHARLES HENRY HULL, Ph. D., 1908–1911.
FRANKLIN LAFAYETTE RILEY, A. M., Ph. D., 1909–1912.
EDWIN ERLE SPARKS, Ph. D., LL. D., 1909–1912.
JAMES ALBERT WOODBURN, Ph. D., LL. D., 1910–1913.
FRED MORROW FLING, Ph. D., 1910–1913.
HERMAN VANDENBURG AMES, Ph. D., 1911–1914.
DANA CARLETON MUNRO, A. M., 1911–1914.
ARCHIBALD CARY COOLIDGE, Ph. D., 1912–1914.
JOHN MARTIN VINCENT, Ph. D., LL. D., 1912–1915.
FREDERIC BANCROFT, Ph. D,, LL. D., 1913–1915.
CHARLES HOMER HASKINS, Ph. D., 1913–1916.
EUGENE C. BARKER, Ph. D., 1914–1917.
GUY S. FORD, B. L., Ph. D., 1914–1917.
ULRICH B. PHILLIPS, Ph. D., 1914–1917.
LUCY M. SALMON, A. M., L. H. D., 1915–1919.
SAMUEL B. HARDING, Ph. D., 1915–1919.
HENRY E. BOURNE, A. B., B. D., L. H. D., 1916–1920.
CHARLES MOORE, Ph. D., 1916–1917.
GEORGE M. WRONG, M. A., 1916–1920.
HERBERT E. BOLTON, B. L., Ph. D., 1917–1920.
WILLIAM E. DODD, Ph. D., 1917–1920.
WALTER L. FLEMING, M. S., Ph. D., 1917–1920.
WILLIAN E. LINGELBACH, Ph. D., 1917–1920.
JAMES T. SHOTWELL, Ph. D., 1919–
RUTH PUTNAM, B. Litt., 1919–
ARTHUR L. CROSS, Ph. D., 1920–
SIDNEY B. FAY, Ph. D., 1920–
CARL RUSSELL FISH, Ph. D., 1920–
CARLTON J. H. HAYES, Ph. D., 1920–
FREDERIC L. PAXSON, Ph. D., 1920–
ST. GEORGE L. SIOUSSAT, Ph. D., 1920–

OFFICERS AND COMMITTEES 1921

President.—Jean Jules Jusserand, the French Embassy, Washington, D. C.
First vice president.—Charles H. Haskins, Harvard University, Cambridge, Mass.
Second vice president.—Edward P. Cheyney, University of Pennsylvania, Philadelphia, Pa.
Secretary.—John S. Bassett, Smith College, Northampton, Mass.
Treasurer.—Charles Moore, Library of Congress, Washington, D. C.
Assistant secretary-treasurer.—Patty W. Washington, 1140 Woodward Building, Washington, D. C.
Editor.—Allen R. Boyd, Library of Congress, Washington, D. C.

EXECUTIVE COUNCIL

(in addition to above)

Elected members.—Arthur L. Cross, 705 South State Street, Ann Arbor, Mich.; Sidney B. Fay, 32 Paradise Road, Northampton, Mass.; Carl Russell Fish, 244 Lake Lawn Place, Madison, Wis.; Carlton J. H. Hayes, Columbia University, New York, N. Y.; Frederic L. Paxson, 2122 Van Hise Avenue, Madison, Wis.; Ruth Putnam, 2025 O Street NW., Washington, D. C.; James T. Shotwell, 407 West One hundred and seventeenth Street, New York, N. Y.; St. George L. Sioussat, University of Pennsylvania, Philadelphia, Pa.

Ex-presidents.—James Ford Rhodes, 392 Beacon Street, Boston, Mass.; John Bach McMaster, 2109 Delancy Place, Philadelphia, Pa.; Simeon E. Baldwin, 69 Church Street, New Haven, Conn.; J. Franklin Jameson, 1140 Woodward Building, Washington, D. C.; George Burton Adams, 57 Edgehill Road, New Haven, Conn.; Albert Bushnell Hart, Harvard University, Cambridge, Mass.; Frederick J. Turner, 7 Phillips Place, Cambridge, Mass.; William M. Sloane, Princeton, N. J.; William A. Dunning, Columbia University, New York, N.Y.; Andrew C. McLaughlin, University of Chicago, Chicago Ill.; George L. Burr, Cornell University, Ithaca, N.Y.; Worthington C. Ford, 1154 Boylston Street, Boston, Mass.; William Roscoe Thayer, 8 Berkeley Street, Cambridge, Mass.; Edward Channing, Harvard University, Cambridge, Mass.

STANDING EXECUTIVE COMMITTEES OF THE COUNCIL

Committee on agenda.—Charles H. Haskins, chairman (ex officio); Jean Jules Jusserand, Edward P. Cheyney (ex officio), John S. Bassett (ex officio), Charles Moore (ex officio), Arthur L. Cross, Sidney B. Fay, Carlton J. H. Hayes, Frederic L. Paxson.

Committee on meetings and relations.—John S. Bassett, chairman; Edward Channing, Carl Russell Fish, James T. Shotwell, Ruth Putnam.

Committee on finance.—Charles Moore, chairman; John S. Bassett, Sidney B. Fay, Frederic L. Paxson, St. George L. Sioussat.

Committee on appointments.—Jean Jules Jusserand, chairman; John S. Bassett, Edward P. Cheyney, Carl Russell Fish, Carlton J. H. Hayes.

Committee on disposition of records.—Waldo G. Leland, chairman, 1140 Woodward Building, Washington, D. C.; H. Barrett Learned, 2123 Bancroft Place, Washington, D. C.; C. O. Paullin, 1025 Fifteenth Street NW., Washington, D. C.

Committee to formulate rules for the George L. Beer prize.—William A. Dunning, chairman, Columbia University, New York, N. Y.; Marshall S. Brown, 19 Fairview Street, Yonkers, N. Y.; Edward S. Corwin, 115 Prospect Avenue, Princeton, N. J.

Committee on nominations.—Frank H. Hodder, chairman, 1115 Louisiana Street, Lawrence, Kans.; Henry E. Bourne, Western Reserve University, Cleveland, Ohio; William E. Dodd, 5757 Blackstone Avenue, Chicago, Ill.; Eloise Ellery, Vassar College, Poughkeepsie, N. Y.; William E. Lingelbach, University of Pennsylvania, Philadelphia, Pa.

Committee on program for the thirty-sixth annual meeting.—Evarts B. Greene, chairman, University of Illinois, Urbana, Ill. (appointed for one year); Charles Seymour, 127 Everit Street, New Haven, Conn. (appointed for two years); Walter L. Fleming, Vanderbilt University, Nashville, Tenn. (appointed for three years); Thomas M. Marshall, Washington University, St. Louis, Mo.; Norman M. Trenholme, University of Missouri, Columbia, Mo. Ex officio: Nils Andreas Olsen, secretary of the Agricultural History Society, Bureau of Farm Management, Department of Agriculture, Washington, D. C.; John C. Parish, secretary of the Conference of Historical Societies, State Historical Society of Iowa, Iowa City, Iowa.

Committee on local arrangements, thirty-sixth annual meeting.—William K. Bixby, chairman, Kings Highway and Lindell Avenue, St. Louis, Mo.; Mrs. Nettie H. Beauregard, Jefferson Memorial Building, St. Louis, Mo.; Ralph P. Bieber, Washington University, St. Louis, Mo.; Stella M. Drumm, Jefferson Memorial Building, St. Louis, Mo.: David R. Francis, 214 North Fourth Street, St. Louis, Mo.; Benjamin Gratz, Rialto Building, St. Louis, Mo.; John H. Gundlach, 3615 North Broadway, St. Louis, Mo.; Breckinridge Jones, 45 Portland Place, St. Louis, Mo.; Mrs. Robert McKittrick Jones, 6 Westmoreland Place, St. Louis, Mo.; Breckinridge Long, 5145 Lindell Boulevard, St. Louis, Mo.; Mrs. N. A. McMillan, 23 Portland Place, St. Louis, Mo.; Thomas M. Marshall, Washington University, St. Louis, Mo.; Charles P. Pettus, American Trust Co., St. Louis, Mo.; George R. Throop, Washington University, St. Louis, Mo.

Board of editors of the American Historical Review.—J. Franklin Jameson, managing editor, 1140 Woodward Building, Washington, D. C. (term expires 1925); Guy Stanton Ford, chairman, University of Minnesota, Minneapolis, Minn. (1926); Archibald C. Coolidge, 4 Randolph Hall, Cambridge, Mass. (1924); Williston Walker, Yale University, New Haven, Conn. (1923); Carl Becker, Cornell University, Ithaca, N. Y. (1922); Claude H. Van Tyne, 1942 Cambridge Road, Ann Arbor, Mich. (1921).

Historical manuscripts commission.—Justin H. Smith, chairman, 7 West Forty-third Street, New York, N. Y.; Annie H. Abel, 811 North M Street, Aberdeen, Wash., Eugene C. Barker, University of Texas, Austin, Tex.; Robert P. Brooks, University of Georgia, Athens, Ga.; Logan Esarey, Bloomington, Ind.; Gaillard Hunt, Department of State, Washington, D. C.

Committee on the Justin Winsor prize—Clive Day, chairman, Yale University, New Haven, Conn.; Isaac J. Cox, Northwestern University, Evanston, Ill.; Thomas F. Moran, Purdue University, West La Fayette, Ind.; Bernard C. Steiner, Enoch Pratt Free Library, Baltimore, Md.; William W. Sweet, 632 East Washington Street, Greencastle, Ind.

Committee on the Herbert Baxter Adams prize.—Conyers Read, chairman, 1218 Snyder Avenue, Philadelphia, Pa.; Charles H. McIlwain, 19 Francis Avenue, Cambridge, Mass.; David S. Muzzey, 492 Van Cortlandt Park Avenue, Yonkers, N. Y. Nellie Neilson, Mount Holyoke College, South Hadley, Mass.; Bernadotte E. Schmitt, 1938 East One hundred and sixteenth Street, Cleveland, Ohio; Wilbur H. Siebert, Ohio State University, Columbus, Ohio.

Committee on publications (all ex officio except the chairman).—H. Barrett Learned, chairman, 2123 Bancroft Place, Washington, D. C.; Allen R. Boyd, secretary, Library of Congress, Washington, D. C.; John S. Bassett, Smith College, Northampton, Mass.; J. Franklin Jameson, 1140 Woodward Building, Washington, D. C.; Justin H. Smith, 7 West Forty-third Street, New York, N. Y.; Rodney H. True, secretary Agricultural History Society, Macfarlane Hall of Botany, University of Pennsylvania, Philadelphia, Pa.

Committee on membership.—Thomas J. Wertenbaker, chairman, 111 Fitz Randolph Road, Princeton, N. J.; Louise Fargo Brown, 263 Mill Street, Poughkeepsie, N. Y.; Eugene H. Byrne, 240 Lake Lawn Place, Madison, Wis.; A. C. Krey, University of Minnesota, Minneapolis, Minn.; Frank E. Melvin, 737 Maine Street, Lawrence, Kans.; Richard A. Newhall, 353 Ellsworth Avenue, New Haven, Conn.; Charles W. Ramsdell, University of Texas, Austin, Tex.; Arthur P. Scott, University of Chicago, Chicago, Ill.; J. J. Van Nostrand, jr., University of California, Berkeley, Calif.; James E. Winston, Sophie Newcomb College, New Orleans, La.; George F. Zook, Bureau of Education, Washington, D. C. Associate members: Milledge L. Bonham, jr., Hamilton College, Clinton, N. Y.; Henry E. Bourne, Western Reserve University, Cleveland, Ohio; Julian P. Bretz, Cornell University, Ithaca, N. Y.; Robert P. Brooks, University of Georgia, Athens, Ga.; Sarah A. Dynes, State Normal School, Trenton, N. J.; Austin P. Evans, Columbia University, New York, N. Y.; J. Montgomery Gambrill, Teachers College, Columbia University, New York, N. Y.; Sheldon J. Howe, Princeton University, Princeton, N. J.; M. Berna Hunt, 127 Summit Avenue, Jersey City, N. J.; Laurence M. Larson, University of Illinois, Urbana, Ill.; John H. Logan, Rutgers College, New Brunswick, N. J.; Margaret J. Mitchell, University of Oklahoma, Norman, Okla.; Laurence B. Packard, University of Rochester, Rochester, N. Y.; George Petrie, Auburn, Ala.; Walter Prichard, Baton Rouge, La.; Charles H. Rammelkamp, Illinois College, Jacksonville, Ill.; Morgan P. Robinson, 113 South Third Street, Richmond, Va.; Louis M. Sears, Purdue University, West La Fayette, Ind.; Augustus H. Shearer, the Grosvenor Library, Buffalo, N. Y.; Earl E. Sperry, Syracuse University, Syracuse, N. Y.; David Y. Thomas, University of Arkansas, Fayetteville, Ark.; Frederic L. Thompson, 63 South Pleasant Street, Amherst, Mass.; Norman M. Trenholme, University of Missouri, Columbia, Mo.; James A. Woodburn, Indiana University, Bloomington, Ind.; Jesse E. Wrench, 1815 University Avenue, Columbia, Mo.; John P. Wynne, Agricultural College, Miss.

Conference of historical societies.—George S. Godard, chairman,[1] Connecticut State Library, Hartford, Conn.; John C. Parish, secretary State Historical Society of Iowa, Iowa City, Iowa.

COMMITTEES APPOINTED BY THE CONFERENCE

Committee on bibliography of historical societies.—Joseph Schafer, chairman, State Historical Society of Wisconsin, Madison, Wis.; Julius H. Tuttle, Massachusetts Historical Society, Boston, Mass.; A. P. C. Griffin, Chief Assistant Librarian, Library of Congress, Washington, D. C.

Committee on handbook of historical societies.—George N. Fuller, secretary of Michigan Historical Commission, Lansing, Mich.; Solon J. Buck, superintendent of Minnesota Historical Society, St. Paul, Minn.; John C. Parish, State Historical Society of Iowa, Iowa City, Iowa.

Committee on national archives.—J. Franklin Jameson, chairman, 1140 Woodward Building, Washington D. C.; Charles Moore, Library of Congress, Washington, D. C.; Col. Oliver L. Spaulding, jr., United States Army, Chief of Historical Branch, General Staff, Washington, D. C.

---

[1] Elected at the business meeting of the conference of historical societies.

Committee on bibliography.—George M. Dutcher, chairman, Wesleyan University, Middletown, Conn.; William H. Allison, Colgate University, Hamilton, N. Y.; Sidney B. Fay, 32 Paradise Road, Northampton, Mass.; Augustus H. Shearer, the Grosvenor Library, Buffalo, N. Y.; Henry R. Shipman, 27 Mercer Street, Princeton, N. J.

Subcommittee on the bibliography of American travel.—Solon J. Buck, Minnesota Historical Society, St. Paul, Minn.; M. M. Quaife, State Historical Library, Madison, Wis.; Benjamin F. Shambaugh, State University of Iowa, Iowa City, Iowa.

Public archives commission.—Victor H. Paltsits, chairman, 48 Whitson Street, Forest Hills Gardens, Long Island, N. Y.; Solon J. Buck, Minnesota Historical Society, St. Paul, Minn.; R. D. W. Connor, North Carolina Historical Commission, Raleigh, N. C.; Waldo G. Leland, 1140 Woodward Building, Washington, D. C.; Arnold J. F. van Laer, 433 Western Avenue, Albany, N. Y.

Committee on obtaining transcripts from foreign archives.—J. Franklin Jameson, chairman, 1140 Woodward Building, Washington, D. C.; Charles M. Andrews, 424 St. Ronan Street, New Haven, Conn.; Waldo G. Leland, 1140 Woodward Building, Washington, D. C.

Committee on military history.—Brig. Gen. Eben Swift, United States Army, retired, chairman, 1823 Nineteenth Street NW., Washington, D. C.; Allen R. Boyd, Library of Congress, Washington, D. C.; R. B. House, North Carolina Historical Commission, Raleigh, N. C.; Eben Putnam, Wellesley Farms, Mass.; Col. Oliver L. Spaulding, jr., United States Army, Chief of Historical Branch, General Staff, Washington, D. C.

Committee on hereditary patriotic societies.—Dixon R. Fox, chairman, Columbia University, New York, N. Y.; Natalie S. Lincoln, editor D. A. R., Memorial Continental Hall, Washington, D. C.; Harry Brent Mackoy, Covington, Ky.; Mrs. Annie L. Sioussat, Arundel Club, Baltimore, Md.; R. C. Ballard Thruston, 1000 Columbia Building, Louisville, Ky.

Committee on service.—J. Franklin Jameson, chairman, 1140 Woodward Building, Washington, D. C.; Elbert J. Benton, Western Reserve University, Cleveland, Ohio; Clarence S. Brigham, American Antiquarian Society, Worcester, Mass.; Worthington C. Ford, Massachusetts Historical Society, 1154 Boylston Street, Boston, Mass.; Arthur C. Howland, University of Pennsylvania, Philadelphia, Pa.; Albert E. McKinley, University of Pennsylvania, Philadelphia, Pa.; James Sullivan, State Education Building, Albany, N. Y.

Board of editors of The Historical Outlook.—Albert E. McKinley, managing editor, University of Pennsylvania, Philadelphia, Pa.; Edgar Dawson, Hunter College, New York, N. Y.; Sarah A. Dynes, State Normal School, Trenton, N. J.; Daniel C. Knowlton, the Lincoln School, 646 Park Avenue, New York, N. Y.; Laurence M. Larson, University of Illinois, Urbana, Ill.; William L. Westermann, 116 Schuyler Place, Ithaca, N. Y.

Committee on history teaching in the schools.—Henry Johnson, chairman, Teachers College, Columbia University, New York, N. Y.; Henry E. Bourne, Western Reserve University, Cleveland, Ohio; Philip P. Chase, 241 Highland Street, Milton, Mass.; Guy Stanton Ford, University of Minnesota, Minneapolis, Minn.; Daniel C. Knowlton, the Lincoln School, 646 Park Avenue, New York, N. Y.; Albert E. McKinley, University of Pennsylvania, Philadelphia, Pa.; Eugene M. Violette, Kirksville, Mo.

SPECIAL COMMITTEES OF THE ASSOCIATION

Committee on bibliography of modern English history.—Edward P. Cheyney, chairman, University of Pennsylvania, Philadelphia, Pa.; Arthur L. Cross, 705 South State Street, Ann Arbor, Mich.; Roger B. Merriman, 175 Brattle Street, Cambridge, Mass.; Wallace Notestein, 237 Goldwin Smith Hall, Ithaca, N. Y.; Conyers Read, 1218 Snyder Avenue, Philadelphia, Pa.

Committee on the historical congress at Rio de Janeiro.—Bernard Moses, honorary chairman, care London Co. and Westminster Bank, 22 Place Vendome, Paris, France; Percy A. Martin, acting chairman, Leland Stanford Junior University, Stanford University, Calif.; Julius Klein, secretary, Bureau of Foreign and Domestic Commerce, Department of Commerce, Washington, D. C.; Charles Lyon Chandler, Corn Exchange National Bank, Philadelphia, Pa.; Charles H. Cunningham, University of Texas, Austin, Tex.; Manoel de Oliveira Lima, 3536 Thirteenth Street NW., Washington, D. C.; Edwin V. Morgan, American Embassy, Rio de Janeiro, Brazil; Constantine E. McGuire, Inter-American High Commission, Washington, D. C.; William L. Schurz, 606 East Ann Street, Ann Arbor, Mich.

Committee on the documentary historical publications of the United States.—J. Franklin Jameson, chairman, 1140 Woodward Building, Washington, D. C.; Charles Moore, Library of Congress, Washington, D. C.

Committee on the writing of history.—Ambassador Jean Jules Jusserand, chairman, French Embassy, Washington, D. C.; Charles W. Colby, 253 Broadway, New York, N. Y.; Wilbur C. Abbott, 219 Livingston Street, New Haven, Conn.

Committee to cooperate with the Peoples of America Society in the study of race elements in the United States.—John S. Bassett, chairman; Frederic L. Paxson.

ORGANIZATION AND ACTIVITIES

The American Historical Association is the national organization for the promotion of historical writing and studies in the United States. It was founded in 1884 by a group of representative scholars, and in 1889 was chartered by Congress. Its national character is emphasized by fixing its principal office in Washington and by providing for the publication of its annual reports by the United States Government through the secretary of the Smithsonian Institution. The membership of the association, at present about 2,500, is drawn from every State in the Union, as well as from Canada and South America. It includes representatives of all the professions and many of the various business and commercial pursuits. To all who desire to promote the development of history—local, national, or general—and to all who believe that a correct knowledge of the past is essential to a right understanding of the present the association makes a strong appeal through its publications and other activities.

The meetings of the association are held annually during the last week in December in cities so chosen as to accommodate in turn the members living in different parts of the country, and the average attendance is about 400. The meetings afford an opportunity for members to become personally acquainted and to discuss matters in which they have a common interest.

The principal publications of the association are the annual report and the American Historical Review. The former, usually in two volumes, is printed for the association by the Government and is distributed free to all members who desire it. It contains the proceedings of the association, including the more important papers read at the annual meetings, as well as valuable collections of documents, edited by the historical manuscripts commission; reports on American archives, prepared by the public archives commission; bibliographical contributions; reports on history teaching, on the activities of historical societies, and other agencies, etc.; and an annual group of papers on agricultural history contributed by the Agricultural History Society. The American Historical Review is the official organ of the association and the recognized organ of the historical profession in the United States. It is published quarterly, each number containing about 200 pages. It presents to the reader authoritative articles, critical reviews of important new works on history, notices of inedited documents, and the news of all other kinds of historical activities. The Review is indispensable to all who wish to keep abreast of the progress of historical scholarship, and is of much value and interest to the general reader. It is distributed free to all members of the association.

For the encouragement of historical research the association offers two biennial prizes, each of $200, for the best printed or manuscript monograph in the English language submitted by a writer residing in the Western Hemisphere who has not achieved an established reputation. The Justin Winsor prize, offered in the even years, is awarded to an essay in the history of the Western Hemisphere, including the insular possessions of the United States. In odd years the Herbert Baxter Adams prize is awarded for an essay in the history of the Eastern Hemisphere.

To the subject of history teaching the association has devoted much and consistent attention through conferences held at the annual meetings, the investigations of committees, and the preparation of reports. The association appoints the board of editors of The Historical Outlook, thus assuming a certain responsibility for that valuable organ of the history-teaching profession. At the close of the war a special committee was appointed on the revision of the historical program in all schools under college grade.

The association maintains close relations with the State and local historical societies through a conference organized under the auspices of the association and holding a meeting each year in connection with the annual meeting of the association. In this meeting of delegates the various societies discuss such problems as the collection and editing of historical material, the maintenance of museums and libraries, the fostering of popular interest in historical matters, the marking of sites, the observance of historical anniversaries, etc. The proceedings of the conference are printed in the annual reports of the association.

The Pacific Coast Branch of the association, organized in 1904, affords an opportunity for the members living in the Far West to have meetings and an organization of their own while retaining full membership in the parent body. In 1915 the association met with the branch in San Francisco, Berkeley, and Palo Alto in celebration of the opening of the Panama Canal. The proceedings of this meeting, devoted to the history of the Pacific and the countries about it, have been published in a separate volume.

From the first the association has pursued the policy of inviting to its membership not only those professionally or otherwise actively engaged in historical work, but also those whose interest in history or in the advancement of historical science is such that they wish to ally themselves with the association in the furtherance of its various objects. Thus the association counts among its members lawyers, clergymen, editors, publishers, physicians, officers of the Army and Navy, merchants, bankers, and farmers, all of whom find material of especial interest in the publications of the association.

Membership in the association is obtained through election by the executive council, upon nomination by a member or by direct application. The annual dues are $3, there being no initiation fee. The fee for life membership is $50, which secures exemption from all annual dues.

Inquiries respecting the association, its work, publications, prizes, meetings, memberships, etc., should be addressed to the assistant secretary of the association at 1140 Woodward Building, Washington, D. C., from whom they will receive prompt attention.

HISTORICAL PRIZES

WINSOR AND ADAMS PRIZES

For the purpose of encouraging historical research, the American Historical Association offers two prizes, each prize of $200—the Justin Winsor prize in American history and the Herbert Baxter Adams prize in the history of the Eastern Hemisphere. The Winsor prize is offered in the even years (as heretofore), and the Adams prize in the odd years. Both prizes are designed to encourage writers who have not published previously any considerable work or obtained an established reputation. Either prize shall be awarded for an excellent monograph or essay, printed or in manuscript, submitted to or selected by the committee of award. Monographs must be submitted on or before July 1 of the given year. In the case of a printed monograph the date of publication must fall within a period of two years prior to July 1. A monograph to which a prize has been awarded in manuscript may, if it is deemed in all respects available, be published in the annual report of the association. Competition shall be limited to monographs written or published in the English language by writers of the Western Hemisphere.

In making the award the committee will consider not only research, accuracy, and originality, but also clearness of expression and logical arrangement. The successful monograph must reveal marked excellence of style. Its subject matter should afford a distinct contribution to knowledge of a sort beyond that having merely personal or local interest. The monograph must conform to the accepted canons of historical research and criticism. A manuscript—including text, notes, bibliography, appendices, etc.—must not exceed 100,000 words if designed for publication in the annual report of the association.

The Justin Winsor prize.—The monograph must be based upon independent and original investigation in American history. The phrase "American history" includes the history of the United States and other countries of the Western Hemisphere. The monograph may deal with any aspect or phase of that history.

The Herbert Baxter Adams prize.—The monograph must be based upon independent and original investigation in the history of the Eastern Hemisphere. The monograph may deal with any aspect or phase of that history, as in the case of the Winsor prize.

Inquiries regarding these prizes should be addressed to the chairmen of the respective committees, or to the secretary of the association, 1140 Woodward Building, Washington, D. C.

The Justin Winsor prize (which until 1906 was offered annually) has been awarded to the following:

1896. Herman V. Ames: "The proposed amendments to the Constitution of the United States."

1900. William A. Schaper: "Sectionalism and representation in South Carolina"; with honorable mention of Mary S. Locke: "Antislavery sentiment before 1808."

1901. Ulrich B. Phillips: "Georgia and State rights"; with honorable mention of M. Louise Green: "The struggle for religious liberty in Connecticut."

1902. Charles McCarthy: "The Anti-Masonic Party"; with honorable mention of W. Roy Smith: "South Carolina as a royal province."

1903. Louise Phelps Kellogg: "The American colonial charter: A study of its relation to English administration, chiefly after 1688."

1904. William R. Manning: "The Nootka Sound controversy"; with honorable mention of C. O. Paullin: "The Navy of the American Revolution."

1906. Annie Heloise Abel: "The history of events resulting in Indian consolidation west of the Mississippi River."

1908. Clarence Edwin Carter: "Great Britain and the Illinois country, 1765–1774"; with honorable mention of Charles Henry Ambler: "Sectionalism in Virginia, 1776–1861."

1910. Edward Raymond Turner: "The Negro in Pennsylvania: Slavery—servitude—freedom, 1639–1861."

1912. Arthur Charles Cole: "The Whig Party in the South."

1914. Mary W. Williams: "Anglo-American Isthmian diplomacy, 1815–1915."

1916. Richard J. Purcell: "Connecticut in transition, 1775–1818."

1918. Arthur M. Schlesinger: "The Colonial Merchants and the American Revolution, 1763–1776." (Columbia University Studies in History, etc., No. 182.)

From 1897 to 1899 and in 1905 the Justin Winsor prize was not awarded.

The Herbert Baxter Adams prize has been awarded to:

1905. David S. Muzzey: "The Spiritual Franciscans"; with honorable mention of Eloise Ellery: "Jean Pierre Brissot."

1907. In equal division, Edward B. Krehbiel, "The Interdict: Its history and its operation, with especial attention to the time of Pope Innocent III"; and William S. Robertson, "Francisco de Miranda and the revolutionizing of Spanish America."

1909. Wallace Notestein: "A history of witchcraft in England from 1558 to 1718."

1911. Louise Fargo Brown: "The political activities of the Baptists and Fifth Monarchy men in England during the Interregnum."

1913. Violet Barbour: "Henry Bennet, Earl of Arlington."

1915. Theodore C. Pease: "The leveller movement"; with honorable mention of F. C. Melvin: "Napoleon's system of licensed navigation, 1806–1814."

1917. Frederick L. Nussbaum: "G. J. A. Ducher: An essay on the political history of mercantilism during the French Revolution."

1919. Williams Thomas Morgan: "English political parties and leaders in the reign of Queen Anne, 1702–1710."

The essays of Messrs. Muzzey, Krehbiel, Carter, Notestein, Turner, Cole, Pease, Purcell, Miss Brown, Miss Barbour, and Miss Williams have been published by the association in a series of separate volumes. The earlier Winsor prize essays were printed in the annual reports.

AMERICAN HISTORICAL ASSOCIATION STATISTICS OF MEMBERSHIP

DECEMBER 15, 1920

I. GENERAL

'otal membership	2,524
Life	106
Annual	2,202
Institutions	216
'otal paid membership, including life members	2,074
)elinquent (total)	450
Since last bill	442
For one year	8
,oss (total)	206
Deaths	37
Resignations	64
Dropped	105
;ain (total)	285
Life	3
Annual	266
Institutions	16
otal number of elections	271
'et gain or loss	79

II. BY REGIONS

'ew England: Maine, New Hampshire, Vermont, Massachusetts, Rhode Island, Connecticut	403
'orth Atlantic: New York, New Jersey, Pennsylvania, Delaware, Maryland, District of Columbia	774
,outh Atlantic: Virginia, North Carolina, South Carolina, Georgia, Florida	138
'orth Central: Ohio, Indiana, Illinois, Michigan, Wisconsin	507
,outh Central: Alabama, Mississippi, Tennessee, Kentucky, West Virginia	74
/est Central: Minnesota, Iowa, Missouri, Arkansas, Louisiana, North Dakota, South Dakota, Nebraska, Kansas, Oklahoma, Texas	289
acific coast: Montana, Wyoming, Colorado, New Mexico, Idaho, Utah, Nevada, Arizona, Washington, Oregon, California	240
erritories: Porto Rico, Alaska, Hawaii, Philippine Islands	5
ther countries	94
	2,524

III. By States

	Members	New members, 1920		Members	New members, 1920
Alabama	12	5	New Jersey	69	4
Alaska			New Mexico	7	1
Arizona	6	1	New York	360	33
Arkansas	6		North Carolina	28	
California	139	21	North Dakota	8	2
Colorado	18	3	Ohio	125	26
Connecticut	88	6	Oklahoma	14	3
Delaware	11	2	Oregon	18	3
District of Columbia	105	14	Pennsylvania	172	12
Florida	6		Philippine Islands	3	
Georgia	22	5	Porto Rico	2	
Hawaii			Rhode Island	21	
Idaho	7	1	South Carolina	18	1
Illinois	178	16	South Dakota	12	3
Indiana	54	7	Tennessee	17	4
Iowa	46	4	Texas	45	2
Kansas	28	4	Utah	8	2
Kentucky	22	1	Vermont	11	4
Louisiana	15	2	Virginia	64	18
Maine	13	1	Washington	23	1
Maryland	57	7	West Virginia	19	3
Massachusetts	242	17	Wisconsin	63	6
Michigan	87	15	Wyoming	3	
Minnesota	50	6	Canada	31	2
Mississippi	4		Cuba	2	
Missouri	43	2	South America	5	
Montana	6	1	Foreign	56	6
Nebraska	22	1			
Nevada	5		Total	2,524	235
New Hampshire	28	2			

PROCEEDINGS OF THE THIRTY-FIFTH ANNUAL MEETING OF THE AMERICAN HISTORICAL ASSOCIATION

Washington, D. C., December 27-30, 1920

Counting 2 meetings which where held partly in Washington and partly in Baltimore, Md., and Richmond, Va., respectively, 12 of the 35 annual meetings of the American Historical Association have been held in the National Capital—that of 1886, presided over by the venerable George Bancroft, and those of 1888–1891, inclusive, of 1894 and 1895, of 1901, 1905, 1908, 1915, and 1920. The act of January 4, 1889, incorporating the society, provides that it shall have its principal office at Washington, though it may hold its annual meetings where it pleases. Other provisions of the act, concerning relations with the Smithsonian Institution, emphasize the Washington connection, and the association is always entitled to consider itself more distinctly at home in Washington than in any other city, and to meet there without specific invitation, though always assured of cordial welcome by the resident members. Under such circumstances, if the resident members are obliged to feel that they have done less for the entertainment of their fellow members on occasion of the annual meeting than has been done in some other cities, they console themselves with the reflection that Washington is the society's legal home, that every citizen of the United States has his or her share in its ownership, and that the city has many intrinsic attractions of its own, independent of whatever pleasures might be devised to accompany a professional gathering of historical scholars. Not the least of these attractions is a winter climate milder than that of most of the cities where the association has met; but there are also the buildings and other sights of Washington, and, an attraction having especial drawing power for historians, the printed and manuscript treasures of the Library of Congress and the archives—if in their present condition they deserve to be called archives—of the National Government.

By whatever attractions drawn, the number of members attending the thirty-fifth meeting, December 28–30, 1920, was much greater than had been expected. At the Washington meeting of 1915 the registration was 430; but railroad fares have grown higher since then, teachers poorer. Moreover, the railroads proved as unwilling this year as the United States Railroad Administration had been in the year preceding to make any concessions as to reduction of railroad fares for such

---

[1] This account of the Washington meeting is taken, with some modifications and abridgments, from the American Historical Review for April, 1921.

an occasion. They could not be persuaded to class the American Historical Association's meeting among "meetings of religious, educational, charitable, fraternal, or military character." Most members it is hoped, found the meeting both educational and fraternal; at all events, members came in unexpected numbers. The registration amounted to 360. The other societies meeting at the same time—the American Political Science Association, the American Sociological Society, the American Catholic Historical Association, the Mississippi Valley Historical Association, and the Agricultural History Society— also had gratifying numbers registering. The subscription dinner in which all the societies joined, had an attendance of 300, and the breakfast conferences and luncheon conferences for informal discussion of themes or projects asssumed to have a special interest for merely a limited number of members had on this occasion so embarrassing a number of attendants that at meetings hereafter held it will seem difficult to combine the feeding of the multitude with preaching of the word.

The subscription dinner deserves a special comment. Such functions are expensive, and the association had seldom ventured to have them; but this particular dinner, a joint affair of all the societies amply justified itself. No one who heard the incisive remarks of the French Ambassador on historical processes and modern events, or the Secretary of War's penetrating and brilliant discussion of the relation of history to the Great War, or Dr. J. J. Walsh's witty speech on historical assumptions respecting progress, is likely ever to forget the occasion. Doctor Walsh spoke as representative of the American Catholic Historical Association, of which he had that day been elected president. Others who spoke were Dr. Paul S. Reinsch, president of the American Political Science Association, and Dr. Edward A. Ross for the American Sociological Society. At the beginning, graceful words of welcome on behalf of the municipal government were spoken by Miss Mabel Boardman, one of the Commissioners for the District of Columbia.

Other occasions on which there was union of societies were the joint session with the Mississippi Valley Historical Association, presided over by the president of that society, Prof. Chauncey S. Boucher, of the University of Texas; the joint session with the Agricultural History Society, at which its president, Dr. Rodney H. True, of the Department of Agriculture, acted as chairman; and three joint sessions with the American Political Science Association. The first of these three was the occasion when the presidents of the two societies delivered their annual addresses, Dr. Herbert Putnam, Librarian of Congress, presiding. The thoughtful address of Prof. Edward Channing, of Harvard, as president of the American Historical Association, entitled "An historical retrospect," was printed in the January (1921) issue of the Review. The address of Doctor Reinsch was entitled "Secret diplomacy: How far can it be eliminated?"

The second of these joint sessions was concerned with Pan American political and diplomatic relations, and was held, appropriately, under the chairmanship of Dr. Leo S. Rowe, the new Director of the Pan American Union, and in the Union's beautiful building (nearly all other meetings were held in the New Willard Hotel, the association's headquarters). In both this session and the luncheon conference on the history of Latin America, which preceded it, the same tendency was noticeable that has been seen on previous occasions when the association has made provision for the consideration of Hispanic American history, the tendency, namely, to turn away from that history to the consideration of present-day problems of the mutual relations between the Latin American Republics and the United States. The truth is that while interest in these present relations is acute and extensive, and while the history of those portions of the present United States that were once under Spain is being cultivated with exceptional ardor, the historical study of the regions to the southward of our boundaries is still in its infancy among us.

The third of these joint sessions occurred on the last evening, when, under the chairmanship of Baron Korff, formerly of the University of Helsingfors but now of Washington, papers were read on aspects of recent European history and politics. At the close of the session, Baron Korff in graceful words expressed thanks on behalf of the association to the committees who had been in charge of the meeting and to those who, as hosts, had entertained the members. In the Historical Association, the chairman of the committee of local arrangements was Dr. H. Barrett Learned, the secretary Dr. George F. Zook, of the Bureau of Education. The chairman of the committee on the program was Prof. Carlton J. H. Hayes, of Columbia University. The entertainments included a "smoker" at the Cosmos Club, an evening reception by the National Club House Committee of the Association of Collegiate Alumnæ, and a most pleasant afternoon reception at the French Embassy by Ambassador and Madame Jusserand.

The "luncheon conferences" were four. One was composed, as has already been mentioned, of persons chiefly interested in Latin America; another of those interested in the history of the Far East; another was devoted, with excellent results, to practical considerations respecting the study and teaching of economic history. In this conference formal papers were read. Prof. Clive Day, of Yale University, who presided, spoke on the recognition of economic history as a distinct subject, reviewing its history, and discriminating between those elementary courses in which its fusion with general history is desirable and those more advanced stages of instruction to which separate and special courses are more appropriate. Prof. Abbott P. Usher, of the School of Business Administration in Boston University, spoke on the field for the teaching of economic history in colleges and secondary schools. It appears that in most colleges and universities where economic history finds a place the chief provision for it consists in a course which gives one semester to the economic history of Europe and one to that of America. Many difficulties, especially in the intricate subjects of medieval agriculture and commerce, are avoided by beginning the European part of the course with the Industrial Revolution, but such a procedure sacrifices too much of what is stimulating to the student, to whom the contrast between medieval and modern conditions, medieval and modern forms of social organization, especially in the field of industry, is sure to be highly instructive. Within the last few years economic history has become an important subject in the curricula of business schools, especially their undergraduate divisions, now rapidly growing. Here, little other history can be taught; economic history must give elementary training in both historical and statistical method, and must be coordinated with the work descriptive of industries and, in general, of present-day economic organization. The speaker doubted the wisdom of trying to extend economic history into the field of secondary and vocational education.

In the same conference, Professor Hayes, of Columbia University, spoke on the relation of courses in economic history to courses in history and in economics, respectively; Prof. Frank T. Carlton, of De Pauw University, on the history of labor as a field for historical research, with especial emphasis on the need for comparative study of the structure and operation of different types of labor organizations, considered as social forces.

Much the most numerously attended of these luncheon conferences was that which was concerned with the opportunities for historical research in Washington. By the courtesy of the Librarian of Congress, it took place in the Library. The circumstances confined the speakers—Dr. Gaillard Hunt, of the Department of State, Mr. Charles Moore, chief of the Division of Manuscripts in the Library of Congress, Mr. Theodore Belote, curator of American history in the National Museum, and Prof. Frederick J. Turner—to the elements of the subject, but it was impressive and most gratifying to see the eager interest with which their hearers, mostly young graduate students, absorbed these elements of knowledge and incitement concerning the historical treasures of Washington. Would that some adequate appreciation of the opportunities presented here might be diffused among the members of the historical profession, and all others who are interested in history! How do they escape the knowledge that

Washington is far the best place for the study of most of the really important parts of American history? Certainly no city in the world so richly provided with historical materials is so little resorted to for purposes of historical writing. From a country of such enormous wealth, there should be, outside the number of those who earn their living in Washington by the teaching of history or other historical work, and the occasional professors who come on leave of absence, at least 50 scholars able to vivere suo who have settled down in Washington to lead the historical student's life and exploit this wonderfully opulent mass of material. There are not five. But apparently the well-to-do young American, though nowadays he goes or is sent to college, seldom acquires from either parents or teachers the conviction that there is an inviting career in further study. He is not found in the graduate school. Yet historical writing has never been a poor man's pursuit, but always a pursuit of the well-to-do or the endowed—and in America, with no Congregation of St. Maur, the endowed class has embraced only professors of history, and them only in the happy years from 1880 to 1914, when professors still had some free time!

But to return to the meeting. Before proceeding to those papers which can best be taken into consideration individually, one should speak of two sessions which had more the character of "experience meetings," or of free conferences unencumbered by meals, than of assemblages for the reading of formal papers—the usual annual meeting of the Conference of Historical Societies and the conference which met to discuss the report of the committee on history and education for citizenship in the schools. The former, presided over by Dr. James Sullivan, State historian of New York, was given the shape of a joint meeting of the representatives of historical societies and of the National Association of State War History Organizations. For the latter body, which now embraces some 15 of the organizations which States have formed for the collection and preservation of their records of service in the Great War, Mr. Karl Singewald, of the historical division of the Maryland Council of Defense, presented a report of "Progress in the collection of war records by State war history organizations"; Prof. Albert E. McKinley, secretary of the Pennsylvania War History Commission, a paper of "Suggestions and plans for State and local publications of war history." The materials chiefly collected are, first, the service records of individuals; secondly, other military records, such as histories of units, diaries, rosters, photographs, etc.; thirdly, various materials relating to economic participation in the war, and to welfare and morale work. The projected publications correspond—histories of military participation, histories of economic effort, histories of the welfare movements.

In respect to the work of historical societies, the main subject was that of cooperation of societies within the individual State. Dr. Joseph Schafer, superintendent of the State Historical Society of Wisconsin, described the intensive survey of the settlement of that State which is being carried on by the cooperative efforts of that society and of the local historical societies, and to which has been given the appropriate title of the Wisconsin Domesday Book; Dr. Worthington C. Ford and Dr. James Sullivan described, respectively, the work of the Bay State Historical League in Massachusetts, and of the various county and regional federations of historical societies in New York, and dwelt upon the stimulus given to local societies by the contacts afforded by these groupings.

At the close of the session the conference of historical societies, which enjoys a certain autonomy under the auspices of the association, held its annual business meeting. Mr. George S. Godard was reelected chairman for the present year and two special committees were appointed, one to publish, if possible, a handbook of historical societies, the other to consider a continuation of the bibliography of historical societies compiled to 1905 by Mr. A. P. C. Griffin and printed as Volume II of the annual report of the association for that year. Dr. Dunbar Rowland made a report as chairman of the committee appointed by the conference in 1907, on cooperation among American historical societies and State departments of history. The project undertaken by the committee, namely, the calendaring of all documents in Parisian archives relating to the Mississippi Valley, for which the societies and departments of that region had raised a fund of $3,000, has been substantially completed, so far as the gathering of material for it is concerned. Doctor Rowland recommended that the offer of the Department of Historical Research in the Carnegie Institution of Washington to edit and publish the calendar be accepted and that the special committee be discharged. This recommendation was adopted.

The committee on history and education for citizenship in the schools was constituted in 1918, first by the National Board for Historical Service and later by the association, in order to consider those extensive modifications in the methods of historical teaching in schools which, it was then felt, must be brought about as a result of the Great War, in order that history might do its full part in training the minds of the young for proper service to a new era. The history of the committee's work may be traced in these pages and in those of the Historical Outlook, where also preliminary reports from it have been printed.[2] Many obstacles have delayed the presentation of its final report. The object of the present conference

---

[2] See American Historical Review, XXIV, 351–353, 746; XXV, 372–373; Historical Outlook, X, 273–281, 349–351, 448–451; XI, 73–83, 111–115.

was the discussion of portions of its proposals, already made known by some of its previous publications.

In the first of the two formal addresses presented, both of them by members of the committee, Prof. Henry Johnson, of Teachers College, Columbia University, discussed the questions of "Local and American history in grades II–VI" and "World history in the high school." He described three groups of dominant ideas respecting the aims and subject matter of history as a theme of instruction—(1) that the past should be used, as needed, to elucidate the present, without regard to boundaries of subjects, such as geography, literature, economics, history, etc.; (2) that there should be systematic study of history, but that the selection of subjects or events to be studied should be determined solely by present interests; (3) that there should be a study of history for its own sake, because it represents what the past was and how the present came to be. The work of the committee was based on the last conception. Professor Johnson then gave concrete illustrations of methods of teaching pupils in the grades. The central idea was that of so presenting material as to lead pupils to do constructive thinking; to use the historical method in implanting the idea of change, in evaluating evidence, and in forming conclusions. The speaker approved the proposal of a course in world history in the high schools.[3]

The secretary of the committee, Mr. Daniel C. Knowlton, outlined the proposed course in modern history for grade X, consisting of a preliminary course of one semester in ancient and medieval history and a semester in modern history. Main topics and subtopics were enumerated, chosen for the purpose of showing the progress toward democracy in Europe, for grade X, to be followed by a course in American history with a similar purpose, for grade XI, and one in problems resulting from the growth of democracy, for grade XII. Miss Harriet Tuell, president of the New England History Teachers' Association, criticized the committee's plan as inadequate, as running beyond the capacity of the average high-school pupil, and as laying undue emphasis on one phase of European development—the growth of democracy.

In view of the transfer of the chairman of this committee, Professor Schafer, from Oregon to a new occupation in Wisconsin, and of other changes of occupation by other members, the committee asked to be discharged and to have its work reviewed and concluded by a fresh committee. The council acceded to this request and appointed a new committee to be called the committee on history teaching in schools, of which the chairman is Professor Johnson.

---

[3] Mr. Johnson's address, together with a preliminary report by Mr. Schafer, will be found in the Historical Outlook for March, 1921, XII, 87–97.

Another session having a special character was that devoted to the history of science. Its chairman, Dr. Robert S. Woodward, the retiring president of the Carnegie Institution of Washington, welcomed the attitude of the American Historical Association toward the history of science, emphasized the need of breaking down the artificial barriers which separate one department of learning or science from another, and recalled plans of earlier years for a general history of the inductive sciences. Of the three papers read, the first was one by Dr. Fielding H. Garrison, librarian of the Surgeon General's Office, on "Recent realignments in the history of medieval medicine and science." While the most important medical texts of classical antiquity and the Middle Ages were issued in type by the renaissance printers, much of the scientific and medical literature of those times remained in manuscript, and it was not till quite recent years that either the early printed books or the thousands of medical and other scientific manuscripts have been subjected to careful examination. The result has been to show that the medieval physicians were weak in anatomy and in physiology; that internal medicine was with them a matter of tradition, both as to theory and as to practice; but that in surgery and in hygiene their accomplishment was considerable. Other branches of science developed in the Middle Ages chiefly through the pursuit of practical inventions.

The second of these papers in the history of science was one on "Developments in electromagnetism during the last hundred years," by Prof. Arthur E. Kennelly, of Harvard.[4] The occasion of this survey was the hundredth anniversary of Oersted's discovery of the connection between electricity and magnetism—of the deflecting of the magnetic needle by an electric current. The development of the subject was traced, from Ampère's epochmaking paper of the same year, 1820, through his subsequent researches, through Faraday's discovery of electromagnetic induction, through the applications to telegraphy, ocean cables, and the telephone, through Clerk Maxwell's researches into the relations between electricity and light, the subsequent investigation of radioelectric waves, and the study of the electron theory of matter. This session concluded with a paper by Prof. James H. Robinson, of the New School of Social Research, in New York, on "Free thought, yesterday and to-day." Treating his subject with characteristic wit and pungency of statement, from the point of view of the student of intellectual history, he compared especially the modes of thought of the eighteenth century deists and other philosophers with our own, and set forth the gains to modern thinking derived from the scientific advance of the last century.

---

[4] Printed in a modified form in the Boston Transcript of Jan. 26, 1921.

Proceeding now to the main body of substantive papers, or papers read as contributions to history, it must be said that on the whole they seemed to be of less importance or excellence than the average of what has been brought forward on such occasions in the past, yet some were of exceptionally high quality. The most convenient plan for giving some notion of what the papers not already mentioned contained is perhaps to deal with them in the chronological order of their subjects, beginning with ancient history. In the session devoted to that field, the first paper was read by Dr. Donald McFayden, of the University of Nebraska, on the "Growth of autocracy in the Roman Empire." Its main features were an argument that the powers granted to the princeps in 23 B. C. did not include a legal majus imperium over the senatorial provinces, and, derived from this, a theory of the evolution of the princeps' relation to the administration of justice. Contrary to the accepted view, he held that under the Augustan Constitution the princeps possessed no jurisdiction except over the imperial provinces, that the activities of his judicial court and of that held by the praefectus urbi as his deputy were technically unconstitutional, and that the appellate jurisdiction of the princeps was simply an outgrowth of the tendency to refer all difficult problems to his arbitrament—to make him the chief jurisconsult of the empire. Hadrian's action in organizing a council of eminent jurisconsults to assist him in rendering his decisions fixed him in that position. The extra-legal origin of the jurisdiction exercised by the princeps and his deputies was held to explain the relatively informal character of their procedure, while the alliances between the empire and the professional lawyers impregnated the later Roman law with the spirit of absolutism.

Next followed an important paper on the "Origin of the Russian state on the Dnieper," by Prof. Mikhail Rostovtsev, formerly of the Petrograd Academy of Sciences, now of the University of Wisconsin. In the ninth century, when the Russian annals begin to give a systematic record, we find Russia to have already a civilization of its own and a well-defined political, social, and economic structure, having for its basis a group of commercial city-states, defended and in part ruled by alien princes invited from without, one of whom, in that century, succeeded in uniting the whole group of cities under one dynasty and into one State, with its capital at Kiev. The problem of the paper was to account for this form of organization, so strikingly different from the agricultural and feudal form prevalent at that epoch in western Europe. It was to be solved only by taking into consideration that earlier history of south Russia of which a portion was treated by Professor Rostovtsev in an article printed in our last number.[5] The civilization depicted in that article as

---

[5] Pp. 203–224, above.

prevailing under the joint influence of the Greek colonial cities and the Iranian-Scythian empire was not destroyed when the Sarmatian power-replaced the Scythian, nor when Celtic and after them Germanic invaders came. They took over, as it was their interest to do, the commercial relations which they found; and when the Germans passed on into the Roman Empire and the west, the Slavs, in the main, simply took their place, founded a State of the same type, took over their towns, their trade relations, and their civilization— not a Germanic, nor thereafter a Slavonic, civilization, but the ancient Graeco-Iranian civilization of the Scythians and Sarmatians, with slight modifications. The Slavonic is but one of the epochs in the evolution of Russia, but with this difference, that the Slavs made Russia their final aim and home.

A paper on "The problem of control in medieval industry,"[6] by Dr. Austin P. Evans, of Columbia University, addressed itself to questions made timely by the recent tendency to extol medieval economic organization as worthy of imitation in our time. The author showed how medieval theories respecting property and value left the Government, of State or city, free to control the production and sale of goods. As to the warmly debated question, whether guilds freely controlled industry, whether guilds were everywhere under the control of civil authorities of State or town, or whether guilds had a larger measure of autonomy while the civil authorities maintained residuary power, Mr. Evans held that most commonly the guilds were under the ulterior control of the State, but he deprecated sweeping generalizations in a field marked by so much variety, and also all tendency to idealize the economic organization prevalent in the Middle Ages.

The only other paper in medieval history was one by Prof. Louis J. Paetow, of the University of California, on "Latin as an international language in the Middle Ages." Modern civilization, he pointed out, rests on the achievements of Latin Christendom in that period, yet, though the Latin language was the chief engine of civilization throughout those ages, so little effort has been applied to the scholarly study of medieval Latin that Du Cange's Glossarium, published in 1678 and augmented largely in the eighteenth century, is still referred to as its standard dictionary. Made international by the Western Church, that speech remained the common medium of communication and literature throughout western Europe, its chief bond of union, until the Italian humanists, while enthusiastically awakening classical Latin to new life, fatally checked the development of the current Latin as a living and international language. Recent efforts to restore Latin to that position were described.

[6] Printed in the Political Science Quarterly, Vol. XXXVI, No. 4, December, 1921.

The paper of Prof. George M. Dutcher, of Wesleyan University, on "The enlightened despotism," opened with a brief analysis in which the enlightened despotism was characterized as based upon the authority of reason and not upon humanitarianism. Next the origin of the movement in Prussia, rather than in the more progressive nations, England and France, was explained. Conditions in the German lands at the close of the Thirty Years' War were sketched with special reference to the situation of the Hohenzollern possessions, and the constructive policy and work of the Great Elector were outlined as the earliest manifestation of the enlightened despotism, whose foremost exponent was that prince's great-grandson, Frederick the Great. Special emphasis was laid upon Frederick's achievement in internal administration during the 10 years' truce beginning in 1745, and its imitation by Maria Theresa, in the rival campaigns of preparedness preceding the Seven Years' War. The priority of these reforming activities in administration to the appearance of the famous writings on government by the French philosophical thinkers was brought out as evidence that the enlightened despotism developed as a practical achievement, not as a response to the stimulus of political theorists. In short, it was an effort at administrative efficiency designed for the aggrandizement of the State, which was conceived of as an entity above rulers as well as above subjects and as founded on the authority of reason rather than on divine right.

Later periods of European history were traversed in a summary survey of "The break-up of the Hapsburg Empire," by Prof. Archibald C. Coolidge, of Harvard University, and in a paper on "Sinn Fein," by Prof. Edward R. Turner, of the University of Michigan. Dr. Ralph H. Lutz, of Stanford University, narrated the history of "The Spartacist uprising in Germany," of which he had been an eyewitness in Berlin. Miss Ruth Putnam, in a paper entitled "The aspirations of one small State," described the evolution of the grand-duchy of Luxemburg from the time when it first obtained the opportunity of self-determination, after the armistice of November, 1918, to recent days. This paper, too, was based in large part on the data of an eyewitness. Problems of labor, finance, railroads, and economic affiliation with the neighboring countries were described, and some account given of the course and achievements of parties under a new constitution providing for woman suffrage and proportional representation.

In a paper on "The establishment of a new Poland," Col. Lucius H. Holt, of the United States Military Academy, traced the establishment of a new government, and political events in Poland from the outbreak of the war in 1914 to the present date. The paper emphasized the work of the supreme national committee during the years from 1914 to 1916. It traced briefly the influences which led the Central Powers to recognize Poland in the autumn of 1915, and the subsequent incidents which revealed the duplicity of Germany and turned the Poles against that country. It summarized the points in the allied recognition of Poland in 1918. It outlined the clash of conflicting political forces in Poland during the armistice period and the result, spoke of the elections of January, 1919, and closed with a statement of the progress made by the Polish Assembly upon the draft of a constitution.

The last of the papers which we may describe as bearing on the history of the Old World was that of Dr. Stephen P. Duggan, director of the Institute of International Education, on "Syria, Palestine, and Mandates."[7] When the Great War broke out the Allies found strong support among the Syrian patriots and leaders who, under the rule of the Young Turks, or exiled by them, had been contending for an autonomous or independent Syria administered by Arabs with Arabic as official language. Unfortunately, the agreement of October 25, 1915, made between the Sherif of the Hejaz and the British High Commission at Cairo, conflicted with the provisions of the Sykes-Picot treaty between France and Great Britain as to the disposition of the Arab lands of the Ottoman Empire. Moreover, that treaty was considered by the Arabs to be superseded by the Anglo-French declaration of November 8, 1918. When, therefore, after the occupation of the territory by General Allenby, mandates were given by the Supreme Council to Great Britain for Palestine and to France for Syria, the Arab nationalists considered that they had been deceived, opposed the erection of a Zionist commonwealth in Palestine, and entered on a course of conflict with the British in Palestine and of warfare with the French elsewhere in Syria.

At the end of this last session, Dr. Victor Andrés Belaunde, of the University of San Marcos of Lima, Peru, read a brief paper on "The communistic system of the Incas," and the comparison between its features and those of Russian communism under Lenin and Trotzky.

Passing now to the papers in American history, it is to be noted that, appropriately to the date, one session was devoted to commemorating the tercentenary of the arrival of the Pilgrim Fathers. In this session three papers were read, of which the first by Prof. Clive Day, of Yale University, dealt with "Capitalistic and socialistic tendencies in the Puritan colonies." Its special object was to consider a view recently advanced by the late Prof. Max Weber, of Heidelberg, that in the development of the modern capitalist and of a capitalistic society, as set forth in Sombart's familiar analysis, an essential source

---

[7] Printed in the Journal of International Relations, April, 1921, under the title, "The Syrian Question."

of the capitalist spirit is to be found in the religious beliefs and ethical principles of the Puritans. Confining himself to the Puritans of New England, the speaker set forth the results of a careful examination of their sermons and laws as expressions of their ethical ideals. He did not find that encouragements to industry and thrift bulked large in their sermons and concluded that whatever urgency was manifest toward the accumulation of capital, greatly needed in the colonies, was social rather than individual and capitalistic in its motives.

Mr. Lincoln N. Kinnicutt, of Worcester, followed with a paper entitled, "The settlement of Plymouth contemplated before 1620." Its thesis was that Sir Ferdinando Gorges desired a settlement at Plymouth Harbor and did what he could to guide the Pilgrims thither, supplying them with information and endeavoring to arrange that Captain Dermer and Tisquantum should be at hand to point their way, possibly also making private arrangements with Captain Jones of the *Mayflower*.

Thirdly, Prof. David S. Muzzey, of Columbia University, in a paper on "The heritage of the Puritans," after acknowledging the defects characteristic of Puritanism but urging that all estimates of these should be based on comparisons with contemporaneous phenomena rather than with those of the present time, set forth in admirable style three principal portions of our inheritance from the Puritans and Pilgrims—the results of their political philosophy, with its insistence on covenant as the basis of civil relations; the influence of the New England town, primordial cell of local self-government; and the emphasis which the Puritans permanently placed upon unremitting education for responsibility.

The paper on "The slave trade into South Carolina before the Revolution," by Miss Elizabeth Donnan, of Wellesley College, a product of researches conducted on behalf of the Carnegie Institution of Washington, derived its information for the first third of the eighteenth century from offical papers, dealing with those aspects of the trade in which British officials and British merchants concerned themselves, such as the import taxes imposed by the colony, payment of debts to British merchants, and monopoly by the Royal Co. From 1732 we have the files of the South Carolina Gazette and from 1748 the business letters of Henry Laurens. From these two sources much can be learned concerning the actual process of buying and selling the black cargoes, which were handled by importing merchants, prominent in Charleston society, who were giving to their British principals copious information concerning weather, crops, prices, and other factors which influenced the market. The paper described in detail such matters as the terms of contract between principal and factor and between factor and purchasing planter, the methods of the auction sales, the range of territory covered, and the risks and difficulties which the factor encountered.

The paper which was read by Prof. Fiske Kimball, of the University of Virginia, on "Architecture in the history of the Colonies and of the Republic," in which he traversed several current notions as to the influence of pioneer conditions on American colonial building, and emphasized the American elements in the development of classical architecture in the early years of the Republic, appears in the October (1921) issue of the Review.

The paper entitled "John Wesley, Tory," by Prof. William W. Sweet, of De Pauw University, treated of the activities and influence of Wesley during the American Revolution. In the 10 years beginning with 1768 Wesley published 10 political pamphlets. The first 3 were caused by the excitement concerning the case of John Wilkes, and took the side of King and Government; the fourth was devoted to the slave trade, of which Wesley was one of the earliest opponents. The remaining 6 have to do with the American Revolution, the first and most important of them being "A calm address to our American Colonies" (1775). In all of them Wesley invariably supports the King and Government. The reasons for his course are complex—he was born and bred a High-Churchman and a Tory; he believed in the divine right of kings, for that theory seemed to him the most religious; he was a firm supporter of law and order; he hated rebellion; the King had been kindly disposed toward the Methodists; the King's private life and his court were free from scandal; Lord Dartmouth was a leader in the Evangelical movement. Wesley's position on the American war led to some suspicion and even persecution of American Methodists as Tories, but at the close of the war he was wise enough to recognize the result as providential and set about to organize the American Methodists into an independent church.

In the paper by Prof. Homer C. Hockett, of the Ohio State University, on "The American background of federalism," the endeavor was to show the part played by American influences in the development of the two chief modern federations, the American Union and the British Empire. He held that the immediate background of our own federalism lay rather in the relations of the Colonies to one another than in the previous practices of the British Empire; that while the modern British imperial organization, as a league of autonomous commonwealths, was foreshadowed by the American position in the controversy preceding the Revolution, British policy was not changed by the American contention; but that the essential change in that policy resulted rather from the undermining of mercantilism, and thus of the old colonial system, by Adam Smith's political economy, and from the aggressive demands of the Canadians for responsible government. Of the papers on American history in the early part of the nineteenth century, that of Prof. Louis M. Sears, of Purdue University, on "Philadelphia and the embargo of 1808,"[8] adverted first to the ambiguous position of that city in respect to economic status at that time. As a commercial city, Philadelphia was subject to the distress entailed by the embargo upon all sections of the commercial population. But Philadelphia, in common with Baltimore and other ports of the Middle States, possessed an incitement to manufactures in her proximity to the new trans-Alleghany settlements. She seized her opportunity, actually developed a considerable manufacturing industry, and won prosperity for a greater number of her citizens than the embargo had impoverished. The material expression of this prosperity was a building boom involving the construction of over a thousand houses. The political expression was a continued confidence in the Democratic party and in the wisdom and goodness of Thomas Jefferson, Philadelphia being, according to one's point of view, either the shining exception to the folly of the Jeffersonian system, or else the shining example of its wisdom.

In the joint session held with the Agricultural History Society, Prof. Percy W. Bidwell, of Yale University, read a paper, which we shall later have the privilege of presenting in full to our readers, on 'The agricultural revolution in New England, 1815–1860," showing how the development of New England manufactures and the creation of factory villages began a transition from farming for a living to farming for profit, how the building of railroads, just as this transition to commercial agriculture was well under way, subjected the New England farmer to disastrous competition from the westward, and how he carried out the readjustment of his economic system which was thus forced upon him.

In the same joint session, Mr. Herbert A. Kellar, of the McCormick Library, Chicago, read a paper on "The influence of the agricultural fair upon American society, 1830–1851," and Mr. Rudolf A. Clemen, of Northwestern University, one on " The economic bases of the American system of large-scale meat packing." Sketching the earlier history of the American trade in livestock and meat and that of the period when Cincinnati was the center and pork the staple, Mr. Clemen devoted his attention chiefly to the period since the establishment of the Chicago stockyards in 1865, and to the economic results of the four chief factors, all introduced about 1870–1875, which gave the meat industry the form it has since borne—the system of ranges and ranches in the far West, the extention of routes of transportation to

---

[8] An outline of this paper appears in the Quarterly Journal of Economics for February, 1921, pp. 54-359.

the sources of supply, the development of refrigeration and of the refrigerator car, and the rise of the great organizers of distribution.

There was but one paper relating to the period of the Civil War, that of Prof. Charles W. Ramsdell, of the University of Texas, on "The control of manufacturing by the Confederate government." He showed that while the strong individualism of the South prevented the Confederacy from regulating manufactures as a feature of its civil policy, a rigorous control was established over the production of cloth and leather through military agencies, particularly the quartermaster's bureau. By means of the conscription and impressment laws, the supplies of labor, wool, hides, and railway transportation came under the control of the War Department, which was able to force the factories and tanneries to contract almost exclusively with the government when they preferred the higher profits of the public market. The State government of North Carolina, however, interposed successfully to prevent Confederate control of manufactures in that State and to preserve their products for the exclusive use of North Carolina troops.

Only two papers bore on the history of the United States between 1865 and 1900, none on our history in the twentieth century. Both of these two bore on aspects of that period which derive their significance from the economic problems which emerged with the growth of capitalism after the Civil War and which are still unsolved. The first was a paper by Prof. John D. Hicks, of Hamline University, Minnesota, on "The political career of Ignatius Donnelly," who figured in the politics of Minnesota and of the Nation, throughout the period named, as the champion, ardent but unpractical, of every movement that gave promise of bettering the lot of the ordinary man and securing his rights against the claims of property. Indifferent to party—by turns Anti-Monopolist, Greenbacker, Democrat, Republican, Farmers' Alliance man, Populist, Middle-of-the-Roader—he sought his cherished reforms most commonly through third-party movements. His final rejection of opportunist tactics was exhibited when the main body of Populists adopted the policy of fusion with the Democratic Party in 1896.

In a paper on "Agrarian discontent in the South during the eighties and nineties of the last century," Prof. B. B. Kendrick, of Columbia University, dwelt on only two of the causes of that discontent. The primary cause, social, lay in the fact that the southern farmer occupied in 1890, in the economical, the political, and especially the social life of the country, a position much lower than he had in 1860. The principal economic cause of his unrest lay in the lien-law system—an evil peculiar to the southern farmer—under which the farmer was almost a serf to the city merchant to whom he happened to be indebted.

Other elements in the southern situation were not peculiar to that section, but were such as, in the case of the West, have been adequately treated in the books of Buck, Haines, Garland, White, and others; but the history of the southern farmer in that period still awaits systematic investigation.

Papers on "Pan American political and diplomatic relations"—the general theme of one of the sessions held jointly by the Historical and the Political Science Associations, fall last to be described. That of Prof. Herman G. James, of the University of Texas, on "Recent constitutional changes in Latin America," is printed in full elsewhere.[9] That of Prof. Julius Klein, of Harvard, entitled "The Monroe doctrine as a regional understanding," was, so far as historical content is concerned, devoted to an interesting exposition of the ways and extent in which the period of the Great War has brought to the South American Republics appreciation of their own capacity for self-development, promoted international cooperation within South America in economic and social matters, enhanced the application of South American capital to industrial and commercial enterprises, and furthered economic independence of Europe while multiplying contacts with North America. The probable bearing of all this on the development of the Monroe doctrine was described.[10]

Prof. Manoel de Oliveira Lima, the eminent Brazilian scholar who has lately become a member of the Catholic University of America, concluded this series with a paper on "Pan Americanism and the League of Nations," in which, after reviewing some earlier attempts at forming leagues which had originated in South America, he advocated, as the most desirable feature of any league of nations, a supreme court to deal with differences, interpretations, and controversies, and dwelt on the "Pan American conscience," the consciousness of the need of union in the New World, and its common respect for public law, as secure foundations for any closer relations between its members.

It remains to narrate the transactions of the annual business meeting. The delay in the printing of our January number made it possible to insert in that number, on pages 411 and 412, some account of these transactions, but a fuller narrative is, according to custom, expected in this place, and may be given in spite of some repetition necessarily involved.

The secretary's report showed a membership of 2,524, a gain of 79 since the preceding year; the gain is to be attributed to the activity of the committee on membership. The treasurer's report showed

---

[9] "Constitutional tendencies in Latin America," Current History, February, 1921.

[10] This paper and that of Dr. Oliveira Lima, next mentioned, appeared in the May, 1921, number of the Hispanic-American Historical Review.

receipts of $10,483, expenditures of $9,786; but the cost of printing the American Historical Review has increased to so extraordinary a degree, especially in the latter months of the year, that drastic measures will be necessary in order to avoid a deficit for the year 1921. These costs of manufacture have been steadily rising since the year before the Great War. The publishers' estimates seem to show that in 1921 they will surpass those of the year last mentioned by more than 80 per cent. Instead of paying to the Macmillan Co. 50 cents per copy for copies supplied to members of the association as required by the present contract, it becomes necessary to pay hereafter 70 cents, or per annum $2.80, nearly the total sum paid to the association by each member as his annual dues. Therefore the association voted to submit to the next annual meeting an amendment to the constitution increasing the annual dues from $3 to $5 (and the life-membership fee from $50 to $100), and in the meantime to authorize the treasurer, when sending out the bills in September, to invite voluntary contributions of from $2 to $5 additional to the dues. The text of the proposed amendment to the constitution is given in the appendix to this article. Provision was also made for a committee on increase of the endowment, which now stands at $31,639.

The special committee on policy, appointed three years ago, submitted an elaborate report. Many of its recommendations require additional funds for their execution. Such as could be carried into effect under existing conditions were adopted. Thus, in order to secure permanence and continuity of policy of the committee on program, it was voted that three members of that committee should serve for terms of three years so arranged that one member should retire each year, while the other members were to serve for terms of one year and be selected with reference to locality. Other recommendations of the committee on policy, adopted by the Association, provided for continuance or revival of the public archives commission, the committee on bibliography, and the committee on the documentary historical publications of the United States Government; for the discharge, at its own request, as mentioned on a previous page of the present committee on history and education for citizenship in the schools and the substitution of a new committee on history teaching in schools; and for the establishment of a standing committee on military history, whose chief function should be to cooperate with the Historical Branch of the General Staff of the United States Army, and other governmental agencies, national and State, engaged in preparing historical works relative to the recent war. As a means of carrying out the desires which have at times been expressed for a special journal of European history, or an organ for the publication of brief monographs in that field, the committee on policy recommended the establishment, when means are at hand, of a series of historical studies; the details were referred to a committee.

The budget proposed by the council is printed on a later page, in connection with an outline of the treasurer's report.

Under the terms of the will of the late George Louis Beer a prize was established, to be known as the George Louis Beer prize, for the "best work upon any phase of European international history since the year 1895"; a committee was appointed to shape rules for its award. The prize offered in military history, to which the council had appropriately given the name of the Robert M. Johnston prize, was awarded to Mr. Thomas R. Hay, for an essay on Hood's Tennessee campaign. It was announced that the committee on the Justin Winsor prize had been unable to agree, and the three essays most regarded were referred to a new committee on that prize appointed for the biennium 1921–22.

A special committee was appointed by the council at the instance of the secretary, to consider the general subject of historical writing (as distinguished from historical research) in the United States and to report as to what means, if any, may be adopted to stimulate the better writing of history. The committee appointed consists of Mr. Jusserand, Dr. Charles W. Colby, and Prof. W. C. Abbott; its report on this exceedingly important subject will be awaited with much interest.

A committee of which Prof. George M. Dutcher is chairman had been appointed at the preceding annual meeting to prepare a manual of historical literature to replace the well-known work by the late Dr. Charles K. Adams. One of the breakfast conferences held during the sessions was organized in order that those who are to take part in the preparation of this manual might hear a report of progress and discuss various questions of policy. The committee's plan involves some further chapters additional to those in Doctor Adams's book, the inclusion of at least half as many more titles, but with somewhat briefer reviews, in order to keep the size of the volume not much larger, and the assignment of each of the proposed 29 chapters to an expert in its field, as chapter editor, with assistance from other specialists. It is anticipated that the new work, which was originally suggested by the American Library Association, will find its largest usefulness in public libraries and high schools, but that it will not be without value for teachers and students in colleges and universities. Most of the titles will be of works which have appeared since the publication of Doctor Adams's book, and there will be a somewhat larger proportion of books in English treated.

It was voted, on a hospitable invitation from St. Louis, that the next annual meeting should be held in that city. The dates will probably be December 28, 29, and 30.

The annual elections followed precisely the list presented by the committee on nominations. His excellency the French ambassador, Mr. Jusserand, was chosen president for the ensuing year, Prof. Charles H. Haskins first vice president, Prof. Edward P. Cheyney second vice president. Prof. John S. Bassett and Mr. Charles Moore were reelected secretary and treasurer, respectively. The election to the executive council also followed precisely the committee's list, except that Professor Becker withdrew his name, preferring to continue as a member of the board of editors of the Review, whereupon the committee substituted the name of Professor Sioussat. The councilors elected were: Miss Ruth Putnam, Profs. Arthur L. Cross, Sidney B. Fay, Carl R. Fish, Carlton J. H. Hayes, Frederic L. Paxson, James T. Shotwell, and St. George L. Sioussat. The council elected Prof. Guy S. Ford a member of the board of editors of the Review in the place of Prof. J. H. Robinson, whose term had expired, and Prof. Archibald C. Coolidge in the place of Professor Cheyney, who resigned after being elected a vice president. For the committee on nominations, to be presented next autumn, the association chose Profs. Henry E. Bourne, William E. Dodd, Eloise Ellery, Frank H. Hodder, and William E. Lingelbach; the committee has since chosen Professor Hodder as chairman. A full list of the committee assignments for 1921 follows this article.

In view of the small number of the ballots which had been received in the autumnal "primary," and by which the committee on nominations had been guided, the outgoing chairman of that committee, Mr. Victor H. Paltsits, proposed for consideration next year an amendment of by-law No. II which would abolish the provision for this formal balloting and would leave it to the committee to nominate, with only such indications from other members as letters received from them, or their conversations, might supply. Meantime it was voted that the preliminary ballot should be omitted in 1921. It may, however, properly be pointed out that it would be possible to maintain the present machinery of balloting and nominating committee, yet to instruct the committee, or leave it to understand, that, while deriving whatever instruction it can from the results of the ballot, it is not bound to follow rigidly, without discretion, its numerical results.

PROGRAM OF THE THIRTY-FIFTH ANNUAL MEETING HELD IN WASHINGTON, D. C., DECEMBER 27-30, 1920

Monday, December 27

9.30 a.m.: MEETING OF THE EXECUTIVE COUNCIL. 1140 Woodward Building, Fifteenth and H Streets.

8.15 p.m.: MEETING OF THE AMERICAN SOCIOLOGICAL SOCIETY. Washington Hotel. Chairman, Edward A. Ross, University of Wisconsin. "Eudemics; a science of national welfare," James Q. Dealey, Brown University, president of the American Sociological Society. "A theory of social interest," Roscoe Pound, Harvard University.

Tuesday, December 28

10 a.m.: MODERN EUROPEAN HISTORY. Large ball room, north end. Chairman, William E. Lingelbach, University of Pennsylvania. "The enlightened despotism," George M. Dutcher, Wesleyan University. "Sinn Fein," Edward R. Turner, University of Michigan. "The aspirations of one small nation," Ruth Putnam, Washington, D. C. "The establishment of a new Poland," Col. Lucius H. Holt, United States Military Academy.

10 a.m.: ANCIENT AND MEDIEVAL HISTORY. Large ball room, south end. Chairman, George L. Burr, Cornell University. "The growth of autocracy in the Roman Empire," Donald MacFayden, University of Nebraska. "The origin of the Russian state on the Dnieper," M. I. Rostovtzeff, University of Wisconsin. "The problem of control in medieval industry," Austin P. Evans, Columbia University. "Latin as an international language in the Middle Ages," Louis J. Paetow, University of California.

10 a. m.: JOINT MEETING OF THE CONFERENCE OF HISTORICAL SOCIETIES AND THE NATIONAL ASSOCIATION OF STATE WAR HISTORY ORGANIZATIONS. Room 1003. Chairman, James Sullivan, historian of the State of New York. "Progress in the collection of war records by State war history organizations," Karl Singewald, historical division, Maryland Council of Defense. "Suggestions and plans for State and local publications of war history," Albert E. McKinley, University of Pennsylvania. "Coördination of historical societies within the State," Joseph Schafer, State Historical Society of Wisconsin. Discussion: Worthington C. Ford, Massachusetts Historical Society; Harlow Lindley, Earlham College; Edmond S. Meany, University of Washington.

12.30 p. m.: Luncheon conference: Opportunities for historical research in Washington. Library of Congress. Chairman, J. Franklin Jameson, director of the Department of Historical Research, Carnegie Institution of Washington. Discussion: Gaillard Hunt, Department of State; Charles Moore, Library of Congress; Theodore Belote, curator of American history in the National Museum; William A. Dunning, Columbia University; Frederick J. Turner, Harvard University; W. F. Willoughby, Institute for Government Research.

53

3.30 p. m.: Business meeting of the National Association of State War History Organizations. Room 1003.

4 p. m. GENERAL SESSION COMMEMORATING THE PILGRIM TERCENTENARY. Large ball room. Chairman, Edward Channing, Harvard University. "Economic precept and practice of the Puritans," Clive Day, Yale University. "The Settlement at Plymouth contemplated before 1620," Lincoln N. Kinnicutt, Massachusetts Historical Society. "The heritage of the Puritans," David Saville Muzzey, Columbia University.

6.15 p.m.: SUBSCRIPTION DINNER OF THE MISSISSIPPI VALLEY HISTORICAL ASSOCIATION. New Ebbitt Hotel. Open to members of the other associations and to others interested in American history. Chairman, Chauncey S. Boucher. Address by Frederick J. Turner, Harvard University.

8.15 p.m.: PRESIDENTIAL ADDRESSES. Large ball room. Joint session with the American Political Science Association. Chairman, William A. Dunning, Columbia University. "An historical retrospect," Edward Channing, president of the American Historical Association. "Secret diplomacy: How far can it be eliminated?" Paul S. Reinsch, president of the American Political Science Association.

9.30 p. m.: Smoker for members of all the associations. Cosmos Club.

9.30 p. m.: Reception by the National Club House Committee of the Collegiate Alumnæ Association to all the members of the associations, at the National Club House, 1607 H Street.

Wednesday, December 29

8.15 a. m.: Breakfast conference: The proposed manual of historical literature. New Ebbitt Hotel. Gold room. Chairman, George M. Dutcher, Wesleyan University.

10 a. m.: CONFERENCE ON THE REPORT OF THE COMMITTEE ON HISTORY AND EDUCATION FOR CITIZENSHIP IN THE SCHOOLS. Large ball room. Chairman, Joseph Schafer, State Historical Society of Wisconsin. "Local and American history in grades II–VI; world history in the high school," Henry Johnson, Teachers' College, Columbia University. "Modern European history in grade X," Daniel C. Knowlton, secretary of the committee. Discussion: Harriet Tuell, president of the New England History Teachers' Association. "Topical study of American history for the national period in grade XI," Joseph Schafer. Discussion: Albert E. McKinley, University of Pennsylvania. "Civics in schools, with special reference to grades IX and XII," Arthur W. Dunn, director of Junior Red Cross.

10 a. m.: AMERICAN HISTORY. Joint session with the Mississippi Valley Historical Association. Large ball room. Chairman, Chauncey S. Boucher, University of Texas, president of the Mississippi Valley Historical Association. "The American background of Federalism," Homer C. Hockett, Ohio State University. "The political career of Ignatius Donnelly," John D. Hicks, Hamline University. "John Wesley, Tory," William W. Sweet, De Pauw University. "Manufacturing activities of the Confederate Government," Charles W. Ramsdell, University of Texas.

10 a. m.: AGRICULTURAL HISTORY. Joint session with the Agricultural History Society. Room 1003. Chairman, Rodney H. True, president of the Agricultural History Society. "The agricultural revolution in New England, 1810–1860," Percy W. Bidwell, Yale University. "The influence of the agricultural fair upon American society, 1830–1851," Herbert A. Kellar, McCormick Library, Chicago. "The internal grain trade of the United States, 1860–1890," Louis B. Schmidt, Iowa State College.

12.30 p. m.: Luncheon conference on economic history. New Ebbitt Hotel. Gold room. Chairman, Clive Day, Yale University. "The recognition of economic history as a distinct subject," the chairman. "The field for courses in economic history," Abbott Payson Usher, Cornell University. "The relation of courses in economic history to courses in history and economics," Carlton J. H. Hayes, Columbia University. "Fields of research in economic history—Agriculture," Louis B. Schmidt, Iowa State College; "Labor," Frank T. Carlton, De Pauw University.

3 p. m.: ANNUAL BUSINESS MEETING. Small ball room, tenth floor. Reports of officers and committees, election of officers, announcement of committee appointments, miscellaneous business.

7 p. m.: SUBSCRIPTION DINNER. Large ball room. For members of all the associations and their friends. Chairman, J. Franklin Jameson, director of the Department of Historical Research of the Carnegie Institution of Washington. Speakers, the French Ambassador; the Secretary of War: Miss Mabel Boardman, Commissioner of the District of Columbia; Hon. Paul S. Reinsch, late minister to China; President Frank J. Goodnow of Johns Hopkins University; Dr. James J. Walsh of Cathedral College, New York; and Prof. Edward A. Ross of the University of Wisconsin.

Thursday, December 30

10 a. m.: AMERICAN HISTORY. Large ball room, south end. Chairman Marshall S. Brown, New York University. "The slave trade into South Carolina," Elizabeth Donnan, Wellesley College. "Architecture in the history of the Colonies and of the Republic," Fiske Kimball, University of Virginia. "Philadelphia and the embargo of 1808," Louis M. Sears, Purdue University. "Agrarian discontent in the South in the eighties and nineties," Benjamin B. Kendrick, Columbia University.

10 a. m: HISTORY OF SCIENCE. Large ball room, north end. Chairman, Robert S. Woodward, president of the Carnegie Institute of Washington. "Recent realignments in the medieval medicine and science," Dr. Fielding H. Garrison, librarian, Surgeon General's Office. "Developments in electro-magnetism during the past hunderd years," Arthur E. Kennelly, Harvard University. "Free thought, yesterday and to-day," James Harvey Robinson, New School for Social Research. "Science in Virginia," Lyon G. Tyler, president emeritus of the College of William and Mary.

12.30 p. m.: Luncheon conference on the history of the Far East. New Ebbitt. Gold room. Chairman, Hon. Paul S. Reinsch, Washington.

12.30 p. m.: Luncheon conference on Latin America. New Ebbitt. Gold room. Chairman, William R. Shepherd, Columbia University.

3 p. m.: PAN AMERICAN POLITICAL AND DIPLOMATIC RELATIONS. Joint session with the American Political Science Association. Pan American Building. Chairman, Leo S. Rowe, director of the Pan American Union. "Recent constitutional changes in Latin America," Herman G. James, University of Texas. "The Monroe doctrine as a regional understanding," Julius Klein, Harvard University. "Pan Americanism and the League of Nations," Manoel de Oliveira Lima, Catholic University of America.

4.30 p. m.: Reception to the members of the associations by His Excellency the French Ambassador and Madame Jusserand at the French Embassy, 2460 Sixteenth Street.

8.15 p. m.: RECENT EUROPEAN HISTORY AND POLITICS. Joint session with the American Political Science Association. Large ball room. "The Spartacan uprising in Germany," Ralph H. Lutz, Leland Stanford Junior University. "The breakup of the Hapsburg Empire," Archibald Cary Coolidge, Harvard University. "Syria, Palestine, and mandates, Stephen P. Duggan," Institute of International Education, New York.

MINUTES OF THE ANNUAL BUSINESS MEETING HELD IN THE SMALL BALL ROOM OF THE NEW WILLARD HOTEL, WASHINGTON, D. C., ON DECEMBER 29, 1920

The meeting was called to order at 3.15 p. m., President Edward Channing presiding.

The secretary of the association presented his annual report (printed in full in the appendix to these minutes). It was voted that the secretary's report be accepted and placed on file.

The treasurer of the association presented his annual report and expenditures (printed in full in the appendix).

The president appointed Mr. Herman V. Ames and Mr. James M. Callahan a committee to audit the treasurer's report. This committee reported that they had examined the treasurer's report and the audit thereof by the American Audit Co. and had found them to be correct.

It was voted that the report of the treasurer be accepted and placed on file.

The treasurer presented the budget as voted by the executive council for the ensuing years, which was adopted as follows:

APPROPRIATIONS FOR 1921

Secretary and treasurer	$3,000
Pacific Coast Branch	50
Nominating committee	100
Committee on membership	100
Committee on program	300
Committee on local arrangements	50
Conference of historical societies	25
Committee on publications	700
Council committee on agenda	300
American Historical Review	7,000
Historical manuscripts commission	20
Justin Winsor prize	200
Writings on American history	200
American Council of Learned Societies	150
Committee on bibliography	250
Committee on the writing of history	75
	12,520

ESTIMATED INCOME

Annual dues	7,000
Registration fees	150
Publications	100
Royalties	50
Interest	1,400
Miscellaneous	50
	8,750

Mr. George L. Burr announced that at the annual meeting of 1921 he would move an amendment to the constitution as follows:

That, in article III there be substituted for "$3," "$5"; and for "$50," "$100"; so that the article shall read:

Any person approved by the executive council may become a member by paying $5, and after the first year may continue a member by paying an annual fee of $5. On payment of $100 any person may become a life member, exempt from fees. Persons not residing in the United States may be elected as honorary or corresponding members and be exempt from the payment of fees.

The secretary of the association presented the report of the executive council (printed in full in the appendix to these minutes).

It was voted that the report be accepted and placed on file.

Mr. Charles H. Haskins presented with explanatory comment the report of the special committee on policy which the council had voted to transmit to the association with its approval. It was voted that the report be accepted (the report is printed in full in the minutes of the executive council).

It was voted that, in acceptance of the invitations extended by Washington University, by the mayor of St. Louis, and by the Governor of Missouri, the thirty-sixth annual meeting of the association should be held in St. Louis during the last week in December, 1921.

The secretary read by title the reports which the committees of the association had submitted to the executive council. No request having been made from the floor for the presentation in full of any of the reports it was voted that they be accepted and placed on file.

The secretary submitted a list of the members who had died during the year.[1]

Mr. John M. Vincent offered a memorial of the late James Schouler, the twelfth president of the association, which was ordered to be spread upon the records of the association (printed in the appendix to these minutes).

It was voted that a memorial of the late George Louis Beer be prepared and spread upon the records of the association (see appendix to these minutes).

Mr. Victor H. Paltsits, chairman of the committee on nominations, presented as the report of the committee the following nominations for officers, members of the executive council, and members of the committee on nominations for the ensuing year:

President, Jean Jules Jusserand.
First vice president, Charles H. Haskins.
Second vice president, Edward P. Cheyney.
Secretary, John Spencer Bassett.
Treasurer, Charles Moore.
Members of the executive council: James T. Shotwell, Ruth Putnam, Carl Russell Fish, Carl L. Becker, Carlton J. H. Hayes, Sidney B. Fay, Frederic L. Paxson, Arthur L. Cross.
Committee on nominations: Frank H. Hodder, Eloise Ellery, William E. Dodd, Henry E. Bourne, William E. Lingelbach.

Mr. Paltsits announced that Mr. Carl L. Becker, nominated for election to the executive council, had withdrawn his name from nomination and that the nominating committee had not been able to make another nomination in order to fill the vacancy. He therefore offered from the floor the nomination of Mr. St. George L. Sioussat for election to the council in the place of Mr. Carl L. Becker.

No other nominations being made from the floor, it was voted by unanimous consent that the secretary of the association be requested to cast the ballot of the association for the persons nominated by the nominating committee, Mr. St. George L. Sioussat being substituted for Mr. Carl L. Becker in the nominations for the council.

The secretary reported that he had cast the ballot as instructed, and the persons nominated were declared duly elected.

Mr. Channing then vacated the chair, and in the absence of the newly elected president and first vice president, it was taken by Mr. Edward P. Cheyney, the second vice president.

Mr. Paltsits offered the following amendment to by-law II, to be acted upon at the annual meeting of 1921:

The word "nomination," line 1, be changed to "nominating," and the sentence beginning "at such," line 3, and ending "be chosen," line 7, be omittted. Change "one day," line 14, to "two days"; so that by-law II will read as follows:

A nominating committee of five members shall be chosen at each annual business meeting in the manner hereafter provided for the election of officers of the association. It shall publish and mail to each member at least one month prior to the annual business meeting such nominations as it may determine upon for each elective office and for the next nominating committee. It shall prepare for use at the annual business meeting an official ballot containing, as candidates for each office or committee membership to be filled thereat, the names of its nominees and also the names of any other nominees which may be proposed to the chairman of the committee in writ-

---

[1] See list of deceased members, p. 60.

ing by 20 or more members of the association at least two days before the annual business meeting, but such nominations by petition shall not be presented until after the committee shall have reported its nominations to the association as provided fo in the present by-law. The official ballot shall also provide, under each office, blank space for voting for such further nominees as any member may present from the floor at the time of the election.

On motion of Mr. Paltsits, the following resolution was adopted:

Resolved, That the operation of the sentence in by-law II, beginning in the third line with the words "at such convenient time" and ending in the seventh line with the words "then to be chosen,"[2] namely, the operation of a preliminary referendum, be suspended during the year 1921.

The list of persons appointed by the executive council to serve on committees during the year 1921 was read by the secretary (see minutes of the executive council for the list of appointments).

There being no further business the meeting adjourned.

JAMES SCHOULER

The American Historical Association desires to place upon its minutes its tribute to the memory of James Schouler, LL. D., former member and officer of that body. The society long ago gave expression to its esteem by election to the highest offices in its gift, but these honors were but one manifestation of the warm personal relations which were for many years maintained between him and the members of the association.

As a soldier he fought for the unity of his native land; as a lawyer he contributed much to the literature of American jurisprudence; as an historian he devoted a large part of his life to the study of his country from its federal foundation; as a benefactor he provided, both during his lifetime and hereafter, for the continuation of historical studies in a prominent university.

His volumes will stand upon their merits with the general public, while to many students of American history and to the younger members of the profession his sympathetic interest and helpfulness will remain a source of inspiration and of grateful remembrance.

GEORGE LOUIS BEER

In the death of George Louis Beer at the height of his powers historical scholarship has suffered a painful loss, a sad sense of which this executive council desires to have expression in its records. His brief life exhibited the best traits of the gentleman, the scholar, and the citizen. Graduated from college at the age of 20, he received from Prof. H. L. Osgood the impulse that centered his interest on the commercial policy of Great Britain toward her American Colonies. For 20 years he devoted himself with singleness of aim and untiring industry to study of the historical antecedents of this policy, till by 1912 he had embodied in four published volumes a complete history of the British colonial system from 1578 to 1765. By this work Beer took, at the age of 40, high rank as a historian. In thoroughness of research among hitherto unknown or neglected sources, in freshness of interpretation and clarity of presentation, he furnished a model of historiography on its more technical side, and a massive support for the view that the revolt of the American Colonies was the result rather of transient political and economic differences among Britons than of permanent antipathies between Britons and Americans. Firmly convinced

---

[2] This is the second sentence in by-law II and reads as follows: "At such convenient time prior to the 15th of September as it may determine it shall invite every member to express to it his preference regarding every office to be filled by election at the ensuing annual business meeting and regarding the composition of the new nominating committee then to be chosen."

of the truth of this view, Beer became active in promoting good relations between the two peoples and in strengthening the bonds between Great Britain and her dominions. With the development of the World War, his wide and accurate knowledge, sound judgment, and practical sagacity came very actively into public service. At the Peace Conference he was one of the most trusted of the American experts, and when the League of Nations was organized he was named to an important position on its staff. Death took him before he could assume his duties.

In·Beer's personality the dominant note was modesty and self-effacement. No man of his learning and wisdom ever seemed less conscious of them than he. In the affairs of the American Historical Association he evaded prominence, but his loyalty to its purposes was deep and sincere. It is some poor mitigation of our grief over his untimely death to reflect that in the spirit of his writings and in the prize that he has established his influence will abide and grow mightily through generations.

REPORT OF THE SECRETARY

My residence in Washington during a sabbatical half year beginning with February 1, 1920, enabled me to gain much valuable information from Mr. Leland, my predecessor in office. I gladly take this opportunity to acknowledge his helpfulness, and to express my great admiration for the ability with which he has conducted the office, as revealed to me in my examination of the records and frequent consultations with him in regard to matters that have come up for action.

My residence in Washington enabled me to avail myself of the services of the assistant secretary, Miss Washington, whose readiness to help me is gratefully acknowledged. By reason of this help it was possible to carry on the.work of my office during this period without extra expense to the association. During the autumn, when I have been in Northampton, the expenses have been reduced to a sum of less than $20 up to December 1. In that sum are included the cost of a brief visit to Branford, Conn., to attend the meeting of the committee on policy.

Membership.—The total number of members December 15, 1920, was 2,524, as compared with 2,445 in 1919 and 2,519 in 1918. This showing probably means that the downward tendency in membership since 1915 has been stopped and progress upward has been resumed. The losses for the current year were 206, against 282 in 1919 and 285 in 1918, and they are nearly the same as in 1914, when they were 205. At no time between 1914 and 1920 have the losses been as low as in 1920. The total gain for the year was 285, more than in any year since 1915, when it was 290. Finally, this is the first year since 1915 when the membership has not shown a net decrease. It is interesting to observe the regional distribution of the net increase of 79. New England gained 6, the North Atlantic division lost 5, the South Atlantic division gained 16, the North Central division gained 30, the South Central division gained 2, the West Central division gained 11, the Pacific Coast States gained 8, and foreign countries gained 11. The largest net gain, therefore, was in the North Central division, where the net gain was 30, and the next largest was in the South Atlantic division, where it was 16. As to the new members during the year, New York led with 33, Ohio came next with 26, and California next with 21.

This favorable report on membership is due chiefly to the present committee on membership, Professor Wertenbaker, chairman. The committee has divided the country into districts, with associate members appointed by the committee. The chairman feels that the organization is not yet perfect, but that it can be improved and made to yield still better results. In order that it may best serve the ends it was created to reach, the committee should have a long term of office, with power to appoint associates as it sees fit.

Gifts to the association.—During the year the association has received a portrait of James Schouler, an ex-president of this association, a bequest in Mr Schouler's will.

The portrait is now in the office of this association in the Woodward Building, Wash ington, D. C. It is for the council to determine what disposition shall be mad of it.

By the will of the late George L. Beer the sum of $5,000 was bequeathed to th association to found a prize for the best essays in the history of the internation relations of modern Europe. It is suggested that a committee be appointed to fo mulate rules for making award of the prize.

Questionable societies.—A committee consisting of the president, secretary, an treasurer of the association considered the question referred to them by the counc of bringing suit against certain questionable societies. The committee was of th opinion that the expenses of such a suit were likely to be heavy and while they wer in sympathy with the idea that such societies should be hindered by all possibl legal means, they did not think it wise to use the funds of the association in su porting suits. The action of the committee has been approved by the council.

Affiliations.—The association is affiliated with the American Council of Learne Societies, and is represented in that body by Prof. Charles H. Haskins and Prof. J Franklin Jameson. Professor Haskins has been elected chairman of the America Council. The work of this organization in obtaining the coordination of work by th various learned societies in the United States is highly important and it is felt tha it should be supported to the extent of the ability of this association. The Ameri can Council of Learned Societies is affiliated with the Union Académique Interna tionale.

Vignaud.—November 24, the following cable message was sent to Henry Vignaud in Paris, on his ninetieth birthday:

American Historical Association sends greetings, congratulations, best wishes.

Mr. Vignaud replied as follows:

Your complimentary cable reached me on the eve of my ninetieth birthday. I am much touched by this attention coming from an association where contributions to historical researches are invaluable and to which I am proud to belong. Very weak physically, I am otherwise in good health and still able to work. Please accept my thanks for your friendly cable and believe me, gratefully yours, Henry Vignaud.

JOHN S. BASSETT, *Secretary.*

DECEASED MEMBERS, 1920

Mrs. Robert Abbe.
George Louis Beer.
Edwin Cortland Bolles.
Helen Boyce.
Richard McCall Cadwalader.
Richard M. Colgate (life member).
Abner H. Cook.
Franklin Bowditch Dexter (life member).
William Sherman Doolittle.
Walter B. Douglas.
Joseph Elkinton.
James F. Failing.
Charles Allcott Flagg.
Sameul Swett Green (life member).
Charles F. Gunther.
Francis W. Halsey.
Edith Shutte Hurst.
Grenville Mellen Ingalsbe.
Robert Matteson Johnston.

Lester Maxwell.
Robinson Locke.
Thomas Hooker Loomis
Jesse Macy.
Anna Lenore Monroe.
Joseph Eugene Moore.
Henry S. Oppenheimer.
Thomas McAdory Owen.
Charles Lawrence Peirson.
Thomas R. Proctor.
Virginia Morgan Robinson (Mrs. J. End- ers Robinson).
Frederic Schenck.
James Schouler (life member).
William H. Seward.
Arley Barthlow Show.
Francis W. Smith.
John William Venn-Watson.
Homer J. Webster.

REPORT OF THE TREASURER, NOVEMBER 30, 1920

The annual dues of the American Historical Association amount to $7,000. The interest on invested funds $1,400; and from miscellaneous sources comes about $150. The total receipts available for expenses are $8,550.

The expenses of the secretary's and treasurer's office are $3,000; the regular committees require $650; the publication committee uses $700; and the Historical Review, under the new prices, costs $8,000; making a total of $12,350. Added to this are the payments of $700 for prizes and the projects undertaken by the association, making a grand total of $13,050.

On this basis the deficit is $4,500. This deficit is made up of $3,000 increased cost of the Review over the cost for the current year: $700 increase in the office expenses; and $800 increase in the items of publications, program, and policy committees and the like.

If it were not for the increase in the cost of the Review, the voluntary contributions, amounting this year to $1,652.60, would cover the deficit. This increase of 3,000 may be partially offset in several ways. The Review receives payments by the publishers of $2,400 a year; it expends for contributions $1,500, leaving a balance of $900 which might be used toward the increased cost. The advertising may yield 1,000 under the new arrangement with the publishers recently entered into by the editors. This will still leave $1,100 to be raised from other sources

In the judgment of the treasurer, the Review should be left unhampered. Essentially it is the association, because to three-quarters of the membership it stands as their only connection with the organization. Only as a temporary expedient should payments be made from the editorial funds of the Review, and then only on the advice and consent of the board of editors. The advertising, however, is a field hitherto unworked. It is not capable of producing large revenues, but it may be made to bring in between one and two thousand dollars a year.

The ideal situation financially would be to have the dues pay for the Review and the running expenses of the association, leaving the income to be used for the projects undertaken by the association. As matters now stand, the dues do not cover the cost of the Review.

The expedient of asking a voluntary contribution of $1 has sufficed during the last two years; but even were the request to be made for $2 and were the response equally wide, their would still be a deficit.

If the dues were raised to $5 a year and the association suffered a loss of 500 members, the income would be:

From dues	$10,000
From investments	1,400
From miscellaneous sources	150
Total	11,550

The expenditures would be:

Review	6,400
Office	3,000
Committees, prizes, and projects	2,050
Total	11,450
Leaving a balance of	100

FINANCIAL STATEMENT NOVEMBER 30, 1920

Receipts:

Annual dues	$6,990.27
Life membership dues	150.00
Registration fees	107.87

Receipts—Continued.

Interest on investments	$1,330.21	
Interest on bank account	39.64	
Voluntary contributions	1,652.60	
Royalties	49.70	
Sales of publications—		
Prize essays	60.23	
Papers and reports	24.40	
Writings on American History	12.75	
Directory	13.95	
Miscellaneous	51.50	
		$10,483.1
Gift from National Board for Historical Service (Andrew D. White fund)		1,000.0
Total receipts		11,483.1
Cash balance Dec. 1, 1919		5,184.7
		16,667.8

Expenditures:

Secretary and treasurer	$2,754.43	
Pacific Coast Branch	45.05	
Committee on nominations	103.00	
Committee on membership	71.35	
Committee on program	259.30	
Committee on local arrangements	50.00	
Conference of historical societies	23.15	
Committee on publications	674.37	
American Historical Review	5,087.85	
Historical manuscripts commission	20.00	
Herbert Baxter Adams prize	200.00	
Writings on American History	200.00	
American Council of Learned Societies	122.85	
London headquarters	31.45	
Committee on policy	133.68	
American Council on Education	10.00	
		9,786.4
Liberty bonds purchased (par value, $2,000)		1,835.8
Accrued interest on Liberty bonds to date of purchase		14.4
Total expenditures		11,636.6
Cash on hand Nov. 30, 1920		5,031.1
		16,667.8

(Excess of net receipts over net expenditures, $696.64.)

Assets:

General—

Bank balance	$5,031.16	
Liberty bonds (par value, $31,450)	29,848.60	
Accrued interest on Liberty bonds	93.59	
Cash in Central Trust Co. of New York (endowment fund)	188.91	
		35,162.2
Publications in stock, estimate	6,195.00	
Furniture, office equipment, books, estimate	425.00	
		6,620.0

American Historical Review:

Bank balance	1,321.40	
Liberty bonds (par value, $1,200)	1,131.64	
Accrued interest on Liberty bonds	6.38	
		2,459.42
		44,241.68

AMERICAN HISTORICAL REVIEW—ANNUAL REPORT OF THE TREASURER,
NOVEMBER 30, 1920

:eipts:
Received from the Macmillan Co. for editorial expenses, as
 per contract... $2, 400. 00
Interest on investments................................. 51. 00
Interest on bank account................................ 23. 56

                            $2, 474. 56
Cash balance Dec. 1, 1919... 967. 42

  Total receipts.. 3, 441. 98

penditures:
Petty cash 138. 18
Printing, stationery, and supplies....................... 142. 75
Binding... 10. 25
Publications 34. 07
Travel 190. 38
Payments to contributors to Review—
  January number................................... 349. 00
  April number..................................... 369. 75
  July number...................................... 397. 25
  October number................................... 367. 00
Additional payments to the Macmillan Co. of 5 cents per
 copy on account of July number of Review sent to mem-
 bers of the American Historical Association............. 121. 95

                            2, 120. 58
Cash balance Nov. 30, 1920.. 1, 321. 40

                            3, 441. 98

: assets of the Review in cash and securities are·
Cash on hand in Union Trust Co.. 1, 321. 40
Liberty bonds (par value, $1,200) 1, 131. 64
Accrued interest on Liberty bonds....................... 6. 38

                            2, 459. 42

                CHARLES MOORE, *Treasurer.*

REPORT OF THE AMERICAN AUDIT CO.

:RICAN HISTORICAL ASSOCIATION,   DECEMBER 20, 1920.
     Washington, D. C.

EAR SIRS: We have audited your accounts and records from December 1, 1919,
Iovember 30, 1920. Our report, including three exhibits, is as follows:
xhibit A.—Assets at November 30, 1920.
xhibit B.—Statement of receipts and disbursements, general.
xhibit C.—Statement of receipts and disbursements, American Historical Review.
'e verified the cash receipts, as shown by the records, and the cash disbursements
1 the canceled checks and vouchers on file, and found the same to agree with the
surer's report.

he cash on hand in the different funds was reconciled with the bank statements.·
he Liberty bonds of the association were submitted for our inspection, and found
e as called for by the records.
espectfully submitted.

          THE AMERICAN AUDIT CO.
AL.]   By C. R. CRANMER, *Resident Manager.*
pproved:
 HARRY M. RICE, *Vice President.*
ttest:
 C. W. GORTCHINS, *Assistant Secretary.*

EXHIBIT A.—*Assets at November 30, 1920*

General:
Cash on hand..	$5, 031. 16	
Liberty bonds (par value $31,450)	29, 848. 60	
Accrued interest on Liberty bonds	93. 59	
Inventories (not verified by the American Audit Co.)—		
Publications (estimate)	6, 195. 00	
Furniture, office equipment, books (estimate).......	425. 00	
		$41, 593. 35

American Historical Review:
Cash on hand..	1, 321. 40	
Liberty bonds (par value $1, 200).......................	1, 131. 64	
Accrued interest on Liberty bonds......................	6. 38	
		2, 459. 42

Endowment fund
Cash on hand..		188. 91
		44, 241. 68

NOTE—No liabilities are reported other than small current bills, the amount of which is not known at this time.

EXHIBIT B.—*Receipts and Disbursements, December 1, 1919, to November 30, 1920*

Receipts:
Annual dues..		$6, 990. 27
Life memberships		150. 00
Registration fees		107. 87
Voluntary contributions................................		1, 652. 60
Publications		111. 33
Royalties		49. 70
Interest—		
Liberty bonds....................................	$1, 330. 21	
Bank account	39. 64	
		1, 369. 85
Miscellaneous		51. 50
Gift from National Board for Historical Service (Andrew D. White fund)....................................		1, 000. 00
Total receipts.......................................		11, 483. 12
Cash on hand Dec. 1, 1919.............................		5, 184. 72
		16, 667. 84

Disbursements:
Secretary and treasurer...............................		2, 754. 43
Pacific Coast Branch..................................		45. 05
Committee on nominations.............................		103. 00
Committee on membership..............................		71. 35
Committee on program.................................		259. 30
Committee on local arrangements......................		50. 00
Committee on historical societies....................		23. 15
Committee on publications............................		674. 37
Committee on policy..................................		133. 68
American Historical Review...........................		5, 087. 85
Historical manuscripts commission....................		20. 00
Herbert Adams Baxter prize...........................		200. 00
Writings on American History.........................		200. 00
American Council of Learned Societies................		122. 85
London headquarters..................................		31. 45
American Council on Education........................		10. 00
Liberty bonds purchased (par value $2,000)...........		1, 835. 80
Accrued interest Liberty bonds to date of purchase......		14. 40
Total disbursements..................................		11, 636. 68
Cash on hand Nov. 30, 1920...........................		5, 031. 16
		16, 667. 84

EXHIBIT C.—*American Historical Review Receipts and Disbursements, December 1, 1919, to November 30, 1920*

Receipts:

The Macmillan Co., per contract		$2,400.00
Interest—		
Liberty bonds	$51.00	
Bank account	23.56	
		74.56
Total receipts		2,474.56
Cash on hand Dec. 1, 1919		967.42
		3,441.98

Disbursements:

Petty cash	138.18
Stationery, printing, and supplies	142.75
Contributors to Review	1,483.00
Binding	10.25
Publications	34.07
Traveling expenses	190.38
Macmillan Co. additional payment on account of July number of Review	121.95
Total disbursements	2,120.58
Cash on hand Nov. 30, 1920	1,321.40
	3,441.98

REPORT OF THE AUDIT COMMITTEE

The undersigned have examined the above report of the treasurer of the American Historical Association as audited by the American Audit Co. and have found the same correct.

HERMAN V. AMES,
J. M. CALLAHAN.

DECEMBER 29, 1920.

REPORT FROM THE EXECUTIVE COUNCIL

The council has held one meeting during the year, beginning at 9.30 a. m., December 27. Through the omission of the meeting formerly held about Thanksgiving a large amount of business had been thrown over to this one meeting. It was necessary to hold five sessions of this meeting, in order to complete the work that came before the council. Provision made in accordance with a recommendation of the committee on policy, to be explained later in the report of that committee, will enable the council to take certain parts of its work in a form that may be disposed of without the necessity of crowding so much work in sessions held while the annual meetings are in progress.

By a vote of the association in 1915 the reports of the committee are submitted to the council, for approval or rejection, and then brought into the annual business meeting where they can be called up specifically by 10 members of the association. In accordance with this rule the reports of committees are present in this room. The following references are made to the contents of these reports:

The committee on London headquarters reported that the rooms occupied in London had been closed, and a balance of $16.27 returned to the treasurer of this association. The committee is discharged.

The board of editors of the American Historical Review reported progress through the year. On account of the resignation of Prof. D. C. Munro, Prof. Williston Walker was appointed to a place on the board.

97244°—25——5

No report was received from the board of editors of The Historical Outlook.

The committee on the Justin Winsor prize reported that it was unable to agree upon an award. The council ordered that the three highest papers be submitted to the committee appointed for 1921 with the request that they report as early as possible.

The committee on publications reported that the annual report for 1917 is about to be distributed. Materials for the report of 1918, in two volumes, should be ready for distribution within two months. The directory of membership will appear in Volume I of this report. The writings on American history, 1918, will also appear in this report. Separates of the directory and the writings will be issued at nominal prices. The annual report for 1919 will include the first instalment of the Stephen B. Austin paper's, edited by Prof. Eugene C. Barker, and designed as the fifteenth report of the historical manuscripts commission. On account of the slow sale of the prize essays, the total receipts of which were only $60.23 during 1920, the council authorized the committee on publications to dispose of the stock of these essays in the best manner possible. For storing and insuring these essays the cost for the year was $113.08.

The secretary of the committee on the historical congress at Rio de Janerio reported progress and the report was accepted.

The committee on the military history prize reported that the prize was awarded to Thomas Robson Hay for his essay on "Hood's Tennessee campaign."

The committee on membership reported the results of their efforts to enlarge the membership of the association, resulting in a net gain of 79 members. This is the first net gain in membership since 1915. The chairman of the committee, Professor Wertenbaker, was authorized to enlarge the membership of the committee by appointing associate members acting in conjunction with the secretary of the association. .

The committee on bibliography of modern English history reported progress.

The committee on a manual of historical literature reported that plans have been made and cooperating bibliographers have been obtained to carry on the work vigorously. The council decided, in accordance with the recommendation of the committee on policy, to revive the committee on bibliography and to combine with it the present committee upon the manual of historical literature.

The council decided, in view of invitations previously extended, to accept the invitation to hold its annual meeting of 1921 in St. Louis. Considerations prompting this decision were the centennial celebration in St. Louis and the geographical position of that city, which makes it advisable that the next meeting of the association should be west of the Alleghany Mountains.

The historical manuscripts commission reported that the Stephen B. Austin papers to be published in the annual report of the association were being prepared, and an instalment had been delivered to the committee on publications.

The committee on history and education for citizenship in the schools made its report. The council voted that in discharging the committee at its own request the council desires to record its high appreciation of the committee's laborious service. The council referred the report of the committee to the new committee on history in schools.

The report of the conference of historical societies was received and approved.

No reports were received from the committees on the Herbert Baxter Adams prize and on bibliography, which were inoperative during the year.

The council recommends the creation of the following standing committees:

On obtaining transcripts from foreign archives.
On military history.
On patriotic societies.
On service.

and the following special committees:

On the documentary publications of the United States Government.
On the writing of history.
To formulate rules for the George L. Beer prize.
To cooperate with the Peoples of America Society in studying race elements in the United States.

REPORT OF THE COMMITTEE ON POLICY

Introduction.—The committee on policy was appointed by the council in 1917 for the purpose of preparing for consideration by the council a comprehensive program of scientific activities which the association might appropriately maintain or undertake. By reason of the various services which its members were called upon to perform in connection with the war and with the peace conference, the committee was prevented from entering actively upon its duties until the present year. A meeting of the committee was held at Branford, Conn., on September 13 and 14, 1920, the following members being present: Messrs. Haskins, Becker, Munro, and there being also present, by request of the committee, Messrs. Bassett, Moore and Leland, respectively secretary, treasurer, and ex-secretary of the association. The committee had before it a summary of the past and present activities of the association, prepared by Mr. Leland; a statement of the financial condition of the association, prepared by Mr. Moore; a letter of suggestions from Mr. G. S. Ford, an absent member of the committee; and a proposal by Mr. L. G. Connor respecting an enterprise in agricultural history.

The committee held four sessions and agreed upon the following conclusions and recommendations. By request of the committee Mr. Leland served as secretary.

1. *Annual meetings.*—The committee does not recommend any change in the present practice of the association with respect to the place and time of holding the annual meetings. It should, however, be observed that the practice of holding the meeting during the Christmas holidays is attended by certain difficulties, such as congestion of railroad travel, exposure to inclement weather, and interruption of family reunions, which would be obviated if some more favorable period were selected as a common vacation time by all educational institutions.

The committee believes that the meetings would benefit from the appointment of a standing committee on program. Such a committee might be composed of five members (it should not be much larger), three of whom should serve for terms of three years, so arranged that one member would retire each year, the other two to be appointed for a term of one year and to be selected with reference to the locality of the meeting during their term of service. It is believed that such a committee would be able to maintain such a degree of continuity or progression in the subject matter of the meetings as might be desirable. It should also anticipate significant historical anniversaries, not only in American history but in general history, and should especially endeavor to stimulate research by arranging sessions on research in the various fields of history, commencing with American history.

2. *Annual report.*—The annual report of the association has the status of a public document and is widely distributed, going not only to members of the association but also to the depository libraries in the United States and to the libraries, societies, and institutions in foreign countries which are included in the International Exchange Service. It is highly important that the report should be as representative as possible of the best work of the association. At present the report contains the following material:

The proceedings of the association, including the account of the meetings that appear in the April number of the Review, the minutes of the business meetings of the association and of the council, and the reports of officers and committees.

Proceedings of the Pacific Coast Branch.

Presidential address, reprinted from the Review.[3]

Papers read at the annual meeting which are not printed elsewhere and which are accepted by the committee on publications.

Papers read before the Pacific Coast Branch and offered by the executive com. mittee of the branch.

Report of the public archives commission, with proceedings of the conference of archivists.

Report of the historical manuscripts commission.

Proceedings of the conference of historical societies.

Writings on American history.

Contribution of the Agricultural History Society.

The committee has no radical change to suggest in the contents of the report except in one particular. The number of papers read at meetings which find pub. lication elsewhere than in the report appears to be increasing, with the result that the comparatively few papers which are included in the annual report are less and less representative. The committee recommends therefore that in place of the papers read at the meetings now printed and in place also of the general account of the meetings reprinted from the Review there be prepared and printed a scholarly sum- mary or abstract of all the papers read at the meetings and not printed in the Review or in the report, and that the space thus saved be devoted to the publication of more fully developed contributions, such as have sometimes been printed in the past, which are too long for presentation in a periodical such as the Review.

The committee also recommends that writings on American history be again divorced from the annual report as soon as other arrangements for its publication can be made (see below, sec. 9), and it suggests that the report, rather than the Review, is the appropriate place for the publication of the presidential address, provided always that it is found possible to bring out the annual report within a reasonable time after the annual meeting. The present policy of indexing the reports with a view to publishing a cumulated index at suitable periods, say of 10 years, should be maintained. The committee especially urges the importance of making every effort to publish each annual report within as short a time as possible after the meetings to which it appertains, and in any event before the next annual meeting.

3. *Historical manuscripts commission.*—Soon after its establishment the council define the function of the historical manuscripts commission as the location, cal- endaring, and printing of historical manuscripts of historical significance which are in private hands and which are not likely soon to be placed in public depositories. This policy has not been consistently followed, for the commission has printed several collections which are in public depositories and has even printed groups of archival documents which do not fall within the category of historical manuscripts. The committee believes that the function of the commission as originally defined is the proper one, and that the location and calendaring of historical manuscripts should receive special attention, while the printing of material in public depositories should be avoided. The committee recommends that the commission make an especial effort to cooperate with the Library of Congress in locating material suitable for acquisi- tion by the Manuscript Division. The committee also recommends that the commis- sion give further consideration to the plan, set forth in its report of December, 1916, of locating and publishing fugitive Revolutionary material in private hands. Other classes of material to which attention might be given are the letters of American historians, the records of home missionary societies, etc.

4. *Public archives commission.*—The public archives commission has completed, so far as practicable, its original program of preparing and printing reports on the

---

[3]Now omitted from the report.

archives of the several States. The committee believes that the commission should be continued for the practical service it can render to the development of archive economy and practice in the United States. The commission should serve as a clearing house of information respecting archival matters and its reports should contain a summary of American legislation respecting archives, together with notes of important developments both in this country and abroad. The commission should continue to organize annual conferences of archivists, as part of the annual meetings of the association, and should be charged with the preparation of the primer of archive economy now confined to a special committee.

5. *Committee on the national archives.*—The erection in Washington of a building for the national archives and the organization of their administration are matters of the utmost importance to all students of American history, and the association has from its earliest days frequently manifested its deep interest therein. The present standing committee on the national archives, consisting of members residing in Washington, should be maintained and should receive the utmost support that the association can give it.

6. *Committee on securing transcripts from foreign archives.*—The Library of Congress is engaged in securing from the archives of foreign countries transcripts of those documents most important for the history of the United States. In this work the Library has at various times asked for the advice of members of the association, and the program of copying in the British archives was drawn up by a subcommittee of the public archives commission. The chief of the Manuscript Division has requested that the association appoint a permanent advisory committee to aid the division in the selection of material to be transcribed. The committee accordingly recommends that such a committee be established, composed, naturally, of those members of the association who have the fullest acquaintance with the material in question.

7. *Committee on the documentary historical publications of the United States Government.*—In 1908 a special committee of the association prepared an elaborate report on the systematic publication by the National Government of series of historical documents. This report was printed as Senate Document 714, Sixtieth Congress, second session, and was distributed to members of the association; the committee on policy believes that, if possible, results should be obtained from the important and exceedingly valuable work of this committee. It is recommended, therefore, that the committee be reappointed and charged with the consideration of methods by which its program, or some part thereof, may be carried out.

8. *Bibliography.*—The committee recommends that the standing committee on bibliography be continued and that it be charged with completing and publishing the bibliography of American travel which has been long in process of compilation. The committee should also be charged with the part which the association has, in cooperation with the American Library Association, in compiling a manual of historical literature to take the place of the manual, now out of date, compiled by C. K. Adams. While the selection of new enterprises in bibliography must mainly be left to the discretion of the committee, it is nevertheless recommended that work be commenced on a check list of collections in American libraries relating to the World War; that the committee consider the desirability of continuing the bibliography of the publications of American and Canadian historical societies, compiled to 1905 by Mr. A. P. C. Griffin; and especially that the committee should institute a series of bibliographical notices of special collections of historical material, printed or in manuscript, in American libraries, at the same time undertaking or otherwise providing for the preparation of catalogues or calendars of certain classes of material.

The committee also recommends that the work of compiling and publishing, in cooperation with English scholars, a bibliography of modern English history, be pushed to completion in charge of the special committee which now has it in hand.

9. *Writings on American History.*—The committee believes most strongly in the continuance of the annual bibliography of Writings on American History which is perhaps the best annual national historical bibliography currently published. It is to be regretted that the recent publishers of the volume feel unable to carry it on and the committee feels that it should not be printed in the annual report if some other means of publication can be found. The committee recommends that the various questions connected with the compilation and publication of Writings, especially its financial support both from contributions and from sales, be fully considered anew and that every effort be made by the association to make this enterprise as self-sustaining as possible and to discover some dependable means of guaranteeing any avoidable deficit. The committee especially urges that every effort be made to insure the prompt publication of the volume, feeling that the delay it now suffers seriously detracts from its value and makes more difficult the question of its support.

10. *History teaching in the schools.*—The committee has a strong sense of the importance of maintaining the interest of the association in the various problems connected with the teaching of history in schools. Having in mind the influence which the reports of the associations's committees have had in this field, the committee is of the opinion that the standing committee on history in the schools should be reconstituted in order that the association may have a body to which may be referred for report the various questions with respect to history teaching which come before it. Such a committee should be not only a committee of reference but should also initiate investigations appropriate to its field. Emphasis is laid, however, on the desirability of requiring the committee to submit to the council any report which it is proposed to put forth embodying the findings or opinions of the committee, and inferentially of the association. This rule should also be applied with respect to the special committee on history and education for citizenship in the schools, which is now engaged in the preparation of its report.

11. *Historical societies.*—The committee desires to emphasize the importance of maintaining cordial, sustained, and effective relations with the various State and local historical societies of the country. The conference of historical societies which was inaugurated in 1904 as a regular feature of the annual meetings should be continued. The reorganization of the conference which was agreed upon in 1916, the details of which are to be found in the annual report of that year (pp. 232–235), was designed to stimulate the conference to greater activity and to provide for a larger degree of cooperation with historical societies. The committee has no specific recommendations to make under this head, thinking it better to wait until the effect of the reorganization referred to can be known.

12. *Patriotic societies.*—A conference of hereditary patriotic societies was held as part of the meetings of 1916, which requested the council to appoint a committee composed of representatives of the societies and of the association for the purpose of preparing definite suggestions respecting cooperation in the various lines of historical work. The council appointed a special committee of three, one of whom has since died. The committee has not as yet presented a report. It is strongly recommended, in view of the possibilities of important and effective work, that the committee be reconstituted and charged with the preparation of a report in the near future.

13. *Military history.*—Having in mind the recognition given by the agencies of the Government to the claims of history, as attested by such developments as the creation of the Historical Branch of the General Staff, the committee recommends that there be appointed a standing committee on military history, the chief function of which should be to advise and cooperate with the Historical Branch and with other governmental agencies, national and State, which are engaged in preparing histories

of the war. The committee should include a representative of the Historical Branch and a representative of the National Association of State War History Organizations.

14. *Agricultural history.*—The committee favors the maintenance of the existing arrangement with the Agricultural History Society, although it hopes that the time will come when the society may be able to maintain a publication of its own instead of depending upon space in the annual report of the association. The committee has considered a proposal laid before it by Mr. L. G. Connor, of the Agricultural History Society, for the establishment of a central bureau for gathering, compiling, and editing data relating to American agricultural history. The committee believes that the association should authorize this enterprise, provided the necessary degree of cooperation with the Department of Agriculture can be secured, and provided that the considerable funds necessary for so large an undertaking can be obtained without any obligation upon the association.

15. *Historical studies.*—The committee has taken into consideration the desire expressed by many members of the historical profession for some means of publishing historical studies which because of their length, technical character, or special nature are unsuited to existing historical periodicals; the committee has also considered the proposal, developed at some length in 1916, for the establishment of a review devoted to European history. The committee is strongly of the opinion that a further medium of publication of historical contributions is desirable; that such a medium should be established and maintained by the association; and that it should attract largely but not exclusively contributions in European history. The committee is, however, convinced that it is not expedient to establish a European history review. Such a review would inevitably duplicate in certain of its departments the work now satisfactorily performed by the organ of the association, the American Historical Review, and the committee believes that it would be preferable to devote the corresponding additional energy and financial support to enlarging the present Review. The committee proposes that there be established, by means of subscriptions and a guarantee fund, a quarterly publication bearing some such title as "Historical Studies," or "American Studies in History," or "Studies of the American Historical Association," which, omitting reviews and notes, shall be devoted exclusively to historical contributions of the highest scholarship, but of rather more technical or special character than the articles usually published in the Review and not subject to the limitations as to length which it is necessary to apply to the articles in the Review.

16. *Prizes.*—The committee recommends that the prize in military history offered this year be known as the Robert M. Johnston prize, in memory of the late Professor Johnston, whose generosity and interest in military history made the offering of the prize possible. The committee recommends that the prize hereafter to be offered annually, in accordance with the Beer bequest, for an essay in the history of recent European international relations be known as the George Louis Beer prize, in memory of the distinguished donor.

The committee raises the question whether further modification of the rules governing the competition for the Winsor and Adams prizes may not be desirable in order more specifically to encourage research by those who have already obtained the doctorate.

17. *American Council of Learned Societies.*—The committee believes that the association is to be congratulated on the part it has been able to take in the organization of the International Union of Academies and of its American member, the American Council of Learned Societies. In the opinion of the committee no more effective way can be found for the association to contribute to the advancement of the humanistic studies and to cooperate with other associations of scholars, both abroad and in

this country, than through the union and the council. Both should be supported to the extent of the association's ability, and the Andrew D. White fund, inaugurated by the National Board for Historical Service and turned over to the association for aiding the latter to take part in the enterprises of the union and of the council, should be enlarged as it is found possible to do so. The committee believes that one of the most useful of domestic enterprises which the American Council of Learned Societies could undertake would be the editing of the long-desired Dictionary of American Biography, and the committee recommends that the council of the association call the attention of the association's delegates in the Council of Learned Societies to this matter.

18. *University center for higher studies in Washington.*—In 1916 the council approved the plan drawn up by a special committee for establishing in Washington a residential center for higher studies in history, economics, and political science, which should be under the control of those departments of the various universities contributing to the support of the center. The committee believes that this plan is the best that has been proposed for encouraging historical research in Washington, and trusts that means may be found for putting it into execution.

19. *Advisory committee on activities.*—The committee recommends that the council appoint a standing advisory committee, the function of which should be to lay before the council from tim? to time proposals to the end that the association may always be possessed of a well-considered, balanced program of appropriate activities. The advisory committee should meet at least once a year, in addition to any meetings it might hold during the annual meetings of the association, and should invite the secretary and treasurer of the association to meet with it.

20. *Committee on service.*—In accordance with the previous note of the council there should be established a standing committee on service, the chairman of which should, in the absence of a salaried secretary of the association, be chosen from among the members residing in Washington. The function of the committee should be to establish relations of service with the various departments of the National Government, to answer such queries relating to historical matters as may be reviewed from time to time by the association, and in general to make more available to the public the services of the association and of historical scholarship.

21. *Finance*—The committee realizes keenly that it is of little use to plan a program of scientific activities unless adequate financial support is assured. In the present state of the association's exchequer the annual income from dues is entirely absorbed by the payments for the American Historical Review and by expenses of administration. The only income available for scientific work is that derived from the invested funds, which now amount to a little over $30,000. It is clear that a vigorous and sustained campaign for an increased endowment must be entered upon. The association should have a salaried secretary who could devote all his time to its affairs, and for this alone a special endowment of at least $100,000 is needed. Further endowment sufficient to assure an income of $10,000 for scientific activities alone should be secured. These are, perhaps, ideals difficult of attainment, but they should never be lost from sight, and every year should see the association appreciably nearer to them. In the meantime the committee recommends the appointment of a standing committee on endowment which should push immediately and actively, by every possible means, the raising of an adequate endowment for the association's work.

In view of the greatly increased expenses of the American Historical Review, the actual printing expenses of which now cost $2.88 per annum, it is plain that the association must take active measures to increase the income received from each member. The least that can be done would be to raise from $1 to $2 the amount annually requested from each member in addition to his dues. It is for the council to decide whether this is sufficient or whether it may not be necessary to advance at once the annual dues to $5.

CHARLES H. HASKINS, *Chairman.*
CARL BECKER.
WILLIAM E. DODD.
GUY STANTON FORD.
DANA C. MUNRO.

DECEMBER 11, 1920.

APPENDIX

ACTIVITIES OF THE AMERICAN HISTORICAL ASSOCIATION 1884–1920

MEMORANDUM FOR THE COMMITTEE ON POLICY

By Waldo G. Leland

[September, 1920]

1. *Pacific Coast Branch.*—The Pacific Coast Branch was organized in 1903, in order that members of the association living in the far West might have more convenient opportunities for holding meetings than those afforded them by the annual meetings of the association. The branch, which embraces the membership of the association residing in the Mountain and Coast States, chooses its own officers and committees, arranges for its own meetings, and carries on such activities as it sees fit. Its members however, pay their annual dues into the general treasury, which in turn makes a small annual appropriation for the administrative expenses of the branch. The executive committee of the branch selects certain of the papers read before it for inclusion in the annual report of the association.

2. *Agricultural History Society.*—The Agricultural History Society was organized in Washington in 1919, with the aid of local members of the association. A temporary arrangement has been effected between the society and the association whereby the principal literary meeting of the former is held as a session of the annual meetings of the latter. The association has agreed to publish in its annual report from 200 to 300 pages of material supplied by the society, subject to the approval of the committee on publications. The society is represented informally in the council and on the program committee of the association.

3. *American Society of Church History.*—In 1896 the American Society of Church History united with the association as a church history section. The arrangement was not wholly satisfactory, partly because the membership of the church history section was largely of the East, and the annual meetings of the association were not always conveniently located for it, but more especially because the governmental connection of the association made it impossible for the latter to print in the annual reports papers dealing with church or religous history. The section was dissolved in 1903 and the American Society of Church History was reorganized as an independent organization, being incorporated under the laws of New York. A joint session of the two societies was held during the annual meetings of 1917.

4. *Mississippi Valley Historical Association.*—In 1907 the newly organized Mississippi Valley Historical Association applied to the council to be made a branch of the association similar to the Pacific Coast Branch, but the council voted that it was inexpedient to establish a branch in the Mississippi Valley. The only relation between the two organizations is an arrangement whereby they hold a joint session presided over by the president of the Mississippi Valley Association as part of the annual meetings of the American Historical Association.

5. *Southern History Association.*—In 1890 a joint committee of the American Historical Association and the Southern History Association reported to the council a plan for the discontinuance of the latter, the transfer of its records and publications to the American Historical Association, and the merging of the membership of the smaller body in that of the larger by the payment of the usual membership dues. The association was to maintain a standing committee for the promotion of historical study in the South. No action was taken in the matter.

6. *Foreign headquarters.*—In 1913 headquarters were established in London in the building occupied by the Royal Historical Society, the association assuming a proportionate part of the rental of the building, at an annual cost of $150. The purpose of this move was to provide an attractive center for American students in England and for English students interested in American history. With the establishment on a permanent basis of the American University Union this object was attained in another way and the headquarters were discontinued early in the present year (1920). Plans were on foot in 1914 to establish similar headquarters in Paris, where the Minister of Public Instruction had offered accommodations, but the war prevented them from being carried out.

7. *American Council of Learned Societies.*—The association is a member of the American Council of Learned Societies organized in 1919–20 for the purpose of enabling American societies devoted to the humanistic studies to have an effective participation in the International Union of Academies, in the organization of which body the delegates of the association had had an important part. The association has two delegates in the council, one of whom is the present chairman of that body, and pays an annual fee of 5 cents for each member. The association has received from the National Board for Historical Service a fund of $1,000, known as the Andrew D. White fund, the income of which is to be devoted to aiding it to carry on its share of the work of the council. Ten other societies are at present members of the council.

8. *Meetings.*—The annual meetings of the association have always been regarded as one of its most important activities. Thus far meetings have been held in Saratoga, Boston, Providence, New Haven, New York, Philadelphia, Baltimore, Washington, Richmond, Columbia, Charleston, New Orleans, Buffalo, Detroit, Cleveland, Cincinnati, Indianapolis, Chicago, Madison, and San Francisco. Until 1895 the meetings were usually held in Washington, but since then they have been held in rotation in such a way as best to suit the convenience of the members of the association. The rotation of East, West, and Washington, adapted in 1898 was abandoned, so far as Washington was concerned, in 1909. The attendance at the meetings ranges from 300 to 500, the larger figures generally being secured in Boston, New York, Washington, and Chicago.

The first program committee was appointed for the meetings of 1890, when for the first time the practice of grouping the papers according to subject was adopted. In 1895 was inaugurated the practice of holding simultaneous sessions, in order to accommodate the increasing variety of interests. In 1904 so-called round-table conferences were instituted for the purpose of providing opportunity for informal discussion. Dinner and luncheon conferences are a more recent innovation, and have become a regular part of the meetings.

The subjects to which sessions are devoted vary from year to year and reflect the current or temporary interest of the public and of the historical profession. What may be called a normal program, however, usually includes sessions or conferences on ancient, medieval, modern European, English, and American (including Latin-American) history, as well as conferences of archivists, of historical societies, and of teachers of history, and joint sessions with the Mississippi Valley Historical Association and with the Agricultural History Society.

9. *Historical congresses.*—The association has taken part, by sending delegates (at their own expense), in various historical congresses, notably the international congresses of Rome, 1903, Berlin, 1908, and London, 1913, the Congress of Archivists in Brussels, 1910, the historical congress of the Norman Millenary in Rouen, 1911, and various congresses of the Americanists. Of South American congresses, now being held with increasing frequency, the association has been represented at the Congress of History and Bibliography in Buenos Aires in 1916, and has accepted an invitation to take part in the congress to be held in Rio Janeiro in 1923 in celebration of the one hundredth anniversary of Brazilian independence.

10. *Historical celebrations.*—The association has not pursued any definite policy with regard to the celebration of historical anniversaries. The annual meetings of important anniversary years have generally included papers pertinent to the occasion, but only once does the association appear to have taken the initiative in calling attention to an approaching anniversary; in 1886 a special committee waited upon President Cleveland to ask him to represent to Congress the desirability of a suitable celebration of the Columbian quartercentenary. Participation in anniversary celebrations has usually been upon invitation from their organizers.

11. *Annual report.*—The annual report of the association has the status of a public document. It is transmitted to the Secretary of the Smithsonian Institution, who submits it, or such part of it as he may see fit, to Congress for publication. The association is allowed 2,000 copies. The Smithsonian Institution distributes it to foreign libraries and institutions through the International Exchange Service, and the Superintendent of Documents distributes it to the depository libraries in this country.

The annual report usually contains from 1,000 to 1,200 pages and is generally printed in two volumes. The association has been allowed such reprints from the report as it may have required. The publication of the report is under the direction of the committee on publications and is the chief function of the editor of the association, who serves as secretary of the committee. A cumulative index to papers and reports was printed as Volume II of the report for 1914, and the current indexes are now being made with a view to their cumulation at intervals of 10 years. At present the annual report normally contains the following:

Proceedings of the association, including the account of the meetings printed in the Review, the minutes of the business meeting and of the council, and the reports of officers and committees.
Proceedings of the Pacific Coast Branch.
Presidential address.[4]
Papers read at the annual meeting which are not printed elsewhere, and which are accepted by the committee on publications.
Papers offered by the executive committee of the Pacific Coast Branch.
Report of the public archives commission, with proceedings of the conference of archivists.
Report of the historical manuscripts commission.
Proceedings of the conference of historical societies.
Writings on American history.
Contributions of the Agricultural History Society.

12. *Historical manuscripts commission.*—The historical manuscripts commission was established in 1895 after an unsuccessful effort to secure congressional legislation creating a governmental commission. The policy of the commission, so far as it has been defined, has been to locate, calendar, and print historical manuscripts of national significance in private hands, not likely soon to be placed in public depositories. This policy has not been consistently followed. Since the first years of the commission's existence no systematic effort has been made to locate collections of papers in private hands, and there has been almost no calendaring of the

[4] Printed in the Review. Now omitted from the report.

sort that characterizes the reports of the Royal Historical Manuscripts Commission. Of the collections of documents printed in the annual reports several do not fall within the category of historical manuscripts in private hands. Two of them, the Texan Diplomatic Correspondence and the Despatches of the French Commissioners to the United States, are public archives rather than historical manuscripts. Other collections, such as the Chase papers, the Van Buren autobiography, and the Austin papers, are in public depositories and might conceivably have been published by other agencies. The Calhoun, Bayard, and Hunter, and the Combs, Stephens, and Cobb collections are, however, well within the category indicated.

At the present time the commission has in press the Van Buren autobiography and the first of three volumes of Austin papers, and has in preparation a volume of letters to Calhoun. Some years ago the commission formnlated a plan for collecting as widely as possible and printing Revolutionary letters and papers in the possession of individuals, but this plan has not been carried out.

The commission joined with the Library of Congress some years ago in preparing and printing a set of suggestions for the editing and publication of original documents.

13. *Public archives commission.*—The public archives commission was organized in 1899, its function being to report on the character of the historical archives of the several States and of the United States, and on the means taken for their preservation and publication. After an unsuccessful effort to secure an appropriation of $5,000 from Congress for carrying on its work the commisson decided to confine its attention to the archives of the States. Adjunct members were appointed to represent the commission in the various States and they undertook to prepare descriptive reports on State archives. In this way reports have been made on the archives of over 40 States. These reports vary greatly in character, from the most summary accounts to detailed inventories. The work has been done without remuneration other than the reimbursement of expenses incurred in travel and for clerical assistance.

The commission has also published several bibliographies of printed archival material and lists of special classes of documents, such as Bibliography of the Printed Archives of the Original States; List of Representations and Reports of the Board of Trade; List of the Journals and Acts of Colonial Legislatures; List of Commissions and Instructions to Colonial Governors, etc.

Through a subcommittee the commission has directed the work of transcribing documents from the British archives for the Library of Congress.

Since its establishment the commission has carried on a persistent propaganda for appropriate legislation respecting archives designed to insure their preservation and their proper administration and utilization, and it is not too much to credit the commission with most of the advance in such matters that has been achieved in the United States during the last 20 years. Furthermore, the commission has been able, through participation in the Congress of Archivists in Brussels in 1910 and through the annual conferences of archivists which it instituted in 1909, to inculcate and encourage in this country the best methods of archive administration.

The commission has never published documentary material, the council having decided adversely in that matter.

At present the commission is in a state of suspended activity. A primer of archive economy, planned by the commission, is now being prepared by a special committee of two, one of whom is the chairman of the commission.

14. *Federal archives.*—The association has, from its first meeting in Washington, been concerned for the safe-keeping, proper administration, and historical utilization of the Federal archives. Special committees have been appointed on the subject, and Congress has frequently been memorialized. There is reason to hope that a national archives' building may be erected in the not too distant future. The

association has a standing committee whose principal function is to watch the situation in Washington and exert whatever influence it may have to secure proper provision for the archives. The committee consists of the chiefs of the Department of Historical Research in the Carnegie Institution, of the Manuscript Division in the Library of Congress, and of the Historical Branch of the General Staff.

15. *United States historical documentary publications.*—In 1908 a special committee was appointed, which received the status of a subcommittee of the governmental committee on department methods, to consider the question of systematic publication by the Government of historical documents from its archives. The committee drew up a plan for such publication and embodied it in a careful and comprehensive report which was presented to Congress by President Roosevelt and printed. No further action has been taken in the matter.

16. *Bibliography.*—The bibliographical output of the association has been varied and large. It commenced with bibliographies, 1889–1892, of members of the association compiled first by Paul Leicester Ford and later by A. Howard Clark; A. P. C. Griffin's Bibliography of Historical Societies was commenced in the annual report for 1890, its final edition being printed as Volume II of the report for 1905. In 1894 the council voted to expend not more than $500 in securing "systematic bibliographies representing the progress and condition of American historical science."

In 1898 a standing committee on bibliography was appointed, and under its direction were compiled most of the bibliographies which have appeared in the annual reports. It was influential in securing the compilation and publication of J. N. Larned's Literature of American History; it published a trial edition of a Union List of Collections on European History in American Libraries (Princeton, 1912) and took charge of the Bibliography of American Travels, which was commenced by a special committee and which now, comprising about 4,500 titles, is awaiting final editing and publication. The committee commenced work on a finding list of historical periodicals in American libraries, a task which has been taken over by the Library of Congress, and prepared a list of American historical periodicals which was published in the annual report for 1916. The committee has been suspended for lack of funds to enable it to carry on any systematic work, but the chairman of the committee has been authorized to cooperate with the American Library Association in the compilation of a new bibliography of general history to take the place of the Manual of Historical Literature published by C. K. Adams.

17. *Writings on American history*—Writings on American History is an annual bibliography compiled and published since 1906 under the auspices of the association, which subscribes $200 each year to a fund to which other historical societies and some individuals also subscribe. The compilation is under the direction of Dr. J. F. Jameson and is performed by Miss Grace G. Griffin. For some years the Yale Press has brought out the annual volume at a net loss, but it has now been obliged to give up its publication, and the bibliography will appear as part of the annual report of the association.

18. *Bibliography of modern English history.*—A conference on research in English history, held during the meetings of 1908, requested the council to appoint a committee on the preparation of a bibliography of modern English history along the lines of the work by the late Charles Gross for the earlier period. The council appointed such a committee, which at once secured the cooperation of a group of English scholars, and the work of compilation was planned and commenced. By 1914 the American collaborators had completed their contribution to the first two of the three volumes which it was proposed to publish, but the project was interrupted by the war, and the committee was authorized by the council to suspend its activities. In 1919 the chairman of the committee was authorized by the council to secure if possible the resumption of work on both sides and to push for the comple-

tion of the bibliography. The association holds in trust a gift of $125 which the committee secured toward the expense of publication.

19. *History teaching in schools.*—(a) Committee of seven. In 1896 the association appointed a committee of seven to prepare and recommend to the National Education Association a plan of historical studies in secondary schools. The final report of the committee was published in 1899, The Study of History in Schools (Macmillan), and has had an influence of first importance upon history teaching.

(b) Committee of five. In 1907 the committee of review of college entrance examinations asked for a new definition of the field of ancient history and for the reconsideration of certain other points in the report of the committee of seven concerning college admission requirements. A committee of five was appointed to deal with the request and in general to review the report of the committee of seven. The new committee prepared a report which was accepted by the council and was published as a supplement to the report of the committee of seven, and also in the annual report of the association for 1910.

(c) Committee of eight. A conference on the teaching of history in the elementary schools which was held as part of the meetings of 1904 requested the council to appoint a committee to investigate and report to the association on a course of history for the elementary schools and on the proper training of teachers. In response to this request the committee of eight was appointed which held conferences at successive meetings of the association and presented a report which was published in 1909, The Study of History in the Elementary Schools (Scribner's Sons).

(d) Committee on qualifications of teachers of history. In 1910 a conference of teachers of history in normal schools and teachers' colleges requested the council to appoint a committee on the qualifications of teachers of history in high schools. As a result of this request, a committee was appointed the principal activity of which was to encourage discussion of the subject by teachers' associations and similar bodies. The committee did not attempt to establish any standard qualifications for history teaching and presented no formal report. It was discontinued in 1913.

(e) Committee on history in schools. In 1914 a standing committee on history in schools was appointed for the purpose of dealing with any matters in its field that might come before the association. The first matter to be referred to it was the request from the College Entrance Examination Board for a fuller definition of the requirements in history. The committee held various conferences and carried on much correspondence, but the war interrupted its work, and it did not present any report. It was suspended in 1919.

(f) Joint committee on history and education for citizenship in the schools. In the early part of 1919 the National Board for Historical Service, at the request of the National Education Association, appointed a "reconstruction" committee on history in the schools. The object of the committee was to prepare a complete report on the study and teaching of history in all schools below the grade of college, having in mind the conditions brought about by the war. This committee, with additions, was adopted by the council as a committee of the association. The National Board having ceased to exist, the committee is no longer a joint one. The committee has held a large number of conferences in various parts of the country and has presented tentative reports. It is expected to present its complete report at the coming meeting of the association.

20. *History teaching in colleges and universities.*—No systematic consideration has been given to the subject of the study and teaching of history in colleges and universities. Frequent conferences have been held in connection with the annual meetings for discussing certain aspects of the subject, such, for example, as the first year in history, the requirements for the doctorate, the teaching of oriental history, etc. Two informal dinner conferences in 1917 and 1919 have discussed the teach-

ing of the history of the Far East, and a committee appointed at these conferences has had the subject under consideration, but this is an activity within rather than of the association.

21. *Historical Outlook.*—The History Teacher's Magazine was founded in 1909 as a private enterprise. In 1911, on recommendation from the board of editors of the American Historical Review, the association took the magazine under its auspices, giving it an annual subsidy of $600, securing an equal amount for it from other sources, and appointing an advisory editorial board. In return for this support the publisher supplied the magazine at half rate to the members of the association and of the history teachers' associations. This arrangement was continued, but the subsidy was later diminished to $400 and then to $200. During the war, with the aid of the National Board for Historical Service the magazine became self-supporting and the subsidy of the association was withdrawn, as was also the reduction in the subscription rate to members of the association. The title of the magazine was changed to Historical Outlook in order that the pedagogical element in the publication might not appear too prominent. In 1919 the council, at the request of the editor, appointed a board of editors.

22. *Historical societies.*—In 1885 the association voted to urge upon its members residing in the newer parts of the United States the desirability of organizing and maintaining local historical societies; thus from its beginning the association has displayed the keenest interest in the welfare of State and local historical organizations. In 1889 a list of historical societies was printed in the papers, and in the same year the council directed the officers to communicate with the State historical societies expressing the desire of the association to cooperate with them and to exchange publications, inviting them to send representatives to the next meeting of the association, and requesting of each society a brief account of its origin, history, organization, publications, collections, and activities in general.

In 1897 a special session of the meetings was devoted to historical societies, and a plan of affiliation between State and local societies and the association was offered to the council but was not acted upon. In 1898 the general committee was established, one of whose functions was to consider the relations between the association and other historical societies. In 1904 a subcommittee of the general committee was authorized to prepare a report on the best methods of organization and work on the part of state and local historical societies. This report, carefully prepared, was published in the annual report for 1905.

The most important development in the relations of the association with local and State societies was the inauguration, in 1904, of the annual conferences of historical societies for the discussion of problems and for the planning of cooperative activities. The conference is now a semi-independent body, electing its own officers, except for the secretary who is appointed by the council and who ranks as a committee chairman, preparing the program of its meetings, and in general conducting its own affairs, always under the auspices of the association. This reorganization of the conference dates from 1917 but has not yet been fully effected, especially as regards financial support from the societies which belong to the conference. The conference particularly desires the publication of a handbook of American historical societies and agencies and the continuation of A. P. C. Griffin's bibliography to the present date. The proceedings of the conference are at present printed in the annual report of the association.

The principal cooperative activity undertaken by the conference has been the calendaring of documents in French archives relating to the Mississippi Valley. A fund of $4,000 was raised for this work; the exploration of the archives has been practically completed and the calendar is being edited by the Carnegie Institution, which proposes to publish it.

23. *Patriotic societies*—A conference of patriotic societies was held in connection with the meetings of 1916 and requested the council to appoint a committee to prepare definite suggestions for methods of cooperation between the association and the patriotic societies in various lines of historical work. A committee of three was appointed in 1917.

24. *European historical societies.*—In 1910 a committee was appointed to consider the preparation of a report on the work of European historical societies. The committee printed in the annual report for 1911 a list of European societies but with no details respecting them. The committee reported that in its opinion a list of European societies with such information respecting their organization, governmental connection, publications, activities, etc., as might be useful to American societies and scholars was a desideratum.

25. *Military history.*—A conference on military history was held as part of the meetings of 1912 and appointed a committee on military history. This committee was confirmed by the council and became one of the committees of the association. The committee arranged a second conference on military history as part of the meetings of 1913 and presented a report on the status of the study of military history in the United States. The committee was enlarged to be a committee on military and naval history, but it made no further reports and was discontinued in 1915. The committee, or at least certain members of it, should be credited with the founding of the Military Historian and Economist which was edited for a short time by the late Professor Johnston and Col. A. L. Conger and which was suspended in 1917 when the editors were sent overseas in the military service. The committee also had an important part in preparing the way for the establishment, in 1917, of the Historical Branch of the General Staff.

26. *Revolutionary records.*—Following action by the council in 1913 and the holding of a special conference in Washington in 1914, a committee of five was appointed to act in an advisory capacity to the National Government in locating, copying, and publishing the military and naval records of the Revolution. The committee functioned for about a year, rendering valuable service to the War and Navy Departments, until the failure of appropriations caused the work to be stopped. Much material was gathered, largely from the archives of the original States, but none of it has been published.

27. *Prizes.*—(a) Justin Winsor and Herbert Baxter Adams prizes. In 1895 the association voted to offer a prize of $100 for the the best historical monograph, exclusive of university dissertations, based on original investigation; and also voted to establish a medal of equal value to be awarded at suitable intervals for the best published work of historical research. The second vote was not carried into effect, but the prize of $100 was awarded in 1896 to Dr. Herman V. Ames. The offer of a cash prize was renewed and thereafter it was called the Justin Winsor prize. Upon the death of Herbert B. Adams, who left an unrestricted bequest of $5,000 to the association, the Herbert Baxter Adams prize in European history was established. Thereafter each prize was increased to $200 and they were awarded in alternate years for unpublished essays only. The essays were at first printed in the annual reports, but in 1909 their publication in a separate series was commenced. The cost of publication increased rapidly while the sales of essays tended to remain at a low figure, so that after a short time the association found itself incurring an annual deficit of between $500 and $1,000. Publication of the essays was discontinued in 1917, unless by consent of author and the committee on publications they should be included in the annual report, and printed essays were admitted to the competition.

(b) Military history prize. The late Prof. R. M. Johnston made an anonymous gift to the association of $250, to be used as a prize for the best monograph in the field of military history that should be offered in a competition held by the association.

The competition has several times been extended but was finally closed on July 1 of the present year.

(c). George L. Beer prize. The late George L. Beer left a bequest of $5,000 to the association on condition that the income from it should annually be offered as a prize for the best essay dealing with European international relations since 1895.

28. *Aids to research.*—In 1912 the council appointed a committee to consider methods of promoting research in American and European history. The committee recommended the establishment of a standing committee on aids to research and of a special committee on the formation of a research fund. It was proposed that the former should prepare a list of funds available for historical research, should receive and pass on applications for aid, should recommend applicants to institutions having funds, and should allot grants from funds which might be secured for the purpose by the special committee. The committee was discharged in 1915 and no further action was taken in the matter.

29. *Historical studies in Washington.*—The association has long concerned itself with encouraging historical research in the governmental collections in Washington. In 1901 a committee was appointed to consider a proposal by Dr. J. F. Jameson for the establishment of a school for historical studies in Washington. This committee reported and was discharged, its place being taken by a committee on the promotion of historical research in Washington. At this time (1902) the Carnegie Institution of Washington was founded and the members of the committee, together with the board of editors of the American Historical Review, succeeded in securing the establishment in the institution of the Deparment of Historical Research. No provision was made, however, for bringing students to Washington or for giving them instruction.

In 1915 a conference was called at Columbia University which resulted in the formation of a plan for the establishment in Washington of a university center for higher studies in history, economics, and political science, which should serve as an adjunct to those departments in the contributing universities. The plan has been approved by the councils of the historical and political science associations, but it is held in abeyance until adequate funds can be secured.

30. *Colonial entries in the Privy-Council register.*—In 1907 the association contributed $250 toward the expense of transcribing and publishing the colonial entries in the register of the Privy Council.

31. *Original narratives of early American history.*—In 1902 the council approved the publication, under the auspices of the association but without expense to it, of the series of reprints since published by Scribner's Sons under the title "Original Narratives of Early American History." The general editor was Dr. J. F. Jameson, who made annual reports to the association while publication was in progress.

32. *Reprints relating to European history.*—In 1907 the council appointed a committee to consider the policy of publishing a series of reprints relating to European history similar to the series of Original Narratives noted above. No report was made.

33. *Calendar of printed letters relating to American history.*—In 1908 a committee was appointed on the compilation of a calendar of printed letters relating to American history, with instructions to draw up a plan of work and to secure the necessary cooperation. No report was made.

34. *Documentary history of the States.*—In 1913 Prof. E. S. Meany presented to the council a project for the publication of a documentary history of the States, one volume for each State, for which the prospective publishers desired the support of the association. The project was referred to the executive committee of the Pacific

Coast Branch for consideration and report as concerns the Pacific States only. No report has been made.

35. *Legal history.*—In 1897 a committee was appointed to inquire into the "feasability of instituting a section devoted to historical jurisprudence or legal history," but no further action was taken in the matter.

36. *Historic sites.*—In 1906 the general committee commenced an inquiry into the marking of historic sites, but did not conclude it. In 1909 a special committee of five was appointed which gathered considerable material relating to various sections of the country, but which did not complete its report. The material gathered and the partial reports were turned over to the secretary of the association, and the committee was discharged.

37. *Historic highways.*—In 1915 a committee of one was appointed at the request of the National Highways Association to cooperate with that body in selecting appropriate names for the historic highways of the country. The committee was successful in securing a considerable degree of cooperation from the various States historical societies and agencies.

38. *Historical study of colonies and dependencies.*—From 1898 to 1900 there was a special committee on the historical study of colonies and dependencies. It cooperated with a similar committee of the Economic Association, outlined a series of reports, and held a conference during the meetings of 1899. It reported its inability to carry out the program it had set for itself, and was discharged. The net results of its activities consist of a few papers printed in the annual reports and the Review, to which may be added as a collateral result the volume by Prof. A. L. Lowell on Colonial Civil Service.

39. *American year book.*—In 1909 Prof. A. B. Hart was appointed a committee of one to confer with representatives of other associations respecting the publication of an American yearbook of history, economics, and politics. The project was carried through and the volume has appeared annually since 1910.

40. *Monographic history of the United States.*—In 1900, after favorable report by a special committee, the council recommended that a committee of five be appointed to arrange for the publication under the auspices of the association of a cooperative monographic history of the United States. The proposal met with opposition in the business meeting and was abandoned so far as the association was concerned. It was after carried through as a private enterprise.

REPORT OF THE BOARD OF EDITORS OF THE AMERICAN HISTORICAL REVIEW

The principal question apart from routine that occupied the board this year is the cost of production of the Review. The Macmillan Co. reported that under our contract with them they had published the Review during the last three years at a loss of approximately $3,000. This, of course, can not continue. The possible means of retrenchment are a considerable reduction of the size of the Review, the use of cheaper paper, or less payment for articles and reviews. The first of these, a reduction in the size of the Review, has already been made. The other two measures the board did not feel to be wise. Some increase in the income from advertising seemed possible and steps have been taken to secure this addition. None of these are, however, adequate to restore the balance, and the board recommends to the executive council an increase in payment to Macmillan to 70 cents per number delivered to the members of the association.

The board takes pleasure in reporting an increase in the productivity of American historical scholarship, so far as this can be tested by the number of articles submitted for publication in the Review, as compared with the paucity of articles during the war years. In this connection the board calls attention to the series of three articles analyzing much of the recently published documentary materials concerning the outbreak of the war, prepared at their request by Prof. S. B. Fay.

The board begs to remind the council that the term of Prof. J. H. Robinson as one of the editors of the Review expires at this time.

Respectfully submitted.

E. P. CHEYNEY, *Chairman.*

REPORT OF THE HISTORICAL MANUSCRIPTS COMMISSION

The work of the commission was completed some time ago for a considerable time in advance, and therefore it has been unnecessary to take any action recently.

The manuscript of Doctor Barker's first volume was placed in the hands of the committee on publications some months ago, as I understand, and he is doubtless at work on the second volume.

Respectfully submitted.

JUSTIN H. SMITH, *Chairman.*

NOVEMBER 18, 1920.

REPORT OF THE COMMITTEE ON THE JUSTIN WINSOR PRIZE

The committee on the Justin Winsor prize has been reduced from five to four members, by the inability of Professor Hodder to serve. The four remaining members have given careful examination to four essays submitted in the competition, and are unable to agree that any one of them is entitled to receive the award.[5]

FREDERIC L. PAXSON, *Chairman.*

DECEMBER 20, 1920.

REPORT OF THE COMMITTEE ON PUBLICATIONS

Mr. Allen R. Boyd, as editor, has submitted to me a statement covering his first year's work, the substance of which I give in the two following paragraphs.

The annual report for 1917 is about to be distributed. Materials in the annual report for 1918 will fill two volumes and should be ready for distribution within two months. Besides the records and articles to which attention was called in my last report, Volume I will contain the first careful directory of our membership printed since 1911 and the annual bibliography "Writings on American History, 1918," compiled by Miss Grace Gardiner Griffin. The bibliography by Miss Griffin is the thirteenth number of a continuous series, opening with 1906. Six independent volumes, bibliographies for 1912, 1913, 1914, 1915, 1916, and 1917, have appeared, it will be remembered, through the public-spirited efforts of the Yale University Press. Last spring, however, the Yale University Press decided to abandon the project. Accordingly your committee concluded that the annual report might readily be utilized to carry on this useful aid to American historical scholarship. Separates of both the directory and the "Writings" will be issued at nominal prices. Separates of the other contents of Volume I have already been issued in advance of the completed volume. The annual report for 1919 will fill two volumes, for, besides containing materials afforded by the Cleveland meeting, it will include (in Volume II) the first instalment of the Stephen F. Austin papers edited by Prof. Eugene C. Barker and designed as the fifteenth report of the historical manuscripts commission.

Owing to the great increase of expense in printing, Mr Boyd calls attention to the need of watching closely the size of our volumes. The committee must consequently be granted authority to exercise its judgment in cooperation with the editor in this matter and to eliminate, if necessary, or to restrict some things offered for publication.

---

[5] The council decided to defer action on the award until the next meeting.

In view of the large amount of time spent by the editor on this year's work—a great mass of material having accumulated—I ask that an additional sum of $100 be given him for this, his first year's labor. Mr. Boyd has been tireless in his reading of proof, giving freely of his time to a multitude of details, and has proved in a variety of ways to be a most conscientious and efficient editor.

The Herbert Baxter Adams prize of $200 was awarded in 1919 to Dr. William Thomas Morgan, assistant professor of European history in Indiana University, for his monograph entitled, "English Political Parties and Leaders in the Reign of Queen Anne, 1702–1710" (New Haven, Yale University Press, 1920, pp. 427). Efforts are still being made to have published without expense to the association Dr. F. L. Nussbaum's essay on "E. J. A. Ducher," which was awarded the Adams prize in March, 1918. If these efforts prove unsuccessful, the association will be bound, I think, to print the book. This will mean, according to very recent estimates, an appropriation of $1,000.

Figures on the sale of our publications for the year are not encouraging, as the following comparisons show:

Publications sold 1916–17, $542; 1917–18, $260.06; 1918–19, $503.59; 1919–20, $161.03. Of the total receipts only $60.23 came from the sale of our prize essays. Against these small receipts is this year's cost of storing and isuring the prize essays—$113.08. In other words, we are losing this year $52.85 on this item. I recommend that the chairman of your committee, the editor, and the treasurer of the association act as a special committee of three in disposing of this stock of prize essays promptly, giving to the 10 authors first an opportunity of taking over all but 10 copies of their respective essays at a low cost such as may seem fair to the special committee. By this means we may be able to settle a problem which is something of a menace constantly to our treasury. The annual appropriation of your committee was $750. Of this amount $674.37 has been spent in various ways, leaving a balance of $75.63.

The projected volume of historical essays in commemoration of 25 years' services of the American Historical Review (1895-1920) has had to be abandoned. The special committee fulfilled last year its assigned task of making selection for the volume. But in May, 1920, it was found to be impossible to secure its publication without expense to the association, owing to the conditions existing in the book trade.

Respectfully submitted.

H. BARRETT LEARNED, *Chairman.*

REPORT OF COMMITTEE ON MEMBERSHIP

The committee on membership began its activities in April, 1920. Since the geographical distribution of the committee made a meeting impracticable, Mr. Leland, Professor Bassett, Professor Zook, and the chairman met in conference in Washington March 8 to decide upon a plan of campaign.

The first step was to divide the country into districts and to assign one to each member of the committee. Thus each commstteeman was held responsible for the task of increasing the membership in his own district. To Prof. L. F. Brown was assigned New York; to Prof. E. H. Byrne, Wisconsin and Iowa; to Prof. A. C. Krey, Minnesota, North Dakota, South Dakota, and Wyoming; to Prof. F. E. Melvin, Kansas, Missouri, Nebraska, and Colorado; to Prof. R. A. Newhall, Connecticut and Rhode Island; to Prof. J. S. Orvis, Massachusetts, Vermont, New Hampshire, and Maine; to Prof. C. W. Ramsdell, Texas, Louisiana, Oklahoma, and Arkansas; to Prof. J. C. Randall, Virginia, Kentucky, Tennessee, North Carolina, South Carolina, Georgia, Alabama, Mississippi, and Florida; to Prof. A. P. Scott, Ohio, Indiana, Illinois, and Michigan; to Prof. E. J. Van Nostrand, California, Oregon, Washington, Utah, Nevada, Idaho, New Mexico, Arizona, and Montana; to Prof. G. F. Zook, Pennsylvania, Delaware, Maryland, and West Virginia; to Prof. T. J. Wertenbaker, New Jersey.

Since the plan outlined entailed a large amount of work it was suggested that each member of the committee appoint as many associate members to assist him as he deemed advisable. As with the committeemen, so the associate members were to be made to feel that they were personally responsible for a certain part of the work, either in a geographical district or with a certain group of persons.

Especial efforts were directed toward securing recruits among graduate students, and it was suggested that graduate teachers in the larger universities, especially in the summer schools, would be the proper persons to work this field. An attempt was made also to increase the membership of the association among persons not teachers or writers of history but who are deeply interested in its study. It was thought certain that there are many men and women in the country, persons of leisure often, who are voluminous readers of history, or are especially interested in some phase of history who, if properly approached, would gladly join the association.

To facilitate this work Mr. Leland and Professor Bassett revised and brought up to date a short sketch of the association published some years ago. A number of copies of this pamphlet with a supply of application blanks were sent to each member of the committee.

To supplement this work, upon the advice of the secretary, a list of names was selected from Writings on American History for 1917, to whom copies of the sketch of the association and application blanks were sent out from the secretary's office.

Although the results obtained during the year were not all that had been desired on the whole encouraging progress has been made. For the first time since 1916 a step has been put to the annual loss in membership and a substantial gain recorded in its place. The total number of additions from December 31, 1919, to December 6, 1920, was 266, while the total loss was 205, leaving a net gain of 61. In 1916 there was a net loss of 187, in 1917 of 85, in 1918 of 35, in 1919 of 74. It is, then, a matter for congratulation that the tide has definitely turned, and that a beginning has been made in the important work of repairing the losses attendant upon the war. It is to be hoped that another year will see more substantial progress and that soon the record total of 2,926 members attained in 1915 will be equaled or even surpassed.

Respectfully yours,

T. J. WERTENBAKER, *Chairman.*

REPORT OF THE CONFERENCE OF HISTORICAL SOCIETIES

The secretary of the conference of historical societies has been concerned during the past year with three lines of activity: (1) The preparation of a program for the meeting of the conference in connection with the annual meeting of the American Historical Association at Washington, D. C., in December, 1920; (2) the circularizing of the societies for the sake of obtaining funds and information; (3) the effort to make constructive plans for rhe future of the conference.

A joint session with the National Association of War History Organizations was planned for 1920; and, cooperating with Dr. Albert E. McKinley, secretary of the latter association, a joint program was formed. Believing that the question of federation of historical societies within the States is most vital to the interests both of the conference and its individual members, Dr. Joseph Schafer, of the Wisconsin State Historical Society, has been asked to read a paper on this subject. Discussion will be participated in by Mr. Worthington C. Ford, of the Massachusetts Historical Society, Prof. Harlow Dindley, of Earlham College, Indiana, and Prof. Edmond S. Meany, of the University of Washington, thus representing three geographical sections of the country.

In accordance with the annual custom of the conference, a circular letter and a questionnaire have been sent out, with the kind assistance of the general office of the American Historical Association. The letter includes an invitation to the societies to send delegates to the meeting at Washington (for which preliminary programs have been enclosed) and also calls attention to the provision of the constitution regarding the financial support of the conference through assessment upon the member societies. The questionnaire asks for the usual data upon the organization and activities of the individual societies. The secretary hopes to be able to report to the conference at its meeting on December 28 an encouraging response to this letter, both in financial returns and information.

With regard to the future, the question of organization deserves first attention. The secretary believes the present constitution, drawn up in 1916, contains a satisfactory working plan for the conference. The actual financial support received is going to depend somewhat upon the evidence which the conference gives to the societies of its value to them. The value of its services likewise is going to depend much on the financial support received. The secretary has faith that the two factors can be made to stimulate each other rather than interfere with each other.

He feels, however, that organization can be pushed one step further to advantage, although not through formal addition to the constitution. The four to five hundred societies scattered over this country and Canada have potentially much in common, but practically make few points of contact. The conference strives to give them a common focus, but close relationship is impossible especially with the smaller local societies. The secretary believes that for the good of the conference as a whole, and for the more vital functioning of the societies individually, there should be a bond organized between the societies within each State and Province. The conference need not cease dealing directly with the small society, but in many cases, for example in the preparation of bibliographical material or in making a survey of any kind, the officers of a federation within a State could render invaluable service to the Conference in an advisory capacity, and often in securing information or action from the smaller societies which the secretary of the conference might never obtain. Furthermore, the historical interests of each State would profit greatly by such a federation. This principle is not a new one before the conference. It has been made the subject of an earlier meeting, but it is, in the opinion of the secretary, of too great importance to be neglected. It is with this in mind that Doctor Schaefer's paper was arranged and it is hoped that the paper and its discussion may have definite results.

Probably the most difficult problem of any historical organization is that of publication. The secretary feels strongly that the proceedings of the annual meetings of the conference, together with the data collected from the societies, should be published in separate form and without delay. The publication of this material by the American Historical Association in its annual reports is greatly appreciated, but it is doubtful if the interest of the societies in sending in answers to the questionnaires can be sustained without earlier report both of the proceedings and data. This is the first publication duty of the conference and should have prior claim on the finances.

Two other projects have been for some years before the conference—a handbook of information regarding the societies and a continuation of the Griffin Bibliography of American Historical Societies. Each is important and each is a somewhat formidable undertaking.

These two projects were broached in 1916 and efforts were made to procure data for their preparation; the Newberry Library agreeing to allow Mr. A. H. Shearer, then secretary of the conference, the time to devote to this work. But financial, military, and other circumstances prevented consummation of the plans year after year. In December, 1919, when the present secretary took office, there existed an unusually large collection of data sent in by the societies in answer to questionnaires of 1917 and 1918 and in anticipation of the publication of a handbook. It seemed wise rather than hold this longer, to publish it in the report of the American Historical Association for 1917, and the retiring secretary kindly agreed to send the reprint of this report out to the societies explaining that this increased collection of statistics, covering over 400 societies, was the nearest approach possible to a handbook under the present conditions, and announcing the change of officers of the conference. Owing to the delay in the appearance of the report this letter was not sent out, but the reprints have recently been mailed to the societies.

It is the opinion of the secretary that a fresh start should be made in the direction of both handbook and the Griffin continuation.

The secretary has received a letter from his predecessor in office to the effect that he is sending a collection of material relative to the conference with regard to these two and other projects. In this, he states, there is material collected by him from Iowa and Virginia toward the Griffin bibliography, and he has had promises from Minnesota, New York, and Illinois. Thus a start has been made.

It seems, however, as if the wisest thing to do would be to ask the conference to name a carefully chosen committee of three to act with the secretary of the conference in planning the details of a handbook and in compiling and publishing it, and to name a similar committee to act with the secretary of the conference in compiling a continuation of the Griffin bibliography. These committees should have working chairmen and the committees could each divide their work as was done in the preparation of the survey of the work of historical societies made in 1905 by a committee consisting of Messrs. Thwaites, Shambaugh, and Riley.

The secretary of the conference could act as a coordinating agency between the two committees, could assist both committees, very materially in connection with sending out questionnaires and in the collection of data, and, as far as his other duties would permit, in every way possible.

With regard to the financing of these publications, it must be said that the treasury of the conference justifies little outlay, and the returns from the societies are a matter of prophecy. The secretary believes that a sufficient amount will be received, together with the balance on hand, to get out the proceedings and annual data in separate form and take care of the circularizing of the societies at least once during the coming year.

If the handbook and the continuation of Griffin's bibliography are printed in the reports of the American Historical Association, the expense to the conference will not be great and can probably be handled by the receipts from the societies if they become assured of definite and satisfactory publication results.

It is believed that more satisfactory returns will be secured if two circular letters are sent out annually, one in the early part of the year giving a general report of the December meeting, announcing the publication of the annual survey and other activities, and calling for the annual dues; and a second one in November announcing the December meeting and requesting information based on a questionnaire. In this way the request for dues will be associated with the objects for which financial support is necessary, and will be freed from the complication of the return of questionnaire data.

For the year 1921, in view of the fact that the certainty of adequate returns from the societies is not yet assured, it is requested that the American Historical Association again make an appropriation of $25 for the conference.

FINANCIAL STATEMENT

The secretary has received from his predecessor in office, Mr. Augustus H. Shearer, $26.74, which sum remains on deposit in an account opened for the conference of historical societies. The conference was also granted in December, 1919, by the American Historical Association, an appropriation of $25. This sum has not been drawn, but expenses connected with the sending out of the circular letter and questionnaire to the societies have been paid by the general office of the American Historical Association as follows:

Duplication of letter and questionnaire (paper supplied by duplicating company) $18. 15
Postage... 5. 00
                                                                                23. 15

It is understood that these items have been charged against the appropriation of $25 on the books of the American Historical Association. The assistant secretary of the association states that an additional small bill for services in connection with the circular letter—probably about $5—was due but had not yet come in when the books were closed. This will be taken care of in 1921.

Aside from the above there have been no disbursements. The call for dues was sent out in the circular letter of December 1, 1920, and as yet no returns have been received with the exception of the sum of $10 from the State Historical Society of Iowa. The actual amount in the treasury of the conference is therefore the balance brought forward from 1919 plus the above item, or $36.74.

JOHN C. PARISH, *Secretary.*

REPORT OF COMMITTEE ON NATIONAL ARCHIVES

In the last session of Congress it was found impossible to persuade the House Committee on Appropriations to make any appropriation for the national archive building. In the session now begun a more hopeful situation appears to exist, due mainly to the efforts of Mr. Moore, of this committee. There appears to be a disposition in Congress to institute a regular program of building operations in Washington, and in framing it to follow the recommendations of the building commission. That commission has given a foremost place to the national archive building in its suggestions as to a proper order for the erection of buildings, and Senator Smoot, in recent remarks in the Senate, speaking for that commission, declared strongly in favor of taking up the erection of that building first.

Respectfully submitted.

J. F. JAMESON, *Chairman.*

REPORT OF THE COMMITTEE ON A BIBLIOGRAPHY OF MODERN ENGLISH HISTORY

The committee on a bibliography of modern English history regrets that it is not in a position to make a definitive report. Shortly after the committee was reconstituted at the last meeting of the association, correspondence was begun with Mr. George W. Prothero, who had been appointed general editor and who had collected much material for the first volume just before the outbreak of the war. Mr. Prothero asked for a postponement of decision in plans until he had fulfilled some postwar responsibilities toward the British Government, which he thought would be by the autumn. With the completion of this work Mr. Prothero's health suddenly failed, and he was ordered to enter upon an immediate and complete rest for six months. It was impossible for the American committee to decide upon a policy before Mr. Prothero left England, and the chairman's last letter to him remains unanswered. Nothing has therefore been done to block out a course of action for the immediate future.

It is evident, however, that something should be done to examine and arrange the materials Mr. Prothero has left in London and to prepare them for his resumption of work. The committee believes that a grant of $150 from the association for the coming year, if it can be made, will enable them to bring the materials now in existence into order ready for a resumption of active preparation for the publication of the first volume of the work.

Respectfully submitted.

E. P. CHEYNEY, *Chairman.*

FINAL REPORT OF THE COMMITTEE ON THE MILITARY HISTORY PRIZE

It will be recalled that at the Charleston meeting, in 1913, it was announced that a friend had donated $250 to the association, to be awarded as a prize for the best essay in American military history, the details of the competition to be determined by the association. The council appointed the following committee to prepare plans and conduct the contest: Capt. A. L. Conger, Army Service Schools, Fort Leavenworth, chairman; Milledge L. Bonham, jr. (then of Louisiana State University, Baton Rouge); Allen R. Boyd, Library of Congress; Fred M. Fling, University of Nebraska; and Albert Bushnell Hart, Harvard University.

A circular was prepared and distributed, announcing the contest for 1915. Five essays were submitted, none of which, in the opinion of the committee, was worthy of the award. Accordingly it was recommended to the association at the Washington meeting of 1915 that no award be made. This recommendation was adopted and the same committee was continued in the service to conduct another contest.

In consequence of Captain Conger's being ordered to join his regiment on the Mexican border in May, 1916, a vacancy was created, which was filled by the appointment, by the council, of Prof. Robert M. Johnston, of Harvard, editor of the Military Historian and Economist, as chairman.

Another circular was prepared, arranging for a contest in 1918. But in June, 1918, Professor Johnston was appointed a major in the Historical Section of the General Staff, United States Army, and sent to France. He resigned from the committee and Mr. Bonham was appointed chairman, and the vacancy filled by the appointment of Prof. Frank M. Anderson, of Dartmouth College.

As every member of the committee was engaged in war work of some sort, and the historical profession was not then primarily interested in previous military events, it was unanimously decided to postpone the contest until after the war.

After the armistice was signed, the committee resumed its work, and upon the suggestion of Mr. Boyd wide publicity was given to the announcement of the contest and an effort made to interest officers of the allied armies in this contest. A circular was distributed, fixing July 1, 1920, for the closing of the contest. At the Cleveland meeting of 1919, the committee met and decided upon plans for handling the essays. The chairman, meanwhile, had removed to Hamilton College.

By July 1, 1920, eight essays were submitted, on subjects ranging from the colonial wars to the World War. Seven of the contestants were men, one a woman. Both the historical profession and the Army were represented, as well as the business world.

From July 1 to December 15, 1920, the essays were being carefully considered by the members of the committee. After much correspondence, and at least one personal conference between members, it was decided, after some hesitation, that in view of the fact that this was not a permanent competition, and because of the probability of the fund being covered into the treasury if not awarded, that a decision had better be made.

The committee awarded the prize to Mr. Thomas Robson Hay, of Pittsburgh, Pa., for his essay, "Hood's Tennessee Campaign." Mr. Hay was advised to make certain revisions before publishing it. A sketch of Mr. Hay has already been sent to the secretary of the association. Honorable mention was accorded to the following essays: "The Texas Rangers in the Mexican War," by Prof. Walter Prescott Webb, of the University of Texas; "What Happens in Battle," by Capt. John Nesmyth Greely, General Staff, United States Army.

Notice of this decision was given to the council by Mr. Boyd during the Washington meeting of 1920. The result has since been reported by the chairman to the contestants, and the essays are being returned to them.

All of which is respectfully submitted by the committee, with the request that it be discharged.

In conclusion, I desire to express my appreciation of the zeal and scholarly attitude of the other members of the committee, and to thank the council and other officers of the association for their courteous and efficient cooperation with the committee.

A statement of the expenses connected with this contest is enclosed.

Respectfully submitted.

MILLEDGE L. BONHAM, Jr., *Chairman.*

Expenditures of the members of the committee:

Mr. Anderson: For dispatching the essays to Mr. Hart	$1. 00
Mr. Boyd: For dispatching the essays to Mr. Anderson	. 83
Mr. Hart: For dispatching the essays to Mr. Fling	1. 20
Mr. Bonham: For correspondence as chairman, 1918–1921	$3. 75
For dispatching essays to Mr. Boyd, July 2, 1920	. 45
For dispatching essays to Mr. Boyd, August 21	. 35
For return of essays from Mr. Fling, Jan. 12, 1921	1. 07
	5. 62

REPORT OF THE COMMITTEE ON THE HISTORICAL CONGRESS AT RIO DE JANEIRO

Although there has been no meeting of the committee in the course of the past year owing to the absence of some of its members from the United States, there has nevertheless been considerable headway made by correspondence. In the absence of Prof. Bernard Moses, the chairman of the committee, it was deemed advisable to designate Prof. P. A. Martin, of Stanford University, as acting chairman. The committee has been in close touch with various officials of the Government who are interested in the proposed congress and have given valuable assistance in the preparation of our plans. We have been particularly indebted in this regard to. Dr. L. S. Rowe, Director General of the Pan American Union, Mr. Sumner Welles, acting chief of the Division of Latin American Affairs of the Department of State, and Ambassador Edwin V. Morgan, who has been made a member of the committee and has taken an active part in its work thus far.

I had the pleasure of a brief visit in Rio early in June and was then able to confer at length with the officials of the Instituto Historico which has charge of the arrangements. The plans for the congress have been laid out along rather broad lines to include geographic and economic as well as historical investigations. This has evidently been thought desirable in view of the interests of the Instituto in the fields mentioned. It may be noted incidentally that the library of that organization is unusually strong in the literature on explorations and discoveries; hence the desire to include geographic contributions. It is to be hoped, therefore, that the American delegation to the congress may have among its members one or two geographers, and your committee is endeavoring to facilitate such an arrangement.

While the Instituto has thus far received acceptances from only six or seven national historical associations of as many American republics, it has ample assurances that the attendance at the congress will be large and comprehensive. There are some 30 sections or sessions on the tentative program, one of which is devoted to the history of the United States. It is suggested, however, that so far as possible the papers submitted shall emphasize the relations between the United States and Brazil.

Your committee is now considering the designation of delegates and the suggestion of topics for papers. It was originally hoped that some contribution toward the expenses of the delegation might be secured from the Government, and tentative representations were made along that line. It now seems unlikely, however, that such assistance will be forthcoming, and for that reason the delegates who will actually make the trip to Rio in September, 1922, will probably be compelled to meet their expenses from their own resources or from those of institutions with which they are connected.

Respectfully submitted.

JULIUS KLEIN, *Secretary.*

REPORT OF THE COMMITTEE ON HISTORY AND EDUCATION FOR CITIZENSHIP IN THE SCHOOLS

Your committee on history and education for citizenship in the schools, which reported progress at the meeting of the council in Cleveland on December 29, 1919, desires at this time to make a supplementary report covering the activities of the committee since the Cleveland meeting.

During the sessions of the American Historical Association at Cleveland your committee held several meetings which resulted in the adoption of decisions concerning its future work, which decisions were published in the Historical Outlook for March, 1920, volume 11, no. 3, pages 111–112. A summary of these decisions would be as follows:

1. It was agreed that the committee should prepare, as Part I of its final report, recommendations for the four-year high-school course.

2. *Minimum requirements.*—That these should include, as a minimum requirement for graduation on the part of all pupils taking a four-year course:

(a) A course in modern world history (except America), beginning aproximately at the middle of the seventeenth century and extending to the present.

(b) A course in American history, treated topically, covering mainly the period from 1789 to the present, with special emphasis on the period since the Civil War. This course should be primarily political, but it should take full account of economic, industrial, and social factors which explain political movements.

3. *Allocation in grades.*—That the above courses should be given, preferably, in grades 10 and 11, respectivly.

4. *Other social studies.*—In addition to this minimum requirement, the committee recommends, as additional required courses, where practicable:

(a) For the ninth grade a course in industrial organization and civics which shall include "the development of an appreciation of the social significance of all work, of the social value and interdependence of all occupations, of the opportunities and necessity for good citizenship in vocational life, of the necessity for social control, governmental and otherwise, of the economic activities of the community, of how government aids the citizen in his vocational life and of how the young citizen may prepare himself for a definite occupation." In this connection, we suggest the study of 10 great industries, as follows: The fisheries and fur trade; lumbering; meat, hides and wool; wheat; corn; cotton; iron and steel; coal; gold, silver and copper; and oil.

(b) For the twelfth grade a course in the problems of American democracy. This should include some of the basic principles of economics, political science and sociology, stated in elementary terms, but should consist mainly of the study of concrete present-day problems illustrating these principles.

The committee hopes to secure the cooperation of organizations of economists, political scientists, and sociologists in preparing syllabi for the above courses.

5. *Electives in history.*—It is by no means the intention of the committee to suggest a reduction in the time usually alloted to history in the high-school program. It is rather the intention, while retaining in full force and effect the list of history offerings in the high school, to increase the positive requirements in social studies for graduation as a guaranty of citizenship training. In addition, therefore, to the above required courses, the committee recommends the offering in the future as in the past of a variety of elective courses in history and the other social studies. It is not necessary that elective history courses should be taken in strictly chronological order.

The following are the courses suggested:

(a) The ancient world to about 800 A. D. This course should be so placed in the program as not to interfere with the required courses outlined above.

(b) A survey of ancient medieval history to approximately the middle of the seventeenth century. If convenient, this should be taken before the required course in modern world history of the tenth grade.

(c) The history of England and the British Empire.

(d) A course involving an intensive study of local, State, or regional history, or of some particular period or movement in the history of the Americas.

(e) A similar course involving an intensive study of some particular period or movement in European history. This might well take the form of the study of the background and history of the Great War.

(f) An intensive study of the recent history of the Far East.

6. *Syllabi.*—For the proposed required courses the committee agreed to prepare syllabi containing list of topics, references for the use of the teacher, and reading list for the pupils. No such syllabi were contemplated for the suggested elective courses, the committee agreeing, however, to facilitate as far as possible the publications and use of syllabi already in existence covering such courses.

Other recommendations.—By reference to the detailed statement in the Historical Outlook as cited, it will be seen that the committee covered in its decisions at Cleveland the question of the junior high school, the first eight grades, and insurance in civics. It was decided to defer the preparation of courses for the first eight grades and for the junior high school—apart from the work of the ninth grade, which is applicable both to the last year of the junior high school and the first year of the four-year high school—to a later time, meantime setting out to prepare the syllabi covering the four years of the high school, to be published as Part I of the final report.

On account of the preoccupation of the members of the committee with other pressing work for which they were responsible, it became evident early in the summer of 1920 that it would be necessary to employ some assistance if the committee expected to have its promised syllabi ready for final revision at the time of the Washington meeting. In consultations held on the subject it was agreed to employ Miss Frances Morehouse, of the University of Minnesota, to work particularly upon the ninth grade course in civics and in industries and upon the eleventh grade course in American history. These are the two courses for which the chairman of the committee made himself responsible, but which, after the assumption of his new duties as superintendent of the State Historical Society of Wisconsin, it was impossible for him to work out unaided. The chairman therefore outlined the two courses briefly, indicating the plan which he understood the committee to have authorized in each case. These notes were placed in the hands of Miss Morehouse, and she, in consultation with the chairman, worked out the courses in detail. It was agreed, after conference with Mr. Leland, who was secretary and treasurer of the National Board for Historical Service, to pay to Miss Morehouse for her services the sum of $300 out of the funds which had been appropriated by the American Historical Association for the use of this committee. I respectfully suggest that the council make provision for the payment to Miss Morehouse of the sum so stipulated.

Of the other required courses, Mr. Knowlton, of our committee, made himself responsible for the tenth grade course in modern world history. My advices are that Mr. Knowlton will be prepared to present to the committee at Washington a syllabus covering his recommendations for that course.

Mr. Knowlton has also been experimenting at the Lincoln School of Teachers College, Columbia University, with a civics course for ninth-grade pupils. He will probably present a syllabus covering his conception of that course, which, in that case will be considered as an alternative to the course prepared by Miss Morehouse under the suggestions of the chairman of the committee.

It has been the hope of our committee that some other committee, or some individual, would prepare a course suitable for the suggested social science work of the twelfth grade. It is understood that Miss Morehouse and others at the University of

Minnesota have been at work upon a course of that description, and there are reports, that others also have had such courses under preparation. It is possible, but not certain, that at the Washington meeting we shall be apprised of the existence of a course which may meet the approval of our committee so that it can be recommended or use in connection with the courses for which the committee holds itself directly responsible.

The courses for the earlier grades and the junior high school.—The chairman has been creditably informed that Prof. Henry Johnson, on whom the committee has relied very largely in making its suggestions for the earlier years, has already prepared courses covering portions of the first eight years, and that the publication of these courses has been contracted for. More definite information, however, will doubtless reach the committee during the Washington session.

The proposed history investigation.—It has been suggested, in letters from the treasurer of the association and from Mr. Leland, former secretary, that there is now a prospect of securing a considerable fund for the scientific investigation of history teaching. If the council or the association shall take steps to procure such a fund, the question of the relation of the present committee to the proposed investigation will need to be settled, probably at the Washington meeting. The chairman has not conferred, except incidentally, with other members of our committee relative to this subject. However, he is convinced that in case such a fund is secured and an investigation undertaken, it ought to be undertaken by a new committee, the members of which shall be so situated as to be able to devote a considerable portion of their time to the work, since under those circumstances they can be compensated for their time. It is possible that some members of our committee might desire to be continued on the new basis. But certainly the majority are men who are fully occupied in work which precludes the employment of any considerable portion of their time in such an investigation, and for these members others would have to be substituted. The most economical plan and the one which the chairman will recommend to the committee will be to ask the American Historical Association to discharge the present committee on history and education for citizenship and to provide for the appointment of a new committee to be constituted as the association may determine.

Conservation of the work which has been done.—With reference to the courses which have been prepared, in the form of syllabi, in so far as these may be approved by the committee for publication with a view to their introduction into the schools of the country, I hope the council may feel disposed to favor their publication for temporary use until such time as the new committee, if appointed, shall be prepared to substitute more scientifically prepared courses for them. Your committee has, in the past two years, devoted considerable time, thought, and energy to the preparation of these high-school courses, and it would seem uneconomical to allow all of this work to be dissipated, particularly at a time when high schools in many parts of the United States are clamoring for leadership in the organization of their history and civics courses.

Summary.—To summarize I should say:

1. The committee hopes to agree upon at least three courses at the Washington meeting.

2. These three courses will be the courses for the ninth, tenth, and eleventh years.

3. In case of agreement, these three courses should be subjected to editorial preparation for publication, and should be published.

4. Such editorial preparation for publication might well be left to the new committee which it is presumed will be appointed by the American Historical Association to conduct a scientific investigation into the subject of history teaching.

5. The present committee of eight should be discharged.

JOSEPH SCHAFER, *Chairman.*

Resolved, That the committtee ask the council for permission to publish its fins report to embody: (1) A fairly definite outline of the reorganized program for the 1 years as embodied in the June, 1919, issue of the Historical Outlook; (2) a straight forward statement justifying the program; (3) syllabi of certain selected topics and courses embodied in the program which will be put forth not as final recommenda tions but merely as suggestive of the detailed treatment that might be accorded to the various parts of the program.

REPORT OF THE COMMITTEE ON A MANUAL OF HISTORICAL LITERATURE.

After considerable correspondence conducted with representatives of both the American Historical Association and of the American Library Association in 1919, the present committee was formally appointed at the Cleveland meeting in December, 1919, to assume charge of the work. The American Library Association is represented on this committee by Doctor Shearer, who is also a member, by appointment, for the American Historical Association. The American Library Association is ready to cooperate in any way desirable in the work, but is willing to leave the prosecution of the enterprise in the hands of this committee of the American Historical Association.

At the meeting in Cleveland the committee was able to hold several conferences and to plan the general organization of the work. They then held a conference of those persons present at the meeting whom they had been able to secure as chapter editors. Since then editors have been secured for all the proposed chapters except possibly two, which relate to fields in which few Americans have specialized. Tentative lists of titles to be included have been prepared for all the proposed chapters, about 30 in number. These lists have been carefully canvassed and criticized by the committee in two sessions, one held in New York in May and one in Middletown, Conn., in November. The members of the committee have divided the chapters among themselves for special study and have been in correspondence with the chapter editors concerning their respective lists in the light of the committee criticisms and suggestions.

The attached memoranda which have been sent to the chapter editors indicate in some detail the plans worked out by the committee. Unfortunately progress has, for many reasons, been much slower than we had hoped, but it is the purpose of the committee to prosecute the work with all possible diligence. The delay may not prove unfortunate if it shall permit publication under more advantageous conditions as regards costs.

The committee purposes to meet in Washington and to utilize all possible time during the sessions of the American Historical Association. It has arranged with the program committee for a breakfast conference with the chapter editors and all others interested on Wednesday morning, December 29.

The question of publication has been taken up with Mr. F. S. Crofts, representing Harper & Bros., who were the publishers of Dr. C. K. Adams's Manual of Historical Literature, of which they still hold copyright. Mr. Crofts has assured the committee of the desire of Harper & Bros. to publish the proposed manual and to arrange the most favorable terms practicable.

The work of the preparation of this manual involves a very large amount of correspondence and will necessarily require frequent meetings of the committee. The expenses of the members in attending the two meetings held in New York and Middletown were as follows:

	Railroad fares	Pullman	Hotel	Meals
Professor Fay:				
New York	$9.80	$3.20	....	$1.40
Middletown	6.50	....	....	....
Professor Shipman:				
New York	5.12	....	$2.50	1.40
Middletown	9.62	....	2.50	2.60
Doctor Shearer:				
New York	13.99	....	3.00	2.96
Middletown	34.78	8.10	....	2.00
Professor Dutcher:				
New York	6.40	....	2.00	2.00
Middletown	....	....	....	....
Total	86.21	11.30	10.00	12.36

In addition, there is due to Wesleyan University for—

Stenographic service $30
Multigraphing 6
Stationery 9
Postage 5

Total 50

No exact account has been kept of the cost of these items, but the figures given are considerably inside the actual expenditures, and the amount was agreed upon with the Wesleyan authorities as satisfactory.

These total costs, then, at a minimum figure, represent a considerable excess over the grant of $75 which, it is understood, was placed at the disposal of this committee for the current year, and which has not yet been drawn upon. Ultimately, these expenditures should be reimbursed from the profit on the publication, and appropriations for the committee at the present time should be considered merely as advances and not as absolute grants. If the work is to be carried forward during the coming year, the cost will be considerably greater than during the past year.

The abolition of the former committee on bibliography of the association and the creation of the present committee on the Manual of Historical Literature has resulted in leaving at least one enterprise of a bibliographical character, prosecuted under the direction of the association, uncompleted, and provision should be made by the association for the appointment of a separate committee to take up this enterprise and carry it to completion. The task is the preparation of a bibliography of American travel. The large mass of materials thus far accumulated is at present in the hands of Doctor Shearer.

Respectfully submitted.

GEORGE M. DUTCHER, *Chairman.*

MANUAL OF HISTORICAL LITERATURE

C. K. Adams's Manual.—At the suggestion of the American Library Association, the American Historical Association has appointed a committee to replace the Manual of Historical Literature prepared by Charles Kendall Adams and published in 1882 by Harpers (third edition in 1888). The work of Adams was divided into 13 chapters, besides the introduction, and contained criticisms varying in length from 100 to 300 words on about 970 titles. In addition, there were appended to each chapter a few pages of suggestions to students and readers, in which courses of reading were outlined with a considerable number of additional titles mentioned, sometimes with a few words of comment.

Purpose of the new manual.—The public to which this book will be addressed will include primarily public libraries and high schools and academies with their teachers of history. The book is to be prepared by experts in a thoroughly scholarly manner, but intended for distinctly popular use. The selection of titles and the character of the comments will, in considerable measure, be determined by the nature of the public addressed. The volume will also have its value for the scholar who wishes guidance in fields other than his own.

As the volume will serve for guidance to public libraries in their purchase of works in history, an arrangement will be made to suggest selected lists for libraries adapted to their size and resources. Assuming that the large libraries will have or purchase nearly all the works reviewed, about 40 to 50 per cent of the titles will be marked by an asterisk as desirable for libraries of moderate size, and about 20 to 25 per cent of the titles will be marked by a double asterisk as desirable for the smaller libraries.

Content of new manuals.—Owing to the lapse of time since the final edition of Adams's work it is practically necessary to abandon his list of titles and to prepare an entirely new list. Further, the events of the past half century and the expansion of historical activities have made necessary chapters on numerous topics not included by Adams. The committee proposes a list of 26 chapters dealing with from 25 to 100 titles each, in accordance with the importance of the subject concerned, giving a total of about 1,300 titles. In large measure, the selection will be made from works now on the market or generally available. These titles are to be entirely of publications in English which have appeared within the last 50 years (1870–1920, inclusive) or have appeared in English translation or in a new edition within that period. To these there will be devoted comments varying from 100 to 300 words with a preference for the shorter comments, the longer comments being usually reserved for those books whose contents require some detailed outline because the title is not sufficiently indicative thereof.

Each chapter will usually include, in addition to this major list, a list of a few titles of standard English works which have not been reprinted within the last 50 years and also of outstanding works in French and German. To titles in these classes comments of from 20 to 50 words will be appended. In the case of a few chapters relating to specific countries which are represented in the American population by a considerable body of immigrants, a few titles of books in the language of the country will be added with similar brief comments.

To each chapter there will be added a somewhat brief section of suggestions to students and readers, which shall refer primarily to the titles included in the chapters rather than being devoted to outlining detailed courses of reading or citing additional titles. The tentative list of chapters, chapter editors, and apportionment of titles is included herewith.

Method of preparation.—Each chapter will be assigned to an expert in the field concerned, who will act as chapter editor. He will assume primary responsibility for selecting the titles which will be submitted to a selected list of librarians and other scholars in the field, for criticism, and additional suggestions, on the basis of which the chapter editor will prepare his final list. The chapter editor will then distribute the titles of works in his chapter among a considerable group of other scholars to prepare the comments, which will be revised and harmonized by the chapter editor. The chapter editor will also be expected to prepare the section on suggestions to readers and students. The arrangement of titles under each chapter should probably be by a partially chronological order under subheadings, the French and German and older English works being interspersed in their proper order among the English of recent date to which the major comments are given.

The work as a whole will be under the direction of a committee of the American Historical Association, which will pass finally upon the lists to be included in the several chapters and will edit the work as a whole. It is desired that the chapter editors submit to the committee their preliminary list not later than February 15, 1920, so that the list may be circulated for criticism and suggestions and then revised by the chapter editor in time for consideration and revision by the committee at a meeting to be held about March 10, 1920, in order that they may approve the list and adjust any overlapping. The chapter editors are requested to furnish the committee, prior to that date, a list of scholars who may be asked to prepare the criticisms of some of the works included in their respective chapters. It is desired that the criticisms of the volumes shall all be in the hands of the chapter editors as early in the summer as practicable, certainly not later than July 15, so that the chapter editors may complete their work and submit it to the committee not later than September 1. The committee may thus be able to arrange for the completion of the editorial work before the close of the calendar year.

Geography.—A very few titles of works of a geographical and descriptive sort should be included in each chapter. These should be general in scope rather than related to a special section or topic. Perhaps these titles would best be incorporated in the suggestions to the reader.

Bibliography.—Each chapter shall include, perhaps in the suggestions to the reader, reference to the most important general bibliographies relating to its subject. In connection with each title mention will be made of special critical bibliographies, if they are contained in the work. The Library of Congress card number will be printed following each title, which shall be given in the form used on the Library of Congress cards.

Articles in periodicals.—As public libraries usually have only a limited number of sets of periodicals, and as the size of the work must be limited, articles in periodicals will not normally be included in the list of titles, save in exceptional cases where there is an important article in a generally accessible periodical covering a subject not adequately handled in an available book. The suggestions to readers and students will sometimes include references to periodicals and periodical articles. Book reviews of unusual value will occasionally be mentioned in connection with the titles to which they relate, but this practice must necessarily be limited by the small number of files of reviewing periodicals in public libraries.

Compensation.—There are no funds available to compensate anyone for any work in preparing this volume, except that the American Historical Association has placed $75 at the disposal of the committee to cover necessary traveling expenses to committee meetings and to cover postage, multigraphing, etc. On the other hand, the volume ought to yield a considerable royalty, and it is suggested that the royalty be paid in such proportions as may be agreed on, to the American Library Association (which it is hoped will forego any claim), and to the American Historical Association. It is suggested that such money as shall thus come to the American Historical Association shall become a permanent fund known as the Charles Kendall Adams fund for historical bibliography, whose income shall be used alone for the promotion of the preparation and publication of works of historical bibliograghy.

The committee will welcome criticisms and suggestions on any matter connected with the work and the details of the plan. The committee also solicits the judgment of the chapter editors on the following problems:

I. Shall the comments be signed with the initials or names of the writers? In my judgment the initials should be used and the names of the coworkers in each chapter should follow that of the chapter editor at the head of the chapter, it being understood that the chapter editor shall feel free to suggest modifications of comments to the original writer where he regards the nature of the comments as distinctly contrary to his own views or as essentially incorrect. It should be understood that the real responsibility for the criticism will rest upon the person whose initials are appended thereto, while the chapter editor assumes responsibility for the general character of the chapter, particularly with reference to the selection of titles and the suggestions to the student and reader. Another possibility is to include the list of names of coworkers at the head of the chapter as I have indicated and to leave all the comments unsigned. This would leave a sort of distributed responsibility and would perhaps leave the chapter editor a certain amount of discretion and freedom in revising the comments of any particular writer on any particular title. In this case the chapter editor would clearly assume a larger responsibility for the character of the comments on all titles in his chapter. This question is obviously of considerable importance.

II. Ought there to be a chapter of introduction more or less similar to that of Adams's, perhaps reprinting sections of that chapter, or should an introduction of an entirely different character be prepared? If there is to be an introduction, who should be asked to write it?

GEORGE M. DUTCHER, *Chairman,*
Wesleyan University, Middletown, Conn.
SIDNEY B. FAY,
Smith College, Northampton, Mass.
AUGUSTUS H. SHEARER,
Grosvener Library, Buffalo, N. Y.
HENRY R. SHIPMAN,
Princeton University, Princeton, N. J.
Committee of the American Historical Association.

97244°—25——7

GENERAL SCHEME OF CHAPTERS

About 1,300 titles (Adams had 970) plus "suggested titles" and cross references.

Chapter	Editor	Titles
General history	C. H. Hull	50
History and auxiliary sciences	G. L. Burr	50
Ancient history	Olmstead	30
Greece	Westerman	40
Rome	Boak	40
Medieval	Paetow	60
Modern—1500 to 1870	Lingelbach	75
Last 50 years	F. M. Anderson	80
Colonial expansion of Europe to 1815	W. C. Abbott	40
Since 1815	Coolidge	50
England	Cross	100
France	Bourne	100
Spain and Portugal	Merriman	30
Italy	T. F. Jones	50
Germany	Fay	100
Netherlands and Belgium	Jameson	25
Scandinavia	Larsen	25
Russia and Poland	Lord	50
Southeastern Europe	Kerner	40
Ottoman Empire	Lybyer	30
India and Middle East	Dennis	30
Far East	Treat	40
Oceania	Blakeslee	25
Africa	Beer	60
United States	To be arranged	
Latin America	Cox	50
Canada	Wrong	30

To the Chapter Editors:

At a meeting of the committee held recently in Middletown it was decided, in order to advance the work, to apportion the chapters among the four members of the committee for special study and for correspondence with the chapter editors and others as might be desirable, particularily in the next few weeks.

It was decided to arrange for a breakfast conference at the American Historical Association meeting in Washington, at 8 a. m., December 29, in the New Ebbitt House. It is hoped that the chapter editors will, as far as possible, plan to attend this conference.

In the study of the lists of titles submitted for the several chapters it has been found necessary to adhere rigidly to the policy of assigning each book to only one chapter and that the chapter to which it most clearly and logically belonged. It was, however, decided that some system of cross reference should later on be arranged.

With regard to the arrangement of titles within the chapters the following policy was approved: (1) Bibliography. (2) Geography and ethnography. (3) General books. (4) Books on periods. (5) Books on special topics.

Under these several headings briefs of books or outlines should be placed first and the major works last. In other cases where this policy does not serve, a chronological arrangement should be followed, as in the subdivision on periods.

Books published prior to 1870 and books in foreign languages should be incorporated at their proper place in the main lists. Their number, however, should be kept as low as reasonably possible, and it is to be understood that any notations on these titles shall usually be kept under 50 words. It is probable that these titles and annotations will be printed in a smaller type than the titles in the main English list.

Where two or more books by the same author are cited in the same chapter they should be treated as one number and given a review together unless such procedure should be quite incongruous. This practice will save space and permit the insertion of a larger number of titles.

In case brief outlines or textbooks are listed, it will be wise, as a rule, to select the one preferred for chief mention and review and then to give just passing mention under the first title to so many additional titles as might be desirable. Thus in English history, after citing as the main title Cross, reference could be made in the briefest fashion to Tout, Cheyney, Wrong, Gardiner, etc.

In order that the list of reviewers may be completed and approved by the committee at the meeting in Washington, will you please, at your earliest convenience, send in a list of names of persons you would suggest to cooperate with us in reviewing books in your chapter? If you know of persons whom you would especially recommend to assist in any other chapters, such suggestions will also be appreciated by the committee.

NOVEMBER 23, 1920.

REPORT OF THE COMMITTEE ON A PRIMER OF ARCHIVES

Mr. Leland and I have found it impossible, notwithstanding our best intentions and correspondence, to meet together during the year for the purpose of working out an apportionment of the primer, and we are able to report at this time that we shall hope to be able to do better next year, if no unexpected illness or other mishaps interpose themselves. Personally, I have given so much time as chairman of the nominating committee this year that I could give no more to the committee on the primer.

Respectfully submitted.

VICTOR H. PALTSITS, *Chairman.*

REPORT OF COMMITTEE ON NOMINATIONS

Article VII of the constitution provides that: "This constitution may be amended at any annual meeting, notice of such amendment having been given at the previous annual meeting *or the proposed amendment having received the approval of the executive council.*" A majority of the members of the present nominating committee, namely, Miss Ellery, and Messrs. Fish, Hamilton, and Paltsits, strongly recommend to the executive council approval before the forthcoming annual meeting of the association of an amendment of Article II of the by-laws, as marked on the exhibit herewith; that is, to change error in the second word, so as to read "nominating" for "nomination"; to omit the words in brackets, namely, the referendum feature beginning with "at such convenient time" and ending with "then to be chosen"; and allowing two days instead of only one before the annual business meeting for the printing of additional nominations as provided otherwise by the by-law in question.

Mr. Hodder seemed disinclined to join the rest of us in our strong appeal for the elimination of the unworkable and costly referendum, which does not at all bring about the results it was supposed would come from it. It has proven itself a fiasco. I have elaborate data, which I am ready to submit to the executive council on behalf of the nominating committee, as information concerning the absurdities of the whole matter. Mr. Hodder found himself hampered by university work at the time when my elaborate analysis was sent to him, as well as to the rest of the committee members. His reply to me as chairman came only after a second request, and I judged from what he wrote that he had not read the entire docket carefully. I have since asked him to submit a minority report. He has not done so; therefore I am not able to know whether he still holds his former judgment or whether a careful reading of the docket has convinced him, as it has the rest of us, that an immediate abrogation of the useless referendum feature is for the best interests of the American Historical Association and its members. The letters from Professors Ellery, Fish, and Hamilton, giving expression of their wishes through me as chairman, are on file and are the command of the executive council, together with everything else that the executive council may wish from the nominating committee as to the duties performed by the said committee in carrying out its trust.

Respectfully submitted.

VICTOR H. PALTSITS, *Chairman.*

FINAL REPORT OF THE CHAIRMAN OF THE COMMITTEE ON THE LONDON HEAD-
QUARTERS OF THE ASSOCIATION

Upon recommendation of the committee, it was voted by the executive council on December 27, 1919, that notice should be given of the termination of the agreement of our association with the Royal Historical Society whereby our association has possessed a room in the building of the Royal Historical Society as a subtenant under that organization; that the treasurer of our association should make such payments to the Royal Historical Society as would be required to meet our legal obligations; that the furniture of the room should be disposed of by giving to the American University Union whatever articles it could use and by selling the rest; that the books should be given to the library of the American University Union; and that messages of thanks should be sent to those who have acted as officers of our London Branch.

These votes were immediately acted upon by the chairman of the committee. On January 2, 1920, Mr. H. P. Biggar, honorary treasurer of the London branch, was notified of the action of the council. After consultation with the officers of the Royal Historical Society termination of the lease was effected on the next quarter day, March 25. The books and all the furniture, excepting the carpets and the fire implements, were turned over in January to the American University Union. Later, Mr. Biggar reported that the Royal Historical Society had bought the fixtures remaining in the rooms. On July 16 Mr. Biggar was instructed to buy from the Macmillan Co. in London copies of any numbers of the American Historical Review which were lacking from the set kept in the library of the Royal Historical Society and to hold for the present whatever balance of the funds of the association remained in his hands.

His final report, filed herewith, indicates a balance remaining in his hands on October 31, 1920, of £4 12s. This sum was paid into the treasury of the association on December 22, being reckoned at $16.27. The directions of the council have now been all carried out and the history of the London branch may be regarded as ended. The committee would wish to be discharged.

Respectfully submitted for the committee.

J. F. JAMESON, *Chairman.*

MINUTES OF THE MEETING OF THE EXECTIVE COUNCIL HELD AT 1140 WOODWARD BUILDING, WASHINGTON, D. C., DECEMBER 27, 1920

The council met at 10.30 a. m. Present: President Channing, presiding; Messrs. Bourne, Burr, Haskins, Jameson, Jusserand, Lingelbach, McMaster, Moore, Miss Putnam, and the secretary. There also attended Mr. Allen R. Boyd, editor; Miss P. W. Washington, assistant secretary-treasurer; Mr. H. B. Learned, chairman of the committee on publicatons; and Mr. Joseph Schafer, chairman of the committee on history and education for citizenship in the schools.

The secretary presented his report, which showed a total membership of 2,524, as against 2,445 a year ago. The number whose dues were paid on December 15, 1920, was reported as 2,074, as against 2,032 on December 18, 1919. The net gain in membership was 79, this being the first year since 1915 in which the membership has shown a net gain.

The secretary reported that the will of the late James Schouler, of Intervale, N. H., former president of the association contained a bequest to the association in the following terms:

To the American Historical Association I give and bequeath the framed oil portrait of myself (a replica by Corner) which now hangs in the parlor of my house at Intervale; the same to be used, loaned, given away, or sold, at the discretion of the council of said association.

The council voted to authorize the secretary to lend the portrait of Mr. Schouler to the United States National Museum.

The secretary reported that the will of the late George Louis Beer contained a bequest to the association in the following terms:

I give, devise, and bequeath to the American Historical Association of Washington, D. C., a corporation duly incorporated and existing by act of Congress, January 4, 1889, the sum of five thousand dollars ($5,000.00), to be held by said corporation as a special fund in trust for the following purposes only: The said sum of $5,000.00 is to be invested by the officials of the said American Historical Association and the net income thereof is to be paid annually to a citizen of the United States who submits "the best work upon any phase of European international history since the year 1895"; the award to be made each year and the judges to be selected in accordance with the rules and regulations adopted by the said American Historical Association.

The council voted to authorize the creation of a prize to be awarded in accordance with the terms of Mr. Beer's bequest and to be known as the "George L. Beer prize."

The council voted to appoint a special committee to prepare rules for the award of the George L. Beer prize.

It was voted to instruct the secretary to secure the preparation of memorials of the late James Schouler and George L. Beer to be spread upon the records of the association.

The special committee, consisting of the president, secretary, and treasurer, which had been authorized to investigate the activities of certain so-called historical societies and to take the appropriate legal action as might be deemed advisable, reported that, while the activities of these societies were clearly shown to be of a commercial character, of no historical value, and in some instances of doubtful legality, it was, in the opinion of the committee, inexpedient for the association to initiate legal action against the organizations. It was voted to accept the committee's report and to discharge the committee. The secretary reported that the Peoples of America Society had requested the association to appoint two representatives to cooperate with that society for the study of racial elements in the United States.

The council voted that the delegates be appointed.

Upon motion by the secretary it was voted to appoint a committee on the writing of history for the purpose of studying the general question of history writing and of reporting on the appropriate means to be adopted for its stimulation and improvement.

Mr. Jameson reported for the committee on London headquarters that, in accordance with the vote of the council on December 27, 1919, the rooms occupied by the association in London had been vacated and an unexpended balance of $16.27 had been turned into the treasury.

It was voted to discharge the committee.

The report of the board of editors of the American Historical Review was presented by the secretary.

It was voted to accept it.

The secretary reported that no report had been received from the board of editors of the Historical Outlook.

The secretary presented the report of the Historical Manuscripts Commission.

It was voted to accept it.

The secretary reported that the committee on the Justin Winsor prize reported its inability to agree upon the award. It was voted that the essays of Messrs. Cunningham, Benns, and Wood be submitted to the Justin Winsor prize committee for 1921 with the request that the committee make the award as early as possible.

Mr. Learned reported for the committee on publications. It was voted to give the committee full power to dispose of the stock of prize essays and to make arrangements for the publication of Mr. Nussbaum's essay on "G. J. A. Ducher: An Essay on Commercial Policy in the French Revolution," to which was awarded the Adams prize of 1917.

Mr. Leland appeared before the council to report for the committee on the disposition of the records of the association. It was voted to authorize the committee to destroy such records of purely routine character as were in its judgment possessed of no value to the association and to deposit with the Library of Congress such records as were selected for preservation and should be deemed of no further use in the transaction of the business of the association.

The secretary presented the report from the committee on the historical congress at Rio de Janeiro, which it was voted to accept.

A statement from the committee on the military history prize was presented to the effect that eight essays had been submitted but that the award had not yet been made. It was voted to give the committee an extension of time and to instruct it to report its award to the secretary as soon as it should be made.

The report of the treasurer was read and accepted.

The report of the committee on history and education for citizenship in the schools, together with its request to be discharged, was presented by the secretary. After discussion it was voted to defer action in the matter and to request Mr. Bourne to attend the conference of the committee on December 29 and to report to the council such recommendations as may seem to him appropriate.

The council adjourned to meet at 2 p. m.

The council met at 2 p. m. Present: President Channing, presiding; Messrs. Bolton, Bourne, Burr, Haskins, Jameson, Lingelbach, Moore, Miss Putnam, and the secretary. There also attended Mr. Allen R. Boyd, editor; Miss P. W. Washington, assistant secretary-treasurer; Mr. George M. Dutcher, chairman of the committee on a manual of historical literature; and Mr. T. J. Wertenbaker, chairman of the committee on membership.

It was voted to recommend to the association that the next meeting be held at St. Louis in acceptance of invitations extended by Washington university, the Governor of Missouri, and the mayor of St. Louis.

The report of the committee on membership was presented by its chairman, Mr. Wertenbaker. It was voted to accept the report and to authorize the chairman to enlarge the committee by appointing associate members.

The report of the committee on a bibliography of modern English history was presented by the secretary. It was voted to accept the report and to refer the committee's request for an appropiation of $150 for 1921 to the committee on finance.

The report of the committee on a manual of historical literature was read by the secretary. It was voted to accept the report, except for the proposal that the major list should be composed exclusively of books printed in English, and to refer the matter of an appropriation for the committee to the committee on finance.

The secretary presented the report of the chairman of the conference of historical societies. The report was accepted.

The council then proceeded to consider the report of the committee on policy as presented by its chairman, Mr. C. H. Haskins. The report was read in full and was then considered section by section, action being taken as follows:

Section 21.—It was voted that, "pending the consideration of an amendment of the constitution raising the annual fees from $3 to $5, members are invited to make special contributions of from $2 to $5 in addition to the present dues."

Section 1.—It was voted that of the program committee three members shall serve three-year terms, so arranged that one member retires each year, the other members to have one-year terms and be selected with reference to locality.

Section 2.—It was voted that scholarly summaries or abstracts of all papers read at the meetings and not printed in the Review shall appear in the annual reports of the association.

Section 3.—It was voted to approve the recommendations of the committee on policy respecting the historical manuscripts commission.

Section 4.—It was voted to continue the public archives commission and to charge it with the preparation of the primer of archive economy, now assigned to a special committee.

Section 5.—It was voted to continue the present standing committee on the national archives.

Section 6.—It was voted to establish a committee on securing transcripts in foreign archives.

Section 7.—It was voted to reestablish a committee on the documentary historical publications of the United States Government.

Section 8.—It was voted to continue the standing committee on bibliography, to charge it with completing and publishing the bibliography of American travel, with continuing, in cooperation with the American Library Association, the compilation of the Manual of Historical Literature, and with the consideration of the other bibliographical projects (except the bibliography of modern English history) enumerated in section 8 of the report of the committee on policy.

Section 9.—It was voted to request the editor to report on some dependable means for carrying on the publication of Writings on American History without incurring a deficit. It was the opinion of the council that Writings should be published in the annual report until it can be brought out separately.

Section 10.—It was voted to comply with the request of the present committee on history and education for citizenship in the schools for the discharge of the said committee, and that the president, the two vice presidents, and the secretary be empowered to appoint a committee on history teaching in the schools.

Section 12.—It was voted to reconstitute a committee on hereditary patriotic societies.

Section 13.—It was voted to appoint a standing committee on military history whose chief function should be to advise and cooperate with the Historical Branch of the General Staff and with other governmental agencies, national and State, which are engaged in preparing histories of the war.

The council adjourned at 5.30 p. m. to meet at the New Willard Hotel on December 28 at 9 a. m.

MINUTES OF MEETING OF THE EXECUTIVE COUNCIL HELD AT THE NEW WILLARD HOTEL, WASHINGTON, D. C., ON DECEMBER 28, 1920

The council met at 9 a. m. Present: President Channing, presiding; Messrs. Bolton, Bourne, Burr, Haskins, Jameson, Lingelbach, Moore, Miss Putnam, and the secretary. There also attended Mr. Allen R. Boyd, editor, and Miss P. W. Washington, assistant secretary-treasurer.

The council continued its consideration of the report of the committee on policy.

Section 15.—It was voted that the proposal for establishing a series of historical studies be approved in principle and that the matter be referred for further report to the committee (D. C. Munro, chairman) which was appointed by the informal conference on the establishment of a journal of European history held at Cincinnati during the annual meetings of the American Historical Association in December, 1916.

Section 16.—It was voted to approve the recommendation of the committee respecting the Robert M. Johnston prize and the George Louis Beer prize.

Section 17.—It was voted to authorize the payment from the treasury of the association of traveling expenses of the association's delegates to the meetings of the American Council of Learned Societies.

Section 18.—It was voted to approve the plan for a university center for higher studies in Washington and to appoint representatives to confer with the representatives of other organizations interested in the enterprise.

Section 19.—It was voted to change the name of the committee on docket to committee on agenda, and that the two vice presidents, the secretary, and the treasurer should be ex officio members of the committee. It was voted to authorize the payment from the treasury of the association of the traveling expenses incurred by the members of the committee on agenda in attending one meeting of the committee each year.

Section 20.—It was voted to establish a standing committee on service.

It was voted to adopt the report of the committee on policy as a whole, subject to the changes involved in the votes of the council relating thereto and to present it to the association with the recommendation that it be adopted.

The council then proceeded to consider the recommendations of the committee on appointments with respect to committee assignments. It was voted to make the following appointments:

STANDING COMMITTEES

(Names of new members are printed in italics

Committee on program for the thirty-sixth annual meeting.—*Evarts B. Greene,* chairman (appointed for one year); *Charles Seymour* (appointed for two years), *Walter L. Fleming* (appointed for three years), *Thomas M. Marshall, Norman M. Trenholme;* and ex officiis, N. A. Olsen, secretary of the Agricultural History Society, John C. Parish, secretary of the conference of historical societies.

Historical manuscripts commission.—Justin H. Smith, chairman; *Annie H. Abel,* Eugene C. Barker, *Robert P. Brooks,* Logan Esarey, Gaillard Hunt.

Committee on the Justin Winsor prize.—*Clive Day,* chairman; *Isaac J. Cox, Thomas F. Moran, Bernard C. Steiner, William W. Sweet.*

Committee on the Herbert Baxter Adams prize.—Conyers Read, chairman; Charles H. McIlwain, *David S. Muzzey,* Nellie Neilson, Bernadotte E. Schmitt, *Wilbur H. Siebert.*

Committee on publications.—H. Barrett Learned, chairman; and, ex officiis, John S. Bassett, Allen R. Boyd, J. Franklin Jameson, Justin H. Smith, R. H. True.

Committee on membership.—Thomas J. Wertenbaker, chairman; Louise Fargo Brown, Eugene H. Byrne, A. C. Krey, Frank E. Melvin, Richard A. Newhall, Charles W. Ramsdell, Arthur P. Scott, J. J. Van Nostrand, jr., *James E. Winston,* George F. Zook.

Conference of historical societies.—John C. Parish, secretary (chairman to be elected by the conference).

Committee on national archives.—J. Franklin Jameson, chairman; Charles Moore, Col. Oliver L. Spaulding, jr.

Committee on bibliography.—George M. Dutcher, chairman; Sidney B. Fay, Augustus H. Shearer, Henry R. Shipman, (it was voted to authorize the chairman in consultation with the secretary of the association to appoint additional members).

Public archives commission.—Victor H. Paltsits, chairman; *Solon J. Buck, R. D. W. Connor, Waldo G. Leland, Arnold J. F. van Laer.*

Committee on obtaining transcripts from foreign archives.—*J. Franklin Jameson,* chairman; *Charles M. Andrews, Waldo G. Leland.*

Committee on military history.—Brig. Gen. Eben Swift, chairman; *Allen R. Boyd, R. B. House, Capt. Eben Putnam, Col. Oliver L. Spaulding, jr.*

Committee on hereditary patriotic societies.—(It was voted that this committee should be appointed by a special committee consisting of the secretary, the treasurer, and Mr. Leland.)

Committee on service.—J. Franklin Jameson, chairman. (It was agreed that the other members of the committee should be appointed by the secretary of the association and the chairman of the committee in consultation.)

Committee on bibliography of modern English history.—Edward P. Cheyney, chairman; *Arthur L. Cross, Roger B. Merriman, Wallace Notestein, Conyers Read.*

Committee on the historical congress at Rio de Janeiro.—Bernard Moses, honorary chairman; Percy A. Martin, acting chairman; Julius Klein, secretary; Charles Lyon Chandler, Charles H. Cunningham, *Constantine E. McGuire, Ambassador Edwin V. Morgan, Manoel de Oliveira Lima, W. L. Schurz.*

Committee on the documentary historical publications of the United States Government.—J. Franklin Jameson, chairman; *Henry Cabot Lodge, Charles Moore.* (It was voted to authorize the committee to add to its numbers.)

Committee to formulate rules for the George L. Beer prize.—William A. Dunning, chairman; *Marshall S. Brown, Edwin S. Corwin.*

Committee on the writing of history.—Ambassador Jean Jules Jusserand, chairman; *Wilbur C. Abbott, Charles W. Colby.*

Upon nomination by the committee on appointments the council elected Mr. G. S. Ford a member of the board of editors of the American Historical Review for the full term of six years ending in December, 1926.

Upon nomination by the committee on appointments the following were elected a board of editors of the Historical Outlook to advise with the managing editor: Edgar Dawson, Laurence M. Larson, William L. Westermann, Sarah A. Dynes, and Daniel C. Knowlton.

The council adjourned to meet at 1140 Woodward Building on December 29 at 9.30 a. m.

MINUTES OF THE MEETING OF THE EXECUTIVE COUNCIL HELD AT 1140 WOODWARD BUILDING, WASHINGTON, D. C., ON DECEMBER 29, 1920.

The council met at 9.30 a. m. Present: President Channing, presiding; Messrs. Bolton, Burr, Haskins, Jameson, Lingelbach, Moore, Miss Putnam, and the secretary. There also attended Mr. Allen R. Boyd, editor, and Miss P. W. Washington, assistant secretary-treasurer.

Mr. Dana C. Munro and Mr. Waldo G. Leland were appointed a committee to confer with representatives of other associations on the organization of a university center for higher studies in Washington.

Mr. Allen R. Boyd reported that the committee on the military history prize had awarded the Robert M. Johnston prize to Mr. Thomas Robson Hay for his essay, "Hood's Tennessee campaign," with honorable mention to Mr. W. P. Webb for his essay "The Texas Rangers in the Mexican War," and to Maj. J. N. Greely for his essay, "What happens in battle."

The treasurer presented the report of the finance committee on the budget for 1921. It was voted to accept the report and to approve for adoption by the association the following budget:

APPROPRIATIONS

Secretary and treasurer	$3,000
Pacific Coast Branch	50
Nominating committee	100
Committee on membership	100
Committee on program	300
Committee on local arrangements	50
Conference of historical societies	25
Committee on publications	700

Council committee on agenda	$300
American Historical Review	7,000
Historical manuscripts commission	20
Justin Winsor prize	200
Writings on American History	200
American Council of Learned Societies	150
Committee on bibliography	250
Committee on the writing of history	75
Total	12,520

ESTIMATED INCOME

Annual dues	7,000
Registration fees	150
Publications	100
Royalties	50
Interest	1,400
Miscellaneous	50
Total	8,750

The committee on history and education for citizenship in the schools submitted, in addition to the report previously presented, the following resolution:

Resolved, That the committee ask the council for permission to publish its final report, to embody: (1) A fairly definite outline of the reorganized program for the 12 years as embodied in the June, 1919, issue of the Historical Outlook; (2) a straightforward statement justifying the program; (3) syllabi of certain selected topics and courses embodied in the program which will be put forth not as final recommendations but merely as suggestive of the detailed treatment that might be accorded to the various parts of the program.

After consideration of the request by the committee on history and education for citizenship in the schools the council voted to adopt the following statement:

In discharging the committee at its own request, the council desires to record its high appreciation of its laborious services. In view of the incomplete nature of the report and of the fact that a considerable difference of opinion seems to exist among the members of the association respecting the recommendations of the committee on history and education for citizenship in the schools, the council is apprehensive that formal publication of the report by the committee would appear to commit the association prematurely, and therefore the council thinks it wise to refer the whole subject to the new standing committee on history teaching in the school.

It was voted to authorize the treasurer to pay from the appropriation of the committee on history and education for citizenship in the schools for 1920 the sum of $300 to Miss Frances Morehouse for services rendered to the committee.

The secretary reported a request that was made to him informally by Mr. George Grafton Wilson for the appointment of a committee to cooperate with the historical section of the Navy Department. It was voted to authorize the committee on service to appoint a committee of three to cooperate with the Historical Section of the Navy Department in such manner as may be desired by the chief of the section. It was also voted to authorize the committee on service to meet similar requests in a similar way.

It was voted to authorize the committee on appointments to appoint two representatives of the association to cooperate with the Peoples of America Society in accordance with the previous vote of the council.

The council adjourned to meet at 1140 Woodward Building on December 30 at 9.30 a. m.

MINUTES OF THE MEETING OF THE EXECUTIVE COUNCIL HELD AT 1140 WOODWARD BUILDING, WASHINGTON, D. C., ON DECEMBER 30, 1920

The council met at 9.45 a. m. Present: First Vice President Haskins, presiding, Messrs. Bourne, Burr, Cheyney, Cross, Fay, Hayes, Jameson, Moore, Sioussat, Miss Putnam, and the secretary. There also attended Mr. Allen R. Boyd, editor, and Miss P. W. Washington, assistant secretary-treasurer.

Mr. Bourne reported that, in compliance with the request of the council, he had attended the conference on the report of the committee on history and education for citizenship in the schools. After discussion it was found to be the sense of the council that the request of the committee respecting the publication of its report should be disposed of in accordance with the statement adopted by the council in the session of December 29.

It was voted to request Mr. Robert S. Brookings, of St. Louis, to serve as chairman of the committee on local arrangements for the St. Louis meeting.

Mr. Archibald C. Coolidge was elected a member of the board of editors of the American Historical Review for the unexpired term of Mr. E. P. Cheyney, who resigned from the board following his election as second vice president of the association.

It was voted that the committee on agenda consist of the president, the vice presidents, the secretary, the treasurer, and four other members of the council to be designated.

Mr. Daniel C. Knowlton was elected a member of the board of editors of the Historical Outlook in place of Mr. Sioussat, who resigned following his election to the executive council.

It was voted to establish a committee of five on endowment. The treasurer was appointed chairman of the committee with authority to appoint the other members in consultation with the secretary.

It was voted that the secretary and treasurer, in consultation with the committee on bibliography, be authorized to make arrangements for the publication of the Manual of Historical Literature.

It was voted that the secretary, with such consultation as he may desire, be authorized to make appointments for 1921 to the ordinary standing committees of the council.

It was voted to suggest to the committee on local arrangements for the St. Louis meeting that the sessions commence on Wednesday, December 28, and last three days.

Mr. Waldo G. Leland was appointed a committee of one to confer with representatives of other learned societies in order to obtain reduced railroad rates for the annual meetings of these societies.

The secretary was instructed to extend the thanks of the council to the committee on local arrangements for the Washington meeting, to the Librarian of Congress, to the Women's City Club, and to the Association of Collegiate Alumnæ for services, courtesies, and hospitalities in connection with the present meetings of the association. The secretary was authorized to write a letter to the Secretary of War in appreciation of his address at the dinner on December 29.

The council adjourned.

PROCEEDINGS OF THE EXECUTIVE COUNCIL ADOPTED BY CORRESPONDENCE WITH THE MEMBERS

APPOINTMENTS TO COMMITTEES OF THE COUNCIL

Committee on Agenda.—Charles H. Haskins (ex officio), chairman; John S. Bassett (ex officio), Edward P. Cheyney (ex officio), Arthur L. Cross, Sidney B. Fay, Carlton J. H. Hayes, Jean Jules Jusserand, Charles Moore (ex officio), Frederic L. Paxson.

Committee on meetings and relations.—John S. Bassett, chairman; Edward Channing, Carl Russell Fish, Ruth Putnam, James T. Shotwell.

Committee on finance.—Charles Moore, chairman; John S. Bassett, Sidney B. Fay, Frederic L. Paxson, St. George L. Sioussat.

Committee on appointments.—Jean Jules Jusserand, chairman; John S. Bassett, Edward P. Cheyney, Carl Russell Fish, Carlton J. H. Hayes.

APPOINTMENTS TO STANDING COMMITTEES OF THE ASSOCIATION

Committee on history teaching in the schools.—Henry Johnson, chairman; Henry E. Bourne, Philip P. Chase, Guy Stanton Ford, Daniel C. Knowlton, Albert E. McKinley, Eugene M. Violette.

Committee on service.—J. Franklin Jameson, chairman; Elbert J. Benton, Clarence S. Brigham, Worthington C. Ford, Arthur C. Howland, Albert E. McKinley, James Sullivan.

Committee on membership, associate members (appointed by the chairman).—Milledge L. Bonham, jr., Henry E. Bourne, Julian P. Bretz, Robert P. Brooks, Sarah A. Dynes, Austin P. Evans, J. Montgomery Gambrill, Sheldon J. Howe, M. Berna Hunt, Laurence M. Larson, John H. Logan, Margaret J. Mitchell, Laurence B. Packard, George Petrie, Walter Prichard, Charles H. Rammelkamp, Morgan P. Robinson, Louis M. Sears, Augustus H. Shearer, Earl E. Sperry, David Y. Thomas, Frederic L. Thompson, Norman M. Trenholme, James A. Woodburn, Jesse E. Wrench, John P. Wynne.

Committee on hereditary patriotic societies.—Dixon R. Fox, chairman; Natalie S. Lincoln, Harry Brent Mackoy, Mrs. Annie L. Sioussat, R. C. Ballard Thurston.

Committee on local arrangements for thirty-sixth annual meeting.—William K. Bixby, chairman; Mrs. Nettie H. Beauregard, Ralph P. Bieber, Stella M. Drumm, David R. Francis, Benjamin Gratz, John H. Gundlach, Breckinridge Jones, Mrs. Robert McKittrick Jones, Breckinridge Long, Mrs. N. A. McMillan, Thomas M. Marshall, Charles P. Pettus, George R. Throop.

Committee on bibliography of American travel.—Benjamin F. Shambaugh, chairman; Solon J. Buck, M. M. Quaife.

APPOINTMENTS TO SPECIAL COMMITTEES OF THE ASSOCIATION

Committee to cooperate with the Peoples of America Society in the study of race elements in the United States.—John S. Bassett, chairman; Frederic L. Paxson.

Register of Attendance at the Thirty-fifth Annual Meeting at Washington, D. C.

A

Abel, Annie Heloise.
Adams, Randolph G.
Adams, Victoria A.
Allison, William H.
Ambler, Charles H.
Ames, Herman V.
Anderson, D. R.
Anderson, Frank Maloy.
Andrews, Charles M.
Andrews, George Gordon.
Appleton, William W.

Arnett, Alex Mathews.
Asakawa, K.
Atkeson, Mary Meek.

B

Baldwin, Alice M.
Baldwin, James F.
Barclay, Thomas S.
Barnes, Harry E.
Barss, Katharine G.
Bassett, John Spencer.
Becker, Carl.

Belmende, Victor Andrés.
Belote, Theodore.
Benton, E. J.
Berry, Sarah.
Best, Harry.
Betten, Rev. Francis S.
Beveridge, Albert J.
Bieber, Ralph P.
Bigelow, Col. John.
Black, J. William.
Bolton, Herbert E.
Bond, Beverley W., jr.

Crouse, N. M.
Curtis, Eugene Newton.

D

Dargan, Marion.
Davenport, Frances G.
David, Charles Wendell.
Day, Clive.
DeForest, Sarah S.
Dodd, William E.
Donnan, Elizabeth.
Drane, Rev. Robert Brent.
Duncan, D. Shaw.
Dutcher, George M.

E

Eckenrode, H. J.
Ellery, Eloise,
Ellis, Ellen Deborah.
Emerton, Ephraim.
Evans, Austin P.

F

Fairbanks, Elsie D.
Farr, Shirley.
Faÿ, Bernard.
Fay, Sidney B.
Ferrin, Dana H.
Ferry, Nellie Poyntz.
Fitzpatrick, J. C.
Flick, Alexander C.
Flippin, Percy Scott.
Flournoy, F. R.
Fogdall, S. P.
Ford, Worthington C.
Foster, Herbert D.
Fox, Dixon Ryan.
Fox, George L.
Fuller, George N.

G

Gallagher, Katharine
    Jeanne.
Gardner, Elizabeth.
Garfield, H. A.
Gaskill, G. E.
Gaus, John Merriman.
Gazley, John G.
Gibbons, Lois Oliphant.
Gipson, Laurence H.
Godard, George S.
Gosnell, C. B.
Gould, Clarence P.
Graves, W. Brooke.

Gray, Helen.
Greenfield, Kent Roberts.
Greve, Harriet C.
Grizzell, E. D.
Grose, Clyde L.
Grouard, Maria Louise.
Guilday, Rev. Peter.

H

Hamilton, J. G. de Roulhac.
Haring, Clarence H.
Harrison, Fairfax.
Haskins, Charles H.
Hayden, Joseph R.
Hayes, Carlton J. H.
Hayes, Mercy J.
Haynes, George H.
Hazard, Blanche Evans.
Healy, Patrick J.
Hearon, Cleo.
Heckel, Albert K.
Hedger, George A.
Heston, Hiram.
Hickman, Emily.
Hicks, J. D. H.
Higby, Chester P.
Hill, Henry W.
Hockett, Homer C.
Hodder, F. H.
Hodgdon, Frederick C.
Holt, Lucius H.
Hoover, Thomas N.
Hoskins, Halford Lancaster.
House, R. B.
Hull, Charles H.
Humphrey, E. F.
Hunt, Gaillard.
Husband, W. W.

I

Irby, Louise.
Irons, Mrs. W. S.
Isanogle, A. M.

J

Jackson, W. C.
James, Alfred P.
Jameson, J. F.
Jenison, Marguerite E.
Jernegan, M. W.
Johnson, Allen.
Johnson, Edward P.
Jones, C. K.
Jones, Theodore F.

K

Kellar, Herbert A.
Kellar, Mrs. Herbert A.
Kellogg, Louise Phelps.
Kendrick, Benjamin B.
Kennelly, A. E.
Kennelly, Mrs. A. E.
Kerner, Robert Joseph.
Kilgore, Carrie B.
Kincaid, Marion B.
Kinchen, Oscar A.
Kinnicutt, Lincoln N.
Klein, Julius.
Klingenhagen, Anna M.
Knapp, Charles M.
Knauss, James Owen.
Knowlton, Daniel C.
Kollock, Margaret P.
Konkle, Burton Alva.
Korff, Baron S. A.
Korff, Baroness S. A.
Kull, Irving S.

L

Latané, John W.
Learned, H. Barrett.
Leavenworth, Charles S.
Leland, Waldo G.
Lerch, Alice Hollister.
Lewis, Hazel R.
Lima, M. de Oliveira.
Lingelbach, William E.
Lonn, Ella.
Lough, Susan M.
Lunt, W. E.
Lutz, Ralph H.

M

MacCarthy, Charles Hallan.
MacDonald, William.
McDougle, Ivan E.
McDuffie, Penelope.
Mace, W. H.
McFayden, Donald.
McGuire, C. E.
McKinley, Albert E.
McMaster, John Bach.
Manhart, George B.
Manning, William R.
Marshall, Thomas Maitland.
Martin, A. E.
Martin, Percy Alvin.
Mereness, Newton D.

Merritt, Elizabeth.
Minot, Jesse.
Mitchell, Margaret J.
Mitchell, Samuel Chiles.
Moffett, Edna V.
Mohr, Walter H.
Moore, Charles.
Morgan, Williams Thomas.
Morriss, Margaret S.
Munro, Dana Carleton.
Musser, John.
Muzzey, David Saville.

N

Nash, Elizabeth Todd.
Neilson, N.
Newhall, Richard A.
Nichols, Roy Franklin.
Nichols, Mrs. R. F.
Nicolay, Helen.
Norwood, J. Nelson.
Notestein, Wallace.
Noyes, Edmund S.
Nussbaum, Frederick L.

O

Oakes, George W. Ochs.
Oldfather, C. H.
Ott, Mary Castle.
Owen, Mrs. Marie Bankhead.

P

Packard, Laurence B.
Paetow, Louis J.
Paine, Mrs. Clarence S.
Paltsits, Victor Hugo.
Parish, John C.
Park, Julian.
Pasvolsky, Leo.
Patterson, David L.
Paullin, C. O.
Pearson, C. C.
Pearson, Henry G.
Pease, Theodore C.
Perkins, Dexter.
Pershing, B. H.
Phillips, Ulrich B.
Porcher, Isaac de C.
Priddy, Mrs. Bessie Leach.
Prince, L. Bradford.

Purcell, Richard J.
Putnam, Bertha Haven.
Putnam, Herbert.

R

Rammelkamp, C. H.
Ramsdell, Charles W.
Randall, J. G.
Randall, Mrs. J. G.
Randolph, Bessie C.
Read, Conyers.
Rees, Col. Robert I.
Reeves, Jesse S.
Reuter, Bertha Ann.
Rhodes, James Ford.
Richardson, Mrs. Hester Dorsey.
Richardson, Lula M.
Ridgate, Thomas H.
Riley, Franklin L.
Rippy, James Fred.
Robertson, James A.
Robinson, Morgan P.
Rosenberry, M. B.
Rosenberry, Mrs. M. B.
Rostovtzeff, Michael T.
Rowland, Dunbar.
Russell, Elmer Beecher.

S

Sanborn, Bernice.
Schafer, Joseph.
Schlesinger, Arthur Meier.
Sears, Louis M.
Shaw, Caroline B.
Shepherd, William R.
Sherwood, Henry Noble.
Shipman, Henry R.
Shoemaker, Floyd C.
Siebert, W. H.
Simmons, Lucy.
Sioussat, Mrs. Albert
Sioussat, St. George L.
Skeel, Mrs. Roswell, jr.
Spaulding, Col. Oliver L., jr.
Stevens, Earnest N.
Stevens, Wayne E.
Stilwell, Lewis D.
Stites, Mary A.
Stock, Leo F.

Stockton, Rear Admiral Charles H.
Stone, Mrs. Mary Hanchett.
Sullivan, James.
Sweet, William W.

T

Tall, Lida Lee.
Tanner, Edwin P.
Taylor, Col. John R. M.
Thompson, Frederic L.
Thorndike, Lynn.
Tschan, Francis J.
Tuell, Harriet E.
Turner, Edward Raymond.
Turner, Frederick J.
Turner, Morris K.

U

Ullrick, Laura F.

V

Van Bibber, Lena C.
Van Tyne, C. H.
Vaughn, Earnest V.
Vaux, George, jr.
Vincent, John Martin.

W

Ware, Edith E.
Washburn, Albert H.
Washburne, George A.
Weber, Nicholas Aloysius.
Wendell, Hugo C. M.
Wertenbaker, T. J.
Wertheimer, Mildred S.
West, Warren Reed.
Wheeler, Benjamin W.
White, Elizabeth B.
Whitney, Cornelia.
Wilkinson, William J.

Williams, Clarence R.
Williams, Judith B.
Williams, Mary Wilhelmine.
Wilson, George G.
Wilson, J. Scott.
Wilson, Lucy L.
Wing, Herbert, jr.
Wittke, Carl.
Wood, George A.
Woodfin, Maude Howlett.
Wriston, Henry M.
Wyatt, Frank S.

Y

Yoder, Bertha A.

Z

Zéliqzon, Maurice M.
Zook, George F.

II. PROCEEDINGS OF THE SIXTEENTH ANNUAL MEETING OF THE PACIFIC COAST BRANCH OF THE AMERICAN HISTORICAL ASSOCIATION

CLAREMONT AND LOS ANGELES, CALIF., NOVEMBER 26–27, 1920

97244°—25——8

The sixteenth annual meeting of the Pacific Coast Branch of the American Historical Association was held on Friday morning and Friday afternoon, November 26, at Pomona College, and on Saturday morning, November 27, 1920, at the University of Southern California. The annual dinner Friday evening was held at the Hotel Clark, Los Angeles, Calif., Prof. Herbert E. Bolton presiding. The presiding officers of the sessions were as follows: Friday morning, Prof. Waldemar C. Westergaard; Friday afternoon, Prof. R. G. Clelland; Saturday morning, Mr. W. F. Bliss, of the San Diego State Normal School.

The general topic for the Friday morning session was "Opportunities for historical research." The first paper of the session was presented by Prof. R. H. Lutz, of Stanford University, who described the Hoover collection at Stanford University. Professor Lutz prefaced his remarks with the statement that the Hoover collection may be approached for study and historical research from almost any angle. He limited his remarks, however, to a discussion of three general phases—(1) the gathering of material; (2) its classification; (3) the most important fields for historical research.

(1) The idea and general plan of starting the Hoover collection was first brought to the attention of Mr. Herbert Hoover almost at the beginning of the World War, when it was pointed out to him that a collection of war documents on all phases of the war would be of inestimable value in later years. The active gathering of documents, pamphlets, and papers of all kinds was started under the direction of Mr. Hoover at the beginning of the work of the Committee for the Relief of Belgium. His chief assistants were Profs. E. D. Adams and Lutz. Documents were collected from every source possible, large collections of invaluable material being secured in London, Brussels, and Paris, and all through the eastern European States, whole collections of private documents sometimes being purchased containing material which now can not be duplicated in the original. The process of gathering material for the Hoover collection still continues, as there remains much to be collected. It must be secured within the next few years or else be lost. This work is now going on all over the world, in every country which was at all affected by the war, and material is constantly coming in.

Contents: The Hoover collection is one of the largest of its kind in the world, being one of three great collections similar in character, the other two being that of the Library of Congress at Washington and the Musée de la Guerre at Paris, France. The collection contains over 80,000 titles and has a value roughly estimated at $200,000.

(2) In classifying the material, five main groups have been established.

(a) Government documents of all kinds bearing on the period of the war from 1914 to 1919. These include records and reports relating to the economic, industrial, and food conditions during the war in practically every country in the world. In addition, this group contains a great wealth of documents of a military and educational nature, nearly every government having gladly sent in whole collections of documents and other material on these subjects, giving a very complete history of that country in practically all its different phases of life during the war.

(b) Delegation propaganda at the time of the Peace Conference. This includes the publications and propaganda of all kinds from over 70 delegations with their claims which were represented before the Peace Conference. It also includes propaganda material of an unauthentic nature issued or published by opposing delegations to further their interests and injure those of their opponents, as in the case of Italy. From Italy came considerable propaganda purporting to be the claims of Yugoslavia, and Yugoslavia in turn published propaganda purporting to be the claims of Italy. A similar case was that of the Zionists and the Anti-Zionists. Reliable and authentic material containing the claims of these nations was secured by going direct to the various delegations themselves.

(c) Society publications of all kinds. This group includes the publications of the French war societies, very complete in nature and of great historical value; publications of 300 British societies; of 200 societies in the United States; also other miscellaneous publications from societies all over the world, in both neutral and belligerent countries; others are yet to be secured. The group includes also the publications of some societies which were afterwards suppressed.

(d) The complete archives and files of the Committee for the Relief of Belgium. The Belgium Government was very grateful for the services rendered by this commission and has given an immense amount of material to the Hoover collection. Documents from this source still continue to come in.

(e) Miscellaneous material of all kinds pertaining to the war. This includes odds and ends of picturesque publications; propaganda sheets in Belgium and in Germany and in Italy; Hungarian propaganda sheets; propaganda of the Bolsheviki in eastern Europe; trench papers and other similar curiosities; also a selected bibliography of books on the World War, written in the United States, England, France, and in other countries throughout the world.

(3) The fields of research may be divided into eight general classes, in all of which the Hoover collection offers a vast amount of original material:

(a) The social, political, and economic phases of the war as affecting England, France, and Belgium. The Government of Belgium has sent in practically everything published in that country.

(b) Political, economic, and social life of Germany, Austria, and Bulgaria during the war.

(c) The study of government documents illustrating the change in the life of European governments during the war.

(d) The psychology of the Peace Conference; its plans, claims of the delegations, their desires and antagonisms, with a comparison of their claims and adjustments as shown by the peace treaty.

(e) The history of the birth of new states: There is sufficient material now at Stanford University on which to write extensive monographs.

(f) The field of international law and diplomacy.

(g) The study of newspaper collections, of which there is a complete catalogue of the most prominent papers in the United States and in Europe during the entire period of the war. There is also the library of the British War Office. Both contain a wealth of propaganda material, offering an intensely interesting study.

(h) The field of philanthrophy and the war; the record of how the United States fed a great part of Europe; this being one of the largest fields for research.

The second speaker, Prof. P. A. Martin, of Stanford University, presented "The opportunities for historical research in Latin American history," stating that the field of Latin American history until recent years has been largely neglected, most of the research work that has been done lying chiefly in the field of diplomacy. At the present time there is already considerable material for research study at Stanford University in the great number of documents of the period of the World War, secured from all the Latin-American countries for the Hoover collection. Similar documents on early periods have been secured from most of the South American Governments.

Materials for the study of Latin American history: Besides the immense amount of source material now to be found in the Hoover collection, there are a number of other collections at Stanford. A fine collection of material on Brazil from the time of its independence from Portugal has been secured through the indefatigable efforts of Dr. J. C. Branner, of Stanford University, who spent many years there. There is also an entire set of the Brazilian Historical Review from its first issue in 1842. There are in addition a complete set of laws and Government publications from the time of the independence of Brazil from Portugal in 1822, and other publications of an economic and social nature. The aim is to build up a collection of original source material on Portugese-American history at Stanford.

Another collection has been made by Professor Coolidge, of Harvard University, which consists of the private library of the librarian of the Government of Chile, which is very complete in nature, being valued at $125,000. Still another collection of materials for research study is that which has been secured by Prof. Hiram Bingham, at Yale University, on the wars of independence of the South American Republics. Other collections of material in this country are those of the Library of Congress, the University of Texas, and the complete library of Dr. Oliveira Lima, former ambassador from Brazil to the United States, on Brazilian history, which is now in the possession of the Catholic University at Washington and is considered the finest collection of its kind outside of Brazil. Further, there are the archives of the Department of State, rich in material, but which are closed at present.

THE FIELDS FOR RESEARCH IN LATIN-AMERICAN HISTORY.

The colonial period of South American history; a great many topics yet to be developed; a great deal of material also to be had at Mexico City.

The study of institutions, their growth and development in Latin-American history, e. g., the Audiencia.

The study of vice-royalties, of captaincies-general, of royal patronage, and of the early financial systems.

The Spanish-American wars for independence. This includes the study of famous leaders such as Bolivar, San Martin, Cortez.

Nationalism and the development of the new states: Opportunities for research as to the lives and achievements of the great leaders of this period, Maximilian in Mexico; the lives of Presidents of the South American Republics, as Sarmiento; all these topics remain to be developed. There are ample opportunities for further research in the fields of economics, sociology, and political science, the slave trade in Brazil offering a vast field in this connection.

There is at present a great demand for the services of men who are fitted for this type of work to assist not only in making these investigations but in offering assistance both to the United States and to the various Latin-American Governments in establishing closer relations between these countries.

Opportunities for the publication of all research work of this character are offered not only in the publications of this country but also in South America in such publications as the Hispanic American Historical Review and others.

The Huntington Library collection of American history was described by Doctor Cole, curator. The collection of American history material in the Huntington Library, which is soon to be open to the public and for research work, is of immense value. . Although complete in itself, it forms but a small part of the great collection which is now being placed in the Huntington Library. The American history collection is classified as follows:

(a) The period of discovery and exploration:
    (1) A number of original source books, which begin with the first Latin edition of the letters of Columbus.
    (2) The letters of Vespucius.
    (3) The Cortez letters, both the Latin and also one French edition.
    (4) The Las Casas tracts.
    (5) The works of Peter Martyr.
(b) The period of colonization and settlement:
    (1) The MSS. of Elliott's Indian Bible and translations.
    (2) The first almanacs printed in New York—the works of Bradford, etc.
    (3) Materials on the settlement of Virginia—Captain John Smith's History of Virginia, with maps.
(c) The Revolutionary period:
    (1) The original MSS. of the letters of George III to his Privy Councilors regarding the independence of the American Colonies; the minutes of the Privy Council.
    (2) Eight hundred Tory pamphlets issued in New York during the Revolutionary War period.
(d) The War of 1812:
    (1) A complete collection of original materials, military, political, and economic in character.
(e) The period of the Civil War:
    (1) The MSS. of Union and Confederate generals; their letters and diaries.
    (2) A complete bibliography of books on the war in all its phases.
(f) Other original MSS. material:
    (1) The letters of John Fiske.
    (2) The letters of Sherman, and letters and writings of Abraham Lincoln.
(g) Materials on the history of California:
    (1) The collection of Mr. Alexander MacDonald—supplementing to a great degree the Bancroft collection at the University of California.
    (2) Old Spanish and Mexican MSS.

Lack of time prevented the reading of the following paper, "A brief statement of the opportunities for historical research in Hawaii," by Prof. K. C. Leebrick, of the University of Hawaii:

Hawaii offers an unusually unique and rich field for the historical student. The source materials are well preserved. Most of them are gathered together in or about Honolulu so that they are easily accessible and ready for study. A guide to the materials and archives is one of the tasks that needs be undertaken at once.

The primitive and unwritten history of the Hawaiian Islands can be studied from unusually large collections of material remains of all kinds. The Bishop Museum has carefully collected almost everything that will help to preserve the life and customs of the Hawaiian people or throw light upon the past history of the people and the country. A large staff of well-trained men and women are constantly at work collecting, arranging, and recording materials. The museum with its rich collections, its reports, and its library, gives the student materials admirably arranged and preserved for this use. There are other lesser collections. The original dwellings, settlements, and other remains are within easy reach of the worker.

The entire written history of the Hawaiian people and islands lies within a very recent period. The Spanish knew of the existence of the islands, but so far little has been found of record as to this early discovery. From the time of Captain Cook's discovery of the islands in 1778, very good descriptions of the people and the islands have been made at frequent intervals by observers, of several nationalities, and by trained searchers in almost every field of knowledge. These records are here. Thus there is a very complete record of the people before their lives and history were altered by contact with another civilization. Europeans from the very first have endeavored to make a complete record of this people, of their traditions and folklore, and of their political history.

The political union of the islands was only achieved in 1795, after the coming of Europeans, and very largely by their aid and advice. There is a considerable body of original manuscript material, in English, covering this most vital period, which saw not only the unification of the archipelago but the modification of the customs and institutions of the people, due to European influence.

The Hawaiian people were given a written language by the missionaries who arrived in the islands in 1820. They had been sent out by the American Board of Commissioners for Foreign Missions. Since that time the missionary has been the chief factor in the development of the people and the islands. There is a complete official record of the activities of this society in the English language. Other missionary societies soon came into the field; their records are also complete and available in English, French, and Latin. The various depositories, official and private, have an almost complete record of all official and vital private documents from this early date to the present. Complete files are available of most public documents; of all newspapers, magazines, books, and pamphlets printed here since the people had a written language. These are generally to be had in both English and Hawaiian. This is most unusual. There is a considerable amount of this material printed for the entire period. The first printing was done in the Hawaiian language in January, 1822, and printing in both Hawaiian and English has been continuous since that date. I am informed that complete files are available for almost all public documents and books printed from the very beginning.

Something has been done to collect documents and copies dealing with the relations with other countries. This will throw light upon the Hawaiian documents, which are almost absolutely complete.

Official documents have been unusually well kept and generally well preserved. This is especially true from 1845, when Mr. Wyllie became Minister of Foreign Affairs. A commission was appointed by the legislature in 1892 to arrange and preserve all official records. This commission did its work well. The oldest documents are English and are dated 1790.

The Hawaiian Historical Society was founded in 1892 and has done much to preserve and record public and private historical material of Hawaii. The "Reports" and "Papers" of the society are preserved in complete files and have just been carefully indexed. The society has built up a good working library of voyages to the islands; complete files of the missionary publications; of many of the books printed in Hawaii, in both Hawaiian and English; and of books printed about Hawaii. There is also a considerable quantity of pamphlet material; there are almost complete files of all newspapers and magazines; and there is some manuscript material, but it is not completely catalogued or arranged. The collection is well housed in the beautiful Territorial Public Library. There are excellent opportunities for the research student.

Shortly after the annexation of the Hawaiian Islands to the United States, Mr. W. C. Ford, of the Library of Congress, came to Hawaii to investigate the archives and to have at least a part of them transferred to Washington. He was urged to recommend that the archives remain here because of their local value; that he did on the condition that they be properly housed and cared for by the Territorial government. In accordance with this recommendation, the legislature of 1903 provided money for a building; the legislature of 1905 passed an act providing for a board of commissioners of public archives. Active work began on the collection and preservation of the documents May 11, 1905. Since that time an excellent fireproof building has been erected on the capitol grounds and close to the Territorial library. Here are found the public records and documents of the Territory of Hawaii well arranged and stored so as to insure their preservation. The librarian, Mr. Robert C. Lydecker, has performed his duties well and is a mine of information regarding the records and history of Hawaii. The archive building is an excellent place to work. I think it sufficiently important to justify me in referring my readers to Mr. Lydecker's paper on "The Archives of Hawaii," printed in "Papers of the Hawaiian Historical Society," No. 13, 1906.

Since the organization of the College of Hawaii in 1907 as an agricultural and scientific college, the library of that institution has been a depository for the United States public documents. The College of Hawaii, now the University of Hawaii (1920), therefore has part of the official United States documents from about the year 1908. Every effort is being made to complete the files and to obtain as many of the volumes before this period as are available.

In addition to these sources one should call attention to the fact that many of the men who took the government into their hands in 1893 and organized an efficient government and opened the negotiations that led to annexation by the United States in 1898 are still living, and that they and their libraries are the best sources for this most interesting period. The writer wishes to acknowledge his indebtedness to the Hon. S. B. Dole, former President of the Republic of Hawaii and the first governor fter the annexation by the United States, for his advice and friendship. Acknowledgment is also due to the librarians of the libraries mentioned and to many of the "elder statesmen" of Hawaii.

The business session was called to order at 2 p. m., with President L. E. Young in the chair.

The committee on resolutions, Prof. P. A. Martin, chairman, presented the following resolutions which were adopted:

(1) Whereas, by the death of Prof. Arley B. Show, of Stanford University, this association has lost one of its oldest members and the profession an able and conscientious scholar who throughout his long years of special work in the training of history teachers not only was a careful and stimulating instructor of those who came under his guidance but also displayed a warm personal interest in their later individual progress, doing much to elevate the standards of history teaching by inspiring the members of the profession with his own enthusiasm for accurate scholarship and for sympathetic and thorough teaching: Be it

Resolved, That this association place on record its high appreciation of the unique and valuable service which Mr. Show rendered to the profession of history teaching on the Pacific coast, and the sense of loss, personal as well as collective, which his death has brought to them; and be it further

Resolved, That copies of this resolution be sent to the president of Stanford University and to Mr. Show's family.

(2) Resolved, That the funds so generously provided by the State board of education for libraries in the elementary schools be supplemented by other funds, or be so administered that the intermediate schools or high schools may obtain some of the advantages accruing from this source.

The auditing committee, Professor Clelland, chairman, reported that it had examined the statement of account with vouchers of the secretary-treasurer and found the statement correct. The report was approved.

The committee on nominations, Prof. R. H. Lutz, chairman, presented as candidates: For president, R. C. Clark; vice president, P. J. Treat; secretary treasurer, J. J. Van Nostrand, jr. For the council, in addition to the above, W. C. Westergaard, Miss Sara L. Dole, W. F. Bliss.

On motion, the nominations were closed and the secretary was instructed to cast the ballots for those nominees who were declared elected. On motion of the secretary, Prof. L. E. Young was appointed delegate of the branch to attend the meeting of the council of the American Historical Association at Washington D. C.

The business session then adjourned, to be followed immediately by the general session of the afternoon.

The first speaker was Prof. R. D. Hunt, of the University of Southern California, whose subject was "The contribution of political science to education." A résumé of Professor Hunt's address follows:

History, with man as its subject, is surely one of the subjects very intimately connected with human society. This being so, it is a subject that requires expert handling. It can not be confined to any restricted area or put in water-tight compartments and still be a subject dealing with life. More than this, education itself can not be considered liberal unless it has the broadest of foundations. No teacher can confine his work or his thinking to any one narrow field.

The end of our education is intelligent citizenship. The educated man is the broad man sharpened to a point; and this is the type of men that America needs to-day, as citizens, more than ever before in her history. And not only does America need this new strength, but Europe needs it even more urgently. The civilization in practically every country of Europe is at such a low ebb that in innumerable places it is at the point of death. Austria, as an example, subsists through charity alone. This condition offers a challenge to opulent America.

At such a time as this, America must not become the victim of the diseases of Spain or Rome. She must be strong in intellectual and spiritual life, and the college men must be the ones to furnish this strength for America. At the present time our people of all classes are obsessed with a spirit of lawlessness which must be overcome. Democracy is never safe in the hands of its enemies. In President Wilson's words, "What we seek is the reign of law, based upon the consent of the governed, and sustained by the organized opinion of mankind." But higher than law—the letter of which we can comply with—is the reign of *moral* law. America must learn to appreciate the value of morality.

Doctor Hunt gave several suggestions which should apply to the teaching of civics and citizenship as well as political science.

Stress fundamental principles. There is much ignorance of our economic fundamentals to-day.

Teach social science through social service. This point of view is a necessity for society's future leaders. Service is the aim.

Preach and practice political idealism. The common man must have his rightful place in political life, and that place must be elevated.

Restore a new type of Puritanism; "he that prays best and preaches best will fight best."

Put principle before expediency. We are all too much concerned with "putting it over" and too little with service of the public.

Exalt the spiritual meaning of life. Spirituality is the leaven of truth hidden in human thought, feeling, and action. Great grasp of religion will give to the historian insight and vision. In our education, the kind of education that a student gets matters more than the quantity of it. He must have that which is quickened by spiritual life. In order to give this, a teacher must be a dynamic creative personality as well as a scholar, and college teachers must lead in spiritual, humanitarian vision. To do this will be to follow in the steps of the world's greatest teachers, for all of them have placed the emphasis on *life*.

The second speaker, Dr. George S. Sumner, took as his subject, "The importance of economics in the training and teaching of history."

Résumé: What does it profit a man to deal simply with the facts of history? The vital thing is *movement*. We must try to ascertain the motivating forces in all cases. To do this, a study of the fundamental facts of economics is necessary. Doctor Sumner would not say that the economic treatment of history is the only one to be given attention; but he does feel that of the various forces that are behind history, the economic force is the strongest. Next to this, will probably come the psychological force.

Thus, history is a means to the twofold end of vitalizing the movements of life and of giving application to present-day problems as they are seen in relation to the past.

Then, economics must not be given a separate treatment; it must be placed in its proper position with respect to the great movements of humanity. The fall of Rome had its economic problem above everything else; Turkey's condition can be explained largely from an economic viewpoint; the Spanish War of 1898 had its economic causes. We must get the benefit in our present life of the economic mistakes of the past. The actual economic condition in the past, as well as in the present, and not a theoretical condition, must be the basis of all of our present study of economics.

Mr. Victor Farrar, of the University of Washington, then spoke on "The United States policy with regard to Alaska."

Mr. Farrar gave in outline an account of his study with reference to the Alaskan question. In brief, he said that the treaty with Russia of 1824 did not define the boundary of Alaska and ended in our denial of Russia's title to Alaska. In 1838 we had not admitted Russia's title more than to say that she had a sphere of influence. Unless Russia acquired the title before 1840, she did not have it in 1867, for we know that she did not acquire it after 1840. The British negotiations suggest that such title was never obtained. But at any rate we cleared the title when our Government purchased the Alaskan Territory.

The meeting than adjourned.

The annual dinner was attended by 28 members. All present were inspired by the presidential address of Professor Young, who impressed us with his eloquent and forceful remarks. Speaking as he did out of the fullness of his experience and study and not from notes,

the president suffers at the hands of an untrained reporter.   The su[l]
ject, "Religious influences in the history of the West," was chose[l]
because the speaker had come to believe that there was somethir[l]
fundamentally deep in the spirit of the pioneer.   The religious inst[i]
tutions of the West express one phase of this depth of feeling.   A[r]
and music are later expressions of this same idealism.   Its emphas[is]
upon education has been constant from the beginning.   A spirit [s]
many-sided in expression can not be neglected by the historian wh[o]
wishes to interpret fully the age of the pioneer.

The teachers' session, held on Saturday, November 27, 1920, 9.3[0]
a. m. at the University of Southern California considered the gener[al]
topic: "The social sciences and education for citizenship in th[e]
schools."   Mr. W. F. Bliss, State Normal School, San Diego, presi[d]
ing, said:

To sum up in a phrase the central idea of thought so far, I should say the busine[ss]
of the historian is to seek ultimately for the idealism of the people he is writing abou[t]
and describing, as expressed in economic activities and in other activities and inst[i]
tutions; and it is the business of the teacher to bring the pupils into contact wit[h]
these ideals and to inspire them to live up to them in their life activities.   It is i[n]
keeping with that thought that the program for to-day has been arranged.

Proposed programs.—Prof. E. Dawson, Hunter College, New Yor[k]
City:

As a university and college teacher, I am convinced that we have a tendency i[n]
America, and even in the West, to be academic.   We have a tendency not to mak[e]
use of our scientific knowledge for practical purposes.   I am a political scientis[t]
Mr. Richard S. Childs says: "There is such a thing as political science, but no re[d]
red-blooded American will confess it."   When speaking to some one of my friend[s]
here this morning, I said something about teaching elementary political science i[n]
the high schools.   He said, "Elementary?"   Some think there is nothing in polit[i]
cal science teachable in secondary schools.   If that is true, I am in favor of elim[i]
nating it from the university.   Political science is the organization of democrati[c]
government.

The purpose of teaching social studies is to introduce the graduates of our hig[h]
schools to the problems which confront our community, in order that we may hav[e]
leadership in the solution of these problems on the basis of scientific knowledge[.]
The twelfth year course in problems of democracy is thought of by the commissio[n]
as a course in the introduction of the solution of the problems of democracy throug[h]
some knowledge of scientific economics on the one hand and scientific politics on th[e]
other.   As I understand it, we have not a solution as yet.

If political science is to present to us an organization based on scientific study o[f]
human psychology and human practices in past democratic efforts, then our task i[n]
teaching political science in the schools is to present them, not with a description o[f]
the constitution of the State of California or of the State of New York, two instru[-]
ments of which any civilized people ought to be ashamed, but the principle is t[o]
improve those instruments in order that our Government may no longer be wha[t]
Elihu Root called "An invisible government."   Our political science is academic[.]
A very distinguished political science teacher recently said: "Not a single construc[-]
tive book on political science has been written by a university professor in the las[t]
five years."

In the fourth year work of the high school, as is suggested by this bulletin, elemen-ary economics and elementary political science is to be given. What has that course o do with the course in American history, which immediately precedes it, and the course in European history, which lies one year below? What kind of European his-ory ought we to teach in the high school, after we have walked 10 blocks down the he streets of Los Angeles and seen the people? What do we want them to know?

The result of whatever history we teach should be to lead the student toward a hopeful evolution of the human race. I am confident that we have not reached, as President Butler said, "the top of the curve of western civilization." But unless ve teach optimistic, constructive organization, we may possibly become pessimists. Therefore, the European history is the background of world history, into which we want to fit American history as the next step; that is, the people who wrote that report thought of those three years, not as three different courses, but as one course, beginning with whatever kind of foundation or basis we must lay down to introduce he person to American history and whatever there is about American history to help one understand the problems which confront us.

Discussion opened by Mr. R. L. Ashley, Pasadena High School:

It seems to me that after all this problem is a very much larger one than we have been making it. It is a problem of education of a group of boys and girls passing through a certain physical and mental stage in their existence. There are two bases upon which we can place this problem for the analysis or study of it. Professor Moose said: "You are not teaching algebra; you are not teaching history; you are not teaching English. You are teaching John and you are teaching Sally." As a matter of fact, here we have a problem. These boys and girls come to us in their teens. In talking over the problems as to what we shall give them, what consider-tion do we give to the adolescent age, to mental and physical development, to psychical reactions?

Community civics is a study of group organization and functioning approached from the standpoint of the individual in his relation to the community or communities in which he lives. I believe the only way to organize the material in social science, which we are trying to present to the students, must be to take it up from the stand-point of civics—present-day institutions, present-day activities—and study the past from that angle. We must integrate the courses. I think not more than one year of social science ought to be required in the three years of the upper high school.

We must know more about the boys and girls we are teaching, because we don't know what to give them until we know something about them. When we know something about them we can group them. They are probably varying from 8 to 9 years, mental age, to 16 or 17. The student who is mentally 16 lives in an entirely different world from the 8-year-old. The first point which I wish to contend is this—that we shall study these students and get some kind of mental measurements. Let us find something about the mental age and classify according to mental age and different capacities.

The children have had a very direct reaction to their environment, to the studies they have had. They have been growing rather rapidly up to 10 and then rather owly to 13. Their memories are probably good and formations within the brain are developing with such rapidity that if habits are formed at that time they are ever forgotten, and if not formed, are probably never formed. The teaching of vics in the grades is almost absolutely a failure, probably because we are trying to teach the kind of civics we teach in high school. The brains of these students have ot formed yet and it is impossible for them to get new points of view. Before this me they are in direct relation with those with whom they have immediate dealings. They can not see the relationship between themselves and any other group. At this

point, when students are just beginning to develop other-selfness, getting new view
points in connection with religion, themselves, the suggestion is made that they tal
up the study of group organization and the relation of the individual to the grou
This seems to me one of the difficulties which the student can not possibly overcom
I think it will be possible only to take this up after students have developed th
new sense of relationship.

Discussion continued by Miss Anna Stewart, Los Angeles Hig School:

I feel that the salvation of democracy lies with the leaders and not with th
average.

My reaction to Bulletin No. 28 is this: A strong desire to come to the defense
history; and it seems to me that Mr. Ashley has laid the foundation for the defens
of history. I am in full accord with making the social sciences function.

The bulletin says: "History, as it is usually taught, is not adapted to the needs
pupils of the ninth grade." The conclusion is: Teach social science instead. Th
bulletin further reads: "Children live in the present and not in the past. The pa
becomes educational to them only as it is related to the present." Then they dra
the conclusion that history must be set aside or used only occasionally. "Here st
ries and pioneer stories are of use in the early grades because children react naturall
to them." Children do react to these stories. So do I; so do you. I have thre
books at home that I am just reading. They are all biographies. Curiosity is a par
of human nature and it seems to me we may depend upon children of the eighth an
ninth grades being interested in these biographies. History is a record of huma
experience, and human experience is necessarily based on our instincts and interest
How can you teach history? For example, I would present to an American histor
class some such topic as this: "The strange way in which Egyptians raised thei
food." I would then ask them to compare this with the way in which Californi
raises its food. Or I might ask them to compare present-day fighting with the fight
ing of the Assyrians. But no, this is too simple! We must rip up the course o
study! This is a course on the art of fighting or this is a course on food study.

The bulletin says "Civics should precede later history courses." Why? Does i
not carry its own interpretation? I should absolutely reverse that statement. Th
Los Angeles elementary schools are shot through with community civics. All tha
can be taught of human relationships is being taught throughout the elementar
grades. We need a good strong socializing course in the normal schools for th
preparation of our teachers to teach these subjects as they should be taught.

If we are going to presume that students will drop out at the end of the ninth o
tenth year, what shall we offer them after civics? I would suggest a reading course
teaching them how to read magazines and books and how to use a library.

Knocking chronology seems to be the pastime of social science writers. The bul
letin says to teach crusades chronologically if you want to, but when it comes t
institutions it is necessary to describe them. Why do we care about descriptions o
the church as an institution? Only because it played an important part in a grea
historical drama. The same might be said about feudalism. Feudalism is a part o
the great movement of the Middle Ages, and its rise, supremacy, and decline are o
interest to us.

Chronology functions horizontally as well as vertically. Chronology function
horizontally when we are studying parallel contemporary movements. For example, in studying slavery, can I take just slavery? No; I have to say slavery and
the need for a great labor supply. Chronology functions vertically when we take
things in sequence order. Grover Cleveland is quoted: "I do not understand any

ry unless I know how it came to be; I do not understand any problem unless I
v how it came to be." That is chronology.

am going to speak in defense of ancient history. It offers us an easier approach
gogically and presents fewer details. The factors and viewpoints stand out and
these that give us our ladder to the social sciences. We have a spiritual kin-
with Judea, Greece, and Rome. Ancient history challenges attention. Things
lifferent and arouse our curiosity. What was the cause of the recent war? I
k you will find it in the heart of the ancient world as much as anywhere else.
merman, in Nationality and Government, writes: "It is not the principle of
nality that would bring peace and good government to Europe, but the prin-
of toleration."

hy should chronology be put in opposition to sociology? I believe they are
ese twins, myself. A social worker recently said: "First we locate the
ly—ancestry, time, place, circumstances, etc." Historically speaking, it is
nology that does that for us. "Until we place the family, we can do nothing
hem," continued the social worker. I conclude, then, that as to the chronolog-
plan there are no gaps that are more serious than any other plan. The social
is easier pedagogically. It offers all that any other plan offers and something
. That something more is the very essence of history itself.

rning to the California situation, and recognizing that it may be unlike that of
r places, how shall we organize the high school? I think four years can be used
ry great advantage. There should be a citizenship course every term. I am
ure the social science department should always get it. The English depart-
t, I believe, should sometimes have it. In our high school, in B-9, they have
iotic ballads and debates. In the A-10 there are courses on vocational guidance.
ady the English department is doing very definite work. I should like to see
ore definite.

lletin No. 28 does not wholly apply to California. Ninth-year civics is undesir-
because it eliminates twelfth-year civics. It is practical and definite, not
ely socializing. We need leadership, but we can't get it from the man with the
er pail or from the newsboy. We can get it from the high-school students. I
t think we spend much time on the dry outlines of the constitution. It is always
nforming principle that we are concerned with. In handling our material we
ld have our approach vary; otherwise, the thing becomes monotonous. In the
r year it might be approached in this manner: First, state the problem;
adly, survey it historically. In organizing a course of study I have always been
ed by the one keynote, "integration." In the selection of material it has been
nterpretation of experience. What do I mean by "integration"? I mean this:
n't have a current events class, but every single social science class uses current
ts in one way or another—events related in some way to the subject under
ideration.

III. PROCEEDINGS OF THE SIXTEENTH ANNUAL CONFERENCE OF HISTORICAL SOCIETIES

Washington,.December 28, 1920

Reported by

JOHN C. PARISH

Secretary

Reported by JOHN C. PARISH, *Secretary*

‏he sixteenth annual session of the conference of historical societies
t at Washington, D. C., in joint session with the National Associ-
‏n of War History Organizations, on Tuesday morning, December
1920, with Mr. James Sullivan, State historian of New York, in
chair. Three papers were presented to the conference. Mr. Karl
gewald, of the Maryland War Records Commission, read a care-
survey of "Progress in the collection of war history records by
te war history organizations." Mr. Albert E. McKinley, of the
‏versity of Pennsylvania, followed with a paper on "Suggestions
‏ plans for State and local publications on war history." The
‏d paper was presented by Mr. Joseph Schafer, of the State His-
cal Society of Wisconsin, on the subject of "Coordination of
‏orical societies within the States." The discussion of this paper
‏ led by Mr. Worthington C. Ford, of the Massachusetts Historical
‏iety, and was participated in by various delegates to the confer-
‏e. The text of these papers and an account of the discussion
‏ch followed are given in the later pages of these proceedings.
‏he meeting was followed by a business session presided over by
‏ chairman of the conference, Mr. George S. Godard, State librarian
‏Connecticut. Mr. John .C. Parish, secretary of the conference,
‏rted informally on activities for the year. Announcement of the
‏ting was sent out in November to all the societies, together with
‏stionnaires as to conditions and activities and a reminder of
‏abership dues, upon which the conference was largely dependent
‏its existence. At the time of the meeting about 90 replies from
questionnaires had been received and dues had come in sufficiently
over the expenses of the year and leave $73.24 in the treasury.
‏secretary, in his report to the council of the American Historical
‏ociation, had asked for a renewal of the appropriation of $25 from
‏ body, which was granted.
‏he secretary stated that it was the intention to publish the pro-
‏ings of the conference in separate form during the year without
‏ing for the reprint from the annual report of the American His-
‏al Association. The proceedings for the year 1917 had been dis-

. 131

tributed to the societies and included reports on over 400 societies, the largest number yet listed.

It was recommended by the secretary that the conference proceed definitely to the carrying forward of two movements which have long been agitated and to that end he proposed that two active committees be appointed, one to take steps for the publication of a handbook of historical societies, the other to take action with reference to a continuation of Griffin's Bibliography of American Historical Societies.

The following motions were then carried by the conference:

Moved, that a committee of three be appointed by the chairman of this conference to lay plans and provide media for the compilation and publication of a handbook of American historical societies.

Moved, that a committee of three be appointed by the chairman of this conference to lay plans and provide media for the compilation and publication of a continuation of the 1905 volume of Griffin's Bibliography of American Historical Societies through the year 1920.

The chairman later appointed the following members of these committees:

The committee on the handbook.—Mr. George N. Fuller, of the Michigan Historical Commission; Mr. Solon J. Buck, of the Minnesota Historical Society; Mr. John C. Parish, of the State Historical Society of Iowa.

The committee on the Griffin bibliography.—Mr. Joseph Schafer, of the State Historical Society of Wisconsin; Mr. Appleton P. C. Griffin, of the Library of Congress; Mr. Julius H. Tuttle, of the Massachusetts Historical Society.

Mr. Dunbar Rowland, chairman of the committee on cooperation of historical societies and departments presented the following report which was adopted by the conference:

To the Conference of Historical Societies:

The committee on cooperation of historical departments and societies submits this its seventh and final report.

At the 1907 meeting of the association held in Madison this committee was appointed for the purpose of bringing about cooperation among historical agencies having common interests and holding membership in the American Historical Association.

The first report of the committee was submitted in 1908 at the Richmond meeting. The following recommendations made in that report were adopted by the conference:

"First. That the historical agencies of the Mississippi Basin join in a cooperative search of the French archives for historical material relating to the States embraced in that territory.

"Second. That a complete working calendar of all materials in the French archives relating to the Mississippi Basin be prepared by an agent appointed by the representatives of the conference having the matter in hand.

"Third. That the calendar when completed be published and distributed under the representatives of the conference.

"Fourth. That the necessary money for the preparation, publication, and distribution of the calendar be raised by voluntary contributions from the historical agencies represented in the conference."

The annual reports of 1909, 1910, 1911, 1912, 1913, and 1914 which appear in the annual reports of the American Historical Association for those years give a detailed account of the progress of the work, the sums contributed, and the expenditures of the fund to 1914.

In August, 1914, as the work of the committee in the French archives was nearing completion, France was invaded by the armies of Germany, and the state of war, which continued until November, 1918, compelled the postponement of the undertaking until the return of peace. For that reason no reports have been made to the conference since the meeting of 1914.

As soon as practicable after the defeat of Germany the work in the French archives was resumed. The work of editing and preparing the calendar for publication was also put in operation by the Department of Historical Research of the Carnegie Institution, and this important task is now nearing completion.

The fund for calendaring this collection of archives concerning the history of the great Mississippi Basin was subscribed through the generosity of the following historical agencies: Alabama Department of Archives and History, Chicago Historical Society, Indiana State Historical Society, State Historical Society of Iowa, Kansas State Historical Society, Louisiana Historical Society, Michigan Historical Society, Mississippi State Department of Archives and History, State Historical Society of Missouri, Texas Historical Society, Wisconsin State Historical Society, and Clarence M. Burton.

The sums subscribed by each contributor appear in the report of the committee of 1913. In round numbers $3,000 was subscribed. There is now in the hands of the treasurer of the committee $355.69, and that amount is sufficient to complete the work.

The annual reports of the committee have made frequent mention of the expert service freely extended by the Carnegie Institution of Washington. We can not express too often our obligation to Dr. J. F. Jameson and Mr. W. G. Leland of the Department of Historical Research of that institution—to Doctor Jameson for securing the cooperation of the Carnegie Institution, and to Mr. Leland, the representative of the committee in direct charge of the work in Paris.

Your committee recommends the acceptance of the proposal of the Carnegie Institution to edit, publish, and distribute the calendar. In no other way could that part of our undertaking be done quite so well. The details of the proposal will be presented to the conference at this meeting by a representative of the Department of Historical Research of the Carnegie Institution. The progress of editing, publishing, and distributing the calendar will be reported to the conference by those having in charge that part of the work.

May we again express our great obligation to the historical agencies which made possible the success of our undertaking by making liberal and unselfish subscriptions to the calendar fund.

The principle of cooperative work along such lines is most helpful and beneficial to the societies engaging in it. Such work should by all means be continued.

We hope we may be permitted to say in this final report that the successful completion under the direction of this conference of the work of calendaring the French archives, in so far as they concern the Mississippi Valley, is of very great importance to the historians of the country. To have undertaken and finished a task of such magnitude is an achievement worthy of the highest praise.

It has been a privilege for the committee to act as the representative of the conference. You have made our duties most pleasant and agreeable. We thank you for
giving us the opportunity to serve you. We report that our work is done, request the
release of the committee, and file this our final report.

Respectfully submitted.

DUNBAR ROWLAND, Chairman.
WORTHINGTON C. FORD.
EVARTS B. GREENE.
J. F. JAMESON.
B. F. SHAMBAUGH.
EUGENE C. BARKER.

DECEMBER 28, 1920.

The following is a partial list of the delegates present at the session:

Abbot, Mrs. Louis A., State historian, District of Columbia.
Ambler, Chas. H., West Virginia University.
Belote, Theodore T., United States National Museum.
Bond, Beverly W., jr., University of Cincinnati.
Boyd, Wm. K., Trinity College, New York.
Callahan, J. M., West Virginia University.
Clark, William Bell, Pennsylvania War History Commission.
Conlan, Mrs. Michael, Oklahoma Historical Society.
Connor, R. D. W., North Carolina Historical Commission.
Doane, Rev. R. B., North Carolina.
Eaton, Allen, Russell Sage Foundation.
Eckenrode, H. Z., Southern Historical Society.
Fitzpatrick, J. C., Library of Congress.
Ford, Worthington C., Massachusetts Historical Society.
Fox, Dixon Ryan, New York State Historical Association.
Fuller, George N., Michigan Historical Commission.
Godard, George S., Connecticut State Library.
Handman, M. S., University of Texas.
Heckel, A. K., Lafayette College.
Hoover, T. N., Ohio Historical Commission on War Material.
House, R. B., North Carolina Historical Commission.
Husband, W. W., Vermont Historical Society.
Jenison, Marguerite E., Illinois Historical Library.
Latané, Edith, Mary Baldwin Seminary, Staunton, Va.
Latanè, John H., Johns Hopkins University.
Latané, Lucy T., Maryland War Records Commission.
Leland, Waldo G., Carnegie Institution of Washington.
McKinley, Albert E., Pennsylvania War History Commission.
Paine, Mrs. Clara S., Mississippi Valley Historical Association.
Palsits, Victor H., New York Public Library.
Parish, John C., State Historical Society of Iowa.
Parker, H. Gilbert, Office of adjutant general of Delaware.
Pease, T. C., Illinois State Historical Library.

Robinson, Morgan P., Virginia State Library.
Rowland, Dunbar, Mississippi Historical Society.
Ryan, Daniel J., National Catholic War Council.
Schafer, Joseph, State Historical Society of Wisconsin.
Schlesinger, Arthur M., State University of Iowa.
Shoemaker, Floyd C., State Historical Society of Missouri.
Sioussat, Mrs. Albert, Maryland Society of the Colonial Dames of
    America.
Steiner, Bernard C., Enoch Pratt Free Library, Baltimore, Md.
Spaulding, Col. Oliver L., Historical Branch, General Staff, United
    States Army.
Stokes, Horace W., Frederick A. Stokes Co., publishers.
Sullivan, James, New York State Historical Association.
Vincent, John Martin, Johns Hopkins University.
Wilson, J. Scott, Virginia War History Commission.

Upon consultation with the handbook committee, which has laid
plans and begun work on the preparation of a handbook of the societies, it has seemed best not to publish in the proceedings at this time
the data secured in November and December, 1920, from approximately 90 of the societies. This material will be used by the committee in the preparation of the more comprehensive publication.

PAPERS AND DISCUSSION.

PROGRESS IN THE COLLECTION OF WAR RECORDS BY STATE WAR HISTORY ORGANIZATIONS[1]

By KARL SINGEWALD
Secretary, Maryland War Records Commission

The article, "The collection of State war records," by Franklin F.
Holbrook, secretary of the Minnesota War Records Commission,
printed in the American Historical Review, October, 1919, is a con-
spectus of the origin, organization, and activities of the various State
war history agencies, although not arranged by States, but topically.

The collection of material relating to the war was carried on, of
course, to some extent from the beginning of the war by all active
State historical commissions, historical societies, libraries, etc. The
compilation of war records in a thorough way, however, in most cases
could not be done by such institutions without a great extension of
their activities, requiring special appropriation and extra staff. Those
agencies that were able to take up the undertaking in a thorough way
from the beginning were in a most fortunate and advantageous posi-

[1] In connection with the preparation of this paper, questionnaires were sent to all of the States
addressed to the agencies known to be engaged in war history work. Replies were received from 20 States.
Some information was already in hand in regard to the work in most of the States. All comparisons
made in this paper must be qualified as being based upon the incomplete information available.

tion. States reporting systematic collection of material during the war include Alabama, Iowa, New York, and Ohio.

General realization of the importance of the compilation of war records, and financial provision for this purpose, came after the first year of our participation in the war. Action was largely through the State councils of defense, pursuant to recommendation by the Council of National Defense, at the instance of the National Board for Historical Service. In a few States the war history committees appointed were to function independently, but in the great majority of States they were to act through or in conjunction with existing State agencies—historical commissions, historical societies, State libraries, or universities.

The next stage was legislative action. In practically all of the States where the historical work was under way it was continued by legislative enactment and appropriation. At present nearly all of the States are engaged to some extent in the undertaking. A number of the States are known to be working in a large way—with a comprehensive program and somewhat adequate facilities. These States are Alabama, California, Connecticut, Illinois, Indiana, Iowa, Kentucky, Maryland, Michigan, Minnesota, Nebraska, New Jersey, New York, North Carolina, Ohio, Pennsylvania, Texas, Virginia, and Wisconsin.

In carrying on the undertaking the State agencies very generally have enlisted county and local cooperation. In most cases special historical committees have been named, but local historical societies and libraries also have been utilized. In New York the act of April 11, 1919, provided for appointment of local historians by local appointing boards. Approximately 1,500 appointments were authorized thereby, and about 50 per cent have been made. In some States, including California, Illinois, Indiana, Michigan, Minnesota, New Jersey, New York, Pennsylvania, and Wisconsin, appropriations for the local work have been made by local governments, usually small in amount—$100 to $500, but large amounts, in some cases; for instance, the city of Buffalo, $40,000. Illinois reports that in several counties sufficient funds have been available to employ some one to take charge of the work. Pennsylvania states that local provision was made very generally either by public appropriation or by turning over balances of welfare or welcome funds. In many of the States supplies have been furnished by the State office, and in a few States small allowances made for local expenses.

The general experience with the local committees is that they are very uneven in their work. In the majority of cases the results are not very satisfactory. Large results are obtained only where some qualified person is found willing to give considerable time and attention to the work. The following States report more than ordinary success in the local work: Illinois, a number of excellent county collections and several published histories; Indiana, complete reports covering the organizations as scheduled in Bulletin No. 10 from more than half of the 92 counties in the State; Michigan, county committees working pretty generally; Pennsylvania, a considerable number of counties doing excellent work. Naturally, the importance of the local war history is recognized, and the compilation of the records taken up effectively, in greater degree where the counties and cities are of considerable size and importance. The city of Buffalo, for instance, appropriated $40,000 and has published a war history.

A survey of war history work State by State would be of great interest, but is impracticable in this paper, both on account of limitation of space and of incompleteness of information in hand. It will be possible herein merely to discuss briefly the larger phases of the undertaking and to indicate roughly the progress made in some of the States.

INDIVIDUAL MILITARY RECORDS

In a few States, including New Hampshire and Rhode Island, record was kept systematically during the progress of the war of those who entered the military and naval forces. Generally, however, this was not done, and the later efforts to compile State rosters have proven very difficult.

No part of the war records work was so generally undertaken by the States as that of obtaining the records of the soldiers and sailors. In most of the States forms were prepared and campaigns were conducted with wide publicity. Cooperation of patriotic organizations was enlisted and local committees employed.

In general, the success of these efforts has not been very marked. The indifference of the men has proven a serious obstacle. A few States report unusally large results. A statement from New Hampshire, as of March, 1920, reported 85 to 90 per cent obtained. In South Dakota, by act of legislature, the assessors were instructed to make a canvass throughout the State, without extra compensation, however. In this way, about one-third of the records were obtained. This was followed up by a systematic campaign through the schools, with good results. South Dakota now reports a roster containing names beyond the number credited to the State by the departments in Washington, but no statement is in hand of the percentage of records filled out. Maryland has obtained nearly one-half of the records. For Baltimore city, the percentage is over one-half, due largely to active cooperation by the police department. In Minnesota, the administration of the bonus act was utilized as an opportunity to obtain the records. Minnesota reports over 80,000 records out of 108,000 applying for the bonus. **Pennsylvania reports over 37,000** in the State files, 45,000 in the hands of the Philadelphia committees, and thousands in the hands of other local committees. In Philadelphia canvass was made by the police department.

California has pressed the collection of these records, especially through the local committees. Results are very incomplete, but arrangements have been made for the American Legion to conduct a systematic campaign whereby it is hoped to obtain most of the records. Kentucky plans binding the service record sheets for each county into a volume, to be placed in the county clerk's office when completed and to be protected by being recorded as permanent county records.

Special attention, naturally, has been given to the compilation of rosters and records of those who died in the service, and of those who received decorations and citations. Most of the States have this part of the work pretty well up.

In most of the States effort has been made to obtain—along with the records—photographs and such material as diaries, letters, and narratives. Results obtained in this way have not been conspicuously large. Illinois, however, reports a large collection of soldiers' letters, through special effort and cooperation of organizations such as the Service Star Legion. New York has collected thousands of letters through a clipping service. Pennsylvania reports 8,000 photographs, thousands of letters, and a few diaries.

The entire aspect of this matter of individual military records was changed greatly when it became assured that the departments in Washington would furnish to the several States abstracts of the service records. The Adjutant General of the Army was given an appropriation for this purpose by the act of July 11, 1919. Thus far the records of casualties have been sent to the States. A similar appropriation was made to the Bureau of Navigation, Navy Department, by the act of June 4, 1920. It is expected that the work will be completed by the end of the fiscal year. The Marine Corps, also, is preparing records for the States.

These official records are being sent to the adjutants general of the States. A number of the States plan publication of military rosters. Such publication generally is to be by the adjutant general or in conjunction with his office. In view of these official records, some of the State war history agencies have concluded to leave the matter of the individual military records entirely with the adjutants general. It may be remarked, however, that the records furnished from Washington are brief abstracts of the service records, with very little of the further biographical information called for by the forms used by the State agencies.

The basis followed by the War and Navy Departments in crediting men to the several States is the home addresses given at the time of entering the service. The records furnished to a State, therefore, will not include former residents who were living elsewhere at the time of entering the service, nor persons living in the State at the time of entering the service, but who gave their addresses in the State of their former residence and family connections. Moreover, of course these records will not include those who served in the military forces of the Allies. Pennsylvania, it may be mentioned, reports having obtained a list of 3,583 men from the State who entered the British service.

In addition to the problems suggested in the last paragraph, there are other questions of inclusion arising in compiling the military roster to include those who served on the Mexican border in 1916. A little nearer is the case of service in the National Guard on Federal duty after April 6, 1917, but prior to the incorporation of the National Guard into the United States Army, August 5, 1917. The United States Public Health Service, in terms of the act of Congress, was made a part of "the military forces of the United States." A part of the personnel of the Lighthouse Service, by virtue of act of Congress, was transferred to the jurisdiction of the Navy Department, but is not counted as part of the Navy. Even the United States Coast Guard records are not in the possession of the Navy Department, although the entire personnel was enrolled in the Naval Reserve Force.

Altogether, unless the State roster is based simply upon service in the United States Army, Navy, or Marine Corps according to the official records furnished from Washington, the task of compilation will be very difficult and the results at best not entirely complete. The only way to obtain the names not included in the records sent from Washington is by building up a State roster systematically from local sources.

MILITARY UNITS AND ESTABLISHMENTS

Much attention is being given to the collection of material relating to military units composed largely of men from the respective States, and to camps and other military establishments located in the State during the war.

There are, of course, two sources of such material—(1) local sources; (2) the records in Washington. In respect to military units, the records obtainable from what may be termed local sources include:

Histories. (a) Manuscript histories of nearly all units were prepared under official direction before demobilization. These are usually short and sketchy. (b) Printed histories of many units have been published, in many cases under the auspices of veterans' organizations of the respective units.

Diaries, narratives, etc., by members of the units.

Copies of official papers—orders, reports, maps, etc.—retained by members of the units.

Newspapers or news bulletins issued by the units.

Photographs and other exhibits.

A number of States have been very active in collecting such material from the returned service men. It may be mentioned that Pennsylvania has obtained copies of a large part of the orders and messages of the Seventy-ninth Division.

The records in Washington are, of course, of prime importance. Every unit, upon demobilization, was required to pack up all of its records and ship them to The Adjutant General in Washington. Here should be complete sets of official papers and documents of the units, whereas records collected from local sources are generally fragmentary. Thus far, very little use has been made of the records in Washington by the State agencies. The photographs taken by the Signal Corps of the Army are the most important general source of photographs.

In the case of camps and military establishments, the classes of material and the sources are similar to those of military units. A number of States report considerable collections of historical reports, camp newspapers, photographs, etc. Here, again, there has been little use as yet of the great store of records in Washington.

INDIVIDUAL CIVILIAN RECORDS

A number of States, in the compilation of the individual military records, have included records of those who served with the military or naval forces as workers under the welfare organizations—Red Cross, Y. M. C. A., etc.

Maryland has undertaken on a more comprehensive basis the compilation of individual civilian records. The purpose has been to include the names of all Marylanders who rendered service of more than ordinary importance in relation to the war in a civilian capacity, whether in Government position, in industry, profession, relief activities, etc. The index includes the officers and leading workers of the principal war agencies in the State and in the several counties. Some idea of the degree of inclusion may be given by the statement that the index contains about 2,500 names for the entire State, as compared with about 62,000 in the military service. The persons whose names are in this index are requested to fill out a form of record and to furnish reports of their work.

California, also, has given special attention to obtaining full accounts of services of individual Californians in relation to the war in a civilian capacity. Some of the local committees have made use of questionnaires for this purpose. Mention should be made, also, of

Virginia's plan of selecting a roll of 100 Virginians who rendered the most distinguished war service. The records of the 100 will be published in the war history.

NONMILITARY WAR AGENCIES AND ACTIVITIES

Apart from the distinctly military activities, there were a number of agencies of prime importance conspicuously known as war agencies and activities, such as the Council of National Defense, War Industries Board, Shipping Board, Railroad Administration, War Loan Organization, Food Administration, Fuel Administration, American Red Cross, and the seven big welfare agencies operating under the supervision of the Commission on Training Camp Activities. These, however, are only the most conspicuous. The number of agencies, emergency and permanent, governmental and private, national and local, performing services of great importance in relation to the war is very large. Then, if we look beyond the more important agencies and activities, it is a fact that practically every organization and individual in the country did something in the general war effort.

In the endeavor to compile the war records, therefore, the problem is ever present of how far to go. In the widest scope, anything and everything pertaining to the life and activities of the people during the war period is part of the war record. The question of what to include arises both in respect to what organizations and activities to cover, and also as to what classes of records to gather.

In respect to organizations included, Pennsylvania has doubtless covered the field more extensively than any other State. About 105,000 pieces of mail have been sent out to about 65 groups, the organizations covered including not only the important war agencies, but also churches, schools, libraries, clubs and societies, banks, insurance companies, industrial and commercial establishments. Some 4,300 reports are in hand, including 1,081 reports from banking institutions and 961 from industrial establishments. Indiana, also, has requested reports from churches, fraternal orders, clubs, banks and manufacturing establishments, with "fairly satisfactory" results. In most of the States, the matter of obtaining reports from individual local organizations, such as churches, schools, clubs, banks, etc., has been left to the local committees.

In respect to material to be gathered, there is the broad general consideration that the State war history agencies are interested particularly in material of special State concern. In the case, however, of activities within the State that are part of the operations of organizations of a national scope, the States are interested in material relating to the national organization, as well as in material especially concerning the particular State.

Most of the State war history agencies have sets of formal publications of United States Government departments and services bearing on the war, whether collected specially or as part of the regular acquisitions of the institutions with which they are connected. The same is largely true of formal publications of the principal nongovernmental agencies of national scope performing service in relation to the war. When it comes to lesser material, such as pamphlets, periodicals, bulletins, circulars, posters, etc., and to the publications of the hundreds of less important agencies, the State collections are necessarily fragmentary. Alabama engaged in collection from the beginning of the war, and reports a very complete set of all material issued by the principal war agencies. Iowa and Pennsylvania also have important collections of material. Texas reports over 1,500 pamphlets relating to the war. The number of such publications issued altogether would run into the hundreds of thousands,

The problems in respect to gathering material issued by agencies of national scope may be understood from a few illustrations. Any collecting agency would eagerly receive such important acquisitions as a set of publications of the Committee on Public Information, or the war bulletins of the American Red Cross, or of the Y. M. C. A. A complete set, however, of books, pamphlets, periodicals, bulletins, circulars, etc., issued by Red Cross during the war would fill several shelves. Then there is a vast quantity of material not relating especially to the war, but of increased interest during the war. For instance, the bulletins of information and of instruction issued by the Department of Agriculture are regular publications, but during the war were of special use in stimulating food production. Publications, also, of the hundreds of religious, professional, trade, and other organizations of national scope are of some interest from the standpoint of war history. There is certainly no clear line of limitation in regard to such material, and, as already remarked, the collection of such material by the State war history agencies is rather desultory.

In regard to agencies and activities within the State, there is, of course, greater reason for systematic effort to make a complete collection of material. The distinctive effort in this field is to obtain historical reports, both of state-wide activities and of local activities. In a large percentage of cases it is necessary to have these reports specially prepared for the historical records. The reports by the States, generally, indicate a very fair measure of success along this line. Pennsylvania and Illinois have done especially well in obtaining reports from members of the draft boards.

A number of the States are making special efforts to secure the deposit of files and records of war agencies in the war records collections. Some of the most important records were required to be shipped to Washington—notably, of the draft boards, Food Administration, and Fuel Administration. Minnesota reports, however, having obtained the files relating to war activities of the Y. M. C. A., Y. W. C. A., A. L. A., J. W. B., W. C. C. S., U. W. W. C., and some of the branch offices of the United States Employment Service in the State. Texas, also, reports a very fair measure of success in obtaining the files of war work organizations such as the Liberty loan, war savings, Red Cross, Y. M. C. A., Y. W. C. A., K. of C., W. C. C. S., and Salvation Army. Generally speaking, the most important files of war activities within the States are those of the State councils of defense or committees of safety. These files, of course, are in official possession of the States, and in a number of cases have come into the custody of the war history agencies The files of the women's section, Maryland Council of Defense, are an extremely valuable mass of material. The women's section was an exceptionally efficient organization, coordinating all women's activities in relation to the war, and the files containing regular, systematic reports of all departments and of the county chairmen.

WAR INDUSTRIES

The subject of war industries does not appear to have been taken up generally with any degree of thoroughness. In a number of States this is being left largely to the local committees.

Pennsylvania, where the industrial contribution was probably the most marked, has gone further than any other State in the compilation of the records. By considerable effort and expense, a list was compiled in Washington of Pennsylvania firms having Government war contracts. There were 2,732 Pennsylvania firms having direct war contracts. Questionnaires were mailed to the firms on this list. In the case of the most important industrial establishments, this was followed up by personal visit and research. Reports are in hand from 961 establishments. Excellent reports have been received from nearly all of the important establishments.

Illinois also reports having compiled a list of firms having war contracts, by assistance of the bureaus in Washington and of the Illinois Manufacturers Association. A questionnaire was sent out and a large percentage of returns received. Maryland, similarly, has compiled a list of firms, and is just sending out questionnaires.

PHOTOGRAPHS, POSTERS, AND OTHER EXHIBITS

A few words may be devoted especially to the subject of photographs, posters, and other exhibits. Many of the States report large collections of photographs—of individuals, of military units, camps, or other military activities, and of civilian activities in relation to the war. Texas has acquired 15,000.

Posters are of two classes—those used generally throughout the country, and those of local origin. Those of the first class are, of course, the more conspicuous, but those of the second class are of greater significance for the State collections. Illinois reports a collection of about 800 posters; Indiana, "a complete collection for all of the State drives"; New York, a collection of all important posters; Pennsylvania, 866 posters; Texas reports a collection of about 2,000 posters, broadsides, etc.—1,200 American, the rest foreign. The method of exchange has been utilized to good advantage.

Only a few of the State war history agencies appear to have given much attention to the collection of other exhibits. Minnesota states that, in cooperation with the museum department of the historical society, a noteworthy collection has been gathered of war relics and mementos, including military equipment and insignia, service flags, etc. Ohio, also, reports a large collection of emblematical material.

NEWSPAPERS

Fortunately, libraries very generally preserve newspaper files. In most States, therefore, files of newspapers with state-wide circulation and of some of the local newspapers are to be found in State libraries, and files of most local newspapers in local libraries. New York, for instance, reports that the State library maintains files of the principal newspaper of each county and of the leading city newspapers.

Most of the State agencies have made special efforts to obtain files for the war period of as many as possible of the newspapers published in the State. Such files, however, are difficult to obtain. Very few newspapers keep back copies other than a single file of their own, and a great many small local newspapers lack even a single complete file. California reports that several county committees have submitted complete files of local newspapers. The State war history department has over 50,000 clippings of war interest. Illinois has obtained a number of complete or partial files for 1917–18 besides the files regularly kept by the library. Indiana reports special effort, with fairly satisfactory results, to secure a complete file of at least one newspaper of each county for 1917–18. Items of war interest are clipped and mounted.

In addition to general newspapers, some attention has been given to the collection of special newspapers and periodicals. Ohio, especially, reports a very large collection of religious periodicals, trade, labor, and agricultural papers, and racial newspapers.

Generally speaking, excellent progress has been made in the work of the State war history agencies, but a great deal remains to be done in the collection of records, apart from the matter of publication. In California, the war history department is to be discontinued as a separate department of the State historical survey commission in January, 1921. In some States, on the other hand, the increased facilities necessary for effective work have but recently been provided. In most of the States the work is proceeding actively, with prospect of continuance for some time to come.

There are it may be mentioned, a number of important special collections of material that are of direct interest to the States. These include the war records compiled by the National Catholic War Council, by the American Jewish Committee, and by the denominations of the Protestant Church. ˋA description of such collections, however, is not within the scope of this paper.

PROGRESS IN THE COLLECTION OF WAR HISTORY RECORDS BY STATE WAR HISTORY ORGANIZATIONS

By ALBERT E. McKINLEY

Secretary of the Pennsylvania War History Commission

The topic of to-day embraces plans and suggestions for war histories by official State bodies. It excludes on one side the publication plans of the War and Navy Departments and other branches of the National Government, and on the other the more or less elaborate plans for more or less accurate histories by private publishing concerns.

Consideration of plans for publication came almost as early as the realization of the necessity for collecting data relating to the war history of our several States. In some cases publication was held consciously in view from the start. Thus the State Historical Society of Iowa stated in its publication "Iowa and War" (No. 19, January, 1919, p. 3), "Collection without compilation is fruitless, and compilation without publication is useless. The collection of the materials of war history should accompany the writing of that history, and the writing of the history should accompany the collection of the materials."

With this concept of the interrelation of collection, compilation, and publication, the Iowa society proceeded to outline a tentative plan for a history of Iowa's part in the World War, and also prepared a similar outline for a local or county history. At least four other States—Minnesota, Virginia, California, and Pennsylvania—have issued somewhat similar outlines, either for local or State histories, or both, which in some cases were based upon the Iowa outline.

It early became apparent that there were really three classes of historical material in which a State might be interested: (1) Service records of individuals, including casualties and citations in the military and naval service; (2) histories, narrative and documentary, of units in the Army, Navy, and Marine Corps, composed largely of

97244°—25——10

citizens of the interested State; (3) the internal history of the State in war time, including the operations of the National Government in the State, the activities of the State government, and the work of civilian individuals and organizations. Plans for publication in the several States from which reports have been received differ greatly in the attitude toward these three classes and in the agencies to which were intrusted the work of preparation for publication.

Individual service records.—At the outset of their work many of the war history bodies in the several States, basing their decision upon the experience of the Civil War, prepared service record blanks to be filled in by soldiers' families or, after return from the field, by the soldiers themselves. Such records might admittedly be inaccurate or incomplete, but they might contain material not included in The Adjutant General's Office, and until the records of the latter office were available they would be valuable for local historical purposes.

The action of Congress in the summer of 1919 in providing funds for sending transcripts of service records to the States and in directing that these records be sent to the adjutant general in each State has had several influences. In the first place, it promises to place at the disposal of the States the service records of their citizens much more quickly and at less expense to the States than was anticipated. It has tended to discourage the distribution, filling out, and collection of the local record blanks within the States, and it has placed in the hands of the adjutant general of each State the personal records of its citizens.

It is but natural, therefore, from the character of the usual duties of a State adjutant general and the records now being received from Washington, that plans for publication of individual war records should center largely in the offices of the adjutants general. The following statement from Delaware illustrates this policy:

The Governor of Delaware has requested the adjutant general of this State to collect all available data in regard to the part played by the service men of this State in the World War, which includes biographies and photographs of the men who made the supreme sacrifice and the personal, family, and military records of the remainder of the men, and at the coming session of the general assembly next month to introduce such a bill to put in book form the above information, with, of course, separate chapters for those who died or were wounded or cited.

Indiana reports that the manuscript of a "gold star volume" is now ready for the press; and that the adjutant general will prepare for publication a State roster containing the names of all Indiana service men and the units to which they were attached. Iowa, with its roster commission, composed of the governor and the adjutant general, organized by act of assembly early in 1919, is probably better prepared than any other State to push the work of publication as soon as the records are received from Washington. The adjutant general of Illinois has in contemplation the publication of a roster, which will occupy, according to estimates, 42 volumes. Missouri has a similiar work under consideration. For the two largest States —New York and Pennsylvania—the publication of an adequate roster is a stupendous task. Our presiding officer, Doctor Sullivan, estimates that 100 volumes would be necessary for the Empire State's records, and Pennsylvania's would not fall far behind that figure.

It thus appears that publication plans for individual service records are largely in the hands of the respective adjutants general, and that the ultimate decision upon publication is dependent upon the speed at which records are received from Washington (on December 1, 1919, only 11 per cent of the Army records had been received), upon the force at the disposal of the adjutants general for compilation and comparison, and upon the appropriation of funds for publication.

Histories of combatant units in which States are largely interested.— Most interest naturally centers in those Army units into which the State militia went. The militia companies and regiments had been a matter of local pride before the World War; their records up to 1917 are preserved in the offices of the adjutants general of the several States; their members were anxious to bring back with them an adequate record of what their units accomplished. Hence local patriotism combined with what is relatively an abundance of historical data makes the preparation and publication of unit histories of the militia comparatively a simple matter. Illinois has already sent to the press a history of the Thirty-third Division, prepared by Col. Frederick L. Huidekoper, who was division adjutant. The history will comprise three volumes, of which the first will contain a narrative history of division operations, and the other two will be devoted to maps and reports. Twenty thousand copies of the first volume will be distributed free to members of the division. An appropriation of $50,000 was made for this publication. In a similar manner the States of Michigan and Wisconsin made appropriations for a history of the Thirty-second Division.

But far more difficult is the preparation of a history of the units into which the selective service men entered. The men had no previous historical or personal associations with the unit; the officers were drawn from all over the Union; and the men themselves, or the officers did not usually show the same interest in bringing back the records of the units which is so apparent in the militia divisions and regiments. While a number of regimental and divisional organizations of the selective service units have been formed, and a considerable body of publications has been privately printed, yet to the writer's knowledge there is not as yet any definite plan for official State publications relating to any of these units.

With regard to the agencies directing the publication of unit histories, it seems true that this work is not considered so purely a duty of the adjutants general as are the individual service records. And it is to be hoped that adequate historical supervision and editorship will be retained in each State over the preparation and publication of such unit histories.

The regularly established or specially created historical bodies in the several States have taken as their peculiar field the collection, compilation, and in some cases, the publication of matter relating to the internal history of the State in war time. As Mr. Singewald has pointed out, these bodies have principally bent their energies to collecting material, and few of them are ready to-day to announce plans for publication. This reluctance may be due partly to the present incomplete character of their collections, partly to the absence of available funds for editorial purposes, partly to the lack of the "leave to print" which is given to most of the regularly constituted State departments, and partly to the unwillingness of legislatures to commit the States to a regular plan of war history publications. To these reasons may be added an indifference to the history of the war which we have all found to exist in many quarters.

The State Historical Society of Iowa, with its funds for publication, its ability to secure trained investigators and writers, and its determination to collect, compile, and publish, is more favorably situated than any other State. Within the last month it has issued the first of its Iowa Chronicles of the World War, a volume upon Welfare Campaigns in Iowa, by M. L. Hansen. Four other manuscripts are ready for the printer: Welfare Work in Iowa, The Red Cross in Iowa, The United States Food Adminstration in Iowa, and The Sale of War Bonds in Iowa. The topics selected for this series will follow in a general way the subjects proposed in the Tentative Outline For a State War History; but no set order will be adhered to, and modifications may be made from time to time.

Other definite plans for publication include a manuscript already completed for the Indiana Historical Commission upon the history of the five Liberty loans in Indiana, and two volumes proposed by the war records section of the Illinois State Historical Library, dealing respectively with "Statistics relating to Illinois and the war" and "Documents relating to Illinois and the war."

More indefinite projects or simply suggestions are as follows: New York, a three-volume work, including general material under subject headings, and material arranged by counties, towns, incorporated villages and cities throughout the State outside of New York City. Minnesota, an eight-volume history, including three devoted to a roster, two to military matters, one to material resources, one to home defense and civilian morale, and one a "narrative summary of the whole story."

Maryland, three volumes—one to be a roster, one military history, and one the record of nonmilitary activities.

From these facts concerning actual plans for publication certain deductions are possible.

1. Owing to the character of the records and their deposition in the offices of the adjutants general of the several States it seems logical that the preparation and publication of individual service records should be left in the hands of these officials. This is particularly true in the larger States, where a very extensive force and great expenditure of money will be necessary before publication can be completed.

2. There may be some competition between the State adjutants general and the State historical bodies with reference to the compilation and publication of unit histories in which the State is interested. Such histories should be prepared and edited in the light of the best historical scholarship. A wealth of information is now, or soon will be, at the disposal of historical scholars for the preparation of such histories. Whether the actual work of publication is done by the adjutants general or by purely historical bodies, there ought to be cooperation in order to secure an historically accurate account. Such unit histories should, of course, be well illustrated with photographs and maps.

3. The histories of civilian activities require research skill of the highest character, including the ability to use with discrimination newspapers, current correspondence, and personal reminiscences. Such work can best be directed by regularly established historical organizations.

4. Omitting from our view individual service records, the following is presented as an outline for a State's war history in moderate compass.

Military and naval participation of the State, including the history of units in which the State is most interested; the history of the preparation and organization of the selective-service machinery; and the United States camps and other establishments within the State limits.

Economic participation in the war, including agriculture and food production, industries, transportation and communication, war finance, trade and commerce.

Civilian welfare and morale work, including financial campaigns for welfare work, the actual conduct of welfare work, the war activities of professional classes, educational organizations, religious bodies, and means for maintaining public morale through the press, patriotic organizations, and other means.

A summary in one volume containing a general review of the State's contributions to the victory of the country.

Such an analysis can readily be extended by larger States into a considerable series of volumes, while in the smaller communities it could be placed in three or four volumes.

The paper presented by Mr. Joseph Schafer, of the State Historical Society of Wisconsin, dealt with the subject of "Coordination of historical societies within the State." He told of cooperation in Wisconsin between the State Historical Society of Wisconsin and the county and other local agencies, by which the State is being mapped out and subjected to an intensive historical survey particularly along the line of settlement and land tenure, a project frequently referred to as the Wisconsin Domesday Book. This topic has been discussed in print by Mr. Schafer in the Wisconsin Magazine of History for September and December, 1920, and a third paper will be published by the Minnesota Historical Society.

Mr. Worthington C. Ford, of the Massachusetts Historical Society, opened the discussion. He said that there was little to discuss in the propositions so clearly laid down by the speakers. The plans and methods described seemed pertinent and adequate, worthy of trial and application. The conditions of historical societies in the East and the West were different, too different to be brought into a common rule. In the West the State historical society is the model, but in the East the private society, incorporated but not aided by the State, still prevails. There are also the questions of age and opportunity. The account given by Mr. Schafer of material permitting the history of almost every acre in his State from its first survey to be related made the mouth water, for there is no such material in the older communities. In Massachusetts, for example, grants were made to townships and to individuals, but in such general terms as to defy exact description or location. Then, too, the history of the eastern conmunities has become fixed in the local history of more than half a century ago, ponderous volumes, compiled on no method, by writers inexperienced in historical presentation, and intended to laud the town and its people irrespective of its relative importance among the towns of the State or section. Such volumes are distinguished rather by what they omit than what they contain; and the same dreary details, crudely thrown together and connected by little sequence or relation, have made that form of history distasteful. Later came commercialized history, compiled for personal reasons and made possible by those willing to pay for notice which they could have in no other way. Professor Turner has shown in his "Frontier in American History" how negligible for historical purposes the State boundaries are; they rather confuse, if observed, for being artificial they do not mean distinctions in race, territory, or natural conditions. So the eastern town history indicates little of the general questions of institutions, people, or economy. Genealogy is not race; a farm is not apt to be a type; and a township is not a national unit unless historically treated by a master. I except two works which can well be taken as examples of what local history can be: Three Episodes of New England History, by Charles Francis Adams, and The History of the Town of Southampton (N. Y.) by James Truslow Adams.

In Massachusetts alone there are more than 300 societies engaged in collecting or in handling historical material. Hardly a town of size is without its historical society, busily engaged in collecting what it can, and eager to prove its right to exist by a publication, more or less occasional, and naturally of widely varying merit. In the wish to introduce some method into this active ferment, the Bay State League of Historical Societies was formed and now welcomes at stated times in the year delegates from the 75 societies that have become members. Historical pilgrimages to various towns, a light spread, a paper of not too solid content, and social intercourse serve to create a spirit of solidarity, and it is hoped this spirit will be developed further so as to give the means of directing local activities and even of controlling publications. This would prevent the duplication of publication, waste of funds in printing the trivial or unimportant, and introduce better and more uniform practices in preparing material for the press. At present the high cost of printing acts as a safety valve, checking a natural tendency to print merely for the sake of printing.

The favorable drift of societies toward combination and union has been somewhat modified, if not checked, by the World War. Formerly each society gathered its books and manuscripts of local origin and had a modest museum containing subjects few in number but clothed with local interest and with pertinency to the real objects of a museum. Each town could show something different from what could be seen elsewhere. Owing to the war these little collections have been swamped by war relics and become "standardized." But a German helmet, fragment of a shell, a gun or war medal has little pertinency to local or State history. The effect has been to revivify local phases of history. Each town, institution, or company is intent upon getting what may tend to glorify its part in the war. This has always been the effect of war—to cultivate the local historical interest. What is wanted is to encourage progress toward general history. Mr. Ford doubted if this could be accomplished for some years, so strong had the local feeling become. Each State, town, and institution must get out its ".war records" before due attention will be given to general history, and to exert a supervising influence in the East will be difficult. This should not hinder attempts toward that end. A State historical society is in a better situation to accomplish good in control than where the State takes no active part in historical study or in supporting a historical activity;

but it yet remains to be proved that the incorporated society is less efficient in the main lines than a State organization, and it is less under direction, less easily influenced.

The secretary of the conference urged the importance and value of federation of historical agencies within each State and Province of the United States and Canada. Mrs. Albert Sioussat, of the National Society of Colonial Dames, and Mr. George S. Godard, of Connecticut, commented on the subject of the relation of patriotic societies to such federations. Mr. Godard mentioned the work which such societies had done in listing the old homes of the early Connecticut settlers. Mr. James Sullivan spoke on the forms which such cooperation had taken in the State of New York in regional leagues of local historical societies. He called attention to the Federation of Historical Societies of the Genesee County in the western part of New York State; the Mohawk Valley Historical Association, which is a league of all of the local historical societies in the Mohawk Valley; and the contemplated leagues such as were being planned in Long Island, the lower and upper Hudson valleys, the Champlain district, and the like.

IV. CONFERENCE ON ECONOMIC HISTORY

Washington, December 29, 1920

NOTE.—This conference was held after a luncheon at the New Ebbitt Hotel on Wednesday, December 29, 1920. It afforded several brief papers and an abstract which are sufficiently significant to be included in the printed records of the association.

THE RECOGNITION OF ECONOMIC HISTORY AS A DISTINCT SUBJECT

By CLIVE DAY

Economic history first received prominent recognition as a distinct subject in this country in 1892, when W. J. Ashley was called to Harvard and given the title of professor of economic history.

An examination of the prospectus of courses of American colleges and universities 10 years later, which was far from covering the whole field, but included most of the institutions of prominence, showed that courses in economic history were offered in 43 institutions. As a rule a single course was given combining the economic history of England and of the United States. Sometimes the economic history of those countries was treated separately, and occasionally a course was offered on some special aspect of economic history—commerce, colonization, or industry. The total number of courses given was 68.

An examination of the announcements of these same institutions in 1920 showed that 9 had dropped the course in economic history. The total number of courses given in the subject was 73. The increase in the courses given had not kept pace with the increase in courses given in other subjects.

There are indications, however, that the attention given to economic history had increased not only absolutely but relatively. Courses which do not bear the title economic history include a consideration of the subject. Notably is this true of courses given in the department of history, according to the description of these courses given in the prospectus.

Economic history, if we can trust this evidence, is being studied more extensively than ever, but it is being studied in connection with other subjects, with which it is fused. The indications that it is being absorbed by other subjects raises the question whether it does or does not deserve recognition as a distinct subject.

In elementary instruction I believe the prevailing tendency is wholesome and should be encouraged. Students should be introduced to an understanding of economic development by a study

155

of economic facts in relation to facts of another kind but of the same time and place. The divorce of economic and political history has been harmful to both.

At a certain stage in the course of instruction the need arises for specialization, and then the study of economic history by itself is profitable and should be encouraged. In advanced work, courses in this subject offer an opportunity for training in method which can not so effectively be supplied by the study of any other subject.

To the student of economics the work in economic history offers the most effective means to acquire that "historical point of view" which is so intangible as to defy definition, but which is indispensable to any sound work in social science.

To the student of history the work in economic history offers connection with a social science which insists that facts are useful only as they lead to generalizations. Some corrective is needed for the worship of the bare fact, which is apt to be inculcated in some stages of historical training. Some experience should be afforded in those processes of historical synthesis which involve general hypotheses and lead to general formulas. For purposes of this kind, the subject of economic history is peculiarly fitted.

THE FIELD FOR THE TEACHING OF ECONOMIC HISTORY IN COLLEGES AND SECONDARY SCHOOLS

By Abbott Payson Usher

Although a number of colleges have separated the teaching of the economic history of the United States from the teaching of the economic history of Europe, it is becoming common to find instruction in economic history divided into two semester courses, concerned respectively with the economic history of England or Europe and with the economic history of the United States. A course in the economic history of the United States is frequently given in institutions which offer no instruction in the economic history of Europe, and at times such a course is offered to undergraduates in colleges which provide excellent facilities for the study of European conditions by graduate students. On the whole, however, the two courses are closely associated, constituting a consecutive year's work.

Economic history makes a wide appeal to the interest of the public at the present time, and this disposition to give more attention to the subject can be utilized if its intrinsic difficulties are not forced on the students. The place of the course in the curriculum will thus depend ultimately upon the purposes and ideals of the instructor—it will become a large and important course if it is not made too severe; it will be a small course pursued by graduates and seniors of high standing if it is given with sumptuous critical scholarship and with equal emphasis upon all the phases of the subject.

Some difficulties can be eliminated by restricting the introductory course in the history of Europe to the period of the Industrial Revolution, leaving all discussion of medieval conditions to the advanced course. This policy has been very generally adopted. But from the larger point of view this is not the best solution of the problem. A course that omits all discussion of conditions prior to 1750 foregoes by necessity all possibility of its largest usefulness. The contrast between modern and medieval conditions is the most stimulating interpretative material in the field of economic history, and, if we were to presume that introductory courses should be dominated by general interpretative problems, it would be essential to treat the Middle Ages at sufficient length to bring out the chief features of difference between the social organization of that period and modern times. The public and the general student body are concerned with economic history only in so far as it bears significantly upon the judgment of the large issues of social organization raised by the radical groups. There is in economic history so little of the dramatic and heroic interest that we can not wisely compete with political and military history in those appeals. Our strongest claim lies in the field of social philosophy. We must emphasize what Professor Farnam called the laboratory facilities afforded by history to the social sciences. Economic history can throw light upon the worth of our existing social institutions, both by affording better appreciation of the existing structure and by stimulating comparison with other possible orderings of society. The appeal made to history by the socialists, too, places us under special obligations to deal critically with the large generalizations that have become current through socialistic efforts. Economic history, like all history, is not primarily a bare record of ascertained fact, but primarily a way of thinking about society. The mass of careful, critical work leads to conclusions and interpretations, and it would seem that in the end it will prove to be more important to make these results widely known than to teach the beginning class the factual detail of the recent period.

In so far as difficulties must be eliminated it is perhaps better to omit the harder features of the subject than to omit entirely a period like the Middle Ages. Many features of the economic history of the Middle Ages could not be presented with success in an introductory undergraduate course. Much in the history of commerce and agriculture must be omitted, but the general outlines of the industrial organization of that period can be presented effectively—some appreciation of these generalities is, indeed, essential to any thorough treatment of the Industrial Revolution. The predominant interest to-day in industry, rather than agriculture or commerce, makes it easier to attract the students to a study of industrial history than to economic history in general. Division of the material by topics rather than by periods would thus strengthen the introductory course and add to its importance in the college curriculum.

Within the last few years economic history has become an important subject in the curricula of business schools, more especially of the undergraduate schools. The function of the course is complex; it serves in part as general training of frankly nonvocational character, in part as grounding in facts and methods of direct vocational significance. The course is very closely related to the work in marketing, commercial geography, and business organization. It takes the place of the course in freshman history in the arts college, as there is seldom time for a purely general course in history. The students are correspondingly less developed than the average college students who elect the work in economic history. Much general training in methods of work must thus be done in connection with this course, and, like the course in freshman history, this becomes inevitably one of the purposes of the course.

The work of the first term in the history of England and Europe differs little from work that might be offered in any arts college, but we are planning at Boston to coordinate the work on the history of the United States with the work in marketing and some of the other special courses offered by the department. Much of the general description of the various industries can be presented in the course on economic history, leaving more time for the discussion of merchandizing problems in the course on marketing. The work in railroads and tariff problems can likewise be made more advanced by careful presentation of the historical background of the current issues. In both courses the students are given training in the handling of simple statistical material by graphic methods, using both arithmetic and the logarithmic scales.

In view of the rapid increase in the registration of the business schools, these required courses in economic or commercial history are becoming numerically more important than the somewhat more advanced courses in the arts colleges. They are thus the outstanding feature of the recent expansion of the field for the teaching of economic history, and it is likely that they may serve to emphasize the opportunity that lies before such elementary courses. The development of this work in the colleges has been influenced by the belief that it must needs be severe; it would seem that severity is not inevitable and unescapable.

The secondary and especially the vocational schools present a possible field, but the policy of extending instruction in economic history to schools of this grade can hardly be deemed well established in fact or theory. The benefits derived from the teaching of economic theory in the secondary schools are dubious, and economic history ought to be classed with theory in connection with the problem of pedagogy. Some teachers have, no doubt, achieved success with economic history in the secondary schools. But is this subject really as important to these students as the subjects which it must displace wholly or in part? More instruction in language might be given, more instruction in geography, science, or mathematics. It is a delicate question, and it is perhaps less important now to reach a conclusion than to stimulate thorough discussion. I doubt the possibility of teaching the distinctive generalizations of economic history to the pupils of the secondary schools. It is not necessary to teach annals by memory processes as in the case of our national history, and for this reason there is no proper parallel between the claims of political and economic history for a place in the school curriculum. It may be that the secondary school should equip its students with a mature philosophy of life, as Mr. Wells suggests in his New Macchiavelli, but when we consider the modest attainments of our college graduates there is little to encourage us in any struggle toward such an ideal.

FIELDS OF RESEARCH IN ECONOMIC HISTORY: LABOR

By Frank T. Carlton.

Omitting from the classification such revolutionary organizations as the Industrial Workers of the World and the Workers' International Industrial Union, American labor organizations may be classed under two groups: the old-line trade or craft union and the new unionism of the industrial type. To the right of the first group are such organizations as the Brotherhood of Locomotive Engineers and the International Typographical Union; to the left of the latter group is the Amalgamated Clothing Workers. Certain amalgamated organizations—of which the remodeled Brewery Workers, now called the Brewery, Flour, Cereal and Soft Drink Workers, is an example— lie in the borderland between the two groups.

In the judgment of the writer, the most important piece of research in labor history now awaiting exploitation is that of tracing carefully the development of the philosophy, strategy, and structure of typical representatives of the two classes of labor organizations; such, for example, as the Amalgamated Clothing Workers, the United Mine Workers, the Brotherhood of Locomotive Engineers, the International Molders' Union, and the Brotherhood of Carpenters and Joiners. What were the conditions and incident forces which evolved the policies and programs for which the conservative trade-unions stand? Why have these organizations stood firmly for the policy of business unionism, of immediate gains, and of little emphasis upon farsightedness?

Again, what are the other types of influences which have produced such powerful industrial unions as the United Mine Workers and the Amalgamated Clothing Workers? Do differences in ideals and methods of strong labor organizations develop out of differences in the industrial environment, in the use of machinery, in the relative numbers of recent immigrants in the union, in the type of workers who go into the various industries, or in the character of leadership? What are the fundamental causes of the great variety in union structure and functions? To what extent are the ideals and the strategy of certain well-known conservative unions out of step with the industrial situation of to-day? How far do they still bear the stamp of the frontier and of small-scale industry?

Studies of specific labor organizations such as are herein approved should be little concerned with dates, strikes, or spectacular details; but these investigations should disclose the play of forces industrial, psychological, and social, which have molded the unions into their present forms and have determined their programs. These studies may also give aid in answering such pertinent questions as: To what extent have industrial conditions in the last few decades cut across or inhibited the fundamental instincts of men? What modifications are feasible which will tend to make industry square with the instinctive inherited mechanism of the human organism? A union of psychology, sociology, and the newer type of historical research which is interested in social forces rather than in chronology is required to obtain the results which are being pointed out as desirable.

And what are the qualifications of the men who are fitted to undertake this work? The investigators, in addition to being students of history and economics, should have a reasonable amount of training in sociology and psychology. They ought not to be out of sympathy with organized labor; but a definite bias in favor of the union element will tend to color their conclusions and impair the usefulness of their results. Obviously, the investigator in this bitterly contested field must be able to take a detached position.

Careful studies, such as these briefly outlined, of a score or more of labor organizations will enable the students of labor problems to speak authoritatively in regard to the desirability of modifications in the practices of employers and employers' associations. Studies of specific organizations will also disclose or aid in disclosing to what extent the unreasonable and antisocial practices of labor unions, such as restriction of output and the closed shop with the closed union, are the products of practices of employers and employers' associations. If, as the writer suspects, these policies are in no small degree the inevitable reaction from the policies of antiunion employers, even the most stiff-necked employer may be forced by educated public opinion to change his tactics.

The highest mission of historical research is to render efficient assist-
cc in clearing away the mists which surround the opening of a new
a in human progress. Historical studies of labor organizations will
t disclose the future status of industrial relations; but studies of
e .sort outlined should aid in reducing to a minimum the friction
ident to industrial changes, and practically remove the dangerous
ssibility of revolutionary modifications. May we soon have skilled
rkers in this fertile and neglected field of economic history.

Only one other suggestion will be offered. The well-known History
Labor in the United States, written by Professor Commons and
sociates, ends with the year 1896. The history of the quarter of a
ntury, 1896-1921, should now be written in an adequate manner.
iis 25-year period marks an important epoch in the history of Ameri-
n labor organizations. The significant features of the period have
en outlined by the writer in his Organized Labor in American
story.

AGRICULTURE AS A FIELD FOR HISTORICAL RESEARCH[1]

By Louis B. Schmidt

The agricultural history of the United States has not received its
oportionate share of emphasis in the study of American economic
velopment. The time has come when more attention must be
en to this subject if we are to have a well-rounded out history of
is country. In this respect English and European historians, who
ve given due emphasis to the place of agriculture in the history of
ose countries, may well be emulated.

The reasons for giving special attention to agriculture as a field for
torical research in the United States may be stated as follows:
Agriculture has always been the fundamental basis of our pros-
rity. (2) The agricultural history of the United States is indis-
nsable to a correct understanding of much of our political and
lomatic history. (3) It furnishes the background for the study of
icultural economics. (4) It affords an opportunity for the study
the lives and services of eminent men who have had a great
luence on our agricultural development. (5) It is essential to the
velopment of a sound and farsighted rural economy.

Among the subjects which this field offers for investigation may be
ntioned the history of the public land question; of specific leading
icultural industries; of agriculture in States and larger regions like

bstract based on a paper entitled "The economic history of American agriculture as a field for study
at the annual meeting of the American Historical Association held in Washington, D. C., in December,
   Doctor Schmidt's paper war printed in the Mississippi Valley Historical Review, June, 1916, III,
,

the Middle West; of agricultural commerce and markets; of agricultural labor; of farm machinery; of farmers' organizations; of the relation of the farmer to politics and legislation. It should be emphasized, finally, that the economic history of American agriculture does not constitute a distinct phase of historical research separate from the other fields for historical research which are being considered at this meeting. On the contrary, it is very closely interrelated with these various fields. It constitutes rather, to be specific, a new point of view in American economic development. On this account it should enlist the sympathy of both the historian and the economist.

V. THE ORIGIN OF THE RUSSIAN STATE ON THE DNIEPER

THE ORIGIN OF THE RUSSIAN STATE ON THE DNIEPER

By Mikhail Rostovtsev

In the ninth century when the Russian annals first begin to give us a systematic record of the Russian people and their princes, Russia appears to us as a well-shaped body, as an organized state, with its own peculiar political, social, and economic structure, and endowed with a high and flourishing civilization. Russia of the ninth century consisted of many important commercial cities, situated partly on the Dnieper and its tributaries, partly in the far north on Lake Ilmen, and partly in the east on the upper Volga. Each of these cities possessed a large territory populated by different Slavonic tribes and had its own self-government, with a popular assembly, a council of the eldest and elected magistrates. For the purpose of defending its flourishing trade the population of each town invited a special body of trained and well-armed warriors, commanded by a prince. To this prince each city intrusted also the task of collecting tribute from the population, and of fulfilling some administrative and judicial duties. These princes with their retinues generally were German, especially Normans, who were called in Russia Varanguians. One of these princes of the ninth century succeeded in uniting under the rule of one dynasty all the Russian cities, and in forming out of them one state, although not a very firmly established one with a capital on the Dnieper—Kiev.

Nothing similar to this kind of federation of large, commercial, self-governing cities, ruled by an invited—i. e., hired—dynasty, existed at that time in western Europe, with her well-known feudal structure. In the history of the formation of the Russian state, all is peculiar and original—the exclusively commercial character of the cities, the great sway of the Russian commerce which reached Constantinople in the south, central Asia, China, and India in the east, and the Baltic and White Sea in the north, the sharp difference between the self-government of the cities and the primitive tribal organization of the country, the contrast between the prehistoric manner of life of the country population and the high standard of civilized life in the cities, and—last but not least—the unparalleled combination of foreign military power and well-organized self-rule in the frame of the same city-state.

All these peculiarities of Russian origins and the appalling differences between Russia and western Europe are still unexplained. Why should Russia begin its evolution with commerce and city life, western Europe with agriculture and the so-called feudal state-estate? What is the reason for Russia's developing the same form of state-estate much later, not earlier than in the thirteenth century, when western Europe had already begun to supercede this form? Why even then had the Russian feudalism assumed peculiar and original forms so dissimilar to the same phenomena in western Europe?

In spite of many attempts made both by Russian and west European scholars to solve this problem, it remains still unsolved. The main reasons for this failure are as follows: It was a mistake to begin the history of Russia with the Russian annals; i. e., with the ninth century; i. e., to confound the history of Russia with the history of the Slavonic race. The history of Russia as an economic and political organism is much more ancient than the first testimonies about the Slavonic race. Russia, as the land, existed much earlier than the ninth century, and formed a part of the civilized world even in the classical period and in the period of migrations. At this epoch the main lines of the future evolution were already definitely shaped. Therefore we must treat the history of Russia not as the history of the Slavonic race, but as the history of the Russian land. I am convinced that if we treat the history of Russia from this point of view, many of the alleged difficulties will disappear at once, and the history of Russia in general will appear before us in an entirely new light. Let me go more into detail and explain from this point of view the political and social structure of the Kievan princedom in the ninth and tenth centuries.

Civilized life in south Russia started much earlier than is generally accepted. Already at the dawn of history, in the so-called prehistoric period, the valleys of the Dnieper, the Don, and the Kuban can not be separated, as regards their civilized life, from the three main focuses of human culture in general; that of Central Asia and the nearer East, that of middle Europe, and especially the Danube Basin, and that of the Mediterranean. In the so-called copper age the valley of Kuban produced a civilization similar to the contemporary civilization of Mesopotamia, Turkestan, and Egypt. At the same epoch a branch of the middle European civilization flourished on the Dnieper. The first steps of cultural development in the Aegean are closely connected with the cultural development on the shores of the Black Sea. The population of the valleys of the Kuban and the Dnieper at this epoch had already begun to develop a settled agricultural life, and its first large townlike settlements date from the same period. The same period witnessed also the formation of the great commercial highways leading to Russia, the caravan road from Central

Asia to the mouth of the Don and to the Azov Sea, the maritime way along the shores of the Black Sea to the shores both Asiatic and European of the Aegean, and the great riverway from the Black to the Baltic Sea, the way of the amber trade.

The first millennium B. C. was a great epoch in the history of Russia. At this time both civilized life and international commerce took firm root in south Russia. To this phenomenon the existence on the shores of the Black Sea of two well-organized and centralized states, both of Indo-European origin, largely contributed. I mean the Thraco-Cimmerian state in the tenth and ninth centuries, B. C., and the Irano-Scythian state in the eighth to the third centuries, B. C. The very existence of these states in south Russia attracted to the shores of the Black Sea the main bearers of civilized life of this time—the Greeks; and thus Russia became connected by evermore solid ties to the cradle of western European civilization—the shores of the Aegean. Exceedingly intensive was civilized life in south Russia during the long existence of the great Scythian state—the minor brother of the Persian world monarchy. This state succeeded in evolving a highly developed military organization, comparable to that of the Spartan state, and thus in uniting under its power all the tribes between the Volga and the Danube by securing to these tribes the full possibility of developing their economic production and an ever-increasing opportunity of selling the products of their economic activity through the intermediary of the Greek colonies on the Black Sea to the Greek world. Grains, fish, and hides were supplied by the partly settled, partly nomadic population of the south Russian steppes. The great Russian rivers brought to the Greek harbors enormous quantities of valuable furs (beavers, sables, etc.), honey and wax, products of the forest industries of the Finnish hunters in central and northern Russia. The caravan trade of Central Asia carried to the mouths of the Don and the Kuban precious metals and stones from the Orient. As a result of the multisecular existence of the Scythian state and of the ever-increasing exchange of goods between Russia and Greece, settled life took firm root on the banks of the great Russian rivers and spread evermore toward the north. The archæological investigations in the valleys of the Dnieper and the Don showed that in both regions the ancient prehistoric settlements developed into important fortified cities, certainly big centers of commerce. While on the mouths of the Russian rivers these settlements were due to the Greek initiative, the large cities on the middle courses were of purely native origin. It is noteworthy that most of these towns are situated in the region which later became the center of the Dnieper-Russia, in the actual provinces of Kiev, Poltava, and Chernigov, on the rivers Dnieper, Desna, Sula, and Psiol. I have every reason to suppose that the main cities of the Dnieper-Russia—Kiev, Chernigov, Pereiaslavl—

developed out of these ancient native settlements. No one of the above-mentioned towns has been systematically investigated. But their large cemeteries, carefully excavated, yielded enormous quantities of precious gold and silver objects, of valuable pieces of furniture, of amphoræ full of wine and oil, all these showing that the prosperity of these cities depended entirely on their trade, which of course assumed the forms of barter, as no Greek or Oriental coins were ever found in the graves.

The Scythians were replaced in the prairies of south Russia, beginning with the third century, B. C., by a sequence of Sarmatian tribes, of the same Iranian stock. They succeeded with the help of some Thracian and Celtic tribes which invaded south Russia from the west, in destroying the mighty Scythian state, but they did not succeed in forming in its place their own united state. They remained divided into different tribes, which constantly moved to the west until they were stopped at the threshold of the mighty Roman Empire. But their appearance in south Russia did not change the whole aspect of life there. Like the Scythians, the Sarmatians understood the importance of keeping alive the international trade and of protecting the big commercial cities, both Greek and native, on the shores of the Black Sea and on the banks of the Russian rivers. But the destruction of the Scythian united state and the substitution for it of many comparatively week tribal formations had a far-reaching influence on the development of Russia. It opened the doors of south Russia to the western neighbors—the Celtic and German tribes. The former of course only hooked on to Russia in their movement toward the rich regions of the Balkan Peninsular and Asia Minor. But the Germans who followed them later on—especially beginning with the first century, B. C.—met with different conditions. Their movement toward the south and the west was barred by the strong legions of the Roman Empire and was stopped at the very threshold of the civilized world, on the line of the Rine and Danube. The only way for their southward expansion was therefore the old commercial way of the Dnieper. Consequently German tribes from the north and the west gradually poured into south Russia and occupied one place after another. This is shown with full evidence by the substitution in south Russia of the Scythian and Sarmatian graves by graves of quite different forms and content identical with graves of the German tribes. But we have no reason whatever to suppose that the German invaders radically changed the whole aspect of life in south Russia. Their graves are of course poorer than those of the Scythians and Sarmatians. But they also are full of products of classical art and industry, and moreover we often find in these graves Roman silver and gold coins. We must not forget that the German tribes in their native country were in constant trade relations with the Roman lands and became accustomed to their system of exchange based on money. No wonder if beginning with the first century, A. D., treasures of Roman coins are of constant occurrence on all the Russian river ways as far as the Baltic shore, and that products of Roman industries and Roman coins penetrated on the same ways as far as the western slopes of the Ural Mountains and the steppes of western Siberia. It is evident therefore that the Germans took over the ancient commercial relations, and even that they developed these relations in teaching the German merchants in Scandinavia and eastern Germany to use as one of the main ways of their trade the system of the Russian rivers. We have no ground, either, to suppose that the Germans destroyed the city life on the Dnieper. They needed these cities as much as their predecessors. I am rather inclined to think that they developed this city life and created new trade centers, especially in the north. Novgorod on the Ilmen, for example, had perhaps this origin.

In the light of this constant filtering of the German tribes into Russia we may better understand the so-called Gothic invasion of Russia in the third century, A. D. It was only the logical consequence of a long process. In the third century the Germans finally reached the shores of the Black Sea and succeeded in unitiug all the German tribes in Russia into one state under the leadership of two mighty tribes—the Visigoths and the Ostrogoths. But on these shores they did not destroy either commerce or civilized life. Of course, they burned down Olbia, but they kept the more important Panticapæum, and used it as the starting point for their commerce and military expeditions against the Roman Empire.

The Germans—warriors and keen sailors—were always attracted by the wealth of the Roman Empire. As soon as they felt that the mighty organism of the empire in the critical period of the third century began to weaken and to disintegrate, they renewed their attacks on the Roman Provinces. The weakest point in the Roman Empire was, of course, the Danube frontier, long and difficult as it was, without a civilized hinterland. But to surmount the superstitious fear of the Germans before the legions of Rome, then supposed to be invincible, and to transform scattered attacks into a mighty movement, a strong push from behind was needed. This shock was given to the German tribes in Russia by the first Mongolian invaders of Europe—the mighty Huns. Under their pressure, a part of the German and Iranian tribes with whom the Germans lived in a kind of federation—the Visigoths and the Alains—rushed first into the Roman Empire. The results are well known and I need not review them. Soon after, the Huns, themselves, under Attila, dragging with them the Ostrogoths, the Alains, and scores of Germanic and Iranian tribes, followed the victorious march of their predecessors. I do not need to elaborate this point.

The results of these events were of the utmost importance for Russia. In the fifth and sixth centuries Russia was swept clean of her German, Iranian, and Mongolian rulers and inhabitants. Small splinters of the Alains remained on the Kuban, where they still dwell under the name of Ossetes. Some tribes of the Goths still occupied a part of the Crimea and of the Tauric Peninsula. Scattered hordes of Huns came back, after their disaster, to the Russian steppes. But no one of these splinters played any part in the future destinies of Russia. The place of the Germans soon was occupied by a new European people—the Slavs. They dwelt originally—as far as our knowledge reaches—on the northern slopes of the Carpathians toward the Vistula and the Baltic Sea. According to Ptolemy and to Jordanes they were well known to the Romans and were divided in three parts—the Veneds, the Sclavenes, and the Antes. During the domination of the Goths in south Russia they were vanquished by them and formed a part of the Gothic Empire and endured a kind of vassalage. But in the sixth century the same Jordanes, a Goth himself, who knew very well the conditions of northeastern Europe, knew likewise of the continuous settlements on the Dnieper and of the occupation of the steppes as far as the Black Sea. It is evident, therefore, that the Slavs repeated the movement of the Germans and replaced them in south Russia. Thus they founded in south Russia a state of the same type as the Germans before them and naturally inherited from them their towns, their trade relations, and their civilization. This civilization was of course not a German civilization, but the ancient Greco-Iranian civilization of the Scythians and the Sarmatians with slight modifications. At the very dawn of their life in south Russia they were threatened by a great danger. New conquerors of the same stock as the Huns—the Avars—tried to swallow them and to drag them into western Europe. But the new Slavonic federation was strong enough to repulse this attack and to annihilate the Avars. Thence the old Russian saying preserved to us by our annals: "They perished like the Avars."

The Slavs took firm root on the Dnieper and spread widely to the north and to the east, occupying all the old highways of commerce. In the north they developed Novgorod, in the east they founded Rostov, in the south—opposite Panticapæum—Tmutarakan. The conditions were favorable for them. Their ancient relations with the Germans secured to them the military help of wandering Norman chieftains, who were prepared to serve and to fight for anybody, provided that they had good opportunities to enrich themselves. The Germans helped the Slavs to find the ancient way to Constantinople and to protect their trade fleet on the Dnieper. The domination in the south of the new rulers on the Volga—the Mongolian tribe of the Khazars—a peaceful domination of a trading people, guaranteed for them the oriental market. So they grew strong and rich and developed a lively trade with the German north, the Finnish northeast, the Arabic southeast, and especially with the Byzantine south. This trade was, as before, the main source of their civilization and their wealth, and dictated to them the forms of their political and social life. Their centers were, as before, the great cities on the Dnieper, and the most important of these cities was, of course, Kiev, thanks to her wonderful geographic situation in the middle of the Dnieper Basin, just midway between the Baltic and the Black Seas.

History knows of no pauses and interruptions in its evolution. Nor are there any in the history of Russia. The Slavonic is one of the epochs in the evolution of Russia as such. But the Slavonic race succeeded in accomplishing one cardinal thing, which neither the Iranians nor the Germans could or wanted to achieve. For the Iranians and the Germans, Russia was an expedient to achieve their main aim, the conquest of western Europe. For the Slavs, Russia was their final aim and became their country. They bound themselves forever to the country, and to them, of course, Russia is indebted not only for her name but also for her peculiar statehood and civilization.

RECENT REALIGNMENT IN THE HISTORY OF MEDIEVAL MEDICINE AND SCIENCE

FIELDING H. GARRISON, M. D.

Surgeon General's Office

Washington, D. C.

RECENT REALIGNMENT IN THE HISTORY OF MEDIEVAL MEDICINE AND SCIENCE

By Fielding H. Garrison, M. D.

Up to the beginning of the twentieth century it was assumed by most historians that science was persecuted and suppressed during the Middle Ages. This was due in part to religious prepossessions, to the aversion to dogmatic theology which sprang up under the liberal teachings of Darwin and Huxley, to the tendency of the human mind to follow tradition, but more particularly to ignorance of the basic documents and their content. Until recently little was known of the contents of the earlier printed books on science, and the scientific manuscripts were practically unknown. Intensive study of the older writings has been the order of the later period, and the manuscripts are now in process of being photographed, catalogued, collated, and studied. It is now taken for granted that the Middle Ages were a period of race absorption and formation of new nations, a period in which the popular mind was paralyzed by the long succession of wars following the downfall of the Roman Empire, in which, as in Russia to-day, life was endangered by the aggressions of wandering outlawry and in which the only stabilizing powers and protectors of learning were the church and the state. In the earlier centuries of the Middle Ages Greek thought was moribund, while western European culture underwent a long process of Latinization, followed by a period of Arabic domination; that is, of Greek culture filtered through Arabic translations, prior to the extensive circulation of the actual Greek texts after the invention of printing. The effect of this Latinizing process upon medicine was peculiar. In the first century of the Christian era the Roman and also the Greek physicians living in Rome began to make huge compilations or encyclopedias of everything known about medicine. We need only mention Celsus, Pliny, Galen, Aretæus, Soranus, and Dioscorides. This tradition was maintained by the Byzantine writers of the sixth and seventh centuries A. D., and was carried straight into the Renaissance period and beyond it. The effect was to make internal medicine a matter of cut and dried doctrine as to theory, and of tradition as to practice. The big books on practice were excellently arranged, divided into chapters and even indexed, but, short of a few original observations, contained

175

little that was not already known. Meanwhile the traditions of rational bedside practice, derived from the Greeks, was maintained at a solitary outpost of Greek culture, the medical school at Salerno. Little was known of medieval anatomy until Sudhoff exhumed, photographed, and published the manuscripts and manuscript illustrations. His findings go to show that the earlier medieval anatomists were, in the main, blind followers of tradition, their descriptions being often based upon the earlier dissections of apes and swine, their illustrations servile copies of crude diagrams which originated, perhaps in the Orient, hundreds of years before. Just before the Renaissance period, as Streeter has shown, the Florentine painters made more dissections and did better anatomical illustration than the professional anatomists themselves. Modern anatomy began with the wonderful hand drawings of Leonardo da Vinci (1510) and the textbook of Vesalius (1543). There was no physiology to speak of between Galen and Harvey. The medieval physicians, then, were weak in anatomy and physiology, and not particularly remarkable in internal medicine. Their main accomplishment was in surgery and public hygiene. Of surgeons there were two classes—the educated, scientific surgeons like Roger, Roland, Hugh, Theodoric, Saliceto, Lanfranc, and Guy de Chauliac, who were protected by prince and prelate; and the wandering outcast surgeons, who operated for cateract, hernia, and stone, and sometimes cast discredit upon the guild by malpractice. Hugh, Theodoric, and Mondeville taught the principles of aseptic surgery, as originally stated by Hippocrates. Guy discredited it. The medieval surgeons used sleeping draughts or anæsthetic inhalations, and their operative skill was considerable. Saliceto knew of suture of nerves and intestines, crepitus in fractures, renal dropsy, venereal contagion, and used mercurial salves and prophylactic ablutions. The many manuscript pictures of surgical practice which have been published by Giacosa, Sudhoff, van Leersum, and others give us a good notion of medieval procedure and etiquette, and from the number of them we can surmise the amount of operating which was done in spite of the many interdictions. In the Renaissance period, due to the development of didactic anatomy by Vesalius, surgery made even greater advances, culminating in the work of Paré.

Adequate knowledge of public medicine in the Middle Ages is of recent date, and is based upon the exhumation, collation, and publication of unprinted public documents and manuscripts, mainly by Sudhoff and his pupils. The development of universities by the state; of hospitals, nursing, and charitable care of the sick by the church; the model law of Frederick II for the regulation of medical practice (1224), were known to earlier historians. Sudhoff has exhumed and published a great number of sanitary ordinances, and fugitive tracts on syphilis, plague, and leprosy, showing the efforts made to prevent these diseases, and the interdiction of the adulteration of food, the sale of poisons, the accumulation of refuse, etc. The Mosaic principle of isolation of diseases thought to be contagious was extended in a city ordinance of Basel (1350) to eight diseases, viz, plague, phthisis, scabies, erysipelas, leprosy, anthrax, trachoma, and epilepsy. Through the severe and rigorous isolation of lepers, leprosy was ultimately stamped out. Quarantine of ships against bubonic plague was first instituted by the Venetian Republic (1374); detention for a month was practiced at Ragusa (1377), and this *trentina* was extended to a *quarantina* (40 days) at Marseille (1383) and applied to infected areas by Venice in 1403. The investigations of early public health documents and tracts on syphilis by Sudhoff go to show that the disease was already known in the time of Columbus and that civil authority was making efforts to prevent its spread. We have to reflect that the Greeks had no definite knowledge or theory of contagion, combating major epidemics not by isolation of patients but by prayers and sacrifices to angered gods. This knowledge came from the Hebrews, and is clearly stated in Leviticus (XIII–XV) and elsewhere in the Bible. The isolation of epileptics, and the existence of an isolation hospital for epileptics at Rufach (Upper Alsace) as late as 1486, was a solitary survival of the Assyro-Babylonian doctrine that the disease is contagious, and of the ancient Greek theory that the major neuroses were in the nature of "miasms" or stains cast upon the soul by the infernal (chthonian) gods, which was ridiculed in the Hippocratic writing "On the Sacred Disease."

As Allbutt has shown, theoretical science was much hampered in the Middle Ages through the opposition between Realists who believed that all things proceed from God (Theism), and Nominalists who maintained that God exists in all things (Pantheism). This opposition led to persecution of freethinkers, tended to make all reasoning deductive, and held but little encouragement to followers of induction and experiment. But such practical inventions as printing, gunpowder, the mariner's compass, astronomical tables, spectacle lenses, and sundry devices in operative surgery were immediately taken up, and it is to this tendency to evaluate an investigation, discovery, or invention by its practical bearings that we owe the development of modern experimental or laboratory science. The medieval physicians devised most of the school arithmetic and grammars of the period. The association of physicians, painters, and apothecaries in the same guild led to the interest of the artists in practical anatomy and made extensive dissecting possible (Streeter). Vesalius and Harvey gained ground through the practical importance of their work; and, in a later period, even such a complex phase of mathematics as the theory of differential equations was developed to solve problems in mechanics and physics. The best phases of medieval science—invention, sanitation, surgery—were away from bald theorizing and in the direction of the practical. The keynote of modern scientific education is that chemistry and physics are best taught in the laboratory, anatomy in the dissecting room, pathology in the deadhouse, surgery in the operating theater, internal medicine in the clinic and at the bedside. Science, as Woodward has said, actually thrives by opposition. This phase of medieval science, the dying out of ancient culture, the development of practical handcraft and redecraft, has been defined by Singer as "the pathology and embryology of human thought."

The status of the scholastic literature of the Middle Ages was never better stated than by Doctor Johnson in his Tour of the Hebrides:

Learning was then rising on the world; but ages so long accustomed to darkness were too much dazzled with its light to see anything distinctly. The first race of scholars in the fifteenth century, and some time after, were, for the most part, learning to speak rather than to think, and were, therefore, more studious of elegance than of truth. The contemporaries of Boethius thought it sufficient to know what the ancients had delivered. The examination of tenets and of facts was reserved for another generation.

This critical examination and study of documents, begun by the medical philologists of the Renaissance period, is now going forward. While the most important medical texts of classical antiquity and the Middle Ages were issued in type by the Renaissance printers, much of the scientific and medical literature of the time remained in the category of "published not printed," i. e., circulated in manuscript. Mrs. Dorothea Waley Singer has catalogued and classified no less than 30,000 scientific manuscripts of the Middle Ages in England alone, and of these, 15,000 are medical. This will give some idea of the enormous amount of scientific literature existing in the Middle Ages, and little of this has been examined to date. Sudhoff has devoted most of his life to the photography, study, and publication of medieval medical manuscripts and manuscript illustrations found in libraries, monasteries, palaces, and elsewhere on the continent of Europe. By collation and comparison of these, he has been able to alter many facts and dates, e. g., the determination of the approximate date of the famous *Regimen sanitatis* of Salerno, by using some 80 manuscripts of the poem as controls. In the textual study of medieval medicine, those who have done most are Choulant, Haeser, Pagel, Sudhoff, Neuburger, Nicaise, Wickersheimer, and Singer. In the United States only two physicians have thus far devoted much attention to this phase of medieval medicine, namely, Dr. James J. Walsh (New York) and Dr. Edward C. Streeter (Boston).

II. LATIN AS AN INTERNATIONAL LANGUAGE IN THE MIDDLE AGES

By LOUIS J. PAETOW

University of California

LATIN AS AN INTERNATIONAL LANGUAGE IN THE MIDDLE AGES

By Louis J. Paetow

The outstanding feature of general history since the fall of the Roman Empire has been the ascendancy of western Europe. In times to come, when historians shall have discarded the fantastic and illogical division of history into medieval and modern times, they will probably designate the period from the decline of the Roman Empire to the beginning of the Great War in 1914 as the period of the dominance of western Europe. Perhaps the opening of this period will be set about 1100 A. D., for in the formative era from the fifth to the eleventh centuries western Europe was still on the defensive against its many foes, and the world was dominated by the Byzantines and the Mohammedans. But beginning with the first crusade, the west of Europe took the offensive, and ever since has dominated the world of thought and of action.

Medieval western Europe fell heir to two extremely important factors in the ancient Roman Empire—the Roman Catholic Church and the Latin language. In the period from the crusades to the age of oceanic discoveries leadership in the world was secured in western Europe by men who called themselves Latins (*Latini*). In short, modern civilization rests flatly upon the achievements of Latin Christendom.

Latin was the dominant note of the culture of western Europe when it emerged as the mistress of the world. Wherever Roman Christianity penetrated, there the Latin language became the bond of union amalgamating the efforts of the most progressive peoples on the globe. Latin was the international language in the Middle Ages not only among the Romanic and Germanic peoples; it had penetrated far into Slavic lands; it was heard in Iceland and Greenland, and perhaps on the shores of North America; it was widespread in eastern Europe and western Asia in the days when there was a Latin kingdom of Jerusalem and a Latin empire of Constantinople; and it had reached the Pacific Ocean in the oriental bishopric of Peking.

One would naturally suppose that so tremendous an engine for civilization as was Latin in the Middle Ages would have been studied and appraised to the last detail by modern scholarship. But what do we see? Almost utter neglect. No adequate history of post-classical Latin; very fragmentary histories of its literature; most of its monuments still unedited, or edited badly; and worst of all, in this age of dictionaries and books of reference, no satisfactory dictionaries for those who concern themselves with the Latin writings of medieval and modern times. If Du Cange could appear among us to-day nothing would surprise him more than that his Glossarium ad scriptores mediae et infimæ latinitatis, written in 1678 and augmented largely in the eighteenth century, is still referred to as the standard dictionary of medieval Latin. Strictly speaking, it is not a dictionary at all, but, as its very title indicates, a glossary of uncommon and technical terms, especially in the domain of politics and law. In many respects it is more a dictionary of medieval antiquities than a true lexicon.

Historians, and medievalists in particular, are much concerned with postclassical Latin and should have a full understanding of its unmerited fate. On the whole, historians have done more than philologists to draw due attention to this form of Latin. Du Cange himself was a historian rather than a linguist. The strange eclipse of medieval Latin in modern times can be understood only when illuminated by the full light of history. Thus the task of awakening interest in the Latin of Latin Christendom should be the joint work of philologists and historians.

Latin was a truly international language in the ancient Roman world. The break-up of the Empire in the fourth and the fifth centuries threatened its total dissolution into a number of Romanic tongues. That danger was averted by the Roman Church. Although Christianity was introduced into western Europe through a Greek medium, by about 400 A. D., western Christendom was thoroughly Latin. St. Augustine could afford to forget the Greek which he had learned as a schoolboy under the master's lash, and St. Jerome sealed the triumph of Latin in the Vulgate. Thus Latin was given a distinctly ecclesiastical stamp and also the stamp of the language of the common people, for Christianity in its earlier stages was a popular religion.

By means of a church which established its center in Rome, the language of ancient Latium was thus preserved as an international language, and soon penetrated into distant woods and swamps of western Europe where the Roman eagles had never been seen.

True, it was not the language of all the inhabitants of western Europe. It was mastered only by the clergy, the learned class, and by others who engaged in international business, including many members of the governing classes and even some merchants. In the early Middle Ages the state of culture was not high enough and the facilities for schooling were so poor that it was impossible to hold the common people to the Latin of books and international intercourse, and so they were left to develop their vernaculars without help or hindrance. Until about the twelfth century, however, there was practically no writing done in western Europe except in Latin.

. It was in this early period that a form of Latin script was developed which rapidly became standard throughout Latin Christendom—the so-called Caroline minuscule. To-day, the use of these letters is well-nigh world-wide. The modern typewriter has done much to make us appreciate the chaste beauty and serviceability of the Caroline minuscule. We usually call it the Roman alphabet, but that is, strictly speaking, a misnomer. If Cæsar could appear among us to-day, he would be unable to read his Commentaries from an ordinary printed edition. Only the capital letters would appear familiar to his eyes. Most of the small letters would perplex him exceedingly. Our alphabet is a medieval Latin product of Carolingian times, originating chiefly in northern France, in that fruitful portion of western Europe which later brought forth Gothic architecture and the medieval university. Bismarck refused to read books printed in "Latin" type, insisting on the Gothic type which he looked upon with national pride as a German product, until it was pointed out to him that the supposedly characteristic German type was merely a survival of a degenerate or baroque form of medieval writing which most of the other nations of Europe had discarded in favor of the Caroline minuscule. This illustrates how seriously the advancement of learning can be hindered by ignorance and prejudice in high places.

The Christian Church thus carried Latin through perilous times. In the twelfth and thirteenth centuries it was borne aloft triumphantly by the medieval university movement. Latin naturally became the sole medium of expression in one of the most remarkable intellectual revivals which the world has ever seen. Now Europe witnessed the interesting spectacle of truly international universities—masters and students flocking to the famous centers of learning from all corners of Europe regardless of the vernaculars which were their mother tongues; books written in remote cells of monasteries becoming at once, without translations, common property of the intellectual class throughout western Europe.

Internationalism is put to the hardest test by war. According to a letter of John of Salisbury, dated 1168, King Louis VII of France complained of the German students in Paris who, with grand and boastful phrases, mocked him because he lived like a plain citizen and had none of the barbaric splendors of a tyrant, constantly surrounded by armed guards. Louis VII actually expelled some foreign students, but John of Salisbury considered that action very exceptional in hospitable France, "the kindliest and most civilized of all nations" (omnium mitissima et civilissima nationum). The powerful and warlike Philip Augustus was very tolerant toward students who were alien enemies. The same is true of his great namesake, Philip IV (the Fair). On February 25, 1297, he sent an order to all his justices and ministers to watch with special care over the students in Paris and Orleans who had come from Flanders. War had broken out with the Count of Flanders, and he feared that under this pretext many might be tempted to molest the members of the university who had come from those parts. As long as they conducted themselves properly in France they were to be under the special care of the king; they were allowed to go to Flanders and to return freely, and messengers with money and supplies were to be allowed to pass between them and their homes.[1] A similar order was issued in 1315 by his successor when war had broken out between France and another Count of Flanders.[2]

Thus Latin was acting most effectively as a bond of union in western Europe when the foundations of modern civilization were laid in parliament, in the jury, and in the university. Apparently the question was never raised as to whether Latin should endure as the international language. Men simply took for granted that it always would endure, for its advantages were so obvious. Roger Bacon never dreamed that the day would come when university lectures would be delivered at Paris in French.[3]

In this very cocksure attitude of the men of the medieval universities there lurked great danger for Latin. They used it with the utmost freedom, which bordered on abandon, in expressing the subtlest distinctions in philosophy and theology. Latin was in large measure remade in these institutions of learning and a new epoch opened in the history of the language. We would suppose that one of the foremost branches in medieval universities would have been the study of Latin itself. If we were to develop an international language to-day, it would at once become the object of the most painstaking study to determine its theory and practice. But medieval universities were so engrossed in other things that they paid practically no attention to the study of Latin language and literature. They had a precious jewel and they handled it as if it were a clod.

Let it be remembered, however, that there is an honorable list of men of the twelfth and thirteenth centuries who advocated the study of Latin language and literature and who foretold the evil consequences which would follow neglect. There were those who pleaded for a sympathetic study of the ancient classical masterpieces of Latin, and others who realized that new and improved grammars and hand-

---

[1] *Chartularium universitatis Parisiensis,* edited by Denifle and Chatelain, II, 75, No. 601.
[2] Ibid., 175, No. 719.
[3] See, e. g., his *Compendium studii,* ed. Brewer. in Fr. Rogeri Bacon *Opera quaedam hactenus inedita,* I (Rolls Series, 15 466), also his *Opus majus,* ed. Bridges, I, 67.

)ooks were necessary to teach Latin in an up-to-date way. It is notorious that for centuries the books of Donatus and Priscian were used to teach medieval Latin to children whose training and mental attitude differed radically from those of the boys for whom these books were written. In the twelfth and thirteenth centuries some valiant efforts were made to correct this evil. The most successful new grammatical text was the famous versified *Doctrinale* of Alexander de Villa Dei.

Alexander was an obscure student in Paris who wrote his book in 199, at the behest of the Bishop of Dol, to tutor his two grandchildren. The grammar is not without its merits, especially in its chapters on syntax, but the astounding thing about it is that so indifferent a book acquired such a wonderful reputation. At least one professor in the University of Paris, John Garland, spent endless efforts in the first half of the thirteenth century decrying the *Doctrinale* or trying to improve it, but to no avail. The sad truth is that the enlightened thirteenth century was satisfied with the *Doctrinale* as a text for teaching Latin. The great medieval universities, which should have fostered the study of their precious international language with utmost care, stultified themselves by resting content with Priscian and the *Doctrinale*.

The inevitable reaction came in the fourteenth century when the Italian humanists turned away from the traditional subjects of the schools and fairly reveled in the study of Latin language and literature in the pages of the ancient classical authors. Laurentius Valla c. 1406–1457), in his *Elegantiæ linguæ Latinæ*, sounded the keynote of this new era in the history of Latin. For hundreds of years, he said, no one had spoken Latin, no one had even been able to read real Latin. Then he contrasted the sad centuries which failed to produce a single scholar with his own happy generation which had recovered the Roman language and set up as its ideal of intellectual achievement Ciceronian eloquence.

This curse of Valla and his followers darkened the Middle Age for centuries; it utterly blighted medieval Latin which had served so wonderfully as an international language. The humanists believed that they had awakened Latin to a new life. They did reawaken classical Latin and thus did scholarship immeasurable benefit by opening up the ancient world. But by condemning all things medieval without discrimination they killed Latin as a living and international language. It was not long before the vernaculars encroached upon the old precincts of Latin and divided former Latin Christendom into many rival linguistic groups at the very time when it was winning the world by means of oceanic discoveries.

Can Latin come back? Can it once again become an international language such as it was for so many centuries of the world's history? Such a question can not be answered offhand in the negative. It is

too important to be brushed aside; it deserves to be investigated.
Ever since the beginning of this century there have come insistent
demands that the problem of a world language must be faced squarely.
Daily in this age of rapid progress distances are shrinking, old barriers are disappearing, our neighbors are coming closer and growing
more numerous, the burden of learning many foreign languages is
becoming more and more intolerable.   We must devise some means of
understanding each other.   This great problem has been approached
largely in a desultory way by miscellaneous groups often working in
a very amateurish and visionary fashion.   The great universities
and other learned bodies have held themselves aloof from it almost
as completely as medieval universities neglected the study of Latin
language and literature.   The late war interrupted the quest for an
international language, but now it has been taken up with renewed
vigor.   The war itself and the Peace Conference forcibly emphasized
the need of a common means of communication.

In July, 1919, the International Research Council, meeting in
Brussels, appointed a committee on international auxiliary language.
This committee has been very active.   At its suggestion the British
Association for the Advancement of Science appointed a committee
"to study the practicability of an international language."   The
Modern Language Association of America has appointed a similar
committee.   The American Classical League has a committee on
"Latin as an international language for scientific purposes."   The
British Classical Association also has a committee.

Is not the time ripe for the American Historical Association to
take some action in this matter?   Medievalists should be especially
anxious to give Latin a proper hearing.   Dense shades of ignorance
still hang about the history of the Latin language and especially about
medieval Latin.   Any investigation of this question would redound
to the benefit of medieval studies.   It is by no means a wild surmise
that the Sphinxlike Middle Ages may reveal the answer to the long
quest for an international language, for they can teach us by the
experience of a time when a practical form of Latin was the international language of Europe among Romanic, Germanic, Slavic, and
Magyar peoples.

VIII. THE ENLIGHTENED DESPOTISM

GEORGE MATTHEW DUTCHER

Wesleyan University

THE ENLIGHTENED DESPOTISM

GEORGE MATTHEW DUTCHER

The most important development in governmental practice on the
ntinent of Europe in the eighteenth century prior to the outbreak
the French Revolution was the enlightened despotism. This
vement has sometimes been miscalled the benevolent despotism
those who emphasize certain of the humanitarian reforms which
aracterized it, without considering the circumstances and motives
ich lay back of these reforms. In fact, so far as I am aware,
iters have hitherto confined their attention to registering certain
s of the enlightened despotism without attempting to analyze that
nifestation.

The element which was new in enlightened despotism was not des-
tism but enlightenment. The word "enlightenment" as used in
s connection as well as its German equivalent *aufklärung* signified
a very definite sense rationalism or, more correctly, the recognition
the authority of reason. The philosophical eighteenth century re-
ted divine right as the foundation of the state in favor of reason—
ightenment as the basic authority. Enlightenment, in this sense,
ile primarily an intellectual movement, found practical applica-
n in the fields of both religion and government. In the field of
gion it expressed the reaction against mysticism and pietism. It
s represented in England by the Deistic school culminating in Bo-
ъbroke and Hume; in France by Voltaire and the Encyclopedists;
Germany most distinctively by Wolff. This movement did not
essarily limit itself to the ideas propounded by the Deistic group but
luded various forms of refusal to submit to authority in matters of
rch and of personal religion. In the relations of state and church
ignified the supremacy of the state in all matters not clearly of a
itual character. In this respect the movement culminated in the
pression of the Society of Jesus in the Catholic lands.

n the side of government the problem appeared in its simplest
n in England where the conditions, arising after the Restoration
centering in the Revolution of 1688, developed the theories of
resistance and of passive obedience. The significance of these
ories, which are so puzzling to the present-day mind, is that out
he conflict between king and parliament there came the recogni-

189

tion of the supremacy of the state quite apart from any individual, even though that individual were the monarch. Even the extreme Tory, Bolingbroke, recognized as the one valid aim the union of all in the service of the state, though he looked to the "patriotic king," not to parliament, for leadership in that union.

In France the development of the movement prior to the Revolution was very largely on the theoretical rather than the practical side, and nowhere was the discussion so broad in its scope or carried with clearer conviction to its logical conclusions. In Germany the result was the reverse of that in England. There, too, the logical development was a recognition of the supremacy of the state, but owing to the lack of properly developed self-governing institutions the leadership in the state was without question vested in the monarch. In Germany, too, thanks to Wolff, the frank and full application of the rationalistic principles to both church and state was most clearly set forth, and, thanks to the practical genius as well as the philosophical instinct of Frederick the Great, it received its most complete demonstration in the enlightened despotism of that prince.

In matters of government the enlightened despotism operated primarily in three fields. The first was in the development of the supremacy of law as a natural correlative to the supremacy of the state. This involved the development of uniformity of law and the consequent movement toward codification, to which Frederick gave particular attention. The second phase was in the tendency toward equality before the law, both of territorial areas and of classes of the population. This movement looked toward centralization and uniformity in administration, and toward the minimizing, if not the abolition, of privilege. The third field was that of administrative efficiency which involved the development of systematic administration, as increased powers came with the progress of centralization in authority. Administration had to respond to the demands and tests of reason by seeing that the government produced for the state the goods which reason approved, especially in matters diplomatic, military, financial, and economic. The characteristic form of administrative system thus developed was bureaucracy. After this brief and inadequate survey or analysis of the enlightened despotism, it is my purpose to undertake to trace not the development of theory, but the practical working out of events which culminated in the enlightened despotism of Frederick the Great and of Maria Theresa and to show how Prussia and Austria, rather than the more advanced nations, England and France, became the birthplace of the enlightened despotism.

In England the civil strife of the Wars of the Roses had wiped out large numbers of the nobility and weakened their power. The Tudor monarchy which rested on the firm basis of popular

upport, devised and executed measures which destroyed the last
lements of power and privilege of the medieval feudal nobility.
These results had been achieved before the religious schism of the
Protestant Revolution reached England, so that king and commons were able to carry into effect a series of ecclesiastical reforms
which destroyed the ecclesiastics, as a privileged class, with no more
erious opposition than such local and spasmodic affairs as the
Pilgrimage of Grace, or Ket's Rebellion, or Wyatt's Insurrection, or
he Rising of the North. Because the Wars of the Roses had de-
troyed the possibility of feudal organization and leadership of an
opposition, and because of the shrewd policy of national unification
of the Tudor monarchs, England escaped the disaster of a series of
wars of religion and enjoyed the opportunity for steady political development free from the strife of Catholic and Protestant. England's
insularity, furthermore, permitted a policy of political isolation and
neutrality so that in Tudor times England kept free from the civil
wars of religion in France and in Stuart times from the Thirty Years'
War in Germany. The traditional emphasis upon the so-called
Tudor absolutism has exalted the success of the royal policy and
he growth of monarchical power, but has ignored the no less signifi-
ant fact of not merely the continued existence, but the steady
growth of the power of the commons. From Anglo-Saxon days,
moreover, the English people had been accustomed to the practice
of local self-government, and the control of local administration was
never centralized. While not producing a uniformly effective and
erfect system, it did provide one that responded to the popular
intelligence and will, and yielded the results the nation required. It
rained the citizen in responsibility and afforded scope for his
initiative.

In England it naturally came to pass that, after the elimination of
eudal privilege in the Wars of the Roses and of ecclesiastical privilege in the Reformation, the commons were able to wage uncompli-
ated and effective war on royal prerogative in the great Civil War
nd the Revolution of 1688, and to enter the eighteenth century with
England fully and clearly organized as a constitutional monarchy,
thoroughly unified and nationalized to participate in the struggle for
world empire. Neither royalty nor nobility nor clergy but the com-
monalty of the realm won for England the splendid triumph sealed
y the peace of Paris in 1763.

With this development in England there stand in contrast the contemporary changes and results in France and in the lands on which
rested the shadow rather than the yoke of the Holy Roman Empire.

France, in the fifteenth century, emerged victorious from its Hun-
red Years' War with England and triumphant in the efforts of the
royal power against the forces of feudal provincialism; but, without

awaiting the completion of the task of national consolidation, plunged rashly into wars of conquest in Italy and of rivalry with Charles V. Ere those wars were ended the Reformation had come to add ecclesiastical strife and afford the restless nobility an opportunity, through the civil wars of religion, to undermine the royal authority and recover political power for their selfish advantage. Henry IV asserted the principles of religious toleration and of the supremacy of national interests and authority, in order that he and his successors might give themselves to the task of humbling the feudal nobility and of exalting the royal power. The double success of Mazarin in the treaties of Westphalia and in compassing the collapse of the Fronde assured the triumph of the royal power and of nationalism, but did not involve the annihilation or even decimation of the feudal nobility, or the abolition or diminution of their privileges. The nobility and the clergy alike were compelled to accept the royal authority and to find their grandeur no longer in their own glory but in reflecting the splendor of royalty. The royal power in France was built upon substantial geographical, racial, and linguistic unity and upon an historical tradition of success and of realization of national ambitions. In contrast with England, however, royalty alone, in France, reaped the political fruits of the victory of the alliance of king and people against the nobility, for the states-general failed to develop from a feudal into a popular representative body or into an effective governmental institution, and from 1614 onward really ceased to exist.

The intelligence of the French people, the development of education, the policy of employing successful business men in administrative capacities, and the organization of local administration were such as to furnish the Bourbon monarchy with an efficient staff of officials in the various stages of the administrative system. On the whole, the provincial and local administrations were more intelligent, progressive, and efficient than the national ministries, which were permeated with favoritism and servility. Intendants found such scope for initiative that they achieved in their provinces reforms which the national government dared not undertake, or undertook only to fail, as in the case of Turgot.

In France, therefore, the royal power became the sole institutional expression of the unity, aims, and action of the nation. It was absolute in the field and its field was the best in Europe. At 1660 no state on the European continent could compare with France in its territorial compactness and its advantageous geographical situation, or in the homogeneity of its population and the solidarity and efficiency of its governmental system, or in the extent and exploitation of its economic resources.

The French monarchy of Louis XIV could readily command unquestioning national support in the twofold ambition of securing national strategic frontiers and of achieving the paramountcy in the European system and hence the leadership in world empire. Monarchy in France faced no opposition, was confronted by no political institutions or moral authority or compelling necessity that would hold it to account. Consequently, prior to the humiliations of the Seven Years' War embodied in the treaty of Paris of 1763, even the criticisms and protests of the intellectual leaders had passed almost unheeded. Now, as the historian looks back over the period following the loss of Louisburg in 1745, he can detect many indications of the impending collapse, besides the presentiments of the Montesquieus, Diderots, Voltaires, Rousseaus, Argensons, and Quesnays of the inadequacy and faultiness of the existing system.

The output of the French mind on political, social, and economic questions in the 15 years beginning with the publication in 1748 of Montesquieu's Spirit of the Laws, and culminating in 1762 in the appearance of Rousseau's Social Contract, was destined not merely to compass the downfall of the French monarchy but to remake the political life of Europe. In those very years when France was formulating the thought of the coming age, two monarchs, the Prussian and the Austrian, were developing policies of efficiency in monarchical administration because war had taught them its necessity in the struggle for existence and for empire.

While it is notorious that the two most intelligent and progressive countries, England and France, did not exemplify the enlightened despotism, that movement had its home and did its most notable work in the lands nominally comprised in the Holy Roman Empire.

By the fifteenth century the Holy Roman Empire had fallen permanently into the hands of the Hapsburgs with their narrow dynasticism which negatived any movement toward sound national growth and unification. In face of the dilatory pettiness of Frederick III and the shallow knight errantry of Maximilian, every personage down to the humblest in the feudal hierarchy not merely asserted to the full his proper rights but also grasped greedily for further privileges and added powers. To such members of the nobility of the German nation Luther's famous address was an incomprehensible appeal, but the break with Rome was an opportunity eagerly seized for feudal aggrandizement and territorial expansion. That they enjoyed this liberty in full measure was due to the preoccupation of Charles V with multitudinous and world-wide interests such as previous emperors had never contemplated. What Charles V might have accomplished, had his hands been free, was forever too late when his weaker successors assumed their narrowed realms. While the emperors were

---

[1] It is remarkable that the wars of 1740 to 1763 led the Elder Pitt in England and Choiseul in France to concentrate governmental effort on the international situation to the almost complete neglect of internal interests, even of their possible effect in increasing the international efficiency of the state.

too distracted or too weak to erect a unified German national state
at the expense of the striving feudal princelings, those same princelings
were wresting every vestige of popular liberties from their subjects.

The peace of Augsburg of 1555 not only failed, as every effort to
stabilize society always has, in the purpose of maintaining permanently the religious *status quo*, but its restrictive character bound
the hands of the emperors from undertaking any nationalizing policy,
while the disintregrating process of feudal aggrandizement persisted
unchecked. The resulting civil wars of religion, known as the Thirty
Years' War, afforded opportunity for each duke or count to seek his
own fortune, even at the expense of treating with the neighboring
nations and utilizing their intervention in German affairs.

The treaties of Westphalia, while establishing a revised and rigid
ecclesiastical status for the German states, accorded to the various
intervening neighbors the control of certain German lands and peoples
and of the country's economic gateways. Thus, at the very time that
England and France were entering upon careers of great maritime
trade and colonial expansion, Germany saw its strategic districts
expropriated and its once powerful Hansa wrecked. The left bank
of the Rhine passed under French possession or influence and its
lower course, as well as that of the Meuse, and the left bank of the
Ems, was confirmed to the declining power of the Dutch. The
mouths of the Weser, the Elbe, the Oder, and the Vistula fell into the
hands of the Danes, Swedes, and Poles whose inadequate powers were
wasted in internecine strife. The nominal limits of the Holy Roman
Empire were greatly narrowed and the authority of the emperor and
of the imperial institutions was reduced to a negligible, almost to an
absurd, minimum. No one of the numerous, practically independent
principalities within Germany was left with an area or resources that
promised self-sufficiency, not to mention the possibility of effective
development and leadership. The Hapsburg emperor abandoned in
despair any hope of developing effective power in the empire on the
basis of his Germanic and Slavic lands, and henceforth turned his
attention to the recovery of the ancient limits of his Hungarian kingdom and the development of his new territorial interests in Italy.

Germany was left a helpless prey to its ambitious neighbors and to
its own unconscionable and incompetent princes. Church and state
had broken down and the anarchy of decadent feudalism alone
remained. The condition of the people was hopeless. War and
pestilence had reduced the population by half, and left some districts
almost depopulated. The devastation of the country had been such
that two centuries had to elapse before agricultural life was restored
to its condition prior to the Thirty Years' War. The ruin of the
towns was such that only 50 free cities, of which but few could boast
of 10,000 souls, remained to preserve the memory rather than the

reality of the once vigorous town life. No institution of popular government—national, provincial, or municipal—remained to form a nucleus for new political growth. There was dearth of individuals with training or experience to fill the administrative posts. Even the universities had barely survived the catastrophe and must pass through a long period of convalescence before they could once more make their contribution to the re-creation of national life. Finally, and worst of all, the Thirty Years' War had left the nation in moral collapse. Materials, men, and principles were equally lacking for the process of reconstruction.

Yet, amid this havoc and squalor, one sordid creature had set himself with grim craft and patient guile to rehabilitate his wasted inheritance and to procure title to other lands. Almost alone among German princes, Frederick William, Margrave-Elector of Brandenburg, contrived to extract from the congresses of Westphalia, not merely guarantees of his ancestral possessions undiminished, but also the recognition of a strange assortment of claims to scattered morsels of territory. Thus his possessions, actual or claimed, were the most extensive within the empire, though they were scattered widely and held under a curious diversity of titles. Out of this assortment of territorial and political junk he had the shrewd insight and dogged persistence to begin the organization of a consolidated state.

Where no element or principle of unity existed, Frederick William evolved in his own mind the idea of a state to whose creation he gave himself unsparingly, and relentlessly required that every subject should do likewise. Every element and process in the operation were crassly material. Men were not free creatures endowed with intelligence, wills, and desires; they were but pawns or slaves to the fixed purpose, and that without exception of child, or wife, or self. Moral scruple or question of principle was never allowed to cross the path. As the historian follows step by step the devious ways of the Great Elector he finds his moral sense protesting against almost every act, and yet he can not withhold recognition of the resultant achievements of territorial extension and consolidation, of unified and absolute monarchical power, of the army steadily developed in numbers and effectiveness, of state treasure amassed, of economic resourses steadily developed, and of population both recruited from abroad and once more expanding by natural growth. Here were the conditions out of which grew the enlightened despotism, the elemental processes of its development, and the basic factors in its character.

Despite their weaker characters, lesser abilities, and peculiar foibles, the son Frederick I and the grandson Frederick William I carried forward the work with definite though modest contributions to the fixed purpose. The great-grandson, Frederick II, was first of these Hohenzollerns with the genius and daring for aggressive measures.

In his first and second Silesian wars he risked the whole achieve-ment of three generations on the chance of a conspicuous conquest, and won, as much by his ruthless diplomacy as by military ability.

None the less this experience confirmed Frederick in the Hohen-zollern conception of the state and of the methods of its enhancement. He realized that the life and growth of the state were dependent upon the maintenance of an effective military machine, which in turn could be maintained and operated only with large and readily available financial power, which could alone be drawn from the fullest exploi-tation of the state's economic resources by the steady hard work of its subjects.

The ten years' truce which followed the treaty of Dresden (1745) might be described as the adolescent period of the enlightened des-potism. It still awaits proper study from this point of view, which is more important than the diplomatic one which has customarily held the attention. While Frederick devoted himself unremittingly during this interval to the improvement of his army and finances and to the development of the economic resources of his dominions, his defeated opponent, Maria Theresa, was not blind to the lessons of de-feat and set herself likewise with indefatigable earnestness to achieve in similar ways such results for Austria that the struggle might be re-newed, the lost provinces retrieved, and the national honor redeemed.

In his task Frederick conceived of himself as the first servant of the state. Unlike the Bourbon who could identify himself with the state, the Hohenzollern had been forced to conceive of the state as an entity apart from himself or his subjects though including them. The state was something above persons and more permanent and enduring than individuals. Such a concept could scarcely have been developed in England or France, while it was not an unnatural adaptation from the theory of the universal and paramount state which, rather than any concrete realization thereof, had subsisted for centuries as the Holy Roman Empire.

It appears, therefore, that the first efforts to practice as a deliber-ate policy the basic principles of the enlightened despotism began prior to the appearance of any of the important French writings mentioned previously and had been interrupted by the Seven Years' War before some of the more significant of them had appeared. This earliest phase of enlightened despotism was, then, little more than two parallel national campaigns of preparedness in two rival states, between two rival dynasties, in anticipation of a desperate military struggle for leadership within the German lands. On either side the purpose was the strengthening and girding of the state for aggrandizement; on the one hand to hold a recently captured prov-ince, on the other to recover that lost province, which each regarded as the key to the situation. Each side considered that the outcome of the struggle would be determined by the effectiveness of the marshaling of the resources of the state in support of its military program. The results justified the policy, for Frederick's own efforts retained the province which the consistent policy of his predecessors had made it possible for him to seize and it left him in the position of primacy in Germany. On the other hand, while Maria Theresa failed in these purposes, she emerged from the struggle with her powers greatly strengthened in her remaining dominions and in a position to recoup military losses in Germany through political gains in Italy and Poland.

It is also important to note that in both cases the monarch was dealing with lands devoid of geographic unity and awkwardly situated so that they lacked the natural and strategic frontiers which, in whole or in large measure, characterized England and France. Military power was essential to offset the lack of nature's gifts, in which matter Prussia labored under the more serious handicap. Furthermore, neither state could compare with England or France in the racial and linguistic homogeneity of its population, though in this respect the handicap of Austria was the more serious. In still other matters both states were at serious disadvantage as compared with England and France. Neither could enjoy the advantage of a compact and harmoniously developed and organized political system, for geography denied it to Prussia and race withheld it from Austria. Nor could either utilize the priceless heritage of historic solidarity with a venerable record of national cooperation in enduring severe tests and effecting glorious achievements which constitutes such powerful challenge to each new generation to maintain the honor of the national name and the security of the national estate. Then, again, neither Frederick nor Maria Theresa could rely upon their prestige, whether as individuals or as the hereditary chiefs of their respective dynasties, to rally their subjects to their support.

In each case, therefore, the consolidation of subjects and resources had to be achieved by other means. Policy must serve where nature and history failed. It was impossible to bide the time which should prove to each province and people its better welfare and larger opportunity within the state to which it happened to belong than might be its lot in any other possible state. The monarch must prejudge such decision and act for himself and his subjects on the assumed truth of such conclusion. He must not leave the question open to the slightest doubt; he must think and plan and act for himself and his subjects, and compel his subjects to cooperate in action without thinking. It was not the part of the subject to think, but only to obey as if under martial law. Popular or constitutional government was impossible of consideration. Neither the church nor feudalism could be relied upon as voluntary or self-convinced associates, for apparent self-interest might readily lead them to other conclusions. Despotism was the only possible solution, and it must follow a policy so obviously reasonable—enlightened—that it should not arouse any doubts but should secure, with a minimum of friction or delay, the maximum result.

Neither the monarch nor the monarchy, but the state, was the ultimate entity to which all else must be subordinate. The state was an utterly intangible and unembodiable thing but none the less extremely real. It was that policy which comprehended the necessities and ideals whose attainment bound sovereign and subjects alike to service for their realization as the absolute general welfare for the present and even more for the future. For the attainment of the ends of the state, coin or commodity, toil or life were alike things to be expended with frugality or with abandon, as circumstances might require. No benevolent sentiment or humane motive, but sheer cold reason—enlightenment, was to determine the methods to be pursued, or was to be considered as an end for which the state existed, though humanitarianism might very possibly chance to be incidental to both methods and aims. The ends sought were the permanency, security, and aggrandizement of the state, for these were the sole safeguards in the struggle for existence which lands and peoples so situated as Prussia and Austria have ever felt compelled to seek.

In conclusion, I can only emphasize the priority in the development of the policies of Frederick the Great and Maria Theresa to the appearance of the great creative writings of the French political and economic thinkers to whom has customarily been ascribed the initiative for the enlightened despotism. The exaltation of the state rather than of the monarch, the undermining of provincial rights and class privileges, the effort to secure uniformity in the incidence of governmental authority, the demand on the administrative system for efficiency, the efforts for codification of law and the reform of the judicial system, the aggressive instead of intriguing diplomacy, the more comprehensive demands for military service, the improved military organization, the more thorough systematization of the finances, the fuller recognition that government finances are dependent upon sound economic conditions—these all appeared in Frederick's policy in the first decade of his reign and were promptly copied with more or less success by Maria Theresa. On the religious side, the enlightenment was a personal, scarcely a governmental, interest with Frederick, and altogether abhorrent to Maria Theresa. It was only with Joseph II that this element developed as not merely a personal interest but also as a wide-reaching governmental policy.[1]

---

[1] In this paper no account has been taken of the reforming or enlightened ministers of the eighteenth century prior to 1763, for their interesting activities were only accidentally related to the enlightened despotism and belong properly to the history of political adventure, e. g. Law, Alberoni and Pombal.

IX. THE ESTABLISHMENT OF A NEW POLAND

By COL. LUCIUS H. HOLT, U. S. A.
United States Military Academy

THE ESTABLISHMENT OF A NEW POLAND

By Lucius H. Holt

The purpose of this paper is to discuss a single phase of the general subject. No attention will be paid, accordingly, to military, territorial, economic, and social issues, except as passing reference may be necessary to sketch in a background. I shall give a simple, direct narrative of Poland's efforts to solve her political problem. My object, then, more strictly defined, is: The reestablishment of a Polish government.

During the long period of subjection to foreign powers Polish leaders had never lost the hope that an opportunity might present itself to strike for an independent Poland. Two divergent policies existed—the first for a revived Poland under the good auspices of Austria-Hungary, whose government had extended liberal political rights to Galicia; the second for a revived Polish state living in friendship with the great Slav Russian nation. Both policies were, of course, directed toward ultimate independence for Poland.

The outbreak of the Great War was recognized by the Polish leaders as Poland's opportunity. Two important committees were at once formed to represent Polish interests, the first a Polish national council at St. Petersburg, with Wielopolski and Dmowski, Polish representatives in the Russian Duma, as organizers; and the second a supreme national committee at Cracow in Galicia, first with Doctor Leo and soon afterwards with Jaworski at its head, both men being Polish deputies to the Austrian Parliament.

So far as we are concerned, the activities of the Wielopolski-Dmowski group during the early years of the war need not delay us long. Its importance in the Russian theater was cut short after the Russian Revolution in 1917 and the subsequent break-up of Russia as a power. It later reorganized as the Polish national committee in Lausanne, Switzerland, August 15, 1917, with Dmowski as chairman, and Paderewski, Sobanski, Skirment, Zamojski, Piltz, and Fronczak as influential members. Later it moved to Paris. The part which this committee played in the closing scenes of the war and in the political affairs in Poland after the armistice we shall mention in due time.

We turn now to trace events within the boundaries of the distinctively Polish territories.   Jaworski's supreme national committee
received the support of important political groups in Galicia, and,
though not officially recognized by Austria-Hungary, became the
spokesman for the Polish policies and ideals.   In collaboration with
this committee, General Pilsudski undertook the recruiting of Polish
legions to engage against Russia in conjunction with the Austro-
Hungarian armies.   The committee's first manifesto ended with
these words:

Under Polish command, and in close connection with the chief direction of the
Austro-Hungarian army, the Polish legions will enter the struggle in order that they
may also throw upon the scales of the greatest war a deed worthy of the Polish nation,
as a condition and beginning of a brighter future.

Notice two facts with respect to this supreme national committee
and its activities.   In the first place, though it had the support of
influential groups in Galicia, it failed to receive general Polish recognition, largely because the people feared that its pro-Austrian policy
might defeat the ultimate object of Polish independence and leave
Poland at the end of the war bound to Austria and her ally, Germany.
In the second place, the cooperation of the Polish legions with the
Austro-Hungarian armies did not imply Polish sympathy with the
general cause and policies of the Central Powers.   The effort of the
Polish legions was directed against Russia, not to achieve victory for
the Germans, but to free Poland from one of the worst systems of
tyranny the modern civilized world has known.   Under agreement
with the Austro-Hungarian government, the Polish legions were to
be maintained as a separate military unit and were to be used only
against Russia.

For more than two years the supreme national committee in Poland
continued its existence, though always unauthorized and unofficial.
During this period, as we know, Poland became the cockpit of the
eastern theater of war.   The Russian hordes surged across the country both to the north and to the south, and were met and hurled
back by the German and Austrian armies.   In their retreat, the
Russians, on the plea of military necessity, devastated the land.   It
was not until the autumn of 1915 that the German-Austrian armies
established their lines along the eastern Polish boundaries.

With their country under German-Austrian control, the members
of the supreme national committee turned to the governments of the
Central Powers for recognition, but received little encouragement.
The German-Austrian armies held the lines, the German-Austrian
civil authorities took over the entire civil administration of the country, German-Austrian agents superintended the systematic requisi-
tioning of supplies, and the Central Governments began to exert
pressure upon the Poles to enlist in the German-Austrian bodies for

service on any front. Neither Germany nor Austria entertained favorably any idea of Polish independence so long as the country yielded supplies and there remained a chance of drawing recruits.

In the autumn of 1916 two prominent Poles, one in political and the other in military life, took steps to hasten the recognition of Polish independence. By the middle of August, Pilsudski requested permission to resign his command of the legionaries; following this request August 30 with a memorial to the supreme national committee requesting its cooperation in his plan to separate the legionaries from the Austro-Hungarian armies and to make them an autonomous independent Polish army. September 20, 1916, the Central Powers agreed to the principle of Pilsudski's memorial. In the meanwhile Ignace Daszynski, a prominent Socialist deputy in the Austrian Parliament, resigned early in September from the Polish Parliamentary Club at Vienna in the endeavor to influence the members of that important political club to demand from the Austro-Hungarian government a statement of its intentions with respect to the creation of an independent Polish state. A few days later the club did present such a memorial to the Austrian Parliament, and Daszynski, September 19, rejoined the club.

The action of Daszynski and Pilsudski convinced the German-Austrian governments, not only that nothing further was to be gained by delay, but that Polish sentiment might be swayed in their favor by a decided change of front. They therefore hastened negotiations. November 5, 1916, the Austro-Hungarian Emperor and the German Emperor issued a joint manifesto announcing that they had "resolved to form of these (Polish) territories an independent State with a hereditary monarchy and a constitutional government." ▪ This manifesto was greeted cordially as the first step toward achieving independence for a united Poland. A Polish provisional regent, known as the Marshal of the Crown, was appointed; and a council of state was organized, composed of all political parties, religious creeds, and social classes. On January 15, 1917, the new council of state met for the first time. The Polish legions, released by Austria from their allegiance, pledged their loyalty to the provisional Polish government and became the nucleus of the new Polish army. All political, civil, and religious bodies in Poland likewise pledged themselves to support the new government.

The leading Poles realized, however, that their dreams of a united Poland were still far from fulfillment. Germany indicated that Posnania was not to be a part of the new State; and Austria-Hungary announced new political powers to Galicia in a statement which showed that Austro-Hungarian control was to be maintained over that province. And further, the German governor general remained in Poland, interfered in Polish affairs, seized food supplies, transported thousands of Polish laborers to Germany, and demanded that the new Polish government raise a large army to fight under German command against the Allies. Pilsudski, followed by the bulk of the legionaries, not only refused to enlist to aid Germany, but began secretly to organize a new military force to act as opportunity offered against Germany. He was seized and imprisoned in the fortress of Magdeburg. The provisional government, disaffected by the turn of events and the lack of sympathy on the part of the Central Powers with Polish ambitions, was replaced by a new government September 12, 1917, composed of a regency council of three (Archbishop Kakowski, Prince Lubomirski, and Count Ostrowski) and a cabinet headed by Kucharewski. Whatever of prestige had remained for the supreme national committee was fatally weakened, for this committee was considered responsible for the relations between Poland and the Central Powers.

The climax to German perfidy, however, came in the treaty negotiation between the Central Powers and Russia at Brest-Litovsk in February, 1918. Without consulting the Poles, Germany ceded the Polish district of Kholm to the new state of Ukrainia in return for promised food supplies. All Poland protested at this conscienceless barter. The manifesto of November 5, 1916, was fully discredited; evidently it was but a "scrap of paper" in the sight of the Emperor. Kucharewski's cabinet resigned; the regency council published a bitter protest to the Central Powers; the Polish delegates in the German Reichstag introduced a resolution of protest there; and the Polish delegates in the Austro-Hungarian Parliament withdrew their support of the von Seydler cabinet, and von Seydler was forced to resign. Though the transfer of Kholm was never consummated, knowledge of the intention of the Central Powers was sufficient to destroy their credit with the Poles. The supreme national committee, its prestige now wholly destroyed, passed out of existence.

One good effect, however, the German-Austrian manifesto had. It forced the Polish problem upon the attention of the Allied Powers. These powers could not well promise less than the Central Powers had promised. Consequently, on January 8, 1918, President Wilson included the independence of Poland as number 13 of his famous fourteen points; and five months later (June 3, 1918) the representatives of the Entente Powers at Versailles issued a statement favoring "a free and independent Poland with access to the sea."

The tumult of the armistice period was now at hand. We all remember how suddenly the Austro-German power crumbled. Poles took immediate advantage of the new situation. During the confused days in late October and early November, 1918, separate governments were speedily organized in the three great divisions of Poland as the grip of the Central Powers relaxed. In Russian Poland, Pilsudski, returning November 10 from his German prison to receive the universal acclaim of his countrymen, accepted from the regency council the mission as chief of state to carry his country through to a constitutional government. A Socialist government, formed by Daszynski November 14, gave way a week later to a Socialist cabinet with Moraczewski as premier. In conjunction with Pilsudski, this cabinet bent all its energies to defending Poland against its most pressing enemies and to securing internal peace and order. In Galicia the Polish deputies to the old Austrian Parliament met at Cracow October 28, declared Austrian-Poland a part of the Polish State, and effected a temporary organization. This Galician group refused later, however, to recognize the Socialist government organized at Warsaw. In Posnania the Polish deputies to the old Reichstag and the Polish members of the Prussian chamber met November 18, arranged for a meeting of trusted representatives of the public December 3, and effected a temporary organization. This Posnanian group could not bring itself to recognize Pilsudski and the existing Warsaw government. It thereupon announced its recognition of the Polish national committee in Paris as representative of the interests of German Poland.

Pilsudski's problem was immeasurably increased in difficulty for the moment by the existence of these other Polish governments. He set himself resolutely to the task of establishing in Russian Poland a representative government, announcing November 28, 1918, that elections would be held January 26, 1919, for a constitutional assembly, and that every citizen of Poland, without distinction of race, religion, nationality, or sex, would have equal political rights and would be qualified to participate in the elections. At the same time he continued negotiations with the leaders in the other sections of Poland with the object of coming to a satisfactory agreement and achieving unity.

Before the date set for these elections in Russian Poland, the unendurable political situation had partially been cleared. Pilsudski and his Socialist government had the advantage of being established in what was universally recognized must be the heart and capital of the new Poland; but the Dmowski group, associated with whom was now the world-famous Paderewski, had the allegiance of Posnania and much sympathy in Galicia. Paderewski served as the agent in bringing about a compromise. When he entered Posnania in late December, 1918, the warmth of his welcome indicated the political complexion of the people as well as his own personal popularity. With this support, and with the common knowledge that his group was favored and recognized by the Allies, he passed over into Russian Poland, entered Warsaw the first of the new year, and conferred with Pilsudski. Just what passed between the two is not known, but it is suspected that Paderewski opened negotiations on the basis of the dismissal of Moraczewski and of certain other of the Socialist ministers. While negotiations were continuing, a group of men, led by Prince Sapieha and Colonel Januszajtis, and inspired by hostility to the social-ist tendencies of the Pilsudski-Moraczewski government, attempted on the night of January 4–5 a coup d'état. The coup was an opéra bouffe affair. The conspirators arrested the ministers, but the man sent to arrest Pilsudski failed, and the one sent to arrest the chief of staff of the army was himself put under arrest by that general. The follow-ing day Pilsudski at once secured the release of his ministers and him-self imprisoned a few of the suspects, among them Prince Sapieha. This attempted coup was not allowed to interfere with the progress of the negotiations, and a few days later Paderewski was invited to form a cabinet on a coalition basis. Paderewski accepted the mission and himself took office as Premier and Foreign Minister January 18, 1919, just eight days before the elections.

All interest was now centered upon these elections. Deputies to the number of 524 were to be chosen from the whole of Poland. Actually, of course, the elections could be held only in those parts of Poland under Polish control. To meet this situation, it was agreed that exceptional steps should be taken for the other parts of Poland. For Galicia 77 deputies were elected, and 94 were called from the old Austrian Parliament. In Posnania the election of the 112 deputies assigned was not held until June 1, the Posnanian deputies in the old German Reichstag sitting in the meanwhile. In Russian Poland, all the 241 deputies were elected. The representation of minorities was guaranteed by the adoption of a system of proportional representation.

The results of the election justified the high hopes of those who had confidence in the orderly political development of Poland. The National Bloc in support of the Paderewski government polled by far the largest number of votes. In Warsaw itself this bloc polled 150,000, the Jewish parties 74,000, and the Socialists only 42,000 votes, the bloc electing both Paderewski and Dmowski among their candidates. Of the total number of 318 representatives elected, the National Bloc had 109. Two weeks later, February 9, 1919, the first meeting of this constitutional assembly was inaugurated by religious ceremonies at the Church of St. John in Warsaw; and February 21, 1919, official announcement was issued that the Allies recognized the Polish government headed by Pilsudski as President and Paderew-ski as Premier.

These steps marked the completion of one distinct stage in Poland's progress toward the establishment of a new government. Her peo-ple had chosen a representative assembly, and her government had received the recognition of the victorious Allies. Much, however, still remained to be done. Perhaps, if we summarize briefly the gen-eral situation, the difficulties will be more apparent.

In the first place, Poland was surrounded by active enemies each of whom claimed territory which Poland regarded as distinctively Polish. The Germans had not given up Posnania; the Czechoslovaks were disputing the possession of the Teschen district; a shadowy Ukrainian government was holding eastern Galicia; the Soviet lines were still drawn too near Warsaw; and the Lithuanians expected Wilna. The allied recognition had contained no assurance of Poland's boundaries, so the Government felt it necessary to take active measures to secure what it considered to be Polish rights. Add to this territorial question the social unrest both among the laboring classes and among the peasantry; the racial antagonisms engendered by the presence of large self-conscious units of different blood and customs, as Jews, Ruthenians, and Germans; and throw over the whole scene the pall of a universal economic distress so paralyzing that we in this fat country can not appreciate it; and you may gain some faint conception of the general situation that confronted the Polish Government in the spring of 1919.

Although the Assembly had as its original purpose the creation of a constitution, the necessities of the situation prevented it from proceeding at once to this task. Through the spring and summer of 1919, all attention was concentrated upon the proceedings of the Peace Conference at Paris and Versailles. It was essential that Poland's boundaries should be assured before Poland's constitution could be drawn. Paderewski in person argued the Polish cause before the representatives of the Powers. Once, discouraged, he tendered his resignation to the Assembly (May 13, 1919), but the Assembly expressed its confidence in him and he retained his position. As Premier he signed the treaty of June 28, 1919, unsatisfactory as it appeared to be. During July he presented the treaty to the Assembly. July 31, 1919, the Assembly duly ratified the treaty. Poland's position was thus secured by an international covenant, signed by friends and enemies alike.

Even after the ratification of this treaty the Assembly found it impossible to proceed rapidly to the work of framing a constitution. Territorial questions were still to be settled, some by plebiscites and some by the Powers in the future; economic conditions presented constantly new problems calling for consideration and action; and military operations, especially on the Russian front, continued on a large scale. December 7, 1919, Paderewski resigned, being succeeded a week later by Skulski.

In the spring and summer of 1920 came the terrific Polish-Bolshevik campaign. At its height, Skulski was forced to resign June 9 in favor of a cabinet headed by Grabski. A month later, July 9, Grabski resigned and was succeeded by the peasant premier, Witos. We know how the Bolshevik menace was turned back, and how negotiations for a Russian-Polish peace were finally carried to a successful conclusion.   During all this troubled period, of course, slight progress could be made toward framing a permanent constitution.

Our story of the reestablishment of a Polish government must, then, be incomplete, for at the present date the constitution has not been adopted. Since the Russian-Polish armistice, however, the Assembly has been able to devote more time to its chief task.   The document under consideration contains 6 chapters and 131 articles. Chapter 1, containing articles 1 and 2, states the form of government, which will be that of a republic.   Chapter 2, containing articles 3 to 38, inclusive, deals with the legislature and prescribes a bicameral body.   Chapter 3, containing articles 39 to 75, inclusive, deals with the executive and his functions and powers.   Chapter 4, including articles 76 to 88, inclusive, deals with the judiciary.   Chapter 5, including articles 89 to 130, inclusive, deals with citizenship and the general rights and duties of citizens.   Chapter 6, containing a single article, prescribes the method of amending and changing the constitution.   Of the entire document, 113 of the articles have been agreed upon by the Assembly and have passed two readings.   Articles 35 and 36, concerning the upper house of the legislature, and article 39, concerning the election of the President of the Republic, are at present under discussion.

With this statement, which brings the story up to include the latest available information, I leave my outline of Poland's measures to reestablish a government.   The country's many other problems—territorial, military, social, and economic—still present the utmost difficulties, but the problem of a government is almost solved.

X. THE SETTLEMENT AT PLYMOUTH CONTEMPLATED BEFORE 1620

By LINCOLN N. KINNICUTT

Massachusetts Historical Society

97244°—25——14

THE SETTLEMENT AT PLYMOUTH CONTEMPLATED BEFORE 1620

By LINCOLN N. KINNICUTT

Was it by mere chance that the Pilgrims found Plymouth Harbor and Plymouth, or had schemes and plans been made by those most interested in the colonization of New England to attempt to bring them to this very spot? I am inclined to believe that before the *Mayflower* sailed from England Sir Ferdinando Gorges had made plans which, if successful, would lead to a settlement in Plymouth Harbor, a locality about which he was well informed and which he had reasons to believe was the most favorable location on the Massachusetts coast.

We owe much to Sir Ferdinando Gorges, much more than he has ever received, and in speaking of him as the father of New England colonization we give him a title he well deserves. His whole life is an interesting story, full of interesting episodes, stirring events, and narrow escapes from political intrigues and combinations, and even from royal displeasure. A man of sound judgment, of infinite resourcefulness and pertinacity, the motto on his coat of arms "Constans et Fidelis" was more truly symbolical of his character than is often found.

He was the son of Edward Gorges of Wraxall and a descendant of Ranoly de Gorges, who came from Normandy to the conquest of England in 1066. The exact date of his birth is not known but he was born about 1562. His whole life must have been influenced by the corrupt age in which his early manhood was passed, when royal favoritism, intrigue, and bribery, were apparently the only paths to position, power, or wealth.

Very little is known of Sir Ferdinando Gorges until 1588. At that time he was captain in the English army in Flanders, and was taken prisoner by the Spanish, probably at the siege of Sluis, but was immediately exchanged. The next year, 1589, he took part in the siege of Paris, where he was severely wounded. Documents tell us that he was borne from the walls by Henry of Navarre himself. In 1595 he was ordered to take charge of the erection of fortifications at Plymouth, and in 1596 he was appointed captain and keeper of the new fortification and of the island of St. Nicholas. He held this most important post for nearly 40 years, for Plymouth was deemed a vulnerable point for Spanish invasion. Queen Elizabeth, James I, and Charles I thus bore witness to their confidence in his ability and trustworthiness. In this long service there was one interim of three years, probably the most fateful years in his whole life, for he was a close friend of the Earl of Essex and had joined with him, although, I believe, unwillingly, in his conspiracy against the Queen. If he did betray his friend and benefactor, which was the belief and always remained the belief of the Puritans, although to-day doubted by many, it was the blot on his escutcheon.

The Earl of Essex for some incomprehensible reason was the great hero of the Puritans, and they ever remembered that tragic, stormy scene at his trial when Essex, turning to Gorges, said, "I pray you answer me, did you advise me to leave my enterprise?" And Gorges, answering, "I think I did." Essex replied, "Nay, it is no time to answer now upon thinking, these are not things to be forgotten. Did you indeed so counsel me?" And Gorges replying, "I did," he sealed the fate of his friend and forged a weapon that was used many years after to destroy practically his own great ambitions and many of the advantages which he had hoped to obtain in the New World. Essex's despairing final appeal to his judges was never forgotten by the Puritan party: "My Lords, look upon Sir Ferdinando and see if he looks like himself. All the world shall see by my death and his life whose testimony is the truest."

After the execution of Essex, Gorges, while in prison, expecting a sentence of death, wrote a bold, pathetic defense against the charge that he had betrayed Essex, his friend. After one year's imprisonment he was pardoned, and on the death of Queen Elizabeth in 1603 was reinstated in his former command at Plymouth.

If this was an age of intrigue, corruption, and bribery, it was also the age of adventure, discovery, and exploration. Sir Humphrey Gilbert and Sir Walter Ralegh belonged to that age and Gorges was their kinsman through the Champernouns. Spain was reaping a rich harvest from her conquests in Mexico and South America, and Sir Ferdinando had intimate knowledge of the great riches brought into English harbors by captured Spanish ships, for he was one of the commissioners to whose custody these great riches were intrusted.

In 1602 Gosnold returned from Buzzards Bay with a valuable cargo of furs and sassafras. In 1603 Martin Pring came from Cape Cod Bay with glowing accounts of the richness of the country, and in 1605 Weymouth explored a part of the coast of Maine, and on his return brought with him five savages, of whom Sir Ferdinando took charge of three. One of them, he tells us, was Tisquantum (Squanto) who, 15 years later, rendered to the Pilgrims indispensable service. From this time until his death, 40 years later, he devoted his extraordinary energy, his influence, and his wealth to the colonization of New England.

Although some historians have questioned this statement in regard to Tisquantum, nevertheless we certainly have Gorges's own statement that he had Squanto with him for three years in England, and in another part of his Narration, speaking of the letter containing news from Dermer that he had found Tisquantum in Maine, he writes of him as "one of my Indians." By this statement Tisquantum must have been under his care at some previous time. Gorges also tells us, in the same Narration, that he made his Indians give him minute details of their native places, of their rivers, of their lands, their chiefs, and their enemies.

Sir Ferdinando Gorges must have known much about Patuxet (Plymouth) and Plymouth Harbor, and even about Massasoit, for Tisquantum was a native of Patuxet and a subject of Massasoit. It is also reasonable to suppose that Sir Ferdinando had other very early knowledge of Plymouth, for he was indefatigable in searching for, and acquiring, all information possible of northern Virginia, his territory.

We know that Martin Pring was at New Plymouth in 1603, living there for six weeks with 40 of his men, naming it Mount Aldworth and calling the harbor Whitsons Bay. He gave minute descriptions of the place and harbor, of the surrounding country, and of the products of the land.

Samuel de Champlain's account of Plymouth, in which he named it Port de Malabarre, was published in 1613.

In the month of April, 1614, Captain John Smith, with whom we associate Virginia and Pocahontas far more than New England and Plymouth, although he gave New England its name, was sent by a few English merchants to the north part of Virginia "to take whales and make tryalls of a myne of Gold and Copper." In August, 1614, on Smith's return to England he immediately reported his adventures and his discoveries to Sir Ferdinando Georges, "his honorable friende." From this circumstance it is a fair supposition that Gorges had taken much interest in John Smith's comtemplated voyage and may have given him certain instructions in respect to exploring the New England coast.

To Sir Ferdinando Gorges he would have given the description and the name of the various towns afterwards published, and of Plymouth he says, "then came you to Accomack (Plymouth), an excellent good harbor, good landing, and no want of anything but industrious people."

On the map that Captain John Smith published the next year, when English names were substituted, is inscribed "The most remarkable parts thus named by the high and mighty Prince Charles, Prince of Great Britain."

At this time Prince Charles was only 15 years old, and probably the English names adopted were suggested to him by some one much interested in that part of the New World. From whatever source it came, the rechristening of Accomack as Plymouth must have been pleasing to Sir Ferdinando, for he loved old Plymouth well, where he had already spent nearly 20 years of his life.

John Smith's glowing account of New England, with its wonderful climate, its fertile soil and its mineral wealth, the abundance of fish, birds, and animals (he called Massachusetts "the Paradise of all these parts"), aroused the mercantile and venturesome spirit of the English, and spurred Sir Ferdinando to greater efforts to accomplish what had become the chief object of his life—the colonization of New England and the establishing on its shores of at least one plantation.

He had already experienced many failures. His first attempt was in 1605, when he sent a ship under the command of Capt. Henry Challons, with the intention of settling a colony on the coast of Maine. This was a complete failure, owing to Captain Challons' disobedience of orders. In 1607, in cooperation with Chief Justice Popham, Gorges attempted the Popham Colony, so called, the earliest settled colony in New England, for it existed for one year, but, as we know, was abandoned in the fall of 1608.

The attempts were made under the charter of the Plymouth Company, first granted in 1606, which company in 1620 was called the Council of New England. Sir Ferdinando Gorges was practically the Plymouth Company and the Council of New England, for without his leadership and his constant petitions to Parliament and to the throne the Plymouth Colony would probably have been overshadowed by the South Virginia or the London Company.

After receiving the report of Capt. John Smith and after the arrival of Smith's second ship, commanded by Capt. Thomas Hunt, which had also been sent to Plymouth to secure a cargo for the Old World, Sir Ferdinando began more active operations.

Two months after the arrival of Smith at Plymouth Sir John Hawkins, who had been chosen president of the Plymouth Council, attempted a voyage to New England which was unsuccessful, and Gorges opened negotiations with Captain Smith to undertake the planting of a colony on the Massachusetts coast. Smith was supplied with two ships, but, when only a short distance from England, the larger was disabled and he was obliged to return. Repairs being made he again started, but his ship was captured by a French cruiser and he was carried a prisoner into a French port. In 1616 Gorges dispatched another ship under Richard Vines, with the same unsuccessful result. In 1617 Smith, who had returned to England,

as supplied by the council with three small ships to make again a
enture, but the ships were becalmed and after much delay returned
) the harbor and the attempt was given up.

One of the two ships supplied to John Smith in 1615 was under
1e command of Capt. Thomas Dermer, who also was in the employ
f Sir Ferdinando Gorges, and this small vessel reached Newfound-
.nd in safety. We know but little of Captain Dermer for the next
vo years, although it is supposed he remained in Newfoundland,
)r in 1618 Gorges received communication from him in Newfound-
.nd that he had found Tisquantum. Gorges immediately gave
1structions to have Tisquantum sent to him, and in the latter part
f 1618 Captain Dermer, with Tisquantum, arrived in England.
orges states in his Narration that after consulting with Dermer in
lation to "particulars of highest consequence and best considera-
ons," he sent him back as fast as one Gorges's own ships could be
1ade ready, and Tisquantum went with him.

This was early in 1619. Dermer was to meet Captain Rowcroft,
ho had been sent out the year before, and was to carry out certain
)ecific plans and wait for further instructions from Gorges. Dermer
1d not find Rowcroft, but, as Gorges narrates, "so resolved he was
1at he ceased not to follow the designs already agreed upon," part
' which evidently was to explore Tisquantum's own country, Ply-
.outh. From a letter written to Sir Samuel Purchase, dated
ecember 27, 1619 we know Dermer certainly did this important
ork, guided by Tisquantum.

The land in the immediate vicinity of Plymouth he found unoccu-
.ed, for the Patuxet Tribe, whose home it was, had been entirely
vept away by the so-called plague. Tisquantum found not one of
s own tribe remaining. They travelled two days' journey to the
est, and two Indian kings came to visit them, probably Massasoit
1d his brother, Quadaquina.

Evidently Gorges was kept well informed in regard to Dermer's
ovements, for he states that Dermer sent him a journal of his pro-
edings and a description of the coast all along as he passed. From
ymouth he went to Capawac, Marthas Vineyard, probably in search
a mine, and then returned to Monhegan. Leaving Tisquantum in
aine, he went to Virginia, but, returning in the spring of 1620, on
s way north to Monhegan he again visited Plymouth and probably
squantum joined him there. It is this visit which is referred to by
)vernor Bradford in his History of Plymouth Plantation.

This Mr. Dermer was here the same year that these people came, as appears by a
ation written by him and given me by a friend bearing date June 30 Anno. 1620.
d they came in November following, so ther was but 4 months difference. In
ich relation to his honored friend, he hath these passages of this very place.
: will first begine (saith he) with that place from whence Squanto, or Tisquantum,
s taken away; which in Capt. Smiths mape is called Plimoth; and I would that

Plimoth had the like commodities. I would that the first plantation might hear be seated, if ther come to the number of 50 persons, or upward. Otherwise at Charlton, because ther the savages are less to be feared. The Pocanawkits, which live to the west of Plimoth, bear an invetrate malice to the English, and are of more streingth than all the savages from thence to Penobscote. * * * The soil of the borders of this great bay, may be compared to most of the plantations which I see in Virginia.

In the botume of the great bay is store of codd and basse, or mulett, etc. But above all he comends Pacanawkite for the richest soyle, and much open gronnd fitt for English graine, etc.

In 1619 Thomas Dermer remained in Tisquantum's country for five or six days at least, exploring the country about Plymouth.

It would be most interesting to know more about this letter, to know to whom it was written, and for what purpose. Did Governor Bradford see it before he sailed from England? We should like to know the exact contents of the letter, for Governor Bradford omitted part. Probably it was written to Sir Ferdinando Gorges, for Dermer was in his employ, and as the *Mayflower* did not sail from England until September, the letter could have been given to Bradford before that time. Evidently Capt. Thomas Dermer had decided that Plymouth was the place above all others to make a settlement, and from this letter he apparently made a much closer study of the locality and all the surrounding conditions than he had made on his first visit the year before. He speaks particularly about the Pocanawkets. This was the name given to the Indians who comprised the Pocanawket Confederacy, and included at least nine tribes living in Bristol, Plymouth, and Barnstable Counties and part of Worcester County. This confederacy also exercised some authority in Nantucket and Marthas Vineyard, and Massasoit was their chief, and Plymouth and all the land about Plymouth was their territory. Dermer speaks of them as the strongest of all the confederacies and tells of the malice they bore to the English, and the reason. But he also speaks of Squanto, or Tisquantum, as having enough influence among them to save his life, and Squanto was one of their own tribe. After all, Dermer commends Pocanawket, an Indian village two days' journey from Plymouth, for the richest soil and much open ground fit for English grain.

Did he rely on Tisquantum being able to establish friendly relations, should a colony be established at Plymouth? If he did so, he certainly judged wisely, as subsequent events proved.

Sir Ferdinando Gorges, writing in 1622, says of Thomas Dermer: "He remained in the discovery of that coast two years, giving us good content in all his undertakings; and after he had made the peace between us and the savages that so much abhorred our nation for the wrongs done them by others, as you have heard; but the fruit of his labor in that behalf we as yet receive to our great commoditie, who have a peaceable plantation at the present time among them, where our people both prosper, and live in good taking and assuredness of their neighbors." (This was Plymouth.)

This good understanding, however, was in my opinion all accomplished by Tisquantum, for from the first he seemed to have much influence among the Indians. After this visit to Plymouth, Dermer went again to Monhegan and in July or in August again returned to Cape Cod Bay, and Bradford states that Tisquantum was with him.

This brings us to within a comparatively few weeks before the Pilgrims were expected to land on our coast, for their plans had been made for a departure from England about July 23, 1620. As we know, the plans were unexpectedly changed. If they had landed on Cape Cod at the expected time they could scarcely have failed of meeting Captain Dermer.

Capawick (Marthas Vineyard) seems to have been one of the objective points for many of Sir Ferdinando Gorges's ventures, and this was on account of supposed mines which, from Indian tales, he believed would be discovered on Marthas Vineyard or Nantucket.

At this time the first object for which he was striving was to find the most desirable place on the Massachusetts coast to plant a colony and then to establish it; and his second object was to find new sources of wealth in the New World.

In 1619 Captain Dermer had explored every harbor from the Penobscot to Cape Cod, according to Gorges, and had visited Capawick. In 1620 he had again explored the country about Plymouth, had decided it was the best place for a colony and had so written, and then, going to Monhegan, had returned to the Cape Cod coast and to Capawick, where he supposed he had established friendly relations with the Indians.

If Dermer wished for any reason to meet the Pilgrim ship, Marthas Vineyard and Nantucket offered many advantages for obtaining early information of its arrival. It would have been almost impossible for a ship to approach Cape Cod from any direction without it being known, at least by the Indians, and Squanto was with Dermer as an interpreter and intermediator. The distance across the Cape at a point opposite Capawick is very short.

It has been the accepted theory that Captain Jones of the *Mayflower* was bribed by the Dutch to prevent the Pilgrims from landing in the vicinity of the Hudson River, but this suspicion rests solely on the statement of Nathaniel Morton in his Memorial—"That they (the Dutch) had fraudulently hired the said Jones for this purpose." In a note he makes the positive assertion "of this plot between the Dutch and Mr. Jones I have late and certain intelligence." The source of "this late and certain intelligence" has never come to light. The assertion rests on one man's judgment of the value of this intelligence. Morton's Memorial was written 50 years after the landing of the Pilgrims, and it is supposed that he obtained his information from his friend Thomas Willet, who had access to the Dutch archives. Sir Ferdinando Gorges has also been suspected of conspiracy with the commander of the *Mayflower*, and certainly his early education had not failed to teach him that bribery was legitimate and almost a virtue.

Admitting, however, that the captain might have been bribed by the Dutch, this would not preclude the possibility of his being bribed also by Sir Ferdinando, and we must consider how much more valuable the result of this supposed bribery would have been to Gorges than to the Dutch.

No documents or letters have been discovered, so far as I have any knowledge, showing any correspondence between Sir Ferdinando Gorges and the Pilgrims, but there are a few established facts which indicate that there may have been some private understanding between some of the English partners and Sir Ferdinando, and this complete silence on his part, for which there were some very adequate reasons, is in itself suspicious.

In 1619–20 the Puritan party in England had become very strong. The Reform Parliament was almost a Puritan Parliament, for the ghost of Essex was there demanding reparation and reprisal upon Sir Ferdinando Gorges. If the King had not dissolved that Parliament, Sir Ferdinando would have suffered severely in his rights and privileges in the New World, but enough had been accomplished to make him recognize that the past was not forgotten.

Although the Pilgrims or Separatists were only a very small part of the Puritan party, nevertheless they were Puritans, and if it were known that Gorges was attempting to influence them to settle under his charter undoubtedly it would have encountered bitter opposition, and consequently any correspondence or understanding necessarily would have been well guarded.

Sir Ferdinando Gorges must have known all about the negotiations which had been carried on for about three years between the South Virginia Company or London Company and the Pilgrims. Among his sources of information was John Gorges, his eldest son, who had married a daughter of the Countess of Lincoln, who took a decided interest in American colonization; moreover the second patent from the South Virginia Company to the Pilgrims was taken out in the name of John Whincop, a member of the family of the Countess of Lincoln.

It is certainly reasonable to suppose that Sir Ferdinando Georges, knowing the character and standing of the body of men who proposed to establish a colony in the New World, would have had them settle in that territory which came under his charter, and there are a few facts which indicate that there may have been some private understanding between some of the leaders and Sir Ferdinando.

November 10 or 11, 1620, the Pilgrims sighted Cape Cod. On the 11th, only a few hours afterwards, even before they landed, the memorable Compact was drawn up. The preamble follows: "Having undertaken for the glorie of God and advancemente of the Christian faith and honor to our King and countrie a voyage to plant the first colonie in the northern parts of Virginia." This seems to permit a possible understanding with the North Virginia Company, and that New England had been considered before the departure from England or Holland. And Winslow writes in his brief Relation, referring to the first plans of the Pilgrims, "for our eye was upon the most northern parts of Virginia."

If, as it is supposed, the Pilgrims, many months before they left England, had decided to plant their colony near the Hudson River, it seems almost inconceivable that such men as Bradford, Winslow, and Standish would so suddenly have changed their preconceived plans, unless a settlement on the Massachusetts coast had previously been considered. It is certainly not consistant with their known characters. A settlement near the Hudson River would have been in the South Virginia territory.

Almost immediately after it was known that the landing had been made at Plymouth, a patent was issued to them by Sir Ferdinando Georges without, so far as is known, any previous attempt to discuss conditions or privileges, and was immediately accepted by the settlers. And the question still arises, when did Governor Bradford first see that letter written by Dermer to his "honored friend ?"

No doubt can exist that the Pilgrims were well acquainted with Capt. John Smith's glowing description of New England and of that part of the coast where they had first landed, and that they had his map to consult. Also without doubt they knew of Champlain's, Pring's and Gosnold's descriptions, and probably had seen the letter of Capt. Thomas Dermer to Samuel Purchase.

Is it unreasonable to suppose that Capt. Thomas Dermer was on the Massachusetts coast and at Plymouth for some definite object only a short time before the Pilgrims' expected landing ? It certainly would have been a wise move of Sir Ferdinando Gorges to have one of his captains ready to meet them, or to try to intercept them on their approach to this country. He would have been able to give them all the advantage of his knowledge and experience.

If it had not been for unforseen accident, Capt. Thomas Dermer undoubtedly would have met the Pilgrims on their arrival at Cape Cod, and they, judging from their attempts to find a suitable harbor, would gladly have accepted any guidance, even if unexpected, and Dermer undoubtedly would have taken them to Plymouth, the place where he had expressed a wish that "the first plantation might hear be seated."

Taking into consideration that for 14 years, ever since 1606, Sir Ferdinando Gorges had attempted unsuccessfully to settle a colony under the North Virginia charter, would he not have used all the means in his power to establish this Plymouth colony? The project had been considered in England and Holland for three years. He knew the standing and the character of the men who composed it, and who proposed to make this settlement. He knew that their chief aim was not wealth but to secure a permanent home. And would he not most naturally have attempted to influence their leaders or put in their way the means of going? For two years he had been planning just such an enterprise. He had already been much influenced by Capt. John Smith's glowing accounts of Massachusetts, and now Dermer supplemented Smith's story. Pring and Gosnold had told their tales of the country in the vicinity of Cape Cod, and had brought back most substantial results. Sir Ferdinando Gorges had in his possession much valuable information to give to the Pilgrims, and he without doubt took measures to have them receive all the information possible. Champlain's and Smith's maps had both been published, and both described Plymouth Harbor minutely.

If there was any understanding with Sir Ferdinando Gorges, the scheme was almost frustrated by an encounter with the Indians on the Isle of Capawick, where Dermer was so severely wounded that he was obliged to go immediately to Virginia. There he shortly afterwards died from his wounds. But the captain and pilot of the *Mayflower* remained, and Squanto; and if the officers of the ship had been bribed by Gorges to land the Pilgrims on the Massachusetts coast in the vicinity of Cape Cod, Sir Ferdinando would have given them all necessary information that he had received from Dermer in regard to Cape Cod Bay.

Governor Bradford tells us that "on the 6th. of December they sent out their shallop again, intending to circulate that deep bay of Cape Cod," and their pilot, a Mr. Coppin was with them. After thus spending two days "they decided to hasten to a place that their pillot did assure them was a good harbor" of which he had knowledge "and they might fetch it before night." About the middle of the afternoon he told them he saw the harbor, but in encountering the storm the mast of the boat was broken and when finally approaching the entrance to Plymouth Harbor, obscurely seen through the darkness and the storm, Governor Bradford writes that Coppin suddenly exclaimed, "the Lord be merciful unto them for his eyes had never seen that place before," but half blinded by the night and the tempest he probably was himself deceived. He had recognized the harbor only a few hours before the approach of the storm, and it was the only harbor which he could "fetch" in the time he himself had specified. If he was following any instructions or guidance received

fore he left England, he certainly had followed them, for he brought
ə Pilgrims to the exact spot selected by Dermer for a "first colony
be established on the Massachusetts coast," and Dermer had so
itten to those most interested in this colonization. - Call it coinci-
nce if you will, but it was very fortunate for Sir Ferdinando Gorges.
Two months afterwards, when the Pilgrims first met Massasoit at
ymouth, they were met by his two messengers, Samoset and
uanto, with the first cordial greeting of the New World to the Old
ɔrld, "Welcome Englishman."

I can not claim that Sir Ferdinando Gorges was the father of
ymouth, but he had provided for her a habitation, he had provided
her nurses, and I believe he was the consultant physician before
r birth.[1]

: wish to acknowledge my indebtedness to James Phinney Baxter for information derived from his
r Ferdinando Gorges and his Province of Maine," published by The Prince Society in 1890, and to
thington C. Ford for information derived from his notes in "The History of Plymouth Plantation,"
lished by the Massachusetts Historical Society in 1912.

I. CAPITALISTIC AND SOCIALISTIC TENDENCIES IN THE PURITAN COLONIES

By CLIVE DAY

Yale University

CAPITALISTIC AND SOCIALISTIC TENDENCIES IN THE PURITAN COLONIES

By Clive Day

If the Pilgrim of 300 years ago could return to life and survey the
ctivities of the present world, what change would strike him most,
hat features of our life would be to him least intelligible? Human
ature, in the individual, is much the same. He would not agree
ith our theology, and would differ with us on points of ethics, but
e would be well prepared to dispute the points of difference with
s, and might possibly be able to give us advice that would be to
ur advantage. Our politics would seem to him not very different
om his; would seem, maybe, not very much better. Our system of
cial classes has altered in some respects, but it remains still much
ke that in which he lived. Some of our attainments, notably in the
rts and sciences, would indeed astonish him. But that aspect of
ur life which would most surprise him when he saw its superficial
anifestations, and would most perplex him when he sought to
nderstand its operation, would be, I feel sure, our material civiliza-
on. Even when he had become used to the externals—the food
nd drink and clothing and housing; the omnipresent engine, whether
eam or gasoline or electric, and the inevitable machine operated
y it—he would find himself at the threshold of a deeper problem.
; would be his task, namely, to understand an organization far more
aborate and delicate than any machine, the organization of the
man beings by whom and for whom the machines are run. The
mple system of economic cooperation which prevailed in England,
: Holland, or America in the seventeenth century would scarcely
ggest to him the intricacies of the present system. Nor could he
rn to Aristotle for enlightenment, as he might still in a matter of
hics or politics. Economics is still a young science.
Imagine now the amazement of our Pilgrim when he is assured
at he bears a share of personal responsibility for these changes in
onomic life; that he, as a Puritan, was an important contributor
the process of economic revolution. Such is the suggestion soberly
lvanced by a German scholar of standing, Max Weber, who until
s death this past year was professor at Heidelberg. He follows

back the line of development which has led to our present elaborate organization, and his path takes him to early Massachusetts. I do not follow him in his conclusions, as will appear in the course of this paper. To understand his argument, and to criticize it effectively, we must first review the general subject of capitalism, the subject to which he and other German scholars have devoted so much attention in recent years.

"Capitalism" is a vague term, yet I think its meaning is sufficiently obvious for present purposes.[1] It implies a dominance at the present time of capital, just as we might use the terms feudalism or terrorism to suggest the dominance of some other element at another time. It is, I believe, the best word that we can use to characterize the present stage of industrial progress. The whole material equipment of our civilization is capital. Our activities are regulated, to a considerable degree determined, by capitalists. The share of enjoyment that each of us gets from life comes to him not as the immediate product of his own exertions, but as a complex of the products and services of other people; and on every path that leads from producer to consumer stands the capitalist. It is he, more than any other individual, who has made the economic world what it is to-day.

We sometimes refer to the present period as the age of machinery, and the term is sufficiently accurate if we seek merely to describe the technical processes of production. It is superficial and misleading when applied to the vital processes of our economic life. The machines that we see all about us have not grown up of themselves. They have been invented and constructed to the order of the capitalist. They did not make him; he made them.

The Germans are right, therefore, when they have fixed on capitalism as the distinctive mark of our present industrial organization, and they have done good service to history when they have directed attention to the problem of the origins of capitalism. They have followed bold methods in their inquiries, and have propounded conclusions of which some have already been disproved. I shall not enter on the large questions involved, but must sketch briefly their formulation of the problem, to illustrate these methods and at the same time to introduce properly the particular question of the contribution of the Puritan colonies to the capitalistic movement.

The problem of the origin of capitalism is in their view twofold. It involves, first, a study of the conditions of society at any period. Was there in existence a fund of money sufficient to make possible

---

[1] In recent years protests have been made against the loose use of the term "capitalism," which indeed has been applied by different authors in very different meanings. Compare articles by Passow in *Jahrbücher für Nationalökonomie*, October, 1916, vol. 107, p. 433 ff., by Diehl in Schmoller's *Jahrbuch für Gesetzgebung*, 1920, vol. 44, p. 203 ff. It seems unnecessary to seek here to refine the concept.

its active circulation ? Were contracts in terms of money facilitated by the effective administration of a rather advanced code of law ? Was there a considerable group of dependent laborers, the germ of the later "proletariat," forced to seek a livelihood by working for others ? These questions suggest a group of conditions, some of them external and material, all of them more or less objective and unconscious, which must be satisfied before capitalism in its present form could develop. But alone by themselves these conditions do not create capitalism. They make it possible, but not necessary. Capitalism as a living institution must wait until the capitalist himself appears.

There is, therefore, another set of conditions, termed subjective, which must be satisfied before the *idea* of capitalism springs up, before individuals see the opportunity, cast off the inherited notions which would hamper them in exploiting it, and by their success make the idea of capitalism current, and found a class of capitalists. According to this view the capitalist proper is as different from the individual human beings of a preceding period as is the capitalistic society from the simpler society out of which it grew. Let us consider for a moment the typical characteristics of the present-day capitalist as they are presented in Sombart's analysis.[2]

First of all, he must have the qualities of the successful *entrepreneur*, of the man who will undertake great things and who can execute them. He must be an organizer, able to judge men and to coordinate their activities to advance his own ends; he must be a bargainer, with the instinct for making money out of every contract; he must be a conqueror, with ambitious aims and the persistence that does not accept defeat. And he must be something more than all these things. Qualities such as those indicated are dangerously egoistic. They promise, to an individual or a class, a brilliant career, but threaten a short one. They must be balanced by some element which will reduce the strain of motives and will stabilize the capitalist's activities. Such an element Sombart finds in what he calls the bourgeois or middle-class virtues as they are displayed in the life of the conservative business man, the good citizen, the prudent father of a family. Benjamin Franklin is a type of this class; Poor Richard's Almanac is the bible from which its texts are taken.

The capitalist spirit, it will be noted, is a complex of different and contrasting elements. Like other historical phenomena, it must have been the product of slow growth. It must have grown up in a hostile atmosphere. Anything so new and strange as this combination would surely be opposed by all the traditions of a society clinging to its past. The investigator who seeks the origin of the capitalist spirit

---

[2] This summary follows Werner Sombart, Der Bourgeois, Leipzig, 1913, which has been translated by M. Epstein under the title "The Quintessence of Capitalism." Sombart reproduces these views with no great change in the revised edition of Der Moderne Kapitalismus, vol. 1 (1916), p. 322 ff., p. 836 ff.

must explain how the elements that composed it were supplied, and particularly how they were protected in their development by the very society which they were destined eventually to destroy.

Here we come at last to the Puritan, who has been kept so long in the background of this paper. In the religious beliefs and the ethical principles of Protestant sects Weber finds one of the essential sources of the capitalist spirit. He finds the germs of the capitalist spirit long before capitalism itself developed. In the southern colonies of America, in spite of the fact that they were founded by men of property for purposes of gain, he finds the capitalist spirit far less developed than in Massachusetts, which was founded for religious reasons by ministers and college graduates, by simple artisans and yeomen. The capitalist spirit developed there just because it was sheltered by the shield of religion.[3]

The Puritan doctrine, according to this view, harmonized the quest of profit with the quest of God, and gave an ethical basis to the economic standard of worldly success. It did not condemn riches as such, or the pursuit of riches. Riches were, indeed, a danger by inviting to repose, but became an evil only when they were enjoyed. Spending, the enjoyment of wealth, became a vice; saving, the employment of wealth to get more wealth, became a virtue. Is not that, we are asked, the very essence of capitalism?

The particular doctrine of the Puritans which Weber most stresses as a root of the capitalist spirit is the doctrine of the "calling." This gave an ethical, even a religious, basis to the precept that man on earth must not merely work hard; he must work profitably. A few extracts from Baxter's Christian Directory will illustrate the position.[4]

It is for *Action* that God *maintaineth us* and our *abilities*: *work* is the *moral* as well as the *natural* End of *power*. . . . It is *Action* that God is most served and honored by. . . . If God shew you a way in which you may lawfully get more than in another way, (without wrong to your soul or to any other) if you refuse this and choose the less gainful way, you cross one of the ends of your Calling, and you refuse to be God's Steward, and to accept his gifts, and use them for him when he requireth it: You may labour to be *Rich for God*, though not for the *flesh* and sin.

---

[3] Max Weber, "Die protestantische Ethik and der 'Geist' des Kapitalismus," Archiv für Sozialwissenschaft (1905), vol. 20, pp. 1–54, vol. 21, pp. 1–110. An article by P. T. Forsyth, "Calvinism and capitalism," Contemporary Review (1910), vol. 97, pp. 728–741, vol. 98, pp. 74–87, was stimulated by Weber and reproduces many of his views.

[4] Richard Baxter, A Christian Directory: or a Summ of Practical Theologie and Cases of Conscience. Second edition, London, 1678, folio, Tome 1, ch. 10, pt. 1, p. 376 ff., "Direction about our Labour and Callings." Another exposition of this view occurs in an anonymous pamphlet, "Truth, a letter to the gentlemen of Exchange Alley," London, 1733. It is a vice, says the author, to detest and refuse riches. I cite in modernized spelling. "For this is refusing the means and the opportunities of doing good, and putting it out of a man's power to practice many excellent and beneficial virtues. There needs but little consideration to convince us, that the using riches as one ought, and getting an absolute dominion over them is a task much more laborious and difficult than the being content under the want of them; and a prudent and virtuous behaviour in poverty is more attainable than a steady goodness in the midst of plenty." The dedicatory epistle of the pamphlet is signed by F. G., F. R. S., but I find no one with the initials F. G. listed as a member of the Royal Society at the time.

I shall not stop to review the criticisms which Weber's work has called forth from continental scholars. I shall leave aside the questions first whether the doctrine of the "calling" of English nonconformers was peculiar to them, and secondly, whether the aspect of it which I have sketched was really characteristic of them. I shall confine myself to a statement of what I have found in the history of the Puritan colonies.

The sources which I have consulted fall, for the most part, into two categories—sermons and laws. To the sermons of the time I look for an expression of the ethical ideals proclaimed by the spiritual leaders of the people for the guidance of their flocks.[5] In the laws we find a record of the attempts to bring to practical realization such ideals as might be imposed in the form of rules by sovereign authority.

Let us consider that document absurdly advertised as "the first sermon preached in New England,"[6] which certainly was printed in England in 1622 and which purports to be a discourse delivered at Plymouth in New England in 1621. Whether or not the tradition is well founded that ascribes it to Robert Cushman, and fixes the spot in Plymouth where he preached in November or December, 1621, the document is certainly a good source for the study of Puritanism in the Pilgrim colony. To those who seek there the germs of the capitalist spirit the sermon gives cold comfort. It is entitled "The Sin and Danger of Self-Love." It is based on a text from the first epistle to the Corinthians, "Let no man seek his own: But every man another's wealth." These points are not in themselves decisive, for it is of the essence of Weber's argument that concealed under such banners as these the capitalistic spirit was going forth to conquer. Let us therefore look further in the sermon, seeking particularly the Puritan doctrine of the "calling." We find, indeed, a reference to it, when Paul is quoted as criticizing "such as were negligent in their labors and callings." But the point of Paul's criticism, as it appeared to the preacher, was the effect of negligence in limiting charity, its reaction on the consumption of wealth, not on production. The very first to be condemned by the preacher among those who "seek their own" are "such as are covetous, seek their own by seeking riches, wealth, money." The sermon indeed introduces a distinction. "Here is the difference between a covetous worldling and an honest, thrifty Christian; it is lawful sometimes for men to gather wealth, and grow rich, even as there was a time for Joseph to store up corn; but a godly and sincere Christian will see when this time is, and will not hoard up when he seeth others of his brethren and associates to want."

[5] Of the sermons I should estimate that I have consulted several score, but have kept no exact record. Most of them yield nothing for the purpose in view, and I have not attempted to examine even all of those in the Yale Library.

[6] Self-Love, by Robert Cushman, 1621, reprinted by Comstock, New York, 1847.

That is the gist of the sermon on this crucial issue. A man may lawfully gather riches, but nowhere is he exhorted so to do, and the general attitude of the preacher toward those who seek wealth is openly contemptuous. "The greatest scratchers and scrapers and gatherers of riches" are fools.

In the later literature of the Puritans in America, I find, indeed, some doctrines which lend themselves more readily to the support of Weber's view that qualities destined to further the development of a capitalist society were being fostered by religious teaching in the Colonies.

The most complete and systematic treatment of the doctrine of the calling which I have found is contained in the "Compleat Body of Divinity" of Samuel Willard, pastor of the South Church in Boston and vice president of Harvard College.[7] There one finds a detailed discussion not only of the "effectual calling," a theological mystery with which we have nothing to do, but also of the "general calling" in the service of God, and the "particular calling" which treats "the lawful procuring and furthering of our own and our Neighbour's Wealth or outward estate," the "way to prosperity." I will cite a few passages to illustrate his point of view; they are the more significant because Willard is seeking to justify in connection with them the practice of loans at interest.

God hath given to Men their Estates for their outward Benefits. . . . There is therefore an Honest Gain to be moderately sought in the Improvement of such Estates. . . . It is true, our prosperity depends upon God's Favour; but we are to seek it in the Use of *Man's* and that is by *Improvement*; for these are perishable things, and will, without such Care and Endeavour go to decay, as common Experience will daily teach us. That therefore which I shall only here assert in general is, that meerly to advance our Estate by the *turning* of it, is not in itself a *Sin*, but a *Duty* to endeavour it; and that there is an Honest way so to do, and this may be in a Lawful Calling.[8]

The only sermon devoted to this subject, which I have found, is contained in Cotton Mather's "Two brief Discourses. One directing a Christian in his General Calling; Another directing him in his Personal Calling," printed at Boston in 1701. Every Christian has "a *Personal Calling*; or, a certain *Particular Employment* by which his *Usefulness* in his Neighborhood is distinguished," and which must not be allowed to encroach on the duties of his general calling. Every one, even a gentleman, should show a calling; it should be legitimate, agreeable, and entered on with a suitable disposition; every Christian

---

[7] A Compleat Body of Divinity in two hundred and fifty expository lectures on the Assembly's Shorter Catechism, by the Reverend & Learned Samuel Willard, Boston, 1726, folio. The lectures are dated, and those which I cite were written, 1704-1705. It is worth noting that I have examined a number of Willard's separate sermons without finding in them anything more on the subject; this and other negative evidence make it a fair presumption that the subject was not a "live" one at the time.

[8] P. 699, May 29, 1705.

hould be able to give a good account not only of his particular occu-
,ation but also of what he amounts to in it.   He should mind his
ccupation with industry, discretion, honesty, contentment and piety.
.Samuel Willard and Cotton Mather are authorities of the first
nportance by reason of their high position in the world of their time
nd the extent of their influence.   Do their doctrines which I have
;riefly sketched, support Weber's contention that the Puritan moral-
its made it not only man's right but also his duty to acquire wealth?
think that they do.   Neither in these authors nor in any others of
he period have I found such open exhortations to get rich as appear
1 Baxter and other English sources.   The preachers stress, rather,
he other side of the subject, that it is improper to grow poor.   They
ondemn the vices that lead to that result, and urge the correspond-
ig virtues that lead to prosperity and riches, without attending very
much to the results on a man's personal fortunes.   The parable of
he talents is often on their lips.   "Let your *Business* Engross the
Most of your Time," wrote Cotton Mather.   "Avoid all impertinent
Avocations.   Laudable *Recreations* may be used now and then: But,
beseech you, Let those Recreations be used for *Sawce* but not for
Meat." [9]   "Idleness is a sinful waste of our Time," wrote Timothy
Dwight[10] at the close of the colonial period.   "Prodigality is another
'raud, of the same general nature."   By both of these vices property
; effectually wasted."
Certain qualifications are to be noted, affecting the importance
rhich we may ascribe to these doctrines as the germs of a later cap-
;alism.   In the first place these teachings take a subordinate place
1 the sermons of the period.   Industry and thrift, to be sure, are
:equently referred to as commonplace virtues, the propriety of
:hich may be taken for granted; and the German scholar might
rge that this fact proves his contention, and that Puritanism had
itablished its standards.   It appears to me, rather, that the preacher
ad found that self-interest was sufficient stimulant to urge men to
conomic exertion; and he sought to direct men's minds to things
bove them rather than to things around them.   Whatever be the
xplanation, the doctrine of the calling, in the particular not the
eneral sense, receives at best no more than a bare reference in
:rmons which I have seen, aside from that of Cotton Mather, and is
ot treated at all in Dwight's Theology.   One seeks it in vain in
:rmons whose titles seem to promise some economic philosophy, such
; Cotton Mather's "The Serviceable Man," 1690; Solomon Stod-
ard's "God's Frown in the Death of Usefull Men," 1703; Samuel
Vhitman's "Practical Godliness the Way to Prosperity," 1714.

[9] Two Discourses, p. 49.
[10] Theology; explained and defended in a series of sermons.   Middletown, 1818, vol. 4, p. 229, p 282.

Another point to be noticed is the conflict between the encouragement of the accumulation of riches, as expressed in extracts quoted above, and the social philosophy of the Puritans. The class distinctions which they brought with them from England tended to grow weaker, but did not disappear, and were in fact supported by the influence of the ministers. They discourage any seeking after social advancement, and preached contentment in the station in which a man found himself. So Timothy Cutler, in his election sermon at Hartford, 1717, on "The Firm Union of a People," urged the need of "compactness," that every man should keep within the limits of his sphere and station; and Benjamin Colman, preaching the election sermon at Boston the next year, required that "Every one is to act *in his own place*, studying to be quiet and to do his own business, in the Relation Trust and Office which the governing Providence of God assigns him."

Finally, we must inquire into the relation of some of the moral doctrines which we have been considering to the practical policy adopted by the community in the form of laws, and the relation of both doctrine and policy to the material conditions of life. May it not be that some of the precepts which I have quoted were inculcated not so much because the people were Puritans as because they were colonists? This I believe to have been the case.

In one sense the colonists were without question capitalistically inclined—in the sense, namely, that their stock of capital was desperately small, and that they must strive in every way to further its maintenance and its increase. When we study, however, the ways that they chose to further these ends, we find a curious contrast; these ways were distinctly socialistic. I have not in mind here the ill-fated communistic experiment in early Plymouth. There was no attempt later to depart so far from individualism. Samuel Willard, at the end of the seventeenth century, was able to justify private property by reference to all law, both human and divine. Private property was recognized, but its social bearings were emphasized as they have never been in our later life. Capital was wanted, not for the individual who might possess it, but for the group who might benefit by its employment; and the use of capital was closely restricted to serve social ends.

The Pilgrim's compact of 1620, or John Winthrop's Modell of Christian Charity of 1630, show a consciousness of the superiority of the interests of the group above the interests of any individual which was realized so far as practicable in later economic legislation. Acts fixing the wages which artizans might demand were common in the early history of the Puritan colonies, and though they show a few traces of class interests, appear to have been in general an honest attempt to regulate the economic relations of individuals for the ben-fit of the whole society.   When the failure of these general acts, whether administered by the colonial or by a local body, was realized, the government confined its activities to the punishment of individual cases of extortion, and to the regulation of specific trades. Attempts to fix the price of bread were made and abandoned, but regulation of bakers' charges, expressed in an assize of bread, was widespread and was carried out in practice.   The Selectmen's Records and the Town Records of Boston show that the assize of bread was enforced in that town through the later seventeenth and the eighteenth centuries.[11]

Attempts to fix by law prices in exchanges were also common in the early period.   They were likewise soon abandoned, but the motive behind them expressed itself in a great variety of legislation designed to protect the interests of the group from the selfishness of individuals. The establishment of markets was a device to bring together buyers and sellers in such numbers that a fair market price might be fixed and that the individual might thereby be protected from the oppression to which his ignorance or weakness might otherwise expose him.

In most cases the market appears to have resulted in nothing more than this regular concourse of people seeking to trade with each other, but in some cases it became an elaborate institution, with regular officials to enforce the medieval rules against forestalling, engrossing, and regrating.   This was notably the case in Boston, where the question of market regulations became in the eighteenth century a political issue, and led to open riot.[12]   Timothy Dwight, writing of the period shortly after 1800, thought that the greatest evil from which the inhabitants of New Haven suffered was the want of a regular market system.[13]

For a supply of the necessary provisions the people relied as a rule on individual traders attracted to the market.   The colony, and sometimes the town, imposed restrictions on the export of wares which might be wanted by the consumers of the community; and often imposed an embargo on the shipment of provisions, to protect the consumer from the selfish interest of the producer seeking his best market.   Measures of this kind were not always sufficient to satisfy the demand for protection.   Cotton had proposed in 1641 that each town should have its own public grain store,[14] and this

---

[11] The assize of bread was established in Massacusetts by an act of 1646, and was put under control of the towns in 1681, Records of Massachusetts Bay, 2:181, 5:322.   Boston administered the assize more less strictly from 1682 to 1801.   There are scattered references to the assize in other New England towns, it it does not seem to have been administered systematically in any of them.

[12] Boston is in this regard again peculiar in the determination which it showed in attempting to carry to effect the market rules of the medieval town; the question of the market runs through many volumes the town's records.

[13] Travels in New England, I:194.

[14] Hutchinson Papers, Albany, 1865, I:189.

form of "town trading," to use the modern phrase, was practiced on an elaborate scale in Boston in the eighteenth century. A bread riot in that town in 1713 appears to have been the occasion of the system by which the town government purchased grain from public funds and distributed it at a price set to check exorbitant demands on the part of private sellers. The town records show that this system was in regular operation in the town down to the Revolution.[15]

The clearest example of the strong tendency to socialize private capital appears in the public position given the gristmill. In the earliest period the Indian corn which formed the staple food was pounded in a samp mortar, or ground in a hand mill, "quarn," by a laborious process. Bradford says that the Pilgrims pounded their corn for many years. So great, however, were the hardships of this process that the colonists made every effort to obtain a power mill driven by water or by wind. The town sometimes established the mill as a public undertaking, sometimes enlisted private enterprise by offering assistance or by promising a limited monopoly. The mill enjoyed, in any event, a practical monopoly. The miller of a town had the people at his mercy. He could charge what rates he pleased. We find early established, therefore, the doctrine that the mill, even though it were a purely private undertaking, could operate only under conditions laid down by law for the protection of customers. To use the later language of the law, it was "private property affected to a public use," and, like the grain elevators or the railroads of recent times, it was socialized, and it must grind well and duly for specified rates of toll. The struggles of the town with its gristmill present in miniature all the troubles that the Nation was later to undergo in dealing with the railroads—the failure of competition, the inadequacy of regulation, recourse in some cases to municipal ownership as the avenue of escape.[16]

---

[15] A committee appointed in 1774 to inquire into the operation of the granary recommended that it be closed, Town Records, Reports, vol. 18, pp. 156, 170. The building was let to a private person in 1786, Selectmen's Records, Reports, vol. 25, p. 324.

[16] The problem of just price, the rate at which a man may properly exchange his goods or services, is not infrequently raised in the doctrinal literature of the colonial period, but the writers are evidently dependent on the canonist doctrines which tradition had bequeathed to them, and make no original contribution on this puzzling question. Even while they recognized the practical difficulties in the way of establishing the just price in a concrete case they believed that at least some prices could be shown to be unjust; and the courts punished individual cases of extortion.

With regard to the loan at interest, the Puritans reflected the view then prevailing in England, that interest was legitimate, but that it should not be excessive, and that Christian charity required that it be altogether remitted in case of need Cotton proposed in 1641 a positive law forbidding interest on a loan to a poor brother, but the statutes actually adopted merely set a limit to the rate. The Massachusetts act of 1693 expressly excepted transactions in bottomry and foreign exchange, in which the competition of business men might be expected to establish a fair rate. On the whole, however, the colonial usury laws seem to have been designed to lower the rate of interest, to the advantage of the borrower. The colonial community felt a sore need of capital to develop the new country, and passed laws which by discouraging the capitalist may have actually defeated the end in view. Evasion was, however, so easy that the matter is of theoretical rather than of practical importance.

The conclusions of this study in the capitalistic tendencies of the Puritan colonies may be summarized as follows: Puritan religious doctrines did lend themselves, by their insistence on industry and thrift, to the process of saving, which is essential to the accumulation of capital.   The spiritual leaders of the people appear, however, to have aid but little emphasis on the doctrine of the "calling," and to have allowed it to drop far into the background of their interests.   The strength of their appeal for saving was derived not from ethical or religious doctrines, but from the practical needs of a society in a colonial environment.   Capital was wanted for social ends; its accumulation was rigidly governed by precepts and by laws opposing its employment to further selfish interests.   The spirit of the Puritan colonies was, on the whole, rather socialistic than capitalistic.

XII. THE HERITAGE OF THE PURITANS

By DAVID SAVILLE MUZZEY
Columbia University

THE HERITAGE OF THE PURITANS

By David Saville Muzzey

Anniversaries are dangerous. They often tempt to the pious exaggeration of panegyric. As the lamp beneath the retort liberates from certain chemical substances a roseate cloud of vapor, so the flame of patriotism or filial pride warms the heart of orator or poet until it expands and overflows in language that can hardly bear the acid test of historical criticism. Daniel Webster, at Plymouth Rock 100 years ago, praised the spot as that "where Christianity, civilization, and letters made their first lodgment in a vast extent of country"; and 23 years later, at a dinner of the New England Society at the old Astor House in New York, he spoke of "the free nature of our institutions and the popular form of those governments which have come down to us from the Rock of Plymouth." Yet Daniel Webster knew that more than a decade before the Pilgrims landed Christianity and civilization had made a permanent lodgment on the banks of the James, and that more than a year before the *Mayflower* sighted the shores of Cape Cod 22 burgesses from the plantations and hundreds of the Virginia colony had met in the rude church at Jamestown as the first representative body on American soil, the prototype and promise of our "free institutions and popular forms of government." In his Robinson of Leyden, Oliver Wendell Holmes sang of the Pilgrim Fathers:

> And these were they who gave us birth,
> The Pilgrims of the sunset wave,
> Who won for us this virgin earth,
> And freedom with the land they gave.

The meter and the rhyme are faultless, but the lines will not bear the scrutiny of the historian. The Pilgrims did not give us birth, unless by "us" Doctor Holmes means "us descendants of the Pilgrims." And as for winning for us this virgin earth, what of the long procession of explorers, missionaries, traders, pioneers who file in a great pageant before our eyes with their faces toward the sunset! Did the French "coureurs" pass through Plymouth, or the Germans

239

of the Schuylkill and the Juniata, or the Scotch-Irish of the Shenandoah, or the Huguenots of Carolina? Did the men of the western waters carry faces bronzed by the sun and salt of Cape Cod Bay, or were Radisson, La Salle, Daniel Boone, and George Rogers Clark sons of the Pilgrims? Yet it has been too common to indulge in such poetical or rhetorical extravagances from the seventeenth century, when Nathaniel Morton in his New England Memorial saw in the Puritans the vine of Psalm lxxx which God had planted in the wilderness and caused to take deep root and fill the land, to the twentieth century, when Theodore Roosevelt at the laying of the corner stone of the Provincetown Monument said: "The coming hither of the Pilgrims three centures ago shaped the destinies of this continent."

In attempting to estimate our heritage from the Puritans I would not prejudice my case by assuming that they were the sole testators of our country's blessings; nor would I, like Palfrey and other pious New England historians (whatever secret satisfaction I may take in my New England birth and blood), maintain that all that the Puritans bequeathed was good. Their shortcomings have received ample attention. From the coarse ridicule of Butler's Hudibras to Macaulay's stately persiflage in the essay on Milton; from Maverick's courteous declaration of grievances and Roger Williams's stubborn eristics to the delicious satire of the Deacon's One Hoss Shay, all the changes have been rung on the Puritan's defects—his intolerance, his sourness, his hypocrisy, his inhumanity, his conceit, his censoriousness, and so on through the appalling list, down to his ridiculous aversion to mince pies and beer at the Christmas season. And, indeed, there is something uncongenial, to say the least, in the atmosphere of the seventeenth century Puritan. Take Judge Samuel Sewall, for instance, as we see him in his diary—now spending his Christmas in the "awful but pleasing diverson" of arranging the coffins in the family vault, now endeavoring to terrify his young son into a premature experience of grace by strong representations of hell-fire, now pressing the courtship for his third marriage with a slyly amorous pomposity. You and I to-day would not feel any live spirit of "camaraderie" with a seventeenth-century Puritan, for it is a difficult thing to establish a common ground of friendly intercourse with a man who thinks that you are wallowing in original sin. But after all, much of the impatient disgust with the Puritans (like that which found expression in the remark attributed sometimes to an Anglican bishop and sometimes to an Oxford don, namely, that he wished that Plymouth Rock had landed on the Pilgrims), is due to our applying twentieth-century tastes and standards to seventeenth-century men. I imagine that it would be uncongenial also for most of us to associate with a courtier of King James.

Indeed, the application of that elementary but oft-neglected canon of historical criticism, namely, contemporaneity, while by no means freeing the Puritan from all of his unloveliness, would go far toward a proper appreciation of the motives from which he acted. If we saw the difficulties and perils of his situation with the same promptness with which we detect the eccentricities of his character, there would be little danger of our sharing Chesterton's opinion of Puritan New England as "a madhouse where religious maniacs had broken loose and locked up their keepers." Take, for example, the attitude of the Puritan toward the Church of England. To-day, in New England or in any other part of our country, political disqualification or religious persecution of Episcopalians would be bigotry pure and simple. Not so in the troubled decade of the 1630's, when, in John Cotton's virile phrase, "God rocked the three kingdoms" of Britain. The New England Puritans had left their homeland and come to the wilderness not so much to enjoy freedom of worship, as is so frequently stated ("enjoy" being a rather strange word in their vocabulary), as to establish that form of church and magistracy which they believed God laid upon their conscience. They were beset with foes on both sides of the Atlantic, whose purpose was not to secure the admission of the peaceful celebration of the Anglican rites alongside of the sterner Puritan worship, but to destroy the Puritan colony root and branch. Charles I ordered the surrender of the Massachusetts charter in 1634, five years after he had granted it. Sir Ferdinando Gorges, the servant of King Charles, spent his life in the attempt to wreck New England Puritanism. To admit Episcopalians into Massachusetts would not have been simply to tolerate the prayer book and the vestments, but to welcome the political supporters of Charles and Strafford; to make their servants, Mason and Gorges, feel at home; to receive the emissaries of Archbishop Laud, for whom, in Gardiner's classic phrase, the church was not the temple of the Holy Ghost but the palace of an invisible king. To the Puritan the Anglican Church was the palace of a very visible and pestilential king. If Charles and Laud and Gorges had succeeded, there would have been no Puritan New England. You may believe that it would have been better for America if there had been no Puritan New England. "De Gustibus non est disputandum." But it is hardly possible to rejoice in the preservation of Puritan New England and at the same time to blame the Puritans for their self-preservation.

> Intolerant!—They bought
> Their freedom with a price too nobly great
> To lose it lightly. Always in their thought
> A future peril to their children loomed
> With entrance of false doctrine!

It is a "reductio ad absurdum" of the principle of tolerance—as we have had reason to ponder on somewhat deeply in the last few years—to expect any society to admit to its bosom propaganda whose avowed object is its destruction.

You will have noticed that in turning my first page I dropped the Pilgrims and began to speak of the Puritans. And you may have thought on reading the title in the program, "The heritage of the Puritans," that this paper, if read at all, should be postponed to the annual meeting of the association in 1930—when I shall be old and gray. We are well aware, of course, of the distinctions between the Pilgrims and the Puritans—distinctions emphasized in every classroom. Aside from the different circumstances of the migration, there are some notable contrasts (explained to some extent, I believe, by the historical condition to which I have just alluded) in the temper of the settlements. The smaller colony to the south, as we follow its history in the pages of Bradford, did not develop that rigidity which we find among the Massachusetts Puritans. The harshness of the "lord bretheren," as Blackstone calls them with humorous reference to the "lord bishops," is lacking. Also those unlovely habits of "gathering providences" in the shape of God's retributions and judgments. "This day," writes Increase Mather in his diary on November 17, 1675, "I hear God shot an arrow into the midst of this town. The small pocks is in the ordinary of the sign of the Swan. The Keeper is a drunkard . . . His daughter is attacked to show God's displeasure." When some ships were wrecked on the way from Massachusetts to Connecticut, the clergy of Boston said that it was "a correction from God." But Bradford, commenting on the accident, added: "I dare not be so bould with God's judgments in this kind." This sounds more like John Greenleaf Whittier than like John Endicott. When we compare Bradford's portraiture of the sweet reasonableness of Elder William Brewster with the temper of any of the leaders of the northern colony, we realize that there were real contrasts between the two settlements.

Nevertheless, from the broader historical point of view of the influence of New England Puritanism the differences between the two colonies sink into comparative insignificance. Both came to these shores driven by the same "rude impulse." Three thousand miles of water between them and the motherland made them both "separatists." There was no more thought of establishing even a "purified" Anglicanism among the Boston Pilgrims than there was among the Plymouth Pilgrims. Moreover, both in origin and history the two colonies were closely connected. At least half a dozen members of the Massachusetts Bay Company had been prominent among the adventurers in the Plymouth undertaking. Bradford's History shows on many pages a spirit of cooperation and mutual consideration between the two settlements in such matters as trade, Indian policy, and the maintenance of independency in the churches. In fact, the union of the two colonies by the royal charter of 1691 was rather the acknowledgment of an accomplished fact than the enforcement of an unwelcome policy. It was not resisted by Plymouth, as the merger with Connecticut had been resisted by New Haven 27 years before.

The mention of the new charter of 1691 suggests a point too seldom given its weight in our estimate of the contribution of the Puritans, namely, that a great change had come over the face of Puritan New England toward the close of the seventeenth century. Prof. Frederick J. Turner in an address before the American Antiquarian Society at Worcester in October 1919, quoted the amusing insolence of the Mayor of Boston to a member of the Harvard corporation in a conversation held in 1916, when his honor declared that 'the Irish had letters and learning, culture and civilization, when the forebears of New England were the savage denizens of the Hyperborean forests; that the Irish had made Massachusetts a fit place to live in, and that the New England of the Puritan fathers was as dead as Julius Cæsar." This is not the change that had come over New England by the end of the seventeenth century, but a later transformation. However, if the culture of the Irish had not supplanted the savagery of the descendants of the Hyperborean forests, and if the New England of the Puritans was not as dead as Julius Cæsar in 1700, the actual Puritans of the first generation were as dead as Julius Cæsar. A new generation had grown up in America—a generation that knew of bishops' visitations and gunpowder plots and millenary petitions and the king's dragoons only by hearsay. The children's teeth were not set on edge by the sour grapes their fathers had eaten.

So long as there was any danger that the Stuarts might succeed in destroying their chartered liberties or overthrowing their independent churches, the Puritans naturally maintained their wary and zealous orthodoxy. The accession of William of Orange brought the sense of security that was a prerequisite for a saner political development. And the charter which was issued two years later marks, as well as any single event can mark the beginning of an epoch, the change from an essentially religious to an essentially political New England. Three provisions of the charter put an end to the rule of the saints: (1) Religious toleration was extended to all Christians except Roman Catholics; (2) the suffrage was relieved of all restrictions except a small property qualification; and (3) the governor and a great number of officials became royal appointees. Further evidence of the change in the Puritan character at the close of the seventeenth century can be seen in the cessation of the witchcraft obsession in 1692 and the expulsion of the Mathers from the control of Harvard College in 1701. Finally, a silent, steady influence had been flowing back upon the old Puritanism from the "outskirts" of its civilization in the frontier settlements, the "mark colonies," the towns of the Connecticut Valley and New Hampshire, for the interesting details of which I must refer you to Professor Turner's paper in the Proceedings of the Colonial Society of Massachusetts for April, 1914. Puritanism here was incidental to the problems of military defense and economic subsistence. The tendency was more toward the Plymouth type of society. The traditional control of the clergy gave way to the influence of those traits which have ever characterized our western pioneers (for the emigrants to the Connecticut Valley were as truly pioneers as the men who crossed the Alleghanies and the Rockies): Namely, individual initiative, resourcefulness, impatience of distant authorities, pragmatic tests of character, secularism, confidence, hard grips with real things. There was little room for the subtleties of theological debate. The trial and condemnation of Mistress Anne Hutchinson at Cambridge (which seems as remote to us as the trial and condemnation of Nestorius at Ephesus) could hardly have been enacted in the Connecticut Valley.

We can read very plainly in the works of Cotton Mather how the secularism of the frontier villages, "on the wrong side of the hedge" as he characterized them, pained the last champion of the old orthodoxy. In his "Frontiers Well Defended" of 1707, Mather goes a "gathering providences" to show God's punishment of secularism. Remember that it was but three years after Hertel de Rouville's band of Indians had swooped down upon Deerfield, massacring 49 men, women, and children, and carrying 111 into captivity. "The unchurched villages," says Mather, "have been utterly broken up by the war, while those with churches regularly formed were under the more sensible protection of Heaven." Needless to say, Mather's report is somewhat marred by "tendency." It is hard to see what "sensible protection" Heaven gave to the Rev. John Williams of Deerfield whose flock was massacred and himself taken captive by the Indians. Nevertheless, Mather's anxiety was well founded. "By the end of the colonial period," says Professor Turner (and the same might be said with almost equal truth of the end of the seventeenth century), "there were two New Englands, the one coastal and dominated by the commercial interests and the established Congregational churches, the other a primitive agricultural area, democratic in principle and not afraid of innovation." In the seventeenth century John Hampden "sought the Lord" on ship money; in the eighteenth, James Otis sought the law on writs of assistance.

It is a distortion of perspective in estimating the heritage of the Puritans—whether we consider the actual expansion of New England into central New York and the old Northwest, or the influence of New England on our political and social institutions—to confine our view, as so many have been tempted to do by the picturesque manifestations of the so-called New England conscience, to the theological and moral aspects of the Puritan régime. The reign of the saints lasted a scant two generations; the influence of socio-political New England has extended over two centuries. It is to two or three of these latter influences that I wish to call your attention in what remains of this paper.

First, and most important, as I think, is the political philosophy of Puritanism. In an age when, acccording to Mr. Wells, the monarchs were exploiting the principles of Machiavelli for the establishment of the "great powers" as transcendant, super-legal states, the Puritan insisted on the primacy of natural, or God-given, rights and the origin of government in a covenant by the people. This, of course, begins in a religious compact after Calvin's teaching, the Bible itself being a convenant (diathêkê, awkwardly translated by the Latin "testamentum") between God and his people. Note the language of the *Mayflower* Compact: "Wee . . . do by these presents solemnly and mutualy in the presence of God and of one another, covenant and combine ourselves together into a civil body politick for our better ordering and preservation"; or more fully in the famous Exeter Covenant of 1639: "Wee . . . bretheren of the Church of Exeter, situate and lying upon the river Piscataqua . . . considering with ourselves the holy will of God and our own necessity that we should not live without wholesome laws and government amongst us . . . do in the name of Christ and in the sight of God, combine ourselves together to enact and set up amongst us such government as shall be to our best discovering agreeable to the will of God, professing ourselves subject to our sovereign Lord King Charles, according to the liberties of our English colony of Massachusetts." *In cauda venenum!*

That a handful of men could set up a state "agreeable to the will of God" was a direct corollary to the doctrine that two or three could make a church under the divine diathêkê. And both claims were abhorrent and blasphemous in the eyes of the established powers. If you would realize the vast influence on our history of the remark of John Cotton: "It is evident by the light of nature that all civil relations are founded in covenant," think ahead to the American Revolution, based on the doctrines that governments are made by man and made for man's needs, that the individual is prior to the government and has rights beyond the power of government to curtail, that all government is restrained by a superior authority, a fundamental law. If you say: "But this is Thomas Jefferson!" I do not deny it. I disclaimed at the beginning of my paper any disposition to attribute to the Puritan a monopoly of political virtue. I would only suggest that Jefferson was a rebel and a radical in Virginia, who broke with the Blairs and the Pendletons and the other "cyphers of aristocracy" as he called them, and went back to the men of Puritan tradition in England, to Milton and Sidney and Locke, for his inspiration. The political philosophy which he had to fight for in Virginia was normal in New England. You would not find any irate, apoplectic Peyton Randolph rushing out into the lobby of the Massachusetts General Court, shouting that he would have given a hundred guineas for the single vote necessary to defeat the resolutions condemning the Stamp Act. When Charles II, just a century earlier, was commending the Virginians as "the best of his distant children" and quartering the arms of the Old Dominion, his commissioners to Massachusetts were flouted as intruders, and his great minister, Clarendon, wrote that the New England colonies were already "hardening into republics." In other colonies there were protests against this or that governor or act or policy, but the very existence of the Puritan governments was a standing protest and a chronic rebellion against hetero-determination. If some modern historians fail to grasp the full significance of this contrast, at least it was distressingly clear to the British Government of the seventeenth and eighteenth centuries.

The source and inspiration of the Puritan's stark philosophy of political self-determination was, as we have seen, the religious doctrine of government by covenant, with its insistence on individual competency (through the illumination of God's will as revealed in the Scriptures) and collective responsibility. The particular agency by which this philosophy was realized in society was the town. The New England town as a kind of cell in our body politic, as a social, religious, and educational unit, is the second contribution of the Puritan to our American democracy that I would emphasize. Of the compact structure of the New England towns, their completeness and self-sufficiency of function, their propagation through a system by which the land of the colony, instead of being sold for revenue or alloted to settlers by "head-rights", was given to groups of men who were responsible for the maintenance of Puritan institutions and the preservation of Puritan ideals, I have not time to speak. You remember the recipe for making a New England town which John Adams gave to Major Langbourne of Virginia: Town meetings, training days, schools, and ministers. At the time of the Stuart Restoration Samuel Butler ridiculed the pretensions of these towns to religious autonomy. New England was:

A commonwealth of Popery,
Where every village is a see
As well as Rome, and must maintain
Its tithe-pig metropolitan.
And every hamlet's governèd
By's Holiness the Church's head,
More haughty and severe in's place
Than Gregory and Boniface.

Their holinesses the Cottons, Wilsons, Mathers, and Shepards had ceased to play the Gregory and Boniface before the generation of Hudibras had passed; but the towns remained keenly conscious of their individual and several responsibility for the preservation of liberty. For example, John Adams's own town of Braintree, Mass., passed resolutions, September 24, 1765, on the occasion of the Stamp Act, to the effect that "We have clear knowledge and a just sense of our rights and liberties, and with submission to Divine Providence we never can be slaves." The protest of a score or two citizens of Braintree was as stately, formal, and considerable in their eyes as the remonstrance of a Continental Congress. A few Sundays later Parson Wibird, as yet somewhat untried, announced as his text: "Hear O heavens, and give ear O earth! I have nourished and brought up children and they have rebelled against me." John Adams, on his front seat, was immediately alert. "I began to suspect a Tory sermon on the times," he writes in his diary, adding with relief, "but the preacher confined himself to spirituals." Here is the "eternal vigilance" which Daniel Webster called "the price of liberty." When the towns of Massachusetts joined forces, they made the toughest web of resistance that ever authority tried to pierce. Thomas Hutchinson said of the Circular Letter of 1768 that it "had a greater tendency toward a revolution in the Government than any preceding measure in any of the Colonies." And Thomas Jefferson's experience in trying to enforce the embargo is well known. "I felt the ground shaken under my feet," he says, "by the actions of the New England town meetings."

It would take us far beyond the limits of our time to describe even in the most cursory manner the influence of the town polity upon the development of our democracy. I would only refer you to the legislation of the Virginia burgesses in 1701, which substituted for the "quasi manorial grants" of the Beverlys, Smiths, and Byrds, as the best way of protecting the frontiers, "settlements like the New England towns;" to the eventual replacement in the Ohio Valley of the large tracts of land sold to speculative companies by a democracy of small landholders; to the general coincidence of the census settlers of New England ancestry with the preponderance of the free-soil vote in the West and Northwest; to the solicitude of the New England missionaries in the extension of our settlements into Wisconsin, lest the supply of the means of grace might prove "inadequate to the dispersion into remote and still remoter corners of the land." Eventually all the practices of the Puritans, even the most unlovely and inquisitorial, were directed to the noble end of rearing a society of utterly responsible individuals—the only society on which an enduring democracy can rest. For your military power is nothing, your wealth is nothing, your numbers are nothing without the seed from which all greatness come—free and enlightened citizens. Local self-government is the germ cell of democracy. It is of no avail to count our millions if the individuals are ignorant, weak, and venal. Zero multiplied by any conceivable magnitude still results in zero. The so-called democratic empire, like that of Louis Napoleon, is one of the most despicable and dangerous forms of government. There is rhetorical exaggeration, but yet a kernel of profound truth, in the words of Jared Sparks written in 1836: "We owe it to the Puritans that we are not tossed like a shuttlecock from the pikes of an enraged populace to the bayonets of a military police."

So, in the end, our most valuable heritage from the Puritan (and it would be a sort of impiety to conclude my paper without acknowledgment of it) is the emphasis they put upon unremitting education for responsibility. That the education was sought primarily in Holy Scripture by the earlier generation, and that the responsibility was conceived of as a peculiar relation to God, resulted in dogmatism, bigotry, and exclusiveness. But all that, after all, was incidental. More than anything else, intellectual activity works the purgation of its own errors. It is only when thought stops that dogma is fixed. The Puritan educated the individual in order that he might be fit to meet his God in whatever great appointment his God might have for him. For, as Cotton said, "God might enlarge private men with public gift and dispense them to edification." But the mind will not be held in religious or scientific graveclothes when once it has begun to inquire and grow. The Puritans of the seventeenth century would have been scandalized by Emerson and Lowell as the purveyors of "unsound, unsavory, and giddie fancies," like Mistress Anne Hutchinson; yet Emerson and Lowell were their legitimate children. The famous Massachusetts education law of 1647 was passed to circumvent Satan in "one of his chief projects, to keep men from the knowledge of the Scriptures." The preamble to the Massachusetts constitution of 1780 begins: " Wisdom and knowledge, as well as virtue, diffused generally among the body of the people being necessary for the perpetuation of their rights and liberties," etc. To such sane and secular wisdom had the circumvention of Satan led in a century and a half!

I confess that I, for one, am neither sorry to see our attention called back to the Puritans at this time, nor inclined to use the occasion for smart ridicule of the Puritans' peculiar failings. An age which makes a religion of business will naturally look with little sympathy on an age which made a business of religion. And a philosophy that is impatient of absolutisms may need reminding that a thoroughgoing pragmatism would rank a miscarriage of burglary with a misconception of truth. One fault, at least, the Puritan was free from—the fashionable fault of sickness with existence.

> The world for [him] held purport: life [he] wore
> Proudly as kings their solemn robes of state.

XIII. PHILADELPHIA AND THE EMBARGO: 1808

By LOUIS MARTIN SEARS
Purdue University

PHILADELPHIA AND THE EMBARGO: 1808

By Louis Martin Sears

The year of the embargo was critical in the economic history of
he United States. During the Great War in Europe, especially in
he first phase from 1792 to the Peace of Amiens a decade later,
America as the chief of neutrals had built up a carrying trade of vast
proportions. The million[1] or more tons of shipping engaged in this
rade constituted an important interest for the nation, and one
which in predominantly commercial districts like Massachusetts was
paramount.

Among the mercantile community, accordingly, the action of our
Government in replying to the Berlin and Milan Decrees and the Or-
lers in Council of 1806 and 1807, which greatly hampered commerce,
by an embargo which prohibited it wholly, was viewed with conster-
ation. And in proportion as mercantile interests determined the
pinion of the people, the embargo was execrated as the knell of
American prosperity. As a result, something of a tradition has grown
up in American history as to the hard times produced by that "ill
udged" measure.

If the embargo offered small comfort to commerce, it gave a wholly
ew impetus to manufactures. And herein lies the explanation of
sudden prosperity enjoyed by certain commercial cities at the very
ime when their sisters and rivals were most depressed. It was not
hat their shipping was less hit, but rather that their opportunities
or a transfer of capital to manufactures were greater. This seems
o have been especially true of the commercial cities of Pennsylvania
nd Maryland, doubtless in part because of the great demand for
manufactured articles throughout the rapidly developing trans-
Alleghany region. Baltimore is an example of a commercial city sud-
enly widening its field of activities. The Baltimore newspapers
uring the year of the embargo have numerous advertisements of and
ther references to rapidly expanding manufactures. But Philadel-
hia is a more conspicuous example of a commercial city—she had
omething like a twelfth of the shipping tonnage of the United

[1] Boston Gazette Extra; Jan. 11, 1808, puts the American tonnage at 1,200,000. Cf. Richmond Enquirer,
ec. 17, 1808, which estimates American shipping tonnage at 800,000.

States—able by means of manufactures, in spite of the gloom among the purely mercantile elements, to develop a high degree of prosperity.

The present study will attempt to show that industrial gains so far offset commercial losses that the year of the embargo coincided, in Philadelphia at least, with a notable prosperity. It must be conceded, however, that the depression of the shipping interests was grave. So sudden a cessation of commerce spelled ruin to both capital and labor in so far as either was unable to adjust itself to an industrial basis. And one is not surprised that those upon whom the burden of readjustment was imposed felt it keenly. Even granting that new avenues to prosperity lay open for those whose former life was commerce, still the process of readjustment is seldom simple and would ruin some, while enriching others. There is, therefore, in the very nature of things a dark side to Philadelphia life in 1808. It is necessary to take that into account. The merchants and the seamen dependent upon them for a livelihood were the victims of a situation in which manufactures was the only outlet. To such of them as were unable to avail themselves of this outlet the times were, indeed, hard.

The merchants of Philadelphia had some warning of the embargo by the act of April 18, 1806, "to prohibit the importation of certain goods, wares, and merchandise." This act was originally passed as a threat, and stood for many months in abeyance. But fearing that now (December, 1807) the act was finally to be enforced, the Philadelphians petitioned Congress to let it remain a dead letter. Their petition was tabled, however, by a vote of 79 to 50.[2] But to men who opposed mere nonimportation, an embargo in addition was far from pleasing.

It is not surprising, therefore, that Philadelphians were among the first to seek a loophole for evading the new legislation. Undaunted by their former experience with Congress, they now came forward with a second petition, this time for a grant of clearance papers to those vessels already in cargo when the embargo act was published.[3] To grant this would have liberated from 300 to 400 vessels in the various ports of the country, in contravention of the entire purpose of the act, and Congress, after but slight debate, tabled this petition also by the decisive vote of 91 to 16.[4]

These two experiences with Congress practically ended direct action on the part of the merchants. They did, however, make one further protest, this time not against the embargo itself, but against an exception to it, permitted by the President in his executive capacity. A certain Chinese who claimed to be a great mandarin of Canton, by

[2] Annals of Congress xviii, 1179, 1187.
[3] Ibid., xviii, 1272.
[4] Ibid., 1275. Of the approximately 800,000 tons of American shipping in 1808, Pennsylvania, i. e., Philadelphia, possessed 86,723. Cf. Richmond Enquirer, Dec. 17, 1808.

imposing upon the credulity or the internationalism of the President, had obtained permission to proceed in a vessel to Canton, and there to load a return cargo. This was too much for plain American citizens who had no flowing robes and peacock feathers wherewith to unlock the gates of commerce, and a group of Philadelphia merchants wrote to Albert Gallatin, the Secretary of the Treasury, their opinion of the transaction. They assured the Secretary in the first place that men of mandarin rank never emigrated from the Celestial Empire, and in the second, that several of their own number had lived in Canton and personally knew this *soi-disant* mandarin to be a person of no consequence. "To some of us he is known only as a petty shopkeeper in Canton, utterly incapable of giving a credit; and to the remainder he is altogether unknown; which would not be the case were his character and standing in any degree respectable." They considered him an imposter and a tool in the hands of others, and allowed the Government to realize that it had been duped.[5]

But these formal communicatins from rich and conservative merchants were not the only anti-embargo protests which emanated from Philadelphia. Thomas Leiper, a friend and correspondent of Jefferson, described for the latter's benefit the hardships of poor flatboat men under regulations compelling a bond of $300 a ton for little sloops in the coas wise trade; $9,000, therefore, for a vessel of 30 tons, worth all told no more than $300. In the case in point the owner had only a half interest, and Leiper exclaims, "Nine Thousand Dollars, is this *reasonable*, is this *just* to require a man his bond to follow his lawfull business for Nine Thousand Dollars who is only worth One Hundred and Fifty—But he must give it too for his all is in the Flatt and he most (*sic*) keep soul of Body together abstracted from his being able to pay for his other half of his Flat."[6]

On no other class in the community did the embargo weigh more heavily than on the officers of merchant ships, men bred to the sea as a profession, who could not lightly turn to the first new work that offered. Their complaint is full of pathos. In terms the most respectful, they urge Jefferson to keep their situation near his heart, "that means may be had to prevent our Families beging, there (*sic*) subsistance." As for themselves they declare, "We become irksome to our friends; and no means by which we can subsist left us."[7]

The common sailors, too, were wretched enough, and one can not but commiserate them. In one sense, however, their situation was less serious than that of their officers, because they had less to surrender in leaving the sea, and might have been expected to adjust

[5] Jefferson MSS. (Library of Congress), to Albert Gallatin, Aug. 10, 1808.
[6] Ibid. Thomas Leiper to Jefferson. Philadelphia, Jan. 27, 1808.
[7] Jefferson MSS. Library of Congress. Philadelphia petition of Aug. 10, 1808. See also a similar petition of Aug. 8, 1808.

themselves to the lot of a laborer on the land with less difficulty. Be that as it may, their memorial to Jefferson relating their sad condition loses nothing in pathos from the English in which it is couched.

Philadelphia Dat November 14th 1808

We Distrsat Seamen of Philadelphia
Petitioners to you Honoure
Thomas Jeffarison President of the United States. We Humble Bag your Honur to Sum weekly allowance. Sir at as Hard times pon us seamen your Hounr Nos 50 or 60 Coasting vissels will not carry 4 or 5000 seamen. Out of this Port Sir we Humble bag your Honur to grant us destras seamen sum releif for God nos what we will do your Petitioners is at Present utterly destitute of all Employamat We Humble Bag Honur to grant us som employmant.
200 of us mat in the State Hous yard on friday Last we Have all wifes & famlys sir we Humble bags your Honur Pardon of at mis.

(signed) Thomas Truman.[8]

Shipowners, ship captains, common seamen, and longshoremen like the protégé of Leiper, of necessity bore the full burden of the embargo. Their situation was indeed a hard one, and confirms one in thinking that only great prosperity among other classes of citizens would justify an assumption of Philadelphia prosperity in 1808. But this is, of course, only one side of the case. And there is abundant evidence that other classes were actually in the enjoyment of the counterbalancing prosperity. That the city was at any rate far from presenting one unbroken front of misery is plain from the United States Gazette of October 8, 1808, which, though an opposition paper endeavoring to make out the worst possible case, reluctantly admits even a certain degree of prosperity. "The embargo," declares the Gazette, "has as yet produced *comparatively* little inconvenience in this city and its neighborhood. During the last winter, we began to suffer from the domiciliary visits of labourers, *in forma pauperis*, who could not find employment and were obliged to beg; but, generally, the stores laid in by poor men before the embargo were sufficent 'to keep want from their doors' until the spring opened; since when, the unexampled improvements in our city have given constant employment to eight or ten thousand of them."[9] To preserve the proper tone of opposition gloom, the Gazette predicts a hard winter as soon as frost suspends these building operations. Meanwhile, the fact would not down that Philadelphia was in the midst of a wholly unprecedented building boom.

One estimate places the number of houses erected at nearly 400; another at 1,000. The former gives details as to the stimulus thereby contributed to general industry, and declares that "In Philadelphia the embargo, although felt severely, has not produced distress ac-

[8] Ibid. Thomas Truman and others to Jefferson. Philadelphia Nov. 14, 1808.
[9] United States Gazette, Philadelphia, Oct. 8, 1808.

cording to the population. This is owing in a great measure to the buildings now erecting in the city. The capital of the merchants and monied men being withdrawn from commerce, has been appropriated to other purposes. Almost four hundred houses are now erecting in the city, which, allowing twenty men to each house including carpenters, brickmakers, bricklayers, masons, labourers, &c., now give employment to 8,000 of our citizens who would otherwise be severely affected by the embargo. Besides, the banks have continued their discounts, and have, indeed, so much money to lend, that no man who has tolerable personal security to offer will be refused a discount." [10]

A rather playful explanation of this era of construction, involving the building of possibly 1,000[11] new houses at Philadelphia alone in the single year of the embargo, attributes it to the prosperity of the Philadelphia lawyers. To these virtuous citizens the embargo brought a blessing in disguise. The very act which restrained commerce multiplied marine lawsuits, and their effect upon the gentry of the bar is humorously described by Horace Binney, one of its own distinguished ornaments.

The stoppings, seizures, takings, sequestrations, condemnations, all of a novel kind unlike anything that had previously occurred in the history of maritime commerce—the consequence of new principles of national law, introduced offensively or defensively by the belligerent powers—gave an unparalleled harvest to the bar of Philadelphia. No persons are bound to speak better of Bonaparte than the bar of this city. He was, it is true, a great buccaneer, and the British followed his example with great spirit and fidelity, but what distinguished him and his imitators from the pirates of former days was the felicitous manner in which he first, and they afterwards, resolved every piracy into some principle of the law of nations, newly discovered or made necessary by new events; thus covering or attempting to cover the stolen property by the veil of the law. Had he stolen and called it a theft, not a single lawsuit could have grown out of it. The under-writers must have paid and have been ruined at once and outright. But he stole from neutrals and called it lawful prize; and this led to such a crop of questions as nobody but Bonaparte was capable of sowing the seeds of. For while he did everything that was abominable, he always had a reason for it, and kept the world of the law inquiring how one of his acts and his reasons for it bore upon the policy of insurance, until some new event occurred to make all that they had previously settled of little or no application. In many instances the insurance companies got off; in others, though they failed, it was after a protracted campaign in which, contrary to campaigns in general, they acquired strength to bear their defeat. In the mean time, both in victory and defeat, and very much the same in both events, the lawyers had their reward.[12]

It is hardly necessary to remark that although Philadelphia lawyers were reaping a harvest that has made their name a byword for

---

[10] "The Republican and Savannah Evening Ledger," Oct. 28, 1808, quoting Gazette of the United States and New York Public Advertiser.
[11] Annals of Congress, XIX, 100–103.
[12] Charles Chauncey Binney, Life of Horace Binney, pp. 60–61.

shrewdness and success, this could not represent a net gain to the community. The real expansion of Philadelphia lay in industrial enterprise, and progress in this direction appears to have more than compensated for losses commercial.

In the very nature of things the embargo proved a stimulus to manufactures. And nowhere was this stimulus more promptly felt than in Philadelphia. Manufactures were of course not unknown before 1808, but in that year they assumed an altogether fresh variety and significance. The Philadelphia Price Current devoted to them an article which produced a local sensation, and which the editor at once forwarded to Jefferson "to prove that by the Presidents originating partial deprivations, he has ultimately bestowed on his country immense and imperishable benefits."[13]

The inclosure, which must have given keenest satisfaction to the harassed Jefferson, is here quoted in full, notwithstanding its length, as proof conclusive of the manufacturing impetus of the period.

AMERICAN MANUFACTURES

The following new American Manufactures, we quote with pleasure, as an evidence of the increase of public spirit, and a sure pressage of future prosperity and independence.

Floor Cloth carpets of any size with or without border per sq. yard	$2.25	Manufactured by John Dorsey.
The same with three colours	2.00	
The same with two colours	1.75	
The same with one colour	1.50	
The patterns are in great variety and the colours bright, hard and durable.		
Cotton Bagging, per yd. 50 cts	Apply to Maclure & Robertsons.	
Printed Calicoes (war'd fast colours) pr yd.	20c	Manufactured by John Thoburn & Co.
4-4———25 a	27	
Shawls assorted 9-8 per shawl	21	
4-4 do.	32	
5-6 do. 50 a	58	
Bed spreads 10-4	$1.	

EARTHEN WARE.

Yellow—Tea Pots, Coffee Pots and Sugar Boxes per doz.	$3.	Manufactured by Binney & Ronaldson.
Assorted Ware do.	$1.25	
Red-Tea Pots, Coffee Pots and Sugar Boxes per doz.	$2.50	

GLASS WARE.

Green hlf gall. Bottles per doz	$2.	Manufactured by T. Harrison & Co.
Do. quart Do do	1	
Green hlf. gall. Jars do	2.	
Do. quarts Do do	1.	
White hlf. gall. Jars do	7.50	
Do. quart Do do	3.75	
Green Pocket Bottles do	80	
Glass per pound · do	50	

[13] Jefferson MSS. Library of Congress. Editor of the Philadelphia Price Current to Jefferson, Nov. 7, 1808.

Windsor Soap per lb.	35	Manufactured
Fancy do. per dozen	$2 a 3.	by W. Lehman,
Sealing Wax per lb.	50 cts. $3	W. Smith & son.
White Lead per cwt.	$17 a 18	Manufactured
Red Lead do	15	by Dr. Joseph
Litharge do	15	Strong.
		This extensive
Shot B B B 1a 12 per cwt	$11.	manufactory
Do. S G G and Buck	13	(Paul Beck's)
Bar Lead	10.50	goes into oper-
		ation this day.
Shot B B B 1a 10 per cwt	12.	Manufactured
Do. Goose and Buck	10.50	by Bishop & Sparks.
Bar Lead		
Floor Cloths per square yard	$1.75	Apply at Do-
Do. do do	2 a 2.25	mestic Manufac-
Cotton Flannel per yard	47	tory.
Acet. Distillat ....gall	$ 60	
Acid Muriatic ....lb		
Aq. Fortis dup	45	
Alcohol ....gall	2.	
Aq. Amon c Cale ....lb	20	
————— c Tart	22	
Calomel Crud.	1.90	
——Ppt	2.10	
Camphor Refin...................		
Ether Vitriol	1.75	
Liq. Anod. Min. Hoff............	.75	
Lunar Caustic ....oz.	1.50	
Merc. Corros. Sublim............	1.50	
Ol. Vitriol	.15	
Sp. Nitri Dulc....................	34	
—Vitrirol Dulc...................	75	
—Salis. Volat. Arom	75	
—Nitri Fortis		
—Vinos. Rect. G. P. Proof.......gall.	1.50	
—Turpentine	40	
Patent Green ....lb	67	
Vermilion ....lb	1.50	
Tartar Emetic ....lb	1	
Vitriol Roman	25	
Varnish Bright.................gall		

Manufactories of various other articles are in operation, and several rapidly pro-
ressing; we could not, however, for the present number ascertain with precision the
ust denomination of articles or their quotation, but shall soon increase our paper so
s to embody them in the general prices of Domestic Articles, and for that purpose
nvite communications.[14]

It will have been noticed that white lead receives mention in this
Price Current of November, 1808. Yet three months later, in Feb-
uary, 1809, William Dalzell of Philadelphia, apparently ignorant
of the output of Doctor Strong, sent Jefferson "a sample of I believe
he first White Lead ever manufactured in the U. States." He
omplimented the President on the wisdom of the embargo as the
neasure which was making possible the industrial growth on every
and, and concluded with a fervent hope that Congress would adopt
he one means which could insure permanence to these infant indus-
ries, namely a protective tariff.[15]

---

[14] Hope's Philadelphia Price Current and Commercial Record in Jefferson MSS.
[15] Ibid. Wm. Dalzell to Jefferson, Philadelphia, Feb. 10, 1809.

Curiously enough, neither Dalzall nor the Price Current speaks of the heavier manufactures depending upon iron and steel. But an advertisement in Duane's paper, the Aurora, supplies the missing evidence.

AMERICAN MANUFACTURES

The acting committee of the society of Iron-mongers, of the city of Philadelphia give notice, that agreeable to a resolution of the society, they will receive proposals for manufacturing any of the following articles, to wit:

Cast WAGGON BOXES, neatly ground inside.
Cast SAD IRONS, made agreeable to the Dale co. patterns, and neatly ground to the face and edges.
FRYING PANS with long handles.
PLAIN IRONS, Socket and Firmer CHIZELS and GOUGES, Carpenters' ADZES FILES, RASPS, STEELYARDS and HOES.

The proposals must be in writing, stating the probable quantity that can be furnished within a stated period with their price, delivered in this city, and in all cases to be accompanied with samples. Application to be made to either of the subscribers.[1]

The wording of this advertisement is obscure, it must be granted casting some doubts as to whether the articles were to be manufactured in Philadelphia or elsewhere. It is clear, however, that a society of ironmongers existed, and the presumption is strongly in favor of their being in active business.

From time to time, the Aurora contained other advertisements bearing witness to still greater diversity in Philadelphia manufactures. Thus machines for repairing weavers' reeds,[17] felting superior to the imported,[18] satinets, muslinets, cotton stripes, bed tickings,[19] Germantown stockings, socks, and gloves, fleecy hosiery, and cotton and woolen yarns,[20] all contributed to American self-sufficiency, and to the enrichment of their *entrepreneurs.*

It is thus apparent that Philadelphia prosperity in 1808 was not a mere shifting of wealth from merchants to their lawyers, but a genuine progress, resting on an active and diversified industrial basis. As Charles Jared Ingersoll summarized it,

Who that walks the streets of Philadelphia, and sees, notwithstanding a twelve months stagnation of trade, several hundred substantial and elegant houses building and the labouring community employed at good wages, who reads at every corner advertisements for workmen for factories of glass, of shot, of arms, of hosiery and coarse cloths, of pottery and many other goods and wares; who finds that within the last year rents have risen one-third, and that houses are hardly to be had at these prices; that land is worth, as Mr. Brougham observes, much more than it is in Middlesex; in a word, who perceives, wherever he goes, the bustle of industry and the smile of content; who, under such circumstances, that is not too stupid to perceive

16 Aurora, Philadelphia Mar. 21, 1808.
17 Ibid., Apr. 14, 1808.
18 Ibid., June 3, 1808.
19 Ibid., Oct. 18, 1808.
20 Ibid., Nov. 2, 1808.

and too prejudiced to believe when he does perceive, can doubt the solid capital of this country?[21]

Nicholas Biddle also, though he has less to say about the embargo and its effects than one would expect from so important a man of affairs, confirms Ingersoll's estimate of Philadelphia prosperity. Writing to a friend in Paris, he says,

> You would scarcely recognize Philadelphia, so much has it grown and improved. Among your former acquaintances, Cadwalader is always here and prospering. His wife has just presented him with a third child. Chauncey is making a fine fortune, and surely no one deserves it more than he. As for politics, our actual position is not the most agreeable. The embargo presses heavily on the people, but it has been put in execution without difficulty, and as the people is very sane, the session of Congress soon to meet will be peaceably awaited. In spite of this the embargo appears to have wrought some change in New England, where the elections have terminated in favor of the Federalists. There is even an appearance . . . that the Government of the United States will pass once more into the control of the Federalist Party, or at least that the embargo will be raised before very long. In all these matters I do not mingle. After my long absence, it is impossible to become a very zealous partisan, and I am occupying myself with my profession.[22]

Interesting testimony this is as to the possibility of living in 1808 without worrying over the embargo, its wisdom, or its consequences, although no Philadelphian could quite ignore the prosperity his own city was harvesting.

If confirmation of these estimates of Ingersoll and Biddle is needed, it is to be found in a communication of William Short, a friend of Jefferson, to the President. Short possessed a handsome fortune and, like Biddle, would have seen little to recommend in the embargo had it proved as ruinous as its enemies alleged. He writes,

> And this City (Philadelphia) has really acted as the government could wish on the subject of the embargo—I speak of those who are considered as of opposition politics & who are numerous—They frequently & publicly speak their determination to support it, & if on a jury to punish with rigor the violators of it. I have more than once heard it affirmed & not contradicted, that if the merchants of this City were assembled; confined to Federalists alone, nine out of ten would approve the embargo, & of the Tenth disapproving, most of them would be men without capital.[23]

But the best test of the economic situation, better than the enthusiasm of Ingersoll and Short or the contentment of Biddle, was the state of political parties in 1808. Economics and politics are so interrelated that if commercial stagnation had proved ruinous to any considerable proportion of the citizens, popular discontent would have registered itself in the overthrow of the Republican machine. Nothing of the sort occurred. The State legislature passed a resolution

[21] Charles Jared Ingersoll, "A View of the Rights and Wrongs, Power and Policy of the United States of America." (1808), p. 49.
[22] Nicholas Biddle Papers. Library of Congress. I. 1775–1809. Nicholas Biddle to Mr. J. M. de la Grange. Sept. 26, 1808.
[23] Jefferson MSS. Library of Congress. William Short to Jefferson, Aug. 27, 1808.

most reassuring to the Federal authorities.[24]   And although the campaign for the governorship in 1808 was warmly fought, the Federalists thinking that they had even made inroads upon the Irish vote[25] which already by tradition belonged to the Democrats, nevertheless the final victory for Snyder and the party of Jefferson was decisive, the Republican majority being "immense," to use the language of an enthusiastic contemporary.[26]   As one of the President's correspondents in Philadelphia stated it,

A stranger from reading our antirepublican newspapers, might have anticipated a different issue, but we are sound to the core.   We believe the General Government has, by its measures, consulted our true interests, and we wished in the day of election to express that sentiment in the strongest possible terms.[27]

In Congress the Pennsylvania delegation was not wholly united. One of its members, William Hoge, was irreconcilable, being the only man in Congress to vote with Barent Gardenier of New York for a frank submission to the edicts of Great Britain and France.[28]   But his colleague, Smilie, who led the proadministration forces of the State, made in the early debates a strong speech on behalf of the embargo,[29] and consistently maintained his position.[30]   The Pennsylvania record varies only slightly between the 11 to 5 with 2 not voting, for the original embargo act of December 18, 1807,[31] and the 10 to 6 with 2 not voting, for the nonintercourse act which superseded it on February 27, 1809.[32]

Whatever the temptation to oppose the embargo, Congressmen, at least from Philadelphia, were not allowed to forget the favor it enjoyed among the people back home.   As some staunch defenders of the administration expressed it,

We behold in a temporary suspension of our commerce an ephemeral & doubtful evil, producing a great, a growing & a lasting good.   We see arising out of this cause the prolific sources of our internal wealth explored & with industry & ability directed thro' channels, which while they benefit the enterprising, enrich our country with solid wealth & make her more independent & happy.[33]

And when, in January, 1809, the friends of embargo were called for a last rally in its defense for the passage of amendments which would make its operation ironclad, Philadelphians, at least the numerous element among them whom a share in the industrial

[24] Am. State Papers. For. Rel. III, 294, 295.
[25] United States Gazette, Oct. 8, 1808.
[26] The Palladium, Frankfort, Ky. Nov. 3, 1808.
[27] Jefferson MSS, Library of Congress Elijah Griffith to Jefferson, Philadelphia Nov. 14, 1808.
[28] Annals of Congress. XIX, 853.
[29] Ibid., XVIII, 1710.
[30] Ibid., XIX, 574.
[31] Journal of the House of Representatives. VI, 320-321.
[32] Ibid., VI, 565-566.
[33] Jefferson MSS. Library of Congress. Delegates of the Democratic Republicans of the city of Philadelphia to Jefferson. Mar. 1, 1808.

prosperity served to strengthen in their fidelity to party, lent their fullest measure of support. A broadside of the times rings like a bugle call.

ANOTHER
TOWN   MEETING
DEMOCRATIC   REPUBLICANS,
OF THE CITY AND COUNTY OF PHILADELPHIA,

Your duty to your country—your political principles—your attachment to the present Administration—your sacred regard for the Union—and the fair fame of the city and county of Philadelphia, all imperiously call you to the State House on Tuesday next at 11 o'clock in the forenoon.

The Friends of the Constitution, Union and Commerce, are invited to a Town Meeting. Come forth in all your strength. Be ye firm, vigilant, and active. Your enemies are up and doing. January 29, 1809.[34]

In Philadelphia, as we have seen, the ruin of powerful commercial interests brought a real and somewhat widespread distress. But in Philadelphia, much more than in many other localities subject to similar commercial losses, men found compensation, and frequently much more than compensation, in the development of a large-scale industrialism. On this basis was reared the superstructure of building operations which made Philadelphia the wonder of the times, and at least one commercial city toward which Jefferson could point for vindication of his system. A prosperity in which so many types of citizens participated clinched the loyalty of city and State to the political party which sponsored it, and served to hold in the Democratic household of faith a State whose defection would have been peculiarly embarrassing at a time when Federalism was regaining so much lost ground in New England.

But this is drawing larger deductions than the thesis of the present paper undertook to establish. Its more modest task was to demonstrate that in the case of one great commercial city an embargo which should in theory have proved wholly ruinous, served in fact, partly in combination with growing demands from the western market, to stimulate manufactures to a point where prosperity exceeded adversity. It may be that the paper has incidentally demonstrated that the tradition that the hard times in 1808 were attributable solely to the embargo, the weak device of an impractical philosopher, a tradition largely fostered by New England, should not be accepted without a certain degree of caution. For Philadelphia, at least, such an assumption concerning the embargo is untenable.

---

[34] Broadside in the Library of Congress. Vol. 93. Pennsylvania.

XIV. AGRARIAN DISCONTENT IN THE SOUTH: 1880-1900

By BENJAMIN B. KENDRICK
Columbia University

AGRARIAN DISCONTENT IN THE SOUTH: 1880–1900 [1]

By Benjamin B. Kendrick

The causes of agrarian discontent in the South from 1880 to 1900 were both social and economic. Time permits of the discussion of only two phases of these causes. First, the low social status of the southern farmer in 1890, relative to his high status in 1860; second, the lien law system which was a grievance peculiar to the southern farmer of this period and not shared by his brother in the West.

In order to understand the first cause, it is necessary to remind ourselves of the fact that previous to the Civil War the agricultural class in the South was by far the most articulate in that section and even to a certain extent in the United States. Their manners and customs fixed the standard of polite society. They dominated the politics of their counties and States, and until the election of Abraham Lincoln in 1860 they were not without a major share of influence in the National Government. Even in the cities their influence was potent, for what commercial and industrial interests there were did not challenge the dominance of the planters. The merchants depended for their prosperity upon the patronage of the farmers and were distinctly secondary in importance to them. There were not enough manufacturers in the South before 1860 to feel a distinct class interest. Professional men such as lawyers, physicians, clergymen, editors, and teachers were largely drawn from the agricultural classes. Hence their views were reflected in the courtrooms and legislative halls, in the pulpits, in the columns of the newspapers and magazines, in the academies and colleges. At no other period in American history were the ideas and ideals of one class so completely unchallenged as were those of the southern planters during the last three decades of the ante-bellum South.

Certainly not all farmers were large slaveholders, but the small farmer shared in the benefits that accrued to agriculture as a whole because of the dominance of the planters in the county seats, the State capitals, and even in Washington. No greater mistake can be made than to suppose that there was any great social demarcation among southern planters derived from the numbers of acres owned or slaves held. I am referring only to those farmers who depended

---

[1] W. S. Morgan, History of the Wheel ahd Alliance, 1891; C. H. Otken, The Ills of the South, 1894; E. A. Allen, Labor and Capital.

upon cotton as their means of livelihood. The cotton industry was too young to have developed an aristocracy. It must be remembered that there had been only two generations of cotton growers when the Civil War began, and in many sections there had been but one. Even in the counties of western Georgia, where the Creek Indians had lived until the late twenties, and in which section I have made considerable personal investigation, I have found that nearly all the farmers there in 1860 had come with very little wealth in money or slaves. The same thing was true of the newer cotton regions of Alabama, Mississippi, northern Louisiana, Arkansas, and Texas. Even in the older cotton regions of eastern Georgia, western South Carolina, North Carolina, and Tennessee, not more than two generations of cotton growers had lived before 1860. It is idle to suppose that in these regions there were any great marked social differences. Land was cheap and even small farmers owned several hundred acres; so when we say that social and political life in the South was dominated by the agriculturists, we mean all the cotton farmers. We are not considering here the great rice, sugar, and tobacco growers of South Carolina, Louisiana, and Virginia. Here there was, indeed, something of an aristocracy. Nor are we thinking of the so-called poor whites of the great pine barrens or their economic kinsmen of the mountainous country. Among these people hardly any class consciousness existed.

Twenty years after he War between the States closed, the same people or their sons were living in the cotton regions of the South. Some of them owned less land than in 1860, some more. The average size of farms had declined somewhat, because there were more farmers. The estate of a father may have been divided among his sons. There were a few newcomers from the North or from the poorer white classes of the mountains or the pine barrens. A few negroes owned part of the land of their old masters; but essentially the same people or their sons were raising cotton in 1890 as in 1860, and on the same land. But how changed their condition! They were no longer the social leaders. The State governments had generally passed from their hands. They controlled the counties in only those sections where there were no urban communities worthy the name city. Their influence at Washington under a Democratic administration was next to nothing and under a Republican administration was quite nothing at all. Preachers no longer ransacked the Scriptures to find that God wholly approved the interests of agriculture, but preached the gospel according to Henry Ward Beecher and Samuel Smiles. Lawyers found fatter fees serving the interests of railroads, merchants, urban real estate dealers, lumber kings, mining princes and the new manufacturing classes whose enterprise was creating that "New South" hailed first by Henry W. Grady and afterwards by thousands of orators from high-school rostrums to legislative halls.

The prosperity of the South still depended to a large extent upon the size of the cotton crop and the price of the staple, but the growers were no longer the dominant class. Social prestige no longer depended upon ownership of land, but upon the ownership of a merchandising house, city real estate, stock in a manufacturing enterprise or bank, or even upon a managerial or technological position in one of these establishments. To all of these the farmer was socially inferior, no matter if his father had lorded it over half a hundred slaves and owned 2,000 acres of land. Even the $20-a-month clerks in the stores regarded themselves as better than the farmers. The very mechanics or factory operatives, descendants for the most part of the despised poor whites, yielded nothing of social prestige to the farmers. At least they lived in the city and had advantages which the farmers did not have.

This change in social status had been caused by an economic revolution that had taken place in less than 30 years. What were its causes? In the first place, to the farmer, the Civil War and Reconstruction had brought desolation and ruin. In the cities a war followed by reconstruction had accelerated if not caused an industrial revolution similar in character to that which had taken place in England nearly a century before, and in the East 50 years before. The farmer had taken up the burden of making a living in 1865 under most trying circumstances. His stock was killed or stolen, his fences and barns and frequently his dwelling were destroyed or in poor repair, his land had deteriorated from poor management, his slaves were freed, thus tending to confuse freedom from slavery with freedom from any sort of labor. Then came from 5 to 10 years of reconstruction during which the negroes became even more demoralized and disinclined to work for wages. The effort to continue to utilize the negro as the basis of farm labor first gave rise to the so-called black codes, which had for their main purpose the forcing of negroes to take positions as agricultural laborers on the lands of their old masters. It is true that these codes contemplated a sort of peonage for the negro and from that standpoint were indefensible in the North which, so its leading politicians declared, had just fought a four years' war for the purpose of ridding the country of every sort of slavery and serfdom. Hence these codes became null and void through the passage of the Civil Rights Act and the Fourteenth Amendment. From the southern farmer's point of view, these laws were necessary if the land was to continue to support the negroes and themselves, for it was a pretty generally accepted conclusion, tested by a year or more of experience, that the negro was disinclined to render steady service on a freedom of contract wage basis. Even the more conscientious agent of the Freedmen's Bureau admitted that a contract in the eyes of the negroes was not a very sacred document.

Then came the effort to obtain work from the negro by placing at his disposal land ordinarily sufficient to constitute a one-mule farm. This was to be operated on the share basis, usually half and half, the landlord furnishing the house for the tenant as well as his stock and farming implements. Fertilizers and seed were paid for jointly, and the tenant was to pay out of his half at the end of the year whatever the landlord had advanced for his maintenance. Under this so-called "cropping system" the negro was much happier than under the wage system. For the first time in his life he enjoyed the blessing of self-determination as to the disposal of his own time and efforts. He could work when, if, and as he pleased. The landlord was free to give him advice which was usually humbly received with expressions of gratitude and respect and quickly forgotten or quietly ignored.

As long as the southern local and State governments were in the hands of the carpetbaggers, the landlord had little or no redress. But white dominion returned. One of the first acts passed by the redeemed legislatures were lien laws, ostensibly in the interests of the landlords, but, as the event proved, greatly to their detriment. The object of the laws was to give the landlord a mortgage upon the products, both actual and potential, of the tenant, until the end of the year when the settlement was to be made. This would have benefited the farmer if he had had the capital himself with which the tenant produced the crop. But such capital only a very few farmers indeed possessed. They owned land which during the 30 years following the Civil War was very low in value, so low in fact that it frequently happened that they could not obtain any money on it at all even if it were owned free and clear.

We have alreay mentioned the fact that the close of the war left the farmer devoid of all sorts of capital except his land. Hence it became necessary for him to obtain credit from the town merchant, who in turn borrowed from the local banker, who in his turn was under obligations to the central banks, especially New York banks. As a rule the merchant was unwilling to take a mortgage upon the farmer's land, and the farmer seldom could borrow directly from the banker on his land as a security. Neither the banker nor the merchant could afford to tie up capital in securities that had such problematic value and upon which ready cash could hardly ever be obtained. Of all classes in business of any sort, the farmer could obtain credit only on the hardest terms and with the greatest difficulty. Even in case the farmer was able to borrow directly on his land, the terms were so hard and the amount raised so little that it usually was not long before he had consumed all that he had borrowed and was back again applying to the merchant for credit. During the reconstruction period the merchants had lost considerable money by furnishing farmers and their negro tenants on no other security than personal notes. The declining prices and the undependableness of labor had made it very hard for the farmers to come out even after each year's crop; hence it often happened that they were unable to meet their obligations to the merchant, who was thus put to the expense and trouble of a lawsuit. Consequently, when the lien laws were passed the merchant was quick to take advantage of them, and in a very few years it was the customary thing for a merchant to demand of every farmer who asked credit the execution of one of these "ironclad" or "anaconda" mortgages. In return for supplies for himself and tenants the farmer gave the merchant a mortgage on his crop, on his stock, and on his agricultural implements, wagons, buggies, etc.

It was generally provided in the mortgage that the accounts on the merchant's books would be incontestable as to the amounts which the farmer owed the merchant at the end of the year. It frequently happened that the farmer's and his tenants' crops were not sufficient to pay these amounts at the end of the year; consequently the farmer was obliged to continue from year to year in debt to the same merchant under the same galling conditions. For the supplies which the farmer purchased on credit during the spring and summer, the merchant generally charged from 25 to 50 per cent above the local cash prices. The merchant demanded that the farmer and his tenants plant most of their land in cotton. His object in doing this was twofold. In the first place, he would be sure to obtain a commodity which he could turn into money, and in the second place it meant that if the farmer did not raise his own meat and corn he would have to buy these products from the merchant and so increase the latter's sales at very handsome profits. Thus it happened that the farmer's capital, even with the addition of his personal labor, proved hardly sufficient to support himself and family in any sort of comfort. In thousands of cases, during the period of low prices for cotton in the early nineties, it proved altogether insufficient, and the land began to go piecemeal to the merchant. Cotton which during the seventies and eighties had averaged about 11 and 9 cents, respectively, averaged about $6\frac{1}{2}$ cents in the nineties, reaching the low level of 4.6 cents in 1894. A good portion of the land consequently passed into the hands of merchants, who cropped it on their own account with negro or poor white tenants. As a rule negroes preferred to crop the land of merchants, as this removed them still further from any sort of supervision. As a consequence, the merchants were able to obtain for their own land the choice of the negroes, and the farmer saw his better tenants tolled off to the merchant lands and himself left with tenants of second-rate character and intelligence.

Of course, all farmers did not work their land by means of the cropping system. Some hired negroes for what was called standing wages, and many did all or a considerable part of the work themselves. The farmer who did most or all of his work on a relatively small portion of land was usually better off than his neighbor who owned more land, but put it to cultivation in the hands of croppers. That is to say, he was more likely to come out even at the end of the year, and if he was thrifty and a fairly good manager, he might even get ahead sufficiently to run his place on a pay-as-you-go basis. Hence we often hear of men being land poor. But the small farmer suffered from the low prices of the nineties and had in common with the other farmers the grievance against the State taxation system, the poor educational system, the railroads, and, most important of all, the national system of currency and taxation.

Time does not permit me to go into detail concerning the grievances the farmers of the South had in these matters, but it will suffice to say that they were not unlike the same grievances that the farmers of the West had with regard to the same subjects. Prof. Solon Buck and other writers and investigators have stated very well what these grievances were and how the farmers attempted to remove them. The particular grievance of the southern farmer was the lien-law system, which kept him, as he often expressed it himself, the lien-law slave of the merchant.

It has not been my purpose here to state how southern farmers came to organize such societies as the Wheel and Industrial Union and the Farmers' Alliance and finally to agitate for the capture of the Democratic Party to make it serve agrarian purposes or, failing that, to organize a new party, the Populist, to accomplish the same purpose. This sort of thing might serve very well for young southern historical students who are looking for subjects for master's essays or doctoral dissertations. One of my own students has in preparation a doctor's dissertation on the Populist Party in Georgia, and I see no reason why such dissertations might not be prepared on the general social, political, and economic conditions in the other Southern States, covering the period from the point where the monographs on Reconstruction leave off to the close of the nineteenth century. It is my opinion that this period would prove very fertile in material for monographs that would help us to a just appreciation of the unfavorable conditions under which the southern farmer labored, and I am confident that such investigations would shatter the current erroneous notion that the southern farmers continued to dictate the policy of the State governments or the notion that it was their interest which the southern wing of the Democratic Party represented in the eighties and nineties, or for that matter represents at the present time.

XV. THE DEVELOPMENT OF ELECTROMAGNETISM DURING THE LAST HUNDRED YEARS

By A. E. KENNELLY

Harvard University and Massachusetts Institute of Technology.

THE DEVELOPMENT OF ELECTROMAGNETISM DURING THE LAST HUNDRED YEARS

By A. E. KENNELLY

It is just 100 years ago since electricity and magnetism were discovered to be intimately connected. Prior to the year 1820, electricity and magnetism were regarded as distinctly separated sciences. Electricity was produced by friction and also electrochemically by the voltaic cell. Magnetism resided in permanent magnets and was communicated from one steel bar to another by appropriate contact.

In 1820 Hans Christian Oersted was professor of physics at Copenhagen.[1] He had in his laboratory a battery of voltaic cells and a magnetic needle. He knew that a wire carrying the current in a voltaic circuit becomes heated. The idea occurred to him that a metallic wire, heated in this way, might disturb a poised magnetic compass needle. He seems to have had no previous anticipation of the existence of a magnetic field around such a wire. He tried the experiment and found immediately a very marked and definite influence exerted by the wire upon the needle. This was not a thermal, but a magnetic, effect. The needle deflected strongly. In a few minutes of laboratory investigation, the two sciences of electricity and magnetism that had been separate and absolutely distinct in human thought since the night of time, were connected and became interrelated. Electromagnetism was born.

The news of this remarkable discovery spread rapidly among scientists. But this was before the electric telegraph era. Only the semaphore, working visually from hill to hill, transmitted messages along certain main European routes. Oersted's public announcement from Copenhagen bears the date of July 21, 1820, and was in Latin. This seems to have been the last announcement for the physical sciences transmitted in Latin through Europe, although Latin announcements in the botanical sciences have continued down to the present day. The news of the discovery was brought from Geneva to Paris by the French physicist, Arago, who repeated the experiment before the French Academy on September 11, 1820. Among those present was Prof. André Ampère of the École Polytechnique.

---

[1] Oersted, "Experimenta circa effectum conflictus electrici in acum magneticam." Hafn. July 21, 1820.

The demonstration stirred Ampère profoundly. He immediately set up a voltaic battery and some magnetic needles to repeat the experiment. Test followed test successfully and Ampère could scarcely find time for rest. The French Academy was scheduled to meet in Paris on September 18. Within the intervening week, Ampère prepared an epoch-making academy paper, greatly extending the scope of Oersted's discovery.

With the precision and clarity that have made French science famous for centuries, Ampère connected electricity[2] and magnetism so definitely in experiment, in mathematics, and in logic, that ever since the two sciences have been inseparably associated.

The next great step in the knowledge of electromagnetism was furnished by Faraday's first discovery, in 1831, of electromagnetic induction.[3] His researches continued for nearly 25 years, and indicated that electric forces are set up whenever relative motion occurs between a magnetic field and surrounding space. In particular, if relative motion occurs between a magnetic field and a conductor, an electric force is set up in the conductor, which may be utilized for producing an electric current. This discovery lies at the basis of all modern dynamo-electric machinery. Faraday actually constructed the first little dynamo-electric machine with his own hands.

Whereas the Oersted-Ampère researches demonstrated a relation between magnetism and electric flow, involving mechanical forces, Faraday's researches showed that any disturbance of a magnetic field, in time or in space, gave rise to electric phenomena. Researches made since Faraday's time have shown that, reciprocally, any disturbance of an electric field, in time or in space, gives rise to magnetic phenomena. In that sense, both electric and magnetic phenomena have come to be regarded as collateral aspects of any electromagnetic disturbance.

Prior to the year 1840, it may be said that there was no recognized science of energy, or capability of doing work. Energy was perhaps recognized as existing in various forms, such as heat energy, electric energy, magnetic energy, chemical energy and mechanical energy, including both potential and kinetic types; but there was no doctrine of equivalence between these forms. Owing to the work of many scientists during the decade 1840–1850, and particularly of Joule,[4]

[2] Ampère, "Sur l'état magnetique des corps qui transmettent un courant d'électricité". *Ann. Chem Phys.*, Vol. xvi, Paris, 1821.

[3] Faraday, "Experimental Researches in Electricity," Series I. London, 1831.

[4] Joule, James Prescott. Mem. Manchester. Soc. Ser. II, VII 1846, VIII 1848, IX 1851, X 1852. Phil. Tr. 1850, 1852, 1853, 1856. Sturgeon's Annals II 1838, III 1838–39, IV 1839–40, V 1840, VI 1841, VIII 1842. Phil. Mag. Ser. III, XIX 1841, XXII 1843, XXIII 1843, XXIV 1844, XXV 1844, XXVI 1845, XXVII 1845, XXVIII 1846, XXX 1847, XXXI 1847; Series IV, II 1851, III 1852, IV 1852, VI 1853, XII 1856, XIV 1857, XV 1858.

Helmholtz,[5] Colding,[6] Mayer and Kelvin,[7] it came to be recognized that if energy is apparently created at any time and place, it is merely transformed from some preexisting stock. According to this doctrine, which is now generally admitted, energy may be converted from one form to another, upon a definite basis of equivalence, but can neither be created nor destroyed. As a consequence of this doctrine, it would follow that the sum total of all the energy existing in the known universe remains constant. This is the famous doctrine of the conservation of energy. It is regarded to-day as so axiomatic that it is hard to realize how recently the doctrine has been promulgated and accepted.

A somewhat similar doctrine of the conservation of matter was not long since in very general acceptance. It was supposed that the total numbers of atoms of the different elementary substances remained constant, despite changes in their chemical combinations. This doctrine of the conservation of matter, however, has had to be surrendered, or at least considerably modified, as the result of researches on radium during the last few years. It is believed that atoms of radium, and other radioactive elements, occasionally break up spontaneously, as though by internal explosion, into atoms of other and simpler elements. Energy in relatively very large quantities is released by these atomic explosions.

Except for electroplating, the first application of electromagnetics was to telegraphy. The electric telegraph has a long history and a considerable literature prior to 1837; but its industrial introduction dates from about 1838 in England, on the Great Western Railway, using six wires. Very little was known about it publicly until 1845, when the arrest of an escaping murderer was accomplished with the aid of a telegram, thus drawing public attention to the utility of the telegraph. The first telegraph construction company—The Electric Telegraph Co.—was formed in that year.

In America, Joseph Henry published in 1831[8] the results of a series of researches he had made while in the then frontier town of Albany, N. Y., on the design and construction of electromagnets. In 1835 he developed and demonstrated the electromagnetic relay principle, whereby a feeble electric current, received from a distance, may

[5] Helmholtz, Hermann Ludwig Ferdinand: Über d'Erhaltung d'Kraft. Berol, 1847. Überd. Wechselswirkung d.Natur-Krafte und die darauf bezüglichen Ermittlungen d'Physik. Königsberg, 1854. Über d.Dauer u. d. Verlauf der durch Stromesschwankungen inducirten elekr. Strome. Pogg. Ann. 83, 1851.

[6] Colding, Ludwig Augustus. An examination of steam engines and the power of steam. Copenhagen, 1851. Undersögelse over Vanddampene og deres bevaegende Kraft i Dampmaskinen. Danske Vid. Selsk. Skriften, 1852. Undersögelser om de almindelige Naturkräfter og deres gjensidige afhängighed og i särdeleshed om den ved visse faste Legermes Gniding utviklide Varme. Ibid., 1854. Om Magnetens Indvirkning paa det blöde Jern.

[7] Lord Kelvin (Sir William Thomson) "Reprints of papers on electrostatics and magnetism." London, 1872.

[8] Silliman's Journal, 1831, No. 19, p. 400.

cause a delicate receiving electromagnet to actuate a light contact, and thus close the local circuit of a more powerful electromagnet.

Morse demonstrated his electromagnetic telegraph, working over half a mile[9] in 1837, and sought in vain, until the closing hours of the congressional session in 1843[10], for congressional appropriation to build a telegraph line. The first single-wire Morse line was completed from Baltimore to Washington on June 4, 1844.[11] The first published use of the electric telegraph to the determination of longitude, appears to have been between the Capitol at Washington and Battle Monument Square, Baltimore,[12] June 12, 1844.

The first submarine telegraph cable to be put into public use, was laid between Dover and Calais, across the English Channel, in 1851, following a partially successful attempt between Dover and Cape Gris-Nez, in 1850. The first transatlantic cable between Ireland and Newfoundland was laid in 1858, but failed electrically a few weeks after completion, and after having transmitted over 700 messages.[13] The first permanently successful cable between Ireland and Newfoundland was laid in 1866. At the present time there are no less than 15 such cables laid across the Atlantic Ocean.

Returning to the scientific side of the subject, Prof. James Clerk Maxwell showed, in 1867, that the known properties of electricity and magnetism led to the conclusion that electromagnetic disturbances were propagated through nonconductors, in waves, at definite speed.

These electromagnetic waves were also susceptible of being reflected and refracted like waves of light. He put forward the theory[14] that light was merely an electromagnetic disturbance, of such wave lengths as the eye could detect. This celebrated electromagnetic theory of light has since received confirmation and is now generally accepted. According to this doctrine, not only visible light, but all radiation of the thermal type, is electromagnetic. This in turn involves the theory that all luminous and thermally radiating sources are electromagaetically active, and therefore that all bodies are composed of atoms, which, at all working temperatures, are electromagnetically active. In that sense, all the rays of light and heat we receive from the sun are received as electromagnetic waves, across the intervening 150,000,000 kilometers and are steady wireless "messages" from the solar atoms. The electromagnetic theory of light was amply supported by the researches of Hertz, who, in 1888, showed experimentally that the electromagnetic waves emitted

[9] "Life of S. F. B. Morse." S. I. Prime, N. Y., 1875, Chapter XI pp. 473-509.

[10] *Congressional Globe*, Feb. 21, 1843

[11] "Life of S. F. B. Morse, " p. 509.

[12] Ibid.

[13] "Life Story of Sir C. T. Bright." Charles Bright., Rev. 1908.

[14] James Clerk Maxwell, "Method of making a direct comparison of electrostatic with electrodyn, force and the electromagnetic theory of light," London, Phil. Trans. 158, 1869.

by a spark-discharging circuit possessed all the optical properties presaged by Maxwell's theory. It is now generally accepted that the invisible electromagnetic waves emitted from a radio telegraph antenna, or "wireless mast," differ from polarized light waves only as to their length. Radio waves vary from, say 50 meters to 20 kilometers in length. Visible light waves vary in length, approximately from 0.4 to 0.8 micron (millionth meter). The shortest radio wave would contain about 60,000,000 of the longest visible light waves. The long radio waves, however, can, fortunately, bend around the spherical earth's surface and follow its contour; whereas the short optical waves, except under extreme limiting conditions, move forward in straight or very nearly straight lines.

Modern electrochemical researches have led to the view that chemical affinity and chemical forces of molecular union are electromagnetic. This doctrine seems to be rapidly gaining support. It leads to the conclusion that, in a certain sense, chemistry is a branch of electromagnetics, and that chemical combinations can be explained electromagnetically. The explanations, however, are as yet only in an elementary stage.

Moreover, modern electric researches have led to the very generally accepted belief that all the atoms of elementary chemical substances are composed of electric charges called electrons. Just as a molecule of matter is supposed to be built up of atoms, so atoms are supposed to be built up of electrons. It has been estimated that the radius of an atom, assumed as spherical, is about 10^{-10} meter, or, as it has been expressed—if a drop of water were magnified to the size of the earth, the atoms in it might be expected to be about baseball size. But the "radius" of an electron is supposed to be about 10^{-15} meter, or one hundred-thousandth of the atomic radius, so that the atoms magnified into baseballs, might then have their component electrons sufficiently large to be detected by a good microscope.

Moreover, the electrons are commonly supposed to be in planetary or orbital motion around their atomic nuclei, so that, during the last half century, an atom has come to be regarded as a microcosm or planetary system, something like the solar system on an enormously reduced scale. There is at least as much evidence for the existence of the electron to-day, as an individual electromagnetic entity, as there was 50 years ago for the atom as an individual chemical entity. Moreover, the evidence is strong that the electrons in the different chemical atoms are all similar; so that, for example, an atom of hydrogen differs only from an atom of oxygen in the number, grouping, and orbital relations of its component electrons. In other words, the electron theory of the last two decades, as now very generally accepted, claims that electrons are the bricks of the materal world, out of which some 90 different kinds of chemical atoms are built, and that these bricks are electric. Chemical atoms are therefore built up of organized electric charges, and chemistry is the science which teaches their electromagnetic relations, as revealed in combination.

This widespread modern electron theory has appropriated the whole material universe as its own. It claims that all matter is an aggregation of molecules, themselves made up of atoms, which in their turn are microcosms of organized electromagnetic entities; so that in this sense, everything is electricity. The properties of matter, like mass and inertia, thus become electromagnetic properties, and are explainable by the laws of electromagnetism as worked out in the laboratory. As to the fundamental nature of electricity and of magnetism, we have as yet only speculation; but the two are known to be definitely interconnected and related in such a manner that, if either of them could be explained, the nature of the other would thereby become determined.

The development of electromagnetic theoretical science during the last century has therefore led to its absorbing nearly all the other branches of natural philosophy. In the case of gravitation, however, although attempts have been made to find an explanation, by the electron theory, it has not yet been considered as accounted for. Very recently, the Einstein theory of relativity, which has received much scientific attention, seeks to explain gravitational force as a pseudo phenomenon, due to the departure of space from ordinary Euclidian three-dimensional geometry in the neighborhood of matter. It may be one of the tasks of scientific history of the next century to trace the influence of this theory on thought and accomplishment. At present it would seem that the results of the theory have no significance in ordinary business, insignificance in engineering or geodesy, a small but appreciable significance in astronomy, but an enormous significance in philosophy. For instance, all space is claimed to be finite in Einstein theory; but is infinite, or at least has no limits, in Euclidian theory. The Einstein theory, however, claims to be in accordance with, and to be based upon, the geometrical postulates of electromagnetics; so that, in this sense, it is an electromagnetic theory.

Turning once more to electromagnetic applications introduced during the last century, a complete list of them would be very lengthy. The following are important applications: electric lighting, heating, transportation, power transmission and distribution, electrochemical industry and electric furnaces, also electric communication by wire and radio, both telegraphically and telephonically. In wire telegraphy, the total length of working submarine cables on the globe (262,000 nauts) would go around its Equator nearly 12 times; while the total length of telegraph lines (2,520,000 km.) would go round it nearly 63 times. In radio, or wireless telegraphy, signals are now receivable from powerful sending stations all around the world, under favorable conditions. The time required for the passage of any single radio wave to go half-way round the globe to the Antipodes has never yet been measured, but is estimated to be about one-tenth of a second; so that we are all living, according to that belief, on a tenth-of-a-second world of utmost separation in time. The human voice in speech, directed to a telephone transmitter at Arlington radio station near Washington, D. C., has been heard faintly and understood, at a receiver under the shadow of the Eiffel Tower in Paris, and also at a radio station in Hawaii.

Electromagnetism, during its history of the last hundred years, has, as a theoretical science, laid claim to absorb and include the sciences of physics, chemistry, and of the material universe. As an applied science it has been harnessed to many duties. It has destroyed distance and time as an agency of world communication.

Looking backward through the century that has passed, the science of electromagnetism has slowly but steadily advanced, without interruptions, discontinuities or reversals. The internationally accepted experimental facts bearing on the subject make up collectively the sum of human knowledge and experience in this domain. As time has gone on, this sum total has always increased. The interpretations of these facts, or the hypotheses built upon them, have undergone modification from time to time, as new facts have been added, so that electromagnetic theory is thus always, to a certain extent, in a state of flux, whereas electromagnetic knowledge is, in general, only modified by time in the sense of accretion. A very striking example of this contrast is offered by the recent Einstein doctrine of relativity. If future measurements should confirm this theory and lead to its general acceptance, electromagnetic knowledge would be scarcely affected; but our interpretation of this knowledge would be almost revolutionized. Our intellectual relations with the universe, so far as we can know it, would be profoundly modified.

The history also indicates that the study of electromagnetism is materialistic or imaginative or spiritual, according to the viewpoint and philosophy of the student contemplating the admitted facts. If the student has been materialistic, so also has been the electromagnetism he interpreted. If the student has been of an imaginative soul, so also has been the electromagnetic theory which the same facts depicted to his mind. From any aspect, however, electromagnetism is so great a subject that it may be regarded as coterminous only with all creation.

XVI. DESCRIPTION AND TRAVEL AS SOURCE MATERIAL FOR THE HISTORY OF EARLY AGRICULTURE IN PENNSYLVANIA

By RAYNER W. KELSEY
Haverford College

DESCRIPTION AND TRAVEL AS SOURCE MATERIAL FOR THE HISTORY OF EARLY AGRICULTURE IN PENNSYLVANIA

By RAYNER W. KELSEY

INTRODUCTION

It is proposed to illustrate in this paper the type of material for agricultural history that may be gathered from works usually classified in libraries as "Description and travel." This material is fairly distinct from official documents such as customhouse records, agricultural laws, probate-court records, and departmental reports of various kinds. Some material, such as newspaper items, personal memoirs, and account books, does not always classify readily under either of the above headings, but usually in its nature and function belongs in the category of "Description and travel."

This type of material has destinctive value and definite limitations. It constantly supplies data, especially in the early periods of American history, that can be obtained from no other source. On the other hand, it must be used with care, for frequently the author was so shortsighted as not to foresee the obligation of accuracy that would be placed upon historians of later centuries.

For example, the present writer recently secured transcripts from the archives of Basel, Switzerland, of two descriptions of an early land project in South Carolina. They were letters written home by two actual settlers in the same vicinity at the same period. Each one described the climate, soil, products, labor conditions, etc. Then one of them declared the place to be an "earthly paradise," while the other called it "a damned fraud." It was a considerable discrepancy for the historian to wrestle with. Unfortunately the profane conclusion bore up better under the test of historical scrutiny.

In purely travel accounts something can usually be judged from the writer's general equipment for accurate observation. If he was a farmer himself, or for any reason especially interested in farm problems and progressive farming methods, his record is of course greatly enhanced in value. Fortunately, a good many early travelers were themselves farmers, interested in all the vital phases of farm practice.

285

In some cases a writer's accuracy in minor details may be checked at the present day, and thus some gauge be had of the general accuracy of his mental habits.

The present writer recently followed the trail of an eighteenth century traveler in Pennsylvania[1] and measured, by automobile speedometer, the distances indicated between stops. By checking the points covered by the early traveler during 15 days of travel, it was found that he had been surprisingly exact in his statement of distances. So in many other respects his accuracy stood the test. One more example may be cited. The early traveler visited a little lake or pond and recorded that it was "18 feet deep [and] peculiarly full of excellent trout."[2] The modern *voyageur* visited the same pond and made inquiries at the farm on its borders. After some casual remarks he asked the farm wife whether there were any fish in the pond. She answered, "plenty of trout." He then said, "The pond looks deep." "Yes," was the answer, "18 feet at the deepest." After a few such tests as that, one is justified in placing some dependence on the general accuracy of a journalist's observations.

It remains to illustrate in a few topical studies the value and availability of description and travel as source material. In these studies it will be necessary, as it always is, to supplement the account occasionally with materials not to be precisely classified under the above rubric. The main reliance will, however, be upon early travel and description.

SOIL IMPROVEMENT

In the early agriculture of Pennsylvania, as in other parts of America, precious little was thought or written about soil improvement.

It is of interest and value, however, to follow such a topic in order to see the rise of a more progressive practice.

William Penn was forward looking in this matter, as in policies of statecraft. In 1686 he wrote as follows to the man whom he had selected to manage his farming project:

I recommend to thee for the gardens and improvement of the lands, that ashes and soot . . . are excellent for the ground, grass, or corn. Soot may be gotten at Philadelphia for fetching, I suppose; it should be sowed pretty thick for corn, in Spring, not too thick; its best for low lands and such as are moist. Let me desire thee to lay down as much as thou canst with english grass and plow up new Indian fields and after a crop or two they must be laid down so too; for that feeds sheep, and that feeds the ground, as well as they feed and clothe us, and fitts it for grass, corn and wine.[3]

---

[1] Theophile Cazenove. See Cazenove Journal, 1794. Haverford College Studies, No. 13. Haverford, Pa., 1922.

[2] Cazenove Journal, 43.

[3] William Penn to James Harrison, in Penn MSS., Domestic and Misc., 32 (Historical Society of Pennsylvania).

That the father of Pennsylvania had a lively interest in farm problems is shown by his inclusion, in one of his early accounts of Pennsylvania, of a letter to him from Robert Turner. This letter tells of various experiments in farm practice tried by Turner. Among other things he tells of planting some patches of grass seed and using manure on part of it. The patch manured made the poorest growth.[4]

In 1698 Thomas's Account records that although limestone is plentiful and cheap, it is not used as fertilizer because of the natural fertility of the soil.[5] Here is an early admission of the deliberate policy of neglecting the soil and squandering its stored up wealth, the results of which bear heavily upon thousands of Pennsylvania farmers to-day.

From 1700 to 1750 almost nothing has been found on the subject of soil improvement, in an examination of the most promising collections of description and travel, manuscript and printed.

In the middle of the century Peter Kalm observed that there was little manure available because cattle were not housed in winter nor "tended" in the fields. Hence, he says, the fields are allowed to lie fallow a few years, after three years of grain raising.[6]

Near the middle of the century there was some discussion about the value of potash in agriculture, and some private correspondence between Philadelphia and London on the subject of a wonderful, secret fertilizer being perfected by the English writer that will "make Corn Grow in Barren and Sandy Ground."

Between 1775 and 1800 there is a great outcry against wasteful methods of soil exhaustion, and some amendment in this respect. A few scattering items may show the trend of the times:

1773. Alexander Thompson tells of buying a farm and finding the accumulated manure of 11 years piled up and unused. He hauled it to the fields and was rewarded with rich crops of wheat, rye, and Indian corn.[7]

About 1775 a traveler records that John Bartram, of Philadelphia, conducts spring water to his reservoir; then he throws in old lime, ashes, and horse dung and turns the water from the reservoir on his fields twice a week; he also spreads old hay, straw, and fodder on the ground in the fall. Thus he gets 53 hundredweight of hay per acre on land th t would hardly have grown "five fingers" before.[8]

1783. Farmers sometimes use lime and gypsum as fertilizer.[9] Schoepf records, 1783–84, that much lime is used on the land; it costs from 8d. to 13d. per bushel, Pennsylvania currency; on ordinary

[4] "Penn's Further Account" in Pennsylvania Magazine of History, IX, 74.
[5] In Myers Narratives of Pennsylvania, 320.
[6] In Pinkerton, Voyages, XIII, 410.
[7] In Pennsylvania Magazine of History, VIII, 321.
[8] Crèvecoeur, Letters (Everyman's ed.), 188–189.
[9] Pennsylvania Magazine of History, V, 76

upland they use from 15 to 20 bushels per acre; on clayey, low ground more than twice that amount.[10]

From this time forward there are frequent references by Schoepf, Cazenove, Liancourt, and others, to the use of lime, marl, gypsum, and barn manure. Rush says that Jacob Berger first used gypsum some years before the Revolution on a city lot in Philadelphia. Richard Peters indicates that he became acquainted with the use of gypsum in 1770.

A Pennsylvania farmer wrote in 1788 that plaster of Paris, lime, and marl act only as medicines or cordials upon the land; they give it a temporary activity which produces large crops and exhausts the soil; he quotes a German saying that plaster of Paris "makes rich children but poor grandchildren." His conclusion is that such fertilizers should be used only in conjunction with large quantities of stable manure, which he calls the only proper food for the earth.[11] This treatise of 1788 sounds almost like a current number of the Farmers' Bulletin published by the Department of Agriculture at Washington.

Even before the end of the century there is agitation for deeper plowing, better crop rotation, and for the proper preservation of manure. Then when the Memoirs of the Philadelphia Agriculture Society begin publication in 1808 we have available long and, one may say, scientific treatises on the use of all the above-mentioned fertilizers; on the construction of pits and shelters for manure, and on subsoil plowing and the proper rotation of crops.

The beginning, however, of real progress in soil improvement in Pennsylvania is in the last quarter of the eighteenth century.

WAGES AND WHEAT PRICES

A very interesting study would be to measure farm wages at various periods in terms of a representative group of farm products. A little step in that direction is taken here by comparing wages in terms of wheat. There is constant difficulty, because wages and the price of wheat differ considerably at different seasons of the year and in various localities, and it is often difficult to bring together data that represent similar conditions. Some approximate results may, however, be attained.

About 1682 wheat was running at 3s. 6d. per bushel in the neighborhood of Philadelphia. At the same time men could be hired at 15d. per day for clearing land.[12] Such a wage would amount to approximately 22 pounds of wheat, or just a little more than a third

---

[10] Schoepf, Travels (ed. 1911), II, 2–3.
[11] Pennsylvania Gazette, Apr. 9, 1788, p. 2.
[12] Pennsylvania Magazine, 333, 336, Myers, Narratives of Pennsylvania, 252.

of a bushel. Harvest help always came higher, and by comparison with other periods one would say that harvest help probably brought a half bushel of wheat per day, or a little more, in the early days of William Penn's settlement.

Figures for 1698 run almost the same, the maximum for harvest help running at almost exactly 30 pounds or a half bushel of wheat. In that year, however, common labor is quoted as low as 18d. per day, or 12 pounds of wheat.[13]

In 1725 wheat had risen to 4s. a bushel and winter labor would purchase 25 pounds of wheat per day, while a mower in harvest could buy as much as 38 pounds.[14]

In 1760, with wheat at 5s. 6d., labor is quoted at 4s. to 4s. 6d. By this score labor could purchase from 44 to 49 pounds of wheat per day.[15] This was during the French and Indian War and the comment is made in this year that "all prices including labor have risen." It is apparent, however, that labor prices had risen faster than the price of wheat.

For the year 1794 data are quite full for various parts of Pennsylvania. Wheat prices run from 7s. 6d. in Carlisle to 11s. 9d. near the Philadelphia market. An average price within a radius or 50 miles of Philadelphia is 10s. The figures on wages are somewhat uncertain because sometimes it is not specified whether board is included. At one place near Philadelphia wages are 3s. and board "and a pint of whiskey," where 70 years before they were 2s. 6d. "and a pint of rum"—showing small improvement in wages or temperance. On the whole, however, in 1794 labor would buy from 20 to 30 pounds of wheat per day but in most places, it was nearer the former figure.[16]

Thus we may conclude that in the century following the settlement by William Penn labor, measured in terms of wheat, had remained at nearly the same level, and would usually buy a little less than half a bushel. The choice of wheat as a measure is further justified in 1794 by a traveler in Berks County who states that farm laborers demanded payment in wheat.

(Data since 1800 have not been gathered, but it seems evident that in recent times the status of farm labor, as measured by wheat, has improved. By the writer's knowledge of conditions in several parts of eastern Pennsylvania before the Great War, and during the price fluctuations to 1917, a day's labor would buy from a bushel to a

---

[13] Pennsylvania Magazine, XVIII, 247: Myers, Narratives of Pennsylvania, 328.

[14] Pennsylvania Magazine, V, 350.

[15] Pennsylvania Gazette, Feb. 7, 1760, p. 3; Pemberton Papers (MSS., in Library of Historical Society of Pennsylvania), XIV, 71.

[16] Cazenove Journal, 28, 33, 34, 36, 59, 60, 67, 77; cf. "Letters and Documents," in Pennsylvania Magazine, V, 350.

bushel and a quarter of wheat, or more than twice as much as in the colonial period.)

Having illustrated the function of description and travel in two topical studies, it may be useful to close this paper with a cross-section view of one work of travel to show the variety of data that may be found in a single document of the kind.

One of the latest journals of early American travel to become available in print is the record kept by Theophile Cazenove in a journey across New Jersey and Pennsylvania in 1794. Cazenove was a Dutchman of French descent and at the time of his journey was general agent in America for the Holland Land Company. He was a keen observer, with a natural and also a professional interest in farm lands and farm problems of all sorts. Consequently his journal is a document par excellence on the agriculture of that period and on the whole round of life in that country.

Perhaps a fairly definite idea may given of the amount of material on various topics by stating the number of pages that contain items on each topic, with an occasional illustration of the type of information given.

First, some of the crops may be considered. For buckwheat one finds items on 17 pages, including culture, prices, and production per acre. He gives the production per acre in 10 different localities. It runs from 15 to 18 bushels in northern Jersey, and from 25 to 40 bushels in Pennsylvania. He even follows the buckwheat to the stage of buckwheat cakes, which, he says, the German farmers eat largely instead of bread because they are cheaper.[17]

Items on oats are found on 7 different pages; hay, 14 pages; barley, 10 pages; corn, 20 pages; wheat, 32 pages. On the subject of wheat there are 7 items on culture, 10 on prices, and 17 on the amount produced per acre. The production of wheat runs from 10 to 15 bushels per acre in Jersey, and from 15 to 20 bushels on the limestone soils of Pennsylvania. A study of Cazenove's figures in connection with a soil map of the districts traversed creates a strong presumption for the accuracy of the journalist.

There are four references to the ravages of the Hessian fly, the longest one being in the following paragraph on Chester County, Pa.:

An acre of good valley land generally yields 15 to 20 bushels of wheat, but these last 2 or 3 years they have been annoyed in this district by the Hessian fly and this year (1794) by mildew—so they cultivate corn more extensively, and sow their fields in clover, because when there is not enough wheat sown, the Hessian fly attacks barley.[18]

---

[17] Cazenove Journal, 34.
[18] Cazenove Journal, 77.

On various other subjects Cazenove supplies data as follows: Cattle, items on 9 different pages; horses, 9 pages; prices of farm lands, 30 pages; use or nonuse of manure, 5 pages; transportation of produce, 9 pages; farm buildings, 8 pages; butter prices, 10 pages; size of farms, 24 pages; farm wages, 11 pages.

The following is an example of the condensed information given by Cazenove for the vicinity of Lebanon, Pa.:

In Lebanon, flour costs —, butcher's meat 5 pence a pound, fresh pork 6 pence, butter 1 s [hilling]; walnut wood 2 dollars a cord, oak wood 10 s [hillings] a cord.

A workman earns 3 s. per day, and ½ dollar in summer.

For fertilizer, lime, which is plentiful here; plow with two horses.

[Rotation] New ground here:

      1st year, wheat
      2   ,,   wheat again
      3   ,,   oats
      4   ,,   fallow, rest
      5   ,,   wheat
      6   ,,   fallow, etc.

Lands cultivated a longer time:

      1st year, wheat
      2   ,,   barley
      3   ,,   corn, or oats
      4   ,,   fallow, or buckwheat
      5   ,,   if buckwheat the 4th year, then fallow.

The cattle stay in the stables from December to April.

Board per week in private house, 2 dollars.

Now prices are: wheat 9 shillings per bushel, corn 5 s., barley 7-1/2 s., oats 2/6 (the army 3/6); hay £4.10 per ton now, it being in the barn; £3.15 to 4, taken directly from the fields.

([Side endorsement]: The carting of a ton of hay from here to Philadelphia is from £5 to £6, if the road is bad; 2 s./6 for a bushel of grain.)[19]

Of course one finds useful and plentiful data on manners and customs. Description and travel excel particularly in this field. This paper may be closed by a quotation, semiinformational, semiphilosophical, showing Cazenove's reaction to the German farmers of Pennsylvania. Readers who may be of German ancestry will perhaps make allowance for the fact that Theophile Cazenove was of French descent.

The German farmers also manufacture coarse woolen material for coats, skirts, etc.; and all their shirt-linens; they buy only their best clothes, for Sunday, and not many of these, as they are thrifty to the point of avarice; to keep seems ? to be their great passion; they live on potatoes; and buckwheat cakes instead of bread. They deny themselves everything costly; but when there is snow, they haunt the taverns. They are remarkably obstinate and ignorant.

On every farm they cultivate enough flax and hemp and also raise what sheep they need for making their linen and cloth. They have a few gardens, at least for cabbage and carrots, and they all have bee-hives. You always feel like settling in the country when you see the excellent ground and the charm of the country, and also the advantage of farming, but you lose courage when you realize the total lack of education of the farmers, and that it is absolutely necessary to live to yourself, if you

[19] Cazenove Journal, 48-49.

have any education, knowledge and feeling. There ought to be 5 or 6 families living close together in these districts; then they would be very happy, for freedom and abundance are obtained in a thousand places of the United States, if you are sensible and diligent; but for society—*nescio vos.*

All these farmers talk politics; and because they read the papers, they think they know a great deal about the government; they think that government officers are too many and overpaid. One of these was complaining about the government excise and wanted a land-tax, but I pacified him with an argument for those who never generalize ideas—a land-tax, I told him, is against liberty, because every one must pay it if he has land, while the excise can be avoided if you want to—in order to do so, do not distill or drink any intoxicating drinks.[20]

It might be added that Cazenove's advice about avoiding intoxicating drinks was purely philosophical, never practical on his own part. Yet whatever his principles or practices on the temperance question, he has given us a storehouse of information on the farming methods and conditions of his day, and his journal is a worthy example of the source material for agricultural history that may be classified under the heading of "Description and travel."

---

[20] Cazenove Journal, 34–35.

XVII. THE EARLY DEVELOPMENT OF AGRICULTURAL SOCIETIES IN THE UNITED STATES

By RODNEY H. TRUE
University of Pennsylvania

THE EARLY DEVELOPMENT OF AGRICULTURAL SOCIETIES IN THE UNITED STATES

By RODNEY H. TRUE

In the first half of the eighteenth century English agriculture began to reap the harvest resulting from the sowing of the preceding century. The steady passing of the land from the irresponsible, inflexible, community tenure of the Middle Ages to individual ownership had already begun to tell in the increased effectiveness of individual initiative. New crops and methods from the ever efficient Netherlands had given the English farmer clover and turnips; America had contributed the potato. The improvement of roads had increased the ease of communication and thereby speeded up the propagation of new ideas and increased the range of individual observation. Crop rotation, a cardinal feature of farming operations since Roman times, was receiving more intelligent attention, and the fallow, in the old sense, was beginning to be doubted. Stock raising was recognized as a complement to crop growing, not an alternative. Tull had begun his agricultural revolution based on tillage.

In view of the general activity of these times, some kind of united effort would be expected as a natural result. The Scotch apparently secured the priority when in 1723 the Edinburgh Society of Improvers in the Knowledge of Agriculture in Scotland was founded. Lord Stair, taking the lead, organized those interested in the problem of the land. This society became prominent through the publication in 1743 of Maxwell's Select Transactions.

In 1731 Ireland followed Scotland, and the Dublin Society was established under the ægis of government. Not only were communications published, but a farm for the carrying on of experiments was established under the care of an official experimentalist. This advanced step was made possible by the very considerable financial support from the government.

England caught the step in 1754 when the Society for the Encouragement of Arts, Manufactures and Commerce was organized in London. The program of this society was broader than that of the earlier Scotch and Irish societies, but due attention was given to

295

agriculture as a part of the effort.   After some decades (1783) it, too, published its transactions.

In point of time, the next society of this nature that has come to my attention was organized in 1765, in Russia, under direct orders of the Empress Catherine.   The Free Oeconomical Society, as it was called, began immediately to print its treatises.   A large experimental establishment was set up near St. Petersburg under the charge of a Russian clergyman who had studied scientific agriculture in England on Arthur Young's estate.   It was planned that a certain number of young men, later to become priests, were to be brought from different parts of Russia for a training that was to be carried by them to their future parishioners.

In 1766 the government of France took the lead in still another direction, founding the celebrated veterinary school at Charenton, near Paris.   This was later transferred to Rambouillet, where it became world famous.   In 1786 a farm for experimental purposes was annexed to it and four professorships were established; two in rural economy, one in anatomy, and one in chemistry.   (Young's Travels in France, Bohn. Libr. 1912: 99.)

The first American society for the advancement of agriculture, known to the writer, the New York Society for Promoting Arts, was already organized in 1766.[1]   In that year it offered premiums for papers or reports concerning practical work done on specific subjects to which the society wished to direct the attention of the farmers.

England showed great activity in the following decades by developing many county societies, some of special significance, as the Bath and West of England Society in 1777.

Several American societies fall within this period, as the South Carolina Agricultural Society, 1784, the Philadelphia Society for the Promotion of Agriculture, 1785, the New York society, 1791, and others following closely.

It is our task to study the general features of these American organizations, their composition, purposes and methods of operation. In most cases one or more prominent men of a leading city took the initiative and rallied around themselves a group of the well-to-do public-spirited citizens of their neighborhood who took a more or less active interest in the improvement of agricultural conditions.

At the very beginning a cleavage line between the agricultural and manufacturing interests is detected and a conscientious effort seems to have been made in many societies to overcome this by attempts to demonstrate the identity of interests.   These societies were organized to better the circumstances of the overwhelmingly

---

[1] New York Gazette, Mar. 13, 1766: New York Mercury, Mar. 10, 1766: Weekly Post Boy, Mar. 13, 1766.

preponderant agricultural population, but as the political strife raged more and more savagely during the decades following the Revolution traces of political discord are sometimes discoverable in the activities of these groups.   In general, these organizations show a tendency to side with the liberals rather than with the conservatives.   The antagonism between agriculture and manufactures, in spite of diligent efforts at suppression, would at times break out.   While conservatives like Timothy Pickering and John Adams of Massachusetts, were active in the early days, the liberal wing usually took the lead vigorously in later decades.

Passing now to the details of organization, it may be said that, while variations in the minor points of the plan were found, these young American societies followed pretty closely the British pattern as worked out in the county societies.   Membership, while not exclusive, was guarded to the end that members secured would be able and willing to meet the dues, while proposals and consideration for a period prior to election to membership seem to have been the rule.   The members paid into the treasury an annual fee that even in these days would be respectable, thus raising a fund that could be devoted to meeting the modest expenses of the organization and to paying very substantial premiums for the best papers on specific subjects, or for the best production of specified crops grown under indicated conditions.   These premiums were sometimes cash sums, sometimes silver plate.   The latter was quite the rule in the Southern States, but perhaps less often such in the Middle and Northern States.

As specimen subjects for which premiums were offered by the Philadelphia Society for the Promotion of Agriculture for the year 1791 the following may be cited: .

Rotation of crops, having been found capable in England of improving the soil instead of exhausting it, it is deemed important that the farmers of Pennsylvania should acquaint themselves with this mode of husbandry.   Accordingly, for the best experiment of a five years' course of crops a piece of silver plate of the value of $200 is offered, inscribed with the name and the occasion.   For the experiment made of a like course of crops next in merit, a piece of plate likewise inscribed is offered of a value of $100.

The importance of the giving the best shelter to cattle and in such a way as to procure the greatest quantities of manure from within the farm leads the society to offer a gold medal for the best design of farm yard and method of managing it from the points of view noted.   A silver medal is offered for the second best offering.

The best method of raising hogs—gold and silver medals for best and second best plans, respectively.

For the best method of recovering worn-out fields to a more healthy state, within the power of common farmers, without dear or far-fetched manures; but by judicious culture and the application of materials common to the generality of farms; founded on experience—a gold medal and a silver medal as before.

For the best information, the result of actual experience, for preventing the damage to crops by insects, especially the Hessian fly [discovered but a few years before]—gold and silver medals.

For the best comparative experiments on the culture of wheat, broadcast, drilled, or with the seed spaced at equal distances—gold and silver medals.

A vegetable food, easily procured and preserved, that best increases milk in cows and ewes in March and April founded on experiment—gold and silver medals.

For the greatest quantity of ground, not less than one acre, well fenced, producing locust trees growing in 1791 from seeds sown after April 5, 1785, to be of a sort used for posts and trunnels, and not fewer than 1,500 per acre—again medals.

Wishing to emphasize the use of oxen instead of horses in husbandry and other services and the value of improved herds, the society offers a gold medal for the best essay based on experience in the breeding, feeding, and management of cattle for the purpose of rendering them most profitable for the dairy and for beef, and most docile and useful for the draught—a silver medal for the next best plan.

To ascertain the powers of oxen as draught animals when hitched up as horses are hitched, or on some better plan if there is such, when used on plough or loaded carriage—medals are offered; methods and expense of shoeing, harnessing, etc. to be described.

A footnote refers to the common use of oxen in New England, something apparently rare in Pennsylvania.

To find the best method of recovering old gullied fields to a hearty state, or when damaged beyond remedy, how best to use them, as for tree planting—medals.

For the best cheese, not less than 500 pounds—gold medal; not less than 250 pounds—silver medal.

The society, believing that the culture of hemp on some of the low rich lands in the neighborhood of this city may be attempted with advantage, offers a gold medal for the greatest quantity of hemp, not less than 3 tons, grown within 10 miles of Philadelphia. For second greatest quantity, a silver medal.

A final provision allows the successful candidates for prizes to receive either plate or medal, or their cash equivalent.

The society awarded prizes on the basis of written reports properly certified by competent witnesses. The pithy recommendation "That reasoning be not mixed with the facts" accompanies the statement of conditions of competition. It will be noted that premiums were not offered for definite itemized products, but rather for the best solutions of problems of general significance.

Here we have the general type illustrated. Variations in minor particulars are found among the different societies, as the problems to be solved varied with each region concerned.

The leaders of these early American societies seem to have realized that in holding meetings and listening to reports on experiments they were but half accomplishing their object. Greater numbers must be reached through some sort of printed medium. For some years they seem to have used the newspapers, almanacs, and other general periodical literature open to them. In time, several of the stronger organizations, following the conspicuous lead of the Bath and West of England, Highland, Dublin, and other Old World societies, issued volumes of memoirs or transactions, in which selected papers were printed for their membership and indirectly for a wider circle of readers. Among the societies doing so, the following may be cited as examples: South Carolina Agricultural Society (1785); New York Society for Agriculture, Arts, and Manufactures (1792); Massachusetts Society for Promoting Agriculture (1796).[2]

None of the American societies, so far as known, was able to imitate Dublin and the Oeconomical Society of Russia in establishing experimental farms. Institutions founded on the voluntary contributions of a general membership could hardly have expected to undertake an enterprise requiring so large and steady a support.

However, in 1794 a committee of the Philadelphia Society, of which John Beal Bordley, colonial judge of the Admiralty at Annapolis, Md., and in his later years a resident of Philadelphia, acted as chairman, petitioned the State legislature to incorporate a State Society of Agriculture in Pennsylvania, which, among other objects, would establish "pattern farms" in different and convenient parts of the State in charge of competent men. Incidentally this same committee urged that books presenting sound principles and methods of farming be used in the county schools, the masters being enjoined to combine the teaching of agriculture with the other subjects of education.[3] The national farm established by the French government in 1783 was cited as an example of such a pattern farm.[4] The actual establishment of such pattern farms for the general diffusion of information was not accomplished, I believe, in the early days in Pennsylvania or in any other State.

Although the giving of agricultural instruction, carried on very effectively in a private way by Arthur Young, was urged by this committee of the Philadelphia society, the formal teaching of agriculture does not seem to have passed beyond the point of animated discussion even in that State. This idea, however, was generally discussed about this time by many leaders of American thought, Washington and Jefferson among the number.

The general model on which these early agricultural societies was based is to be found in the learned societies of the times. The American Philosophical Society, organized in 1743 at Philadelphia, published many articles on agricultural subjects long before this branch of interest segregated itself. Hence it was natural that the early agricultural societies should preserve somewhat of the aristocratic character of their prototypes and, like them, should fail to reach the men who actually held the plow. How to popularize agricultural improvement and to bring not only the idea but concrete illustrations of it to the men on the land was a problem for the agricultural leaders to solve. One result of the effort to do this took the form of agricultural exhibitions in which the farmers themselves competed for premiums

[2] Phil. Soc. Prom. Agri. 4: xx.
[3] Mem. Phila. Soc. Prom. Agri., 1: xxi.
[4] Ibid., 1: xxv.

offered for specified products. This sort of extension work, in which the principles advocated by advanced thinkers were given the form of more and better grains, fruits, and animals, marked the transition of these societies from the Old World aristocratic type of learned organization to a much larger democratic institution that dealt much less with ideas and much more with everyday realities.

This movement in America ran roughly parallel with a like development in the mother country. Probably the germ of the new thing was to be found in the occasional popular gatherings on the premises of Coke of Holkham, in Norfolk, who from 1778 to 1821 annually gathered his farmers together for consultation on agricultural matters and to study on his highly improved lands the results of better methods. All were welcome from the smallest tenant farmer to His Royal Highness the Duke of Sussex.[5] The exhibition of horses, pigs, and implements of husbandry was followed by the shearing of sheep. Fleeces were weighed and different types of sheep were killed and their mutton value determined. As the climax of the occasion, a grand dinner was served, with toasts drunk in the orthodox manner and with the customary speeches.

This type of demonstration work was imitated in America by several leading citizens. George Washington Parke Custis began his series of annual sheep shearings in 1802 at Arlington, across the Potomac from Washington.[6] Here the model set by Coke was as closely followed as circumstances would permit.[7]

Col. David Humphreys, formerly minister to Spain, and Robert R. Livingstone at a little later date (1810) followed the example of Coke and Somerville and invited gatherings to their premises where sheep were sheared, speeches made, and toasts drunk in good English style.[8] The popularity of these gatherings and their effectiveness as a means of arousing and broadening interest in better agriculture was apparently promptly recognized by the agricultural societies. Many soon organized exhibitions at which not only were sheep sheared but the greater variety of subjects of interest to a farming population was recognized in a program of much broader scope.

The question of priority in holding agricultural exhibitions brings to view one of the most interesting men of those days in the person of Elkanah Watson, a man of wide public experience who was much interested in the improvement of agricultural conditions. In the autumn of 1807 Watson determined to make the arrival of two merino sheep that he had just bought a matter of general interest to the

[5] Curtler, Short History of English Agriculture, 227. For a lively account of the three days' meeting in autumn of 1820, see American Farmer, 2: 217.

[6] Connor, Brief History of the Sheep Industry in the United States, An. Rpt. Am. Hist. Assoc. 1918, I: 99.

[7] Bryan, W. B., A History of the National Capital, I: 597; also Lossing, Benson, J., The American Centenary, 1876: 107.

[8] Agr. Museum 1: 35, 4, 1810.

farmers of Pittsfield, Berkshire County, Mass., where he was then living. He gave notice that he would exhibit these animals under the great elm tree in the public square. He took this occasion to make an enthusiastic speech in the interest of improved stock. An agricultural society was duly chartered in 1810, and in the fall of 1811 held a formal exhibition with an award of about $70 to the most meritorious animals. Other interests than those of livestock were not recognized on account of a lack of funds. Anyone who enjoys a bit of enthusiastic writing should read Watson's account of his exhibition.[9]

It seems clear that unless Watson's speech to the Berkshire farmers over his two merinos, under the great elm in Pittsfield square, constituted an agricultural exhibition in the accepted sense, Massachusetts was anticipated one year by the District of Columbia. Here, on the outskirts of Georgetown, on May 16, 1810, an exhibition was held about which there could be little doubt. Not two sheep and an enthusiastic orator only, but a list of premiums was awarded for sheep to the amount of $240; for domestic manufactures, $260; "for shearing a sheep in the neatest, safest and most expeditious manner" $15 awarded to a resident of the city of Washington. Apparently the palm for priority goes to the District of Columbia.[10]

It is to be noted that in both exhibitions the only animals recognized were sheep. To offset this may be cited another activity of the exhibition type in which cattle were the chief object of interest. Cattle shows were held in England from 1802 onward under the patronage of Lord Somerville.[11] The Smithfield cattle show, begun in 1793, was an effort on a wider basis.[12] In America, too, cattle had their own special appreciation, and that mainly in the Northern and Central States. Here, about the exhibits of fat cattle grouped a variety of features similar to that seen at the southern sheep shearings. In most cases both North and South, as in the District of Columbia, domestic manufactures were given special emphasis.

It will be seen that in these exhibitions, or shows, or shearings, the different elements of the rural life of the times were gradually being brought together. The problem of agricultural implements, even in the early days, appealed to Americans. Jared Eliot, the author of our first American work on agriculture, with the assistance of President Clapp of Yale College, devised a drill plow based on the rather clumsy type developed before 1735 by Tull in England. Eliot sent one of these machines to William Logan in Philadelphia in 1755. Americans, thrown on their own resources in these matters, were forced to

[9] Watson, Men and Times of the Revolution : 368.
[10] Agri. Museum, 1 : 11, 1810.
[11] Agri. Museum, 1: 49, 1810.
[12] Curtler: 218.

make tools to fit their needs.   The plow had always been an object of special difficulty because, until Jefferson's time, each tool was a thing by itself, made of wood on a plan favored by the individual plow-right and finished off with sundry iron parts furnished by the blacksmith.   No two plows were exactly alike.   A favorite implement was kept as long as possible, then duplicated as nearly as might be.

This condition of affairs, in respect to this most important implement and observations, made on the almost Neolithic plows seen at work in 1795 by Jefferson while touring in Lorraine led that statesman to seek some principle of construction that might standardize plows on a rational basis.   He worked on this problem until by 1793 he was able to formulate his principles in terms of mathematics, and to have plows made on his design.[13]   They were used on his Virginia estates and worked admirably.   A discussion of the problem with his solution was presented to the American Philosophical Society in Philadelphia in 1798.[14]   He used a spring dynamometer to ascertain the actual draft of plows of different designs.

It will be readily understood from this explanation how alive the problem of the plow was a decade or so later in the days of these cattle shows, sheep shearings, and agricultural exhibitions.   The plowing match was seen as a regular feature on most of these occasions.   Sometimes contests were held between horses and oxen. Generally plowmakers from several places would enter their handi-work, and, following the example of the patron of the arts and sciences from Monticello, put their products to the strict tests of the dynamometer.

For some years exhibitions of the types described went under a variety of names—sheep shearings, cattle shows, agricultural exhibitions.   After a time another name came to be associated with these, namely—the fair.

Fairs had been established institutions in the Old World from relatively remote times, coming into existence with the improvement of roads and means of conveyance.   About 1600, horse fairs were held at Ripon, Harborow, Wolf Pit, and other places in England.[15] The great market for hops and wool was found at the Sturbridge Fair,[16] the great market for sheep at the Waybill Fair in 1719.[17]   In the day of Coke, St. Faith's Fair near Norwich was a central point for the sale of cattle, some even coming from Scotland to be fattened for the London market.[18]

[13] Randall, Trans. N. Y. State Agr. Soc., 22: 67, 1862.
[14] Trans. Am. Phil. Soc., 4: 313–322, 1799.
[15] Curtler: 105.
[16] Ibid., 171.
[17] Ibid., 172.
[18] Prothero, English Farming, Past and Present, 218.

In America, fairs for the exhibition and sale of livestock, home manufactures, and produce were well known at a relatively early date.   A Virginia act of 1742 sanctioned the holding of semiannual fairs in Alexandria in the spring and fall.   In Maryland the act laying out the town of Georgetown in 1751 gave the same authority to this place. The Virginia enactment indicated that these fairs should afford an opportunity for " the sale and vending of all manner of cattle, victuals, provisions, goods, wares, and merchandises."[19]   After the city of Washington had begun to take shape in 1804, the city council authorized the holding of fairs "for the sale of all kinds of cattle, goods, wares, and merchandise" in May and November of each year. In addition to the opportunities for selling merchandise, premiums were offered for the best specimens of the various kinds of livestock sold during the fair.   Here, along with the exchange feature, the improvement motive had begun to develop before the agricultural societies had adopted it as an extension feature of their more formal and strictly intellectual proceedings.

Even earlier, however, than Virginia and Maryland, Carolina had been holding fairs in the vicinity of Charleston.   The South Carolina Gazette of May 5, 1733, states that "on Tuesday next Strawberry Fair will begin as usual."   In the number of September 28, 1734, occurs the notice of the fair as an annual event at Strawberry.   That real estate, as well as produce and livestock, was also sold at this fair is indicated by a notice in the Gazette of the same date that two "Town lotts in Childsberry alias the Strawberry" would "be sold for ready money to the highest bidder at publick Out-Cry," at the next Strawberry Fair in the month of October.

The Strawberry Fair seems to have been first authorized by an act of 1723, establishing it at Childsberry town in St. John's Parish, in Berkeley County.   Public fairs were to be held "at least twice in every year for exposing for sale horses, cattle, and merchandise." "Anything may be brought there by anybody for sale or barter at such times, hours and seasons as directors or rulers at the Fairs at the time may appoint."   A further most interesting provision follows: "Fairs shall be held with a Court of Pipowder with liberties and customs of Fairs such as are holden in South Britain or England." The duties of the rulers of the fair appointed by the governor of the province in holding court of pipowder are defined.   The further provision is made that "during Fair no one there shall be liable to arrest by virtue of any process except treason, felony or other capital crime, or breach of the peace."

An act of March 16, 1783, is somewhat more explicit concerning this court.   The establishment of a "court of pipowder" is provided

---

[19] Bryan, History of National Capital, I: 60, 1914.

for. A majority of the inhabitants of the town were authorized to elect a person or persons as directors or rulers of the fair, which directors or rulers were authorized to hold a "court of pipowders together with all liberty and free customs to such appertaining, and that they and every one of them may have and hold there, at their respective courts, from day to day and hour to hour from time to time upon all occasions plaints and please of a court of pipowders, together with all summons, attachments, arrests, issues, fines, redemptions and commodities."

The court of pipowder was derived immediately from early English usage, as is indicated in the language of the act. The name, "the court of dusty feet," as well as this form of temporary petty tribunal, came from France, where at maritime points this international emergency court grew up at the fairs held in the Middle Ages. Such was apparently the remote origin of the temporary courts, with their constables, having limited powers of action, named for the duration of the fair.[20]

We get traces of this element in the machinery of agricultural fairs from the beginnings of these institutions down to the present time.

Such was the early origin and character of the fairs that furnished a favorable stock onto which the post-revolutionary agricultural societies grafted their extension operations. Already established as occasions that brought many people together, and therefore popular as social events in days when the social side of farm life had little chance, these societies needed only to guide this activity into the desired channels. By offering premiums for individual animals or articles of definite kinds, the society officers directed the attention of the community toward such objects as seemed to them to be of major importance. By varying the objects for which premiums were offered, or by regulating the sums offered, it was possible to bring new ideas to the front and to point out new needs to be met. Thus the premium lists of any society of long life throw a very strong light on farming conditions as they existed in the beginning and as they changed with time. Thus, also, the fairs, originally, as the name suggests, places of purchase and barter, changed their character as the propaganda spirit took possession of them. They retained, and retain to this day, the name "fair," but the original element gradually vanished before the improving spirit of the agricultural societies that took charge of them.

Another institution that originated independently of the agricultural fairs and finally gravitated to them was the horse race. From very early times horse racing had been a favorite form of amusement, and the elements of popularity were recognized by the early agricul-

---

[20] Holdsworth, The Law Merchant, Select Essays in Anglo-American Legal History, vol. 1, also Selden Society, Select Cases of Law Merchant, 1270-1638, vol. 1. Introduction.

tural organizers as likely to furnish a means of advancing agriculture. Horses were the chief means of travel for all parts of the country from early times, and from saddle use to racing was a short step. The breeding of saddle horses was carried on in the latter half of the seventeenth century, in Rhode Island[21], among other places. This was the possible source of saddle horses advertised for sale in Charleston, S. C., at a somewhat later date. Edward Vanvelsen, in the South Carolina Gazette of September 14, 1734, offered for sale "Two Rhode Island Stallions, Natural Pacers," both 15 hands high. On January 4, 1735, Nathaniel Potter offered for sale "at his store at Mr. William Pinckney's several Rhode Island pacing horses," Molasses, Cyder Potatoes, etc.

At an early date horse racing was already a public institution in Charleston. A race having for a prize a saddle valued at 20 pounds was advertised as an attraction at a fair held in May, 1737, at Ashley Ferry.[22]

Horse racing began in Georgetown, Md., as early as 1769, and in the spring of 1797 a great race of 4-mile heats was run in Washington, the chief contestants being horses owned by Charles Ridgeley of Maryland and Colonel Tayloe of Virginia. A great interstate rivalry made this race one long remembered.[23]

Although racing was thus already established in the area included in the District of Columbia years before the agricultural exhibition held in Georgetown in 1810, the races were not associated with it. Perhaps the agricultural exhibition was still too intent on the serious business for which it was organized to seek the aid of a sport then, as now, not without its shady side. Indeed, it seems to have been decades later before the horse race was drawn into the synthesis, and then often with a sort of half apology.

From what I have outlined here, the following conclusions may be gathered:

With the general awakening to the importance of agricultural improvement in the early seventeen hundreds, organizations intended to forward this movement were formed both in Europe and in America. Membership was limited in number, and the scientific and philosophical organizations of the time formed the prototype. Efforts to widen the circle of influence included the publishing of memoirs and transactions, and the offering of premiums for solutions to problems. A further widening was sought by applying the demonstration principle, the result being exhibits at which products were put in competi-

[21] Weeden, Social and Economic History of New England; 333.
[22] South Carolina Gazette, Apr. 16, 1737.
[23] Bryan, History of National Capital, 1: 304.

tion for prizes.   Other features of popular interest, agricultural in nature, gradually gathered about this exhibit to build up an institution that had a very broad appeal, and through its effect on great numbers of farmers hastened very greatly the dissemination of new information, awakened the spirit of improvement and made concrete the work of intellectual leaders.

As effort centered more and more on the application of principles to practice the intellectual level of these societies declined.   However, they achieved democracy and thereby accomplished a great work.

XVIII. HISTORY OF THE RANCH CATTLE INDUSTRY IN OKLAHOMA

By EDWARD EVERETT DALE

University of Oklahoma

XVIII. HISTORY OF THE RANCH CATTLE INDUSTRY IN OKLAHOMA

By EDWARD EVERETT DALE

University of Oklahoma

HISTORY OF THE RANCH CATTLE INDUSTRY IN OKLAHOMA.

EDWARD EVERETT DALE

This paper deals with that period of time from the beginning of ranching in Oklahoma upon a large scale to statehood in 1907—the period of the ranch cattle industry. The subject is treated from an historical rather than an economic viewpoint, omitting so far as possible statistics and questions of profit and loss in order to devote more space to governmental relations and the influence of cattle raising in Oklahoma upon the development of the West and upon the country as a whole.

It has seemed well to limit the subject in this way, because cattle raising in Oklahoma, during the period named, was far different from that industry in any other State of the Union and its peculiar features had a powerful and far-reaching influence. Broadly speaking, the history of the ranch cattle industry in Oklahoma is merely a part of the history of a much larger movement—that of the conquest of the American wilderness. This movement has been characterized by the appearance of various successive stages of society, that of the hunter, the herder, and the pioneer farmer. The significant thing is that Oklahoma has passed through all of these stages within a single generation, owing to the fact that Oklahoma was a region of retarded development, since it was an Indian territory in which white settlement was for a long time forbidden.

Cattle ranching as a frontier pursuit has existed in America since early colonial days. Once agricultural settlement was firmly planted along the Atlantic seaboard and began its march westward across the continent, pushing before it the broken fragments of various Indian tribes, there was always to be found along its western edge a comparatively narrow rim or border of pastoral life. For a century and more it was there, pushed on steadily west as agricultural settlement advanced, a sort of "twilight zone" with the light of civilization behind it and the darkness of savagery before. It is one of the most remarkable things in American economic history, however, that immediately after the Civil War this comparatively narrow belt of pastoral life, hitherto fairly constant in width and area, suddenly shot out into the wilderness and spread with remarkable rapidity

309

until it covered a region larger than all that part of the United States east of the Mississippi devoted to agriculture.[1]

Among the factors chiefly responsible for this sudden and enormous expansion of the industry were the slaughter of the buffalo, thus leaving vast areas of excellent pasture lands entirely without animals to consume the grass; and the gathering up of the Plains tribes of Indians and the placing of them upon reservations in Oklahoma and elsewhere.[2]

The last was somewhat dependent upon the former. It was virtually impossible to keep the roving tribes of the Plains upon reservations as long as there were plenty of buffalo to be found, a potential supply of food, clothing, and shelter. But by 1880 the buffalo had almost entirely disappeared and after that date it was comparatively easy to keep the Indians upon reservations where they were fed by the Government of the United States.[3] Thus the destruction of the buffalo herds not only opened up a vast pastoral region by leaving the grass formerly consumed by these animals for cattle, but it also made it possible for the ranchmen to occupy that region with some degree of safety, since the Indians could then be controlled and kept upon their own lands.

Even so, it would have been impossible for the ranching industry to have grown to such great proportions so rapidly, because enough animals could not have been found to stock these enormous new ranges, had there not existed in the Southwest a great reservoir from which they might be drawn—the State of Texas. That Commonwealth, with an area greater than the combined areas of the thirteen original States, was an ideal region for cattle raising. Climate, soil, and the land system all combined to make this true. The winters were usually mild so that cattle kept fat upon the open range throughout the year; the soil usually produced a good quality of grass, while the system inherited from Spain of granting out lands in large tracts had made Texas a region of large landed proprietors, most of whom had herds of cattle.[4]

During the four years of the Civil War Texas remained the least touched of any Southern State by that struggle. While the armies of Sherman were laying waste a broad strip through Georgia and the Carolinas, while the border States were being devastated by the troops of both sides, and while the fields of the Cotton Kingdom were lying

---

[1] Nimmo gives the area devoted to the range cattle industry in 1885 as 1,350,000 square miles; a region larger than the combined areas of Great Britain, Ireland, France, Germany, Denmark, Holland, Belgium, Austria (as it then was), Italy, Spain, Portugal, and one-fifth of Russia in Europe. See Nimmo, Range and Ranch Cattle Traffic of the U. S., p. 1.

[2] Some 20 tribes of Plains Indians were brought to western Oklahoma and located upon reservations there between 1866 and 1885.

[3] The disappearance of the buffalo may be traced in the reports of the Indian agents for the western tribes of Oklahoma. See Reports of Commissioner of Indian Affairs, 1876, pp. 46-49; ibid, 1879, p. 65.

[4] The census of 1860, Volume on agriculture, p. 148, gives the total number of cattle in Texas at that time as 3,534,768. Census figures are most unreliable, however, when applied to an industry of this nature, and those of that particular census are especially so.

fallow for want of laborers to till them, the cattle herds of Texas remained undisturbed and were increasing rapidly under the favorable conditions surrounding them. The result was that when the Texas soldiers returned to their homes at the close of the war . they found their ranges overflowing with fine fat cattle for which they had no market though cattle and beef were selling at high prices in the North.[5]

Out of this condition grew the so-called " northern drive." Early in 1866 many Texas ranchmen gathered up herds of fat steers and drove them northward in an effort to reach market. Finding it almost impossible to drive cattle through the settled regions that must be traversed in order to reach Kansas City or St. Louis, they soon began to keep to the west of all settlements and bring their herds to shipping points on the railroads building westward through Kansas and Nebraska, which came to be known as " cow towns. " Here the cattle were loaded on cars and shipped to the northern or eastern markets. [6]

It is estimated that between five and six million head of cattle were driven north from Texas during the 18 years following the Civil War, and it seems probable that this estimate is too low.[7] The fat animals were shipped to the packing centers to be slaughtered; others were sent into the corn belt where they were fed corn for from 60 to 120 days before being consigned to the packers. Also, it was not long until the possibilities of the northern ranges were discovered, with the result that the drive to Abilene, Wichita, or Dodge City frequently became but the first part of a longer drive to Dakota, Montana, or Wyoming. It was found that both the northern and southern plains had their advantages. Texas, because of the low altitude and warm climate, remained the great breeding ground, while the northern plains became the great feeding ground; many men held ranges in both regions.

As time went on the ranch cattle industry grew in popularity. Ranching became almost a fad. Young college men from the East, as the late Theodore Roosevelt, to quote a conspicuous example, came West and engaged in the business. Foreign capitalists invested heavily in ranching ventures, and a number of these, such as Baron Richthofen and the Marquis of Mores, came over from Europe and gave their personal attention to the business. A literature of the cattle country came into existence. Large corporations were formed,

---

[5] In 1866 round steak was retailing in New York at 20 to 25 cents a pound, sirloin at 25 to 35, and rib roast at 28 to 30 cents (New York Tribune, June 23, 1866). On the live stock market of eastern cities cattle were quoted at $5 to $10 per hundredweight the last-named price being refused on the Albany market Dec. 21, 1866, for a choice consignment of Illinois steers (New York Times, Dec. 22, 1866).

[6] See Joseph G. McCoy, Historic Sketches of the Texas Cattle Trade, for a contemporary account of the development of the northern drive.

[7] Nimmo, Range and Ranch Cattle Traffic, p. 28.

in many of which prominent State and national officials held stock. Within 10 years after the close of the Civil War the industry of herding had spread over the entire Plains region and extended from the edge of the agricultural settlements on the east to the Rocky Mountains and even beyond.

In the very center of this great "cow country" lay the Indian Territory, later to become the State of Oklahoma, a region larger than all New England, yet with a population of hardly more than a hundred thousand souls. Obviously it was a "strategic region," since it lay between the breeding grounds of Texas and both the markets and feeding grounds of the North, and in consequence nearly all of the cattle trails leading north crossed it. It was also interesting in itself. The eastern half was occupied by the Five Civilized Tribes of Indians who owned their lands in common and governed themselves almost as though they were five independent republics. These people, through contact with the whites in their old home east of the Mississippi, had passed from the hunting to the pastoral stage of society, but at this point had been driven westward to Oklahoma. Here they had continued the herding industry begun in the old home, but their herds were destroyed by the Civil War and their country so devastated that after that struggle they never reached the point in cattle raising that they had previously attained. The western half of the Indian Territory, with an area as great as that of Ohio, had less than 20,000 half savage blanket Indians living upon large reservations of which they made little use, while certain extensive areas such as Greer County, Old Oklahoma, and the Cherokee Outlet had no Indian inhabitants at all.[8]

White settlement was forbidden in this territory and, as an agricultural population slowly crept westward engulfing it, Oklahoma remained an attractive but little inhabited island of wilderness in the midst of swirling currents of civilization. It was as though a dike had been erected about the Indian country by governmental decree, a dike impervious to the waves of settlement that beat against it.

---

[8] The Indians located in Oklahoma were as follows:
Osage, 1872, 17 Stats. 228.
Kaw, 1872, 17 Stats. 228.
Ponca Sioux, 1877, 21 Stats. 422.
Pawnee, 1876, 19 Stats. 28.
Otoe and Missouria, 1882, 21 Stats. 380.
Tonkawa, formerly Nez Perce Reservation, 1884, 20 Stats. 63.
Sac and Fox, 1867, 15 Stats. 495.
Iowa Executive order, 1883, Kappler, Indian Laws and Treaties, Vol. I, 843.
Kickapoo, Executive order, 1883, ibid. 844.
Potawatomi, 1867, 15 Stats. 591.
Cheyenne-Arapaho, 1869, Executive order, Kappler, Vol. I, 839.
Comanche-Kiowa-Apache, 1867, 15 Stats. 581.
The Wichita and Caddo were given their reservation in 1872 by unratified agreement, but had been living there for a long time before; they themselves said for two centuries.

Through this dike, however, the range-cattle industry at last began to flow. An industry, more fluid in its nature than agriculture, at last began to trickle through a barrier that had proved impenetrable to white settlement in the ordinary sense of the term.

This was not true at first. As long as there was abundant range elsewhere, the cattlemen who occasionally drove herds up the trails leading across Oklahoma did not view the permanent occupation of that region with much favor. True, the range and climate were excellent. Lying between the breeding grounds of Texas and the feeding grounds of the northern plains, Oklahoma had most of the advantages of both and few of the disadvantages of either. The climate was mild enough to enable cattle to live through the winter upon the open range without serious loss, and yet cool and bracing enough so that the animals grew larger and became fatter than they did in the extreme Southwest. The water supply was fairly abundant and the pasturage of the best. Yet there were disadvantages, too. The ever hungry Indians would be certain to prove a constant source of anxiety and of loss, while the Department of the Interior refused to give leases of Indian land for grazing purposes and showed an earnest determination to keep the ranchmen out. Even if it were possible to occupy ranges there by stealth, or with the connivance of Indian agents and their employees, the ranchmen would be in a region entirely without the protection of the law, and so would have little redress when their herds were preyed upon by the barbaric tribes that occupied these reservations, or by white thieves and outlaws. In consequence it was some time before there was any real attempt at permanent occupation of pasture lands in Oklahoma by the ranchmen.

As this great stream of Texas cattle continued to flow north and spread itself over the plains, attractive ranges became increasingly scarce. Cattle companies were paying large dividends, as much as 25 to 35 per cent a year in some cases,[9] and such profits naturally caused the rapid extension of the industry. Beef contractors were permitted to bring herds into Oklahoma and hold them near the agencies for issue to the Indians; ranchmen living along the border in adjoining States permitted their cattle to drift across the line; others, driving herds on the trails across Oklahoma, began in some cases to linger for several weeks or months during the drive, and at last some of these men began to contemplate a permanent occupation of these rich pasture lands.

The first attempts met with little success. The Department of the Interior refused to approve leases or grazing permits, insisting that under the existing law it had no right to do so and called upon the

---

[9] L. A. Allen, Our Cattle Industry Past and Present, pp. 6–7.

War Department to expel all intruders.[10]   The latter made a half-hearted attempt to do this, but soon desisted, claiming it was impossible, and urged the Department of the Interior to permit grazing upon the western reservations in consideration of a reasonable payment for that privilege.[11]   The Department of the Interior refused, and the result was an unseemly altercation between the two departments.

In the meantime more and more cattle were brought upon the Indian reservations.   Some of the Indian agents, finding themselves confronted with a shortage of food for their charges, owing to inadequate appropriations, sought to make up the deficiency by granting to the ranchmen permission to pasture cattle upon Indian lands in exchange for beef.[12]

In the spring of 1883, the agent for the Cheyenne-Arapaho, John D. Miles, called the Indians together in council and secured the consent of the greater part of them to lease nearly all their reservation to seven cattlemen for a period of 10 years at a yearly rental of two cents an acre.   The total amount of land leased was over 3,000,000 acres, for which the Indians were to receive $62,000 a year.[13]

These leases were sent to Washington for approval by the Department of the Interior, accompanied by a letter from Agent Miles describing in glowing terms the benefits that were certain to accrue to the Indians.[14]   This brought the matter of grazing cattle upon Indian lands to a direct issue, since the interests involved were of such magnitude as to demand attention.   The result was that the Secretary of the Interior wrote to Mr. Edward Fenlon, one of the lessees, a letter known as the "Fenlon letter," laying down the policy which the department had determined to pursue.   In this letter the Secretary said in part:

While the department will not recognize the agreement or lease you mention, nor any other of like character, to the extent of approving the same, nor to the extent of assuming to settle controversies that may arise between the different parties holding such agreements, yet the department will endeavor to see that parties having no agreement are not allowed to interfere with those who have.   Whenever there shall be just cause for dissatisfaction on the part of the Indians, or when it shall appear that improper persons, under the cover of such lease or agreement, are allowed in the Territory by parties holding such agreement, or for any reason the department shall consider it desirable for the public interest to do so, it will exercise its right of supervision to the extent of removing all occupants from the Territory without reference to such lease or agreement, on such notice as shall be right and proper under the circumstances under which the parties have entered the Territory and

[10] See Price to Lewis, Sen. Ex. Doc. 54, 48th Cong., 1st sess., Vol. IV, p. 54 (Oct. 20, 1881).   Also Price to Sec. of Int. Jan. 28, 1882, ibid., p. 57, and Kirkwood to Sec. of War, Feb. 1 1882, ibid., p. 58.

[11] Sheridan to Lincoln, Mar. 6, 1882, ibid., p. 60.

[12] Report of Com. of Indian Affs., 1882, p. 68.

[13] See inclosure of Miles to Commissioner of Indian Affairs, Apr. 6, 1883.   Sen. Ex. Doc. 54, 48th Cong., 1st sess., Vol. IV, p. 92.

[14] Miles to Commissioner of Indian Affairs, Apr. 6, 1883.   Sen. Ex. Doc. 17, 48th Cong., 2d sess., Vol. I, p. 92.

have complied with the terms of the agreement and instructions of the department. All parties accepting such agreements should accept the same subject to all conditions herein, and subject to any future action of Congress and this department as herein stated in relation to occupants of such Territory. Instructions will be issued to the agents in accordance with this letter.[15]

Such a policy was little short of absurd. It invited ranchmen to enter the Indian Territory and intrigue with savage tribesmen. It placed a premium upon bribery and corruption and made of every agency employee a person to be flattered, cajoled, and, if possible, bribed by men with large interests at stake. Also, it could not be enforced. Men who had no agreements approved by the agent, but who were friendly with certain small bands of Indians, refused to remove, and their Indian friends, who were receiving more money from these ranchmen than their share of the lease money would amount to, refused to ratify the agreement made by their chiefs, and cut the fences and killed the cattle of the "approved lessees." The latter appealed to the agent for protection, demanding that men without leases be excluded; but the War Department, when called upon for troops, refused to furnish them on the ground that leases had not been approved by the Department of the Interior.[16]

Conditions on the Cheyenne-Arapaho reservation steadily grew worse. Agent Miles resigned and the new agent was unequal to the task imposed upon him. The Indians got beyond control, partly as a result of interference with them by rival groups of cattlemen, and a general outbreak was threatened.[17] The result was that General Sheridan was sent to this reservation with all available troops in the West to quiet the trouble, and the President at last ordered all cattle to be removed from the reservation within 40 days.[18] The number of cattle on the reservation was estimated at 210,000 head, but was possibly much larger. By December, 1885, all had been removed, but range was scarce elsewhere and the winter a severe one. As a result, the losses of cattle by starvation and freezing were frightful throughout the Southwest in this winter of 1885-6, and these losses were no doubt in part due to the placing of these Oklahoma cattle upon the already overstocked ranges of the bordering States.[19]

In the meantine the Cherokee Outlet was also the field of great ranching operations. That region had been given to the Cherokees, and a patent issued to them for it a few years after their removal; but in 1866 they had by treaty agreed to allow United States to

[15] Teller to Fenlon, Apr. 4, 1882. Sen. Ex. Doc. 54, 48th Cong., 1st sess., Vol. IV, p. 99.
[16] Augur to Adjutant General of the Army, Apr. 7, 1884. Sen. Ex. Doc. 17, 48th Cong., 2d sess., Vol. I, p. 97.
[17] Sen. Ex. Doc. 16, 48th Cong., 2d sess., Vol. I.
[18] Proclamation of July 23, 1885, 24 Stats. 1023. The ranchmen later asserted that Cleveland, by compelling immediate removal of herds from the Cheyenne-Arapaho reservation, struck the cattle interests of the United States a blow from which they never recovered.
[19] See Sheridan's report, July 21, 1885. House Ex. Doc. 1, 49th Cong., 1st sess., Vol. II, pt. II, pp. 69-70.

locate friendly Indians there, the title to remain with the Cherokees until such Indians had been so located. Under the terms of this treaty, several tribes had been placed in the Outlet, but the major portion of it, amounting to over 6,000,000 acres, remained unoccupied in the hands of the Cherokees. Trail herds crossing Oklahoma early. formed the practice of lingering there, in some cases spending several months on these rich pasture lands. Ranchmen in Kansas also began to allow their cattle to cross the line into the Cherokee Outlet, and in some cases drove them into that region for the winter when grass was scarce on the Kansas side of the line.

In 1879 the Cherokees awoke to the possibilities of revenue that might be derived from the Outlet and sent a collector there to levy a grazing tax on all cattle.[20] By this time a large portion of the region had been occupied by ranchmen with their herds. Some of these cattlemen held ranges under the cover of the names of Cherokee citizens who had taken up claims under a sort of assumed headright. Others were occupying pasture lands without any shadow of right, the various individuals determining among themselves the boundaries of each man's range under what was known as "cow custom."[21]

Most of these men paid cheerfully the grazing tax of 40 cents a head per year levied by the Cherokees, but a few evaded this payment, so that it was impossible to collect for a large number of the cattle on the Outlet. Men living in Kansas near the border would drive their cattle across the line into the Cherokee Outlet to avoid paying the property tax on them in Kansas and then drive them back into Kansas in order to avoid paying the grazing tax to the Cherokee.

In order to protect themselves and their ranges against these unscrupulous individuals, and also to aid in determining the rights of each man, the ranchmen who were regularly paying the Cherokee for grazing privileges formed, in 1880, a tentative association. The organization was a very loose one and was merely designed to fix the dates and places of round-ups, to provide some method of settling disputes, to take some measures for protection against trespassers, and also to design plans to combat fires, wolves, thieves, and other destructive agencies.[22]

As more and more cattle were brought into the Outlet, fences were erected about many ranges as a convenience in holding the animals. Also, the Cherokees became more efficient in collecting the grazing tax. The treasurer of the Cherokee Nation came each year to Caldwell, Kans., and established an office there for the collection of this money,

[20] Testimony of Ben S. Miller before the Senate investigating committee, Jan. 9, 1885. Sen. Rep. 1278, 49th Cong., 1st sess., Vol. VIII, pp. 79–80.

[21] Ibid.

[22] Testimony of John A. Blair before the Senate investigating committee Jan. 21, 1885. Sen. Rep. 1278, 49th Cong., 1st sess., Vol. VIII, p 180.

but in spite of his best efforts it was impossible to get all that was rightfully due.[23]

In the meantime the fame of the Cherokee Outlet as a desirable field for ranching had spread to such an extent that the Department of the Interior began to receive numerous inquiries relative to the matter of securing grazing privileges in that territory. Replies to some of these referred the inquirers to the Cherokee authorities, with the explanation that the lands in question were in the possession and under the jurisdiction of the Cherokee Nation of Indians, and sometimes added the information that these Indians granted permits for grazing cattle there.[24] However, to inquiries as to whether or not the Interior Department would permit a lease to be negotiated with these Indians for a term of years and would recognize it and protect the lessees, the Commissioner of Indian Affairs returned a reply in the negative.[25]

It was evident that the tenure of these men occupying the Outlet with herds of cattle was very precarious, and late in 1882 their operations were reported to the Department of the Interior, and an order was issued requiring them to remove all fences and other improvements from these lands within 20 days, failing which they would be removed by the military.[26] Fortunately for the ranchmen, the War Department again showed the utmost reluctance to carry out the request of the Department of the Interior. In the meantime, such a storm of protest was aroused that the order was held in suspension and the cattlemen were allowed to try to make some arrangement with the Cherokee authorities for a more permanent occupation of the Outlet.[27]

This they did in the spring of 1883, by forming an organization known as the Cherokee Strip Live Stock Association, and obtaining from the Cherokee National Council a lease of the Outlet for a term of five years at a rental of $100,000 a year.[28]

The association thus formed was perhaps the largest organization in the world for the promotion of the livestock industry. It was chartered under the laws of Kansas, and embraced more than a hundred individuals and firms. Its members held at this time some 300,000 head of cattle upon the Cherokee Outlet and enormous numbers elsewhere. Its surveyors set to work to determine the boundaries of each member's range, and its court of arbitration

[23] The amounts collected each year were as follows: 1879, $1,100; 1880, $7,620; 1881, $21,555.54; 1882, $41,233.81. See Cherokee Advocate, Feb. 6, 1885.
[24] Acting Commissioner Stevens to Alvord and Woodruff, May 6, 1881. Sen. Ex. Doc. 54, 48th Cong., 1st sess., Vol. IV, p. 128. Also, Stevens to Holt, May 20, 1882. Ibid., p. 10.
[25] Price to Strong, Oct. 11, 1881. Ibid., p. 128.
[26] Price to Tufts, Dec. 30, 1882. Ibid., p. 130.
[27] Teller to Price, Mar. 16, 1883. Ibid., p. 150.
[28] Sen. Ex. Doc. 17, 48th Cong. 2d sess. Vol. I, pp. 151-152.

heard and settled questions involving tens of thousands of dollars.[29] Its power and influence were of the greatest. Some of its members drove their herds into the region known as "Old Oklahoma," others occupied some of the reservations to the south. The cattlemen who had been removed from the Cheyenne and Arapaho country gradually came drifting back again, and men belonging to the Cherokee Strip Live Stock Association also took herds into that region. Other associations were formed but not on so large a scale.

These associations were unique. The ranchmen were without any adequate protection of law and in consequence formed these extra legal organizations, not with the object of securing liberty under ideals of individualism as was the case with most earlier frontier organizations, but to protect property—their herds of cattle. Thus they were economic, rather than political, in their nature, and foreshadowed the later associational arrangements of "big business" that sought to act as corporate persons in accordance with frontier ideals.

For more than six years the Cherokee Strip Live Stock Association was a great power in the Southwest. It fenced the remaining lands of the Outlet, improved the breed of cattle, provided better shipping facilities at the various "cow towns," sought diligently to protect the property of its members against thieves, fire, wolves, and disease, and all the while carried on a bitter struggle against a multitude of opposing elements that sought to destroy it. In this struggle the association always proved the victor until it was at last forced to yield to the power of no less an antagonist than the United States Government itself.

Even then it was not through any fault or mismanagement on the part of its directors and members that the association was driven out of this region. It was merely the victim in a struggle between the United States Government and the Cherokees in which the former sought to induce the latter to cede the lands of the Outlet to furnish homes for white settlers. The great corporation which had for years withstood the attacks of many bitter enemies was at last caught and crushed between these two powerful opposing forces. It was the more or less "innocent bystander," or perhaps it would be more correct to say it was the source of food supply of one of the opponents which must be destroyed in order to force the enemy to surrender.

At the expiration of the five-year term for which the Cherokee Outlet had been leased, the association obtained from the Cherokees a new lease for a second period of five years, paying this time the sum of $200,000 a year.[30] But the Government of the United States had

---

[29] Lyons to Eldred, July 21, 1883, Aug. 26, 1883, and Sept. 26, 1883. Chas. Eldred Papers.
[30] Lyons to Eldred, Dec. 8, 1888. Chas. Eldred Papers.

determined to secure a cession of these lands from the Cherokees in order that they might be opened to white settlement, and now, through the Cherokee Commission, appointed for that purpose, offered the Indians $1.25 an acre for all the lands of the Outlet. Since they had already been offered $3 an acre, or a total sum of $18,000,000, for the Outlet, by a cattle syndicate, provided they could get the consent of the United States to sell,[31] the Cherokees naturally refused the offer of the Government and persisted in this refusal in spite of repeated pleadings and bullyings.

Accordingly, after obtaining from the Attorney General an opinion that the Outlet leases had no legal force or validity, President Harrison, about the middle of February, 1890, issued a proclamation forbidding grazing on the lands of the Cherokee Outlet as prejudicial to the public interests, and ordering all cattle to be removed by October 1, 1890, or sooner, if the lands were in the meantime opened to settlement.[32]

The Indians here met with the same attitude on the part of the Government of the United States that they had met in Georgia more than half a century before. Their lands were needed for white settlement, and yet they refused to cede their equity for what the United States officials regarded as a fair price. As a result, and in order to compel this cession, it was decided that they must be deprived of all revenue or benefit from these lands until such time as they were willing to yield.

The removal of the ranchmen from the Outlet and the opening of the latter to white settlement was inevitable sooner or later. But the removal of the cattlemen at just this time was a political rather than an economic step, though the ultimate purpose of the Government was a great economic change in this region through the opening of this land to agricultural settlement. Since this settlement did not take place for more than three and a half years after the issuance of the President's proclamation, and not until almost three years after the ranchmen had been forced out, the conclusion follows that the ranchmen were not removed in order to make room for settlers, but to stop the revenue derived from these lands by the Cherokees, and so induce the Indians to cede this area upon the terms offered. This cession they were at last forced to make, though the price paid was a little more than was at first offered, amounting to about $1.40 an acre.[33]

---

[31] See 25 Stats. 1005, and Sen. Misc. Doc. 80, 50th Cong., 2d sess., p. 20.

[32] See Opinion of Attorney General Miller, 19 Opinions, 499, and 26 Stats. 1557. This opinion of Attorney General Miller merely reaffirmed that of Attorney General Garland given July 21, 1885. See 18 Opinions, 235.

[33] See agreement in Sen. Ex. Doc. 56, 52 Cong., 2d sess., Vol. V, pp. 15–16.

The replacing of the ranchmen on the Cherokee Outlet with an agricultural population was but one chapter in the story of the struggle between the cattlemen of Oklahoma and the pioneer farmers of adjoining States. It was a struggle which had begun almost as soon as cattle had been brought into that territory and was to continue practically without intermission until the herds had been forced out and the entire region given over to farming.

As agricultural settlement advanced steadily westward on either side of Oklahoma and good farming lands became increasingly scarce, the pioneer farmers began to look with longing eyes toward the great reservations of the Indian Territory. The presence there of many ranchmen, while they themselves were excluded, aroused the bitter resentment of the pioneer farmers, who at last began to make determined efforts to secure the opening of these lands to settlement. Naturally these efforts were resisted by the cattlemen, and the hostility of the would-be settlers was greatly increased by this resistance. The ranchmen came to be regarded as wealthy monopolists, and it was alleged that they bribed the United States officials, corrupted the Indians, and intimidated those who sought to oppose them.[34]

Not only did the settlers along the border seek to secure the opening of these lands by act of Congress, but failing in this, they made determined efforts to settle some of them in defiance of law, and when they were removed by the military many of them insisted that the action of the United States Government had been taken at the instigation of the cattlemen. Little newspapers grew up near the border, established apparently for the twofold purpose of "booming" the opening of Oklahoma lands to settlement and of abusing the cattlemen. The press throughout the country took the matter up; the question of opening Oklahoma to settlement found its way into politics, and office seekers, both local and national, with an eye upon the farmer vote, urged it vigorously, and added their voices to the general outcry against the ranchmen. That the occupation of the country by agricultural settlement was inevitable sooner or later must have been obvious to all. The important thing about the whole matter is that the ranchmen in this way received much unfavorable advertising. They were so critcized and abused by these would-be settlers and their sympathizers that along with public opinion favorable to opening the Indian lands to settlement there also grew up, in the same proportion, a public opinion bitterly adverse to the cattlemen. This was especially true because added to this clamor was that of the homesteaders in other Western States and Territories who urged that the ranchmen monopolized the public domain and sought to prevent settlement.

---

[34] Jackson and Cole, Oklahoma, pp. 134–135.

Out of all this there grew up and crystallized a public opinion that has never changed—to the effect that the cattlemen of our western plains were in a great measure selfish, brutal, and domineering, using their great wealth and the power derived from organization to oppress.

It is false in a great measure, but the opinion still persists, because the ranching industry largely disappeared before it had time to live down the charges thus preferred against it. In consequence, there is a widespread popular belief that the cattlemen were among the first "malefactors of great wealth" of the nineteenth century. From these accusations it was but a step to accusations against railways, manufacturers and others, so it may be confidently asserted that the strong public sentiment against combinations of capital and unscrupulous individuals of great wealth which characterized the "Populistic Southwest" was in part due in its origin to this struggle over Oklahoma between the ranchmen and pioneer settlers.

It was a losing struggle for the cattle interests, however, and in time the dike placed about Oklahoma by governmental decree gave way and settlement came pouring through. Even then the replacing of ranching by agriculture in Oklahoma was most peculiar and has no counterpart in any other State. The settling of most Western States by an agriculture population has been like the slow, steady leaking of water into the hold of an old-type ship until it was full. That of Oklahoma was like the sudden bursting of water into the hold of a modern vessel divided into many water-tight compartments. The first region to be opened to settlement in the Indian country was "Old Oklahoma" which was opened in 1889, and almost each succeeding year for the next decade saw one or more areas added to the original nucleus. The Panhandle was added to Oklahoma in 1890 by the organic act; the Sac and Fox, Potawatomi, and Iowa Reservations were opened in 1891; the Cheyenne-Arapaho Reservation in 1892; the Cherokee Outlet in 1893, and various others, one by one until the last one, the "Big Pasture," was settled in 1906.

Long before the last one was settled, the Department of the Interior had adopted a system of leasing Indian lands for grazing purposes, and so as each Indian reservation was opened and settled, in most cases almost in a single day, the ranchmen withdrew their herds into those remaining until with the opening of the last they found there were no longer any pasture lands left to them.

It should be noted that opening these lands to white settlement did not constitute taking the land from the Indian and giving it to the settler. The Indian did not use the land. As an economic factor he was negligible. What really happened was the taking of the land from the ranchmen and the giving it over to agriculture.

97244°—25——21

But few better examples can be found in our history of the complete change in the economic life of large regions through legislation.

It should be observed, too, that the peculiar method of settling Oklahoma proved disastrous to many ranchmen. Large areas were settled in a single day; no time was given for adjustment; crowds of settlers, swarming across lands not yet open to settlement in order to reach others that were, burned the grass, cut the fences, and brought disease to the cattle. Changes came with startling rapidity. The cattlemen unable to adapt themselves to these conditions suffered heavy financial losses, with the result that as the industry passed out many of them found themselves entirely ruined.

Even after some of the reservations were settled, the cattle industry lingered on, in some cases for a year or two, but here it mingles with another story—that of ranching upon the public domain. However there was little of this, and generally speaking the coming of agricultural settlement marked the passing of the ranch cattle industry in Oklahoma.

INDEX

Compiled by H. S. Parsons, Library of Congress

Brown, Marshall S., of com. to formulate rules for Geo. L. Beer prize (1921), 20, 105.
Bubonic plague, 177.
Buck, Solon J., of conf. of hist. socs. com. on hndbk. of hist. socs. (1921), 21, 132; of bibliog. of Am. travel subcom. (1921), 22, 108; of public archives comm. (1921), 22, 104.
Buckwheat, Cazenove journal, 290.
Budget of A. H. A. (1921), 56, 105–106.
Buffalo, N. Y., appropriation for war records, 136, 137.
Bureau of Navigation. *See* U. S. Bureau of Navigation.
Burr, George L., life councilor, A. H. A., 14, 19; present at council meetings, 100, 102, 103, 105, 107.
Burton, Clarence M.. subscription for calendaring French archives, 133.
Butler, Samuel, ridiculed New England towns, 246–247.
Byrne, Eugene H., of membership com. (1921), 21, 104, (1920), 84.
Calendar of printed letters rel. to Am. hist., A. H. A. com. (1908), 81.
California, war records collection, 136, 138, 140; newspapers, 144; war history, 145.
Callahan, James M., of audit com. (1920), 56; report of audit com. (1920), 56, 65.
Calm Address to Our American Colonies, Wesley, 46.
CAPITALISTIC AND SOCIALISTIC TENDENCIES IN THE PURITAN COLONIES, Day, 44–45, 223–235.
Carlton, Frank T., address, 36; FIELDS OF RESEARCH IN ECONOMIC HISTORY, 159–161.
Carnegie Institution, Dept. of Hist. Research to publish calendar of Parisian archives rel. to Miss. Valley, 38, 133; Dept. of Hist. Research established, 81.
Caroline minuscule, 183.
Cattle, HIST. OF INDUSTRY IN OKLA., 307–322.
Cazenove, Theophile, *Journal, 1794*, 290–292.
Celsus, 175.
Central Powers, joint manifesto rel. to independent Poland, 203.
Champlain, Samuel de, account of Plymouth, 213.
Chandler, Charles L., of hist. congress at Rio de Janeiro spec. com. (1921), 23, 105.
Channing, Edward, life councilor, A. H. A., 14, 19; of meetings and relations com. (1921), 19, 108; pres. A. H. A. (1920), 34; *Historical Retrospect*, 35; presides at annual meeting, 56; presides at council meeting, 100, 102, 103, 105.
Chase, Philip P., of hist. teaching in the schools com. (1921), 22, 108.
Cherokee Indians, cattle grazing on lands of, 316–319.
Cherokee Outlet, cattle raising, 315–320; opened to settlement, 321.
Cherokee Strip Live Stock Association, 317–318.
Chester County, Pa., Hessian fly, 290.
Cheyenne–Arapaho Reservation, land leases 314–315; opened to settlement, 321.
Cheyney, Edward P., 2d vice pres. A. H. A. (1921), 13, 19, 52, 57; of agenda com. (1921), 19, 107; of appointments com. (1921), 19, 108; chairman bibliog. of modern English hist. spec. com. (1921), 22,105; report of editors of *Am. Hist. Rev.* (1920), 82–83; report bibliog. of mod. Engl. hist. spec. com. (1920), 88; present at council meeting, 107.

Chicago Historical Society, calendaring French archives, 133.
Christian Directory, Baxter, 228.
Clark, A. Howard, bibliog. of members of A. H. A., 77.
Clark, Robert C., pres. P. C. B. (1921), 15, 121.
Clelland, R. G., presided at P. C. B. meeting (1920), 115; chairman P. C. B. auditing com. (1920), 121.
Clemen, Rudolf A., *Economic Bases of the American System of Large-Scale Meat Packing*, 47–48.
Coast Guard. *See* U. S. Coast Guard.
Coke of Holkham, 300.
Colby, Charles W., of writing of hist. spec. com. (1921), 23, 51, 105.
Colding, Ludwig A., work in electromagnetism, 277.
Cole, *Dr.*, Huntington Library collection of Am. hist., 119.
Collection of State War Records, Holbrook, 135.
College of Hawaii. *See* Hawaii, University of.
Colman, Benjamin, election sermon, 232.
Colonial Civil Service, Lowell, 82.
Colonial entries in *Privy-Council Register*, 81.
Commission on Training Camp Activities, war records, 141.
Committee on Public Information. *See* U. S. Committee on Public Information.
Commons, *Prof.*, *Hist. of Labor in the U. S.*, 161.
Communistic System of the Incas, Belaunde, 44.
Compleat Body of Divinity, Willard, 230.
Confederate Government, Control of Manufacturing by the, Ramsdell, 48.
Conference of historical societies, members (1921), 21, 104; annual meeting (1920), 37–38; policy com. recommendations, 70; account of, 79; report (1920), 85–88; PROCEEDINGS (1920), 129–252.
Conference on economic history, papers (1920), 153–162.
Conger, A. L., editor *Military Historian and Economist*, 80; chairman military hist. prize spec. com. (1913–1916), 89.
Connecticut, war records collection, 136.
Connor, L. G., agricultural hist. proposal, 67, 71.
Connor, R. D. W., of public archives comm. (1921), 22, 104.
Contribution of Political Science to Education, Hunt, 122–123.
Control of Manufacturing by the Confederate Government, Ramsdell, 48.
Coolidge, Archibald C., of board of editors, *Am. Hist. Rev.* (1921), 20, 52, 107; *Break-up of the Hapsburg Empire, 43.*
Cooperation of historical societies and departments, conf. of hist. socs. com. on, report (1920), 132–134.
Coordination of Historical Societies within the States, Schafer, 131, 150.
Coppin, *Mr.*, pilot to Pilgrims, 220.
Corwin, Edward S., of com. to formulate rules for Geo. L. Beer prize (1921), 20, 105.
Council of National Defense. *See* U. S. Council of National Defense.
Cox, Isaac J., of Justin Winsor prize com. (1921), 20, 104.
Crammer, C. R., report of Am. Audit Co. on A. H. A. finances, 63–65.
Crofts, F. S., of Harper & Bros., 94.
Cross, Arthur L., councilor, A. H. A. (1921), 14, 19, 52, 57; of agenda com. (1921), 19, 107; of bibliog. of modern English hist. spec. com. (1921), 22,105; present at council meeting, 107.

CPSIA information can be obtained
at www.ICGtesting.com
Printed in the USA
BVHW051059230119
538451BV00028B/1451/P

9 781528 535922